CLYMER®

MANUALS

SUZUKI

SV650 • 1999-2009

WHAT'S IN YOUR TOOLBOX?

More information available at Clymer.com
Phone: 805-498-6703

Haynes Publishing Group
Sparkford Nr Yeovil
Somerset BA22 7JJ England

Haynes North America, Inc
861 Lawrence Drive
Newbury Park
California 91320 USA

ISBN 10: 1-59969-627-4
ISBN-13: 978-1-59969-627-0
Library of Congress: 2014955805

Common spark plug conditions

NORMAL

Symptoms: Brown to grayish-tan color and slight electrode wear. Correct heat range for engine and operating conditions.
Recommendation: When new spark plugs are installed, replace with plugs of the same heat range.

WORN

Symptoms: Rounded electrodes with a small amount of deposits on the firing end. Normal color. Causes hard starting in damp or cold weather and poor fuel economy.
Recommendation: Plugs have been left in the engine too long. Replace with new plugs of the same heat range. Follow the recommended maintenance schedule.

CARBON DEPOSITS

Symptoms: Dry sooty deposits indicate a rich mixture or weak ignition. Causes misfiring, hard starting and hesitation.
Recommendation: Make sure the plug has the correct heat range. Check for a clogged air filter or problem in the fuel system or engine management system. Also check for ignition system problems.

ASH DEPOSITS

Symptoms: Light brown deposits encrusted on the side or center electrodes or both. Derived from oil and/or fuel additives. Excessive amounts may mask the spark, causing misfiring and hesitation during acceleration.
Recommendation: If excessive deposits accumulate over a short time or low mileage, install new valve guide seals to prevent seepage of oil into the combustion chambers. Also try changing gasoline brands.

OIL DEPOSITS

Symptoms: Oily coating caused by poor oil control. Oil is leaking past worn valve guides or piston rings into the combustion chamber. Causes hard starting, misfiring and hesitation.
Recommendation: Correct the mechanical condition with necessary repairs and install new plugs.

GAP BRIDGING

Symptoms: Combustion deposits lodge between the electrodes. Heavy deposits accumulate and bridge the electrode gap. The plug ceases to fire, resulting in a dead cylinder.
Recommendation: Locate the faulty plug and remove the deposits from between the electrodes.

TOO HOT

Symptoms: Blistered, white insulator, eroded electrode and absence of deposits. Results in shortened plug life.
Recommendation: Check for the correct plug heat range, over-advanced ignition timing, lean fuel mixture, intake manifold vacuum leaks, sticking valves and insufficient engine cooling.

PREIGNITION

Symptoms: Melted electrodes. Insulators are white, but may be dirty due to misfiring or flying debris in the combustion chamber. Can lead to engine damage.
Recommendation: Check for the correct plug heat range, over-advanced ignition timing, lean fuel mixture, insufficient engine cooling and lack of lubrication.

HIGH SPEED GLAZING

Symptoms: Insulator has yellowish, glazed appearance. Indicates that combustion chamber temperatures have risen suddenly during hard acceleration. Normal deposits melt to form a conductive coating. Causes misfiring at high speeds.
Recommendation: Install new plugs. Consider using a colder plug if driving habits warrant.

DETONATION

Symptoms: Insulators may be cracked or chipped. Improper gap setting techniques can also result in a fractured insulator tip. Can lead to piston damage.
Recommendation: Make sure the fuel anti-knock values meet engine requirements. Use care when setting the gaps on new plugs. Avoid lugging the engine.

MECHANICAL DAMAGE

Symptoms: May be caused by a foreign object in the combustion chamber or the piston striking an incorrect reach (too long) plug. Causes a dead cylinder and could result in piston damage.
Recommendation: Repair the mechanical damage. Remove the foreign object from the engine and/or install the correct reach plug.

CONTENTS

QUICK REFERENCE DATA

MOTORCYCLE INFORMATION

MODEL:_____ YEAR:_____

VIN NUMBER:_____

ENGINE SERIAL NUMBER:_____

CARBURETOR SERIAL NUMBER OR I.D. MARK:_____

TIRE SPECIFICATIONS

Item	Front	Rear
Tire type	Tubeless	Tubeless
Size	120/60ZR17 (55W)	160/60ZR17 (69W)
Minimum tread depth	1.6 mm (0.06 in.)	2.0 mm (0.08 in.)
Inflation pressure (cold)*		
Solo	225 kPa (33 psi)	250 kPa (36 psi)
Rider and passenger	225 kPa (33 psi)	250 kPa (36 psi)

*Tire inflation pressure for original equipment tires. Aftermarket tires may require different inflation pressure. The use of tires other than those specified by Suzuki may affect handling.

RECOMMENDED LUBRICANTS AND FLUIDS

Brake fluid	DOT 4
Engine coolant	
Type	Antifreeze coolant compatible with aluminum radiators
Ratio	50:50 with distilled water
Engine oil	
Grade	
1999-2005	API SF or SG
2006-on	API SF, SG or SH, SJ with JASO MA rating
Viscosity	10W-40
Engine oil capacity	
Oil change only	2.3 L (2.4 U.S. qt., 2.0 Imp. qt.)
Oil and filter change	
1999-2002	2.4 L (2.5 U.S. qt., 2.1 Imp. qt.)
2003-on	2.7 L (2.9 U.S. qt., 2.4 Imp. qt.)
When engine completely dry	
1999-2002	2.7 L (2.9 U.S. qt., 2.4 Imp. qt.)
2003-on	3.1 L (3.3 U.S. qt., 2.7 Imp. qt.)
Fork Oil	
Viscosity	
1999-2002	Suzuki No. 10 fork oil or equivalent
2003-on	Suzuki No. 8 fork oil or equivalent

(continued)

RECOMMENDED LUBRICANTS AND FLUIDS

Fork Oil (continued)
  Capacity per leg
    U.S. and California models
      1999-2001   491 ml (16.6 U.S. oz., 17.3 Imp. gal.)
      2002   480 ml (16.2 U.S. oz., 16.9 Imp. gal.)
    All other models
      1999-2001   489 ml (16.5 U.S. oz., 17.2 Imp. gal.)
      2002   478 ml (16.2 U.S. oz., 16.8 Imp. gal.)
    All SV650
      2003-on   490 ml (16.6 U.S. oz., 17.3 Imp. oz.)
    All SV650S, SV650SF
      2003   488 ml (16.5 U.S. oz., 17.2 Imp. oz.)
      2004-on   485 ml (16.4 U.S. oz., 17.1 Imp. oz.)
Fuel
  Type   Unleaded
  Octane
    U.S., California and Canada   87 [(R + M)/2 method] or 91 research octane or higher
    All other countries   91
  Fuel tank capacity, including reserve
    California models
      1999-2002   15 L (4.0 U.S. gal., 3.3 Imp. gal.)
      2003-on   16 L (4.2 U.S. gal., 3.5 Imp. gal.)
    All other models
      1999-2002   16 L (4.2 U.S. gal., 3.5 Imp. gal.)
      2003-on   17 L (4.5 U.S. gal., 3.7 Imp. gal.)

MAINTENANCE AND TUNE-UP TORQUE SPECIFICATIONS

Item	N•m	in.-lb.	ft.-lb.
Cylinder head cover bolt	14	124	–
Engine sprocket nut	145	–	107
Exhaust pipe bolt	23	–	17
Front axle	65	–	48
Front axle pinch bolt	23	–	17
Main oil gallery plug	18	159	–
Muffler mounting bolt	23	–	17
Oil drain plug	21	186	–
Rear axle nut	65	–	47
Rear brake master cylinder locknut	18	159	–
Spark plug	12	106	–
Valve timing inspection plug	23	–	17

COOLING SYSTEM SPECIFICATIONS

Item	Specification
Coolant capacity	
1999-2002	1.6 L (1.7 U.S. qt., 1.4 Imp. qt.)*
2003-on	1.7 L (1.8 U.S. qt., 1.5 Imp. qt.)*
Radiator cap opening pressure	95-125 kPa (13.5-17.8 psi)
Thermostat opening	180° F (82° C)

*Includes reserve tank.

DRIVE CHAIN SPECIFICATION

Type	DID525V8 (continuous)
Number of links	
SV650	110
SV650S	108
21-pin length	319.4 mm (12.6 in.)
Chain free play	20-30 mm (0.8-1.2 in.)

REPLACEMENT BULBS

Item	Specification
Headlight	
SV650	60/55W
SV650S[1]	45/45W
Indicator lights (1999-2002)[2,3]	1.7W
License plate	5W
Position/parking light (if equipped)	5W
Speedometer lights (1999-2002)[3]	
SV650	1.7W
SV650S	0.84W
Taillight/brakelight (1999-2002)[3]	21/5W
Turn signal	21W

1. In some European countries a 55/55W bulb may be used. Check with a dealership.

2. Water temperature indicator light is LED type. On SV650, oil pressure indicator light is LED type.

3. LED type for 2003-on.

INTRODUCTION

Suzuki introduced the SV650 in 1999 and has not looked back. New owners of the rev-happy twin have sung the bike's praises and thanked Suzuki for giving them the much-needed pleasure of riding a motorcycle that does everything.

With an eye on the street and the track, Suzuki threw their hat into the ring with the introduction of the TL-1000 series to compete with the big bore twins from Ducati and Honda. Suzuki looked to gain the same inherent advantages found in a V-twin design: lightweight, narrow profile and tons of low-end torque. Unfortunately, the TL's came with price tags that were as extreme as their V-twin race brethren.

Enter the SV650, an entirely new model design, and an attempt to revive the middle-weight V-twin. Similar in concept to Honda's Hawk GT (1988-1991), the heart of the SV is a 645cc, 90° liquid-cooled power plant. With TL technology and lessons, the double overhead cam engine features four valves per cylinder and an impressive horsepower-to-weight ratio (69 hp/363 lbs. dry). This, combined with a well-matched, six-speed transmission, makes the SV an impressive performer. With judicious amounts of torque across the entire power band, you have a machine that is happy commuting to work or carving up the local racetrack. A testament to this fact is the SV's use at a number of track riding schools.

The front suspension on early models, surely in an effort to reduce costs, is a non-adjustable 41 mm conventional fork. The single rear shock features seven-position adjustability. A state-of-the-art aluminum truss frame with impressive rigidity and a short wheelbase make for an extremely quick turning machine. Large diameter dual discs up front and a single stopper in the rear ensure the package is safely brought to a halt.

Also, like the old Hawk GT, a bike with similar cult appeal, the SV's are born into the world naked. Without bodywork (S model has a half-faring), the attractive aluminum rack and engine are on full display. The lack of covering also makes service easier and reduces repair costs from minor incidents. From picking up groceries at the local market to visiting family hundreds of miles away to breaking a track record, or just introducing new riders to the sport, the SV650 has proven to be the bike for everybody.

NOTE: Refer to the Supplement at the back of this manual for information unique to 2003-on models.

CHAPTER ONE

GENERAL INFORMATION

This detailed and comprehensive manual covers the Suzuki SV650 models from 1999-2009. Hundreds of original photographs and illustrations developed during a complete disassembly of the machine, combined with the hands on text, provide the detail necessary to carry out any procedure safely and efficiently.

A shop manual is a reference tool and as in all Clymer manuals, the chapters are thumb tabbed for easy reference. Important items are indexed at the end of the manual. All procedures, tables and figures are designed for the reader who may be working on the motorcycle for the first time. Frequently used specifications and capacities from individual chapters are summarized in the *Quick Reference Data* at the front of the manual.

Tables 1-7 appear at the end of this chapter.

Table 1 lists vehicle identification number (VIN) codes.

Table 2 lists vehicle dimensions.

Table 3 lists metric tap and drill sizes.

Table 4 lists decimal and metric equivalents.

Table 5 lists conversion formulas.

Table 6 lists technical abbreviations.

Table 7 lists general torque specifications.

MANUAL ORGANIZATION

This chapter provides general information on shop safety, tool use, service fundamentals and shop supplies. The tables at the end of the chapter include general motorcycle information.

Chapter Two provides methods for quick and accurate diagnosis of problems. Troubleshooting procedures present typical symptoms and logical methods to pinpoint and repair the problem.

Chapter Three explains all routine maintenance necessary to keep the motorcycle running well. Chapter Three also includes recommended tune-up procedures, eliminating the need to constantly consult other chapters on the various assemblies.

Subsequent chapters describe specific systems such as engine, transmission, clutch, drive system, fuel and exhaust systems, suspension and brakes. Each disassembly, repair and assembly procedure is given in step-by-step form.

Some of the procedures in this manual specify special tools. In most cases, the tool is illustrated in use. Well-equipped mechanics may be able to substitute similar tools or fabricate a suitable replacement. In some cases, specialized equipment or expertise may make it impractical for the home mechanic to attempt the procedure. Such operations are identified in the text with the recommendation to have a dealership or specialist perform the task. It may be less expensive to have a professional perform these jobs, especially when considering the cost of the equipment.

WARNINGS, CAUTIONS AND NOTES

The terms, WARNING, CAUTION and NOTE have specific meanings in this manual.

A WARNING emphasizes areas where injury or even death could result from negligence. Mechanical damage may also occur. WARNINGS *are to be taken seriously*.

A CAUTION emphasizes areas where equipment damage could occur. Disregarding a CAUTION could cause permanent mechanical damage, though injury is unlikely.

A NOTE provides additional information to make a step or procedure easier or clearer. Disregarding a NOTE could cause inconvenience, but would not cause equipment damage or personal injury.

SAFETY

Professional mechanics can work for years and never sustain a serious injury or mishap. Follow these guidelines and practice common sense to safely service the motorcycle.

1. Do not operate the motorcycle in an enclosed area. The exhaust gasses contain carbon monoxide, an odorless, colorless and tasteless poisonous gas. Carbon monoxide levels build quickly in small enclosed areas and can cause unconsciousness and death in a short time. Make sure the work area is properly ventilated or operate the motorcycle outside.

2. *Never* use gasoline or extremely flammable liquid to clean parts. Refer to *Cleaning Parts* and *Handling Gasoline Safely* in this chapter.

3. *Never* smoke or use a torch in the vicinity of flammable liquids, such as gasoline or cleaning solvent.

4. Before welding or brazing on the motorcycle, remove the fuel tank, carburetor and shocks to a safe distance at least 50 ft. (15 m) away.

5. Use the correct type and size of tools to avoid damaging fasteners.

6. Keep tools clean and in good condition. Replace or repair worn or damaged equipment.

7. When loosening a tight fastener, be guided by what would happen if the tool slips.

8. When replacing fasteners, make sure the new fasteners are the same size and strength as the original ones.

9. Keep the work area clean and organized.

10. Wear eye protection *anytime* the safety of the eyes is in question. This includes procedures involving drilling, grinding, hammering, compressed air and chemicals.

11. Wear the correct clothing for the job. Tie up or cover long hair so it can not get caught in moving equipment.

12. Do not carry sharp tools in clothing pockets.

13. Always have an approved fire extinguisher available. Make sure it is rated for gasoline (Class B) and electrical (Class C) fires.

14. Do not use compressed air to clean clothes, the motorcycle or the work area. Debris may be blown into the eyes or skin. *Never* direct compressed air at anyone. Do not allow children to use or play with any compressed air equipment.

15. When using compressed air to dry rotating parts, hold the part so it can not rotate. Do not allow the force of the air to spin the part. The air jet is capable of rotating parts at extreme speed. The part may be damaged or disintegrate and cause serious injury.

16. Do not inhale the dust created by brake pad and clutch wear. These particles may contain asbestos. In addition, some types of insulating materials and gaskets may contain asbestos. Inhaling asbestos particles is hazardous to health.

17. Never work on the motorcycle while someone is working under it.

18. When placing the motorcycle on a stand, make sure it is secure before walking away.

Handling Gasoline Safely

Gasoline is a volatile flammable liquid and is one of the most dangerous items in the shop. Because gasoline is used so often, many people forget that it is hazardous. Only use gasoline as fuel for gasoline internal combustion engines. When working on a motorcycle, keep in mind that gasoline is always present in the fuel tank, fuel line and carburetor. To avoid a disastrous accident when working around the fuel system, carefully observe the following precautions:

1. *Never* use gasoline to clean parts. See *Cleaning Parts* in this chapter.

2. When working on the fuel system, work outside or in a well-ventilated area.

3. Do not add fuel to the fuel tank or service the fuel system while the motorcycle is near open flames, sparks or where someone is smoking. Gasoline vapor is heavier than air, it collects in low areas and is more easily ignited than liquid gasoline.

4. Allow the engine to cool completely before working on any fuel system component.

5. When draining the carburetor, catch the fuel in a plastic container and pour it into an approved gasoline storage devise.

6. Do not store gasoline in glass containers. If the glass breaks, a serious explosion or fire may occur.

7. Immediately wipe up spilled gasoline with rags. Store the rags in a metal container with a lid until they can be properly disposed of, or place them outside in a safe place for the fuel to evaporate.

8. Do not pour water onto a gasoline fire. Water spreads the fire and makes it more difficult to put out. Use a class B, BC or ABC fire extinguisher to extinguish the fire.

9. Always turn off the engine before refueling. Do not spill fuel onto the engine or exhaust system. Do not overfill the fuel tank. Leave an air space at the top of the tank to allow room for the fuel to expand due to temperature fluctuations.

Cleaning Parts

Cleaning parts is one of the more tedious and difficult service jobs performed in the home garage. There are many types of chemical cleaners and solvents available for shop use. Most are poisonous and extremely flammable. To prevent chemical exposure, vapor buildup, fire and serious injury, note the following:

1. Read and observe the entire product label before using any chemical. Always know what type of chemical is being used and whether it is poisonous and/or flammable.

2. Do not use more than one type of cleaning solvent at a time. When mixing chemicals, measure the proper amounts according to the manufacturer.

3. Work in a well-ventilated area.

4. Wear chemical-resistant gloves.

5. Wear safety glasses.

6. Wear a vapor respirator if the instructions call for it.

7. Wash hands and arms thoroughly after cleaning parts.

8. Keep chemical products away from children and pets.

9. Thoroughly clean all oil, grease and cleaner residue from any part that must be heated.

10. Use a nylon brush when cleaning parts. Metal brushes may cause a spark.

11. When using a parts washer, only use the solvent recommended by the manufacturer. Make sure the parts washer is equipped with a metal lid that will lower in case of fire.

Warning Labels

Most manufacturers attach information and warning labels to the motorcycle. These labels contain instructions that are important to personal safety when operating, servicing, transporting and storing the motorcycle. Refer to the owner's manual for the description and location of labels. Order replacement labels from the manufacturer if they are missing or damaged.

SERIAL NUMBERS

Serial numbers are stamped in various locations on the frame, engine, transmission and carburetor. Record these numbers in the *Quick Reference Data* section in the front of the manual. Have these numbers available when ordering parts.

The VIN (**Figure 1**) is stamped on the right side of the steering tube. Later models also have a sticker on the left-side of the frame.

The engine serial number is stamped on a pad on the side of the crankcase (**Figure 2**).

Refer to **Table 1** for VIN information.

FASTENERS

Proper fastener selection and installation is important to ensure the motorcycle operates as designed and can be serviced efficiently. The choice of original equipment fasteners is not arrived at by chance. Make sure that replacement fasteners meet all the same requirements as the originals.

Threaded Fasteners

Threaded fasteners secure most of the components on the motorcycle. Most are tightened by turning them clockwise (right-hand threads). If the normal rotation of the component being tightened would loosen the fastener, it may have left-hand threads. If a left-hand threaded fastener is used, it is noted in the text.

Two dimensions are required to match the threads of the fastener: the number of threads in a given distance and the outside diameter of the threads.

Two systems are currently used to specify threaded fastener dimensions: the U.S. Standard system and the metric system (**Figure 3**). Pay particular attention when working with unidentified fasteners; mismatching thread types can damage threads.

NOTE
To ensure the fastener threads are not mismatched or cross-threaded, start all fasteners by hand. If a fastener is hard to start or turn, determine the cause before tightening with a wrench.

The length (L, **Figure 4**), diameter (D) and distance between thread crests (pitch) (T) classify metric screws and bolts. A typical bolt may be identified by the numbers, 8–1.25 × 130. This indicates the bolt has diameter of 8 mm, the distance between thread crests is 1.25 mm and the length is 130 mm. Always measure bolt length as shown in **Figure 4** to avoid purchasing replacements of the wrong length.

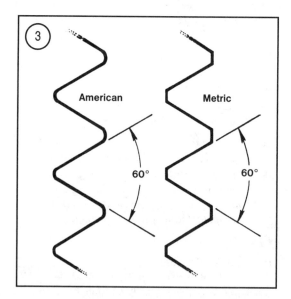

The numbers located on the top of the fastener (**Figure 4**) indicate the strength of metric screws and bolts. The higher the number, the stronger the fastener. Unnumbered fasteners are the weakest.

Many screws, bolts and studs are combined with nuts to secure particular components. To indicate

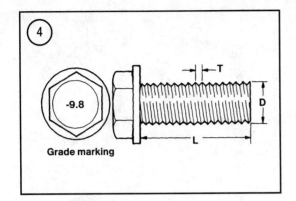

Grade marking

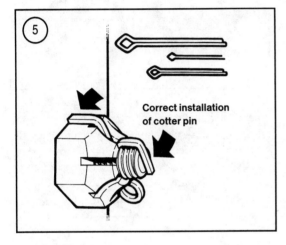

Correct installation of cotter pin

Specifications for torque are provided in Newton-meters (N•m), foot-pounds (ft.-lb.) and inch-pounds (in.-lb.). Refer to **Table 7** for general torque specifications. To use **Table 7**, first determine the size of the fastener as described in *Fasteners* in this chapter. Torque specifications for specific components are at the end of the appropriate chapters. Torque wrenches are covered in the *Basic Tools* section.

Self-Locking Fasteners

Several types of bolts, screws and nuts incorporate a system that creates interference between the two fasteners. Interference is achieved in various ways. The most common type is the nylon insert nut and a dry adhesive coating on the threads of a bolt.

Self-locking fasteners offer greater holding strength than standard fasteners, which improves their resistance to vibration. Most self-locking fasteners cannot be reused. The materials used to form the lock become distorted after the initial installation and removal. It is a good practice to discard and replace self-locking fasteners after their removal. Do not replace self-locking fasteners with standard fasteners.

Washers

There are two basic types of washers: flat washers and lockwashers. Flat washers are simple discs with a hole to fit a screw or bolt. Lockwashers are used to prevent a fastener from working loose. Washers can be used as spacers and seals, or to help distribute fastener load and to prevent the fastener from damaging the component.

As with fasteners, when replacing washers, make sure the replacement washers are of the same design and quality.

Cotter Pins

A cotter pin is a split metal pin inserted into a hole or slot to prevent a fastener from loosening. In certain applications, such as the rear axle on an ATV or motorcycle, the fastener must be secured in this way. For these applications, a cotter pin and castellated (slotted) nut is used.

To use a cotter pin, first make sure the diameter is correct for the hole in the fastener. After correctly tightening the fastener and aligning the holes, insert the cotter pin through the hole and bend the ends

the size of a nut, manufacturers specify the internal diameter and the thread pitch.

The measurement across two flats on a nut or bolt indicates the wrench size.

> *WARNING*
> *Do not install fasteners with a strength classification lower than what was originally installed by the manufacturer. Doing so may cause equipment failure and/or damage.*

Torque Specifications

The materials used in the manufacture of the motorcycle may be subjected to uneven stresses if the fasteners of the various subassemblies are not installed and tightened correctly. Fasteners that are improperly installed or work loose can cause extensive damage. It is essential to use an accurate torque wrench, described in this chapter, with the torque specifications in this manual.

over the fastener (**Figure 5**). Unless instructed to do so, never loosen a torqued fastener to align the holes. If the holes do not align, tighten the fastener just enough to achieve alignment.

Cotter pins are available in various diameters and lengths. Measure length from the bottom of the head to the tip of the shortest pin.

Snap Rings and E-clips

Snap rings (**Figure 6**) are circular-shaped metal retaining clips. They are required to secure parts and gears in place on parts such as shafts, pins or rods. External type snap rings are used to retain items on shafts. Internal type snap rings secure parts within housing bores. In some applications, in addition to securing the component(s), snap rings of varying thickness also determine endplay. These are usually called selective snap rings.

Two basic types of snap rings are used: machined and stamped snap rings. Machined snap rings (**Figure 7**) can be installed in either direction, since both faces have sharp edges. Stamped snap rings (**Figure 8**) are manufactured with a sharp edge and a round edge. When installing a stamped snap ring in a thrust application, install the sharp edge facing away from the part producing the thrust.

Remove E-clips with a flat blade screwdriver by prying between the shaft and E-clip. To install an E-clip, center it over the shaft groove and push or tap it into place.

Observe the following when installing snap rings:
1. Remove and install snap rings with snap ring pliers. See *Snap Ring Pliers* in this chapter.
2. In some applications, it may be necessary to replace snap rings after removing them.
3. Compress or expand snap rings only enough to install them. If overly expanded, they lose their retaining ability.
4. After installing a snap ring, make sure it seats completely.
5. Wear eye protection when removing and installing snap rings.

SHOP SUPPLIES

Lubricants and Fluids

Periodic lubrication helps ensure a long service life for any type of equipment. Using the correct

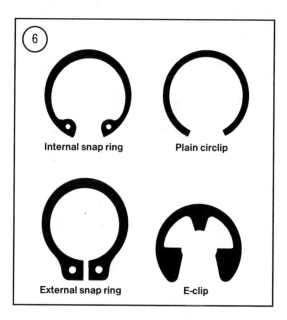

Internal snap ring   Plain circlip

External snap ring   E-clip

type of lubricant is as important as performing the lubrication service, although in an emergency the wrong type is better than none. The following section describes the types of lubricants most often required. Make sure to follow the manufacturer's recommendations for lubricant types.

Engine oils

Engine oil is classified by two standards: the American Petroleum Institute (API) service classification and the Society of Automotive Engineers (SAE) viscosity rating. This information is on the oil container label. Two letters indicate the API service classification. The number or sequence of numbers and letter (10W-40 for example) is the oil's viscosity rating. The API service classification and the SAE viscosity index are not indications of oil quality.

The service classification indicates that the oil meets specific lubrication standards. The first letter in the classification (*S*) indicates that the oil is for gasoline engines. The second letter indicates the standard the oil satisfies.

Always use an oil with a classification recommended by the manufacturer. Using an oil with a different classification can cause engine damage.

Viscosity is an indication of the oil's thickness. Thin oils have a lower number while thick oils have a higher number. Engine oils fall into the 5- to 50-weight range for single-grade oils.

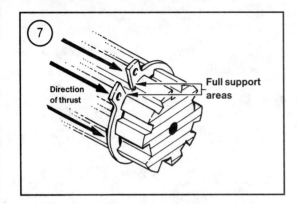

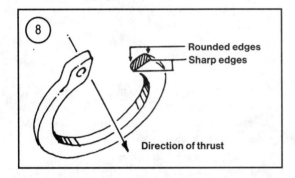

Brake fluid is classified by the Department of Transportation (DOT). Current designations for brake fluid are DOT 3, DOT 4 and DOT 5. This classification appears on the fluid container.

Each type of brake fluid has its own definite characteristics. Do not intermix DOT 3 or DOT 4 with DOT 5 type brake fluid as this may cause brake system failure since the DOT 5 brake fluid is not compatible with other brake fluids. When adding brake fluid, *only* use the fluid recommended by the manufacturer.

Brake fluid will damage any plastic, painted or plated surface it contacts. Use extreme care when working with brake fluid and clean up spills immediately with soap and water.

Hydraulic brake systems require clean and moisture free brake fluid. Never reuse brake fluid. Keep containers and reservoirs properly sealed.

> *WARNING*
> *Never put a mineral-based (petroleum) oil into the brake system. Mineral oil will cause rubber parts in the system to swell and break apart, resulting in complete brake failure.*

Cleaners, Degreasers and Solvents

Many chemicals are available to remove oil, grease and other residue from the motorcycle. Before using cleaning solvents, consider how they will be used and disposed of, particularly if they are not water-soluble. Local ordinances may require special procedures for the disposal of many types of cleaning chemicals. Refer to *Safety* and *Cleaning Parts* in this chapter for more information on their use.

Use brake parts cleaner to clean brake system components when contact with petroleum-based products will damage seals. Brake parts cleaner leaves no residue. Use electrical contact cleaner to clean electrical connections and components without leaving any residue. Carburetor cleaner is a powerful solvent used to remove fuel deposits and varnish from fuel system components. Use this cleaner carefully, as it may damage finishes.

Generally, degreasers are strong cleaners used to remove heavy accumulations of grease from engine and frame components.

Most solvents are designed to be used in a parts washing cabinet for individual component cleaning.

Most manufacturers recommend multigrade oil. These oils perform efficiently across a wide range of operating conditions. Multigrade oils are identified by a (*W*) after the first number, which indicates the low-temperature viscosity.

Engine oils are most commonly mineral (petroleum) based; however, synthetic and semi-synthetic types are used more frequently. When selecting engine oil, follow the manufacturer's recommendation for type, classification and viscosity.

Greases

Grease is lubricating oil with thickening agents added to it. The National Lubricating Grease Institute (NLGI) grades grease. Grades range from No. 000 to No. 6, with No. 6 being the thickest. Typical multipurpose grease is NLGI No. 2. For specific applications, manufacturers may recommend water-resistant type grease or one with an additive such as molybdenum disulfide (MoS_2).

Brake fluid

Brake fluid is the hydraulic fluid used to transmit hydraulic pressure (force) to the wheel brakes.

For safety, use only nonflammable or high flash point solvents.

Gasket Sealant

Sealants are used with a gasket or seal and are occasionally used alone. Follow the manufacturer's recommendation when using sealants. Use extreme care when choosing a sealant different from the type originally recommended. Choose sealants based on their resistance to heat and various fluids, and their sealing capabilities.

One of the most common sealants is RTV, or room temperature vulcanizing sealant. This sealant cures at room temperature over a specific time period. This allows the repositioning of components without damaging gaskets.

Moisture in the air causes the RTV sealant to cure. Always install the tube cap as soon as possible after applying RTV sealant. RTV sealant has a limited shelf life and will not cure properly if the shelf life has expired. Keep partial tubes sealed and discard them if they have surpassed the expiration date.

Applying RTV sealant

Clean all old gasket residue from the mating surfaces. Remove all gasket material from blind threaded holes; it can cause inaccurate bolt torque. Spray the mating surfaces with aerosol parts cleaner and wipe with a lint-free cloth. The area must be clean for the sealant to adhere.

Apply RTV sealant in a continuous bead 2-3 mm (0.08-0.12 in.) thick. Circle all the fastener holes unless otherwise specified. Do not allow any sealant to enter these holes. Assemble and tighten the fasteners to the specified torque within the time frame recommended by the RTV sealant manufacturer.

Gasket Remover

Aerosol gasket remover can help remove stubborn gaskets. This product can speed up the removal process and prevent damage to the mating surface that may be caused by using a scraping tool. Most of these types of products are very caustic. Follow the gasket remover manufacturer's instructions for use.

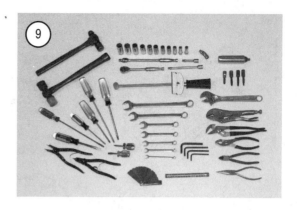

Threadlocking Compound

A threadlocking compound is a fluid applied to the threads of fasteners. After the fastener is tightened, the fluid dries and becomes a solid filler between the threads. This makes it difficult for the fastener to work loose from vibration, or heat expansion and contraction. Some threadlocking compounds also provide a seal against fluid leakage.

Before applying threadlocking compound, remove any old compound from both thread areas and clean them with aerosol parts cleaner. Use the compound sparingly. Excess fluid can run into adjoining parts.

Threadlocking compounds are available in different strengths. Follow the particular manufacturer's recommendations regarding compound selection. Two manufacturers of threadlocking compound are ThreeBond and Loctite. They both offer a wide range of compounds for various strength, temperature and repair applications.

BASIC TOOLS

Most of the procedures in this manual can be carried out with simple hand tools and test equipment familiar to the home mechanic. Always use the correct tools for the job at hand. Keep tools organized and clean. Store them in a tool chest with related tools organized together.

Quality tools are essential. The best are constructed of high-strength alloy steel. These tools are light, easy to use and resistant to wear. Their working surface is devoid of sharp edges and the tool is carefully polished. They have an easy-to-clean finish and are comfortable to use. Quality tools are a good investment.

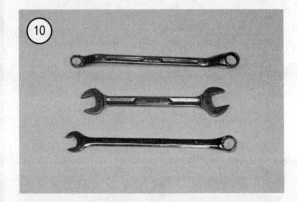

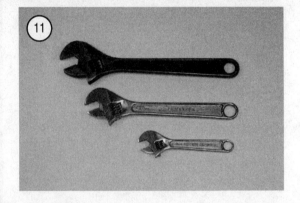

When purchasing tools to perform the procedures covered in this manual, consider the tool's potential frequency of use. If a tool kit is just now being started, consider purchasing a basic tool set (**Figure 9**) from a large tool supplier. These sets are available in many tool combinations and offer substantial savings when compared to individually purchased tools. As work experience grows and tasks become more complicated, specialized tools can be added.

Screwdrivers

Screwdrivers of various lengths and types are mandatory for the simplest tool kit. The two basic types are the slotted tip (flat blade) and the Phillips tip. These are available in sets that often include an assortment of tip sizes and shaft lengths.

As with all tools, use a screwdriver designed for the job. Make sure the size of the tip conforms to the size and shape of the fastener. Use them only for driving screws. Never use a screwdriver for prying or chiseling metal. Repair or replace worn or damaged screwdrivers. A worn tip may damage the fastener, making it difficult to remove.

Torx Drivers

Torx fasteners require specific Torx drivers for removal and installation. These fasteners reduce cam-out and fastener damage, and allow high torque transmission due to the complete enclosure of the driver within the fastener.

Torx screwdrivers in individual sizes, or screwdrivers that accept various bit sizes are available. However, the most practical application is a Torx bit set that accepts various drive types and sizes. A typical set contains T-10 through T40 bits that accept 1/4 and 3/8 in. drive attachments.

Wrenches

Open-end, box-end and combination wrenches (**Figure 10**) are available in a variety of types and sizes.

The number stamped on the wrench refers to the distance between the work areas. This size must match the size of the fastener head.

The box-end wrench is an excellent tool because it grips the fastener on all sides. This reduces the chance of the tool slipping. The box-end wrench is designed with either a 6- or 12-point opening. For stubborn or damaged fasteners, the 6-point provides superior holding ability by contacting the fastener across a wider area at all six edges. For general use, the 12-point works well. It allows the wrench to be removed and reinstalled without moving the handle over such a wide arc.

An open-end wrench is fast and works best in areas with limited overhead access. It contacts the fastener at only two points, and is subject to slipping under heavy force, or if the tool or fastener is worn. A box-end wrench is preferred in most instances, especially when breaking a fastener loose and applying the final tightness to a fastener.

The combination wrench has a box-end on one end and an open-end on the other. This combination makes it a very convenient tool.

Adjustable Wrenches

An adjustable wrench or Crescent wrench (**Figure 11**) can fit nearly any nut or bolt head that has clear access around its entire perimeter. Adjustable wrenches are best used as a backup wrench to keep a large nut or bolt from turning while the other end is being loosened or tightened with a box-end or socket wrench.

Adjustable wrenches contact the fastener at only two points, which makes them more subject to slipping off the fastener. The fact that one jaw is adjustable and may loosen only aggravates this shortcoming. Make certain the solid jaw is the one transmitting the force.

Socket Wrenches, Ratchets and Handles

Sockets that attach to a ratchet handle (**Figure 12**) are available with 6-point (A, **Figure 13**) or 12-point (B) openings and different drive sizes. The drive size indicates the size of the square hole that accepts the ratchet handle. The number stamped on the socket is the size of the work area and must match the fastener head.

As with wrenches, a 6-point socket provides superior holding ability, while a 12-point socket needs to be moved only half as far to reposition it on the fastener.

Sockets are designated for either hand or impact use. Impact sockets are made of thicker material for more durability. Compare the size and wall thickness of a 19-mm hand socket (A, **Figure 14**) and the 19-mm impact socket (B). Use impact sockets when using an impact driver or air tools. Use hand sockets with hand-driven attachments.

> *WARNING*
> *Do not use hand sockets with air or impact tools as they may shatter and cause injury. Always wear eye protection when using impact or air tools.*

Various handles are available for sockets. The speed handle is used for fast operation. Flexible ratchet heads in varying lengths allow the socket to be turned with varying force, and at odd angles. Extension bars allow the socket setup to reach difficult areas. The ratchet is the most versatile. It allows the user to install or remove the nut without removing the socket.

Sockets combined with any number of drivers make them undoubtedly the fastest, safest and most convenient tool for fastener removal and installation.

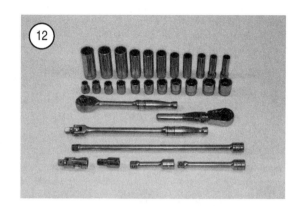

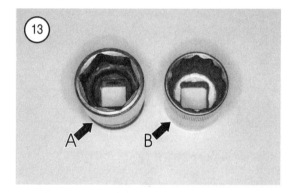

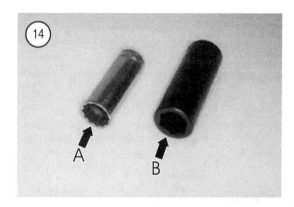

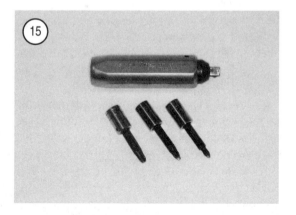

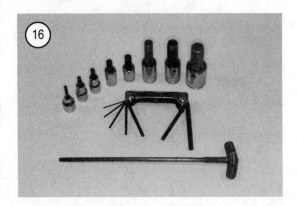

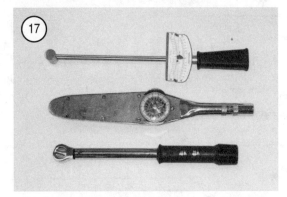

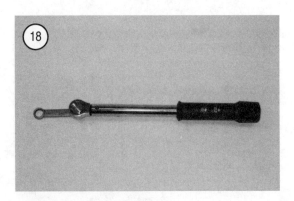

Impact Driver

An impact driver provides extra force for removing fasteners by converting the impact of a hammer into a turning motion. This makes it possible to remove stubborn fasteners without damaging them. Impact drivers and interchangeable bits (**Figure 15**) are available from most tool suppliers. When using a socket with an impact driver, make sure the socket is designed for impact use. Refer to *Socket Wrenches, Ratchets and Handles* in this section.

WARNING
Do not use hand sockets with air or impact tools as they may shatter and cause injury. Always wear eye protection when using impact or air tools.

Allen Wrenches

Allen or setscrew wrenches (**Figure 16**) are used on fasteners with hexagonal recesses in the fastener head. These wrenches are available in L-shaped bar, socket and T-handle types. A metric set is required when working on most motorcycles. Allen bolts are sometimes called socket bolts.

Torque Wrenches

A torque wrench is used with a socket, torque adapter or similar extension to tighten a fastener to a measured torque. Torque wrenches come in several drive sizes (1/4, 3/8, 1/2 and 3/4) and have various methods of reading the torque value. The drive size indicates the size of the square drive that accepts the socket, adapter or extension. Common methods of reading the torque value are the deflecting beam, the dial indicator and the audible click (**Figure 17**).

When choosing a torque wrench, consider the torque range, drive size and accuracy. The torque specifications in this manual indicate the range required.

A torque wrench is a precision tool that must be properly cared for to remain accurate. Store torque wrenches in cases or separate padded drawers within a toolbox. Follow the manufacturer's instructions for their care and calibration.

Torque Adapters

Torque adapters or extensions extend or reduce the reach of a torque wrench. The torque adapter shown in **Figure 18** is used to tighten a fastener that cannot be reached due to the size of the torque wrench head, drive and socket. If a torque adapter changes the effective lever length (**Figure 19**), the torque reading on the wrench will not equal the actual torque applied to the fastener. It is necessary to recalibrate the torque setting on the wrench to compensate for the change of lever length. When a torque adapter is used at a right angle to the drive

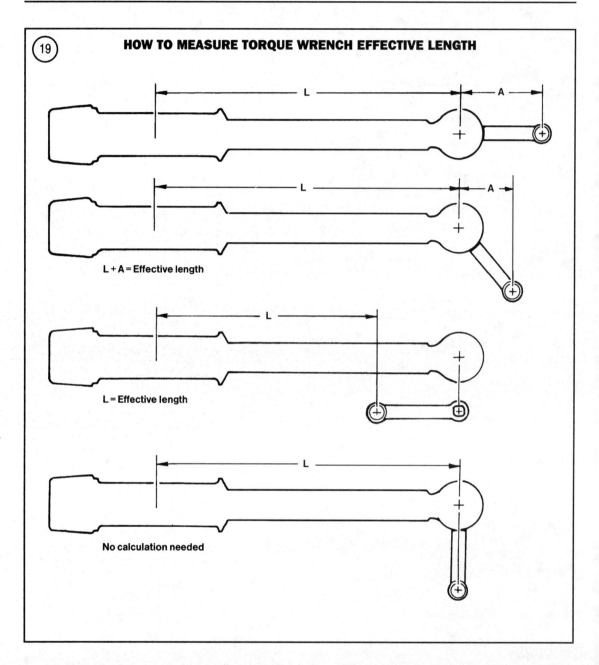

⑲ HOW TO MEASURE TORQUE WRENCH EFFECTIVE LENGTH

L + A = Effective length

L = Effective length

No calculation needed

head, calibration is not required since the effective length has not changed.

To recalculate a torque reading when using a torque adapter, use the following formula and refer to **Figure 19**.

$$TW = \frac{TA \times L}{L + A}$$

TW is the torque setting or dial reading on the wrench.

TA is the torque specification and the actual amount of torque that will be applied to the fastener.

A is the amount that the adapter increases (or in some cases reduces) the effective lever length as measured along the centerline of the torque wrench (**Figure 19**).

L is the lever length of the wrench as measured from the center of the drive to the center of the grip.

The effective length is the sum of L and A (**Figure 19**).

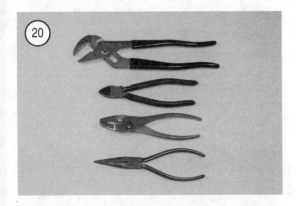

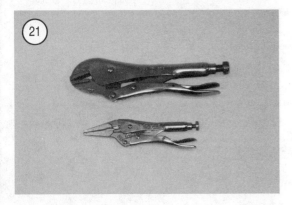

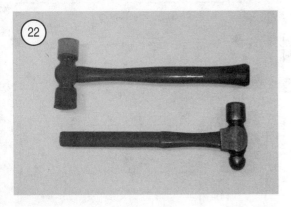

Example:
TA = 20 ft.-lb.
A = 3 in.
L = 14 in.
$$TW = \frac{20 \times 14}{14 + 3} = \frac{280}{17} = 16.5 \text{ ft. lb.}$$

In this example, the torque wrench would be set to the recalculated torque value (TW = 16.5 ft.-lb.). When using a beam-type wrench, tighten the fastener until the pointer aligns with 16.5 ft.-lb. In this example, although the torque wrench is pre-set to 16.5 ft.-lb., the actual torque is 20 ft.-lb.

Pliers

Pliers come in a wide range of types and sizes. Pliers are useful for holding, cutting, bending and crimping. Do not use them to turn fasteners. **Figure 20** and **Figure 21** show several types of useful pliers. Each design has a specialized function. Slip-joint pliers are general-purpose pliers used for gripping and bending. Diagonal cutting pliers are needed to cut wire and can be used to remove cotter pins. Needlenose pliers are used to hold or bend small objects. Locking pliers (**Figure 21**), sometimes called Vise-grips, are used to hold objects very tightly. They have many uses ranging from holding two parts together, to gripping the end of a broken stud. Use caution when using locking pliers, as the sharp jaws will damage the objects they hold.

Snap Ring Pliers

Snap ring pliers are specialized pliers with tips that fit into the ends of snap rings to remove and install them.

Snap ring pliers are available with a fixed action (either internal or external) or convertible (one tool works on both internal and external snap rings). They may have fixed tips or interchangeable ones of various sizes and angles. For general use, select a convertible type pliers with interchangeable tips.

> *WARNING*
> *Snap rings can slip and fly off when they are being removed and installed. Also, the snap ring pliers tips may break. Always wear eye protection when using snap ring pliers.*

Hammers

Various types of hammers (**Figure 22**) are available to fit a number of applications. A ball-peen hammer is used to strike another tool, such as a punch or chisel. Soft-faced hammers are required when a metal object must be struck without damaging it. *Never* use a metal-faced hammer on engine and suspension components, as damage will occur in most cases.

Always wear eye protection when using hammers. Make sure the hammer face is in good condition and the handle is not cracked. Select the correct hammer for the job and make sure to strike the object squarely. Do not use the handle or the side of the hammer to strike an object.

SPECIAL TOOLS

Many of the procedures in this manual require special tools. These are described in the appropriate chapter and are available from either the manufacturer or a tool supplier.

In many cases, an acceptable substitute may be found in an existing tool kit. Another alternative is to make the tool. Many schools with a machine shop curriculum welcome outside work that can be used as practical shop applications for students.

PRECISION MEASURING TOOLS

The ability to accurately measure components is essential to successfully rebuild an engine. Equipment is manufactured to close tolerances, and obtaining consistently accurate measurements is essential to determining which components require replacement or further service.

Each type of measuring instrument is designed to measure a dimension with a certain degree of accuracy and within a certain range. When selecting the measuring tool, make sure it is applicable to the task.

As with all tools, measuring tools provide the best results if cared for properly. Improper use can damage the tool and result in inaccurate results. If any measurement is questionable, verify the measurement using another tool. A standard gauge is usually provided with measuring tools to check accuracy and calibrate the tool if necessary.

Precision measurements can vary according to the experience of the person performing the procedure. Accurate results are only possible if the mechanic possesses a feel for using the tool. Heavy-handed use of measuring tools will produce less accurate results. Hold the tool gently by the fingertips so the point at which the tool contacts the object is easily felt. This feel for the equipment will produce more accurate measurements and reduce the risk of damaging the tool or component. Refer to the following sections for specific measuring tools.

Feeler Gauge

The feeler or thickness gauge (**Figure 23**) is used for measuring the distance between two surfaces.

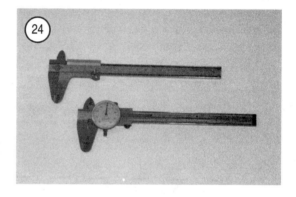

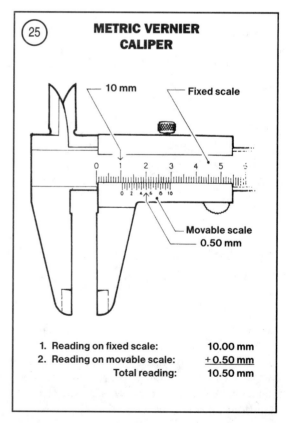

1. Reading on fixed scale:	10.00 mm
2. Reading on movable scale:	+ 0.50 mm
Total reading:	10.50 mm

1

DECIMAL PLACE VALUES*

0.100	Indicates 1/10 (one tenth of an inch or millimeter)
0.010	Indicates 1/100 (one one-hundreth of an inch or millimeter)
0.001	Indicates 1/1,000 (one one-thousandth of an inch or millimeter)

*This chart represents the values of figures placed to the right of the decimal point. Use it when reading decimals from one-tenth to one one-thousandth of an inch or millimeter. It is not a conversion chart (for example: 0.001 in. is not equal to 0.001 mm).

A feeler gauge set consists of an assortment of steel strips of graduated thickness. Each blade is marked with its thickness. Blades can be of various lengths and angles for different procedures.

A common use for a feeler gauge is to measure valve clearance. Wire (round) type gauges are used to measure spark plug gap.

Calipers

Calipers (**Figure 24**) are excellent tools for obtaining inside, outside and depth measurements. Although not as precise as a micrometer, they allow reasonable precision, typically to within 0.05 mm (0.001 in.). Most calipers have a range up to 150 mm (6 in.).

Calipers are available in dial, vernier or digital versions. Dial calipers have a dial readout that provides convenient reading. Vernier calipers have marked scales that must be compared to determine the measurement. The digital caliper uses an LCD to show the measurement.

Properly maintain the measuring surfaces of the caliper. There must not be any dirt or burrs between the tool and the object being measured. Never force the caliper closed around an object; close the caliper around the highest point so it can be removed with a slight drag. Some calipers require calibration. Always refer to the manufacturer's instructions when using a new or unfamiliar caliper.

To read a vernier caliper, refer to **Figure 25**. The fixed scale is marked in 1 mm increments. Ten individual lines on the fixed scale equal 1 cm. The moveable scale is marked in 0.05 mm (hundredth) increments. To obtain a reading, establish the first number by the location of the 0 line on the movable scale in relation to the first line to the left on the fixed scale. In this example, the number is 10 mm. To determine the next number, note which of the lines on the movable scale align with a mark on the fixed scale. A number of lines will seem close, but only one will align exactly. In this case, 0.50 mm is the reading to add to the first number. The result of adding 10 mm and 0.50 mm is a measurement of 10.50 mm.

Micrometers

A micrometer is an instrument designed for linear measurement using the decimal divisions of the inch or meter (**Figure 26**). While there are many types and styles of micrometers, most of the procedures in this manual call for an outside micrometer. The outside micrometer is used to measure the outside diameter of cylindrical forms and the thickness of materials.

A micrometer's size indicates the minimum and maximum size of a part that it can measure. The usual sizes (**Figure 27**) are 0-1 in. (0-25 mm), 1-2

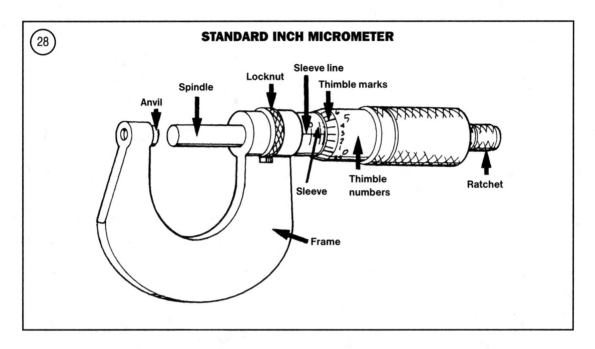

STANDARD INCH MICROMETER

Anvil
Spindle
Locknut
Sleeve line
Thimble marks
Sleeve
Thimble numbers
Ratchet
Frame

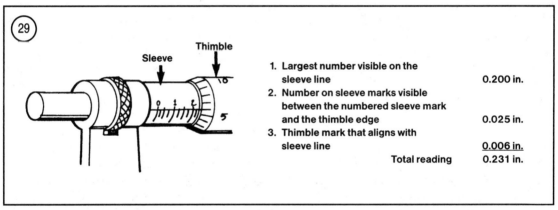

Sleeve
Thimble

1. Largest number visible on the
   sleeve line   0.200 in.
2. Number on sleeve marks visible
   between the numbered sleeve mark
   and the thimble edge   0.025 in.
3. Thimble mark that aligns with
   sleeve line   0.006 in.
                                Total reading   0.231 in.

in. (25-50 mm), 2-3 in. (50-75 mm) and 3-4 in. (75-100 mm).

Micrometers that cover a wider range of measurements are available. These use a large frame with interchangeable anvils of various lengths. This type of micrometer offers a cost savings; however, its overall size may make it less convenient.

Reading a Micrometer

When reading a micrometer, numbers are taken from different scales and added together. The following sections describe how to read the measurements of various types of outside micrometers.

For accurate results, properly maintain the measuring surfaces of the micrometer. There cannot be any dirt or burrs between the tool and the measured object. Never force the micrometer closed around an object. Close the micrometer around the highest point so it can be removed with a slight drag. **Figure 28** shows the markings and parts of a standard inch micrometer. Be familiar with these terms before using a micrometer in the follow sections.

Standard inch micrometer

The standard inch micrometer is accurate to one-thousandth of an inch or 0.001. The sleeve is marked in 0.025 in. increments. Every fourth sleeve

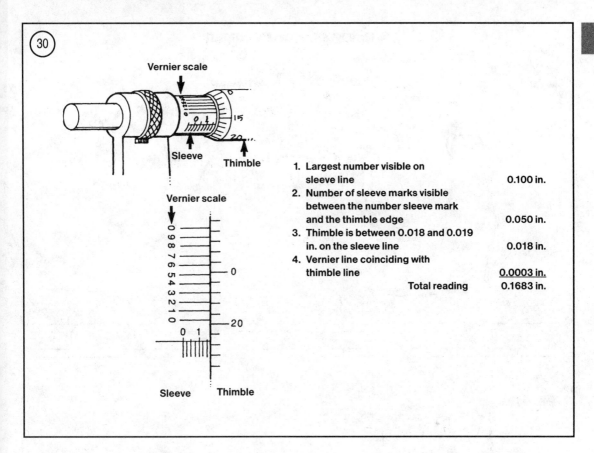

1. Largest number visible on
   sleeve line   0.100 in.
2. Number of sleeve marks visible
   between the number sleeve mark
   and the thimble edge   0.050 in.
3. Thimble is between 0.018 and 0.019
   in. on the sleeve line   0.018 in.
4. Vernier line coinciding with
   thimble line   0.0003 in.
                            Total reading   0.1683 in.

mark is numbered 1, 2, 3, 4, 5, 6, 7, 8, 9. These numbers indicate 0.100, 0.200, 0.300, and so on.

The tapered end of the thimble has twenty-five lines marked around it. Each mark equals 0.001 in. One complete turn of the thimble will align its zero mark with the first mark on the sleeve or 0.025 in.

To read a standard inch micrometer, perform the following steps and refer to **Figure 29**.

1. Read the sleeve and find the largest number visible. Each sleeve number equals 0.100 in.

2. Count the number of lines between the numbered sleeve mark and the edge of the thimble. Each sleeve mark equals 0.025 in.

3. Read the thimble mark that aligns with the sleeve line. Each thimble mark equals 0.001 in.

NOTE
If a thimble mark does not align exactly with the sleeve line, estimate the amount between the lines. For accurate readings in ten-thousandths of an inch (0.0001 in.), use a vernier inch micrometer.

4. Add the readings from Steps 1-3.

Vernier inch micrometer

A vernier inch micrometer is accurate to one ten-thousandth of an inch or 0.0001 in. It has the same marking as a standard inch micrometer with an additional vernier scale on the sleeve. The vernier scale consists of 11 lines marked 1-9 with a 0 on each end. These lines run parallel to the thimble lines and represent 0.0001 in. increments.

To read a vernier inch micrometer, perform the following steps and refer to **Figure 30**.

1. Read the micrometer in the same way as a standard micrometer. This is the initial reading.

2. If a thimble mark aligns exactly with the sleeve line, reading the vernier scale is not necessary. If they do not align, read the vernier scale in Step 3.

3. Determine which vernier scale mark aligns with one thimble mark. The vernier scale number is the amount in ten-thousandths of an inch to add to the initial reading from Step 1.

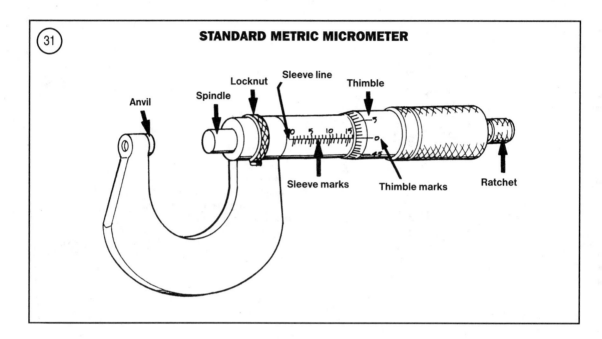

STANDARD METRIC MICROMETER

31

Anvil
Spindle
Locknut
Sleeve line
Thimble
Sleeve marks
Thimble marks
Ratchet

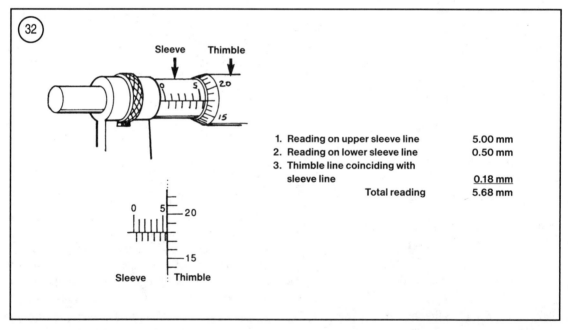

32

Sleeve
Thimble

1. Reading on upper sleeve line   5.00 mm
2. Reading on lower sleeve line   0.50 mm
3. Thimble line coinciding with
    sleeve line   0.18 mm
            Total reading   5.68 mm

Sleeve
Thimble

Metric micrometer

The standard metric micrometer (**Figure 31**) is accurate to one one-hundredth of a millimeter (0.01-mm). The sleeve line is graduated in millimeter and half millimeter increments. The marks on the upper half of the sleeve line equal 1.00 mm. Every fifth mark above the sleeve line is identified with a number. The number sequence depends on

the size of the micrometer. A 0-25 mm micrometer, for example, will have sleeve marks numbered 0 through 25 in 5 mm increments. This numbering sequence continues with larger micrometers. On all metric micrometers, each mark on the lower half of the sleeve equals 0.50 mm.

The tapered end of the thimble has fifty lines marked around it. Each mark equals 0.01 mm. One complete turn of the thimble aligns its 0 mark with

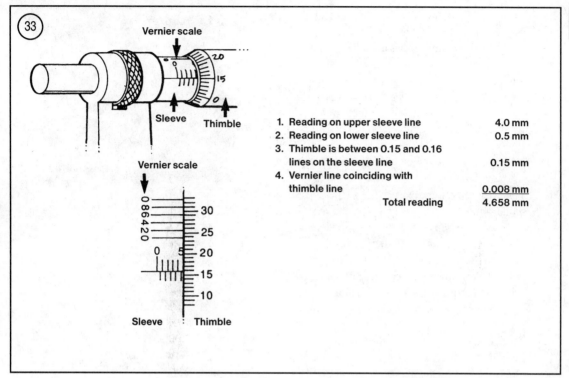

1. Reading on upper sleeve line   4.0 mm
2. Reading on lower sleeve line   0.5 mm
3. Thimble is between 0.15 and 0.16 lines on the sleeve line   0.15 mm
4. Vernier line coinciding with thimble line   <u>0.008 mm</u>

           Total reading   4.658 mm

the first line on the lower half of the sleeve line or 0.50 mm.

To read a metric micrometer, add the number of millimeters and half-millimeters on the sleeve line to the number of one one-hundredth millimeters on the thimble. Perform the following steps and refer to **Figure 32**.

1. Read the upper half of the sleeve line and count the number of lines visible. Each upper line equals 1 mm.

2. See if the half-millimeter line is visible on the lower sleeve line. If so, add 0.50 mm to the reading from Step 1.

3. Read the thimble mark that aligns with the sleeve line. Each thimble mark equals 0.01 mm.

> *NOTE*
> *If a thimble mark does not align exactly with the sleeve line, estimate the amount between the lines. For accurate readings in two-thousandths of a millimeter (0.002 mm), use a metric vernier micrometer.*

4. Add the readings from Steps 1-3.

Metric vernier micrometer

A metric vernier micrometer is accurate to two-thousandths of a millimeter (0.002-mm). It has the same markings as a standard metric micrometer with the addition of a vernier scale on the sleeve. The vernier scale consists of five lines marked 0, 2, 4, 6, and 8. These lines run parallel to the thimble lines and represent 0.002-mm increments.

To read a metric vernier micrometer, perform the following steps and refer to **Figure 33**.

1. Read the micrometer in the same way as a standard metric micrometer. This is the initial reading.

2. If a thimble mark aligns exactly with the sleeve line, reading the vernier scale is not necessary. If they do not align, read the vernier scale in Step 3.

3. Determine which vernier scale mark aligns exactly with one thimble mark. The vernier scale number is the amount in two-thousandths of a millimeter to add to the initial reading from Step 1.

Micrometer Adjustment

Before using a micrometer, check its adjustment as follows.

1. Clean the anvil and spindle faces.

2A. To check a 0-1 in. or 0-25 mm micrometer:
   a. Turn the thimble until the spindle contacts the anvil. If the micrometer has a ratchet stop, use it to ensure the proper amount of pressure is applied.
   b. If the adjustment is correct, the 0 mark on the thimble will align exactly with the 0 mark on the sleeve line. If the marks do not align, the micrometer is out of adjustment.
   c. Follow the manufacturer's instructions to adjust the micrometer.

2B. To check a micrometer larger than 1 in. or 25 mm, use the standard gauge supplied by the manufacturer. A standard gauge is a steel block, disc or rod that is machined to an exact size.
   a. Place the standard gauge between the spindle and anvil, and measure its outside diameter or length. If the micrometer has a ratchet stop, use it to ensure the proper amount of pressure is applied.
   b. If the adjustment is correct, the 0 mark on the thimble will align exactly with the 0 mark on the sleeve line. If the marks do not align, the micrometer is out of adjustment.
   c. Follow the manufacturer's instructions to adjust the micrometer.

Micrometer Care

Micrometers are precision instruments. They must be used and maintained with great care. Note the following:

1. Store micrometers in protective cases or separate padded drawers in a toolbox.

2. When in storage, make sure the spindle and anvil faces do not contact each other or an other object. If they do, temperature changes and corrosion may damage the contact faces.

3. Do not clean a micrometer with compressed air. Dirt forced into the tool will cause wear.

4. Lubricate micrometers with WD-40 to prevent corrosion.

Telescoping and Small Bore Gauges

Use telescoping gauges (**Figure 34**) and small hole gauges (**Figure 35**) to measure bores. Neither gauge has a scale for direct readings. An outside micrometer must be used to determine the reading.

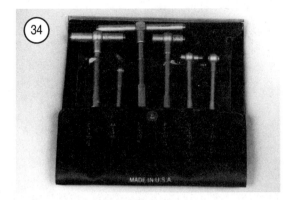

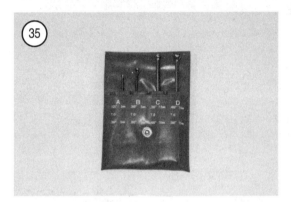

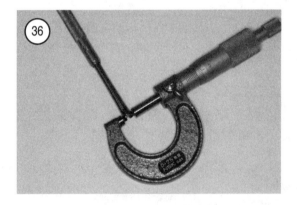

To use a telescoping gauge, select the correct size gauge for the bore. Compress the movable post and carefully insert the gauge into the bore. Carefully move the gauge in the bore to make sure it is centered. Tighten the knurled end of the gauge to hold the movable post in position. Remove the gauge and measure the length of the posts. Telescoping gauges are typically used to measure cylinder bores.

To use a small-bore gauge, select the correct size gauge for the bore. Carefully insert the gauge into the bore. Tighten the knurled end of the gauge to carefully expand the gauge fingers to the limit

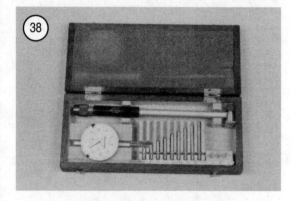

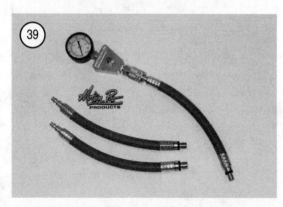

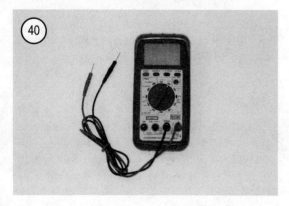

within the bore. Do not overtighten the gauge, as there is no built-in release. Excessive tightening can damage the bore surface and damage the tool. Remove the gauge and measure the outside dimension (**Figure 36**). Small hole gauges are typically used to measure valve guides.

Dial Indicator

A dial indicator (**Figure 37**) is a gauge with a dial face and needle used to measure variations in dimensions and movements. Measuring brake rotor runout is a typical use for a dial indicator.

Dial indicators are available in various ranges and graduations, and with three basic types of mounting bases: magnetic, clamp, or screw-in stud. When purchasing a dial indicator, select the magnetic stand type with a continuous dial.

Cylinder Bore Gauge

A cylinder bore gauge is similar to a dial indicator. The gauge set shown in **Figure 38** consists of a dial indicator, handle and different length adapters (anvils) to fit the gauge to various bore sizes. The bore gauge is used to measure bore size, taper and out-of-round. When using a bore gauge, follow the manufacturer's instructions.

Compression Gauge

A compression gauge (**Figure 39**) measures combustion chamber (cylinder) pressure, usually in psi or kg/cm^2. The gauge adapter is either inserted or screwed into the spark plug hole to obtain the reading. Disable the engine so it will not start and hold the throttle in the wide-open position when performing a compression test. An engine that does not have adequate compression cannot be properly tuned. See Chapter Three.

Multimeter

A multimeter (**Figure 40**) is an essential tool for electrical system diagnosis. The voltage function indicates the voltage applied or available to various electrical components. The ohmmeter function tests circuits for continuity, or lack of continuity, and measures the resistance of a circuit.

Some manufacturers' specifications for electrical components are based on results using a specific test meter. Results may vary if using a meter not recommend by the manufacturer is used. Such requirements are noted when applicable.

Ohmmeter (analog) calibration

Each time an analog ohmmeter is used or if the scale is changed, the ohmmeter must be calibrated.

Digital ohmmeters do not require calibration.

1. Make sure the meter battery is in good condition.
2. Make sure the meter probes are in good condition.
3. Touch the two probes together and observe the needle location on the ohms scale. The needle must align with the 0 mark to obtain accurate measurements.
4. If necessary, rotate the meter ohms adjust knob until the needle and 0 mark align.

ELECTRICAL SYSTEM FUNDAMENTALS

A thorough study of the many types of electrical systems used in today's motorcycles is beyond the scope of this manual. However, an understanding of electrical basics is necessary to perform simple diagnostic tests.

Voltage

Voltage is the electrical potential or pressure in an electrical circuit and is expressed in volts. The more pressure (voltage) in a circuit, the more work that can be performed.

Direct current (DC) voltage means the electricity flows in one direction. All circuits powered by a battery are DC circuits.

Alternating current (AC) means the electricity flows in one direction momentarily then switches to the opposite direction. Alternator output is an example of AC voltage. This voltage must be changed or rectified to direct current to operate in a battery powered system.

Measuring voltage

Unless otherwise specified, perform all voltage tests with the electrical connectors attached. When

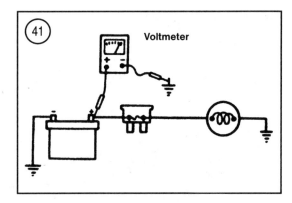

Voltmeter

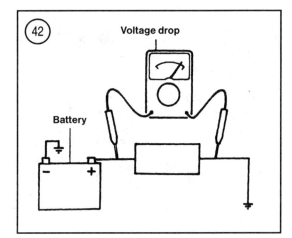

Voltage drop

Battery

measuring voltage, select the meter range that is one scale higher than the expected voltage of the circuit to prevent damage to the meter. To determine the actual voltage in a circuit, use a voltmeter. To simply check if voltage is present, use a test light.

NOTE
When using a test light, either lead can be attached to ground.

1. Attach the negative meter test lead to a good ground (bare metal). Make sure the ground is not insulated with a rubber gasket or grommet.

2. Attach the positive meter test lead to the point being checked for voltage (**Figure 41**).

3. Turn on the ignition switch. The test light should light or the meter should display a reading. The reading should be within one volt of battery voltage. If the voltage is less, there is a problem in the circuit.

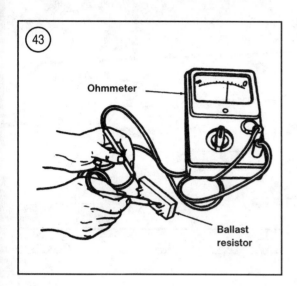

Ohmmeter

Ballast resistor

Voltage drop test

Resistance causes voltage to drop. This resistance can be measured in an active circuit by using a voltmeter to perform a voltage drop test. A voltage drop test compares the difference between the voltage available at the start of a circuit to the voltage at the end of the circuit while the circuit is operational. If the circuit has no resistance, there will be no voltage drop. The greater the resistance, the greater the voltage drop will be. A voltage drop of one volt or more indicates excessive resistance in the circuit.

1. Connect the positive meter test lead to the electrical source (where electricity is coming from).

2. Connect the negative meter test lead to the electrical load (where electricity is going). See **Figure 42**.

3. If necessary, activate the component(s) in the circuit.

4. A voltage reading of 1 volt or more indicates excessive resistance in the circuit. A reading equal to battery voltage indicates an open circuit.

Resistance

Resistance is the opposition to the flow of electricity within a circuit or component and is measured in ohms. Resistance causes a reduction in available current and voltage.

Resistance is measured in a inactive circuit with an ohmmeter. The ohmmeter sends a small amount of current into the circuit and measures how difficult it is to push the current through the circuit.

An ohmmeter, although useful, is not always a good indicator of a circuit's actual ability under operating conditions. This is due to the low voltage (6-9 volts) that the meter uses to test the circuit. The voltage in an ignition coil secondary winding can be several thousand volts. Such high voltage can cause the coil to malfunction, even though it tests acceptable during a resistance test.

Resistance generally increases with temperature. Perform all testing with the component or circuit at room temperature. Resistance tests performed at high temperatures may indicate high resistance readings and result in the unnecessary replacement of a component.

Measuring resistance and continuity testing

CAUTION
*Only use an ohmmeter on a circuit that has no voltage present. The meter will be damaged if it is connected to a live circuit. An analog meter must be calibrated each time it is used or the scale is changed. See **Multimeter** in this chapter.*

A continuity test can determine if the circuit is complete. This type of test is performed with an ohmmeter or a self-powered test lamp.

1. Disconnect the negative battery cable.

2. Attach one test lead (ohmmeter or test light) to one end of the component or circuit.

3. Attach the other test lead to the opposite end of the component or circuit (**Figure 43**).

4. A self-powered test light will come on if the circuit has continuity or is complete. An ohmmeter will indicate either low or no resistance if the circuit has continuity. An open circuit is indicated if the meter displays infinite resistance.

Amperage

Amperage is the unit of measurement for the amount of current within a circuit. Current is the actual flow of electricity. The higher the current, the more work that can be performed up to a given point. If the current flow exceeds the circuit or component capacity, the system will be damaged.

Measuring amps

An ammeter measures the current flow or amps of a circuit (**Figure 44**). Amperage measurement requires that the circuit be disconnected and the ammeter be connected in series to the circuit. Always use an ammeter that can read higher than the anticipated current flow to prevent damage to the meter. Connect the red test lead to the electrical source and the black test lead to the electrical load.

BASIC SERVICE METHODS

Most of the procedures in this manual are straightforward and can be performed by anyone reasonably competent with tools. However, consider personal capabilities carefully before attempting any operation involving major disassembly of the engine.

1. Front, in this manual, refers to the front of the motorcycle. The front of any component is the end closest to the front of the motorcycle. The left and right sides refer to the position of the parts as viewed by the rider sitting on the seat facing forward.

2. Whenever servicing an engine or suspension component, secure the motorcycle in a safe manner.

3. Tag all similar parts for location and mark all mating parts for position. Record the number and thickness of shims as they are removed. Identify parts by placing them in sealed and labeled plastic sandwich bags.

4. Tag disconnected wires and connectors with masking tape and a marking pen. Do not rely on memory alone.

5. Protect finished surfaces from physical damage or corrosion. Keep gasoline and other chemicals off painted surfaces.

6. Use penetrating oil on frozen or tight bolts. Avoid using heat where possible. Heat can warp, melt or affect the temper of parts. Heat also damages the finish of paint and plastics.

7. When a part is a press fit or requires a special tool for removal, the information or type of tool is identified in the text. Otherwise, if a part is difficult to remove or install, determine the cause before proceeding.

8. To prevent objects or debris from falling into the engine, cover all openings.

9. Read each procedure thoroughly and compare the illustrations to the actual components before

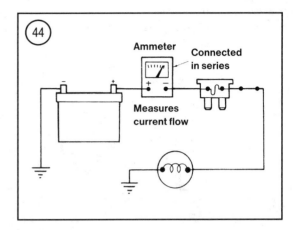

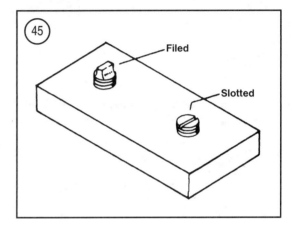

starting the procedure. Perform the procedure in sequence.

10. Recommendations are occasionally made to refer service to a dealership or specialist. In these cases, the work can be performed more economically by the specialist than by a home mechanic.

11. The term *replace* means to discard a defective part and replace it with a new part. *Overhaul* means to remove, disassemble, inspect, measure, repair and/or replace parts as required to recondition an assembly.

12. Some operations require the use of a hydraulic press. If a press is not available, have these operations performed by a shop equipped with the necessary equipment. Do not use makeshift equipment that may damage the motorcycle.

13. Repairs are much faster and easier if the motorcycle is clean before starting work. Degrease the motorcycle with a commercial degreaser; follow the directions on the container for the best results.

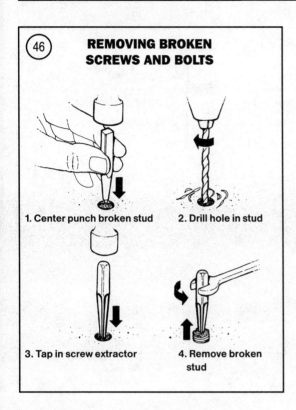

REMOVING BROKEN SCREWS AND BOLTS

46

1. Center punch broken stud

2. Drill hole in stud

3. Tap in screw extractor

4. Remove broken stud

Clean all parts with cleaning solvent as they are removed.

> *CAUTION*
> *Do not direct high-pressure water at steering bearings, carburetor hoses, wheel bearings, and suspension and electrical components. The water will force the grease out of the bearings and possibly damage the seals.*

14. If special tools are required, have them available before starting the procedure. When special tools are required, they will be described at the beginning of the procedure.

15. Make diagrams of similar-appearing parts. For instance, crankcase bolts are often not the same lengths. Do not rely on memory alone. It is possible that carefully laid out parts will become disturbed, making it difficult to reassemble the components correctly without a diagram.

16. Make sure all shims and washers are reinstalled in the same location and position.

17. Whenever rotating parts contact a stationary part, look for a shim or washer.

18. Use new gaskets if there is any doubt about the condition of old ones.

19. If self-locking fasteners are used, replace them with new ones. Do not install standard fasteners in place of self-locking ones.

20. Use grease to hold small parts in place if they tend to fall out during assembly. Do not apply grease to electrical or brake components.

Removing Frozen Fasteners

If a fastener cannot be removed, several methods may be used to loosen it. First, apply penetrating oil such as Liquid Wrench or WD-40. Apply it liberally and let it penetrate for 10-15 minutes. Rap the fastener several times with a small hammer. Do not hit it hard enough to cause damage. Reapply the penetrating oil if necessary.

For frozen screws, apply penetrating oil as described, then insert a screwdriver in the slot and rap the top of the screwdriver with a hammer. This loosens the rust so the screw can be removed in the normal way. If the screw head is too damaged to use this method, grip the head with locking pliers and twist the screw out.

Avoid applying heat unless specifically instructed, as it may melt, warp or remove the temper from parts.

Removing Broken Fasteners

If the head breaks off a screw or bolt, several methods are available for removing the remaining portion. If a large portion of the remainder projects out, try gripping it with locking pliers. If the projecting portion is too small, file it to fit a wrench or cut a slot in it to fit a screwdriver (**Figure 45**).

If the head breaks off flush, use a screw extractor. To do this, centerpunch the exact center of the remaining portion of the screw or bolt. Drill a small hole in the screw and tap the extractor into the hole. Back the screw out with a wrench on the extractor (**Figure 46**).

Repairing Damaged Threads

Occasionally, threads are stripped through carelessness or impact damage. Often the threads can be repaired by running a tap (for internal threads on nuts) or die (for external threads on bolts) through the threads (**Figure 47**). To clean or repair spark plug threads, use a spark plug tap.

If an internal thread is damaged, it may be necessary to install a Helicoil or some other type of thread

1

insert. Follow the manufacturer's instructions when installing their insert.

Stud Removal/Installation

A stud removal tool is available from most tool suppliers. This tool makes the removal and installation of studs easier. If one is not available, thread two nuts onto the stud and tighten them against each other. Remove the stud by turning the lower nut (**Figure 48**).

1. Measure the height of the stud above the surface.
2. Thread the stud removal tool onto the stud and tighten it, or thread two nuts onto the stud.
3. Remove the stud by turning the stud remover or the lower nut.
4. Remove any threadlocking compound from the threaded hole. Clean the threads with an aerosol parts cleaner.
5. Install the stud removal tool onto the new stud or thread two nuts onto the stud.
6. Apply threadlocking compound to the threads of the stud.
7. Install the stud and tighten with the stud removal tool or the top nut.
8. Install the stud to the height noted in Step 1 or its torque specification.
9. Remove the stud removal tool or the two nuts.

Removing Hoses

When removing stubborn hoses, do not exert excessive force on the hose or fitting. Remove the hose clamp and carefully insert a small screwdriver or pick tool between the fitting and hose. Apply a spray lubricant under the hose and carefully twist the hose off the fitting. Clean the fitting of any corrosion or rubber hose material with a wire brush. Clean the inside of the hose thoroughly. Do not use any lubricant when installing the hose (new or old). The lubricant may allow the hose to come off the fitting, even with the clamp secure.

Bearings

Bearings are used in the engine and transmission assembly to reduce power loss, heat and noise caused by friction. Because bearings are precision parts, they must be maintained by proper lubrication and maintenance. If a bearing is damaged, re-

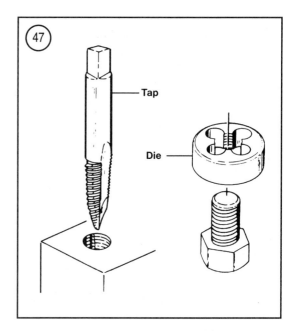

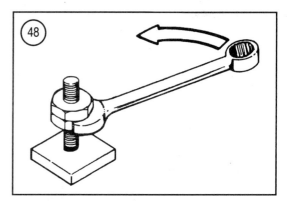

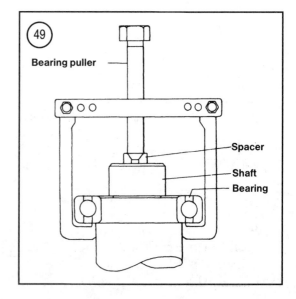

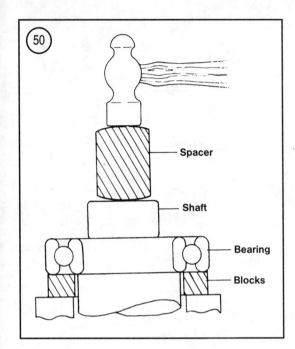

50

Spacer

Shaft

Bearing

Blocks

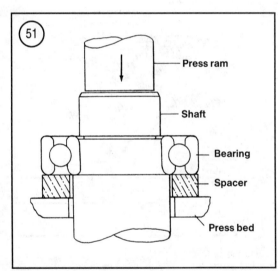

51

Press ram

Shaft

Bearing

Spacer

Press bed

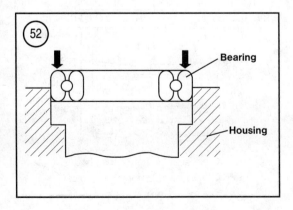

52

Bearing

Housing

place it immediately. When installing a new bearing, take care to prevent damaging it. Bearing replacement procedures are included in the individual chapters where applicable; however, use the following sections as a guideline.

NOTE
Unless otherwise specified, install bearings with the manufacturer's mark or number facing outward.

Removal

While bearings are normally removed only when damaged, there may be times when it is necessary to remove a bearing that is in good condition. However, improper bearing removal will damage the bearing and maybe the shaft or case half. Note the following when removing bearings.

1. When using a puller to remove a bearing from a shaft, take care that the shaft is not damaged. Always place a piece of metal between the end of the shaft and the puller screw. In addition, place the puller arms next to the inner bearing race. See **Figure 49**.

2. When using a hammer to remove a bearing from a shaft, do not strike the hammer directly against the shaft. Instead, use a brass or aluminum rod between the hammer and shaft (**Figure 50**) and make sure to support both bearing races with wooden blocks as shown.

3. The ideal method of bearing removal is with a hydraulic press. Note the following when using a press:

    a. Always support the inner and outer bearing races with a suitable size wooden or aluminum ring (**Figure 51**). If only the outer race is supported, pressure applied against the balls and/or the inner race will damage them.

    b. Always make sure the press arm (**Figure 51**) aligns with the center of the shaft. If the arm is not centered, it may damage the bearing and/or shaft.

    c. The moment the shaft is free of the bearing, it will drop to the floor. Secure or hold the shaft to prevent it from falling.

Installation

1. When installing a bearing in a housing, apply pressure to the *outer* bearing race (**Figure 52**). When installing a bearing on a shaft, apply pressure to the *inner* bearing race (**Figure 53**).

2. To install a bearing as described in Step 1, some type of driver is required. Never strike the bearing directly with a hammer or the bearing will be damaged. When installing a bearing, use a piece of pipe or a driver with a diameter that matches the bearing race. **Figure 54** shows the correct way to use a driver and hammer to install a bearing.

3. Step 1 describes how to install a bearing in a case half or over a shaft. However, to install a bearing over a shaft and into a housing at the same time, a tight fit will be required for both outer and inner bearing races. In this situation, install a spacer underneath the driver tool so that pressure is applied evenly across both races (**Figure 55**). If the outer race is not supported as shown, the balls will push against the outer bearing race and damage it.

Interference fit

1. Follow this procedure to install a bearing over a shaft. When a tight fit is required, the bearing inside diameter will be smaller than the shaft. In this case, driving the bearing on the shaft using normal methods may cause bearing damage. Instead, heat the bearing before installation. Note the following:

    a. Secure the shaft so it is ready for bearing installation.

    b. Clean all residues from the bearing surface of the shaft. Remove burrs with a file or sandpaper.

    c. Fill a suitable pot or beaker with clean mineral oil. Place a thermometer rated above 120° C (248° F) in the oil. Support the thermometer so that it does not rest on the bottom or side of the pot.

    d. Remove the bearing from its wrapper and secure it with a piece of heavy wire bent to hold it in the pot. Hang the bearing in the pot so it does not touch the bottom or sides of the pot.

    e. Turn the heat on and monitor the thermometer. When the oil temperature rises to approximately 120° C (248° F), remove the bearing from the pot and quickly install it. If necessary, place a socket on the inner bearing race and tap the bearing into place. As the bearing chills, it will tighten on the shaft, so installation must be done quickly. Make sure the bearing is installed completely.

2. Follow this step to install a bearing in a housing. Bearings are generally installed in a housing with a slight interference fit. Driving the bearing into the

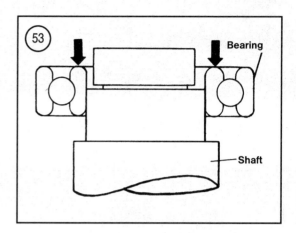

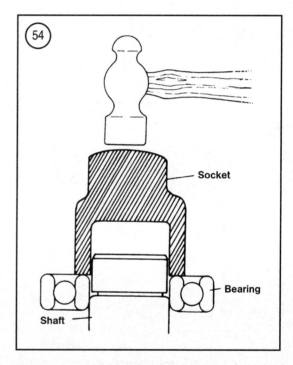

housing using normal methods may damage the housing or cause bearing damage. Instead, heat the housing before the bearing is installed. Note the following:

CAUTION
Before heating the housing in this procedure, wash the housing thoroughly with detergent and water. Rinse and rewash the cases as required to remove all traces of oil and other chemical deposits.

    a. Heat the housing to approximately 212° F (100° C) in an oven or on a hot plate. An easy way to check that it is the proper temperature is to place

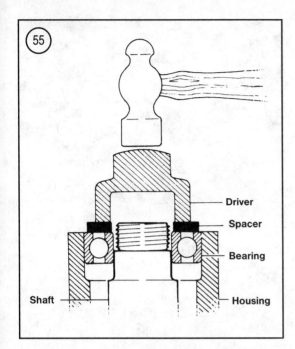

Driver
Spacer
Bearing
Shaft
Housing

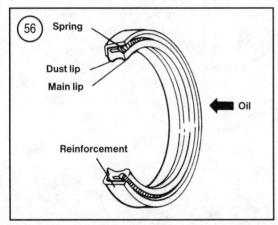

Spring
Dust lip
Main lip
Oil
Reinforcement

kitchen potholder, heavy gloves or heavy shop cloth. It is hot!

NOTE
Remove and install the bearings with a suitable size socket and extension.

c. Hold the housing with the bearing side down and tap the bearing out. Repeat for all bearings in the housing.

d. Before heating the bearing housing, place the new bearing in a freezer if possible. Chilling a bearing slightly reduces its outside diameter while the heated bearing housing assembly is slightly larger due to heat expansion. This will make bearing installation easier.

NOTE
Install bearings with the manufacturer's mark or number facing outward.

e. While the housing is still hot, install the new bearing(s) into the housing. Install the bearings by hand, if possible. If necessary, lightly tap the bearing(s) into the housing with a socket placed on the outer bearing race (**Figure 55**). Do not install new bearings by driving on the inner-bearing race. Install the bearing(s) until it seats completely.

tiny drops of water on the housing; if they sizzle and evaporate immediately, the temperature is correct. Heat only one housing at a time.

CAUTION
Do not heat the housing with a propane or acetylene torch. Never bring a flame into contact with the bearing or housing. The direct heat will destroy the case hardening of the bearing and will likely warp the housing.

Seal Replacement

Seals (**Figure 56**) are used to contain oil, water, grease or combustion gasses in a housing or shaft. Improper removal of a seal can damage the housing or shaft. Improper installation of the seal can damage the seal. Note the following:

b. Remove the housing from the oven or hot plate, and hold onto the housing with a

1. Prying is generally the easiest and most effective method of removing a seal from a housing. How-

ever, always place a rag underneath the pry tool (**Figure 57**) to prevent damage to the housing.

2. Pack waterproof grease in the seal lips before the seal is installed.

3. In most cases, install seals with the manufacturer's numbers or marks face out.

4. Install seals with a socket placed on the outside of the seal as shown in **Figure 58**. Drive the seal squarely into the housing. Never install a seal by hitting against the top of the seal with a hammer.

STORAGE

Several months of non-use can cause a general deterioration of the motorcycle. This is especially true in areas of extreme temperature variations. This deterioration can be minimized with careful preparation for storage. A properly stored motorcycle will be much easier to return to service.

Storage Area Selection

When selecting a storage area, consider the following:

1. The storage area must be dry. A heated area is best, but not necessary. It should be insulated to minimize extreme temperature variations.

2. If the building has large window areas, mask them to keep sunlight off the motorcycle.

3. Avoid buildings in industrial areas where corrosive emissions may be present. Avoid areas close to saltwater.

4. Consider the area's risk of fire, theft or vandalism. Check with an insurer regarding motorcycle coverage while in storage.

Preparing the Motorcycle for Storage

The amount of preparation a motorcycle should undergo before storage depends on the expected length of non-use, storage area conditions and personal preference. Consider the following list the minimum requirement:

1. Wash the motorcycle thoroughly. Make sure all dirt, mud and road debris are removed.

2. Start the engine and allow it to reach operating temperature. Drain the engine oil and transmission oil, regardless of the riding time since the last service. Fill the engine and transmission with the recommended type of oil.

3. Drain all fuel from the fuel tank, run the engine until all the fuel is consumed from the lines and carburetor.

4. Remove the spark plugs and pour a teaspoon of engine oil into the cylinders. Place a rag over the openings and slowly turn the engine over to distribute the oil. Reinstall the spark plugs.

5. Remove the battery. Store the battery in a cool and dry location.

6. Cover the exhaust and intake openings.

7. Reduce the normal tire pressure by 20%.

8. Apply a protective substance to the plastic and rubber components, including the tires. Make sure to follow the manufacturer's instructions for each type of product being used.

9. Place the motorcycle on a stand or wooden blocks, so the wheels are off the ground. If this is not possible, place a piece of plywood between the tires and the ground. Inflate the tires to the recommended pressure if the motorcycle can not be elevated.

10. Cover the motorcycle with old bed sheets or something similar. Do not cover it with plastic material that will trap moisture.

Returning the Motorcycle to Service

The amount of service required when returning a motorcycle to service after storage depends on the length of non-use and storage conditions. In addition to performing the reverse of the above procedure, make sure the brakes, clutch, throttle and engine stop switch work properly before operating the motorcycle. Refer to Chapter Three and evaluate the service intervals to determine which areas require service.

Table 1 VEHICLE IDENTIFICATION NUMBER (VIN)[1,2]

Characters 1-3	Characters 4-8	Character 9	Character 10	Character 11	Characters 12-17
XXX	XXXXX	X	X	X	XXXXX

Characters 1-3: World Manufacturing Identifier (WMI). These characters represent the manufacturer and the type of vehicle.
Characters 4-8: Vehicle attributes. These characters represent make, model and engine type.
Character 9: Check digit. This digit verifies the accuracy of the VIN transcription. The digit is mathematically determined using values assigned to the other characters in the VIN.
Character 10: Model year. The year is assigned to the model by the manufacturer and does not represent the year of manufacture. The letters I, O, Q, U, Z and the numeral 0 are not used in the model year code.
The letter X= 1999, Y=2000.
The number 1= 2001, 2= 2002, and so on until 2010.
The letter A= 2010, B=2011, and so on.
Character 11: Manufacturing plant location.
Characters 12-17: Sequential production number, as assigned by the manufacturer.

1. The VIN consists of 17 characters, with character groups representing the manufacturer and unique information about the motorcycle model.
2. VIN standards are periodically revised by the National Highway Traffic Safety Administration (NHTSA). Refer to their documentation for additional information.

Table 2 VEHICLE DIMENSIONS AND WEIGHT

Dry weight	
SV650	165 kg (363 lb.)
SV650S	169 kg (372 lb.)
Ground clearance	
SV650 and SV650S	140 mm (5.5 in.)
Overall length	
SV650	2070 mm (81.5 in.)
SV650S	2045 mm (80.5 in.)
Overall width	
SV650	750 mm (29.5 in.)
SV650S	740 mm (29.1 in.)
Overall height	
SV650	1060 mm (41.7 in.)
SV650S	1130 mm (44.5 in.)
Seat height	
SV650 and SV650S	805 mm (31.7 in.)
Wheelbase	
SV650 and SV650S	1430 mm (56.3 in.)

Table 3 METRIC TAP AND DRILL SIZES

Metric size	Drill equivalent	Decimal fraction	Nearest fraction
3 0.50	No. 39	0.0995	3/32
3 0.60	3/32	0.0937	3/32
4 0.70	No. 30	0.1285	1/8
4 0.75	1/8	0.125	1/8
5 0.80	No. 19	0.166	11/64
5 0.90	No. 20	0.161	5/32
6 1.00	No. 9	0.196	13/64
7 1.00	16/64	0.234	15/64
		(continued)	

Table 3 METRIC TAP AND DRILL SIZES (continued)

Metric size	Drill equivalent	Decimal fraction	Nearest fraction
8 1.00	J	0.277	9/32
8 1.25	17/64	0.265	17/64
9 1.00	5/16	0.3125	5/16
9 1.25	5/16	0.3125	5/16
10 1.25	11/32	0.3437	11/32
10 1.50	R	0.339	11/32
11 1.50	3/8	0.375	3/8
12 1.50	13/32	0.406	13/32
12 1.75	13/32	0.406	13/32

Table 4 DECIMAL AND METRIC EQUIVALENTS

Fractions	Decimal in.	Metric mm	Fractions	Decimal in.	Metric mm
1/64	0.015625	0.39688	33/64	0.515625	13.09687
1/32	0.03125	0.79375	17/32	0.53125	13.49375
3/64	0.046875	1.19062	35/64	0.546875	13.89062
1/16	0.0625	1.58750	9/16	0.5625	14.28750
5/64	0.078125	1.98437	37/64	0.578125	14.68437
3/32	0.09375	2.38125	19/32	0.59375	15.08125
7/64	0.109375	2.77812	39/64	0.609375	15.47812
1/8	0.125	3.1750	5/8	0.625	15.87500
9/64	0.140625	3.57187	41/64	0.640625	16.27187
5/32	0.15625	3.96875	21/32	0.65625	16.66875
11/64	0.171875	4.36562	43/64	0.671875	17.06562
3/16	0.1875	4.76250	11/16	0.6875	17.46250
13/64	0.203125	5.15937	45/64	0.703125	17.85937
7/32	0.21875	5.55625	23/32	0.71875	18.25625
15/64	0.234375	5.95312	47/64	0.734375	18.65312
1/4	0.250	6.35000	3/4	0.750	19.05000
17/64	0.265625	6.74687	49/64	0.765625	19.44687
9/32	0.28125	7.14375	25/32	0.78125	19.84375
19/64	0.296875	7.54062	51/64	0.796875	20.24062
5/16	0.3125	7.93750	13/16	0.8125	20.63750
21/64	0.328125	8.33437	53/64	0.828125	21.03437
11/32	0.34375	8.73125	27/32	0.84375	21.43125
23/64	0.359375	9.12812	55/64	0.859375	22.82812
3/8	0.375	9.52500	7/8	0.875	22.22500
25/64	0.390625	9.92187	57/64	0.890625	22.62187
13/32	0.40625	10.31875	29/32	0.90625	23.01875
27/64	0.421875	10.71562	59/64	0.921875	23.41562
7/16	0.4375	11.11250	15/16	0.9375	23.81250
29/64	0.453125	11.50937	61/64	0.953125	24.20937
15/32	0.46875	11.90625	31/32	0.96875	24.60625
31/64	0.484375	12.30312	63/64	0.984375	25.00312
1/2	0.500	12.70000	1	1.00	25.40000

Table 5 CONVERSION FORMULAS

Multiply	By:	To get the equivalent of:
Length		
Inches	25.4	Millimeter
Inches	2.54	Centimeter
Miles	1.609	Kilometer
Millimeter	0.03937	Inches

(continued)

Table 5 CONVERSION FORMULAS (continued)

Multiply	By:	To get the equivalent of:
Length (continued)		
Feet	0.3048	Meter
Centimeter	0.3937	Inches
Kilometer	0.6214	Mile
Meter	3.281	Mile
Fluid volume		
U.S. quarts	0.9463	Liters
U.S. gallons	3.785	Liters
U.S. ounces	29.573529	Milliliters
Imperial gallons	4.54609	Liters
Imperial quarts	1.1365	Liters
Liters	0.2641721	U.S. gallons
Liters	1.0566882	U.S. quarts
Liters	33.814023	U.S. ounces
Liters	0.22	Imperial gallons
Liters	0.8799	Imperial quarts
Milliliters	0.033814	U.S. ounces
Milliliters	1.0	Cubic centimeters
Milliliters	0.001	Liters
Torque		
Foot-pounds	1.3558	Newton-meters
Foot-pounds	0.138255	Meters-kilograms
Inch-pounds	0.11299	Newton-meters
Newton-meters	0.7375622	Foot-pounds
Newton-meters	8.8507	Inch-pounds
Meters-kilograms	7.2330139	Foot-pounds
Volume		
Cubic inches	16.387064	Cubic centimeters
Cubic centimeters	0.0610237	Cubic inches
Temperature		
Fahrenheit	(F -32°) 0.556	Centigrade
Centigrade	(C 1.8) + 32	Fahrenheit
Weight		
Ounces	28.3495	Grams
Pounds	0.4535924	Kilograms
Grams	0.035274	Ounces
Kilograms	2.2046224	Pounds
Pressure		
Pounds per square inch	0.070307	Kilograms per square centimeter
Kilograms per square centimeter	14.223343	Pounds per square inch
Kilopascals	0.1450	Pounds per square inch
Pounds per square inch	6.895	Kilopascals
Speed		
Miles per hour	1.609344	Kilometers per hour
Kilometers per hour	0.6213712	Miles per hour

Table 6 TECHNICAL ABBREVIATIONS

ABDC	After bottom dead center
ATDC	After top dead center
BBDC	Before bottom dead center
BDC	Bottom dead center
BTDC	Before top dead center
C	Celsius (centigrade)

(continued)

Table 6 TECHNICAL ABBREVIATIONS (continued)

cc	Cubic centimeters
cid	Cubic inch displacement
CDI	Capacitor discharge ignition
CKP	Crankshaft position sensor
CMP	Camshaft position sensor
cu. in.	Cubic inches
DOHC	Dual overhead cam
F	Fahrenheit
ft.	Feet
ft.-lb.	Foot-pounds
gal.	Gallons
H/A	High altitude
hp	Horsepower
in.	Inches
in.-lb.	Inch-pounds
I.D.	Inside diameter
kg	Kilograms
kgm	Kilogram meters
km	Kilometer
kPa	Kilopascals
L	Liter
m	Meter
MAG	Magneto
MAP	Manifold absolute pressure
ml	Milliliter
mm	Millimeter
N·m	Newton-meters
O.D.	Outside diameter
OE	Original equipment
oz.	Ounces
psi	Pounds per square inch
PTO	Power take off
pt.	Pint
qt.	Quart
rpm	Revolutions per minute
TSSM	Turn signal/security module
TSM	Turn signal module

Table 7 GENERAL TORQUE SPECIFICATIONS

	N·m	in.-lb.	ft.-lb.
5 mm bolt and nut	5	44	–
6 mm bolt and nut	10	88	–
8 mm bolt and nut	22	–	16
10 mm bolt and nut	35	–	26
12 mm bolt and nut	55	–	41
5 mm screw	4	35	–
6 mm screw	9	80	–
6 mm flange bolt (8 mm head)	9	80	–
6 mm flange bolt (10 mm head) and nut	12	106	–
8 mm flange bolt and nut	27	–	20
10 mm flange bolt and nut	40	–	29

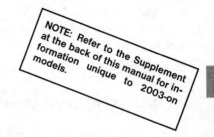

NOTE: Refer to the Supplement at the back of this manual for information unique to 2003-on models.

2

CHAPTER TWO

TROUBLESHOOTING

The troubleshooting procedures described in this chapter provide typical symptoms and logical methods for isolating the cause(s). There may be several ways to solve a problem, but only a systematic approach will be successful in avoiding wasted time and possibly unnecessary parts replacement.

Gather as much information as possible to aid in diagnosis. Never assume anything and do not overlook the obvious. Make sure there is fuel in the tank. Make sure the fuel shutoff valve is in the ON position. If the motorcycle has been sitting for any length of time, fuel deposits may have gummed up the carburetor jets. Gasoline loses its volatility after standing for long periods and water condensation may have diluted it. Drain the old gas and start with a new tank full. Make sure the engine stop switch is in the RUN position. Make sure the spark plug wires are attached to the spark plugs.

If a quick check does not reveal the problem, proceed with one of the troubleshooting procedures described in this chapter. After defining the symptoms, follow the procedure that most closely relates to the condition(s).

In most cases, expensive and complicated test equipment is not needed to determine whether repairs can be performed at home. A few simple checks could prevent an unnecessary repair charge and lost time while the motorcycle is at a dealership's service department. On the other hand, be realistic and do not attempt repairs beyond personal capabilities. Many service departments will not take work that involves the reassembly of damaged or abused equipment. If they do, expect the cost to be high.

If the motorcycle does require the attention of a professional, describe the symptoms, conditions and previous repair attempts accurately and fully. The more information a technician has available, the easier it will be to diagnose.

By following the lubrication and maintenance schedule described in Chapter Three, the need for troubleshooting can be reduced by eliminating potential problems before they occur. However, even with the best of care the motorcycle may require troubleshooting.

OPERATING REQUIREMENTS

An engine needs three basic elements (**Figure 1**) to run properly: correct air/fuel mixture, compression and a spark at the correct time. If any one element is missing, the engine will not run. Four-stroke engine operating principles are described in Chapter Four.

STARTING THE ENGINE

The ignition and starting circuits use a switch interlock system. The position of the sidestand, clutch lever and gear selector affect starting. The engine cannot turn over if the transmission is in gear and the sidestand is down. If the transmission is in gear and the sidestand is up, the clutch must be fully disengaged. To start the engine, refer to the starting conditions that best meet the conditions.

> *CAUTION*
> *The oil pressure warning light should go out a few seconds after the engine starts. If not, stop the engine immediately. Check the oil level as described in Chapter Three. If the oil level is correct, determine whether insufficient oil pressure (Chapter Three) or an electrical problem (Chapter Nine) is the cause.*

Starting a Cold Engine

1. Shift the transmission into NEUTRAL.
2. Set the engine stop switch (A, **Figure 2**) to RUN.
3. Turn the ignition switch ON.
4. Make sure the neutral indicator and oil pressure warning lights are illuminated.
5. Pull the choke lever (A, **Figure 3**) all the way back to the ON position.
6. Pull the clutch lever (B, **Figure 3**) all the way to the handlebar grip and disengage the clutch.
7. With the throttle completely closed, push the START button (B, **Figure 2**).
8. When the engine starts, work the throttle slightly to keep it running.

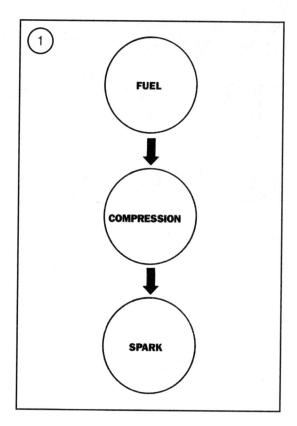

9. Idle the engine for approximately 30-60 seconds or until the throttle responds cleanly, and then push the choke lever all the way forward to the OFF position.

Starting a Warm or Hot Engine

1. Shift the transmission into NEUTRAL.
2. Set the engine stop switch (A, **Figure 2**) to RUN.
3. Turn the ignition switch ON.
4. Make sure the neutral indicator and oil pressure warning lights are illuminated.
5. Make sure the choke lever (A, **Figure 3**) is all the way forward to the OFF position.
6. Pull the clutch lever (B, **Figure 3**) all the way to the handlebar grip and disengage the clutch.
7. Open the throttle slightly and operate the START button (B, **Figure 2**).

Starting a Flooded Engine

If the engine does not start and there is a strong gasoline smell, the engine may be flooded. If so, open the throttle all the way and operate the starter.

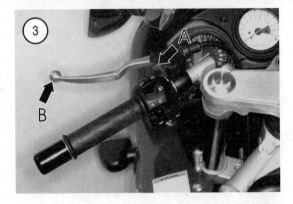

Make sure the choke is in the OFF position. Holding the throttle open allows more air to reach the engine.

NOTE
If the engine refuses to start, check the carburetor overflow hose attached to the bottom of the float bowl. If fuel runs out the end of the hose, the float is stuck open, allowing the carburetor to overfill. If this problem exists, remove the carburetor and correct the problem as described in Chapter Eight.

ENGINE WILL NOT START

If the engine turns over but does not start, check for obvious problems first. Go down the following list step by step. Perform each step while remembering the three engine operating requirements described earlier in this chapter.

If the engine still does not start, refer to the appropriate troubleshooting procedure that follows in this chapter.

1. Make sure the choke lever is in the correct position.

WARNING
Do not use an open flame to check for fuel in the tank. A serious explosion is certain to result.

2. Make sure there is fuel in the tank. Open the fuel filler cap and rock the motorcycle. Listen for the fuel sloshing around. Fill the tank if necessary. If the fuel condition is in doubt, drain the fuel from the tank, and fill it with fresh fuel.

3. If the engine is flooded, open the throttle all the way and operate the START button. If the engine is severely flooded (fouled or wet spark plugs), remove the spark plugs and dry the base and electrode thoroughly with a soft cloth or with an aerosol electrical contact cleaner. Reinstall the plugs and attempt to start the engine.

NOTE
If fuel is reaching the carburetor, the fuel system could still be the problem. The jets (pilot and main) could be plugged from fuel deposits. This is especially true if the motorcycle has not been used recently. However, before removing the carburetors, make sure the ignition provides adequate spark.

4. Make sure the engine stop switch (A, **Figure 2**) is not stuck or working improperly. Also make sure the switch wire is not broken or shorted. If necessary, test the engine stop switch as described under *Switches* in Chapter Nine.

5. Make sure the clutch is disengaged and the clutch switch (**Figure 4**) operates properly.

6. Make sure the spark plug cap is securely on each spark plug. Make sure the spark plug wires are tight. Push on the spark plug caps and slightly rotate them

to ensure a good connection between the plug and the cap.

> *NOTE*
> *If the engine still does not start, continue with the following.*

7. Perform a spark test as described under *Engine Fails to Start (Spark Test)* in this chapter. If there is a strong spark, perform Step 8. If there is no spark or if the spark is very weak, test the ignition system as described under *Ignition System* in this chapter.

8. Check cylinder compression as follows:

> *CAUTION*
> *Ground the spark plug to the crankcase, cylinder or cylinder head. Some covers are made of magnesium and may be damaged by an electrical spark.*

> *NOTE*
> *Refer to Chapter Three for spark plug removal information.*

  a. Remove and ground the spark plug cap against the crankcase.

  b. Put your finger over the spark plug hole.

  c. Operate the start button. When the piston comes up on the compression stroke, pressure in the cylinder should force your finger from the spark plug hole. If your finger pops off, the cylinder probably has sufficient compression to start the engine. Repeat for the other cylinders.

> *NOTE*
> *A compression problem may still exist, even though the cylinder passed the previous test. Check engine compression with a compression gauge as described under* **Tune-up** *in Chapter Three.*

  d. Install the spark plugs and ignition coil/plug caps. Reconnect the vacuum line to the fuel shutoff valve.

Engine Fails to Start (Spark Test)

Perform a spark test to determine if the ignition is producing adequate spark. This test can be per-

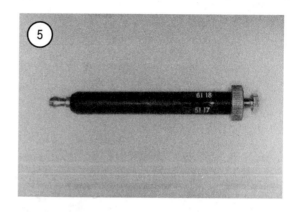

formed with a spark plug or a spark tester. A spark tester (**Figure 5**) is used as a substitute for the spark plug and allows the spark to be more easily observed between the adjustable air gap. The tool shown is available from Motion Pro (part No. 08-0122).

> *CAUTION*
> *Before removing the spark plugs in Step 1, clean all dirt and debris away from the plug base. Dirt that falls into the cylinder causes rapid engine wear.*

1. Refer to Chapter Three and remove the spark plugs.

> *CAUTION*
> *Ground the spark plug to the crankcase, cylinder or cylinder head. Some covers are made of magnesium and may be damaged by an electrical spark.*

2. Insert the spark plug, or spark tester, into its cap and touch the spark plug base against the crankcase to ground it. Position the spark plug so the electrode can be observed.

> *WARNING*
> *Position the spark plug, or tester, away from the spark plug hole in the cylinder so the spark cannot ignite the gasoline vapors in the cylinder. If the engine is flooded, do not perform this test. Fuel that is ejected through the spark plug hole can be ignited by the firing of the spark plug.*

> *NOTE*
> *If not using a spark tester, always use a new spark plug for this test.*

3. Turn the ignition switch ON.

WARNING
*Do **not** hold the spark plug, wire or connector, or a serious electrical shock may result.*

4. Turn the engine over. A fat blue spark should be evident across the spark plug electrode or spark tester terminals. If there is strong sunlight on the plug, shade the plug to improve visability. Repeat for the other cylinder.

5. If the spark is good, check for one or more of the following possible malfunctions:
   a. Obstructed fuel line or fuel filter or a malfunctioning fuel pump.
   b. Low compression or engine damage.
   c. Flooded engine.

6. If the spark is weak or if there is no spark, refer to *Ignition System* in this chapter.

NOTE
*If the engine backfires while starting it, the ignition timing may be incorrect. A loose signal generator or a defective ignition component will change the ignition timing. Refer to **Ignition System** in this chapter for more information.*

ENGINE IS DIFFICULT TO START

The following section groups the three main engine operating systems with probable causes.

Electrical System

The electrical system is a common source of engine starting problems. Trouble usually occurs at the wiring harness and connectors.

1. *Spark plugs:*
   a. Fouled spark plug(s).
   b. Incorrect spark plug gap.
   c. Incorrect spark plug heat range; see Chapter Three.
   d. Worn or damaged spark plug electrodes.
   e. Damaged spark plug(s).
   f. Damaged spark plug cap(s) or wire(s).

NOTE
*Refer to **Spark Plug Reading** in Chapter Three for additional information.*

2. *Ignition coil:*
   a. Loose or damaged secondary or primary wire.
   b. Cracked ignition coil body.
   c. Loose or corroded ground wire.

3. *Switches and wiring:*
   a. Dirty or loose-fitting terminals.
   b. Damaged wires or connectors.
   c. Damaged start switch.
   d. Damaged engine stop switch.
   e. Damaged ignition switch.

4. *Electrical components:*
   a. Damaged signal generator and/or rotor.
   b. Damaged CDI unit.

Fuel System

A contaminated fuel system causes engine starting and performance related problems. It only takes a small amount of dirt in the fuel valve, fuel line, carburetor, or fuel injector to cause problems.

1. *Air filter:*
   a. Clogged air filter.
   b. Clogged air box.
   c. Leaking or damaged air box-to-carburetor boots.

2. *Fuel shutoff valve:*
   a. Clogged fuel hose.
   b. Clogged fuel valve filter.
   c. Clogged or leaking vacuum hose.

3. *Fuel tank:*
   a. No fuel.
   b. Clogged fuel filter.
   c. Contaminated fuel.
   d. Clogged fuel tank breather.

4. *Carburetor:*
   a. Clogged or damaged choke system.
   b. Clogged main jet(s).
   c. Clogged slow jet(s).
   d. Loose slow jet(s) or main jet(s).
   e. Clogged slow jet air passages.
   f. Incorrect float level(s).
   g. Leaking or otherwise damaged float(s).
   h. Worn or damaged needle valve(s).

5. *Fuel pump:*
   a. Leaking vacuum hose.
   b. Damaged diaphragm.
   c. Faulty relief valve.

Engine Compression

Check engine compression with a compression gauge as described in Chapter Three.

1. *Cylinder and cylinder head:*
   a. Loose spark plug(s).
   b. Missing spark plug gasket(s).
   c. Leaking cylinder head gasket.
   d. Leaking cylinder block base gasket.
   e. Excessively worn or seized piston(s), piston rings and/or cylinder walls.
   f. Loose cylinder block and/or cylinder head fasteners.
   g. Cylinder head incorrectly installed and/or torqued down.
   h. Warped cylinder head.
   i. Blown head gasket.
   j. Blown cylinder base gasket.
   k. Loose cylinder fasteners.
   l. No valve clearance.
   m. Incorrect valve timing.
2. *Piston and piston rings:*
   a. Worn piston rings.
   b. Damaged piston rings.
   c. Piston seizure or piston damage.
3. *Crankcase and crankshaft:*
   a. Seized connecting rod(s).
   b. Damaged crankcases.
   c. Damaged oil seals.

POOR IDLE SPEED PERFORMANCE

If the engine starts but off-idle performance is poor (hesitation or cutting out, for example), check the following:

1. Clogged or damaged air filter.
2. *Carburetor:*
   a. Clogged slow jet(s).
   b. Loose slow jet(s).
   c. Damaged choke system.
   d. Incorrect throttle cable adjustment.
   e. Incorrect carburetor adjustment.
   f. Flooded carburetor (visually check carburetor overflow hose for fuel).
   g. Vacuum piston not sliding smoothly in carburetor bore.
   h. Clogged fuel hose.
3. *Fuel:*
   a. Water and/or alcohol in fuel.
   b. Old fuel.

   c. Defective fuel pump or fuel pump relay.
4. *Engine:*
   a. Low engine compression.
   b. Incorrect valve clearance.
   c. Poor valve seating.
   d. Defective valve guides.
   e. Worn tappet/cam surface.
5. *Electrical system:*
   a. Damaged spark plug(s).
   b. Damaged ignition coil/plug cap(s).
   c. Damaged alternator rotor and/or signal generator.
   d. Damaged CDI unit.

POOR MEDIUM AND HIGH SPEED PERFORMANCE

Refer to *Engine is Difficult to Start* in this chapter, then check the following:

1. *Carburetor(s):*
   a. Incorrect fuel level.
   b. Incorrect jet needle clip position (if adjustable).
   c. Clogged or loose main jet(s).
2. Clogged air filter.
3. Defective fuel pump.
4. *Engine:*
   a. Weak valve springs.
   b. Worn camshafts.
   c. Incorrect valve timing.
   d. Incorrect valve adjustment.
5. *Electrical:*
   a. Spark plug gap too narrow.
   b. Insufficient ignition advance.
   c. Defective ignition coil.
   d. Defective spark plug wires/caps.
   e. Defective signal generator or CDI unit.
6. *Other considerations:*
   a. Overheating.
   b. Clutch slippage.
   c. Brake drag.
   d. Engine oil viscosity too high or oil level too high.

STARTING SYSTEM

The starting system consists of the starter motor, battery, starter relay and switch. This section describes procedures for troubleshooting the system. A fully charged battery, ohmmeter and jumper ca-

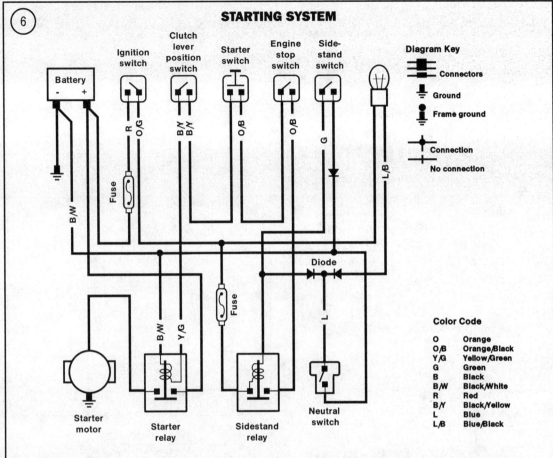

STARTING SYSTEM

For 2003-on models, refer to the appropriate wiring diagram at the back of the manual to verify wire colors and connection points.

bles are required to perform these tests. Refer to the schematic in **Figure 6** throughout the tests.

If the starter does not operate, perform the following. After each test, reconnect any connector that was disconnected before proceeding.

CAUTION
Do not operate the starter motor for more than five seconds. Allow the starter motor to cool for 15 seconds between starting attempts.

1. Make sure the battery is fully charged and the cables are not damaged. Make sure the battery-to-cable connections are clean and secure. Test the battery as described in Chapter Three.

2. Make sure all electrical connections are clean and secure.

3. Inspect the wiring harness and socket connections for damage.

4. Check the main fuse mounted next to the starter relay (**Figure 7**).

    a. Remove the frame covers and front seat as described in Chapter Fifteen.

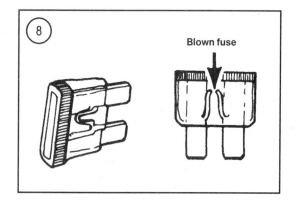

b. Remove the starter relay cover (A, **Figure 7**).

c. Using needlenose pliers, pull out the fuse.

d. Visually inspect the fuse. If the fuse is blown (**Figure 8**), replace it. If the main fuse is good, reinstall it, then go on to the next step.

5. Disconnect the following switches one by one (in the sequence provided) and test them as described in Chapter Nine. If the switch operates correctly, reinstall the switch and test the next one. If the switch does not operate correctly, replace it.

    a. Main switch.

    b. Start switch.

    c. Engine stop switch.

    d. Sidestand switch.

    e. Clutch switch.

6. Inspect the sidestand relay as described in Chapter Nine. Replace the relay if it is defective.

7. Remove the cover from the starter relay. Disconnect the starter relay primary connector (B, **Figure 7**).

8. Disconnect the black starter motor lead and the red battery lead from the starter relay.

9. Connect an ohmmeter and a 12-volt battery to the starter relay terminals as shown in **Figure 9**. When the battery is connected, there should be continuity across the two terminals. When the battery is disconnected, there should be no continuity (infinity).

10. Connect an ohmmeter to the starter relay terminals (**Figure 10**) and measure the resistance across these terminals. The resistance should be 3-6 ohms.

    a. If the starter circuit relay tested correctly, perform Step 11.

    b. If the starter circuit relay did not test correctly, replace the relay and retest.

11. If the starting system problem has not been found, recheck the wiring system for dirty or loose-fitting terminals or damaged wires. Clean and repair the wir-

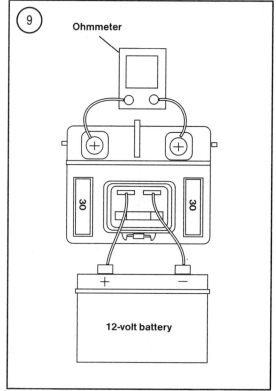

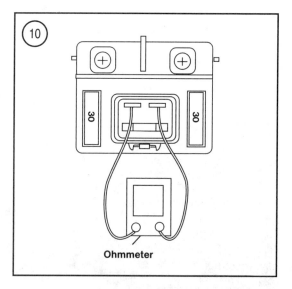

ing/terminals as required. If all the connectors and wires are in good condition, the starter motor is probably faulty. Remove and overhaul the starter motor as described under *Starter* in Chapter Nine.

12. Make sure all connectors disassembled during this procedure are free of corrosion and are reconnected properly.

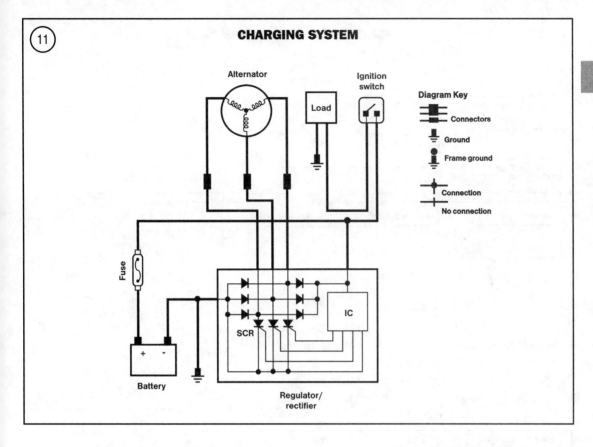

CHARGING SYSTEM

Alternator — Ignition switch — Load

Diagram Key
- Connectors
- Ground
- Frame ground
- Connection
- No connection

Fuse — IC — SCR — Battery — Regulator/rectifier

2

CHARGING SYSTEM

A malfunction in the charging system generally causes the battery to remain undercharged. **Figure 11** shows a schematic of the charging system and its components.

Test each of the following items and refer to the appropriate chapter if applicable.

1. Make sure the battery is fully charged and the cables are not damaged. Make sure the battery-to-cable connections are clean and secure. Test the battery as described in Chapter Three. If the battery cable polarity is reversed, check for a damaged regulator/rectifier.

2. Make sure all wiring and connections between the battery and alternator are clean, secure and undamaged.

3. Perform the *Charging System Output Test* as described in Chapter Nine.

4. Test the regulator/rectifier as described under *Regulator/Rectifier* in Chapter Nine.

IGNITION SYSTEM

All models are equipped with a transistorized ignition system. This solid state system uses no contact breaker points. Because of the solid state design, problems with the transistorized system are rare. If a problem occurs, it generally causes a weak spark or no spark at all. An ignition system with a weak spark or no spark is relatively easy to troubleshoot. It is difficult, however, to troubleshoot an ignition system that only malfunctions when the engine is hot or under load. Use the troubleshooting procedure in **Figure 12** to isolate an ignition system malfunction. Refer to Chapter Nine for specific electrical system tests. The wiring diagrams are at the end of this manual for the specific model and year.

> *WARNING*
> *High voltage is present during ignition system operation. Do not touch ignition components, wires or test leads while cranking or running the engine.*

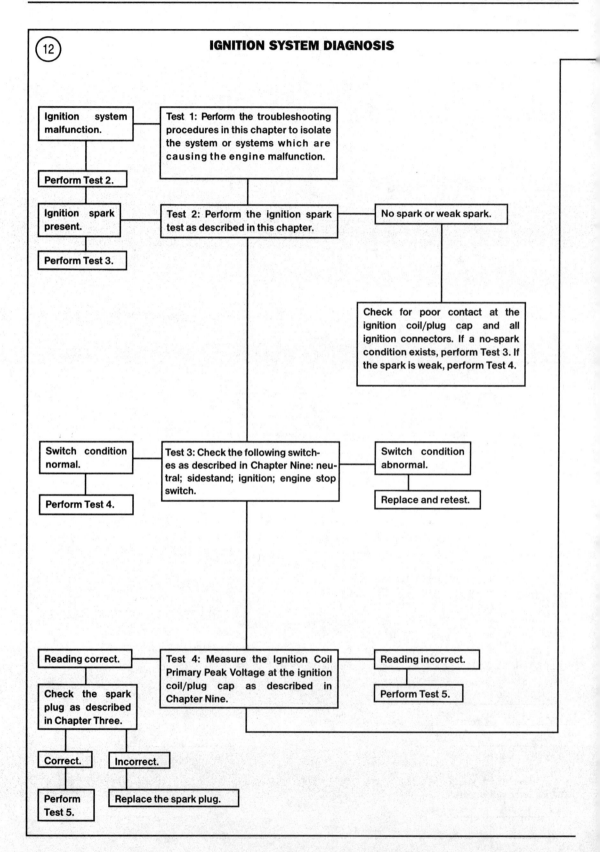

IGNITION SYSTEM DIAGNOSIS

12

Ignition system malfunction.

Test 1: Perform the troubleshooting procedures in this chapter to isolate the system or systems which are causing the engine malfunction.

Perform Test 2.

Ignition spark present.

Test 2: Perform the ignition spark test as described in this chapter.

No spark or weak spark.

Perform Test 3.

Check for poor contact at the ignition coil/plug cap and all ignition connectors. If a no-spark condition exists, perform Test 3. If the spark is weak, perform Test 4.

Switch condition normal.

Test 3: Check the following switches as described in Chapter Nine: neutral; sidestand; ignition; engine stop switch.

Switch condition abnormal.

Perform Test 4.

Replace and retest.

Reading correct.

Test 4: Measure the Ignition Coil Primary Peak Voltage at the ignition coil/plug cap as described in Chapter Nine.

Reading incorrect.

Check the spark plug as described in Chapter Three.

Perform Test 5.

Correct.

Incorrect.

Perform Test 5.

Replace the spark plug.

2

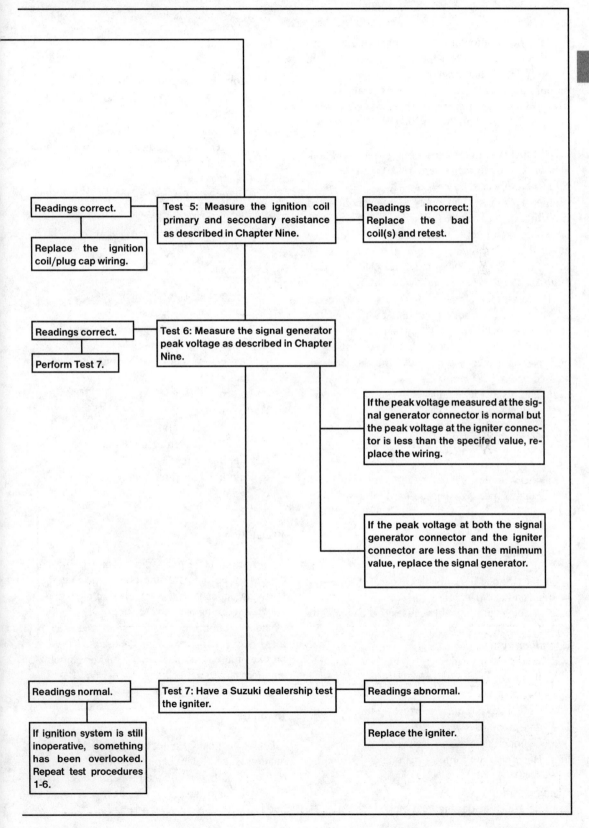

Test 5: Measure the ignition coil primary and secondary resistance as described in Chapter Nine.

Readings correct.

Replace the ignition coil/plug cap wiring.

Readings incorrect: Replace the bad coil(s) and retest.

Test 6: Measure the signal generator peak voltage as described in Chapter Nine.

Readings correct.

Perform Test 7.

If the peak voltage measured at the signal generator connector is normal but the peak voltage at the igniter connector is less than the specifed value, replace the wiring.

If the peak voltage at both the signal generator connector and the igniter connector are less than the minimum value, replace the signal generator.

Test 7: Have a Suzuki dealership test the igniter.

Readings normal.

If ignition system is still inoperative, something has been overlooked. Repeat test procedures 1-6.

Readings abnormal.

Replace the igniter.

FUEL SYSTEM

Many riders automatically assume that the carburetors are at fault when the engine does not run properly. While fuel system problems are possible, carburetor adjustment is seldom the answer. In many cases, adjusting the carburetors only compounds the problem by making the engine run worse.

Start fuel system troubleshooting at the fuel tank and work through the system, reserving the carburetor assembly as the final point. Most fuel system problems result from an empty fuel tank, a plugged fuel filter or fuel valve, fuel pump failure or contaminated fuel. Fuel system troubleshooting is also covered under *Engine Is Difficult To Start, Poor Idle Speed Performance* and *Poor Medium and High Speed Performance* in this chapter.

The carburetor choke system can also present problems. Check choke operation by moving the choke lever back and forth by hand. The choke should move freely without binding or sticking in one position. If necessary, remove the choke as described under *Carburetor Disassembly* in Chapter Eight and inspect its plunger and spring for severe wear or damage.

ENGINE

Engine troubles generally indicate something wrong in a suspect system, such as ignition, fuel or starting.

Overheating

Engine overheating can quickly cause engine seizure and damage. The following section groups five main systems with probable causes that can lead to engine overheating.

1. *Ignition system:*
   a. Incorrect spark plug gap.
   b. Incorrect spark plug heat range; see Chapter Three.
   c. Defective CDI unit/incorrect ignition timing.
2. *Engine compression:*
   a. Cylinder head gasket leakage.
   b. Heavy carbon buildup in combustion chamber.
3. *Engine cooling:*
   a. Improper spark plug heat range.

   b. Incorrect coolant level.
   c. Cooling system malfunction.
   d. Clogged radiator.
   e. Thermostat stuck closed.
   f. Worn or damaged radiator cap.
   g. Fan switch, relay or thermoswitch malfunction.
   h. Damaged cooling fan blades.
   i. Clogged or blocked coolant passages in radiator, hoses or engine.
   j. Oil level low.
   k. Oil not circulating properly.
   l. Valves leaking.
   m. Dragging brakes.
   n. Clutch slippage.
   o. Heavy carbon deposits.
4. *Fuel system:*
   a. Clogged air filter element.
   b. Carburetor fuel level too low.
   c. Incorrect carburetor adjustment or jetting.
   d. Loose carburetor hose clamps.
   e. Leaking or damaged carburetor-to-air box boot(s).
   f. Incorrect air/fuel mixture.
5. *Engine load:*
   a. Dragging brake(s).
   b. Damaged drivetrain components.
   c. Slipping clutch.
   d. Engine oil level too high.
   e. Improper grade engine oil.

Preignition

Preignition is the premature burning of fuel and is caused by hot spots in the combustion chambers. Glowing deposits in the combustion chambers, inadequate cooling or an overheated spark plug(s) can all cause preignition. This is first noticed as a power loss but eventually results in damage to the internal parts of the engine because of higher combustion chamber temperatures.

Detonation

Commonly called spark knock or fuel knock, detonation is the violent explosion of fuel in the combustion chamber before the proper time of ignition. Severe damage can result. Use of low octane gasoline is a common cause of detonation.

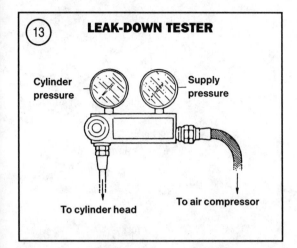

LEAK-DOWN TESTER

Cylinder pressure

Supply pressure

To cylinder head

To air compressor

Even when using a high octane gasoline, detonation can still occur. Other causes are over-advanced ignition timing, lean air/fuel mixture at or near full throttle, inadequate engine cooling, or the excessive accumulation of carbon deposits in the combustion chamber (cylinder head and piston crowns).

Power Loss

Several factors can cause a lack of power and speed. Look for a clogged air filter or fouled or damaged spark plugs. A piston or cylinder that is galled, incorrect piston clearance or worn or sticky piston rings may be responsible. Look for loose bolts, defective gaskets or leaking machined mating surfaces on the cylinder head, cylinder block or crankcase.

Piston Seizure

This is caused by incorrect bore clearance, piston rings with an improper end gap, compression leak, incorrect air/fuel mixture, spark plugs of the wrong heat range or incorrect ignition timing. Overheating may result in piston seizure.

Piston Slap

Piston slap is an audible slapping or rattling noise resulting from excessive piston-to-cylinder clearance. When allowed to continue, piston slap eventually causes the piston skirt to shatter.

To prevent piston slap, clean the air filter on a regular schedule. When piston slap is heard, disassemble the engine top end, measure the cylinder

bore and piston diameter, and check for excessive clearance. Replace parts that exceed wear limits or show damage.

Noises

1. A knocking or pinging during acceleration can be caused by using a lower octane fuel than recommended or a poor grade of fuel. Incorrect carburetor jetting and a too hot spark plug can also cause pinging. Refer to *Spark Plug Heat Range* in Chapter Three. Check also for excessive carbon buildup in the combustion chamber or a defective ignition system component.
2. A slapping or rattling noise at low speed or during acceleration can be caused by excessive piston-cylinder wall clearance. Check also for bent connecting rods or worn piston pins and/or piston pin holes in the pistons.
3. A knocking or rapping while decelerating is usually caused by excessive rod bearing clearance.
4. A persistent knocking and vibration or other noise is usually caused by worn main bearings. If the main bearings are good, consider the following:
   a. Loose engine mounts.
   b. Cracked frame.
   c. Leaking cylinder head gasket.
   d. Exhaust pipe leakage at cylinder head.
   e. Stuck piston ring(s).
   f. Broken piston ring(s).
   g. Partial engine seizure.
   h. Excessive connecting rod bearing clearance.
   i. Excessive crankshaft runout.
   j. Worn or damaged primary drive gear.
5. Rapid on-off squeals can be caused by a compression leak around the cylinder head gasket or spark plug.

CYLINDER LEAKDOWN TEST

A cylinder leakdown test can locate engine problems from leaking valves, blown head gaskets or broken, worn or stuck piston rings. This test is performed by applying compressed air to the cylinder and then measuring the percent of leakage. Use a cylinder leakdown tester (**Figure 13**) and an air compressor to perform this test.

Follow the manufacturer's directions along with the following information when performing a cylinder leak down test.

1. Start and run the engine until it reaches normal operating temperature. Then turn off the engine.

2. Remove the air box as described in Chapter Eight. Open and secure the throttle so it remains in the wide open position.

3. Remove both spark plugs as described in Chapter Three. This makes it easier to turn the engine by hand.

4. Remove the timing inspection plug (A, **Figure 14**).

5. Remove the alternator retaining nut access plug (B, **Figure 14**).

6. Insert a suitably sized socket through the side cover to engage the alternator bolt (**Figure 15**).

NOTE
The alternator rotor has lines marked F or R to indicate top dead center for the front cylinder (F) or rear cylinder (R).

7. Rotate the engine *counterclockwise*, as viewed from the left side of the motorcycle. Rotate the alternator rotor until the F or R line, depending on the cylinder being tested, aligns with the mark on the timing inspection hole as shown in **Figure 16**. To determine if the piston is on the compression stroke, hold a finger in the spark plug hole of the cylinder being tested to feel the compressed gases as they escape.

8. Install the leakdown tester into the cylinder spark plug hole. Connect an air compressor to the tester fitting.

NOTE
The engine may turn over when air pressure is applied to the cylinder. To prevent this from happening, shift the transmission into fifth gear and set the parking brake.

9. Apply compressed air to the leakdown tester. Read the rate of leakage on the gauge. Record the leakage rate for that cylinder.

10. After recording the leakage rate of the cylinder, listen for air escaping from the engine.

    a. Air leaking through the exhaust pipe points to a leaking exhaust valve.

    b. Air leaking through the carburetor points to a leaking intake valve.

    c. Air leaking through the crankcase breather tube indicates worn piston rings.

    d. Air leaking into the cooling system causes the coolant to bubble in the radiator. If this occurs, check for a damaged cylinder head gasket and/or a warped or cracked cylinder head or cylinder block surface.

11. Repeat Steps 7-10 for the remaining cylinder.

    a. For a new or rebuilt engine, a leakage rate of 0 to 5 percent per cylinder is desirable. A leakage rate of 6 to 14 percent is acceptable and means the engine is in good condition.

    b. If testing a used engine, the critical parameter is not each cylinder's actual leakage rate, but the difference in the leakage rates between the cylinders. On a used engine, a difference of 10 percent or less between the cylinders is acceptable.

    c. If the leakage rate of the cylinders differs by more than 10 percent, the engine is in poor condition and further testing is required.

CLUTCH

The two basic clutch troubles are clutch slipping and clutch dragging.

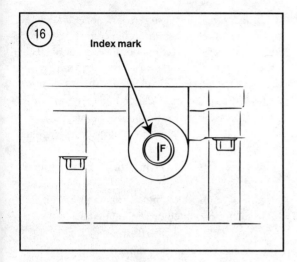

All clutch troubles require partial engine disassembly to identify and repair the problem. Refer to Chapter Six for procedures.

Clutch Slipping

1. *Clutch wear or damage:*
   a. Loose, weak or damaged clutch spring.
   b. Worn friction plates.
   c. Warped steel plates.
   d. Excessively worn clutch hub and/or clutch housing.
   e. Incorrectly assembled clutch.
   f. Incorrectly adjusted clutch.
2. *Engine oil:*
   a. Low oil level.
   b. Oil additives.
   c. Low viscosity oil.

Clutch Dragging

1. *Clutch wear or damage:*
   a. Warped steel plates.
   b. Swollen friction plates.
   c. Warped pressure plate.
   d. Incorrect clutch spring tension.
   e. Incorrectly assembled clutch.
   f. Incorrectly adjusted clutch.
   g. Loose clutch nut.
   h. Damaged clutch boss.
2. *Engine oil:*
   a. Oil level too high.
   b. High viscosity oil.

TRANSMISSION

The basic transmission troubles are difficult shifting and gears popping out of mesh.

Transmission symptoms can be hard to distinguish from clutch symptoms. Make sure that the clutch is not causing the trouble before working on the transmission.

Difficult Shifting

If the shift shaft does not move smoothly from one gear to the next, check the following.
1. *Shift shaft:*
   a. Incorrectly installed shift lever.
   b. Stripped shift lever-to-shift shaft splines.
   c. Bent shift shaft.
   d. Damaged shift shaft return spring.
   e. Damaged shift shaft where it engages the shift drum.
   f. Loose shift return spring pin.
   g. Shift drum positioning lever binding on pivot bolt.
2. *Stopper lever:*
   a. Seized or damaged stopper lever roller.
   b. Broken stopper lever spring.
   c. Loose stopper lever mounting bolt.
3. *Shift drum and shift forks:*
   a. Bent shift fork(s).
   b. Damaged shift fork guide pin(s).
   c. Seized shift fork (on shaft).
   d. Broken shift fork or shift fork shaft.
   e. Damaged shift drum groove(s).
   f. Damaged shift drum bearing.
   g. Worn shift pawls.

Gears Pop Out of Mesh

If the transmission shifts into gear but then slips or pops out, check the following:
1. *Shift shaft:*
   a. Incorrect shift lever position/adjustment.
   b. Stopper lever fails to move or set properly.
2. *Shift drum:*
   a. Excessively worn or damaged shift drum groove(s).
   b. Worn shift pawls.
3. Bent shift fork(s).
4. *Transmission:*
   a. Worn or damaged gear dogs.

b. Excessive gear thrust play.
c. Worn or damaged shaft circlips and/or thrust washers.

Transmission Overshifts

If the transmission overshifts when shifting up or down, check for a weak or broken shift mechanism arm spring or a weak or broken shift drum positioning lever.

DRIVETRAIN NOISE

This section deals with noises restricted to the drivetrain assembly, drive chain, clutch and transmission. While some drivetrain noises have little meaning, abnormal noises indicate a developing problem. The difficulty is recognizing the difference between a normal and abnormal noise. A new noise, no matter how minor, should be investigated.

1. *Drive chain noise*—Normal drive chain noise can be considered a low-pitched, continuous whining sound. The noise will vary, depending on the speed of the motorcycle and the terrain, as well as proper lubrication, wear (both chain and sprockets) and alignment. When checking abnormal drive chain noise, consider the following:
   a. *Inadequate lubrication*—A dry chain gives off a loud whining sound. Clean and lubricate the drive chain at regular intervals; see Chapter Three.
   b. *Incorrect drive chain adjustment*—Check and adjust the drive chain as described in Chapter Three.
   c. *Worn drive chain*—Check the drive chain for wear at regular intervals and replace it when its overall length reaches the wear limit specified in Chapter Three.
   d. *Worn or damaged sprockets*—Worn or damaged engine and rear sprockets accelerate drive chain wear. Inspect both sprockets carefully as described in Chapter Three.
   e. *Worn swing arm/drive chain guide or slider*—A damaged chain guard or worn through buffer will allow the chain to contact the frame or swing arm. If this occurs, the chain will wear rapidly and damage the frame and/or swing arm. Inspect the guard and buffer at regular intervals and replace them if worn or damaged.

2. *Clutch noise*—Investigate any noise that develops in the clutch. First, drain the engine oil, checking for bits of metal or clutch plate material. If the oil is contaminated, remove the clutch cover and clutch (Chapter Six) and check for the following:
   a. Worn or damaged clutch housing gear teeth.
   b. Excessive clutch housing axial play.
   c. Excessive clutch housing-to-friction plate clearance.
   d. Excessive clutch housing gear-to-primary drive gear backlash.
   e. Worn splines on the countershaft or hub.
   f. Distorted clutch or friction plates.
   g. Worn clutch release bearing.
   h. Weakened clutch dampers.

3. *Transmission noise*—The transmission exhibits more normal noises than the clutch, but investigate any new noise. Drain the engine oil into a clean container. Check for the presence of metallic particles. Inspect the drain container for signs of water separation from the oil. Transmission-associated noises can be caused by:
   a. Insufficient engine oil level.
   b. Contaminated engine oil.
   c. Engine oil viscosity too thin. A low viscosity oil will raise the transmission operating temperature.
   d. Worn transmission gear(s).
   e. Chipped or broken transmission gear(s).
   f. Excessive transmission gear side play.
   g. Worn or damaged crankshaft-to-transmission bearing(s).

HANDLING

Investigate handling problems immediately. Minor symptoms can develop into problems that may have an adverse effect on motorcycle control and result in a crash. Check the following items:

1. If the handlebar is hard to turn, check for the following:
   a. Low tire pressure.
   b. Incorrect front brake hydraulic hose routing.
   c. Incorrect throttle cable routing.
   d. Incorrect handlebar switch cable routing.
   e. Steering stem adjustment is too tight.
   f. Bent steering stem.
   g. Improperly lubricated steering stem bearings.
   h. Damaged or worn steering stem bearings.

2. If there is excessive handlebar shake or vibration, check for the following:

   a. Loose or damaged handlebar holder bolts.
   b. Incorrect handlebar holder and bolt installation.
   c. Bent or cracked handlebar.
   d. Loose steering stem nut.
   e. Worn wheel bearing(s).
   f. Damaged tire.
   g. Excessively worn front tire.
   h. Damaged rim.
   i. Loose, missing or broken engine mount bolts and mounts.
   j. Cracked frame, especially at the steering head.
   k. Incorrect tire inflation pressure for prevailing riding conditions.
   l. Imbalance between the left and right fork legs.
   m. Distorted front fork.
   n. Bent front axle.

3. If the rear suspension is too soft, check for the following:

   a. Incorrect shock absorber adjustment.
   b. Damaged shock absorber damper rod.
   c. Leaking shock absorber damper housing.
   d. Sagged shock spring.
   e. Loose or damaged shock mount bolts and nuts.

4. If the rear suspension is too hard, check for the following:

   a. Incorrect shock absorber adjustment.
   b. Rear tire inflation pressure too high.
   c. Shock linkage binding or damaged.
   d. Bent shock absorber shaft.

FRAME NOISE

Noises traced to the frame or suspension are usually caused by loose, worn or damaged parts. Various noises that are related to the frame are listed below:

1. *Disc brake noise*—A screeching sound during braking is the most common disc brake noise. Some other disc brake associated noises can be caused by:

   a. Glazed brake pad surface.
   b. Severely worn brake pads.
   c. Warped brake disc(s).
   d. Loose brake disc mounting bolts.
   e. Loose or missing caliper mounting bolts.
   f. Damaged caliper(s).

   g. Cracked wheel flange or bosses, where the brake disc mounts to the wheel.

2. *Front fork noise:*
   a. Contaminated fork oil.
   b. Fork oil level too low.
   c. Broken fork spring.
   d. Worn front fork bushings.
   e. Loose bolts on the suspension.

3. *Rear shock absorber noise:*
   a. Loose shock absorber mounting bolts and nuts.
   b. Cracked or broken shock spring(s).
   c. Damaged shock absorber.
   d. Loose shock absorber linkage mounting bolts and nuts.
   e. Damaged shock absorber linkage.
   f. Worn swing arm or shock linkage bearings.

4. Some other frame associated noises can be caused by:
   a. Cracked or broken frame.
   b. Broken swing arm or shock linkage.
   c. Loose engine mounting bolts.
   d. Damaged steering bearings.
   e. Loose mounting bracket(s).

BRAKES

The front and rear brake units are critical to riding performance and safety. Inspect the brakes frequently and repair any problem immediately. When replacing or refilling the disc brake fluid, use only DOT 4 brake fluid from a closed and sealed container. See Chapter Fourteen for additional information on brake fluid selection and disc brake service. Use the troubleshooting procedures in **Figure 17** to isolate the majority of disc brake troubles.

When checking brake pad wear, check that the brake pads in each caliper contact the disc squarely. If one of the brake pads is wearing unevenly, suspect a warped or bent brake disc or damaged caliper.

If the brake disc is warped due to overheating, check for the following causes that result in unequal brake pressure:

1. Floating caliper is binding on the caliper mounting bracket shafts.
2. Caliper piston seals worn or damage.
3. Master cylinder relief port is plugged.
4. Master cylinder primary piston cup is worn or damaged.

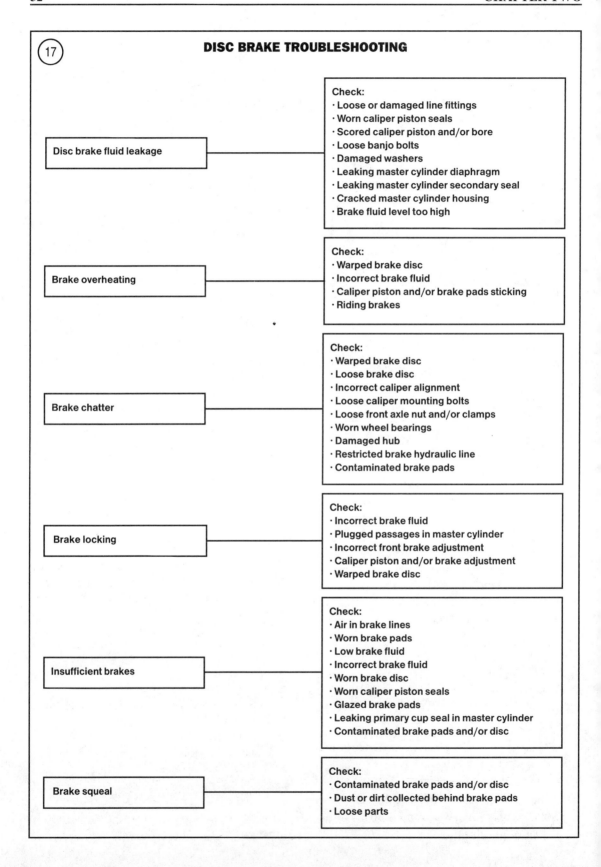

(17) **DISC BRAKE TROUBLESHOOTING**

Disc brake fluid leakage

Check:
- Loose or damaged line fittings
- Worn caliper piston seals
- Scored caliper piston and/or bore
- Loose banjo bolts
- Damaged washers
- Leaking master cylinder diaphragm
- Leaking master cylinder secondary seal
- Cracked master cylinder housing
- Brake fluid level too high

Brake overheating

Check:
- Warped brake disc
- Incorrect brake fluid
- Caliper piston and/or brake pads sticking
- Riding brakes

Brake chatter

Check:
- Warped brake disc
- Loose brake disc
- Incorrect caliper alignment
- Loose caliper mounting bolts
- Loose front axle nut and/or clamps
- Worn wheel bearings
- Damaged hub
- Restricted brake hydraulic line
- Contaminated brake pads

Brake locking

Check:
- Incorrect brake fluid
- Plugged passages in master cylinder
- Incorrect front brake adjustment
- Caliper piston and/or brake adjustment
- Warped brake disc

Insufficient brakes

Check:
- Air in brake lines
- Worn brake pads
- Low brake fluid
- Incorrect brake fluid
- Worn brake disc
- Worn caliper piston seals
- Glazed brake pads
- Leaking primary cup seal in master cylinder
- Contaminated brake pads and/or disc

Brake squeal

Check:
- Contaminated brake pads and/or disc
- Dust or dirt collected behind brake pads
- Loose parts

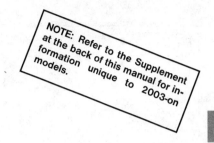

CHAPTER THREE

LUBRICATION, MAINTENANCE AND TUNE-UP

This chapter covers lubrication, maintenance and tune-up procedures. **Figure 1** and **Figure 2** show the locations of various components relating to service. A schedule, specifications, lubricants and capacities are listed in **Tables 1-5** at the end of this chapter.

To maximize the service life of the motorcycle and gain the utmost in safety and performance, it is necessary to perform periodic inspections and maintenance. Minor problems found during routine service can be corrected before they develop into major ones.

This chapter covers lubrication, maintenance and tune-up procedures. **Figure 1** and **Figure 2** show the locations of various components relating to the service procedures.

Refer to **Tables 1-5** at the end of this chapter for the maintenance schedule and specifications.

PRE-RIDE CHECKLIST

Perform the following checks before the first ride of the day. Each check is described in this chapter. If a component requires service, refer to the appropriate section.

1. Check the engine oil level in the oil inspection window (**Figure 3**) located on the clutch cover. The oil level must be between the upper and lower lines.

> *WARNING*
> *When performing any service work to the engine or cooling system, never remove the radiator cap, coolant drain screws or disconnect any coolant hose when the engine and radiator are hot. Scalding fluid and steam will blow out under pressure and cause serious injury.*

2. Check the coolant level when the engine is cold. Check the cooling system for leaks and make

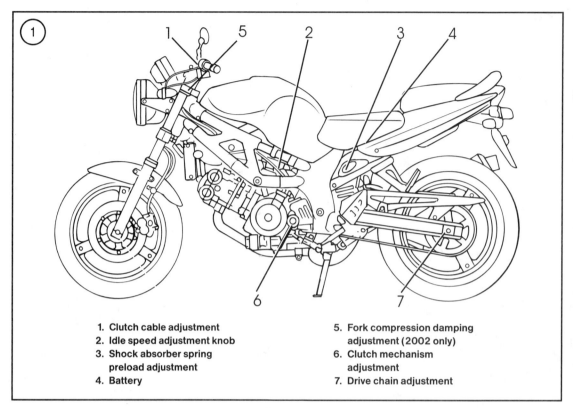

1. Clutch cable adjustment
2. Idle speed adjustment knob
3. Shock absorber spring preload adjustment
4. Battery
5. Fork compression damping adjustment (2002 only)
6. Clutch mechanism adjustment
7. Drive chain adjustment

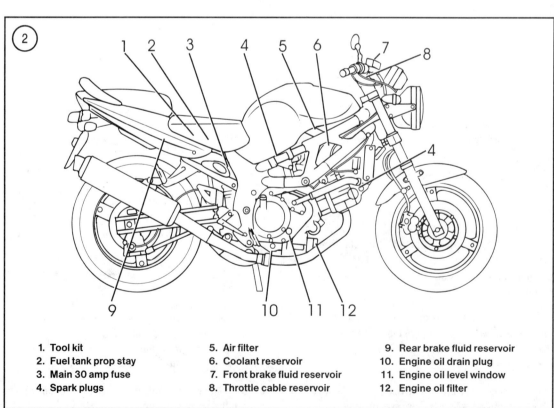

1. Tool kit
2. Fuel tank prop stay
3. Main 30 amp fuse
4. Spark plugs
5. Air filter
6. Coolant reservoir
7. Front brake fluid reservoir
8. Throttle cable reservoir
9. Rear brake fluid reservoir
10. Engine oil drain plug
11. Engine oil level window
12. Engine oil filter

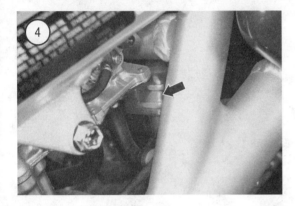

6. Inspect the front and rear suspension. Make sure they have a good solid feel with no looseness.

7. Check both wheels and tires for damage.

8. Inspect the drive chain for wear, correct tension and proper lubrication.

9. Check the drive chain guide for wear or damage; replace if necessary.

10. Lubricate the drive chain.

11. Make sure the air filter element is clean and the air box and carburetor boots are secured tightly.

12. Check tire pressure (**Table 2**).

13. Check the exhaust system for looseness or damage.

14. Check the tightness of all fasteners, especially engine, steering and suspension mounting hardware.

15. Check the rear driven sprocket bolts and nuts for tightness.

16. Make sure the fuel tank is full of fresh gasoline.

17. Inspect the fuel lines and fittings for wetness.

18. Check the brake fluid level in both front and rear brake master cylinder reservoirs. Add fluid if necessary.

sure the coolant is between the FULL and LOW marks on the coolant reservoir (**Figure 4**). If the fluid level is below the LOW mark, add coolant to the reservoir until the fluid level is at the FULL mark. Always add coolant to the reservoir, not the radiator.

3. Turn the handlebar from side to side and check for steering play. Check that the control cables are properly routed and do not interfere with the handlebar or the handlebar controls.

4. Check the throttle operation. Open the throttle all the way and release it. The throttle should close quickly with no binding or roughness. Repeat this step with the handlebar facing straight ahead and at both full lock positions.

5. Check that the clutch and the brake levers operate properly with no binding. Replace damaged levers. Check the lever housings for damage.

> *WARNING*
> *When checking the brake and clutch levers, check the ball on the end of the lever. If it is broken off, replace the lever immediately.*

MAINTENANCE SCHEDULE

Table 1 is a recommended schedule. Strict adherence to these recommendations ensures long service from the motorcycle. However, if the motorcycle is run in an area of high humidity, perform the lubrication and services more frequently to prevent possible rust damage.

For convenience when maintaining the motorcycle, most of the services shown in **Table 1** are described in this chapter. However, some procedures that require more than minor disassembly or adjustment are covered in the appropriate chapter.

TIRES AND WHEELS

Tire Pressure

Check and adjust tire pressure (**Table 2**) to maintain good traction and handling and to prevent rim damage.

> *NOTE*
> *After checking and adjusting the tire pressure, be sure to install the valve*

*stem cap (A, **Figure 5**). The cap pre-*
vents debris from collecting in the
valve stem. This could allow air leak-
age or result in incorrect tire pressure
readings.

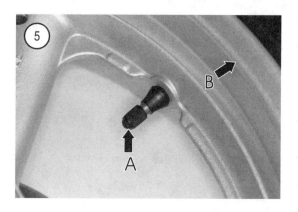

Tire Inspection

Inspect the tires for excessive wear, cuts, or abra-
sions. If an object has punctured the tire, mark its location with a light crayon before removing it. This
will help locate the hole for repairs. Refer to the tire
changing procedure in Chapter Eleven.

Measure the tread depth at the center of the tire
(**Figure 6**) using a tread depth gauge or small ruler.
Replace the original equipment tires when the tread
has worn to the dimensions specified in **Table 2**.

Wheel Inspection

Frequently inspect wheel rims (B, **Figure 5**) for
cracks, warp or dents. A damaged rim may leak or
knock the wheel out of balance. If the rim portion of
an alloy wheel is damaged, replace the wheel. It
cannot be serviced or repaired.

Wheel rim runout is the amount of wobble a wheel
shows as it rotates. Check runout with the wheels on
the motorcycle by supporting the motorcycle with
the wheel off the ground. Slowly turn the wheel
while holding a pointer solidly against a fork leg or
the swing arm with the other end against the wheel
rim. If rim runout seems excessive, measure the runout by following the procedure described in Chapter
Eleven. If the runout is excessive, replace the wheel.

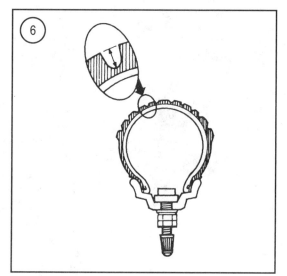

BATTERY

Most electrical system troubles can be traced to
battery neglect. Clean and inspect the battery at periodic intervals. All models are equipped with a
maintenance-free battery. This is a sealed battery, so
the electrolyte level cannot be checked.

When removing the battery, disconnect the negative
cable first, and then disconnect the positive cable. This
minimizes the chance of a tool shorting to ground
when disconnecting the battery positive cable.

Negative Battery Cable

Some of the component replacement procedures
and some of the test procedures in this chapter require disconnecting the negative battery cable as a
safety precaution.

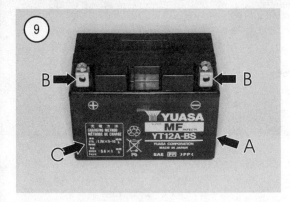

Removal/Installation

1. Remove the front seat as described in Chapter Fifteen.

2. Move the fuse tray/cover above the battery out of the way (**Figure 7**).

3. Remove the bolt and disconnect the negative battery cable (A, **Figure 8**) from the battery terminal.

4. Remove the red protective cap (B, **Figure 8**) from the positive terminal, and disconnect the positive battery cable.

5. Remove the battery.

6. Inspect the cushion pads in the battery compartment for wear or deterioration. Replace any if necessary.

7. Position the battery with the negative battery terminal (A, **Figure 8**) on the right side of the frame.

8. Reinstall the battery into the battery compartment in the frame.

> *CAUTION*
> *Make sure the battery cables are properly connected. The red battery cable must be connected to the positive battery terminal and the black, or black/white, battery cable must be*

connected to the negative battery terminal. Reversing the polarity will damage the rectifier.

9. Connect the positive battery cable to the battery terminal. Tighten the retaining bolt securely.

10. Connect the negative battery cable to the battery terminal. Tighten the retaining bolt securely.

11. Coat the battery connections with dielectric grease or petroleum jelly to retard corrosion.

12. Install the red protective cap (B, **Figure 8**) over the positive terminal.

13. Install the front seat as described in Chapter Fifteen.

Inspection and Testing

The battery electrolyte level cannot be serviced. *Never* attempt to remove the sealing bar from the top of the battery. This bar was removed for the initial filling of electrolyte before delivery of the motorcycle, or the installation of a new battery, and is not to be removed thereafter. The battery does not require periodic electrolyte inspection or water refilling.

Even though the battery is a sealed type, protect eyes, skin and clothing in case the battery is cracked and leaking electrolyte. Battery electrolyte is very corrosive and can cause severe chemical burns and permanent injury. If electrolyte spills onto clothing or skin, immediately neutralize the electrolyte with a solution of baking soda and water, and then flush the area with an abundance of clean water.

> *WARNING*
> *Always wear safety glasses while working with a battery. If electrolyte gets in eyes, call a physician immediately. Force the eyes open and flood them with cool, clean water for approximately 15 minutes and seek medical attention.*

1. Remove the battery as described in this chapter. Do not clean the battery while it is mounted in the frame.

2. Place the battery on a stack of newspapers or shop cloths to protect the surface of the workbench.

3. Inspect the battery compartment cushion pads for contamination or damage. Clean with a solution of baking soda and water.

4. Check the entire battery case (A, **Figure 9**) for cracks or other damage. If the battery case is

warped, discolored or has a raised top, the battery has been suffering from overcharging or overheating.

5. Check the battery terminal bolts, spacers and nuts (B, **Figure 9**) for corrosion or damage. Clean parts thoroughly with a solution of baking soda and water. Replace severely corroded or damaged parts.

6. Clean the top of the battery with a stiff bristle brush, using the baking soda and water solution.

7. Check the battery cable clamps for corrosion and damage. If corrosion is minor, clean the battery cable clamps with a stiff wire brush. Replace excessively worn or damaged cables.

8. Connect a voltmeter between the battery negative and positive terminals. Note the following:

   a. If the battery voltage is 13.0-13.2 volts (at 20° C [68° F]), the battery is fully charged.

   b. If the battery voltage is 12.5 to 12.8 volts (at 20° C [68° F]), the battery is 50-75% charged. Recharge it as described in this chapter.

   c. Once the battery is fully charged, test the charging system as described in Chapter Two.

Charging

Refer to *Battery Initialization* in this chapter if the battery is new.

To recharge a maintenance-free battery, a digital voltmeter and a charger with an adjustable amperage output are required. If this equipment is not available, have the battery charged by a shop with the proper equipment. Excessive voltage and amperage from an unregulated charger can damage the battery and shorten service life.

The battery should only self-discharge approximately one percent of its given capacity each day. If a battery not in use, without any loads connected, loses its charge within a week after charging, the battery is defective.

If the motorcycle is not used for long periods of time, an automatic battery charger (**Figure 10**) with variable voltage and amperage outputs is recommended for optimum battery service life.

> *WARNING*
> *During charging, highly explosive hydrogen gas is released from the battery. Charge the battery only in a well-ventilated area that has no open flames (including pilot lights on some gas home appliances). Do not allow*

> *any smoking in the area. Never check the charge of the battery by arcing across the terminals. The resulting spark can ignite the hydrogen gas.*

> *CAUTION*
> *Always disconnect the battery cables from the battery and remove the battery from the motorcycle before connecting charging equipment. If the cables are left connected, the charger may damage the diodes within the voltage regulator/rectifier.*

1. Remove the battery from the motorcycle as described in this chapter.

2. Set the battery on a stack of newspapers or shop cloths to protect the surface of the workbench.

3. Connect the positive charger lead to the positive battery terminal and the negative charger lead to the negative battery terminal.

4. Set the charger to 12 volts. If the output of the charger is variable, it is best to select the low setting.

> *CAUTION*
> *Never set the battery charger to more than 4 amps. The battery will be damaged if it is charged at a rate exceeding 4 amps.*

5. The charging time depends on the discharged condition of the battery. Use the suggested charging amperage and length of time charge on the battery label (C, **Figure 9**). Normally, a battery should be charged at a slow charge rate of 1/10th its given capacity.

6. Turn the charger ON.

7. After the battery has been charged for the pre-determined time, turn the charger OFF and disconnect the leads.

8. Wait 30 minutes, and then measure the battery voltage. Refer to the following:

 a. If the battery voltage is 13.0-13.2 volts (at 20° C [68° F]), or greater, the battery is fully charged.

 b. If the battery voltage is below 13.0 volts (at 20° C [68° F]), the battery is undercharged and requires additional charging time.

9. If the battery remains stable for one hour, the battery is charged.

10. Install the battery into the motorcycle as described in this chapter.

Battery Initialization

When replacing the old battery, make sure the new battery is charged completely before installing it in the motorcycle. Failure to do so reduces the life of the battery. Using a new battery without an initial charge will result in a battery never holding more than an 80% charge. Charging a new battery after it has been used will not bring its charge to 100%. When purchasing a new battery, verify its charge status. If necessary, have the supplier perform the initial or booster charge to bring the battery up to 100% charge.

> *WARNING*
> *Recycle the old battery. Most motorcycle dealerships accept old batteries in trade. Never place a battery in the household trash. It is illegal to place any acid or lead (heavy metal) contents in landfills. There is also the danger of the battery being crushed in*

the trash truck and spraying acid on the truck or operator.

PERIODIC LUBRICATION

Perform the services listed in this section at the maintenance intervals listed in **Table 1**. If the motorcycle is exposed to harder than normal use with constant exposure to water and high humidity, perform the services more frequently. Refer to *Shop Supplies* in Chapter One for information on lubricants and cleaners.

Engine Oil Level Check

Engine oil level is checked with the oil level gauge located on the clutch cover.

1. If the motorcycle has not been run, start the engine and let it warm up approximately two to three minutes.

2. Park the motorcycle on the sidestand on level ground.

3. Shut off the engine and let the oil settle for two to three minutes.

> *CAUTION*
> *Do not take the oil level reading with the motorcycle on the sidestand, as the oil will flow away from the gauge, giving a false reading.*

4. Have an assistant sit on the motorcycle to hold it vertically on level ground.

5. Check the engine oil level in the oil inspection window (**Figure 3**) on the clutch cover. The oil level must be between the upper and lower lines.

6. If the oil level is low, unscrew the oil filler cap (**Figure 11**) from the clutch cover. Insert a small funnel into the hole. Add the recommended grade and viscosity oil (**Table 3**) to correct the level.

> *NOTE*
> *Refer to **Engine Oil and Filter Change** in this chapter for additional information on oil selection.*

7. Inspect the O-ring seal on the oil filler cap. Replace the O-ring if it is starting to deteriorate or harden.

8. Install the oil filler cap, and tighten it securely.

9. If the oil level is too high, remove the oil filler cap and draw out the excess oil with a syringe or suitable pump.

10. Recheck the oil level and adjust if necessary.

11. Install the oil filler cap, and tighten it securely.

Engine Oil and Filter Change

Regular oil and filter changes contribute more to engine longevity than any other maintenance service. The recommended oil and filter change interval is listed in **Table 1**. This assumes that the motorcycle is operated in moderate climates. If it is operated under dusty conditions, the oil gets dirty more quickly and should be changed more frequently than recommended.

Use only a high-quality detergent motor oil with an API classification of SF or SG. Use SAE 10W-40 weight oil in all models. Use a lighter viscosity oil in cool climates and the heavier viscosity oil in warm climates. Use the same brand of oil at each oil change.

NOTE
Never dispose of motor oil in the trash, on the ground, or down the storm drain. Many service stations accept used motor oil and waste haulers provide curbside used motor oil collection. Do not combine other fluids with motor oil to be recycled. To locate a recycler, contact the American Petroleum Institute (API) at www.recycleoil.org.

1. Start the engine and let it warm for approximately two to three minutes. Shut off the engine.

NOTE
Warming the engine heats the oil so it flows freely and carries out contamination and sludge.

2. Place the motorcycle on the sidestand on level ground.

3. Place a drain pan under the engine.

4. Remove the oil drain plug (**Figure 12**) and gasket from the bottom of the oil pan.

5. Loosen the oil filler cap (**Figure 11**). This speeds up the flow of oil.

6. Allow the oil to completely drain.

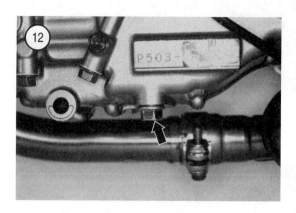

7. Inspect the condition of the drained oil for contamination. After it has cooled, check for any metal particles or clutch friction disc particles.

WARNING
The exhaust system must be completely cool before removing the oil filter.

8. To replace the oil filter, perform the following:
   a. Move the drain pan under the oil filter (**Figure 13**).
   b. Install an oil filter wrench onto the oil filter, and turn the filter *counterclockwise* until oil begins to run out. Wait until the oil stops, then loosen the filter until it is easy to turn.
   c. Remove the oil filter wrench from the end of the filter, then completely unscrew and remove the filter. Hold it with the open end facing up.
   d. Hold the filter over the drain pan and pour out any remaining oil. Place the old filter in a heavy-duty, freezer-grade reclosable plastic bag and close the bag. Discard the old filter properly.
   e. Thoroughly clean the filter-to-crankcase surface. This surface must be clean to prevent leakage.
   f. Apply a light coat of clean engine oil to the rubber seal on the new filter.
   g. Install a new oil filter onto the threaded fitting on the oil cooler.
   h. Tighten the filter by hand until the rubber gasket contacts the crankcase surface, and then tighten it an additional two full turns.

9. Inspect the drain plug gasket for damage. Replace the gasket if necessary.

10. Install the drain plug (**Figure 12**) and its gasket. Tighten the oil drain plug to 21 N•m (186 in.-lb.).

11. Insert a funnel into the oil filler hole and add the quantity of oil specified in **Table 3**.

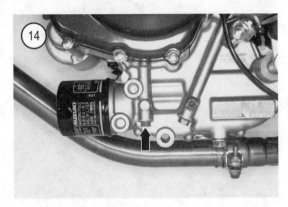

12. Remove the funnel and screw in the oil filler cap securely.

NOTE
If servicing a rebuilt engine, check the engine oil pressure as described in this chapter.

13. Start the engine and let it idle.
14. Check the oil filter and drain plug for leaks. Tighten either if necessary.
15. Turn off the engine and check the engine oil level as described in this chapter. Adjust the oil level if necessary.

WARNING
Prolonged contact with oil may cause skin cancer. Wash hands thoroughly with soap and water as soon as possible after handling or coming in contact with motor oil.

Engine Oil Pressure Test

Perform this procedure after reassembling the engine or when troubleshooting the lubrication system.

To check the oil pressure, a Suzuki oil pressure gauge hose (part No. 09915-74520), gauge attachment (09915-74532) and high pressure meter (09915-77330) are required.

1. Check that the engine oil level is correct as described in this chapter. Add oil if necessary.
2. Start the engine and allow it to reach normal operating temperature. Turn off the engine.
3. Place a drain pan under the main oil gallery plug to catch the oil that drains out during the test.
4. Unscrew and remove the main oil gallery plug (**Figure 14**) from the crankcase.
5. Install the adapter, then install the gauge into the main oil gallery. Make sure the fitting is tight to avoid an oil loss.

CAUTION
Keep the gauge hose away from the exhaust pipe during this test. If the hose contacts the exhaust pipes, it may melt and spray hot oil onto the hot exhaust pipe, resulting in a fire.

6. Start the engine and let it idle. Increase engine speed to 3000 rpm. The oil pressure should be 200-600 kPa (29-87 psi) when the oil temperature is 60° C (140° F).
7. If the oil pressure is lower than specified, check the following:
   a. Clogged oil filter.
   b. Oil leak from oil passageway.
   c. Damaged oil seal(s).
   d. Defective oil pump.
   e. Combination of the above.
8. If the oil pressure is higher than specified, check the following:
   a. Oil viscosity too heavy (drain oil and install lighter weight oil).
   b. Clogged oil passageway.
   c. Combination of the above.
9. Shut off the engine and remove the test equipment.
10. Apply a light coat of gasket sealer to the main oil gallery plug, then install the plug (**Figure 14**) onto the crankcase. Tighten it to 18 N•m (159 in.-lb.).
11. Check oil level and adjust if necessary.

PERIODIC MAINTENANCE

Maintenance intervals are listed in **Table 1**.

General Lubrication

At the service intervals listed in **Table 1**, lubricate the brake and clutch lever pivot points, and the drive chain with engine oil. Lubricate the brake pedal pivot, gearshift lever pivot, footpeg pivots, and the sidestand pivot and springs with waterproof grease.

Control Cable Lubrication
(Non-Nylon Lined Cables)

Clean and lubricate the throttle cables and clutch cable at the intervals indicated in **Table 1**. In addition, check the cables for kinks and signs of wear and damage or fraying that could cause the cables to fail or stick.

The most positive method of control cable lubrication involves the use of a cable lubricator (**Figure 15**). A can of cable lube or an aerosol general lubricant is required. Do *not* use chain lube as a cable lubricant.

1. Remove the fuel tank and air box as described in Chapter Eight.

2. Disconnect both throttle cables from the right handlebar switch. Refer to *Throttle Cable Replacement* in Chapter Eight.

3. Disconnect the clutch cable from the left handlebar switch. Refer to *Clutch Cable Replacement* in Chapter Six.

4. Attach a cable lubricator to the end of the cable following the manufacturer's instructions.

> *NOTE*
> *Place a shop cloth at the end of the cables to catch the oil as it runs out.*

5. Insert the lubricant can nozzle into the lubricator. Press and hold the button on the can until the lubricant begins to flow out of the other end of the cable. If the cable lube will not flow through the cable at one end, remove the lubricator from the cable end. Disconnect the cable from the carburetor assembly or the clutch, and try at the opposite end of the cable.

6. Disconnect the lubricator.

7. Apply a light coat of grease to the cable ends before reconnecting them. Reconnect the cable(s), and adjust them as described in this chapter.

8. After lubricating the throttle cables, operate the throttle at the handlebar. It should open and close smoothly.

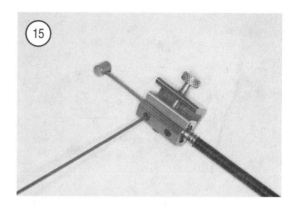

9. After lubricating the clutch cable, operate the clutch lever at the handlebar. It should open and close smoothly.

Drive Chain Lubrication

Clean and lubricate the drive chain at the interval indicated in **Table 1** or whenever it becomes dry. If the drive chain tends to rust between cleanings, clean and lubricate the chain at more frequent intervals. A properly maintained drive chain provides maximum service life and reliability.

1. Place the motorcycle on level ground on the sidestand.

2. Shift the transmission into NEUTRAL.

3. Place a suitable size jack or wooden blocks under the engine to securely support the motorcycle with the rear wheel off the ground.

> *CAUTION*
> *Do not use gasoline or solvent to clean the chain. Only use kerosene. Other fluids can attack the O-rings in the chain.*

Lubricate the swing arm bearing assemblies whenever they are disassembled. Use waterproof grease.

The swing arm must be removed and partially disassembled to lubricate the needle bearings and collars. To clean, examine and lubricate the swing arm bearings and bushings, remove the swing arm as described in Chapter Thirteen. Clean, inspect and lubricate the bearings while they are installed in the swing arm. Do *not* remove the bearings. They will be damaged during removal.

Shock Linkage Lubrication

The shock linkage rocker arm must be removed and partially disassembled to lubricate the needle bearings and collars as described in Chapter Thirteen.

To clean, examine and lubricate the rocker arm bearings and bushings, remove the shock linkage as described in Chapter Thirteen. Clean, inspect and lubricate the bearings while they are installed in the shock linkage component. Do *not* remove the bearings during lubrication. The bearings will be damaged during removal.

Air Filter Cleaning

Remove and clean the air filter at the interval indicated in **Table 1**. Replace the element at the interval indicated in **Table 1** or whenever it is damaged or starting to deteriorate.

The air filter removes dust and abrasive particles before the air enters the carburetors and the engine. Without the air filter, very fine particles will enter the engine and cause rapid wear of the piston rings, cylinder bores and bearings. They also might clog small passages in the carburetors. Never run the motorcycle without the air filter element installed.

1. Raise and support the fuel tank by performing the following:

   a. Remove the front and rear seats as described in Chapter Fifteen.

   b. Remove the fuel tank stay (**Figure 16**) from the tray under the front seat.

   c. Remove the fuel tank mounting bolts (**Figure 17**) from the front of the fuel tank.

   d. Raise the front of the fuel tank, insert the right-angle end of the tank stay into the steering stem and insert the other end into one of the fuel tank mounts (**Figure 18**).

4. Carefully and thoroughly clean the drive chain with kerosene and a soft brush. Dry with clean cloth and then with compressed air.

> *CAUTION*
> *Use SAE 20W-50 weight motor oil to lubricate the chain. Do not use lighter weight oil. It will not stay on the chain as long.*

5. Apply SAE 20W-50 motor oil to the bottom chain run. Concentrate on getting the oil down between the side plates on both sides of the chain. Do not overlubricate the chain. This causes dirt to collect on the chain and sprockets.

6. Rotate the rear wheel and continue lubricating until the entire chain is lubricated.

7. Turn the wheel slowly and wipe excess oil from the chain with a clean shop cloth. Also wipe any oil off the rear hub, wheel and tire.

Swing Arm Bearing Lubrication

Frequent lubrication of the swing arm bearings is vital to keep the rear suspension in peak condition.

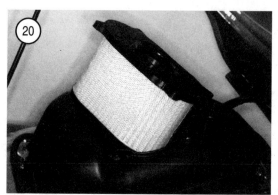

2. Thoroughly clean any debris from the area surrounding the air box cover.

3. Remove the screws securing the top of the air filter (**Figure 19**).

4. Remove the air filter (**Figure 20**) from the air box.

5. Place a clean shop cloth into the opening in the air box to prevent the entry of debris.

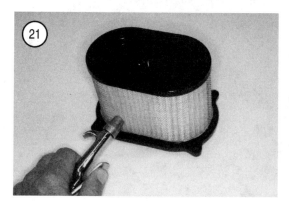

NOTE
If the air filter is extremely dirty or if there are any holes in the element, wipe out the interior of the air box with a shop rag dampened in cleaning solvent. Remove any debris that may have passed through a broken element.

6. Gently tap the air filter to loosen the trapped dirt and dust.

CAUTION
In the next step, do not apply compressed air toward the inside surface of the filter. Air directed at the inside surface forces the dirt and dust into the pores of the element, thus restricting air flow.

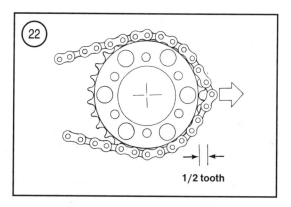

1/2 tooth

7. Apply compressed air to the *outside surface* (**Figure 21**) of the air filter element and remove all loosened dirt and dust.

8. Thoroughly and carefully inspect the filter element. If it is torn or broken in any area, replace the air filter. Do not run the motorcycle with a damaged air filter element. It may allow dirt to enter the engine. If the element is good, use it until the indicated time for replacement listed in **Table 1**.

9. Install the air filter (**Figure 20**). Make sure the filter is properly seated so there is no air leak. Tighten the screws securely.

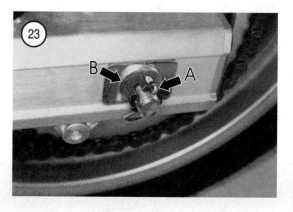

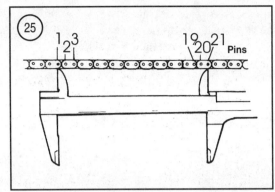

3

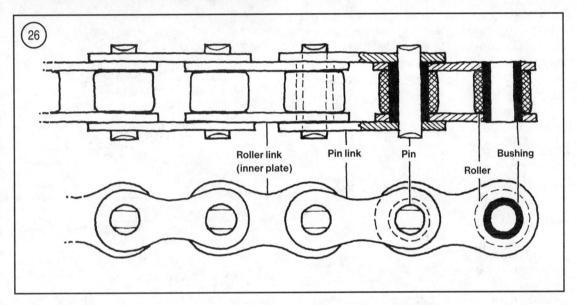

Roller link   Pin link   Pin   Bushing
(inner plate)   Roller

10. Return the fuel tank to its normal position.

Air Box Drain Cleaning

1. Raise and support the fuel tank as described in *Air Filter Cleaning*.
2. Place a rag under the drain on the right side of the air box. Remove the cap, then drain out water and other debris collected in the air box.
3. Reinstall the drain cap. Make sure it is clamped in place.
4. Lower the fuel tank.

Drive Chain and Sprocket Wear Inspection

Check the drive chain frequently and replace it when it is excessively worn or damaged.

A quick check gives an indication of when to actually measure chain wear. At the rear sprocket, pull one of the links away from the sprocket. If the link pulls away more than 1/2 the height of a sprocket tooth as shown in **Figure 22**, the chain is probably worn beyond the service limit. Measure the drive chain wear as described below.

To measure drive chain wear, perform the following:
1. Remove the cotter pin (A, **Figure 23**) from the rear axle nut. Discard the cotter pin. Install a new one during assembly.
2. Loosen the rear axle nut (B, **Figure 23**).
3. On each side, tighten the chain adjusters (A, **Figure 24**) to move the wheel rearward until the chain is tight with no slack.
4. Place a vernier caliper along the chain run and measure the distance between 21 pins (20 links) in the chain as shown in **Figure 25**. If the 21-pin length exceeds 319.4 mm (12.6 in.), install a new drive chain as described in Chapter Thirteen.
5. Inspect the inner plate chain faces (**Figure 26**). They should be lightly polished on both sides. If

they show considerable uneven wear on one side, the engine and rear sprockets are not aligned properly. Excessive wear requires replacement of not only the drive chain but also the engine and rear sprockets.

NOTE
The engine sprocket cover must be partially removed to visually inspect the drive sprocket.

6. To inspect the engine sprocket, remove the engine sprocket cover (**Figure 27**).

7. If the drive chain is excessively worn, inspect both the engine and rear sprockets for undercutting or sharp teeth (**Figure 28**), or broken teeth.

8. If wear is evident, replace the drive chain, the engine sprocket and the rear sprocket as a complete set. If only the drive chain is replaced, the worn sprockets will quickly wear out the new chain. Refer to Chapter Eleven to replace the sprockets.

9. Adjust the drive chain as described in this chapter.

10. Install the engine sprocket cover.

Drive Chain Free Play Adjustment

The drive chain must have adequate play so the chain is not strung tight when the swing arm is horizontal. On the other hand, too much slack may cause the chain to jump off the sprockets with potentially dangerous results.

Check and adjust the drive chain at the interval listed in **Table 1**. A properly lubricated and adjusted drive chain provides maximum service life and reliability.

When adjusting the chain, check the free play at several places along its length by rotating the rear wheel. The chain rarely wears uniformly and as a result will be tighter at some places than at others. Measure the chain free play when the chain's tightest point is halfway between the sprockets.

1. Roll the motorcycle back and forth and check the chain for tightness at several points on the chain. Identify the tightest point, and mark this spot with a piece of chalk.

2. Turn the wheel until this mark is on the lower chain run, midway between the engine and drive sprockets.

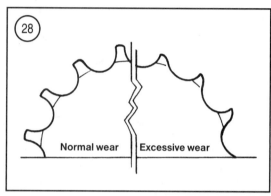

3. Place the motorcycle on the sidestand on level ground.

4. Grasp the chain at the center of the chain run, and move the chain up and down. Measure the distance the chain moves vertically (**Figure 29**). Drive chain free play should be 20-30 mm (0.8-1.2 in.). If necessary, adjust the free play by performing the following.

NOTE
When adjusting the drive chain free play, make sure to maintain rear wheel alignment. A misaligned rear wheel can cause poor handling. All models are equipped with alignment marks on the swing arm and the chain adjusters.

5. Remove the cotter pin (A, **Figure 23**) from the rear axle nut. Discard the cotter pin. Install a new one during assembly.

6. Loosen the rear axle nut (B, **Figure 23**).

7. On each side, loosen the chain adjuster bolts (A, **Figure 24**).

8. Tighten or loosen the adjuster bolt on each side an equal amount until the chain free play is within

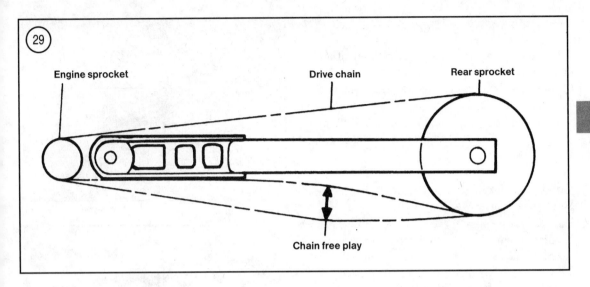

29

Engine sprocket   Drive chain   Rear sprocket

Chain free play

3

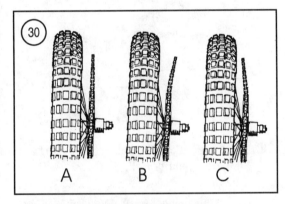

30

A   B   C

31

the specified range. Make sure the edge of each adjuster plate (B, **Figure 24**) aligns with the same mark on each side of the swing arm.

9. When drive chain free play is correct, check the wheel alignment by sighting along the top of the drive chain from the rear sprocket. The chain should form a straight line as it leaves the rear

sprocket and travels to the front sprocket (A, **Figure 30**). If the chain veers to one side or the other (B and C, **Figure 30**), perform the following:

   a. Check that the adjusters are set to the same positions on the swing arm (B, **Figure 24**).

   b. If not, readjust the drive chain so the adjusters are at the same position on both sides and the free play is within specification.

10. Tighten the rear axle nut to 65 N•m (47 ft.-lb.).

11. Install a new cotter pin and bend the ends over completely.

12. If the drive chain cannot be adjusted to the correct measurement, the drive chain is excessively worn and must be replaced as described in Chapter Thirteen. Replace both the engine and rear sprockets when replacing the drive chain. Never install a new drive chain over worn sprockets.

Drive Chain Slider Inspection

Inspect the drive chain slider (**Figure 31**) on the left side of the swing arm for wear. Replace the slider if it is excessively worn.

Routine inspection and replacement of the drive chain slider prevents the drive chain from damaging the swing arm. A chain that is too loose causes rapid wear to the slider. To replace the drive chain slider, remove the swing arm as described in Chapter Thirteen and remove the slider. Whenever the swing arm is removed for slider replacement, inspect and lubricate the swing arm bearings.

Throttle Inspection

Check the throttle operation at the interval indicated in **Table 1**.

Operate the throttle grip. Check for smooth throttle operation from fully closed to fully open and then back to the fully closed position. The throttle should automatically return to the fully closed position without any hesitation.

Check the throttle cables for damage, wear or deterioration. Make sure the throttle cables are not kinked at any place.

If the throttle does not return to the fully closed position smoothly and if the exterior of the cable sheaths appears to be in good condition, lubricate the throttle cables as described in this chapter. Also apply a light coat of grease to the throttle cable spool at the hand grip.

If cable lubrication does not solve the problem, replace the throttle cables as described in Chapter Eight.

Throttle Cable Free Play

Check the throttle cable free play at the interval indicated in **Table 1**. Specified throttle cable free play is 2.0-4.0 mm (0.08-0.16 in.).

In time, the throttle cable free play becomes excessive from cable stretch. This delays throttle response and affects low speed operation. On the other hand, insufficient throttle cable free play can lead to an excessively high idle.

Minor adjustments can be made at the throttle grip end of the throttle cables. If proper adjustment cannot be achieved at this location, the cables must be adjusted at the throttle pulley on the carburetor assembly.

1. Shift the transmission into NEUTRAL.

2. Start the engine and allow it to idle.

3. With the engine at idle speed, slowly twist the throttle to raise engine speed. Note the amount of rotational movement (**Figure 32**) required to increase engine idle speed. This is the throttle cable free play.

4. If throttle cable free play is outside the specified range of 2.0-4.0 mm (0.08-0.16 in.), adjust it by performing the following procedure.

   a. Shut off the engine.

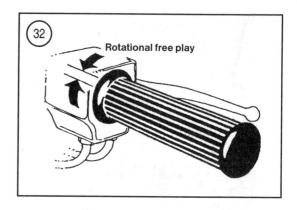

Rotational free play

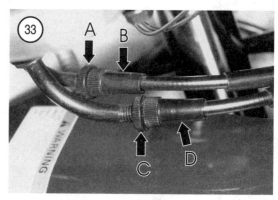

   b. Loosen the locknut on the return cable (A, **Figure 33**) and turn the adjuster (B) all the way in.

   c. Loosen the locknut on the pull cable (C, **Figure 33**) and turn the adjuster (D) in either direction until the correct amount of free play is achieved. Hold the pull cable adjuster, then tighten the locknut securely.

   d. Hold the throttle grip in the fully closed position.

   e. Slowly turn the adjuster on the return cable (B, **Figure 33**) until there is resistance, then stop. Hold the return cable adjuster (B, **Figure 33**) and tighten the locknut (A).

5. Restart the engine and repeat Steps 2-4 to make sure the adjustment is correct.

6. If throttle cable free play cannot be properly adjusted with the adjusters at the throttle grip end of the cables, loosen the locknuts on both cables and turn the adjuster on each cable all the way in toward the throttle housing. Hold the adjuster and tighten the locknut.

7. Raise and support the fuel tank as described in Chapter Eight.

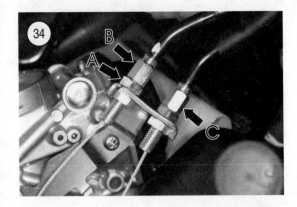

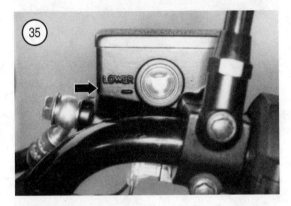

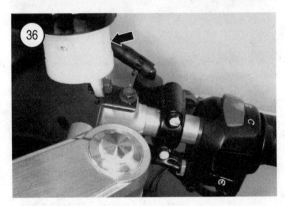

8. At the throttle cables on the carburetor assembly, perform the following:

   a. Loosen both throttle cable adjuster locknuts (A, **Figure 34**) on each side of the cable bracket.

   b. Rotate each adjuster (B and C, **Figure 34**) so the locknut and adjuster are against the bracket.

   c. Rotate the pull adjuster (C, **Figure 34**) in either direction until the correct amount of free play is achieved. Hold the pull cable adjuster, then tighten the locknuts securely.

   d. Hold the throttle grip in the fully closed position.

   e. Slowly turn the adjuster on the return cable (B, **Figure 34**) until there is resistance, then stop. Hold the return cable adjuster (B, **Figure 34**) and tighten the locknuts (A).

9. Recheck the throttle cable free play. If necessary, readjust free play with the adjusters at the throttle grip.

10. If the throttle cable free play cannot be adjusted to specification, the cable(s) is stretched beyond the wear limit and must be replaced. Refer to Chapter Eight for this service procedure.

11. Check the throttle cables from grip to carburetor. Make sure they are not kinked or chafed. Replace as necessary.

12. Lower the fuel tank as described in Chapter Eight.

> *WARNING*
> *With the engine idling, move the handlebar from side to side. If the idle speed increases during this movement, the throttle cables may need adjusting or may be incorrectly routed through the frame. Correct this problem immediately. Do **not** ride the motorcycle in this unsafe condition.*

13. Test ride the motorcycle, slowly at first, and make sure the throttle cables are operating correctly. Readjust if necessary.

Brake Fluid Level

Check the brake fluid in each brake master cylinder at the interval listed in **Table 1**. Also check the brake pads for wear at the same time. Bleeding the system, servicing the brake system components and replacing the brake pads are covered in Chapter Fourteen.

Keep the brake fluid in the reservoirs at the upper line. **Figure 35** shows the front brake reservoir on SV650 models, while **Figure 36** shows the front brake reservoir on SV650S models. **Figure 37** shows the rear brake reservoir for all models. If necessary, correct the level by adding fresh brake fluid.

> *CAUTION*
> *Brake fluid will damage most surfaces it contacts. Immediately wash*

off any spilled brake fluid with soapy water. Thoroughly rinse the area with clean water.

1. Place the motorcycle on level ground on the sidestand.

2. Clean any dirt from the area around the cover before removing the cover.

3A. On SV650 model front master cylinders, perform the following:

    a. Position the handlebar so the front master cylinder is horizontal.

    b. Clean all debris from the top of the master cylinder reservoir.

    c. Remove the screws securing the top cover. Remove the top cover, diaphragm plate and diaphragm.

3B. On SV650S model front master cylinders, perform the following:

    a. Position the handlebar so the front master cylinder is horizontal.

    b. Remove the reservoir cap retaining clip.

    c. Unscrew and remove the top cover, diaphragm plate and diaphragm from the master cylinder reservoir.

4. On the rear master cylinder, perform the following:

    a. Remove the rear seat as described in Chapter Fifteen.

    b. Clean all debris from the top of the master cylinder reservoir.

    c. Remove the screws securing the top cover. Remove the top cover and diaphragm.

> *WARNING*
> *Use DOT 4 brake fluid from a sealed container. Other types may vaporize and cause brake failure. Always use the same brand of brake fluid. Do not intermix different brands. They may not be compatible. Do not use silicone-based (DOT 5) brake fluid. It can cause brake component damage, leading to brake system failure.*

> *NOTE*
> *To control the flow of fluid, punch a small hole into the seal of a new container of brake fluid next to the edge of the pour spout. This helps eliminate fluid spillage while add-*

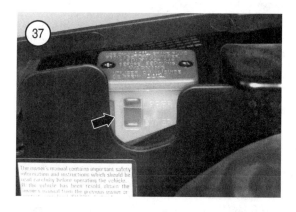

ing fluid to the very small reservoirs.

5. Refill the master cylinder reservoir, if necessary, to maintain the correct fluid level as indicated on the side of the reservoir.

6. On the front master cylinder, perform the following:

    a. Install the diaphragm, diaphragm plate and cover. Tighten the cover securely.

    b. On SV650S models, move the reservoir cap retaining clip back into position and tighten the mounting screw securely.

7. On the rear master cylinder, perform the following:

    a. Install the diaphragm and cover. Tighten the cover screws securely.

    b. Install the rear seat as described in Chapter Fifteen.

Brake Fluid Change

Brake fluid is hygroscopic (absorbs moisture). Moisture in the brake fluid will vaporize at the high temperatures created during hard braking efforts, which will reduce hydraulic pressure. If

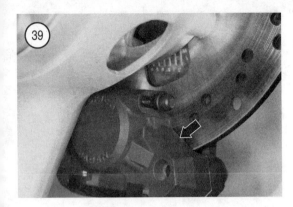

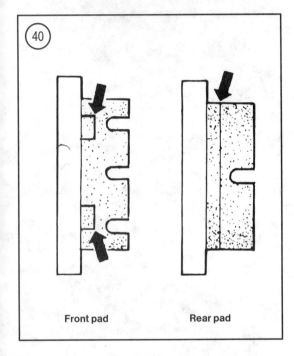

Front pad   Rear pad

this occurs, brake performance will be impaired. Moisture that remains in the system will eventually corrode and damage the internal brake components.

To maintain peak braking efficiency, change the brake fluid at the interval listed in **Table 1**. To change brake fluid, follow the *Bleeding The System* procedure in Chapter Fourteen. Continue adding new brake fluid to the master cylinder and bleed the fluid from the caliper bleeder valve until the brake fluid leaving the caliper is clean.

> *WARNING*
> *Use DOT 4 brake fluid from a sealed container. Other types may vaporize and cause brake failure.*

Always use the same brand of brake fluid. Do not intermix different brands. They may not be compatible. Do not use silicone-based (DOT 5) brake fluid. It can cause brake component damage, leading to brake system failure.

Brake Hose Inspection

Check the brake hoses between each master cylinder and each brake caliper assembly.

If there is any leakage, tighten the connections and bleed the brakes as described in Chapter Fourteen. If tightening the connection does not stop the leak or if the brake hose(s) is obviously damaged, cracked or chafed, replace the brake hose(s) and bleed the system as described in Chapter Fourteen.

Brake Pad Inspection

Inspect the brake pads for wear at the interval indicated in **Table 1**.

On the front brake caliper, look at the brake pads where they contact the brake disc (**Figure 38**) and inspect the brake pads for excessive or uneven wear.

> *NOTE*
> *A small inspection mirror is helpful when viewing the rear brake pads.*

On the rear caliper, look into the caliper from behind the rear wheel (**Figure 39**). Inspect the brake pads for excessive wear.

If any pad is worn to the wear limit (**Figure 40**), replace the pads. Follow the pad replacement procedure in Chapter Fourteen.

> *NOTE*
> *Always replace both pads in each caliper at the same time to maintain even pressure on the brake disc. On the front brakes, replace the brake pads on both calipers at the same time to maintain even braking.*

Rear Brake Pedal Height Adjustment

Adjust the brake pedal height at the interval listed in **Table 1**. The top of the brake pedal should be po-

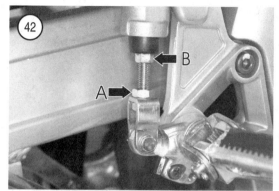

sitioned below the top surface of the footpeg. The distance between the top of the brake pedal and the top of the footpeg (**Figure 41**) should be 55-65 mm (2.2-2.5 in.). If the dimension is incorrect, adjust the brake pedal height by performing the following.

1. Place the motorcycle on level ground on the sidestand.

2. Make sure the brake pedal is in the at-rest position.

3. At the rear brake master cylinder, loosen the locknut (A, **Figure 42**) and turn the pushrod (B) in either direction until the brake pedal height equals the specified dimension.

4. Tighten the rear brake master cylinder locknut to 18 N•m (159 in.-lb.).

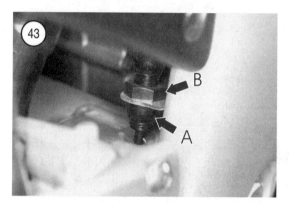

Rear Brake Light Switch Adjustment

1. Turn the ignition switch to the ON position.

2. Depress the brake pedal and watch the brake light. The brake light should come on just before feeling pressure at the brake pedal. If necessary, adjust the rear brake light switch by performing the following.

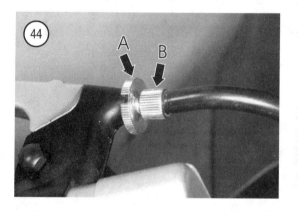

3. To adjust the brake light switch, hold the switch body (A, **Figure 43**) and turn the adjusting nut (B). To make the light come on earlier, turn the adjusting nut and move the switch body *up*. Move the switch body *down* to delay the light coming on.

4. Check that the brake light comes on when the pedal is depressed and goes off when the pedal is released. Readjust if necessary.

5. Turn the ignition switch to the OFF position.

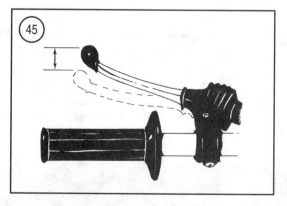

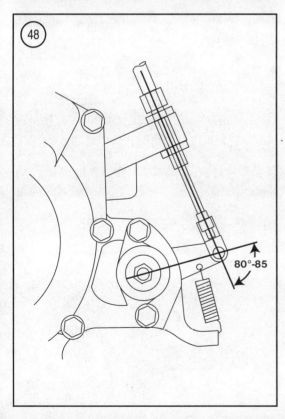

Clutch Lever Free Play Adjustment

Adjust the clutch cable at the interval listed in **Table 1**. For the clutch to fully engage and disengage, there must be free play at the tip of the clutch lever. Specified clutch lever free play is 10-15 mm (0.4-0.6 in.).

For minor adjustments, loosen the locknut (A, **Figure 44**) and turn the adjuster (B) at the clutch lever until the amount of free play at the end of the clutch lever (**Figure 45**) is within the specified range. Retighten the locknut.

If the clutch lever free play cannot be adjusted to within specification at the clutch lever, perform the following.

1. Remove the clutch lever boot.

2. Loosen the locknut (A, **Figure 44**) and turn the adjuster (B) all the way into the clutch lever.

3. Remove the engine sprocket cover (**Figure 46**).

4. Loosen the locknut (A, **Figure 47**) on the clutch release mechanism and turn the adjusting screw (B) two or three turns out.

5. Rotate the locknuts (C, **Figure 47**) so the angle between the clutch release arm and cable is 80-85°, as shown in **Figure 48**.

6. Slowly turn in the clutch release adjusting screw (B, **Figure 47**) until resistance is felt.

7. Turn out the clutch release adjusting screw (B, **Figure 47**) 1/4 turn. Hold the position of the screw with a screwdriver and tighten the locknut (A, **Figure 47**).

8. Install the engine sprocket cover (**Figure 46**).

9. Turn the adjuster (B, **Figure 44**) to obtain the specified clutch lever free play of 10-15 mm (0.4-0.6 in.). Tighten the locknut (A, **Figure 44**).

10. Install the clutch lever boot.

Crankcase Breather Hose Inspection

1. Raise and support the fuel tank as described in Chapter Eight.

2. Inspect the breather hoses (**Figure 49**). If either hose is cracked or deteriorated, replace it. Make sure the hose clamps are in place and are tight.

3. Lower the fuel tank.

Evaporative Emission Control System Inspection (California Models)

The evaporative emissions control system captures fuel vapors and stores them so they will not be released into the atmosphere. The fuel vapors are routed through the charcoal canister (A, **Figure 50**), located on the right side of the rear sub-frame. When the engine is started, these stored vapors are drawn from the canister, through the purge control valves and into the carburetors. Make sure all evaporative emission control hoses (B, **Figure 50**) are correctly routed and properly attached. Inspect the hoses and replace any if necessary as described in Chapter Eight.

PAIR (Air Supply) System Emission Control System (California Models)

The PAIR system introduces fresh air into the exhaust ports to reduce the exhaust emission level.

Refer to *PAIR (Air Supply) System Emission Control System* in Chapter Eight for complete inspection and service procedures.

NON-SCHEDULED MAINTENANCE

Cooling System Inspection

Once a year, or whenever the cooling system requires repeated refilling, check the following items. If the test equipment is not available, the tests can be done by a Suzuki dealership, automobile dealership, radiator shop or competent service station.

> *WARNING*
> *When performing any service work to the engine or cooling system, never remove the radiator cap, coolant drain screws or disconnect any hose while the engine and radiator are hot. Scalding fluid and steam may blow out under pressure and cause serious injury.*

1. With the engine *cold*, loosen the stop screw (A, **Figure 51**), then remove the radiator cap (B).
2. Check the rubber sealing washers on the radiator cap (**Figure 52**). Replace the cap if the washers show signs of deterioration, cracking or other dam-

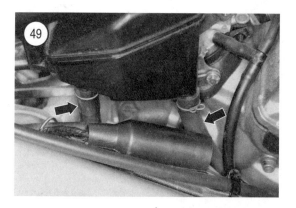

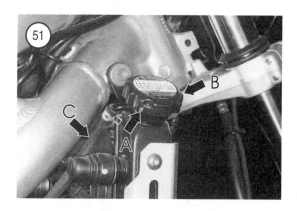

age. If the radiator cap is acceptable, perform Step 3.

> *NOTE*
> *Apply water to the rubber washer in the radiator cap before installing the cap onto the pressure gauge.*

3. Have the radiator cap pressure tested (**Figure 53**). The radiator cap must be able to hold a pressure of 95-125 kPa (13.5-17.8 psi) for at least 10 sec-

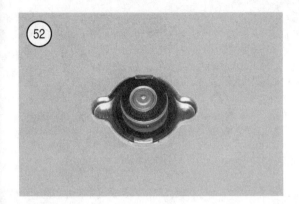

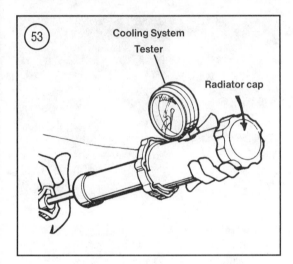

Coolant Type

Use only a high-quality ethylene glycol-based coolant formulated for aluminum radiators and engines. Mix the coolant with distilled water at a 50:50 ratio. Coolant capacity is listed in **Table 3**. When mixing antifreeze and water, be sure to use only soft or distilled water. *Never* use tap water, as this damages engine parts. Distilled (or purified) water can be purchased at supermarkets stores in gallon containers.

Coolant Change

Completely drain and refill the cooling system at the interval listed in **Table 1**.

It is sometimes necessary to drain the coolant from the system to perform a service procedure on some part of the engine. If the coolant is in good condition (and not due for replacement), it can be reused if it remains clean. Drain the coolant into a *clean* drain pan and then pour the coolant into a *clean* sealable container (milk or bleach bottle) and screw on the cap. This coolant can then be reused.

> *WARNING*
> *Antifreeze is an environmental toxic waste. Do not dispose of it by flushing it down a drain or pouring it onto the ground. Place old antifreeze into a suitable container and dispose of it properly. Do not store coolant where it is accessible to children or pets.*

> *WARNING*
> *Do not remove the radiator cap when the engine is hot. The coolant is very hot and under pressure. Severe scalding could result if the coolant contacts skin.*

> *CAUTION*
> *Be careful not to spill coolant on painted, plated or plastic surfaces. It may damage the finish and/or surface. Wash any applicable area with soapy water and rinse thoroughly with clean water.*

onds. Replace the cap if it does not hold pressure or if the relief pressure is too high or too low.

4. Have the radiator and cooling system pressure tested. If the cooling system will not hold pressure, determine the source of leakage and make the appropriate repairs.

5. With the engine cold, remove the radiator cap and test the specific gravity of the coolant. Use an antifreeze tester, following the manufacturer's instructions. This ensures adequate temperature and corrosion protection. Never let the mixture become less than 50 percent antifreeze or corrosion protection will be impaired. Never use a mixture of 60 percent or greater or the cooling efficiency will be reduced.

6. Check all cooling system hoses and the radiator for damage or deterioration as described in Chapter Ten.

7. Install the radiator cap. Turn the radiator cap clockwise to the first stop. Then push down and turn it clockwise until it stops.

Perform the following procedure when the engine is *cold*.

1. Place the motorcycle on level ground on the sidestand.

2. With the engine *cold*, loosen the stop screw (A, **Figure 51**), then remove the radiator cap (B).

3. On the left side, place a drain pan under the water pump housing.

4. Remove the drain screw on the water pump (**Figure 54**) and drain the coolant into the pan.

5. Tip the motorcycle from side to side to drain residual coolant from the cooling system.

> *NOTE*
> *If the coolant is dirty, place another drain pan under the water pump and disconnected coolant hose, and flush the system with clean water. Drain out all water from the system.*

6. Install the water pump drain screw.

7. Detach the reservoir hose from the radiator (C, **Figure 51**) and drain the coolant from the coolant reservoir.

8. If necessary, clean the inside of the reservoir with a liquid detergent. Thoroughly rinse it with clean water.

9. Attach the reservoir hose to the radiator.

> *CAUTION*
> *Do not use a coolant-to-water ratio higher than 50:50. A higher concentration of coolant (60% or greater) actually **decreases** the performance of the cooling system.*

10. Place a funnel into the radiator filler neck and refill the radiator and engine.

11. Use a 50:50 mixture of coolant and distilled water. Slowly add the coolant through the radiator filler neck. Add it slowly so it expels as much air as possible from the engine and radiator. Top off the coolant to the bottom of the filler neck. Do not install the radiator cap at this time.

12. Tip the motorcycle from side to side several times. This helps bleed off some of the air trapped in the cooling system. If necessary, add additional coolant to the system until the coolant level is to the bottom of the filler neck. Do not install the radiator cap at this time.

13. Start the engine and let it run at idle until the engine reaches normal operating temperature. Make sure there are no air bubbles in the coolant and that

the coolant level stabilizes at the bottom of the radiator filler neck. Add coolant as needed.

14. Install the radiator cap.

15. Add coolant to the reservoir tank (**Figure 55**) so the coolant level is between the two lines on the tank.

16. Test ride the motorcycle and readjust the coolant level in the reservoir tank if necessary.

Exhaust System Inspection

1. Inspect the exhaust system for cracks or dents which could alter performance.

2. Check all exhaust system fasteners and mounting points for loose or damaged parts.

3. Make sure all mounting bolts and nuts are tight. If loose, refer to Chapter Eight for torque specifications.

Fuel Line Inspection

Inspect the fuel lines from the fuel tank to the carburetors and other remaining hoses. If any hoses are cracked or deteriorated, replace them. Make sure

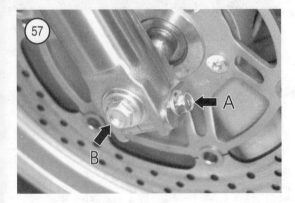

the small hose clamps are in place and holding securely.

> *WARNING*
> *A damaged or deteriorated fuel line presents a dangerous fire hazard to the rider and the motorcycle if fuel should spill onto a hot engine or exhaust pipe.*

Wheel Bearing Inspection

Routinely inspect the front and rear wheel bearings and seals for wear or damage. Clean and repack non-sealed bearings once a year; more often if the motorcycle is operated in wet conditions. The service procedures are covered in Chapter Eleven.

Steering Head Adjustment Check

The steering head on all models consists of upper and lower caged ball bearings. A loose bearing adjustment will hamper steering. In severe conditions, a loose bearing adjustment can cause loss of control.

1. Place the motorcycle on the sidestand on level ground.

2. Place wooden blocks under the engine.

3. Have an assistant sit on the seat to raise the front wheel off the ground.

4. Hold onto the front fork tubes and gently rock the fork assembly back and forth. If there is looseness, adjust the steering head bearings as described in Chapter Twelve.

Handlebar Inspection

Inspect the handlebar assemblies weekly for any signs of damage. Replace a bent or damaged handlebar. Check the tightness of the clamping bolts.

Inspect the handlebar grips for tearing, looseness or excessive wear. Install new grips when required. Use a grip adhesive (ThreeBond Griplock TB1501C, or equivalent) to prevent them from slipping.

> *WARNING*
> *If any of the previously mentioned bolts and nuts are loose, refer to Chapter Twelve for correct procedures and torque specifications.*

Front Suspension Inspection

1. Apply the front brake and pump the front fork up and down vigorously. Check for smooth operation and oil leaks.

2. Make sure the upper and lower steering bracket clamp bolts (**Figure 56**) are tight.

> *NOTE*
> *Figure 57 depicts a SV650S model. The SV650 model is equipped with two front axle clamp bolts.*

3. On the right side, make sure the front axle clamp bolt(s) (A, **Figure 57**) is tight.

4. Check the tightness of the front axle nut (B, **Figure 57**).

> *WARNING*
> *If any of the previously mentioned bolts and nuts are loose, refer to Chapter Eleven or Chapter Twelve for correct procedures and torque specifications.*

Fork Spring Preload Adjustment (2002 Models)

The front fork spring preload can be adjusted on 2002 models. The following procedure describes adjustment.

> *WARNING*
> *Each fork leg must be set to the **same setting**. If the fork legs are set differently, it will adversely affect the handling. Make sure the settings are identical on both fork leg assemblies.*

Adjust the spring preload by turning the spring adjuster (**Figure 58**) on the top of each fork tube. The adjuster is marked with seven (1-7) equally spaced grooves, as shown in **Figure 59**. Position 1 provides the maximum spring preload; position 7 provides the minimum.

The standard setting is when groove No. 6 aligns with the top of the hexagon surface on the fork cap. Turn the spring adjuster clockwise to increase preload. Turn the adjuster counterclockwise to decrease preload. Use the grooves to ensure that the spring preload is set to the same level on each fork leg.

Rear Suspension Inspection

1. Place the motorcycle on level ground on the sidestand.
2. Support the underside of the motorcycle so the rear wheel is off the ground.
3. Push hard on the rear wheel (sideways) to check for side play in the rear swing arm bearings.
4. Refer to Chapter Thirteen and make sure the swing arm pivot bolt is tight. A special tool is required to tighten the locknut.
5. Remove the side covers as described in Chapter Fifteen.
6. Make sure the shock absorber upper (**Figure 60**) and lower (A, **Figure 61**) fasteners are tight.
7. Make sure the shock absorber lever assembly hardware is tight (B, **Figure 61**).
8A. On U.S.A., California and Canada models, make sure the rear axle nut cotter pin (A, **Figure 62**) is in place and that the nut (B) is tight.
8B. On models other than U.S.A., California and Canada, make sure the rear axle nut is tight.

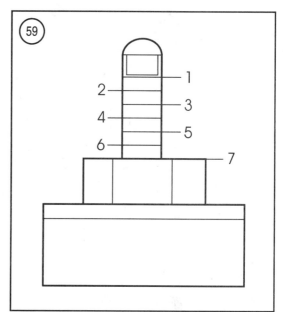

> *CAUTION*
> *If any of the previously mentioned bolts and nuts are loose, refer to Chapter Thirteen for correct procedures and torque specifications.*

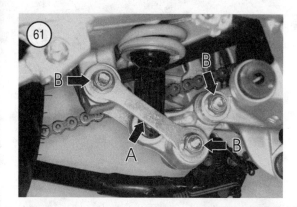

1. Clean or replace the air filter element as described in this chapter under *Periodic Maintenance*.

2. Check and adjust the valve clearances (engine must be cold).

3. Perform a compression test.

4. Check or replace the spark plugs.

5. Check and adjust the carburetor idle speed and synchronization.

Valve Clearance Measurement

The valve clearance for all models is listed in **Table 4**. The exhaust valves are located at the front of the cylinder head on the front cylinder and at the rear of the cylinder head on the rear cylinder. The intake valves are located on the opposite side of the cylinder head from the exhaust valves.

The cylinders are numbered from front to rear. The front cylinder is No. 1; the rear cylinder is No. 2. The left and right sides refer to the position of the parts as viewed by the rider sitting on the seat facing forward.

The figures in this procedure show the engine removed from the frame for clarity; it is not necessary to remove the engine to adjust the valves.

Use a flat metric feeler gauge to check the valve clearance. The engine must be cold (below 35° C [95° F]) to obtain accurate results.

1. Remove the cylinder head covers as described in Chapter Four.

2. Remove both spark plugs as described in this chapter. This makes it easier to turn the engine by hand.

3. Remove the valve timing inspection cap (A, **Figure 64**).

Frame Inspection

Inspect the frame for cracks or other damage. Check all areas where welded sections attach to the main frame spar. Check the tightness of the rear sub-frame mounting bolts (**Figure 63**) and tighten securely, if necessary.

Fastener Inspection

Constant vibration can loosen many of the fasteners on the motorcycle. Check the tightness of all fasteners, especially those on:

1. Engine mounting hardware.
2. Engine crankcase covers.
3. Handlebar and front fork.
4. Gearshift lever.
5. Brake pedal and lever.
6. Exhaust system.

ENGINE TUNE-UP

The following section describes tune-up procedures. Perform these tasks in the following order:

4. Remove the alternator retaining nut access plug
(B, **Figure 64**).

5. Insert a suitably sized socket through the side
cover to engage the alternator bolt (**Figure 65**).

> *NOTE*
> *The alternator rotor has lines marked*
> *F or R to indicate top dead center for*
> *the front cylinder (F) or rear cylinder*
> *(R).*

> *NOTE*
> *The camshaft lobes must point away*
> *from the tappet as shown in either po-*
> *sition A or B, **Figure 66**. Clearance*
> *dimensions taken with the camshaft in*
> *any other position give a false read-*
> *ing, leading to incorrect valve clear-*
> *ance adjustment and possible engine*
> *damage.*

6A. On the front cylinder, rotate the engine *counterclockwise*, as viewed from the left side of the motorcycle. Rotate the alternator rotor until the F line
aligns with the mark on the timing inspection hole.
The camshaft lobes must be in position A as shown
in **Figure 66**. If the camshaft lobes are not as
shown, rotate the crankshaft one complete turn, being sure to realign the F mark.

6B. On the rear cylinder, rotate the engine *counterclockwise*, as viewed from the left side of the motorcycle. Rotate the alternator rotor until the R line
aligns with the mark on the timing inspection hole.
The camshaft lobes must be in position B as shown
in **Figure 66**. If the camshaft lobes are not as
shown, rotate the crankshaft one complete turn, being sure to realign the R mark.

7. With the engine in this position, check the valve
clearance on the valves.

> *NOTE*
> *When checking the clearance, start*
> *out with a feeler gauge of the speci-*
> *fied clearance thickness. If this thick-*
> *ness is too large or small, change the*
> *gauge thickness until there is a drag*
> *on the feeler gauge when it is inserted*
> *and withdrawn.*

8. Check the clearance by inserting the feeler
gauge between the tappet and the camshaft lobe
(**Figure 68**). When the clearance is correct, there
will be a slight resistance on the feeler gauge when

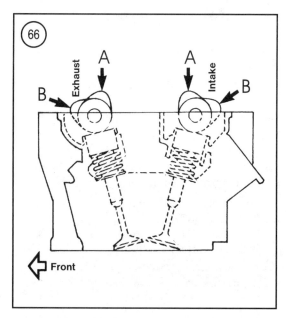

it is inserted and withdrawn. Record the clearance
dimension. Identify the clearance by cylinder
number and by intake or exhaust valve. The clearance dimension is needed if adjustment is necessary.

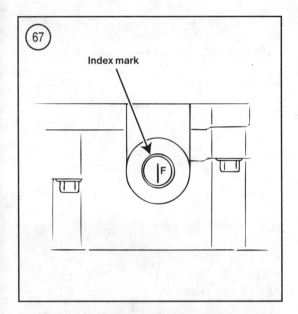

Index mark

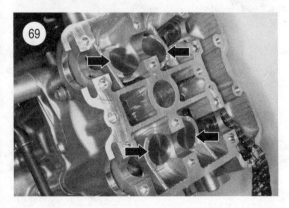

Valve Clearance Adjustment

To adjust the valve clearance, replace the shim located under the tappet with a shim of a different thickness. The camshaft(s) must be removed to gain access to the shims. The shims are available from Suzuki dealerships in thickness increments of 0.05 mm that range from 1.20 to 2.20 mm in thickness.

NOTE
Measure the thickness of the shims that are removed from the engine to confirm their dimensions. If the shim is worn to less than its indicated size, the valve clearance calculations will be inaccurate. Also measure replacement shims to make sure they are correctly marked.

1. Remove the camshaft(s) as described in Chapter Four.

2. To avoid confusion, adjust one valve at a time.

3. Remove the tappet(s) (**Figure 69**) for the valve requiring adjustment.

4. Use needlenose pliers or tweezers to remove the shim(s) (**Figure 70**) from the top of the valve spring retainer.

5. Check the number on the bottom of the shim. If the number is no longer legible, measure the shim with a micrometer (**Figure 71**).

NOTE
Table 4 *lists the valve clearance specification as a range. When performing the calculation in Step 6, use the mid-point of the specified range. For example, the specified intake valve clearance is 0.10-0.20 mm. The mid-point is 0.15 mm.*

9. Measure the clearance of all the valves on the cylinder head before beginning the valve adjustment procedure.

10. If the valves require adjustment, follow the adjustment procedure described below.

6. Using the measured valve clearance, the specified valve clearance listed in **Table 4** and the old shim thickness, calculate the new shim thickness by using the following equation:

$a = (b-c) + d$

Where:

a equals the new shim thickness.

b equals the measured valve clearance.

c equals the specified valve clearance (mid-point of the specified range).

d equals the old shim thickness.

NOTE
*The following numbers are **examples** only. Use the values recorded during the valve clearance check procedure.*

For example: if the measured valve clearance is 0.23 mm, the old shim thickness is 1.70 mm and the specified clearance is 0.15 mm, then:

$a = (0.23 - 0.15) + 1.70 = 1.78$

Because the shims are sold in increments of 0.05 mm, round the calculated shim thickness up to the nearest five-hundredths of a millimeter. In the example, round the 1.78 up to 1.80; therefore, the new shim should be 1.80 mm thick.

NOTE
If the shim thickness exceeds 2.20 mm, check for thick carbon deposits on the valve seat that will require seat refacing.

7. Apply clean engine oil to both sides of the new shim and to the receptacle on top of the valve spring retainer. Position the shim so the side with the printed number faces down, and install the shim(s) (**Figure 70**) into the recess in the valve spring retainer.

8. Install the tappet(s) (**Figure 69**) into the cylinder head receptacle.

9. Repeat this procedure for all valve assemblies that are out of specification.

10. Install the camshaft(s) as described in Chapter Four.

11. Rotate the engine several complete revolutions *counterclockwise*, as viewed from the left side of the motorcycle. This seats the new shims and squeezes any excess oil from between the shim, the spring retainer and the tappet.

12. Recheck all valve clearances as described in the preceding procedure. If there is any clearance

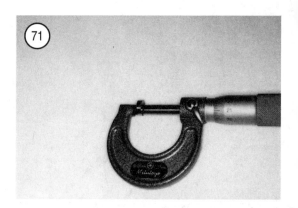

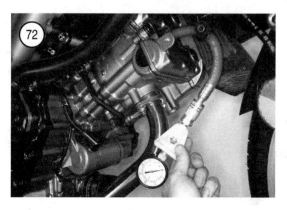

outside the specified range, repeat this procedure until all clearances are correct.

13. Install the cylinder head cover as described in Chapter Four.

Cam Chain Adjustment

An automatic cam chain tensioner assembly is attached to the backside of the cylinder head. Adjustment is neither possible nor required.

Cylinder Compression Test

A cylinder compression test is one of the quickest ways to check the internal condition of the engine, including the piston rings, pistons, and head gasket. Check the compression at each tune-up, record the readings in the maintenance log at the end of the manual and compare them with the readings at the next tune-up. This helps spot any developing problems.

1. Before starting the compression test, make sure the following items are correct:

a. The cylinder head bolts are tightened to the specified torque. Refer to Chapter Four.

b. The valves are properly adjusted as described in this chapter.

c. The battery is fully charged to ensure proper engine cranking speed.

2. Warm the engine to normal operating temperature. Turn the engine off.

3. Remove both spark plugs as described in this chapter.

NOTE
A screw-in type compression gauge with a flexible adapter is required for this procedure. Before using this gauge, check the condition of the rubber gasket on the end of the adapter. This gasket must seal the spark plug hole and cylinder to ensure accurate compression readings. Replace the seal if it is cracked or starting to deteriorate.

4. Install the tip of a compression gauge into the front cylinder (**Figure 72**), following the manufacturer's instructions.

CAUTION
Do not operate the starter more than absolutely necessary. When the spark plug leads are disconnected, the electronic ignition will produce the highest voltage possible and the coils may overheat and be damaged.

5. *Open the throttle completely* and turn the engine over until there is no further rise in pressure. Maximum pressure is usually reached within 4-7 seconds. Record the pressure reading for that cylinder. The recommended cylinder compression and the maximum allowable difference between cylinders is listed in **Table 4**.

6. Remove the compression gauge from that cylinder.

7. Repeat Steps 5-6 for the remaining cylinder and record the readings.

8. Install the spark plugs.

9. Compression between cylinders should not vary by more than the specification in **Table 4** (approximately 15 percent). If the compression between cylinders differs by more than the specification, the low-reading cylinder has a valve or ring problem. To determine which, pour about a teaspoon of engine oil into the spark plug hole of the low-reading cylinder and repeat the procedure. If the compression increases significantly, the piston rings are probably worn. If the compression does not increase, the valves are leaking.

10. Install the spark plugs.

SPARK PLUGS

A spark plug can be used to help determine the operating condition of its cylinder when properly inspected. As each spark plug is removed, note its condition and refer to the *Spark Plug Inspection* section in this chapter.

Front Spark Plug Removal/Installation

1. Detach the horn mounting bracket (**Figure 73**) and tie the horn out of the way.

2. On SV650S models, remove the mounting bolts on each side of the fairing (**Figure 74**) to allow access to the radiator.

3. Remove the lower radiator mounting bolt (**Figure 75**).

4. Loosen the upper radiator mounting bolts (**Figure 76**).

CAUTION
Exercise care when performing Step 5
to prevent damage to the radiator.

5. Swing the radiator forward and wedge a block of wood between the radiator and cylinder head cover to hold the radiator away from the engine (A, **Figure 77**).

CAUTION
Whenever the spark plug is removed,
dirt around it can fall into the plug hole.
This can cause serious engine damage

6. Blow away all loose dirt and wipe off the top surface of the cylinder head cover. Remove all loose debris that could fall into the cylinder head spark plug tunnels.

7. Carefully disconnect the spark plug cap (B, **Figure 77**) from the spark plug. The plug cap forms a tight seal on the cylinder head cover as well as the spark plug. Grasp the plug cap and twist it from side to side to break the seal loose. Carefully pull the plug cap up and off the spark plug. If it is stuck to the plug, twist it slightly to break it loose.

NOTE
Use a special spark plug socket
equipped with a rubber insert that grabs
the side of the spark plug. This type of
socket is included in the standard tool kit
and is necessary for both removal and
installation, since the spark plugs are lo-
cated down deep in their cylinder head
receptacles. Spark plugs cannot be re-
moved or installed by hand.

8. Install the spark plug socket onto the spark plug. Make sure it is correctly seated on the plug. Install an open end wrench or socket handle and remove the spark plug. Label the spark plug with the cylinder number.

9. Inspect the spark plug carefully. Look for a broken center porcelain insulator, excessively eroded electrodes and excessive carbon or oil fouling.

NOTE
Do not clean the spark plug with a
sandblasting type device. Any clean-
ing material left on the plug will fall
into the cylinder during operation
and cause damage.

10. Inspect the plug cap for damage.

11. Install the spark plug using the following procedure.

12. Set the spark plug gap as described in this chapter.

13. Apply a *light* coat of antiseize compound onto the threads of the spark plug before installing it. Do not use engine oil on the plug threads.

CAUTION
The cylinder head is aluminum. The
spark plug hole threads can be easily
damaged by cross-threading of the
spark plug.

14. The spark plugs are recessed into the cylinder head and cannot be started by hand. Attach a length of vinyl or rubber hose to the top end of the spark plug. Screw the spark plug in by hand until it seats. Very little effort is required. If force is necessary, the plug is cross-threaded. Unscrew it and try again. Once the plug is screwed in several revolutions, remove the hose.

15. Use the same tool setup used during removal and hand-tighten the plug until seated. Tighten the plug to 12 N•m (106 in.-lb.).

NOTE
Do not overtighten the spark plug. This only squashes the gasket and destroys its sealing ability.

NOTE
Be sure to push the plug cap all the way down to make full contact with the spark plug post. If the cap does not completely contact the plug, the engine may develop an ignition misfire.

16. Install the plug cap onto the spark plug. Press the plug cap onto the spark plug, rotate the assembly slightly in both directions and make sure it is attached to the spark plug and to the sealing surface of the cylinder head cover.

17. Reinstall the radiator and horn. Tighten the radiator mounting bolts securely.

18. On SV650S models, reinstall the fairing mounting bolts.

Rear Spark Plug Removal/Installation

1. Raise and support the fuel tank as described in Chapter Eight.

CAUTION
Whenever the spark plug is removed, dirt around it can fall into the plug hole. This can cause serious engine damage.

2. Blow away all loose dirt and wipe off the top surface of the cylinder head cover. Remove all loose debris that could fall into the cylinder head spark plug tunnels.

3. Carefully disconnect the spark plug cap (**Figure 78**) from the spark plug. The plug cap forms a tight seal on the cylinder head cover as well as the spark plug. Grasp the plug cap and twist it from side to side to break the seal loose. Carefully pull the plug cap up and off the spark plug. If it is stuck to the plug, twist it slightly to break it loose.

NOTE
Use a special spark plug socket equipped with a rubber insert that grabs the side of the spark plug. This type of socket is included in the standard tool kit and is necessary for both removal and installation, since the spark plugs are located down deep in their cylinder head receptacles. Spark plugs cannot be removed or installed by hand.

4. Install the spark plug socket onto the spark plug. Make sure it is correctly seated on the plug. Install an open end wrench or socket handle and remove the spark plug. Label the spark plug with the cylinder number.

5. Inspect the spark plug carefully. Look for a broken center porcelain insulator, excessively eroded electrodes and excessive carbon or oil fouling.

NOTE
Do not clean the spark plug with a sandblasting type device. Any cleaning material left on the plug will fall into the cylinder during operation and cause damage.

6. Inspect the plug cap for damage.

7. Install the spark plug using the following procedure.

8. Set the spark plug gap as described in this chapter.

9. Apply a *light* coat of antiseize compound onto the threads of the spark plug before installing it. Do not use engine oil on the plug threads.

CAUTION
The cylinder head is aluminum. The spark plug hole threads can be easily

damaged by cross-threading of the spark plug.

10. The spark plugs are recessed into the cylinder head and cannot be started by hand. Attach a length of vinyl or rubber hose to the top end of the spark plug. Screw the spark plug in by hand until it seats. Very little effort is required. If force is necessary, the plug is cross-threaded. Unscrew it and try again. Once the plug is screwed in several revolutions, remove the hose.

11. Use the same tool set-up used during removal and hand-tighten the plug until seated. Tighten the plug to 11 N•m (96 in.-lb.).

NOTE
Do not overtighten the spark plug. This only squashes the gasket and destroys its sealing ability.

NOTE
Be sure to push the plug cap all the way down to make full contact with the spark plug post. If the cap does not completely contact the plug, the engine may develop an ignition misfire.

12. Install the plug cap onto the spark plug. Press the plug cap onto the spark plug, rotate the assembly slightly in both directions and make sure it is attached to the spark plug and to the sealing surface of the cylinder head cover.

13. Lower and secure the fuel tank.

Spark Plug Gap

Carefully gap the spark plug to ensure a reliable, consistent spark. Use a special spark plug gaping tool and a wire feeler gauge.

1. Unscrew the terminal nut (A, **Figure 79**) from the end of the plug. This nut is *not* used.

2. Insert a wire feeler gauge between the center and side electrode of the plug (**Figure 80**). The specified gap is 0.7-0.8 mm (0.028-0.031 in.). If the gap is correct, there will be a slight drag as the wire is pulled through. If there is no drag or if the gauge will not pass through, bend the side electrode with a gaping tool (**Figure 81**) and set the gap to specification.

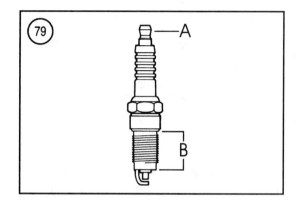

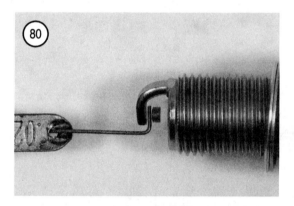

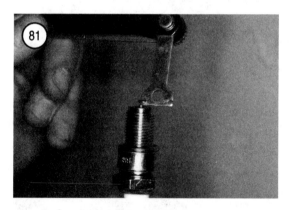

Spark Plug Inspection

Reading the spark plugs can provide a significant amount of information regarding engine performance. Reading plugs that have been in use will give an indication of spark plug operation, air/fuel mixture composition and engine conditions. Before checking the spark plugs, operate the motorcycle under a medium load for approximately 6 miles (10 km). Avoid prolonged idling before shutting off the engine. Remove the spark plugs as described in this chapter. Examine each plug and compare it to those in **Figure 82**.

SPARK PLUG CONDITIONS

(82)

NORMAL

GAP BRIDGED

CARBON FOULED

OVERHEATED

OIL FOULED

SUSTAINED PREIGNITION

3

If the plugs are being read to determine if carburetor jetting is correct, start with new plugs and operate the motorcycle at the load that corresponds to the jetting information desired. For example, if the main jet is in question, operate the motorcycle at full throttle and shut the engine off and coast to a stop.

Spark Plug Heat Range

Spark plugs are available in various heat ranges, hotter or colder than the plugs originally installed by the manufacturer.

Select a plug with a heat range designed for the loads and conditions under which the motorcycle will be operated. A plug with an incorrect heat range can foul, overheat and cause piston damage.

In general, use a hot plug for low speeds and low temperatures. Use a cold plug for high speeds, high engine loads and high temperatures. The plug should operate hot enough to burn off unwanted deposits, but not so hot that it is damaged or causes preignition. To determine if plug heat range is correct, remove each spark plug and examine the insulator.

Do not change the spark plug heat range to compensate for adverse engine or carburetion conditions. Compare the insulator to those in **Figure 82** when reading plugs.

When replacing plugs, make sure the reach (B, **Figure 79**) is correct. A longer than standard plug could interfere with the piston, causing engine damage.

Refer to **Table 4** for recommended spark plugs.

Normal condition

A light tan- or gray-colored deposit on the firing tip and no abnormal gap wear or erosion indicates good engine, ignition and air/fuel mixture conditions. The plug in use is of the proper heat range. It may be serviced and returned to use.

Carbon fouled

Soft, dry, sooty deposits covering the entire firing end of the plug are evidence of incomplete combustion. Even though the firing end of the plug is dry, the plug's insulation decreases when in this condition. The carbon forms an electrical path that by-

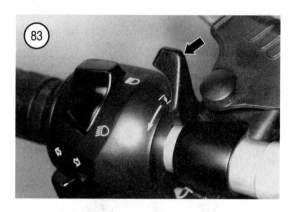

passes the electrodes, resulting in a misfire condition. Carbon fouling can be caused by one or more of the following conditions:

1. Rich air/fuel mixture.
2. Spark plug heat range too cold.
3. Clogged air filter.
4. Improperly operating ignition component.
5. Ignition component failure.
6. Low engine compression.
7. Prolonged idling.

Oil fouled

An oil fouled plug has a black insulator tip, a damp oily film over the firing end and a carbon layer over the entire nose. The electrodes are not worn. Common causes for this condition are:

1. Incorrect air/fuel mixture.
2. Low idle speed or prolonged idling.
3. Ignition component failure.
4. Spark plug heat range too cold.
5. Incomplete engine break-in.
6. Worn valve guides.
7. Worn or broken piston rings.

Oil fouled spark plugs may be cleaned in an emergency, but it is better to replace them. It is important to correct the cause of fouling before the engine is returned to service.

Gap bridging

Plugs with this condition have deposits building up between the electrodes. The deposits reduce the gap and eventually close it entirely. If this condition is encountered, check for excessive carbon buildup or oil entering the combustion chamber.

Make sure to locate and correct the cause of this condition.

Overheating

Badly worn electrodes and premature gap wear are signs of overheating, along with a gray or white blistered porcelain insulator surface. This condition is commonly caused by a spark plug heat range that is too hot. If the standard heat range spark plug is being used and the plug is overheated, consider the following causes:

1. Lean fuel/air mixture.
2. Improperly operating ignition component.
3. Engine lubrication system malfunction.
4. Cooling system malfunction.
5. Engine air leak.
6. Improper spark plug installation (overtightening).
7. No spark plug gasket.

Worn out

Corrosive gases formed by combustion and high voltage sparks have eroded the electrodes. A spark plug in this condition requires more voltage to fire under hard acceleration. Install a new spark plug.

Preignition

If the electrodes are melted, preignition is almost certainly the cause. Check for carburetor mounting or intake manifold leaks and advanced ignition timing. The plug's heat range may also be too hot. Find the cause of the preignition before returning the engine into service. For additional information on preignition, refer to *Preignition* in Chapter Two.

Ignition Timing

The engine is equipped with a fully transistorized ignition system. This solid state system uses no breaker points or other moving parts, and there are no means of adjusting ignition timing. Suzuki does not provide any ignition timing procedures. Because of the solid state design, problems with the transistorized system are rare and adjusting the ignition timing is neither necessary nor possible. If there seems to be an ignition related problem, inspect the ignition components as described in Chapter Nine.

Incorrect ignition timing can cause a drastic loss of engine performance and efficiency. It may also cause overheating.

Idle Speed Adjustment

Before making this adjustment, the air filter element must be clean and the engine must have adequate compression. Otherwise this procedure cannot be done properly. See *Cylinder Compression Test* in this chapter.

1. Make sure the throttle cable free play is adjusted correctly. Check and adjust if necessary as described in this chapter.
2. Start the engine and let it warm approximately two to three minutes. Shut off the engine and make sure the carburetor choke lever (**Figure 83**) is all the way forward in the OFF position.
3. Connect a tachometer, following the manufacturer's instructions.
4. The idle speed knob (**Figure 84**) is on the left side of the motorcycle. Turn the idle speed knob in or out to adjust the idle speed to the specification in **Table 4**.
5. Open and close the throttle a couple of times. Check for variations in idle speed, and readjust if necessary.

> *WARNING*
> *With the engine running at idle speed, move the handlebar from side to side. If idle speed increases during this movement, the throttle cable needs adjusting or may be incorrectly routed through the frame. Correct this problem immediately. Do not ride the motorcycle in this unsafe condition.*

6. Turn off the engine.

7. Disconnect the tachometer.

Carburetor Idle Mixture

The idle mixture (pilot screw) is pre-set by the manufacturer and *is not to be reset*. Do not adjust the pilot screws unless the carburetors have been overhauled. Refer to Chapter Eight.

Carburetor Synchronization

To ensure maximum engine performance, the carburetors must be synchronized. This procedure ensures that each carburetor is opening the same amount throughout the throttle range.

Synchronization tools are available in a number of different styles; some measure engine vacuum with a traditional vacuum gauge or by the movement of mercury within a glass tube, while some perform this function electronically. In addition to the synchronization tool, an auxiliary fuel tank and tachometer are required for this procedure. If this equipment is not available, have a Suzuki dealership or motorcycle specialist perform the operation. Do not attempt to synchronize the carburetors without the proper equipment. Doing so will result in misadjustment and poor engine performance.

NOTE
Prior to synchronizing the carburetors, clean the air filter element and adjust the valve clearance.

1. Start the engine and let it reach normal operating temperature.
2. Adjust the idle speed as described in this chapter, and then shut off the engine.
3. Remove the air box as described in Chapter Eight.
4. Remove the cap on the front carburetor vacuum fitting (**Figure 85**). Connect a synchronization tool hose to the fitting.

NOTE
*A California model is shown in **Figure 86**. Other models are not equipped with the T-fitting shown in the vacuum hose.*

5. Disconnect the vacuum hose from the rear carburetor vacuum fitting (A, **Figure 86**). Connect a synchronization tool hose to the fitting.

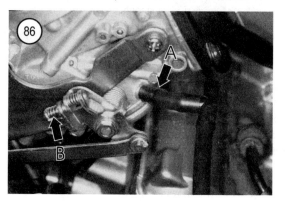

WARNING
If using an auxiliary fuel tank, make sure the tank is secure and all fuel lines are tight to prevent leaks.

NOTE
If using the fuel tank as the source of fuel, connect a vacuum source to the vacuum fitting on the fuel valve. A Mity-Vac hand-operated pump is suitable for this purpose. The vacuum must be 51-102 mm Hg (2.0-4.0 in. Hg).

6. Start the engine and balance the vacuum gauge set, following its manufacturer's instructions, prior to using it in this procedure.
7. Turn the idle speed knob (**Figure 84**) until the engine idles at 1300 rpm.
8. If the carburetors are correctly balanced, the gauge set will have equal readings for each cylinder.
9. If the vacuum is not equal for both cylinders, turn the throttle balance screw (B, **Figure 86**) until the cylinders are balanced.
10. Reset the idle speed to the specification in **Table 4**.

11. Shut off the engine.

12. Disconnect the auxiliary fuel tank and the synchronization tool from the carburetors.

13. Reconnect the vacuum hose (A, **Figure 86**) onto the rear carburetor vacuum fitting.

14. Install the cap on the front carburetor vacuum fitting (**Figure 85**).

15. Install the air box as described in Chapter Eight.

16. Lower and secure the fuel tank.

3

Table 1 MAINTENANCE SCHEDULE

Weekly/gas stop
  Check tire pressure cold; adjust to suit load and speed
  Check condition of tires
  Check brake operation
  Check throttle grip for smooth operation and return
  Check for smooth but not loose steering
  Check axle, suspension, controls and linkage fasteners; tighten if necessary
  Check engine oil level; add oil if necessary
  Check lights and horn operation, especially brake light
  Check for any abnormal engine noise and leaks
  Check coolant level
  Check stop switch operation
Initial 600 miles (1000 km) or 1 month
  Change engine oil and replace oil filter
  Check idle speed; adjust if necessary
  Check throttle cable free play; adjust if necessary
  Clean and lubricate drive chain
  Check brake pads for wear and rear pedal height
  Check brake discs thickness; replace if necessary
  Check brake discs for rust and corrosion; clean if necessary
  Check steering play; adjust if necessary
  Check and tighten exhaust system fasteners
  Check tightness of all chassis fasteners; tighten if necessary
  On California models, synchronize the carburetors
Every 4000 miles (6000 km) or 6 months
  Check air filter element for contamination; clean or replace if necessary
  Check spark plugs; replace if necessary
  Check all fuel system hoses for leakage; repair or replace if necessary
  Change engine oil
  Check idle speed; adjust if necessary
  Check throttle cable free play; adjust if necessary
  Check clutch lever free play; adjust if necessary
  Check radiator and all coolant hoses for leakage
  Check battery charge and condition
  Clean and lubricate drive chain
  Check drive chain and sprockets for wear or damage
  Check drive chain free play; adjust if necessary
  Check brake pads for wear
  Check brake discs thickness; replace if necessary
  Check brake discs for rust and corrosion; clean if necessary
  Check brake system for leakage; repair if necessary
  Check brake fluid level in both reservoirs; add fluid if necessary
  Check tire and wheel rim condition
  Lubricate all pivot points
  Check tightness of all chassis fasteners; tighten if necessary
Every 7500 miles (12,000 km) or 12 months
  All items listed in 4000 miles (6000 km) or 6 months and the following:
    Replace the spark plugs
    Synchronize carburetors

(continued)

Table 1 MAINTENANCE SCHEDULE (continued)

Every 7500 miles (12,000 km) or 12 months (continued)
  Check front fork operation and for leakage
  Check EVAP hoses (California models)
  Check PAIR (air supply) hoses (California models)
  Lubricate control cables
Every 11,000 miles (18,000 km) or 18 months
  All items listed in 7500 miles (12,000 km) or 12 months and the following:
  Replace air filter element
  Replace oil filter
Every 15,000 miles (24,000 km) or 24 months
  All items listed in 7500 miles (12,000 km) or 12 months and the following:
  Check valve clearance; adjust if necessary
Every 2 years
  Replace coolant
  Replace brake fluid
Every 4 years
  Replace all brake hoses
  Replace EVAP hoses (California models)

Table 2 TIRE SPECIFICATIONS

Item	Front	Rear
Tire type	Tubeless	Tubeless
Size	120/60ZR17 (55W)	160/60ZR17 (69W)
Minimum tread depth	1.6 mm (0.06 in.)	2.0 mm (0.08 in.)
Inflation pressure (cold)*		
Solo	225 kPa (33 psi)	250 kPa (36 psi)
Rider and passenger	225 kPa (33 psi)	250 kPa (36 psi)

*Tire inflation pressure for original equipment tires. Aftermarket tires may require different inflation pressure. The use of tires other than those specified by Suzuki may affect handling.

Table 3 RECOMMENDED LUBRICANTS AND FLUIDS

Fuel	
Type	Unleaded
Octane	
U.S.A., California and Canada models	87 [(R + M)/2 method] or research octane of 91 or higher
Non- U.S.A., California and Canada models	91
Fuel tank capacity, including reserve	
California models	15 L (4.0 U.S. gal., 3.3 Imp. gal.)
All other models	16 L (4.2 U.S. gal., 3.5 Imp. gal.)
Engine oil	
Grade	API SF or SG
Viscosity	SAE 10W-40
Capacity	
Oil change only	2.3 L (2.4 U.S. qt., 2.0 Imp. qt.)
Oil and filter change	2.4 L (2.5 U.S. qt., 2.1 Imp. qt.)
When engine completely dry	3.0 L (3.2 U.S. qt., 2.6 Imp. qt.)

(continued)

Table 3 RECOMMENDED LUBRICANTS AND FLUIDS (continued)

Brake fluid	DOT 4
Fork oil	
Viscosity	Suzuki No. 10 fork oil or equivalent
Capacity per leg	
U.S. and California models	
1999-2001	491 ml (16.6 U.S. oz., 17.3 Imp. gal.)
2002	480 ml (16.2 U.S. oz., 16.9 Imp. gal.)
All other models	
1999-2001	489 ml (16.5 U.S. oz., 17.2 Imp. gal.)
2002	478 ml (16.2 U.S. oz., 16.8 Imp. gal.)
Engine coolant	
Type	Antifreeze coolant compatible with aluminum radiators
Ratio	50:50 with distilled water
Capacity	1.6 L (1.7 U.S. qt., 1.4 Imp. qt.)*

*Includes reserve tank

Table 4 MAINTENANCE AND TUNE-UP SPECIFICATIONS

Battery	
Type	YT12A-BS Yuasa Maintenance free (sealed)
Capacity	12 volt 10 amp hour
Spark plug	NGK CR8E, ND U24ESR-N
Spark plug gap	0.7-0.8 mm (0.028-0.031 in.)
Idle speed	
Austria, Switzerland models	1250-1350 rpm
All other models	1200-1400 rpm
Ignition timing	5 B.T.D.C. at 1300 rpm
Valve clearance (cold)	
Intake	0.10-0.20 mm (0.004-0.008 in.)
Exhaust	0.20-0.30 mm (0.008-0.012 in.)
Compression pressure (at sea level)	
Standard	1500 kPa (217 psi)
Service limit	1100 kPa (159 psi)
Maximum difference between cylinders	193 kPa (28 psi)
Engine oil pressure (hot)	200-600 kPa (29-87 psi) at 3000 rpm
Brake pedal height	55-65 mm (2.2-2.5 in.)
Throttle cable free play	2.0-4.0 mm (0.08-0.16 in.)
Clutch lever free play	10-15 mm (0.4-0.6 in.)
Rim runout (front and rear)	
Axial	2.0 mm (0.08 in.)
Radial	2.0 mm (0.08 in.)
Radiator cap release pressure	95-125 kPa (13.5-17.8 psi)
Drive chain 21-pin length	319.4 mm (12.6 in.)
Drive chain free play	20-30 mm (0.8-1.2 in.)
Fork spring preload adjuster (2002 only)	4th groove from top
Rear shock absorber spring preload	
SV650	2nd position
SV650S	4th position

Table 5 MAINTENANCE AND TUNE-UP TORQUE SPECIFICATIONS

Item	N•m	in.-lb.	ft.-lb.
Cylinder head cover bolt	14	124	–
Engine sprocket nut	145	–	107
Exhaust pipe bolt	23	–	17
		(continued)	

Table 5 MAINTENANCE AND TUNE-UP TORQUE SPECIFICATIONS (continued)

Item	N•m	in.-lb.	ft.-lb.
Front axle	65	–	48
Front axle pinch bolt	23	–	17
Main oil gallery plug	18	159	–
Muffler mounting bolt	23	–	17
Oil drain plug	21	186	–
Rear axle nut	65	–	47
Rear brake master cylinder locknut	18	159	–
Spark plug	11	96	–
Valve timing inspection plug	23	–	17

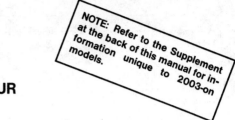

NOTE: Refer to the Supplement at the back of this manual for information unique to 2003-on models.

CHAPTER FOUR

ENGINE TOP END

4

All models covered in this book are equipped with a liquid-cooled, four-stroke, V-twin engine with dual overhead camshafts in each cylinder head. The crankshaft is supported by two main bearings, which are replaceable sleeve type bearings mounted in the vertically split crankcase.

The camshafts are chain-driven from the sprocket on the right end of the crankshaft. The camshaft lobes operate the valves directly.

An oil pump on the right side of the engine next to the clutch delivers oil under pressure throughout the engine. A gear on the clutch drives the oil pump gear. A filter screen on the oil pickup and a disposable oil filter remove contaminants from the oil.

This chapter contains information for removal, inspection, service and reassembly of the top end of the engine. The removal and installation of the engine assembly are covered in Chapter Five.

Table 1 provides general engine specifications and **Table 2** lists top end engine specifications. **Table 1** and **Table 2** are located at the end of this chapter.

Before beginning work, re-read Chapter One of this manual. Work done on the motorcycle will be better with this information fresh in mind.

Throughout the text there is frequent mention of the right and left side of the engine. This refers to the engine as it sits in the motorcycle frame, not as it sits on the workbench. The right and left refers to a rider sitting on the seat facing forward.

ENGINE PRINCIPLES

Figure 1 explains basic four-stroke engine operation. This is helpful when troubleshooting or repairing the engine.

ENGINE COOLING

The motorcycle is equipped with a liquid cooling system to remove engine heat. A water pump located on the right crankcase cover circulates a mixture of water and antifreeze through the engine and

FOUR-STROKE ENGINE PRINCIPLES

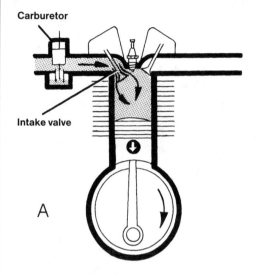

As the piston travels downward, the exhaust valve closes and the intake valve opens, allowing the new air-fuel mixture from the carburetor to be drawn into the cylinder. When the piston reaches the bottom of its travel, (BDC) the intake valve closes and remains closed for the next 1 1/2 revolutions of the crankshaft.

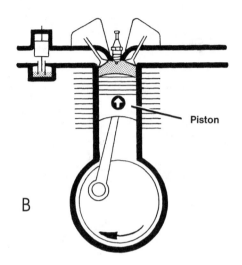

While the crankshaft continues to rotate, the piston moves upward, compressing the air-fuel mixture.

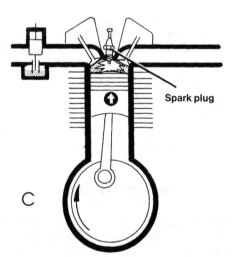

As the piston nears the top of its travel, the spark plug fires, igniting the compressed air-fuel mixture. The piston continues to top dead center (TDC) and is pushed down by the expanding gasses.

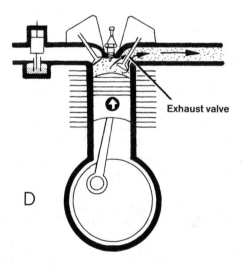

As the piston nears BDC, the exhaust valve opens and remains open until the piston is near TDC. The upward travel of the piston forces the exhaust gasses out of the cylinder. After the piston has reached TDC, the exhaust valve closes and the cycle repeats.

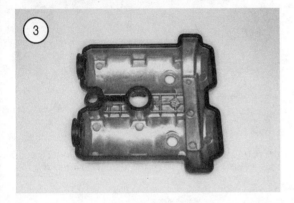

cooling system. Refer to Chapter Three for cooling system maintenance procedures. Refer to Chapter Ten for cooling system repair procedures.

CLEANLINESS

Repairs go much faster and easier if the engine is clean before beginning work. This is especially important when servicing the engine's top end. If the top end is being serviced while the engine is installed in the frame, note that dirt trapped underneath the fuel tank and frame members can fall into the cylinder and crankcase openings. Thoroughly clean the engine and surrounding area prior to starting work on the upper end of the engine.

SERVICING ENGINE IN FRAME

The following components can be serviced while the engine is mounted in the frame (the frame is a great holding fixture for breaking loose stubborn bolts and nuts):
1. Camshaft.
2. Cylinder head.

3. Cylinder.
4. Carburetors.
5. Starter.
6. Alternator.
7. Clutch assemblies.
8. Water pump.
9. Oil pump

CYLINDER HEAD COVERS

The cylinder head covers can be removed with the engine mounted in the frame. However, for clarity, some of the illustrations depict the engine removed.

Removal

> *NOTE*
> *If removing only one cylinder head cover (front or rear), note the steps that provide specific information for that cylinder head cover.*

1. Disconnect the negative battery cable as described in Chapter Three.
2A. *Rear cylinder head cover*—Remove the fuel tank as described in Chapter Eight.
2B. *Front cylinder head cover*—Remove the radiator as described in Chapter Ten.
3. Detach the spark plug lead and move it out of the way.
4. Remove the cylinder head cover retaining bolts (**Figure 2**).
5. Remove the cylinder head cover and gasket.

Inspection and Gasket Replacement

1. Make sure the gasket sealing surface in the cover groove is clean and free of any oil. This surface must be clean and smooth to provide a tight seal.
2. Inspect the cylinder head cover gasket around its perimeter for wear or damage. Replace the gasket if it is not in excellent condition.
3. Remove all old gasket sealer residue from the gasket sealing surface around the perimeter of the cylinder head. Be sure to clean off all old sealer from the crescent-shaped machined surfaces at the end of the cylinder head.
4. Check the cylinder head cover (**Figure 3**) for warp, cracks or damage, and replace if necessary.

5. Inspect the cover bolts for thread damage and rubber/metal sealing rings for damage or hardness. Replace as necessary.

6. Install a *new* gasket onto the cylinder head cover. Make sure it is completely seated around the perimeter.

7. Apply a light coat of Suzuki Bond No. 1207B, or equivalent, to the half-round shaped portions (A, **Figure 4**) of the gasket. This ensures a tight seal between the cylinder head cover and the cylinder head.

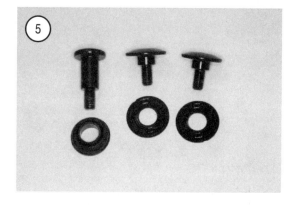

Installation

1. Make sure the gasket is installed correctly in the cylinder head cover.

2. Before installation, be sure to identify the cylinder head covers. The front cylinder head cover is equipped with a threaded radiator mounting hole (B, **Figure 4**).

3. Install the cylinder head cover onto the cylinder head. Make sure the half-round portions of the cover gasket properly engage the crescent shaped areas of the cylinder head.

4. Refer to **Figure 5** and install the correct gasket washer on the cylinder head bolts. If so equipped, position the metal side of the washer next to the bolt head.

5. Install the cover bolts making sure the gaskets are installed under each bolt. Tighten the bolts in a crossing pattern to 14 N•m (124 in.-lb.).

6. Connect the spark plug leads.

7A. *Rear cylinder head cover*—Install the fuel tank as described in Chapter Eight.

7B. *Front cylinder head cover*—Install the radiator as described in Chapter Ten.

8. Connect the negative battery cable as described in Chapter Three.

CAMSHAFT

The procedures for servicing the camshafts on the front and rear cylinders are similar. However, due to the restricted space available around the rear cylinder, follow the additional steps described in the following procedures when servicing the camshafts on the rear cylinder.

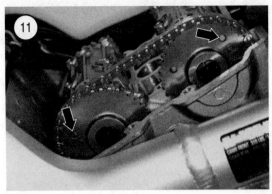

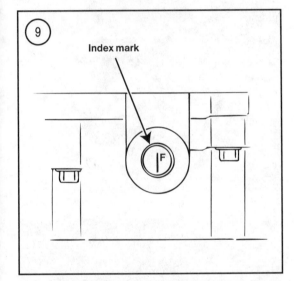

Index mark

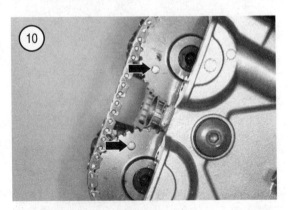

Removal

1. Remove the cylinder head cover as described in this chapter.

2. Remove the spark plugs as described in Chapter Three. This makes it easier to turn the engine by hand.

3. Remove the valve timing inspection plug (A, **Figure 6**).

4. Remove the alternator retaining nut access plug (B, **Figure 6**).

5. Remove the cam chain guide (**Figure 7**).

6A. *Front cylinder*—Correctly position the camshafts as follows:

   a. Insert a suitably sized socket through the side cover to engage the alternator bolt (**Figure 8**). Rotate the engine *counterclockwise*, as viewed from the left side of the motorcycle, until the F line on the alternator rotor aligns with the mark on the timing inspection hole as shown in **Figure 9**.

   b. Make sure the holes marked F on the camshaft sprockets are positioned as shown in **Figure 10**. If the sprocket holes are not positioned as shown, rotate the crankshaft one full revolution (360°) until the sprocket holes are positioned correctly.

   c. If it was necessary to rotate the crankshaft an additional revolution, recheck that the F line on the alternator rotor is once again aligned with the mark on the timing inspection hole (**Figure 9**). Realign if necessary.

6B. *Rear cylinder*—Correctly position the camshafts as follows:

   a. Insert a suitably sized socket throught the side cover to engage the alternator bolt (**Figure 8**). Rotate the engine *counterclockwise*, as viewed from the left side of the motorcycle, until the F line on the alternator rotor aligns with the mark on the timing inspection hole as shown in **Figure 9**.

   b. Make sure the holes marked F on the camshaft sprockets are positioned as shown in **Figure 11**. If the sprocket holes are not positioned as shown, rotate the crankshaft one full revolution (360°) until the sprocket holes are positioned correctly.

   c. If it was necessary to rotate the crankshaft an additional revolution, recheck that the F line on the alternator rotor is once again aligned with the mark on the timing inspection hole (**Figure 9**). Realign if necessary.

7. Remove the cam chain tensioner as described below.

NOTE
Mark the camshaft holder according to cylinder location (front or rear).

8. Using a crossing pattern, loosen and then remove the bolts securing the camshaft holders (**Figure 12**). Pull the holders straight up and off the cylinder head.

NOTE
*There is no need to secure the camshaft drive chain to the exterior of the engine. The cam chain stopper bolt (B, **Figure 7**) prevents the chain from dropping into the crankcase.*

9. Disengage the cam chain from the camshaft sprockets and remove the intake and the exhaust camshafts (**Figure 13**) from the cylinder head one at a time.

CAUTION
If the crankshaft must be rotated while the camshafts are removed, pull up on the cam chain so it properly engages the crankshaft timing sprocket. Hold the chain taut on the timing sprocket while rotating the crankshaft. If this is not done, the cam chain could become kinked, which could cause damage to the chain, timing sprocket and surrounding crankcase area.

Inspection

When measuring the camshafts in this section, compare the actual measurements to the new and wear limit specifications in **Table 2**. Replace parts that are out of specification or show damage as described in this section.

1. Check the camshaft lobes (A, **Figure 14**) for wear. The lobes should not be scored and the edges should be square.

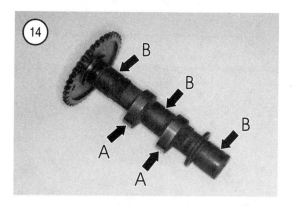

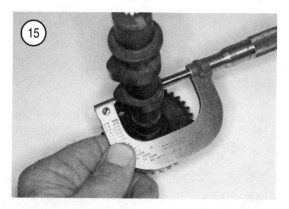

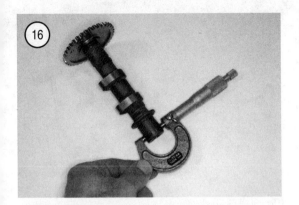

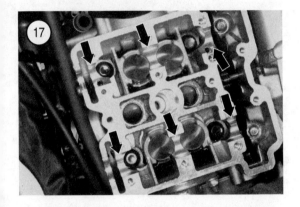

2. Measure the height of each lobe (**Figure 15**) with a micrometer. Replace the camshaft if any lobe is out of specification.

3. Check each camshaft journal (B, **Figure 14**) for wear and scoring.

4. Measure the diameter of each camshaft journal (**Figure 16**) with a micrometer. Record each measurement. It is necessary to have them when measuring camshaft journal oil clearance. Replace the camshaft if any journal diameter is out of specification.

5. If the camshaft journals are excessively worn or damaged, check the journal surfaces in the cylinder head (**Figure 17**) and in the camshaft holders (**Figure 18**). They should not be scored or excessively worn. If any of the journal surfaces are worn or scored, replace the cylinder head assembly and camshaft holders as a set.

6. Place the camshaft on a set of V-blocks (**Figure 19**) and check the runout with a dial indicator. Replace the camshaft if its runout is out of specification.

7. Inspect the camshaft sprocket (**Figure 20**) for broken or chipped teeth. Also check the teeth for cracking or rounding. If the camshaft sprocket(s) is damaged or excessively worn, replace the camshaft. Also, inspect the camshaft timing sprocket mounted on the crankshaft as described in Chapter Five.

NOTE
If the camshaft sprockets are worn, check the cam chain, chain guides and chain tensioner for damage.

8. Inspect the sliding surface of the top cam chain guide (**Figure 21**) for wear or damage. Also check both ends of the guide. Replace the top guide as necessary.

Clearance Measurement

This procedure requires the use of Plastigage. The camshafts must be installed into the cylinder head. Before installing the camshafts, wipe all oil residue from each camshaft journal and from the journal surface of the cylinder head and camshaft holders.

1. Do not install the drive chain onto the camshafts for this procedure.

> *NOTE*
> *The camshafts are identified according to location by embossed letters on each camshaft (**Figure 22**). The identifying letters are IN for the intake camshaft, EX for the exhaust camshaft, F for the front cylinder, and R for the rear cylinder.*

2. Install the camshafts into their respective cylinder head in the correct location. Refer to the marks (**Figure 23**) on each camshaft. On the front cylinder, install the exhaust camshaft in the front of the engine and the intake camshaft in the rear. On the rear cylinder, install the exhaust camshaft in the rear of the engine and the intake camshaft in the front.

3. Place a strip of Plastigage onto each journal (**Figure 24**). The Plastigage must be parallel to the camshaft.

4. Install each camshaft holder in its correct location. Refer to the *IN* and *EX* marks (**Figure 25**) on each holder, as well as the marks made during disassembly to indicate original cylinder location. The groove at the end of each camshaft holder (**Figure 26**) must fit over the flange on the camshaft.

5. Install the camshaft holder bolts fingertight at this time.

> *CAUTION*
> *Failure to tighten the bolts in a crossing pattern will result in damage to the bearing surfaces in the cylinder head and camshaft holders.*

6. Install the bolts and tighten them evenly in a crossing pattern to 10 N•m (88 in.-lb.).

> *CAUTION*
> *Do not rotate the camshafts with the Plastigage in place.*

7. Loosen the bolts in a crossing pattern.

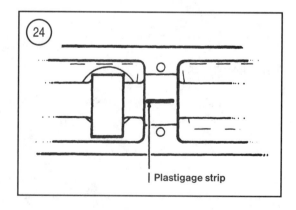

Plastigage strip

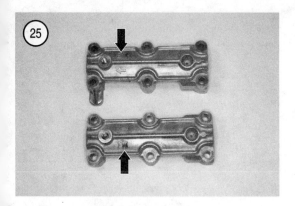

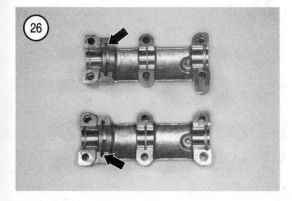

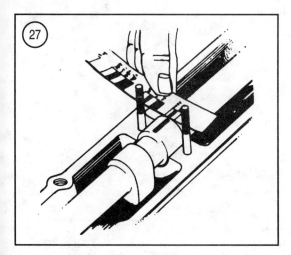

8. Pull straight up and carefully remove the camshaft holders.

9. Measure the flattened Plastigage (**Figure 27**) at the widest point, according to the manufacturer's instructions.

> *CAUTION*
> *Be sure to remove all traces of Plastigage from the camshaft holders*

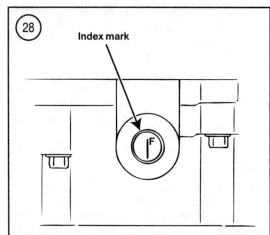

Index mark

and from the camshaft journal. If any of the material is left in the engine, it can plug an oil control orifice and cause severe engine damage.

10. Remove *all* Plastigage from the camshafts and camshaft holders.

11. If the camshaft journal oil clearance is greater than specified in **Table 2**, refer to the camshaft journal outside diameter dimension recorded in *Inspection* Step 4. If the bearing surface is worn to the service limit; replace the camshaft. If the camshaft is within specification; replace the cylinder head assembly.

Installation (Front Cylinder Camshaft)

> *NOTE*
> *The camshafts are identified according to location by embossed letters on each camshaft (**Figure 22**). The identifying letters are IN for the intake camshaft, EX for the exhaust camshaft, F for the front cylinder, and R for the rear cylinder.*

1. Pull up on the cam chain and make sure it is properly meshed with the crankshaft timing sprocket.

> *NOTE*
> *If the crankshaft has not been disturbed since the camshafts were removed, the engine may still be at the correct position for camshaft installation. If the F line on the alternator rotor is still aligned with the mark on the timing inspection hole (**Figure 28**)*

then the engine is in the correct position for camshaft installation. If alignment is incorrect, perform Step 2.

2. Use a suitable wrench on the alternator retaining bolt (**Figure 29**). Rotate the engine *counterclockwise*, as viewed from the left side of the motorcycle, until the F line on the alternator rotor is aligned with the mark on the timing inspection hole (**Figure 28**).

3. Apply a light coat of molybdenum disulfide grease to each camshaft journal (B, **Figure 14**). Coat all bearing surfaces in the cylinder head (**Figure 17**) and camshaft holders (**Figure 18**) with clean engine oil.

4. Set the exhaust camshaft into the cam chain and install the camshaft onto the cylinder head bearing surface (A, **Figure 30**).

5. Lift up on the chain and rotate the exhaust camshaft until the 1F arrow mark (A, **Figure 31**) is level with the top surface of the cylinder head. The No. 2 arrow mark (B, **Figure 31**) is now pointing straight up. Properly mesh the cam chain with the sprocket and install a short cable tie to secure the cam chain to the cam sprocket.

6. Fit the intake camshaft (B, **Figure 30**) through the cam chain and install the camshaft onto the cylinder head bearing surface.

7. Note that the No. 2 arrow on the exhaust cam sprocket points to a pin on the cam chain. This is the first pin (**Figure 32**). Starting at this pin, count back to the 16th pin. Properly mesh the cam chain with the intake cam sprocket so the 16th pin is opposite the No. 3 arrow on the intake cam sprocket (**Figure 32**). Install a short cable tie to secure the cam chain to the sprocket.

CAUTION
Engine damage is likely if the cam chain-to-camshaft installation and alignment is incorrect. Recheck the work several times to make sure alignment is correct.

NOTE
The cam chain is now riding on the crankshaft timing sprocket, the exhaust cam sprocket and the intake cam sprocket. Do not disturb this alignment until the camshaft holders and cam chain tensioner are properly installed.

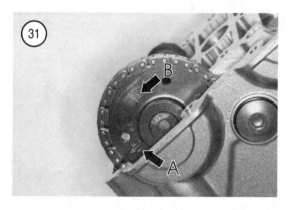

8. Install the camshaft holders onto the correct camshaft. Refer to the *IN* and *EX* marks (**Figure 25**) and install the camshaft holder onto the respective camshaft. The groove at the end of each camshaft holder (**Figure 26**) must fit over the flange on the camshaft.

CAUTION
Do not substitute any other type of bolt for the original camshaft holder bolts. These special bolts are marked with a 9 on the head and are of a supe-

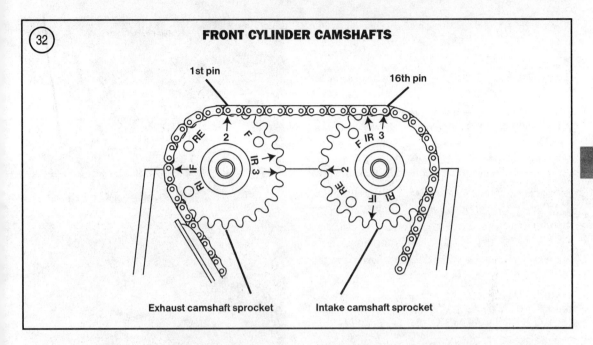

FRONT CYLINDER CAMSHAFTS

1st pin

16th pin

Exhaust camshaft sprocket

Intake camshaft sprocket

4

rior strength grade. Substitute bolts may not have the required strength.

9. Install the camshaft holder bolts fingertight at this time.

CAUTION
Failure to tighten the bolts in a crossing pattern will result in damage to the bearing surfaces in the cylinder head and camshaft holders.

10. Install the bolts and tighten them evenly in a crossing pattern to 10 N•m (88 in.-lb.).

11. Remove the cable ties securing the cam chain to the sprockets.

12. As a final check, insert a finger into the tensioner receptacle in the cylinder, push on the chain and take out the chain slack. Recheck all the timing marks to make sure all marks are still aligned properly as shown in **Figure 32**. If incorrect, reposition the cam chain on the sprockets.

13. Install the top cam chain guide (**Figure 7**) and tighten the mounting bolts to 10 N•m (88 in.-lb.).

14. Install the cam chain tensioner as described in this chapter.

15. Fill the pockets in the cylinder head with clean engine oil.

16. After the tensioner is installed correctly, re-check the alignment as shown in **Figure 32**. If any

of the alignment points are incorrect, repeat this procedure until *all* are correct.

CAUTION
*If there is any binding while rotating the crankshaft, **stop**. Determine the cause before proceeding.*

17. Insert a suitably sized socket through the side cover to engage the alternator bolt (**Figure 29**). Rotate the crankshaft *counterclockwise* as viewed from the left side of the motorcycle. Rotate the crankshaft several complete revolutions and check the operation of the valve train.

18. Adjust the valves as described in Chapter Three.

19. Install the spark plugs as described in Chapter Three.

20. Install the cylinder head cover as described in this chapter.

Installation (Rear Cylinder Camshaft)

NOTE
*The camshafts are identified according to location by embossed letters on each camshaft (**Figure 22**). The identifying letters are IN for the intake camshaft, EX for the exhaust camshaft, F for the front cylinder, and R for the rear cylinder.*

1. Pull up on the cam chain and make sure it is properly meshed with the crankshaft timing sprocket.

2. If the crankshaft has not been disturbed since the front cylinder camshafts were installed, use a suitable wrench on the alternator retaining bolt (**Figure 29**). Rotate the crankshaft 360° *counterclockwise*, as viewed from the left side of the motorcycle, until the F line on the alternator rotor is aligned with the mark on the timing inspection hole (**Figure 28**). Proceed to Step 4.

3. If the crankshaft position is not known, proceed as follows:

   a. If the cylinder head cover on the front cylinder is installed, remove it as described in this chapter.

   CAUTION
   Pull up on the rear cylinder cam chain when rotating the crankshaft to prevent internal damage due to chain binding.

   b. Insert a suitably sized socket through the side cover to engage the alternator bolt (**Figure 29**). Rotate the crankshaft *counterclockwise*, as viewed from the left side of the motorcycle, until the F line on the alternator rotor aligns with the mark on the timing inspection hole as shown in **Figure 28**.

   c. Make sure the holes marked F on the front cylinder camshaft sprockets are positioned as shown in **Figure 10**. If the sprocket holes are not positioned as shown, rotate the crankshaft one full revolution (360°) until the sprocket holes are positioned correctly.

   d. With the crankshaft now positioned properly for the front cylinder, rotate the crankshaft one full revolution (360°) *counterclockwise*, as viewed from the left side of the motorcycle, until the F line on the alternator rotor aligns with the mark on the timing inspection hole as shown in **Figure 28**. The rear cylinder will now be on the compression stroke and in position for installation of the camshafts.

4. Apply a light coat of molybdenum disulfide grease to each camshaft journal (B, **Figure 14**). Coat all bearing surfaces in the cylinder head (**Figure 17**) and camshaft holders (**Figure 18**) with clean engine oil.

5. Set the intake camshaft into the cam chain and install the camshaft onto the cylinder head bearing surface (A, **Figure 33**).

6. Lift up on the chain and rotate the intake camshaft until the 1R (A, **Figure 34**) arrow mark is level with the top surface of the cylinder head. The No. 2 arrow mark (B, **Figure 34**) is now pointing straight up. Properly mesh the cam chain with the sprocket and install a short cable tie to secure the cam chain to the cam sprocket.

7. Fit the exhaust camshaft (B, **Figure 33**) through the cam chain and install the camshaft onto the cylinder head bearing surface.

8. Note that the No. 2 arrow on the intake cam sprocket points to a pin on the cam chain. This is the first pin (**Figure 35**). Starting at this pin, count back to the 16th pin. Properly mesh the cam chain with the exhaust cam sprocket so the 16th pin is opposite the No. 3 arrow on the exhaust cam sprocket (**Figure 35**). Install a short cable tie to secure the cam chain to the sprocket.

CAUTION
Engine damage is likely if the cam chain-to-camshaft installation and

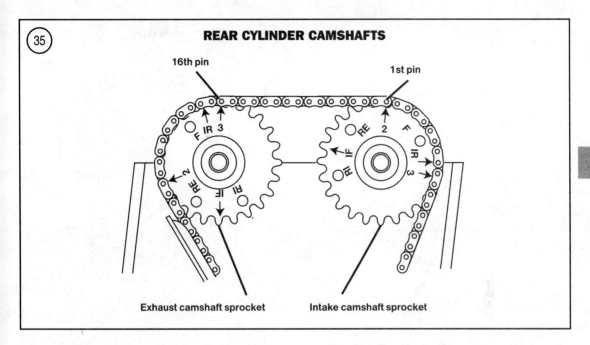

REAR CYLINDER CAMSHAFTS

16th pin

1st pin

Exhaust camshaft sprocket   Intake camshaft sprocket

4

alignment is incorrect. Recheck the work several times to make sure alignment is correct.

NOTE
The cam chain is now riding on the crankshaft timing sprocket, the exhaust cam sprocket and the intake cam sprocket. Do not disturb this alignment until the camshaft holders and cam chain tensioner are properly installed.

9. Install the camshaft holders onto the correct camshaft. Refer to the *IN* and *EX* marks (**Figure 25**) and install the camshaft holder onto the respective camshaft. The groove at the end of each camshaft holder (**Figure 26**) must fit over the flange on the camshaft.

CAUTION
Do not substitute any other type of bolt for the original camshaft holder bolts. These special bolts are marked with a 9 on the head and are of a superior strength grade. Substitute bolts may not have the required strength.

10. Install the camshaft holder bolts fingertight at this time.

CAUTION
Failure to tighten the bolts in a crossing pattern will result in damage to

the bearing surfaces in the cylinder head and camshaft holders.

11. Install the bolts and tighten them evenly in a crossing pattern to 10 N•m (88 in.-lb.).

12. Remove the cable ties securing the cam chain to the sprockets.

13. As a final check, insert a finger into the tensioner receptacle in the cylinder, push on the chain and take out the chain slack. Recheck all the timing marks to make sure all marks are still aligned properly as shown in **Figure 35**. If incorrect, reposition the cam chain on the sprockets.

14. Install the top cam chain guide (A, **Figure 7**) and tighten the mounting bolts to 10 N•m (88 in.-lb.).

15. Install the cam chain tensioner as described in this chapter.

16. Fill the pockets in the cylinder head with clean engine oil.

17. After the tensioner is installed correctly, recheck the alignment as shown in **Figure 35**. If any of the alignment points are incorrect, repeat this procedure until *all* are correct.

CAUTION
*If there is any binding while rotating the crankshaft, **stop**. Determine the cause before proceeding.*

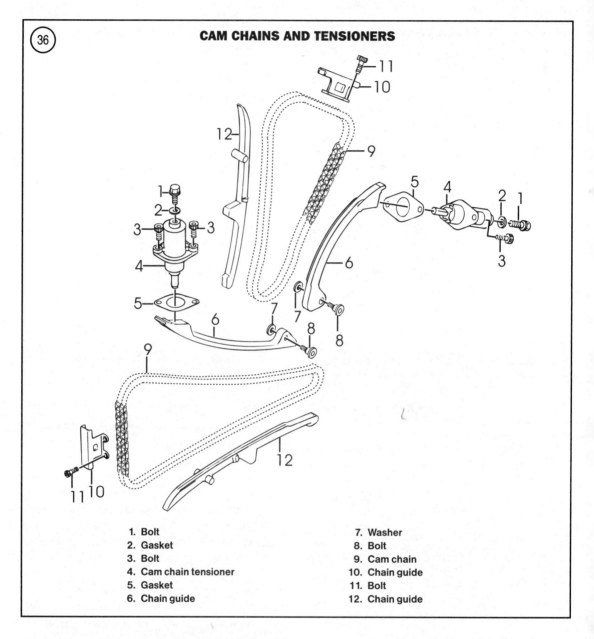

CAM CHAINS AND TENSIONERS

1. Bolt
2. Gasket
3. Bolt
4. Cam chain tensioner
5. Gasket
6. Chain guide
7. Washer
8. Bolt
9. Cam chain
10. Chain guide
11. Bolt
12. Chain guide

18. Insert a suitably sized socket through the side cover to engage the alternator bolt (**Figure 29**). Rotate the crankshaft *counterclockwise* as viewed from the left side of the motorcycle. Rotate the crankshaft several complete revolutions and check the operation of the valve train.

19. Adjust the valves as described in Chapter Three.

20. Install the spark plug as described in Chapter Three.

21. Install the cylinder head cover as described in this chapter.

CAM CHAIN TENSIONER AND GUIDES

The engine is equipped with a cam chain tensioner and guides for each cylinder (**Figure 36**). The cam chain tensioner on the front cylinder is located on the intake side of the cylinder (**Figure 37**) and is relatively accessible. The cam chain tensioner on the rear cylinder is located on the exhaust side of the cylinder (**Figure 38**). While the rear cylinder cam tensioner is accessible, it is difficult to service with the engine in the frame. Before

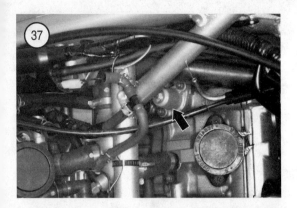

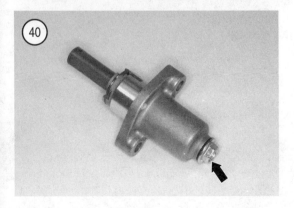

servicing the rear cylinder cam tensioner, particularly if other major work will be performed, read the following procedure as well as the procedure for engine removal and installation. Servicing the cam tensioner with the engine on the workbench may be the better procedure.

**Cam Chain Tensioner
Removal/Inspection/Installation**

> *CAUTION*
> *The cam chain tensioner is a non-return type. The internal push rod will not return to its original position once it has moved out, even the slightest amount. After the tensioner mounting bolts are loosened, the tensioner assembly must be **completely removed** and the pushrod reset. If the mounting bolts are loosened, do not simply retighten the mounting bolts. The pushrod has already moved out to an extended position, and it will exert excessive pressure on the chain leading to costly engine damage.*

Refer to **Figure 36**.

1. If removing the cam chain tensioner on the front cylinder, remove the carburetors as described in Chapter Eight.

2. If removing the cam chain tensioner on the rear cylinder, perform the following to gain access to the cam tensioner:

    a. Remove the two bolts that secure the rear brake pedal assembly and move it out of the way (**Figure 39**).

    b. Remove the rear brake switch.

3. Remove the 5 mm Allen bolts securing the cam chain tensioner. Remove the cam chain tensioner and gasket.

4. Unscrew and remove the bolt (**Figure 40**) and washer from the end of the tensioner.

5. The cam chain tensioner is available only as a unit assembly. Do not attempt to disassemble it. Inspect the housing and rod for damage. Replace the tensioner assembly if necessary.

6. Remove all gasket residue from the cam chain tensioner and cylinder.

> *NOTE*
> *Before installing the cam chain tensioner, the tensioner must be*

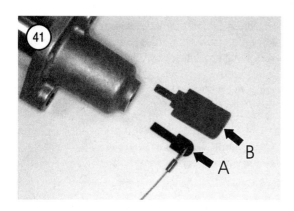

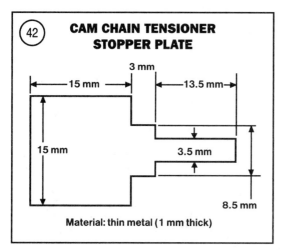

CAM CHAIN TENSIONER STOPPER PLATE

3 mm

15 mm 13.5 mm

15 mm 3.5 mm

8.5 mm

Material: thin metal (1 mm thick)

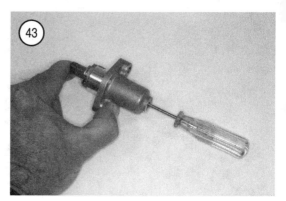

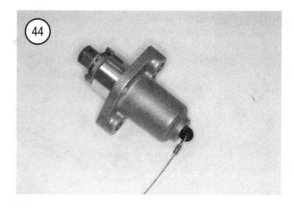

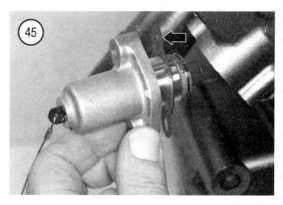

locked in the retracted position using a stopper plate. Suzuki offers tool 09917-62430 (A, Figure 41); however, a stopper plate may be fabricated (B) from a piece of thin metal using the dimensioned drawing in Figure 42.

7. Use a narrow flat-blade screwdriver and turn the inner adjuster *clockwise* to retract the rod (**Figure 43**).

8. Hold the rod in the retracted position.

9. Remove the screwdriver and insert the stopper plate (**Figure 44**) in the grooves of the rod and housing to keep the spring tension locked.

10. Install a new gasket (**Figure 45**) onto the tensioner.

11. Install the tensioner and mounting bolts. Tighten the mounting bolts to 10 N•m (88 in.-lb.).

12. Remove the stopper plate from the tensioner body to allow the rod to extend.

NOTE
*The tensioner should **click** after removing the stopper plate, which indicates the rod has extended. If not, remove the tensioner and check tensioner operation.*

13. Install the sealing bolt and washer (**Figure 46**) and tighten to 8 N•m (71 in.-lb.).

14. If removed, install the carburetors as described in Chapter Eight.

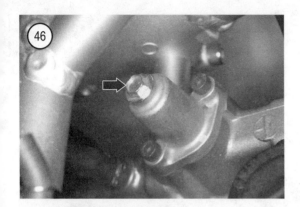

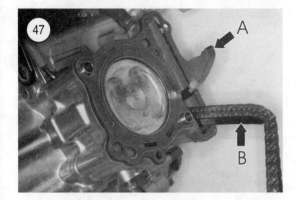

15. If removed, install the rear brake switch and the rear brake pedal assembly.

Cam Chain Guides
Removal/Inspection/Installation

Refer to **Figure 36**. The rear cam chain guide (A, **Figure 47**) on each cylinder is secured at its lower end by a bolt on the side of the crankcase. The front cam chain guide (B, **Figure 47**) on each cylinder rests in pockets in the crankcase and cylinder.

1. Remove the cylinder head as described in this chapter.

2. *Front cylinder cam chain guides*—Remove the starter clutch assembly as described in Chapter Five.

3. *Rear cylinder cam chain guides*—Remove the primary drive gear as described in Chapter Six.

4. Pull straight up and withdraw the front cam chain guide (**Figure 48**).

5A. *Front cylinder*—To remove the rear cam chain guide, remove the bolt and washer (A, **Figure 49**) securing the rear chain guide. A washer sits between the backside of the guide and the crankcase. Do not lose it.

5B. *Rear cylinder*—To remove the rear cam chain guide, remove the bolt and washer (A, **Figure 50**) securing the rear chain guide. A washer sits between the backside of the guide and the crankcase. Do not lose it.

6. Pull straight up and withdraw the rear chain guide.

7. Inspect both guides for wear or damage. Replace as necessary.

8. Make sure the cam chain is properly meshed with the timing sprocket on the crankshaft.

9. Install the rear cam chain guide into position.

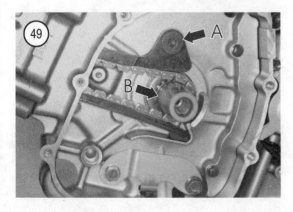

10. Install the bolt (A, **Figure 51**) part way through the guide. Install the washer (B, **Figure 51**) behind the guide and push the bolt the rest of the way through the guide.

11. Tighten the bolt to 10 N•m (88 in.-lb.).

12. Install the front cam chain guide (**Figure 48**) and push it down until it seats in the pockets in the crankcase and cylinder.

13. *Front cylinder cam chain guides*—Install the starter clutch assembly as described in Chapter Five.

14. *Rear cylinder cam chain guides*—Install the primary drive gear as described in Chapter Six.

15. Install the cylinder head as described in this chapter.

CAM CHAINS

The engine is equipped with two cam chains, one for each cylinder. The cam chain in the front cylinder is driven by a sprocket on the crankshaft behind the starter driven gear. The cam chain in the rear cylinder is driven by a sprocket on the crankshaft behind the primary drive gear.

Continuous cam chains are used on all models. Do not cut the chains; replacement link components are not available.

Removal/Installation

1. Remove the cylinder head as described in this chapter.

2. Remove the cam chain guides as described in this chapter.

3. Remove the cam chain from the sprocket (B, **Figure 49** or **Figure 50**) on the crankshaft.

4. Pull the cam chain up through the chain tunnel in the cylinder and remove the chain.

5. If cam chain sprocket service is required, refer to Chapter Five.

6. Install the cam chain by reversing the preceding removal steps.

Inspection

If the cam chain or chain guides are excessively worn, the chain tensioner may not be working properly. Refer to *Cam Chain Tensioner* in this chapter.

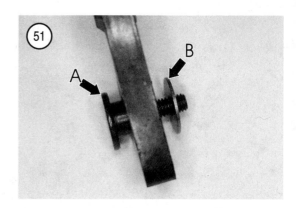

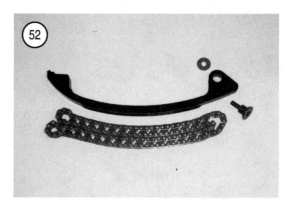

1. Clean the cam chain in solvent. Blow it dry with compressed air.

2. Inspect the cam chain (**Figure 52**) for:

 a. Worn or damaged pins and rollers.

 b. Cracked or damaged side plates.

3. If the cam chain is excessively worn or damaged, inspect the camshaft sprockets (**Figure 20**) and the drive sprocket on the crankshaft (B, **Figure 49** or **Figure 50**) for the same wear conditions. If any of the sprockets show signs of wear or damage, replace them.

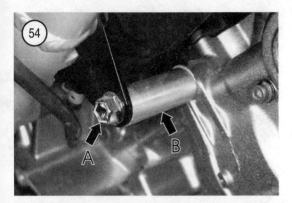

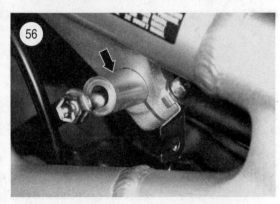

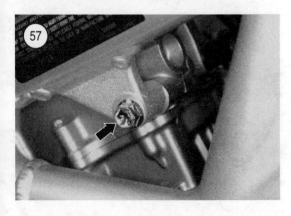

CAUTION
Do not install a new chain onto worn or damaged sprockets. Doing so will quickly wear the new chain.

CYLINDER HEAD

Removal

1. Drain the cooling system as described in Chapter Three.

2. Remove the carburetors as described in Chapter Eight.

3. Remove the exhaust system as described in Chapter Eight.

4. Remove the camshafts as described in this chapter.

5A. *Front cylinder head*—Perform the following:

   a. Remove the left engine mounting bolt (A, **Figure 53**). Loosen the spacer clamp bolt (B, **Figure 53**) and move the spacer (C) away from the cylinder head.

   b. Remove the right engine mounting bolt (A, **Figure 54**) and spacer (B).

5B. *Rear cylinder head*—Perform the following:

   a. Remove the left engine mounting bolt (A, **Figure 55**). Loosen the spacer clamp bolt (B, **Figure 55**) and move the spacer (**Figure 56**) away from the cylinder head.

   b. Remove the right engine mounting bolt (**Figure 57**).

CAUTION
The valve lifters and shims can remain in the cylinder head if it is not going to be serviced. Do not allow the lifters and shims to fall out by turning the cylinder head over or on its side. If these parts fall out, they may be damaged and it will be impossible to return them to their original locations, making it necessary to adjust the valve clearances.

6. If the cylinder head is going to be inspected and/or serviced, remove the valve lifters and shims before removing the head. Refer to *Valve Lifters and Shims Removal and Installation* in this chapter.

7. Tie a piece of wire to the cam chain and secure it so the cam chain cannot fall into the engine.

8. Unscrew and remove the cylinder head side bolt (A, **Figure 58**).

9. Remove the 6 mm cylinder head-to-cylinder Allen bolt (B, **Figure 58**) on the side of the cylinder head.

10. Remove the 6 mm bolts in the cam chain compartment (A, **Figure 59**).

11. In a crossing pattern, remove the 10 mm cylinder head bolts (B, **Figure 59**) securing the cylinder head.

12. Loosen the cylinder head by tapping around the perimeter with a rubber or soft-faced mallet. Do not use a metal hammer.

13. Lift off the cylinder head. Guide the camshaft chain through the opening in the cylinder head and retie the wire to the exterior of the engine. This will prevent the drive chain from falling down into the crankcase.

14. Remove the cylinder head gasket (A, **Figure 60**). Account for the locating dowels (B, **Figure 60**).

15. Place a clean shop cloth into the cam chain opening in the cylinder to prevent the entry of debris.

Inspection

NOTE
*The cylinder heads are not identical. A cavity on each cylinder head contains either an F or R (**Figure 61**) to designate the location of the cylinder head.*

1. If not already removed, remove the valve lifters and shims. Make sure to keep them in order so they can be reinstalled in their original locations. Refer to Step 6 in the cylinder head removal procedure.

2. Remove all traces of gasket residue from the cylinder head (**Figure 62**) and cylinder mating surfaces. Do not scratch the gasket surfaces.

3. Without removing the valves, remove all carbon deposits from the combustion chamber (A, **Figure 63**). Use a fine wire brush dipped in solvent or make a scraper from hardwood. Take care not to damage the head, valves or spark plug threads.

CAUTION
Cleaning the combustion chamber with the valves removed can damage the valve seat surfaces. A damaged or even slightly scratched valve seat causes poor valve seating.

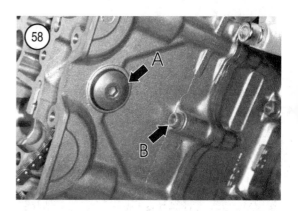

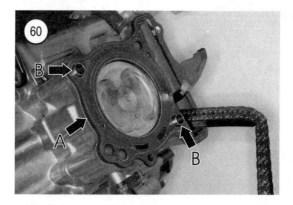

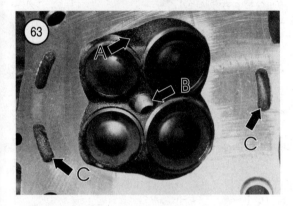

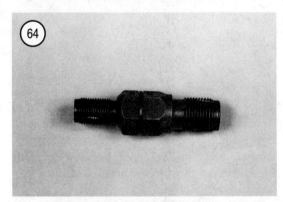

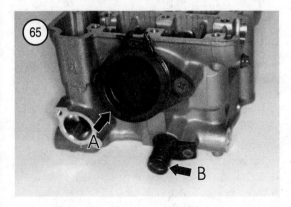

4. Examine the spark plug threads (B, **Figure 63**) in the cylinder head for damage. If damage is minor or if the threads are dirty or clogged with carbon, use a spark plug thread tap (**Figure 64**) to clean the threads following the manufacturer's instructions. If thread damage is excessive, the threads can be restored by installing a steel thread insert. Thread insert kits can be purchased at automotive supply stores or the inserts can be installed by a Suzuki dealership or machine shop.

CAUTION
Aluminum spark plug threads are commonly damaged due to galling, cross-threading and overtightening. To prevent galling, apply an antiseize compound on the plug threads before installation and do not overtighten.

NOTE
When using a tap to clean spark plug threads, coat the tap with an aluminum tap cutting fluid or kerosene.

5. After all carbon is removed from combustion chambers and valve ports, and the spark plug thread hole is repaired, clean the entire head in solvent. Blow it dry with compressed air.

6. Examine the crown on both pistons. A crown should show no signs of wear or damage. If a crown appears pecked or spongy-looking, also check the spark plug, valves and combustion chamber for aluminum deposits. If these deposits are found, the cylinder is overheating from a lean fuel mixture or preignition.

NOTE
*The intake tubes (A, **Figure 65**) are marked according to location. The intake tube for the front cylinder head is marked UPF on the lip of the tube, while the intake tube for the rear cylinder head is marked UPR.*

7. Service the intake tube (A, **Figure 65**) as follows:

    a. Inspect the intake tube for cracks or other damage that would allow unfiltered air to enter the engine.

    b. If necessary, remove the intake tube and install a new O-ring between the intake tube and the cylinder head. Lubricate the O-ring using Suzuki Super Grease A or equivalent.

c. Install the intake tube so the UPF or UPR on the lip of the tube is toward the top of the cylinder head.

d. Apply Threadlock 1342 to the intake tube retaining bolts and tighten them securely.

8. Remove the coolant fitting (B, **Figure 65**). Inspect the fitting for cracks or other damage and replace if necessary. Install a new O-ring onto the fitting. Coat the O-ring with coolant before installing the fitting.

9. Check for cracks in the combustion chamber, intake port and exhaust. Replace a cracked head if it cannot be repaired by welding.

10. On the rear cylinder head, remove the exhaust pipe (**Figure 66**). On both cylinder heads, inspect the threads on the exhaust pipe mounting studs for damage. Clean with a metric die if damaged.

11. Make sure all coolant passageways (C, **Figure 63**) are clear. If necessary, blow the passageways clear with compressed air.

12. Run a tap through each threaded hole to remove any debris accumulation. Make sure the engine mounting bolt holes are in good condition.

13. Thoroughly clean the cylinder head in solvent and then hot soap water.

> *NOTE*
> *If the cylinder head was bead blasted, grit in small crevices can be hard to remove. Any residual grit left in the engine will contaminate the oil and cause premature wear. Repeatedly wash the cylinder head in a solution of hot soap and water to remove this debris.*

14. After the head has been thoroughly cleaned, place a straightedge across the gasket surface at several points. Measure warp (**Figure 67**) by attempting to insert a feeler gauge between the straightedge and cylinder head at each location. The maximum warp limit is 0.05 mm (0.002 in.). A warped or nicked cylinder head surface could cause an air leak and result in overheating. If the warp limit exceeds the specification, the cylinder head must be resurfaced or replaced. Consult a Suzuki dealership or machine shop experienced in this type of work.

Installation

1. Remove the shop cloths from the cylinder.

2. Make sure the cylinder head and cylinder mating surfaces are clean of all gasket residue.

3. If removed, install the two locating dowels (B, **Figure 60**) into the cylinder.

4. Install a new cylinder head gasket (A, **Figure 60**). Make sure all the gasket holes align with those in the cylinder.

5. Position the cylinder head over the cylinder and run the cam chain and its safety wire through the cam chain tunnel. Tie the safety wire to the exterior of the engine.

6. Carefully slide the cylinder head onto the engine and seat the cylinder head onto the cylinder. Make sure the locating dowels engage the cylinder head.

7. Pull up on the cam chain and make sure it is properly engaged with the crankshaft timing sprocket before continuing.

8. Make sure the cylinder head bolt, threads and washers are free of debris. Dirt on the bolt threads or washers may affect bolt torque.

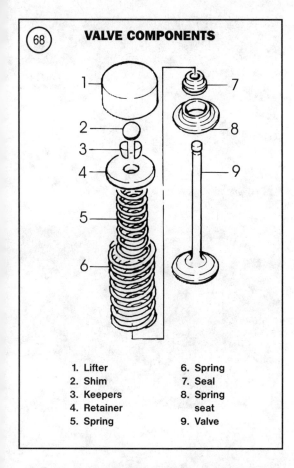

VALVE COMPONENTS

1. Lifter
2. Shim
3. Keepers
4. Retainer
5. Spring
6. Spring
7. Seal
8. Spring seat
9. Valve

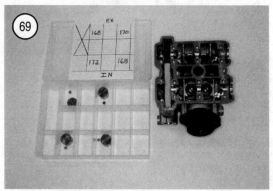

NOTE
Apply clean engine oil to the washers and threads on the cylinder head bolts before installation.

9. Install the 10 mm cylinder head bolts and washers. Tighten the bolts in a crossing pattern. Initially, tighten all the bolts to 25 N•m (18 ft.-lb.), then tighten them to a final torque of 42 N•m (31 ft.-lb.).

10. Install the 6 mm bolts in the cam chain compartment (A, **Figure 59**) and tighten to 10 N•m (88 in.-lb.).

11. Install the 6 mm cylinder head-to-cylinder Allen bolt (B, **Figure 58**) on the side of the cylinder head. Tighten the bolt to 10 N•m (88 in.-lb.).

12. Pull up on the cam chain and install the cylinder head side bolt (A, **Figure 58**) and a new gasket washer. Install the washer so the metal side contacts the bolt head. Tighten the bolt to 14 N•m (124 in.-lb.).

13. Remove the safety wire from the cam chain.

14. If the valve lifters and shims were removed, install them at this time as described in *Valve Lifters and Shims Removal and Installation* in this chapter.

15A. *Front cylinder head*—Perform the following:
   a. Position the spacer (C, **Figure 53**) between the frame and cylinder head, then install the left engine mounting bolt (A). Tighten the bolt to 55 N•m (40 ft.-lb.). Tighten the clamp bolt (B, **Figure 53**) to 23 N•m (17 ft.-lb.).
   b. Install the spacer (B, **Figure 54**) and right engine mounting bolt (A). Tighten the bolt to 55 N•m (40 ft.-lb.).

15B. *Rear cylinder head*—Perform the following:
   a. Position the spacer (**Figure 56**) between the frame and cylinder head, then install the left engine mounting bolt (A, **Figure 55**). Tighten the bolt to 55 N•m (40 ft.-lb.). Tighten the clamp bolt (B, **Figure 55**) to 23 N•m (17 ft.-lb.).
   b. Install the right engine mounting bolt (**Figure 57**). Tighten the bolt to 55 N•m (40 ft.-lb.).

16. Install the camshafts as described in this chapter.

17. Install the carburetors as described in Chapter Eight.

18. Install the exhaust system as described in Chapter Eight.

19. Fill the cooling system as described in Chapter Three.

VALVE LIFTERS AND SHIMS

Removal and Installation

Refer to **Figure 68** when servicing the valves.

If the cylinder head is going to be inspected and/or serviced, remove the valve lifters and shims before removing the head. To avoid mixing the parts, perform this procedure carefully.

1. Make or use a holder for the valve lifters and shims (**Figure 69**). Mark it with the front or rear cylinder, intake or exhaust valve and right or left valve location.

2. Remove the valve lifters (**Figure 70**) and their respective shims (**Figure 71**) and place both of them in the correct location in the holder. Repeat this step for all of the valve lifters and shims.

3. Inspect the valve lifters and shims for wear or heat damage. Service specifications for the outside diameter of the lifter and the inside diameter of the lifter receptacle in the cylinder head are not available. The lifter, with clean oil applied to its sides, should move up and down in the cylinder head with no binding or chatter. If the side of the lifter is scuffed or scratched, replace it.

NOTE
*To avoid mixing the parts, perform Steps 4-7 carefully and work on one cylinder at a time. Position the holder containing the valve lifters and shims (**Figure 69**) with the same orientation as the cylinder head.*

4. Install the shim onto the top of the valve keepers and make sure it is seated correctly.

5. Apply clean engine oil to the side of the valve lifter and install it.

6. Rotate the lifter to make sure it is seated correctly and rotates freely.

7. Install all the shims and lifters.

VALVES AND VALVE COMPONENTS

Refer to **Figure 68**.

Complete valve service requires a number of special tools. The following procedures describe how to check for valve component wear and to determine what type of service is required. In most cases, valve troubles are caused by poor valve seating, worn valve guides and burned valves. A valve spring compressor will be required to remove and install the valves.

Valve Removal

1. Remove the cylinder head, valve lifters and shims as described in this chapter.

2. Install a valve spring compressor (**Figure 72**) squarely onto the valve spring retainer (A, **Figure**

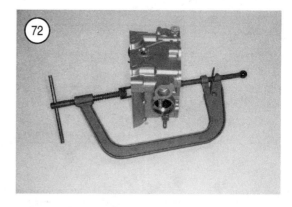

73) and place the other end of tool against the valve head.

CAUTION
To avoid loss of spring tension, do not compress the spring any more than necessary to remove the valve keepers.

3. Tighten the valve spring compressor until the valve keepers (B, **Figure 73**) separate from the valve stem. Lift the valve keepers out through the

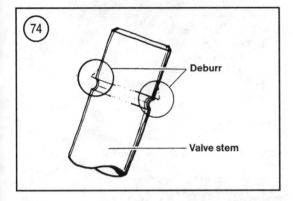

Deburr

Valve stem

valve spring compressor with a magnet or needlenose pliers.

4. Gradually loosen the valve spring compressor and remove it from the cylinder head.

5. Remove the spring retainer and the two valve springs.

> *CAUTION*
> *Remove any burrs from the valve stem groove before removing the valve (**Figure 74**); otherwise, the valve*

guide will be damaged as the valve stem passes through it.

6. Remove the valve from the cylinder while rotating it slightly.
7. Remove the spring seat.
8. Pull the oil seal off the valve guide. Discard the oil seal.

> *CAUTION*
> *All component parts of each valve assembly must be kept together (**Figure 75**). Place each set into a divided carton, into separate small boxes or into small reclosable plastic bags. Label each valve set. Identify a valve set by front or rear cylinder, intake or exhaust valve and right or left location in the cylinder head. This will prevent parts mixing and will make installation simpler. Do not intermix components from the valves or excessive wear may result.*

9. Repeat Steps 2-8 and remove the remaining valves. Keep all valve sets separate.

Valve Inspection

Refer to the troubleshooting chart in **Figure 76** when performing valve inspection procedures in this section. When measuring the valves and valve components in this section, compare the measurements to the new and wear limit specifications listed in **Table 2**. Replace parts that are out of specification or show damage as described in this section.

1. Clean valves in solvent. Do not gouge or damage the valve seating surface.
2. Inspect the valve face (**Figure 77**). Minor roughness and pitting can be removed by lapping the valve as described in this chapter. Excessive unevenness to the contact surface is an indication that the valve is not serviceable.
3. Inspect the valve stem for wear and roughness. Then measure the valve stem outside diameter with a micrometer (**Figure 78**).
4. Remove all carbon and varnish from the valve guides with a stiff spiral wire brush before measuring wear.

> *NOTE*
> *If the required measuring tools are not available, proceed to Step 6.*

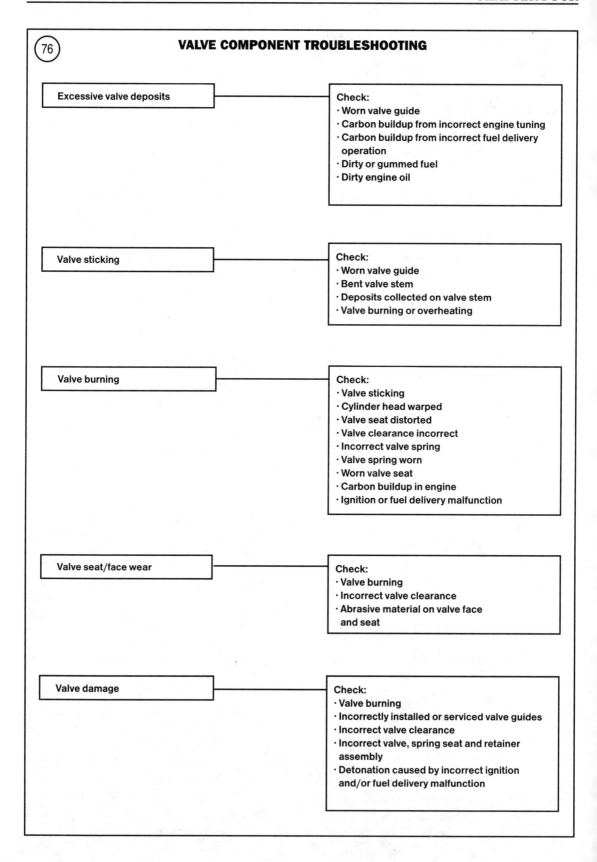

(76) **VALVE COMPONENT TROUBLESHOOTING**

Excessive valve deposits

Check:
· Worn valve guide
· Carbon buildup from incorrect engine tuning
· Carbon buildup from incorrect fuel delivery operation
· Dirty or gummed fuel
· Dirty engine oil

Valve sticking

Check:
· Worn valve guide
· Bent valve stem
· Deposits collected on valve stem
· Valve burning or overheating

Valve burning

Check:
· Valve sticking
· Cylinder head warped
· Valve seat distorted
· Valve clearance incorrect
· Incorrect valve spring
· Valve spring worn
· Worn valve seat
· Carbon buildup in engine
· Ignition or fuel delivery malfunction

Valve seat/face wear

Check:
· Valve burning
· Incorrect valve clearance
· Abrasive material on valve face and seat

Valve damage

Check:
· Valve burning
· Incorrectly installed or serviced valve guides
· Incorrect valve clearance
· Incorrect valve, spring seat and retainer assembly
· Detonation caused by incorrect ignition and/or fuel delivery malfunction

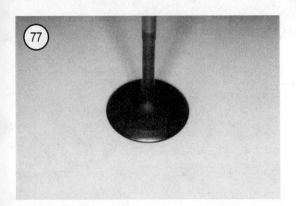

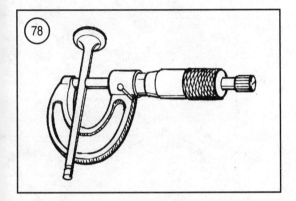

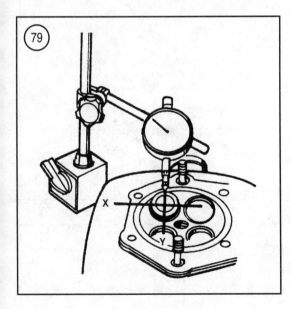

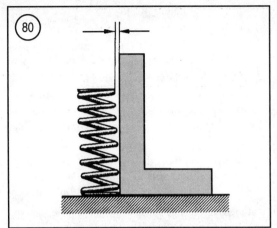

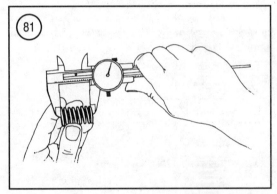

the valve head (**Figure 79**) and check the valve stem deflection. Hold the valve 10 mm (0.4 in.) off its seat and rock it sideways in two directions 90° to each other. If the valve stem deflection in either direction exceeds the service limit in **Table 2**, the guide is probably worn. However, as a final check, take the cylinder head to a Suzuki dealership or machine shop and have the valve guides measured.

7. Check the inner and outer valve springs as follows:

    a. Check each of the valve springs for visual damage.

    b. Use a square and check the spring for distortion or tilt (**Figure 80**).

    c. Measure the valve spring free length with a vernier caliper (**Figure 81**) and compare with the dimension in **Table 2**.

    d. Repeat for each valve spring.

    e. Replace defective springs as a set (inner and outer).

8. Check the valve spring seats and valve keepers for cracks or other damage.

5. Measure the valve guide inside diameter with a small hole gauge. Measure at the top, center and bottom positions. Then measure the small hole gauge and check against the dimension in **Table 2**.

6. If a small hole gauge is not available, insert each valve into its guide. Position a dial indicator against

9. Inspect the valve seats (**Figure 82**, typical) and corresponding valve mating areas with layout fluid. If worn or burned, they may be reconditioned as described in this chapter. Seats and valves in near-perfect condition can be reconditioned by lapping with fine carborundum paste. Remove all layout fluid residue from the seats and valves.

10. Check the valve stem runout with a V-block and dial indicator as shown in **Figure 83**. Replace the valve if the valve stem runout exceeds the service limit listed in **Table 2**.

11. Measure valve head radial runout with a dial indicator as shown in **Figure 84**. Replace the valve if the valve head radial runout exceeds the wear limit in **Table 2**.

12. Measure the valve head margin with a vernier caliper (**Figure 85**). Replace the valve if valve head margin is less than the service limit in **Table 2**.

Valve Installation

Refer to **Figure 86** when performing the following procedure.

1. Clean the end of the valve guide.

2. Install the spring seat around the valve guide.

3. Lubricate the inside of the new oil seal and install it over the end of the valve guide. Push the seal down until it is completely seated on the valve guide.

4. Coat the valve stem with molybdenum disulfide paste. Install the valve part way into the guide. Then, slowly turn the valve as it enters the oil seal and continue turning it until the valve is completely installed.

5. Position the valve springs with their *closer* wound coils (**Figure 87**) toward the cylinder head.

6. Install the outer valve spring and make sure it is properly seated on the spring seat.

7. Install the inner valve spring and make sure it is properly seated on the lower spring seat.

8. Install the spring retainer on top of the valve springs.

> *CAUTION*
> *To avoid loss of spring tension, do not compress the spring any more than necessary to remove the valve keepers.*

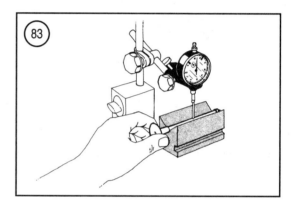

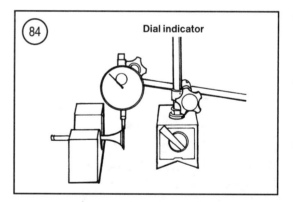

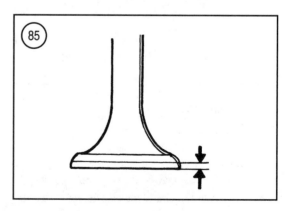

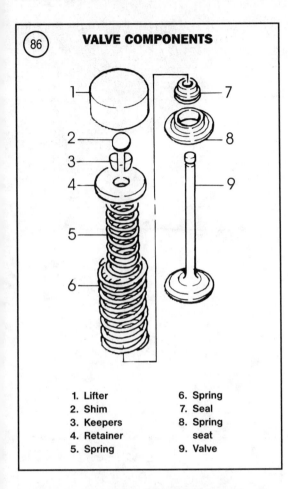

86 VALVE COMPONENTS

1. Lifter
2. Shim
3. Keepers
4. Retainer
5. Spring
6. Spring
7. Seal
8. Spring seat
9. Valve

87

9. Compress the valve springs with a valve spring compressor (**Figure 72**) and install the valve keepers (B, **Figure 73**).

10. Make sure both keepers are seated around the valve stem before releasing the compressor.

11. Slowly release tension from the compressor and remove it. After removing the compressor, inspect the valve keepers to make sure they are prop-

erly seated. Tap the end of the valve stem with a drift and hammer. This ensures that the keepers are properly seated.

12. Repeat Steps 1-11 for the remaining valves.

13. Install the shims and valve lifters as described in this chapter.

14. Install the cylinder head as described in this chapter.

15. Adjust the valve clearance as described in Chapter Three.

Valve Guide Replacement

If the valve stem-to-valve guide clearance is excessive, replace the valve guides and valves. Special tools and experience are required to replace the valve guides. If these tools are not available, it is more economical to have this procedure performed by a machine shop.

Valve Seat Inspection

The most accurate method for checking the valve seat is to use a layout fluid, available from auto parts and tool stores. Layout fluids are used for locating high or irregular spots when checking or making close fits and when scraping bearing surfaces. Follow the manufacturer's directions.

NOTE
Because of the close operating tolerances within the valve assembly, the valve stem and guide must be within tolerance; otherwise the inspection results will be inaccurate.

1. Remove the valves as described in this chapter.

2. Clean the valve seat in the cylinder head and valve mating areas with contact cleaner.

3. Thoroughly clean off all carbon deposits from the valve face with solvent or detergent and dry the valve thoroughly.

4. Spread a thin layer of layout fluid evenly on the valve face. Allow the fluid to air dry.

5. Moisten the end of a suction cup valve tool and attach it to the valve. Insert the valve into the guide.

6. Using the valve lapping tool, tap the valve against the valve seat. Do not rotate the valve.

7. Remove the valve and examine the impression left by the layout fluid. If the impression (on the valve or in the cylinder head) is not even and contin-

uous and if the valve seat width (**Figure 88**) is not within the specified tolerance in **Table 2**, the valve seat must be reconditioned.

8. Closely examine the valve seat in the cylinder head (**Figure 82**). It should be smooth and even with a polished seating surface.

9. If the valve seat is good, install the valve as described in this chapter.

10. If the valve seat is not correct, recondition the valve seat(s).

11. Repeat for the other valves.

Valve Seat Reconditioning

Considerable expertise and specialized equipment are required to recondition valve seats. If these are not available, have the procedure performed by a machine shop that specializes in valve service.

Valve Lapping

Valve lapping is a simple operation which can restore the valve seal without machining if the amount of wear or distortion is not too great.

Perform this procedure only after determining that the valve seat width and outside diameter are within specifications. A lapping stick (**Figure 89**) is required.

1. Smear a light coat of fine grade valve lapping compound onto the seating surface of the valve.

2. Insert the valve into the cylinder head.

3. Wet the suction cup of the lapping stick and stick in onto the head of the valve. Spin the stick in both directions, while pressing it against the valve seat and lap the valve to the seat. See **Figure 90**. Every 5 to 10 seconds, rotate the valve 180° in the valve seat. Continue with this action until the mating surfaces on the valve and seat are smooth and equal in size.

4. Closely examine the valve seat in the cylinder head (**Figure 82**). It should be smooth and even with a polished seating ring.

5. Repeat Steps 1-4 for the remaining valves.

6. Thoroughly clean the valves and cylinder head in solvent or detergent and hot water to remove all valve grinding compound. Dry the components thoroughly.

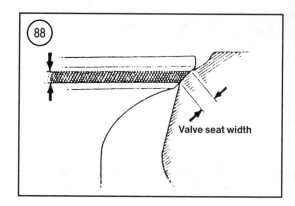

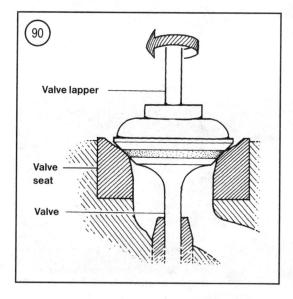

CAUTION
Any compound left on the valves or the cylinder head will contaminate the oil and cause premature engine wear.

7. Install the valve assemblies as described in this chapter.

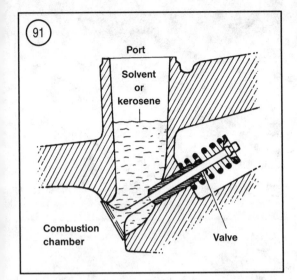

8. After completing the lapping and reinstalling the valves into the head, test the valve seal. Check the seal of each valve by pouring solvent into the intake and exhaust ports (**Figure 91**). There should be no leaking past the seat in the combustion chamber. If leakage occurs, the combustion chamber will appear wet. If fluid leaks past any of the seats, disas-

semble that valve assembly and repeat this procedure until there is no leakage.

> *NOTE*
> *This solvent test does not ensure long-term durability or maximum power. It merely ensures maximum compression will be available on initial start-up after reassembly.*

9. Apply a light coat of engine oil to all bare metal surfaces to prevent rust.

CYLINDER

Removal

> *CAUTION*
> *If it is necessary to rotate the crankshaft, pull up the cam chains so they cannot bind internally.*

1. Remove the cylinder head cover and cylinder head as described in this chapter.

2. On California models, detach the air supply hose from the cylinder (**Figure 92**).

3. Remove the nuts (**Figure 93**) securing the cylinder to the crankcase.

4. Loosen the cylinder by tapping around the perimeter with a rubber or plastic mallet. If necessary, *gently* pry the cylinder loose with a broad-tipped screwdriver.

5. Pull the cylinder straight off the crankcase dowel pins and piston. Work the cam chain wire through the opening in the cylinder.

6. Remove the cylinder base gasket (A, **Figure 94**) and discard it. Remove the dowel pins (B) from the crankcase.

7. Install a piston holding fixture under the piston (**Figure 95**) to protect the piston skirt from damage. This fixture may be purchased or constructed of wood. See **Figure 96** for basic dimensions.

8. Place a clean shop cloth into the openings in the crankcase to prevent the entry of foreign material.

NOTE
*The oil flow valve is located on the top side of the crankcase (**Figure 97**). Refer to **Oil Flow Valve** in this chapter if service is necessary.*

9. Inspect the cylinder as described in this chapter.

Installation

NOTE
*The front and rear cylinders are not identical. Each cylinder is identified with FRONT or REAR embossed on the cylinder (**Figure 98**).*

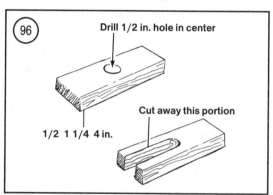

Drill 1/2 in. hole in center

Cut away this portion

1/2 1 1/4 4 in.

1. If used, remove the clean shop cloth from the openings in the crankcase opening.

2. If used, remove the piston holding fixtures.

CAUTION
When rotating the crankshaft, pull up the cam chains so they cannot bind internally. Protect the pistons so they will not be damaged when retracting into the crankcase.

3. Rotate the crankshaft so the piston being serviced is below the crankcase opening.

4. Check that the top surface of the crankcase and the bottom surface of the cylinder are clean.

NOTE
Protect the piston and rings when applying sealer in Step 5.

5. Apply a light coat of Suzuki Bond No. 1207B, or equivalent, to the crankcase mating surface joint on the crankcase-to-cylinder mating surface (**Figure 99**).

6. If removed, install the locating dowels (A, **Figure 100**).

7. Install a new cylinder base gasket (B, **Figure 100**).

8. Rotate the crankshaft so the piston is above the crankcase, then install the piston holding fixture. Be

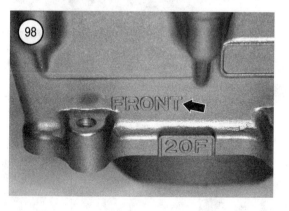

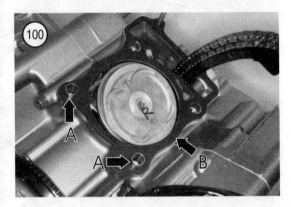

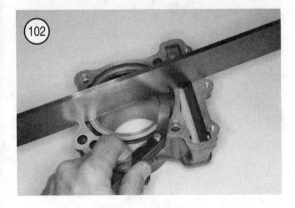

careful when installing the piston holding fixture so the cylinder base gasket is not damaged.

9. Apply a liberal coat of clean engine oil to the cylinder wall, especially at the lower end where the piston will enter.

10. Apply clean engine oil to the piston and piston rings. This will make it easier to guide the piston into the cylinder bore.

11. Make sure the piston ring end gaps are *not* aligned. They must be staggered evenly around the piston circumference.

12. Start the cylinder down over the piston. Compress each piston ring by hand as it enters the cylinder.

13. Push the cylinder down past the piston rings.

14. Carefully feed the cam chain and wire up through the opening in the cylinder and tie it to the engine.

15. Slide the cylinder down until it bottoms on the piston holding fixture.

16. Remove the piston holding fixture and push the cylinder down into place onto the crankcase until it bottoms.

17. Install the lower nuts (**Figure 93**) securing the cylinder to the crankcase and tighten only fingertight at this time. On the rear cylinder, be sure to install the wiring harness clamp on the rear stud (**Figure 101**).

18. Install the cylinder head as described in this chapter.

19. Tighten the cylinder-to-crankcase lower nuts (**Figure 93**) to 10 N•m (88 in.lb.).

20. Install the cylinder head cover as described in this chapter.

21. On California models, connect the air supply hose to the cylinder (**Figure 92**).

Inspection

1. Thoroughly clean the cylinder with solvent. Then, using a *dull* gasket scraper, carefully remove all gasket material from the top and bottom mating surfaces on the cylinder. Do not nick or gouge the gasket surfaces or leakage will result.

2. After the cylinder has been thoroughly cleaned, place a straightedge across the cylinder-to-cylinder head gasket surface at several points. Measure warp (**Figure 102**) by attempting to insert a feeler gauge between the straightedge and cylinder at each location. The maximum warp limit is 0.05 mm (0.002

in.). Replace the cylinder if the gasket surface is warped to or beyond the specified limit.

3. Thoroughly check the bore surface for scratches or gouges. If damaged in any way, the bore will require boring and reconditioning.

4. Determine piston-to-cylinder clearance as described in *Piston Clearance* in this chapter.

5. If the cylinder requires service, such as boring, remove all dowel pins from the cylinder prior to taking it to a dealer or machine shop for service.

6. After the cylinder has been serviced, perform the following:

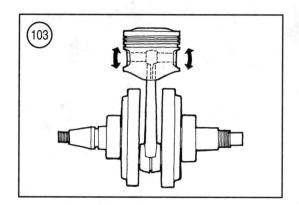

> *CAUTION*
> *A combination of soap and hot water is the only solution that will completely clean cylinder walls. Solvent and kerosene cannot wash fine grit out of cylinder crevices. Any grit left in the cylinder will act as a grinding compound and cause premature wear to the new rings.*

a. Wash the cylinder bore in hot soapy water.

b. Also wash out any fine grit material from the cooling passages surrounding the cylinder.

c. After washing the cylinder wall, wipe the cylinder wall with a clean white cloth. It should *not* show any traces of grit or debris. If the rag is the slightest bit dirty, the wall is not thoroughly cleaned and must be washed again.

PISTON AND PISTON RINGS

The pistons are made of an aluminum alloy. The piston pin is made of steel and is a precision fit in the pistons. The piston pins are secured by a clip at each end.

Piston Removal

> *NOTE*
> *If it is necessary to rotate the crankshaft, pull up the cam chains so they cannot bind internally. Protect the pistons so they will not be damaged when retracting into the crankcase.*

1. Remove the cylinder head and cylinder as described in this chapter.

2. Mark the top of the piston with an identification letter (F or R).

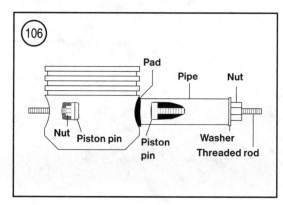

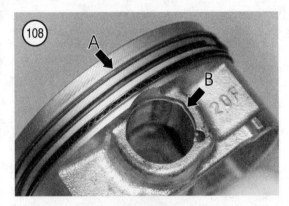

3. Block off the crankcase below the piston with a clean shop cloth to prevent the piston pin circlips from falling into the crankcase.

4. Before removing the piston, hold the rod tightly and rock the piston (**Figure 103**). Any rocking motion (do not confuse with the normal sliding motion) indicates wear on the piston pin, rod bushing, pin bore, or more likely, a combination of all three.

5. Remove the circlip (**Figure 104**) from one side of the piston pin bore.

6. From the other side, push the piston pin (**Figure 105**) out of the piston by hand. If the pin is tight, use a homemade tool (**Figure 106**) and remove it. Do not drive the piston pin out. This action could damage the piston pin, connecting rod or piston.

7. Lift the piston off the connecting rod.

8. Inspect the piston as described in this chapter.

Piston Inspection

1. If necessary, remove the piston rings as described in this chapter.

2. Carefully clean the carbon from the piston crown (**Figure 107**) with a soft scraper or wire wheel mounted in a drill. Large carbon accumulations reduce piston cooling and result in detonation and piston damage. Renumber the piston as soon as it is cleaned.

CAUTION
Be careful not to gouge or damage the piston when removing carbon. Never use a wire brush to clean the piston skirt or ring grooves. Do not attempt to remove carbon from the sides of the piston above the top ring or from the cylinder bore near the top. Removal of carbon from these two areas may cause increased oil consumption.

3. After cleaning the piston, examine the crown. The crown should show no signs of wear or damage. If the crown appears pecked or spongy-looking, also check the spark plug, valves and combustion chamber for aluminum deposits. If these deposits are found, the engine is overheating.

4. Examine each ring groove (A, **Figure 108**) for burrs, dented edges or other damage. Pay particular attention to the top compression ring groove. It usually wears more than the others. Because the oil rings are constantly bathed in oil, these rings and grooves wear little compared to compression rings and their grooves. If there is evidence of oil ring groove wear or if the oil ring assembly is tight and difficult to remove, the piston skirt may have collapsed due to excessive heat. Replace the piston.

5. Check the oil control holes (**Figure 109**) in the piston for carbon or oil sludge buildup. Clean the holes with wire and blow them clear with compressed air.

6. Inspect the piston skirt (**Figure 110**) for cracks or other damage. If a piston shows signs of partial seizure, indicated by bits of aluminum buildup on the piston skirt, it should be replaced to reduce the possibility of engine noise and further engine damage.

> *NOTE*
> *If the piston skirt is worn or scuffed unevenly from side-to-side, the connecting rod may be bent or twisted.*

7. Check the circlip groove (B, **Figure 108**) on each side for wear, cracks or other damage. If the grooves are questionable, check the circlip fit by installing a new circlip into each groove and then attempt to move the circlip from side-to-side. If the circlip has any side play, the groove is worn and the piston must be replaced.

8. Measure piston-to-cylinder clearance as described in *Piston Clearance* in this chapter.

9. If damage or wear indicate piston replacement, select a new piston as described under *Piston Clearance* in this chapter. If the piston, rings and cylinder are not damaged and are dimensionally correct, they can be reused.

Piston Pin Inspection

1. Clean the piston pin in solvent, and dry it thoroughly.

2. Inspect the piston pin (**Figure 111**) for chrome flaking or cracks. Replace if necessary.

3. Lubricate the piston pin with engine oil and install it into the connecting rod (**Figure 112**). Slowly rotate the piston pin and check for radial play.

4. Lubricate the piston pin and partially install it into the piston (**Figure 113**). Check the piston pin for excessive play (**Figure 114**).

5. Measure the piston pin outside diameter with a micrometer. If the piston pin outside diameter is less than the service limit in **Table 2**, replace the piston pin.

6. Measure the inside diameter of the piston pin bore (**Figure 115**) with a small hole gauge. Measure the small hole gauge with a micrometer. If the measurement exceeds the service limit in **Table 2**, replace the piston.

7. Replace the piston pin and/or piston or connecting rod if necessary.

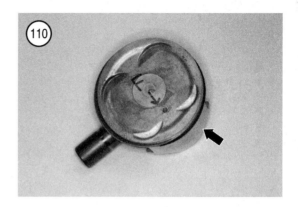

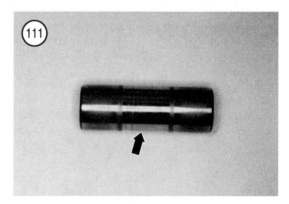

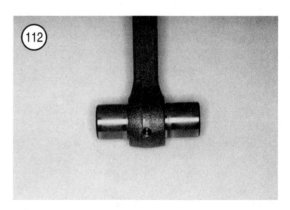

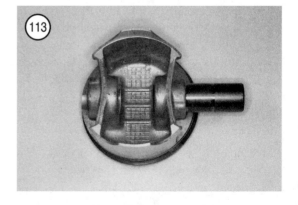

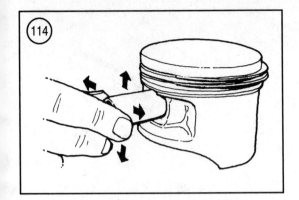

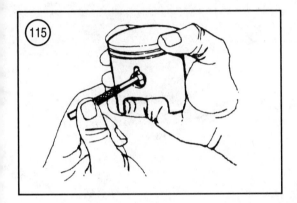

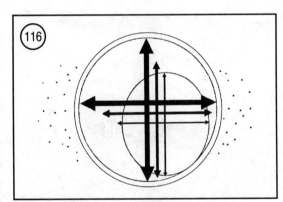

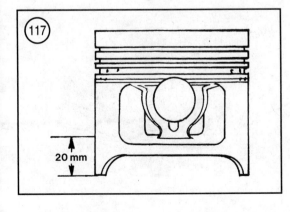

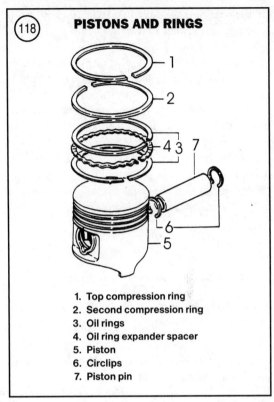

PISTONS AND RINGS

1. Top compression ring
2. Second compression ring
3. Oil rings
4. Oil ring expander spacer
5. Piston
6. Circlips
7. Piston pin

Piston Clearance

1. Make sure the piston skirt and cylinder wall are clean and dry.

2. Measure the cylinder bore with a bore gauge or inside micrometer. Measure the cylinder bore at the three positions shown in **Figure 116**. Measure in line with the piston pin and 90° to the pin. Record the bore inner diameter measurement.

3. Measure the piston outside diameter with a micrometer at a right angle to the piston pin bore. Measure up 20 mm (0.79 in.) from the bottom edge of the piston skirt (**Figure 117**).

4. Subtract the piston outside diameter from the largest bore diameter; the difference is piston-to-cylinder clearance. If the clearance exceeds the service limit in **Table 2**, determine if the piston, cylinder or both are worn. If necessary, take the cylinder to a dealership that can rebore the cylinder to accept an oversize piston.

Piston Ring Inspection and Removal

The piston and ring assembly is a three-ring type (**Figure 118**). The top and second rings are compression rings. The lower ring is an oil control ring assembly consisting of two ring rails and an expander spacer.

When measuring the piston rings and piston in this section, compare the actual measurements to the new and service limit specifications in **Table 2**. Replace parts that are out of specification or show damage as described in this section.

1. Measure the side clearance of each compression ring in its groove with a flat feeler gauge (**Figure 119**). If the clearance is greater than specified, replace the rings. If the clearance is still excessive with the new rings installed, replace the piston.

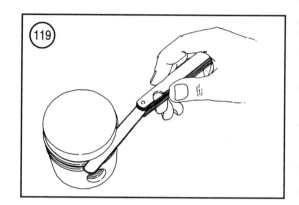

> *WARNING*
> *The piston ring edges are sharp. Be careful when handling them.*

> *NOTE*
> *Store the old rings in the order they were removed.*

2. Remove the compression rings with a ring expander tool (**Figure 120**) or by spreading the ring ends by hand (**Figure 121**).

3. Remove the oil ring assembly by first removing the upper and then the lower ring rails. Then remove the expander spacer.

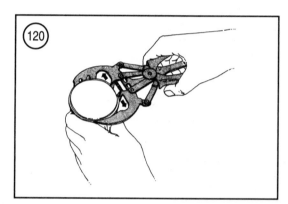

4. Using a broken piston ring, carefully remove carbon and oil residue from the piston ring grooves (**Figure 122**). Do not remove aluminum material from the ring grooves as this increases ring side clearance.

5. Measure each compression ring groove width with a vernier caliper. Measure each groove at several points around the piston. Replace the piston if any groove is outside the specified range.

6. Inspect grooves carefully for burrs, nicks or broken or cracked lands. Replace the piston if necessary.

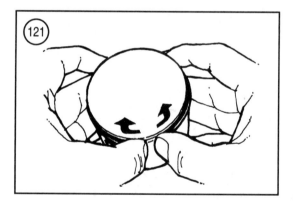

7. Measure the thickness of each compression ring with a micrometer (**Figure 123**). If the thickness is less than specified, replace the ring(s).

8. Measure the free end gap with a vernier caliper (**Figure 124**). If the free end gap exceeds the service limit specified in **Table 2**, replace the ring(s).

9. Insert the ring into the bottom of the cylinder bore and square it with the cylinder wall by tapping it with the piston. Measure the installed end gap with a feeler gauge (**Figure 125**). Replace the rings if the end gap equals or exceeds service limit specified in **Table 2**. Also measure the end gap when in-

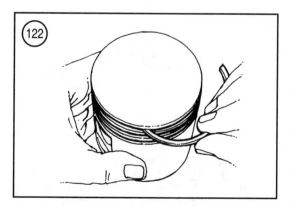

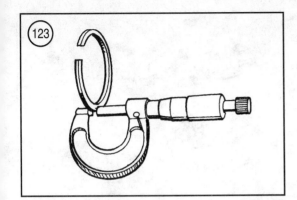

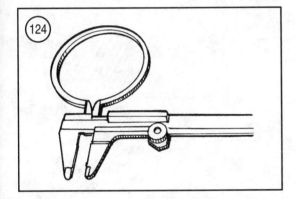

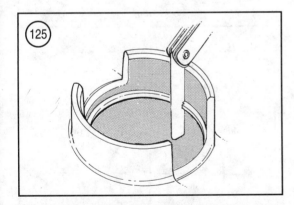

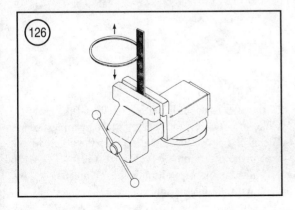

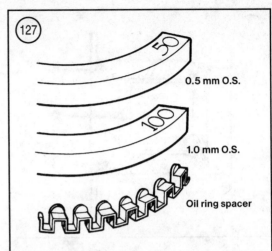

0.5 mm O.S.

1.0 mm O.S.

Oil ring spacer

stalling new piston rings. If the gap on a new compression ring is smaller than specified, secure a small file in a vise, grip the ends of the ring by hand and carefully enlarge the gap (**Figure 126**).

Piston Ring Installation

1. If new rings will be installed, deglaze or hone the cylinder. This helps seat the new rings. Refer honing service to a Suzuki dealership or machine shop. After honing, measure the ring end gap for each compression ring.

2. When installing oversized compression rings, check the ring number (**Figure 127**) to ensure that the correct rings are installed. The ring oversize number should be the same as the piston oversize number.

3. A paint mark on the oil ring spacer identifies oversized oil rings. When installing oversized oil rings, check the color to ensure that the correct sizes are being installed. Standard size rings have no color, 0.5 mm oversize rings are blue, and 1.0 mm oversize rings are yellow.

4. Clean the piston and rings. Dry them with compressed air.

5. Install the piston rings as follows:

WARNING
The piston ring edges are sharp. Be careful when handling them.

NOTE
When installing aftermarket piston rings, follow the manufacturer's directions.

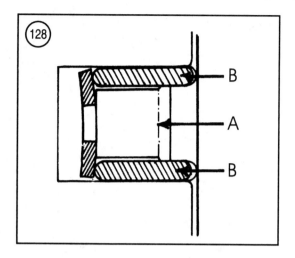

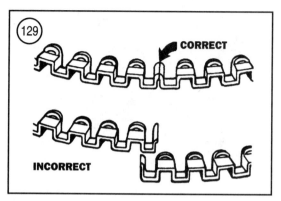

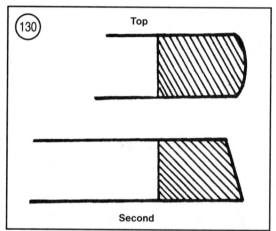

a. Install the oil control ring assembly into the bottom ring groove. Install the oil ring expander spacer first (A, **Figure 128**), and then install each ring rail (B). Make sure the ends of the expander spacer butt together (**Figure 129**). They should not overlap. If reassembling used parts, install the ring rails in their original positions.

b. Install the compression rings with a ring expander tool (**Figure 120**) or by carefully spreading the ring ends by hand (**Figure 121**).

c. Install the second or middle compression ring with the manufacturer's RN mark facing up. This ring has a slight taper (**Figure 130**).

d. Install the top compression ring with the manufacturer's R mark facing up.

6. Make sure the rings are seated completely in their grooves all the way around the piston and that the end gaps are distributed around the piston as shown in **Figure 131**. To prevent compression from escaping past them, the ring gaps must not align.

7. If new parts were installed, follow the *Engine Break-In* procedure in Chapter Five.

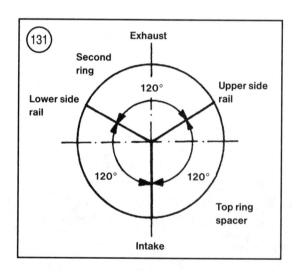

Piston Installation

> *CAUTION*
> *If it is necessary to rotate the crankshaft, pull up the cam chains so they cannot bind internally.*

1. Coat the connecting rod bushing, piston pin and piston with molybdenum grease.

2. Install a *new* circlip into one side of the piston. Make sure it is correctly seated in the piston groove. The circlip ends must not align with the notch adjacent to the piston pin bore (**Figure 132**).

3. Slide the piston pin into the piston until its end is flush with the piston pin boss.

4. Place the correct piston onto the connecting rod so the indexing dot on the piston crown is toward the exhaust side of the engine (**Figure 133**).

5. Align the piston pin with the hole in the connecting rod. Push the piston pin through the connecting rod and into the other side of the piston until it is centered in the piston.

6. Install a *new* piston pin circlip into the other side of the pin boss. Make sure the circlip is seated correctly in the piston groove.

7. If removed, install the piston rings as described in this chapter.

8. Install the cylinder and cylinder head as described in this chapter.

Table 1 GENERAL ENGINE SPECIFICATIONS

Item	Specification
Type	90° V-Twin, four-valve, DOHC
Firing order	Front, then rear cylinder
Bore and stroke	81.0 62.6 mm
	(3.189 2.465 in.)
Displacement	645 cc (39.4 cu. in.)
Compression ratio	11.5 to 1
Compression pressure (at sea level)	Approx. 1500 kPa (217 psi)
Ignition timing	5° BTDC @ 1300 rpm
Lubrication	Wet sump

Table 2 TOP END SPECIFICATIONS

Item	Specification	Service limit
Camshaft		
Journal holder inside diameter	22.012-22.025 mm	–
	(0.8666-0.8671 in.)	
Journal outside diameter	21.959-21.980 mm	–
	(0.8645-0.8654 in.)	
Journal oil clearance	0.032-0.066 mm	0.150 mm (0.0059 in.)
	(0.0013-0.0026 in.)	
Lobe height		
Intake	35.480-35.530 mm	35.180 mm (1.3850 in.)
	(1.3968-1.3988 in.)	
Exhaust	33.480-33.530 mm	33.180 mm (1.3063 in.)
	(1.3181-1.3201 in.)	
Runout	–	0.10 mm (0.004 in.)

(continued)

Table 2 TOP END SPECIFICATIONS (continued)

Item	Specification	Service limit
Connecting rod		
Small end inside diameter	20.010-20.018 mm (0.7878-0.7881 in.)	20.040 mm (0.7890 in.)
Cylinder head warp (max.)	0.05 mm (0.002 in.)	
Piston diameter	80.940-80.955 mm (3.1866-3.1872 in.)	80.88 mm (3.184 in.)
Piston-to-cylinder clearance	–	0.055-0.065 mm (0.0022-0.0026 in.)
Piston pin bore diameter	20.002-20.008 mm (0.7875-0.7877 in.)	20.030 mm (0.7886 in.)
Piston pin diameter	19.992-20.000 mm (0.7871-0.7874 in.)	19.980 mm (0.7866 in.)
Piston rings		
Number of rings		
Compression	2	–
Oil control	1	–
Ring free end gap		
Top	Approx. 9.9 mm (0.39 in.)	7.9 mm (0.31 in.)
Second	Approx. 10.5 mm (0.41 in.)	8.4 mm (0.33 in.)
Ring end gap (in cylinder bore)		
Top & second	0.20-0.35 mm (0.008-0.014 in.)	0.70 mm (0.028 in.)
Ring side clearance		
Top	–	0.180 mm (0.0071 in.)
Second	–	0.150 mm (0.0059 in.)
Ring thickness		
Top	1.17-1.19 mm (0.046-0.047 in.)	–
Second	0.97-0.99 mm (0.038-0.039 in.)	–
Valves and valve springs		
Valve stem outside diameter		
Intake	4.465-4.480 mm (0.1758-0.1764 in.)	–
Exhaust	4.455-4.470 mm (0.1754-0.1760 in.)	–
Valve guide inside diameter		
Intake and exhaust	4.500-4.512 mm (0.1772-0.1776 in.)	–
Stem-to-guide clearance		
Intake	0.020-0.047 mm (0.0008-0.0018 in.)	–
Exhaust	0.030-0.057 mm (0.0012-0.0022 in.)	
Valve stem deflection	–	0.35 mm (0.014 in.)
Valve seat width		
Intake and exhaust	0.9-1.1 mm (0.035-0.043 in.)	–
Valve stem runout	–	0.05 mm (0.002 in.)
Valve head margin	–	0.5 mm (0.02 in.)
Valve head radial runout	–	0.03 mm (0.001 in.)
Valve spring free length (intake and exhaust)		
Inner spring	–	36.8 mm (1.45 in.)

(continued)

Table 2 TOP END SPECIFICATIONS (continued)

Item	Specification	Service limit
Valve spring free length (intake and exhaust) (continued)		
Outer spring	–	39.8 mm (1.57 in.)
Valve spring pressure (intake and exhaust)		
Inner spring	4.2-4.8 kg @ 29.9 mm (9.3-10.6 lb. @ 1.18 in.)	–
Outer spring	17.0-19.6 kg @ 33.4 mm (37.5-43.2 lb. @ 1.31 in.)	–

Table 3 TOP END TORQUE SPECIFICATIONS

Item	N•m	in.-lb.	ft.-lb.
Cam chain guide mounting bolt	10	88	–
Cam chain tensioner mounting bolt	10	88	–
Cam chain tensioner sealing bolt	8	71	–
Camshaft holder bolts	10	88	–
Camshaft top chain guide	10	88	–
Cylinder-to-crankcase nuts	10	88	–
Cylinder head bolts			
6 mm	10	88	–
10 mm*	42	–	31
Cylinder head cover	14	124	–
Cylinder head side bolt	14	124	–
Engine mounting bolts	55	–	40
Engine mounting spacer clamp bolts	23	–	17

* See text.

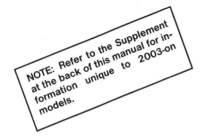

NOTE: Refer to the Supplement at the back of this manual for information unique to 2003-on models.

ENGINE LOWER END

This chapter provides service procedures for lower end components. These include the crankcase, crankshaft and connecting rods, and the oil pump/lubrication system. This chapter also includes removal and installation procedures for the transmission and internal shift mechanism assemblies. However, service procedures for these assemblies are described in Chapter Seven.

Refer to **Tables 1-4** at the end of this chapter for specifications and bearing selection information.

One of the most important aspects of a successful engine overhaul is preparation. Before removing the engine and disassembling the crankcase, degrease the engine and frame. Have all the necessary hand and special tools available. Make sure the work area is clean and well lit. Identify and store individual parts and assemblies in appropriate storage containers (**Figure 1**).

References to the left and right sides refer to the position of the parts as viewed by the rider sitting on the seat facing forward, not how the engine may sit on the workbench.

SERVICING ENGINE IN FRAME

The frame is an excellent holding fixture, especially for breaking loose stubborn bolts and nuts. The following components can be serviced with the engine mounted in the frame:
1. External gearshift mechanism.
2. Clutch.
3. Oil pump.
4. Carburetors.
5. Alternator.
6. Starter motor and gears.

ENGINE

Removal

This procedure describes engine removal and installation. It may be easier in some cases to remove as many engine assemblies as possible before removing the lower end from the frame. Following this method reduces the weight of the engine and al-

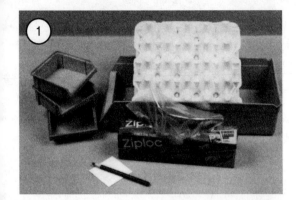

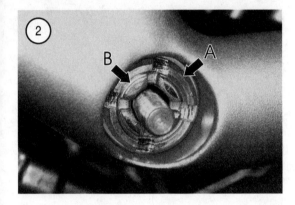

lows the frame to be used as a holding fixture. Disassembling the engine on the workbench without some type of holding fixture can be difficult and time consuming.

CAUTION
The Suzuki engine mounting thrust adjuster socket wrench (part No. 09940-14990) is required to remove and install the engine in the frame. Failure to use the tool will damage the engine mounting fasteners. Read the following procedure before removing the engine.

1. Securely support the motorcycle on level ground.
2. Drain the engine oil and remove the oil filter as described in Chapter Three.
3. Drain the engine coolant as described in Chapter Three.
4. Remove the seats as described in Chapter Fifteen.
5. Disconnect the negative battery cable as described in Chapter Three.
6. Remove the fuel tank as described in Chapter Eight.
7. Remove the exhaust system as described in Chapter Eight.

8. Remove the air box and carburetor assembly as described in Chapter Eight.
9. Disconnect the spark plug leads and secure them out of the way.
10. Remove the radiator assembly and coolant reservoir as described in Chapter Ten.
11. Detach the clutch cable from the engine as described in Chapter Six.
12. Remove the engine sprocket and drive chain from the engine as described in Chapter Eleven.
13. Disconnect the following electrical connectors:
    a. Engine ground cable: (black).
    b. Starter motor lead: (red).
    c. Alternator connector: three-pin (three yellow wires).
    d. Coolant temperature sensor lead: (black/green and black/white wires).
    e. Neutral switch connector: four-pin (blue, yellow/blue, green/blue and black/white).
    f. Oil pressure switch connector: one-pin: (black wire).
    g. Signal generator connector: two-pin (white and green wires).
    h. Sidestand switch connector: two-pin (green and black/white wires).
    i. Speed sensor connector: three-pin (black/white, pink and orange/green wires).
    j. Cooling fan connector: (black and blue wires)
    k. Cooling fan switch: (black/red and black/white wires)
14. If the engine requires disassembly, remove the following sub-assemblies:
    a. Alternator (Chapter Nine).
    b. Clutch (Chapter Six).
    c. Oil pump (this chapter).
    d. Starter motor (Chapter Nine).
15. Move all electrical wires, harnesses and hoses out of the way.
16. Place a floor jack underneath the engine. Raise the jack so the pad just rests against the bottom of the engine. Place a thick wooden block on the jack pad to protect the engine.

CAUTION
*Use the Suzuki engine mounting thrust adjuster socket wrench (part No. 09940-14980) to loosen the engine mounting thrust adjuster locknut (A, **Figure 2**) and mounting thrust adjuster (B). Do not try to loosen these fasteners without this special wrench.*

The fasteners will be damaged. This tool is also required to tighten the fasteners to the correct torque specification during installation.

CAUTION
The locknuts are self-locking and must be discarded after removal. Do not reuse a self-locking nut or substitute another type of locknut.

NOTE
In Step 17 and Step 18, do not remove the lower and upper throughbolts at this time. Leave them in place until the other fasteners are removed.

17. On the upper throughbolt (A, **Figure 3**) and lower throughbolt (B), perform the following:
   a. Remove the engine mounting nut from the throughbolt.
   b. Use the special tool and remove the thrust adjuster locknut (A, **Figure 2**).
   c. Use the special tool and remove the thrust adjuster (B, **Figure 2**).

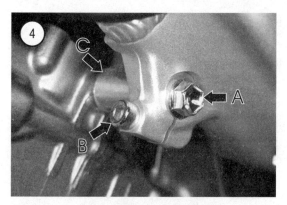

NOTE
If the cylinder heads were removed with the engine in the frame, then the engine mounting bolts in Steps 18 and 19 have already been removed. Proceed to Step 20.

18. Remove the following mounting bolts attached to the front cylinder head:
   a. Remove the left engine mounting bolt (A, **Figure 4**). Loosen the spacer clamp bolt (B, **Figure 4**) and move the spacer (C) away from the cylinder head.
   b. Remove the right engine mounting bolt (A, **Figure 5**) and spacer (B).

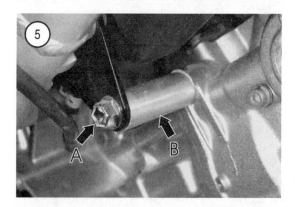

19. Remove the following mounting bolts attached to the rear cylinder head:
   a. Remove the left engine mounting bolt (A, **Figure 6**). Loosen the spacer clamp bolt (B, **Figure 6**) and move the spacer (**Figure 7**) away from the cylinder head.
   b. Remove the right engine mounting bolt (**Figure 8**).

20. Make sure the floor jack is still positioned correctly against the engine.

21. Block the front wheel so the motorcycle cannot roll in either direction.

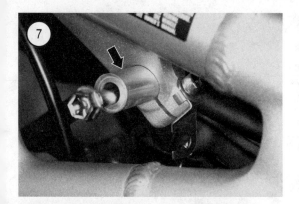

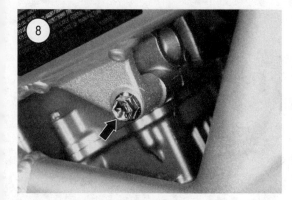

22. Tie the front brake lever to the throttle grip to keep the front brake applied.

23. Remove the center mounting bolt (A, **Figure 9**).

24. Slowly withdraw the upper throughbolt (B, **Figure 9**) from the right side.

25. Have an assistant steady the engine assembly, then withdraw the lower through bolt (**Figure 10**) from the right side.

NOTE
While removing the engine, make sure the exhaust pipe on the rear cylinder head and the drive chain do not obstruct removal.

26. Completely lower the engine from the frame.

27. Place the engine on a workbench.

28. While the engine is removed, check all the engine mounting points on the frame for cracks or other damage. Also check the mounting bolts and holes for thread damage and repair them if necessary.

29. Remove corrosion from bolts and their threads with a wire wheel. Check the threads on all parts for wear or damage. Clean with the appropriate size metric tap or die and clean with solvent.

30. Before installation, spray the engine mounting bolts with a rust inhibitor.

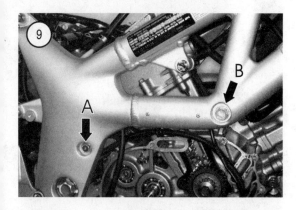

Installation

Installation is the reverse of removal. Follow the installation and tightening sequence described below. Do not tighten any of the engine mounting fasteners until they all have been installed. Install all the engine mounting hardware fingertight, then tighten the hardware to the specified torque.

1. Verify that the center mounting sleeve (A, **Figure 11**) is properly positioned in the frame leg. A

clamp bolt (B, **Figure 11**) secures the sleeve in the frame. Specified tightening torque for the clamp bolt is 23 N•m (17 ft.-lb.).

2. Be sure the engine mounting thrust adjusters (**Figure 12**) are installed in the frame.

NOTE
When installing the engine, place the drive chain around the output shaft.

3. Position the engine into the frame and align the upper and lower throughbolt holes with the frame.

4. Install the lower throughbolt (**Figure 10**) from the right side.

5. Install the upper throughbolt (B, **Figure 9**) and center throughbolt (A).

6A. *Front cylinder head*—Perform the following:
   a. Position the spacer (C, **Figure 4**) between the frame and cylinder head, then install the left engine mounting bolt (A). Tighten the bolt fingertight.
   b. Install the spacer (B, **Figure 5**) and right engine mounting bolt (A). Tighten the bolt fingertight.

6B. *Rear cylinder head*—Perform the following:
   a. Position the spacer (**Figure 7**) between the frame and cylinder head, then install the left engine mounting bolt (A, **Figure 6**). Tighten the bolt fingertight.
   b. Install the right engine mounting bolt (**Figure 8**). Tighten the bolt fingertight.

7. Use the special tool and tighten the engine mounting thrust adjusters (B, **Figure 2**) on the upper throughbolt (A, **Figure 3**) and lower throughbolt (B) to 10 N•m (88 in.-lb.).

8. Use the special tool and tighten the engine mounting thrust adjuster locknuts (A, **Figure 2**) on the upper throughbolt (A, **Figure 3**) and lower throughbolt (B) to 45 N•m (33 ft.-lb.).

9. Tighten the nuts on the upper throughbolt (A, **Figure 3**) and lower throughbolt to 93 N•m (68 ft.-lb.).

10. Tighten the center throughbolt (A, **Figure 9**) to 55 N•m (40 ft.-lb.).

11A. *Front cylinder head*—Perform the following:
   a. Tighten the left engine mounting bolt (A, **Figure 4**) to 55 N•m (40 ft.-lb.). Tighten the clamp bolt (B, **Figure 6**) to 23 N•m (17 ft.-lb.).
   b. Tighten the right engine mounting bolt (A, **Figure 5**) to 55 N•m (40 ft.-lb.).

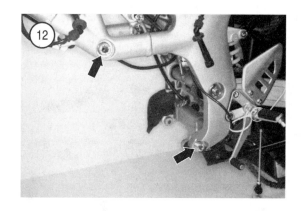

11B. *Rear cylinder head*—Perform the following:
   a. Tighten the left engine mounting bolt (A, **Figure 6**) to 55 N•m (40 ft.-lb.). Tighten the clamp bolt (B, **Figure 6**) to 23 N•m (17 ft.-lb.).
   b. Tighten the right engine mounting bolt (**Figure 8**) to 55 N•m (40 ft.-lb.).

12. Assemble the engine by reversing Steps 2-14 of engine removal. Note the following:
   a. Fill the engine with the recommended type and quantity of engine oil and coolant, as described in Chapter Three.
   b. Adjust the drive chain as described in Chapter Three.

OIL PUMP

The oil pump is mounted behind the clutch on the right side of the engine. The oil pump can be removed with the engine mounted in the frame. Replacement parts are *not available* for the oil pump, with the exception of the oil pump gear. If the oil pump is not operating properly, replace the entire oil pump assembly.

If abnormal oil pressure is suspected, perform the oil pressure test described in Chapter Three.

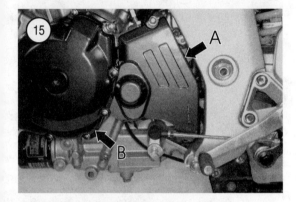

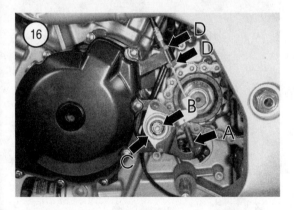

Removal

1. Remove the clutch as described in Chapter Six.

2. Place a clean shop cloth into the crankcase opening to prevent any small parts from falling into the crankcase.

3. Remove the snap ring (A, **Figure 13**) securing the gear, then remove the gear (B).

4. Remove the pin (A, **Figure 14**) and washer (B).

CAUTION
The Phillips head screws have a locking agent applied to them during installation. Use an impact driver or air tool to loosen the screws. The screw heads may be damaged if removal is tried using a hand-held, regular Phillips head screwdriver.

5. Remove the oil pump mounting screws, then withdraw the oil pump assembly (C, **Figure 14**) from the crankcase.

Inspection

The oil pump cannot be disassembled for inspection or service and must be replaced as a unit.

Inspect the oil pump driven gear for wear, chipped or missing teeth. Also inspect the oil pump drive gear on the backside of the clutch housing. Replace either gear if necessary.

Installation

1. If a new oil pump is being installed or the existing oil pump was cleaned in solvent, the oil pump must be primed. Pour fresh engine oil into one of the openings in the backside of the oil pump until it runs out the other opening. Rotate the drive shaft several times by hand to make sure the internal rotors within the oil pump are coated with oil.

2. Reverse the removal steps to install the oil pump. Apply Threadlock 1342 to the oil pump mounting screws and tighten them to 8 N•m (71 in.-lb.).

STARTER CLUTCH AND GEARS

Removal

NOTE
The starter clutch and gears can be removed with the engine installed in the frame. For clarity, the illustrations show the engine removed and partially disassembled.

1. If the engine is in the frame, perform the following:
   a. Remove the engine sprocket cover (A, **Figure 15**).
   b. Detach the clutch release return spring (A, **Figure 16**).

   c. Loosen the clutch adjusting nut (B, **Figure 16**).

   d. Remove the two retaining bolts, then remove the clutch release assembly (C, **Figure 16**).

   e. Loosen the clutch cable mounting nuts (D, **Figure 16**) and separate the cable from the mounting arm on the alternator cover.

   f. Remove the front seat and disconnect the alternator three-wire electrical connector (A, **Figure 17**) and the signal generator two-wire connector (B).

2. Remove the bolts securing the alternator cover (B, **Figure 15**) to the crankcase.

NOTE
Note the path of the wiring harness when withdrawing it in Step 3.

3. Remove the alternator cover. If the engine is in the frame, carefully withdraw the wiring harness from the frame. Do not lose the two locating dowels behind the cover (**Figure 18**).

4. Extract the idler shaft (A, **Figure 19**), then remove the starter idler gear (B).

5. Remove the alternator rotor as described in Chapter Nine.

6. Remove the drive key (A, **Figure 20**).

7. Remove the starter driven gear (B, **Figure 20**).

8. Inspect all components as described in the following section.

9. Install by reversing the preceding removal steps and noting the following:

   a. If removed, install the two locating dowels (**Figure 18**).

   b. Install a new gasket.

   c. Install a new gasket washer onto each of the alternator cover bolts (**Figure 21**).

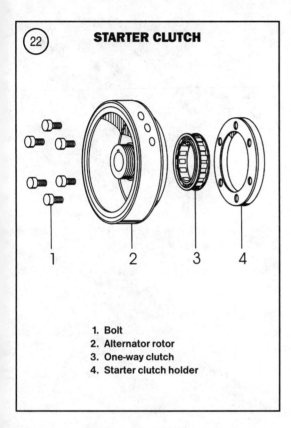

STARTER CLUTCH

1. Bolt
2. Alternator rotor
3. One-way clutch
4. Starter clutch holder

Disassembly/Inspection/Assembly

Refer to **Figure 22** for this procedure.

1. Inspect the starter idle gears and shaft (**Figure 23**) for wear or damage. Replace if necessary.

2. Set the rotor and starter driven gear on the workbench with the rotor facing down.

3. Inspect the one-way clutch as follows:

 a. Attempt to rotate the starter driven gear (**Figure 24**) clockwise; it should not rotate.

 b. Rotate the starter driven gear counterclockwise; it should rotate.

 c. If the one-way clutch fails either of these tests, replace the one-way clutch.

NOTE
The starter driven gear, starter clutch holder and one-way clutch are only available as an assembly.

4. Rotate the starter driven gear (**Figure 24**) counterclockwise and pull it up at the same time. Remove the gear from the backside of the AC generator rotor.

5. Inspect the starter driven gear for wear, chipped or missing teeth (A, **Figure 25**). Replace the gear if necessary.

6. Inspect the starter driven gear bushing (B, **Figure 25**) for wear or damage. The bushing is not available separately from the gear.

7. Inspect the starter driven gear outer surface (C, **Figure 25**) where it rides on the one-way clutch. If the surface is damaged, replace the gear.

8. Inspect the rollers (A, **Figure 26**) of the one-way clutch for burrs, wear or damage. If necessary, remove the one-way clutch as follows:

a. Use a wrench on the hex portion (A, **Figure 27**) of the AC generator rotor or a strap-type wrench (B). Hold the rotor stationary while loosening the Allen bolts in the next step.

CAUTION
The Allen bolts have a locking agent applied to them during installation. Use the correct size wrench to loosen the screws; otherwise, the screw heads will be damaged.

b. Loosen, then remove, the Allen bolts (C, **Figure 27**) securing the starter clutch holder and one-way clutch to the backside of the AC generator rotor.

c. Remove the starter clutch holder (B, **Figure 26**) and the one-way clutch from the backside of the AC generator rotor.

d. If removed, install the one-way clutch so the flanged side fits into the notch on the starter clutch holder. Install the starter clutch holder (B, **Figure 26**) so the stepped side is toward the rotor and align the bolt holes.

e. Apply Threadlocker Super 1303 to the Allen bolt threads prior to installation, then install the bolts (C, **Figure 27**). Use the same tool set up used for loosening the bolts and tighten the bolts to 25 N•m (18 ft.-lb.).

9. To install the starter driven gear onto the alternator rotor, rotate the starter driven gear (**Figure 24**) counterclockwise and push it down at the same time.

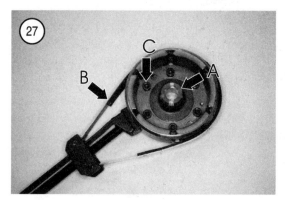

PRIMARY AND WATER PUMP DRIVE GEARS

The primary drive gear is located between the water pump drive gear and rear cylinder cam chain drive sprocket on the right end of the crankshaft. Removing the primary drive gear requires clutch removal.

Removal/Installation

1. Remove the clutch cover as described in the clutch removal section in Chapter Six.

2. To prevent gear rotation when loosening the retaining bolt, the following methods may be used.

a. Place a small gear (A, **Figure 28**) in mesh with the clutch and primary drive gears.

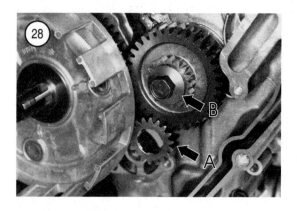

b. Place a soft copper washer, penny or shop cloth into mesh with the gears. This will prevent the primary drive gear from turning in the next step.

NOTE
The primary drive gear retaining bolt has left-hand threads. Loosen it by turning it clockwise.

3. Remove the primary drive gear retaining bolt (B, **Figure 28**) by turning the bolt clockwise.

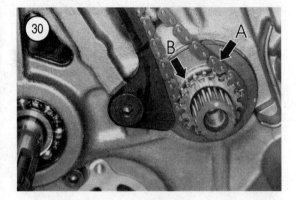

4. Remove the water pump drive gear (A, **Figure 29**).

5. Remove the clutch as described in Chapter Six.

6. Remove the primary drive gear (B, **Figure 29**). The rear cylinder cam chain (A, **Figure 30**) and sprocket (B) are now accessible.

7. Inspect the gears for excessive wear and damage. Replace if necessary.

8. Install the primary drive gear and water pump drive gear by reversing the removal procedure. Clean the threads of any oil, then tighten the retain-

ing bolt to 70 N•m (51 ft.-lb.) by turning it counterclockwise.

CAM CHAIN SPROCKETS

The cam chain in the front cylinder is driven by an integral sprocket on the crankshaft behind the starter driven gear. The cam chain in the rear cylinder is driven by a removable sprocket on the crankshaft behind the primary drive gear.

Proceed as follows to service the removable cam chain sprocket for the front cylinder.

1. Remove the primary drive gear as previously described.

2. Remove the cam chain drive sprocket (A, **Figure 31**).

3. Inspect the sprocket for excessive wear and damage. Replace if necessary.

NOTE
If replacing the drive sprocket, also install a new cam chain.

4. Install the cam chain drive sprocket by reversing the removal procedure. Be sure to align the timing marks (B, **Figure 31**) on the sprocket and crankshaft end when installing the sprocket on the crankshaft.

CRANKCASE

Disassembly of the crankcase (splitting the cases) and removal of the crankshaft assembly require that the engine be removed from the frame. However, many of the attached assemblies should be removed with the engine in the frame.

The crankcase is made in two halves of precision die cast aluminum alloy. To avoid damage, do not hammer or pry on any of the interior or exterior projected walls. These areas are easily damaged. The cases are split vertically down the centerline of the connecting rod. The cases are assembled without a gasket; only gasket sealer is used while dowel pins align the crankcase halves when they are bolted together. The crankcase halves are sold as a matched set only; if one crankcase half is damaged, both halves must be replaced.

Special Tools

The tool requirements vary depending on the condition of the crankcase, the bearings and the crankshaft. In some case the crankcase halves can be separated and the crankshaft removed without the use of special tools. However, if difficulty is encountered, either obtain the required tools or have the procedure performed by a Suzuki dealership. Remember, the crankcase halves can be easily damaged by improper disassembly and assembly techniques. Fabricate and/or obtain the following tools or their equivalents:

1. When handling the crankcase assembly, two 4 × 4 wooden blocks or a wooden fixture of 2 × 4 in. wood as shown in **Figure 32** will assist in engine disassembly and assembly and will help to prevent damage to the crankshaft and transmission shafts.

2. Suzuki crankcase separating tool (part No. 09920-13120), or equivalent. This tool threads into the right crankcase and is used to separate the crankcase halves and press the crankshaft out of the left crankcase. The tool is simple in design and a similar type of tool, such as a steering wheel puller, may be substituted.

Crankcase Disassembly

The procedure that follows is presented as a complete, step-by-step, major lower end rebuild that should be followed if an engine is to be completely reconditioned. However, if replacing a defective part, the disassembly should be carried out only until the failed part is accessible; there is no need to disassemble the engine beyond that point, as long as the remaining components are in good condition and were not affected by the failed part.

Remember that the right and left side of the engine relates to the engine as it sits in the frame, not as it may sit on the workbench.

1. Remove the engine as described in this chapter.

2. Remove all exterior engine assemblies as described in this chapter and other related chapters. Be sure to also remove the following components:

   a. External shift mechanism as described in Chapter Six.
   b. Oil seal retainer (A, **Figure 33**).
   c. Neutral switch, contact pins and springs (B, **Figure 33**) as described in Chapter Nine.
   d. Spacer (C, **Figure 33**).
   e. Cam chains and front cylinder sprocket as described in Chapter Four and this chapter.

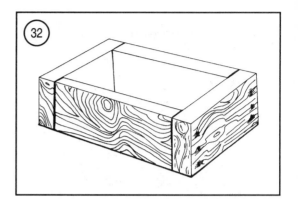

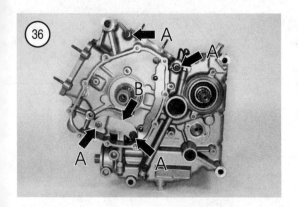

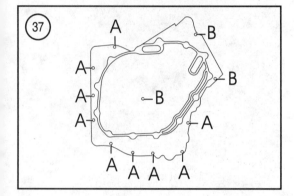

5

f. Oil pipe retainer (**Figure 34**) and oil pipe (**Figure 35**).

3. Remove the four crankcase bolts on the left side as shown at A, **Figure 36**. Loosen the bolts in two steps in a crossing pattern. The lower bolts also secure the oil plate (B, **Figure 36**), which should also be removed.

4. Remove the crankcase bolts on the right side indicated in **Figure 37**. Note the location of the 6 mm bolts (A, **Figure 37**) and 8 mm bolts (B).

CAUTION
Perform the next step directly over and close to the workbench as the crankcase halves may separate easily. Do not hammer on the crankcase halves or they will be damaged.

5. Place the crankcase assembly on the wooden box or wooden blocks with the right side facing up.

6. Install the Suzuki crankcase separating tool (part No. 09920-13120) or equivalent tool (**Figure 38**). If the proper tools are not available, take the crankcase assembly to a dealer and have it separated. Do not risk expensive crankcase damage with improper tools or techniques.

NOTE
Never pry between case halves. Doing so may result in oil leaks, requiring replacement of the case halves as a set.

7. Account for the locating dowels (**Figure 39**) if they are loose in the case. They do not have to be removed from the case if they are secure.

8. Remove the transmission, shift drum and shift fork shaft assemblies as described in Chapter Seven.

9. The crankshaft assembly (A, **Figure 40**) can be removed at this time, if desired. Do not lose the thrust washer (B, **Figure 40**).

10. Inspect the crankcase halves and crankshaft assembly as described in this chapter.

Crankcase Reassembly

1. If the following components were removed, make sure they are properly installed:
   a. Connecting rods.
   b. Main bearings.
   c. Oil strainer and oil regulator.
   d. Oil jets.
   e. Oil seals.
   f. Transmission assembly and bearings.

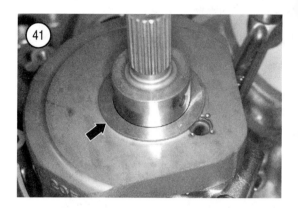

> *NOTE*
> *Set the left crankcase half assembly on wooden blocks or the wooden holding fixture shown in* **Disassembly**.

> *NOTE*
> *Lubricate the lips of all oil seals with clean engine oil.*

2. If removed, install the crankcase dowel pins into the left crankcase half (**Figure 39**).

3. Carefully install the crankshaft into the left crankcase half so the tapered crankshaft end faces the left crankcase half. Position the connecting rods into their respective cylinder openings at the same time.

4. Determine the correct thickness of the thrust washer (**Figure 41**) using the following procedure:

> *NOTE*
> *The following procedure describes a temporary assembly of the crankcase to measure crankshaft end play. Do not apply sealant to the crankcase halves.*

   a. Install the thrust washer (**Figure 41**) so the grooved side contacts the crankshaft thrust surface and the smooth side faces out toward the crankshaft end.
   b. Install the right crankcase half onto the left crankcase half.
   c. Install the crankcase bolts (**Figure 37**) and tighten in a crossing pattern. Tighten the 6 mm bolts to 11 N•m (97 in.-lb.). Tighten the 8 mm screws to 26 N•m (19 ft.-lb.).
   d. Install the oil plate (A, **Figure 42**). Note that the split end (B, **Figure 42**) fits around a rib inside the crankcase. Install the oil plate retaining bolts fingertight. Note the location of

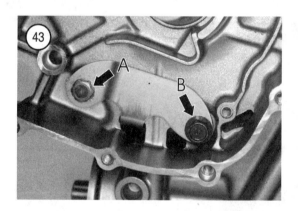

the gold-head bolt (A, **Figure 43**) and green-head bolt (B).

e. Tighten the crankcase bolts on the left crankcase half (**Figure 36**) in a crossing pattern to 26 N•m (19 ft.-lb.).

f. Install the alternator rotor and retaining bolt as described in Chapter Nine.

g. Install the cam chain sprocket, primary drive gear and water pump drive gear onto the crankshaft right end. Tighten the retaining bolt to the specified torque as described in this chapter.

h. Place the engine in its normal operating position. Push the crankshaft toward the right side of the engine. Using a feeler gauge, measure the clearance between the inside of the cam chain sprocket and the crankcase (**Figure 44**). Record the measurement.

i. Disassemble the crankcase assembly until the thrust washer (**Figure 41**) is accessible.

j. Desired crankshaft end play is 0.050-0.110 mm (0.0020-0.0043 in.). If the measured end play is not within the desired end play, measure the thickness of the thrust washer (**Figure 45**) and calculate the thickness of a thrust washer that will provide the correct end play. Obtain the correct thrust washer from a Suzuki dealership.

5. Apply a light coat of molybdenum disulfide grease to the thrust surfaces at both ends on the crankshaft (A, **Figure 46**).

6. Apply a light coat of molybdenum disulfide grease to the main bearing surfaces at both ends on the crankshaft (B, **Figure 46**).

7. Install the selected thrust washer (**Figure 41**) so the grooved side contacts the crankshaft thrust surface and the smooth side faces out toward the crankshaft end.

8. Make sure the dowel pins (**Figure 39**) are installed.

NOTE
Apply a light coat of grease to the O-rings in Step 8 to hold them in place when assembling the crankcase halves.

9. Install the O-rings (**Figure 47**) into the recesses in the left crankcase half.

NOTE
Make sure the crankcase mating surfaces are clean and free of all old sealant material.

10. On early models, install the oil plate into the right crankcase half (**Figure 48**).

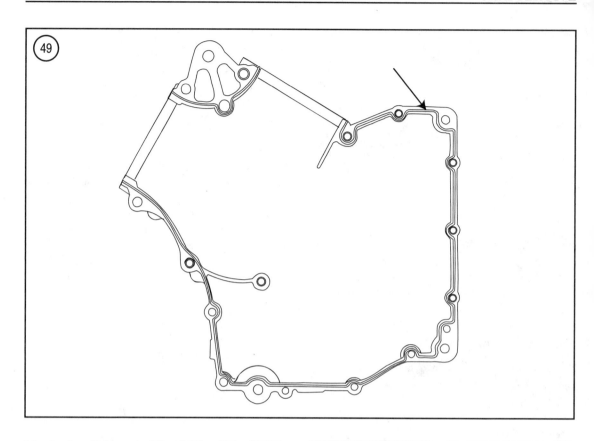

11. Apply a light coat of Suzuki Bond No. 1207B, or equivalent, to the mating surface of the left crankcase half as shown in **Figure 49**.

12. Install the right crankcase half onto the left crankcase half.

13. Install the crankcase bolts (**Figure 37**) and tighten in a crossing pattern. Tighten the 6 mm bolts to 11 N•m (97 in.-lb.). Tighten the 8 mm screws to 26 N•m (19 ft.-lb.).

14. Install the oil plate (A, **Figure 42**). Note that the split end (B, **Figure 42**) fits around a rib inside the crankcase. Install the oil plate retaining bolts fingertight. Note the location of the gold-head bolt (A, **Figure 43**) and green-head bolt (B).

15. Make sure to install the wire clamp onto the upper crankcase bolt (A, **Figure 50**).

16. Tighten the crankcase bolts on the left crankcase half (**Figure 36**) in a crossing pattern to 26 N•m (19 ft.-lb.).

17. If removed, install the oil plate (B, **Figure 50**) onto the left crankcase half.

18. Reassemble the remainder of the crankcase by reversing the removal procedure while noting the following:

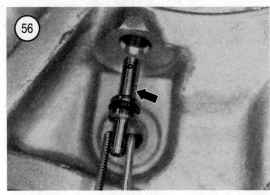

a. Install the oil pipe so the crimped end is out (**Figure 51**). Install the oil pipe retainer as shown in **Figure 52**.

b. Install a new O-ring into the groove into the output shaft spacer (**Figure 53**). Lubricate the O-ring and oil seal, then install the spacer so the grooved end is in and the flat end (**Figure 54**) is out.

Crankcase Inspection

1. Clean the crankcase halves, inside and out, and clean all crankcase bearings with cleaning solvent. Thoroughly dry all components with compressed air. Make sure there is no solvent residue left in the cases as it will contaminate the new engine oil.

2. Using a scraper, *carefully* remove any remaining sealer residue from all crankcase sealing surfaces.

3. Carefully check the sealing surface of both crankcase halves. Check for gouges or nicks that may lead to an oil leak.

4. Service the piston cooling jets as follows:

a. Remove the piston cooling oil jet retainer (**Figure 55**) and the cooling jet (**Figure 56**). Each crankcase half is equipped with a cooling jet.

b. Clean the jet and the jet passage.

c. Install a new O-ring onto the jet before installing it. Lubricate the O-ring with engine oil.

d. Install the jet so the hole in the tip points toward the cylinder opening in the crankcase. Make sure the jet is properly seated in the crankcase.

e. Apply Threadlocker 1342 or equivalent to the threads of the Allen bolt. Tighten the bolt 10 N•m to (88 in.-lb.).

5. Service the oil passage jets as follows:

a. Remove the oil passage jet (**Figure 57**) from the cylinder mating surface. Each crankcase half is equipped with an oil passage jet.

b. Clean the jet and the jet passage.

c. Install a new O-ring onto the jet before installing it. Lubricate the O-ring with engine oil.

d. Install the jet so the slotted end points up toward the cylinder (**Figure 58**).

6. Service the transmission oil jet as follows:

a. Remove the oil passage bolt (**Figure 59**) and the transmission oil jet (**Figure 60**) in the crankcase half.

NOTE
It may be necessary to dislodge the jet by directing a wire into the oil passage behind the jet. Insert the wire through the oil hole in the transmission shaft bore (A, Figure 61).

b. Clean the jet and the jet passage.

c. Install a new O-ring onto the jet before installing it. Lubricate the O-ring with engine oil.

d. Install the jet so the slotted end points inward (**Figure 60**). Insert the jet until it bottoms in the oil passage.

e. Tighten the oil passage bolt to 18 N•m (159 in.-lb.).

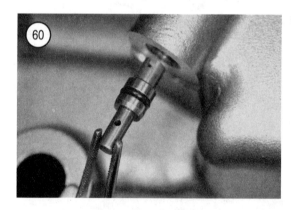

7. Remove the oil passage plugs and washers (**Figure 62**) from the left crankcase half.

8. Direct compressed air to the oil passages and blow out any accumulated residue. If necessary, rinse out the passages with solvent and once again apply compressed air to thoroughly clean out the gallery.

9. Install the oil gallery plugs with new sealing washers and tighten them securely.

10. Inspect the cases for cracks and fractures, especially in the lower areas where they are vulnerable to rock damage. Check the areas around the stiffen-

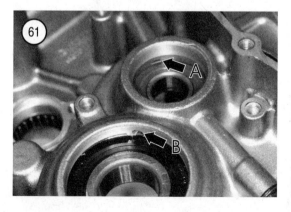

ing ribs, around bearing bosses and threaded holes for damage. If damage is found, have it repaired by a shop specializing in the repair of precision aluminum castings or replace the crankcases as a set.

11. Check the tightness of the shift lever stopper pin (**Figure 63**). If loose, remove the stopper pin. Apply Threadlocker Super 1303 to the stopper pin threads and reinstall it. Tighten the stopper pin to 23 N•m (17 ft.-lb.).

12. Inspect the main bearings (**Figure 64**). Replace the main bearings if damaged or excessively worn. Measure main bearing clearance as described in this chapter.

> *NOTE*
> *The crankcase is equipped with insert-type main bearings in each crankcase half. A Suzuki special tool is required to install the the bearings. If the bearings are excessively worn or damaged, take the crankcase and crankshaft to a Suzuki dealership for bearing installation.*

13. Check the shift drum bearing (**Figure 65**) for wear. Rotate the inner race of the bearing by hand. The bearing must rotate freely with no signs of binding. If necessary, replace the bearing as described in this chapter.

> *CAUTION*
> *If oil seal removal is necessary, be careful not to damage the crankcase bore. When removing the transmission mainshaft or transmission output shaft seal, the crankcase may be damaged if the removal tool snags the adjacent oil passage in the crankcase bore (A or B, Figure 61).*

14. Inspect the oil seals for the transmission mainshaft (A, **Figure 66**), transmission output shaft

(B) and transmission shift shaft (C). Check for hardness, deterioration and wear. Replace if necessary. Install the mainshaft and output shaft seals so they are flush with the crankcase; if installed too deeply, the seals may block the oil passages. Install the shift shaft seal so it bottoms in the crankcase.

Oil Strainer

The oil strainer is contained in a compartment in the right crankcase half (**Figure 67**).

1. Remove the retainer plate (**Figure 67**).
2. Remove the oil strainer (A, **Figure 68**).
3. Thoroughly clean the strainer, retainer plate and crankcase in solvent and dry them with compressed air.
4. Inspect the strainer screen for broken areas or damage. Replace the strainer if damaged or if it cannot be cleaned adequately.

> *NOTE*
> *Perform service to the crankcase halves before installing the oil strainer.*

5. Install the oil strainer into the crankcase half so the projection (B, **Figure 68**) is toward the bottom of the crankcase.
6. Install the retainer plate. Apply Threadlock 1342 to the retainer bolts and tighten them to 10 N•m (88 in.-lb.).

Oil Pressure Regulator

The oil pressure regulator valve is located inside the left crankcase half (**Figure 69**).

> *NOTE*
> *There are no replacement parts for the valve. If damaged, the entire valve must be replaced.*

1. Unscrew the valve (**Figure 69**) from the crankcase.
2. To check the valve operation, use a piece of plastic rod or wood and push down on the piston within the valve. The piston must slide smoothly and return to the fully closed position when released. If piston operation is not smooth, clean the valve in solvent and thoroughly dry it with compressed air.

3. Repeat Step 3 to check valve operation. If cleaning does not solve the problem, replace the valve.
4. Use a small amount of threadlocking compound on the valve threads before installation.
5. Install the valve (**Figure 69**) and tighten it to 27 N•m (20 ft.-lb.).

Bearing Replacement

Before removing a bearing, note and record which side of the bearing has markings on the races. Install the new bearing so the markings appear on the same side with relation to the crankcase.

1. On a bearing so equipped, remove the screws (**Figure 70**, typical) securing the bearing retainer plate(s) and remove the retainer plate(s). If the bearing is not going to be replaced, check the retaining screws for tightness.

> *CAUTION*
> *Before heating the crankcase halves in this procedure to remove the bearings, wash the cases thoroughly with hot water and detergent. Rinse and rewash the cases as required to re-*

move all traces of oil and other chemical deposits.

CAUTION
Even after the cases have been thoroughly washed, there may be a slight residual oil or solvent odor left in the oven after heating the crankcase. This may be undesirable if using a household oven.

2A. The bearings are installed with a slight interference fit. The crankcase must be heated in an oven or hot plate to a temperature of about 215° F (100° C). An easy way to check the proper temperature is to drop tiny drops of water on the case; if they sizzle and evaporate immediately, the temperature is correct. Heat only one case at a time.

CAUTION
Do not heat the cases with a torch (propane or acetylene); never bring a flame into contact with the bearing or case. The direct heat will destroy the case hardening of the bearing and may warp the case.

2B. A hydraulic press may be used instead of heat to remove and install the bearings and oil seals.

3. Remove the case from the oven or hot plate using a kitchen pot holder, heavy gloves or heavy shop cloths—it is hot.

4. Hold the crankcase with the bearing side down and tap it squarely on a piece of soft wood. Continue to tap until the bearing(s) fall out. Repeat for the other case half.

CAUTION
Be sure to tap the crankcase squarely on the piece of wood. Avoid damaging the sealing surface of the crankcase. If the bearings or seals are difficult to remove or install, do not risk damaging the case. Have the work performed by a dealer or competent machine shop.

5. If the bearings are difficult to remove, they can be gently tapped out with a suitable size socket or piece of pipe the same size as the bearing inner race.

6. While heating the crankcase halves, place the new bearings in a freezer if possible. Chilling them will slightly reduce their overall diameter while the hot crankcase is slightly larger due to heat expansion. This will make bearing installation much easier.

NOTE
Prior to installing the new bearing(s) apply a light coat of lithium-based grease to the inside and outside to aid in installation.

NOTE
Install a new bearing so that the manufacturer's name and size code face in the same direction recorded during disassembly. If this information was not noted prior to removing the bearings, install the bearings so that their marks are visible after the bearing has been installed.

7. While the crankcase is still hot, press each new bearing(s) into place in the crankcase by hand until it seats completely. Install the bearings by hand, if possible. If necessary, lightly tap the bearing(s) into the case with a socket placed on the outer race. Do not install new bearings by driving on the inner bearing race. Install the bearing(s) until it seats completely. If the bearing will not seat, remove it and cool it again. Reheat the crankcase and install the bearing again.

5

CRANKSHAFT

Removal/Installation

1. Remove the crankshaft/connecting rod assembly as previously described in *Crankcase Disassembly* in this chapter.
2. Inspect the crankshaft and main bearings as described in this chapter.
3. Install the crankshaft/connecting rod assembly as described in *Crankcase Assembly* in this chapter.

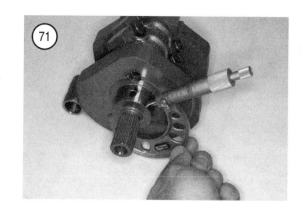

Crankshaft Inspection

1. Clean the crankshaft thoroughly with solvent. Clean the crankshaft oil passageways with compressed air. If necessary, clean them with rifle cleaning brushes, then flush the passageways with solvent. Dry the crankshaft with compressed air, then lubricate all bearing surfaces with a light coat of engine oil.
2. Inspect each crankshaft main journal and each connecting rod journal for scratches, ridges, scoring, nicks or heat discoloration. Very small nicks and scratches may be removed with crocus cloth. Anything more serious must be referred to a machine shop.
3. If the surface finish on each crankshaft main bearing journal is satisfactory, measure the main journals with a micrometer for runout, taper and wear (**Figure 71**). Compare the measurements with the specifications listed in **Table 1**.
4. If the surface finish on each connecting rod journal is satisfactory, measure the journals with a micrometer and check runout, taper and wear. Compare the measurements with the specifications listed in **Table 1**.
5. Inspect the crankshaft outer splines (A, **Figure 72**) and threads (B) on the right end of the crankshaft. If damaged, replace the crankshaft. If the crankshaft splines are damaged, also inspect the inner splines on the cam chain sprocket and primary drive gear.
6. On the left end, inspect the threads (A, **Figure 73**), cam chain sprocket (B) and keyway (C) for wear or damage. If damaged, replace the crankshaft.

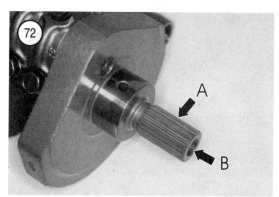

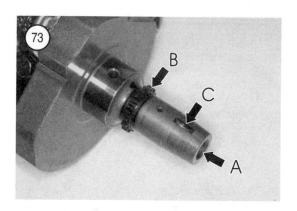

Crankshaft Main Bearings

The crankcase is equipped with insert-type main bearings in each crankcase half. A Suzuki special tool is required to install the the bearings. If the bearings are excessively worn or damaged, take the crankcase

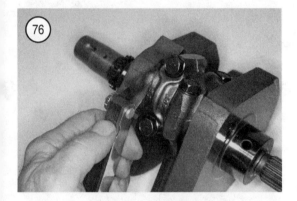

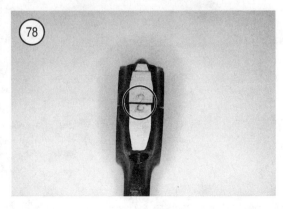

and crankshaft to a Suzuki dealership for bearing installation. Use the following procedure to determine the condition of the crankshaft and bearings.

1. Check each crankshaft main bearing insert (**Figure 74**) for evidence of wear, abrasion and scoring. If the bearing inserts are good, they may be reused. If any insert is questionable, replace the entire set.

2. Be sure the bearing retainer (**Figure 75**) is installed. If removed, install the bearing retainer. Apply Threadlock 1342 to the bearing retainer mounting screws and tighten them to 8 N•m (71 in.-lb.).

3. Clean the bearing surfaces of the crankshaft and the bearing inserts for the crankshaft.

4. Measure the main bearing inside diameter with an inside micrometer. Record the bearing inner diameter measurement.

5. Measure the crankshaft main journal outside diameter with a micrometer (**Figure 71**). Record the main journal diameter.

6. Subtract the crankshaft main journal diameter from the main bearing diameter; the difference is crankshaft main bearing oil clearance. If the clearance exceeds the service limit specified in **Table 1**, the crankshaft, main bearings, or both must be replaced. Take the crankshaft and crankcase to a Suzuki dealership for further service.

CONNECTING RODS

Removal/Installation

1. Remove the crankshaft/connecting rod assembly as described in *Crankcase Disassembly* in this chapter.

2. Insert a flat feeler gauge between the connecting rod and the crankshaft machined surface (**Figure 76**). Compare the measurement to the connecting rod big end side clearance service limit in **Table 1**. Measure each connecting rod. If the measurement is not within the service limit refer to *Connecting Rod Inspection* in this chapter to determine which component requires replacement.

3. Remove the connecting rod cap bolts (**Figure 77**), remove the cap and separate the rods from the crankshaft. Keep each cap with its original rod. The weight mark on the end of the cap should align with the mark on its connecting rod (**Figure 78**).

> *CAUTION*
> *If old bearing inserts are reused, they must be installed in their original lo-*

5

cations. Keep each bearing insert in the connecting rod and cap. If they are removed, label the backside of each insert with a F or R that corresponds to the cylinder location and with rod (R) and cap (C) identification.

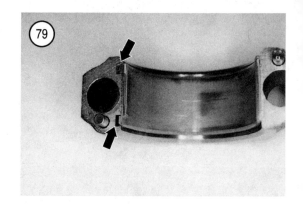

4. Inspect the connecting rods and bearings as described in this chapter

5. If new bearing inserts are being installed, check the bearing clearance as described in this chapter.

6. Apply a light even coat of clean engine oil and molybdenum disulfide grease to the crankpin journals.

7. Make sure the inserts are locked into place (**Figure 79**). Apply clean engine and molybdenum disulfide grease oil to the bearing surface of both bearing inserts.

8. Install each connecting rod onto the crankshaft in the correct location and with the weight mark (**Figure 80**) facing toward the *middle* of the engine. Be careful not to damage the bearing surface of the crankshaft with the sharp edge of the connecting rod and upper insert.

9. Align the weight mark on the end of the cap with the mark on the rod and install the cap onto the rod. Push it on until it contacts the connecting rod.

10. Install the connecting rod cap bolts (**Figure 77**). Initially, tighten the bolts to 35 N•m (26 ft.-lb.), then tighten the bolts to a final torque of 67 N•m (49 ft.-lb.).

11. After installing the connecting rods and tightening the cap nuts tightened correctly, rotate each connecting rod on the crankshaft and make sure there is no binding.

Connecting Rod Inspection

1. Check each connecting rod assembly for obvious damage such as cracks or burns.

2. Make sure the small end oil hole (**Figure 81**) is open. Clean it if necessary.

3. Measure the small end inside diameter with a small hole gauge (**Figure 82**) and measure the gauge with a micrometer. Replace the connecting rod if the small end inside diameter is worn to the service limit specified in **Table 1**.

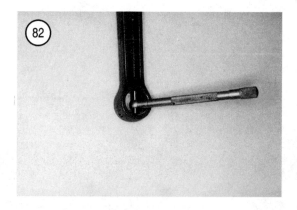

4. Check the piston pin (**Figure 83**) for chrome flaking or cracks. Replace the pin if necessary.

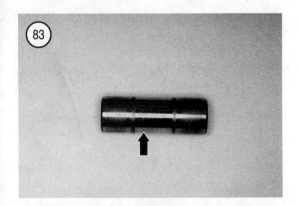

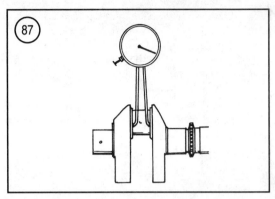

5. Check the piston pin where it contacts the surface of the small end (**Figure 83**) for wear or abrasion.

6. Lubricate the piston pin and install it in the connecting rod (**Figure 84**). Slowly rotate the piston pin and check for radial play.

7. Inspect the alignment of each connecting rod. If there is evidence of abnormal piston or cylinder wear, have the connecting rod inspected at a machine shop. Specialized equipment is required to accurately determine if a rod is bent or twisted.

8. Examine the bearing inserts (**Figure 85**) for wear, scoring or burned surfaces. They are reusable if in good condition. Make a note of the bearing color identification on the side of the insert if the bearing is to be discarded. A previous owner may have installed undersize bearings.

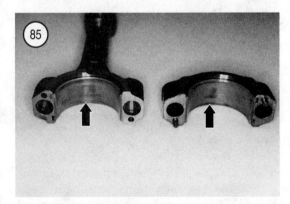

9. If the connecting rod big end side clearance (*Connecting Rod Removal/Installation*) is greater than specified, perform the following:

    a. Measure the width of the connecting rod big end with a micrometer (**Figure 86**). If the width is less than the value specified in **Table 1**, replace the connecting rod assembly.

    b. Measure the crankpin width with a dial caliper or vernier caliper (**Figure 87**) and compare the measurement to the dimension listed in **Table 1**. If the width is greater than specified, replace the crankshaft.

Connecting Rod Bearing Clearance Measurement

1. Inspect each connecting rod insert (**Figure 85**) for evidence of wear, abrasion and scoring. If the bearing inserts are good they may be reused. If any

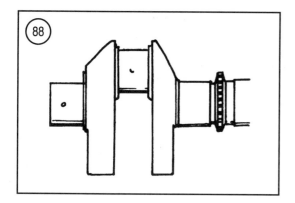

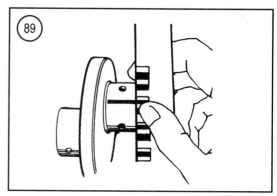

insert is questionable, replace all of the inserts as a set.

2. Clean the crankshaft crankpin (**Figure 88**) and check for damage.

3. If removed, install the existing bearing inserts into the connecting rod and cap. Make sure they are locked into place (**Figure 79**).

4. Install the connecting rods onto the crankshaft in the correct location with the weight mark (**Figure 80**) facing the *middle* of the engine. Be careful not to damage the bearing surface of the crankshaft.

5. Place a piece of Plastigage onto the rod journal. Make sure the Plastigage runs parallel to the crankshaft as shown in **Figure 89**. Do not place the Plastigage material over the oil hole in the crankshaft.

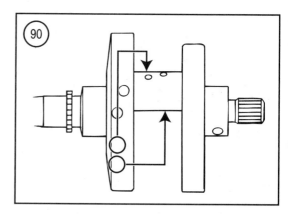

CAUTION
Do not rotate the crankshaft or the connecting rod while the Plastigage is in place.

6. Align the weight mark on the end of the cap with the mark on the rod (**Figure 80**) and install the cap. Install the bolts. Initially tighten the bolts to 35 N•m (26 ft.-lb.), and then tighten the bolts to a final torque of 67 N•m (49 ft.-lb.).

7. Loosen the cap bolts. Carefully lift the cap straight up and off the connecting rod.

8. Measure the width of the flattened Plastigage according to the manufacturer's instructions. Measure both ends of the Plastigage strip (**Figure 89**).

   a. A difference of 0.025 mm (0.001 in.) or more indicates a tapered journal. Confirm the measurement using a micrometer.

   b. If the connecting rod bearing clearance is greater than the wear limit specified in **Table**

1, select new bearings as described in this chapter.

9. Remove all of the Plastigage from the crankshaft rod journals.

Connecting Rod-to-Crankcase Bearing Selection

1. The crankpin is identified by a code (1, 2 or 3) stamped into the counterbalance web on the crankshaft. The codes coincide with the crankpin journal outside diameter as shown in **Figure 90**.

2. The connecting rods are coded with a weight number (1 or 2) marked on the side of the connecting rod (**Figure 78**). The codes coincide with the inside diameter of the connecting rod.

3. Select new bearings by cross-referencing the crankpin outside diameter code (**Figure 90**) in the row across the top of **Table 3** with the connecting rod inside diameter code (**Figure 78**) in the column down the left side of the table. The intersection of the appropriate row and column indicates the color of the new bearing inserts. **Table 4** lists the bearing

color, part number and thickness. Always replace the bearing inserts as a set.

4. After installing new bearing inserts, recheck the clearance by repeating the *Connecting Rod Bearing* *Clearance Measurement* procedure. If the clearance is still out of specification, either the crankshaft or the connecting rod(s) is worn to the service limit and requires replacement.

Table 1 LOWER END SPECIFICATIONS

Item	Specification	Service limit
Connecting rod		
Big end diameter		
Code 1	41.000-41.008 mm (1.6142-1.6145 in.)	–
Code 2	41.008-41.016 mm (1.6145-1.6148 in.)	–
Big end side clearance	0.170-0.320 mm (0.0067-0.0126 in.)	0.5 mm (0.02 in.)
Big end width	20.95-21.00 mm (0.825-0.827 in.)	–
Big end oil clearance	0.032-0.056 mm (0.0013-0.0022 in.)	0.080 mm (0.0031 in.)
Small end inside diameter	20.010-20.018 mm (0.7878-0.7881 in.)	20.040 mm (0.7890 in.)
Crankpin standard diameter	37.976-38.000 mm (1.4951-1.4960 in.)	–
Code 1	37.992-38.000 mm (1.4957-1.4960 in.)	–
Code 2	37.984-37.992 mm (1.4954-1.4957 in.)	–
Code 3	37.976-37.984 mm (1.4951-1.4954 in.)	–
Crankpin width	42.17-42.22 mm (1.660-1.662 in.)	–
Crankshaft end play	0.050-0.110 mm (0.0020-0.0043 in.)	–
Crankshaft main		
bearing journal	41.985-42.000 mm (1.6529-1.6535 in.)	–
Crankshaft main bearing		
oil clearance	0.008-0.035 mm (0.0003-0.0014 in.)	0.080 mm (0.0031 in.)
Crankshaft runout	–	0.05 mm (0.002 in.)

Table 2 LOWER END TORQUE SPECIFICATIONS

Item	N•m	in.-lb.	ft.-lb.
Center engine mounting			
sleeve clamp bolt	23	–	17
Connecting rod bolt			
Initial torque	35	–	26
Final torque	67	–	49
Crankcase bolts*			
6 mm	11	97	–
8 mm	26	–	19
Engine mounting bolts	55	–	40
Engine mounting spacer			
clamp bolts	23	–	17
Engine mounting			
thrust adjuster	10	88	–
Engine mounting			
thrust adjuster locknut	45	–	33
Engine mounting			
throughbolt nut	93	–	68
Main bearing retainer			
plate screws	8	71	–
Oil passage bolt	18	159	–
Oil pressure regulator	27	–	20

(continued)

5

Table 2 LOWER END TORQUE SPECIFICATIONS (continued)

Item	N•m	in.-lb.	ft.-lb.
Oil pump mounting screws	8	71	–
Oil strainer retainer plate bolts	10	88	–
Piston cooling jet retaining bolt	10	88	–
Primary drive gear retaining bolt*	70	–	51
Shift lever stopper pin	23	–	17
Starter clutch bolts	25	–	18
* See text.			

Table 3 CONNECTING ROD BEARING SELECTION

Crankpin outer diameter code		1	2	3
Connecting rod inside diameter code	1	Green	Black	Brown
	2	Black	Brown	Yellow

Table 4 CONNECTING ROD BEARING INSERT COLOR, PART NO., THICKNESS

Color and part No.	Specification
Green 12164-46E01-0A0	1.480-1.484 mm (0.0583-0.0584 in.)
Black 12164-46E01-0B0	1.484-1.488 mm (0.0584-0.0586 in.)
Brown 12164-46E01-0C0	1.488-1.492 mm (0.0586-0.0587 in.)
Yellow 12164-46E01-0D0	1.492-1.496 mm (0.0587-0.0589 in.)

NOTE: Refer to the Supplement at the back of this manual for information unique to 2003-on models.

CHAPTER SIX

CLUTCH AND
EXTERNAL SHIFT MECHANISM

6

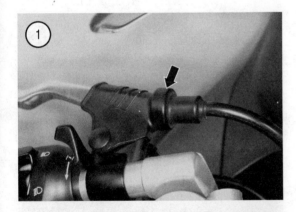

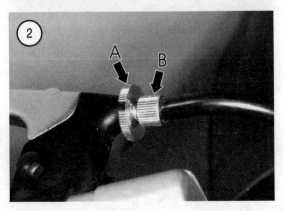

This chapter provides service procedures for the clutch, clutch release mechanism and external shift mechanism. Clutch specifications are in **Table 1** and **Table 2** at the end of the chapter.

The SV650 clutch is a wet (operates in the engine oil) multi-plate design. The clutch assembly is located on the right side of the engine. The clutch hub is mounted on the splines on the transmission input (main) shaft. The outer clutch housing is driven by the primary drive gear on the crankshaft.

Clutch release is accomplished via a pushrod/push piece assembly operating on the pressure plate. The pushrods pass through the transmission input shaft and are activated by the clutch cable pulling on the clutch lifter mechanism mounted in the drive sprocket cover on the left side of the engine. This system requires routine adjustment (Chapter Three) to compensate for cable stretch.

CLUTCH CABLE REPLACEMENT

1. Slide the rubber boot (**Figure 1**) off the clutch hand lever adjuster.
2. At the clutch hand lever, loosen the locknut (A, **Figure 2**) and turn the adjuster (B) all the way in to-

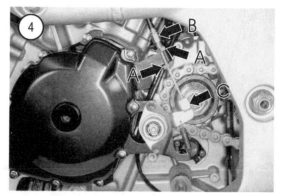

ward the clutch lever holder to allow maximum cable slack. Disconnect the cable from the clutch lever.

3. Raise and support the fuel tank as described in Chapter Eight.

4. Remove the engine sprocket cover (**Figure 3**).

5. Loosen the locknuts (A, **Figure 4**) on the lower cable housing.

6. Rotate the adjuster (B, **Figure 4**) to increase cable slack.

7. Disconnect the clutch cable end from the clutch release arm (C, **Figure 4**).

8. Tie a piece of heavy string onto the lower end of the old cable. Cut the string to a length that is longer than the new clutch cable.

9. Tie the lower end of the string to the frame or engine component.

NOTE
It may be necessary to detach cable clamps to extract or install the cable.

10. Remove the old clutch cable by pulling it from the top (upper cable end). Continue until the cable is removed from the frame, leaving the attached piece of string in its mounting position.

11. Untie the string from the old cable and discard the old cable.

12. Lubricate the new clutch cable as described in Chapter Three.

13. Tie the string onto the bottom end of the new clutch cable.

14. Slowly pull the string and cable to install the cable along the path of the original clutch cable. Continue until the clutch cable is correctly routed through the engine and frame. Untie and remove the string.

15. Visually check the entire length of the clutch cable as it runs through the frame and engine. Make sure there are no kinks or sharp bends. Straighten out if necessary.

16. Connect the upper cable end to the clutch lever.

17. Reattach the lower end of the clutch cable as shown in **Figure 4**. Be sure to bend up the locking tab (**Figure 5**) so the cable end is secured in the swivel fitting.

18. Adjust the clutch cable as described in Chapter Three.

EXTERNAL GEARSHIFT MECHANISM

The external gearshift mechanism is located on the right (clutch) side of the engine. Access to the internal gearshift mechanism requires removing the engine and splitting the crankcase as described in Chapter Five. Internal gearshift mechanism service is described in Chapter Seven.

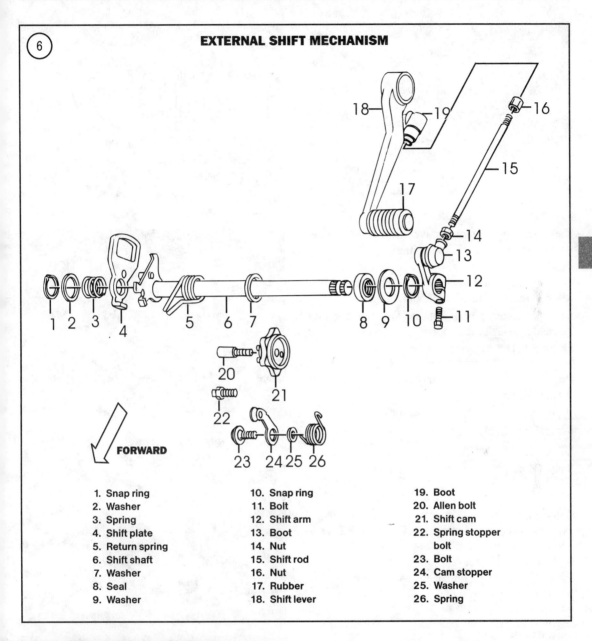

⑥   **EXTERNAL SHIFT MECHANISM**

FORWARD

1. Snap ring	10. Snap ring	19. Boot
2. Washer	11. Bolt	20. Allen bolt
3. Spring	12. Shift arm	21. Shift cam
4. Shift plate	13. Boot	22. Spring stopper
5. Return spring	14. Nut	bolt
6. Shift shaft	15. Shift rod	23. Bolt
7. Washer	16. Nut	24. Cam stopper
8. Seal	17. Rubber	25. Washer
9. Washer	18. Shift lever	26. Spring

Removal

Refer to **Figure 6**.

1. Remove the clamp bolt (A, **Figure 7**) and slide the shift arm (B) off the shift shaft.

2. Remove the clutch assembly as described in this chapter.

3. Remove the snap ring (A, **Figure 8**) and washer (B) from the left end of the shift shaft.

4. On the right side of the engine, withdraw the shift shaft (**Figure 9**) from the crankcase. Reinstall

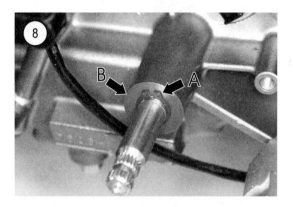

the washer and circlip removed in Step 3 onto the shift shaft to avoid misplacing them.

5. Remove the Allen bolt (A, **Figure 10**).

6. Push back the gearshift cam stopper (B, **Figure 10**) and remove the gearshift cam plate (C).

7. Remove the bolt (A, **Figure 11**), washer, spring (B) and gearshift cam stopper (C). Note the washer (**Figure 12**) located between the stopper and spring.

8. If the locating pins (D, **Figure 11**) in the end of the shift drum are loose, remove them. If not, leave them in place.

9. Inspect the components as described in this chapter.

Inspection

1. Inspect the gearshift shaft (A, **Figure 13**) for bending, wear or other damage; replace if necessary.

2. Inspect the return spring (B, **Figure 13**). If broken or weak, replace it.

3. Inspect the shift cam (A, **Figure 14**) and pins (B) for wear or damage. Replace the shift cam if excessively worn or damaged.

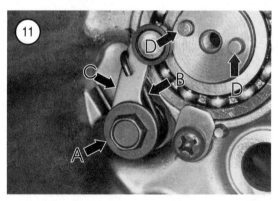

Installation

1. Make sure the locating pins (D, **Figure 11**) are in place in the end of the shift drum.

> *NOTE*
> *If the cam stopper was removed as an assembly and not disassembled, the components may be installed onto the crankcase as an assembly (**Figure 11**) instead of following Steps 2 and 3. Apply Threadlocker 1342 or equivalent to the threads of the bolt. Tighten the bolt 10 N•m (88 in.-lb.).*

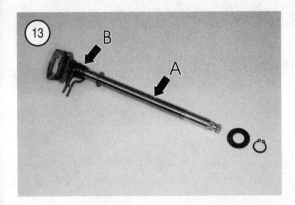

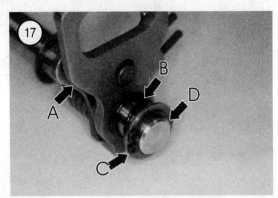

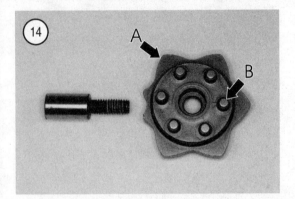

6

2. Assemble the cam stopper components (**Figure 12**) as shown in **Figure 15**. Install the washer between the spring and arm. Note that the spring end must fit into the notch (**Figure 15**) on the back of the cam stopper and force the stopper down.

3. Apply Threadlocker 1342 or equivalent to the threads of the bolt. Install the cam stopper assembly and tighten the bolt 10 N•m (88 in.-lb.).

4. Push up the cam stopper (B, **Figure 10**), then install the shift cam (C) onto the shift drum end while aligning the holes in the shift cam with the locating pins.

5. Apply Threadlocker 1342 or equivalent to the threads of the Allen bolt, then secure the shift cam by installing the bolt (A, **Figure 10**). Tighten the Allen bolt to 10 N•m (88 in.-lb.).

6. Install the spring onto the shift shaft so the spring ends fit around the tab (A, **Figure 16**). Install the washer (B) onto the shift shaft next to the spring.

7. Install the shift plate (A, **Figure 17**), spring (B), washer (C) and snap ring (D) onto the shift shaft as shown in **Figure 17**.

8. Install the shift lever assembly (**Figure 18**). While inserting the shaft, position the legs of the return spring around the shift arm stopper (**Figure 19**).

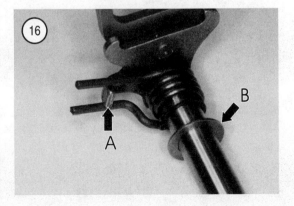

9. Install the washer (B, **Figure 20**) and snap ring (A) onto the left end of the shift shaft.

10. Install the clutch assembly as described in this chapter.

11. Install the shift arm onto the shift shaft.

CLUTCH

Removal/Disassembly

Refer to **Figure 21** when performing this procedure.

NOTE
If only the clutch plates require service, remove the inner clutch cover and perform Steps 8-14.

1. Drain the cooling system as described in Chapter Three.

2. Drain the engine oil as described in Chapter Three.

3. Detach the bypass hose (A, **Figure 22**) from the water pump.

4. Loosen the hose clamp (B, **Figure 22**) and disconnect the inlet hose from the water pump.

NOTE
Different length bolts are used to retain the clutch cover. Note the length and location of the bolts during disassembly.

5. Remove the outer clutch cover retaining bolts, as well as the retaining bolt just below the water pump (**Figure 23**). Note that the three upper left bolts also retain the clutch inner cover.

6. Remove the outer clutch cover.

7. Remove the gasket. Do not lose the dowel pins (**Figure 24**).

8. Using a crossing pattern, gradually and evenly loosen the clutch bolts (**Figure 25**).

9. Remove the bolts and spacers securing the springs to the pressure plate (**Figure 26**).

10. Remove the springs.

11. Remove the pressure plate (**Figure 27**).

12. Remove the washer (A, **Figure 28**), thrust bearing (B) and push piece (C).

13. Withdraw the clutch right pushrod (A, **Figure 29**) from the transmission shaft.

14. Remove all the friction discs and clutch plates (B, **Figure 29**).

15. Use a chisel or screwdriver and bend back the folded portion of the lockwasher (**Figure 30**).

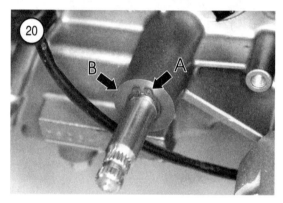

CAUTION
If using the clutch hub holding tool, make sure it is held securely in place. Do not rely on the clutch housing to support the holding tool or the clutch housing will be damaged.

NOTE
*Use an impact wrench to loosen the clutch hub nut. If an impact wrench is not available, a special tool must be used to hold the clutch hub. A simple tool can be fabricated by welding a steel rod to a steel clutch plate, as shown in **Figure 31**. In addition, a universal clutch sleeve holding tool is available from Suzuki (part No.09920-53740) and from accessory companies.*

16. Use the impact tool or the holding tool and wrench and loosen the clutch hub nut (**Figure 32**).

17. Remove the nut and washer.

18. Remove the clutch hub (**Figure 33**).

19. Remove the thrust washer (A, **Figure 34**).

CLUTCH AND RELEASE MECHANISM

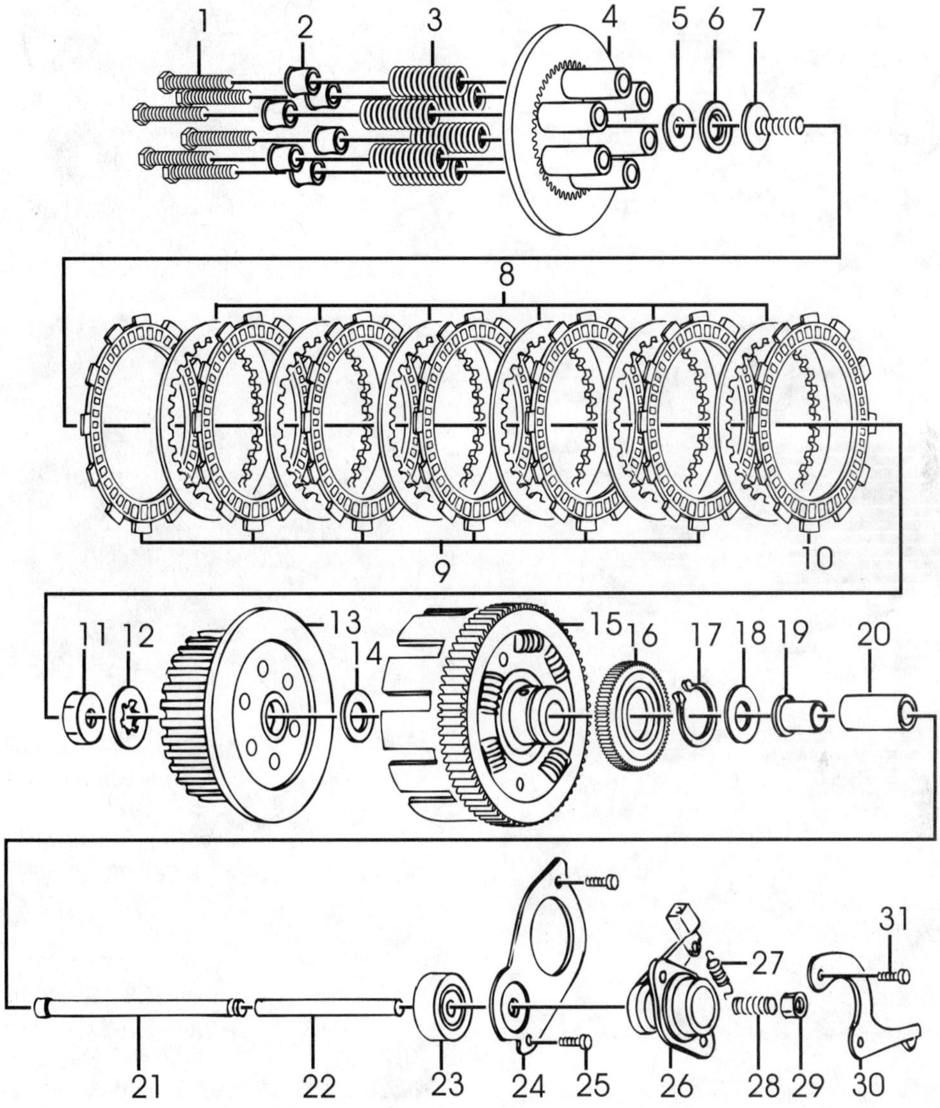

(21)

6

1. Bolts	12. Splined washer	22. Pushrod (left)
2. Spacers	13. Clutch hub	23. Oil seal
3. Springs	14. Thrust washer	24. Oil seal retainer
4. Pressure plate	15. Outer housing	25. Bolt
5. Washer	16. Oil pump drive gear	26. Clutch release
6. Thrust bearing	17. Snap ring	mechanism
7. Push piece	18. Washer (early models)	27. Spring
8. Steel clutch plates (6)	19. Flanged sleeve (later	28. Threaded stud
9. No. 1 friction plates (6)	models)	29. Nut
10. No. 2 friction plate (1)	20. Sleeve (early models)	30. Spring bracket
11. Nut	21. Pushrod (right)	31. Bolt

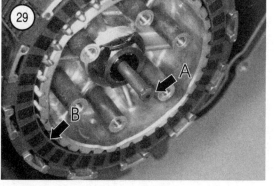

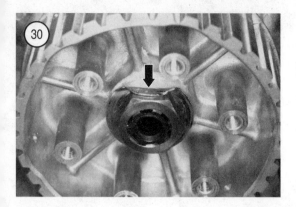

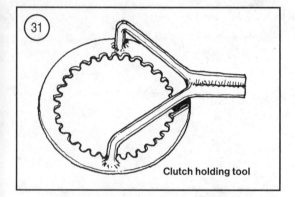

Clutch holding tool

6

20. Remove the clutch housing/primary driven gear assembly (B, **Figure 34**).

NOTE
*On early models, a washer and a sleeve are used in place of the flanged sleeve shown in **Figure 35**.*

21. Remove the flanged sleeve (**Figure 35**).
22. Inspect all parts as described in this chapter.

Inspection

1. Measure the free length of each clutch spring as shown in **Figure 36** and compare to the service limit in **Table 1**. To maintain even clutch pressure and maximum performance, replace all springs as a set if any one is not within the specified tolerance.

2. Measure the friction plate tab width as shown in **Figure 37**. Replace any friction plate worn to less than the service limit specified in **Table 1**.

3. The friction material on the friction plate is bonded to an aluminum plate for warp resistance and durability. Measure the thickness of each friction plate at several

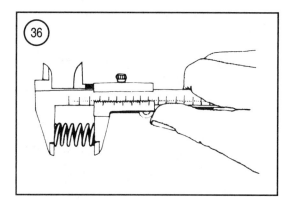

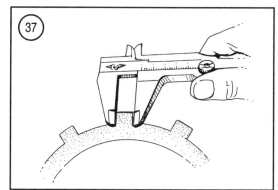

places as shown in **Figure 38**. Replace all plates if any one is worn to less than the service limit in **Table 1**.

4. Place each steel clutch plate on a flat surface, such as a piece of plate glass, and check for warp with a feeler gauge (**Figure 39**). If any plate is warped more than specified in **Table 1**, replace the entire set of clutch plates. Do not replace only one or two plates, as clutch operation will be unsatisfactory.

5. The steel clutch plate's inner teeth mesh with the clutch hub splines. They must be smooth for chatter-free clutch operation. If the sleeve hub splines are worn, check the steel plate teeth for wear or damage as they may also require replacement.

6. The tabs on the clutch friction plates slide in the clutch housing grooves (**Figure 40**). Inspect the groove tabs for cracks or galling. The grooves must be smooth for chatter-free clutch operation. Light damage can be repaired with an oilstone. Replace the clutch housing if required.

7. Inspect the clutch pressure plate splines (A, **Figure 41**) for wear or damage. Replace the pressure plate if required.

NOTE
If the clutch outer housing teeth are damaged, the primary drive gear may also be damaged. Inspect it and replace if necessary.

8. Check the gear teeth (A, **Figure 42**) on the clutch outer housing. Check for damaged, chipped or missing teeth. Remove any small nicks with an oilstone. If damaged, the outer housing must be replaced. Also, check the gear teeth on the primary drive gear as it may also be damaged. Refer to Chapter Five.

9. Inspect the clutch outer housing damper springs (B, **Figure 42**). If they are sagged or broken, replace the housing.

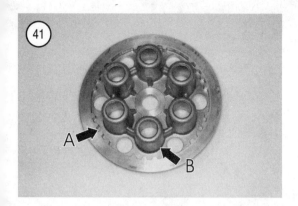

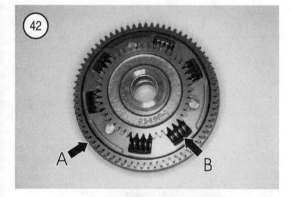

10. Check the inner bushing surface (A, **Figure 43**) of the clutch outer housing. Replace the outer housing if necessary.

NOTE
*On early models, a washer and a sleeve are used in place of the flanged sleeve shown in **Figure 43**.*

11. Inspect the sleeve (B, **Figure 43**) on which the clutch rides. Replace the sleeve if it is galled, excessively worn or otherwise damaged.

12. Inspect the clutch spring bolt studs on the clutch hub (A, **Figure 44**) for thread damage or cracks at the base of the studs. Thread damage may be repaired with a correct size metric tap. Use kerosene on the tap threads. If the bolt stud is cracked or damaged, replace the clutch hub.

13. Inspect the inner splines (B, **Figure 44**) in the clutch hub for damage. Remove any small nicks with a file. Replace the clutch hub if damage is excessive.

14. Inspect the clutch spring towers on the pressure plate (B, **Figure 41**). If any are worn or damaged, replace the pressure plate.

15. Inspect the outer grooves on the clutch hub (C, **Figure 44**). If any are worn or damaged, replace the pressure plate.

16. If necessary, replace the oil pump drive gear as follows:

NOTE
The oil pump drive gear pin may be loose and fall out when the gear is removed.

a. Remove the snap ring (A, **Figure 45**) securing the drive gear and remove the drive gear (B).

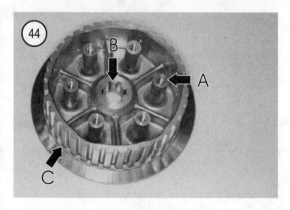

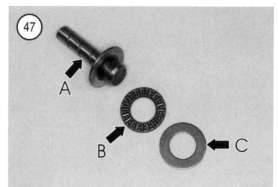

b. If removed, install the locating pin (**Figure 46**) into the clutch outer housing.

c. One side of the drive gear has numbers cast into it. Install the drive gear onto the clutch outer housing so the numbers are visible (C, **Figure 45**). The notch in the drive gear must align with the drive pin.

d. Push the gear down until it bottoms, then install the snap ring with the flat side facing out.

e. Be sure the snap ring is properly seated in the groove.

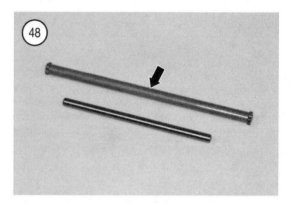

17. Examine the push piece (A, **Figure 47**) for wear or scoring. Install it into the end of the transmission shaft and push it in and out. It should move freely with no hesitation. Replace if necessary.

18. Install the thrust bearing (B, **Figure 47**) and washer (C) onto the push piece and rotate slowly. The bearing must rotate freely with no sign of wear or chatter. Check the thrust bearing needles for wear or damage. Replace the thrust bearing and push piece as a set if necessary.

19. Inspect the right pushrod (**Figure 48**) for bending, wear or damage. Replace if necessary.

Assembly/Installation

NOTE
*On early models, a washer and a sleeve are used in place of the flanged sleeve shown in **Figure 49**.*

1. Install the flanged sleeve (**Figure 49**) onto the transmission shaft.

2. Apply clean engine oil to the inner bushing area of the clutch housing.

3. Install the clutch housing assembly (A, **Figure 50**). Make sure it is meshed properly with the primary drive gear (B, **Figure 50**) and the oil pump

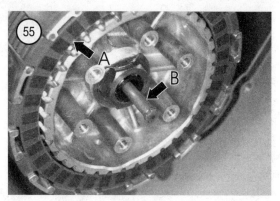

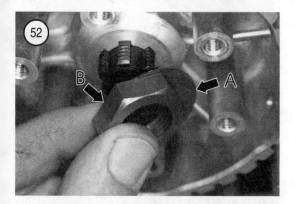

driven gear (C), then push it onto the transmission shaft until it bottoms out. Double check all gear engagements.

4. Install the thrust washer (D, **Figure 50**).

5. Install the clutch hub (**Figure 51**).

NOTE
Install the clutch hub nut so the chamfered side is out.

6. Install a new lockwasher (A, **Figure 52**), then install the clutch hub nut (B).

7. Use the same tool arrangement used in Step 16 of *Removal/Disassembly* and tighten the clutch hub nut (**Figure 53**) to 50 N•m (37 ft.-lb.).

8. Fold over a portion of the lockwasher securely against the nut as shown in **Figure 54**.

NOTE
Lubricate the contact surfaces of the friction plates and steel plates with clean engine oil prior to assembly.

9. Install friction plate No. 2 onto the clutch hub. The thickness of friction plate No. 2 is greater than the thickness of each of the other six No. 1 friction plates.

10. Install a steel plate next to friction plate No. 2.

11. Install a No. 1 friction plate, then continue to install a steel plate, a friction plate and alternate them until all are installed. The last item installed is a friction plate (A, **Figure 55**).

12. Install the right clutch pushrod (B, **Figure 55**) into the transmission shaft. Push it in until it bottoms against the left pushrod still located in the transmission shaft.

13. Install the push piece (A, **Figure 56**) into the transmission shaft.

14. Apply a light coat of clean engine oil to both sides of the washer and thrust bearing.

15. Install the thrust bearing (B, **Figure 56**) onto the push piece, then install the washer (C).

16. Install the clutch pressure plate (**Figure 57**) and push it on until it bottoms.

17. Install the springs, spacers and bolts (**Figure 58**). Start the bolts and tighten only fingertight.

18. To prevent clutch rotation when performing the next step, the following methods may be used.

    a. Place a small gear (**Figure 59**) in mesh with the clutch and primary drive gears.

    b. Place a soft copper washer, penny, or shop cloth into mesh with the gears. This will prevent the primary drive gear from turning in the next step.

19. Tighten the clutch screws in a crossing pattern in two to three stages. Tighten the screws to 5.5 N•m (49 in.-lb.).

20. Make sure the dowel pins (**Figure 60**) are in place and install a *new* clutch cover gasket.

21. Install the outer clutch cover while carefully engaging the water pump gears. Make sure to install the bypass hose (A, **Figure 61**).

22. If the inner clutch cover was removed, install a *new* O-ring into the groove in the cover, then install the clutch inner cover. Place the hose clamp on the lower left inner cover retaining bolt. Tighten the clutch cap retaining bolts fingertight.

23. Apply Threadlock 1342 to the clutch cover retaining bolts and install them.

24. Tighten the inner and outer clutch cover retaining bolts to 10 N•m (88 in.-lb.).

25. The radiator hose is a shaped hose and must be installed properly. Push the hose onto the water pump until it bottoms against the stop on the pump inlet. The paint dot (B, **Figure 61**) on the hose end must be just above the pump inlet centerline.

26. Refill the cooling system with the recommended type and quantity of coolant as described in Chapter Three.

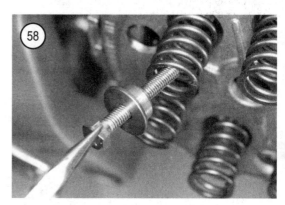

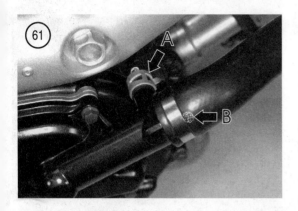

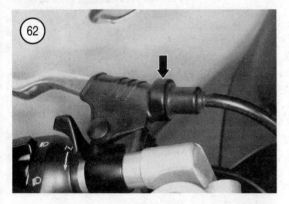

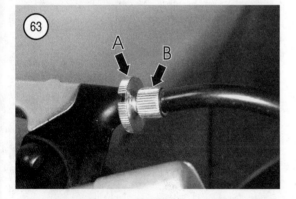

6

27. Refill the engine with oil as described in Chapter Three.

CLUTCH RELEASE MECHANISM

Removal/Installation

1. Slide the rubber boot (**Figure 62**) off the clutch hand lever adjuster.

2. At the clutch hand lever, loosen the locknut (A, **Figure 63**) and turn the adjuster (B) all the way in toward the clutch lever holder to allow maximum cable slack. Disconnect the cable from the clutch lever.

3. Remove the engine sprocket cover (**Figure 64**).

4. Loosen the locknuts (A, **Figure 65**) on the lower cable housing.

5. Rotate the adjuster (B, **Figure 65**) to increase cable slack.

6. Disconnect the clutch cable end from the clutch release arm (C, **Figure 65**).

7. Detach the return spring (A, **Figure 66**) from the spring bracket (B).

8. Remove the mounting bolts (C, **Figure 66**), then remove the clutch release assembly (D).

9. Operate the release mechanism and check for binding or other signs of faulty operation. Inspect the mechanism for damage. Replace if necessary.

10. Install by reversing the removal procedure while noting the following:

   a. Apply lithium multipurpose grease to the spiral splines before assembly.

b. Loosen the stud and nut (**Figure 67**) several turns before assembly.

c. Assemble the mechanism and spring bracket as shown in **Figure 68**.

d. Tighten the mounting bolts securely.

e. Adjust the clutch as described in Chapter Three.

Table 1 CLUTCH SERVICE SPECIFICATIONS

Item	Standard	Service limit
Friction plate thickness		
No. 1	2.92-3.08 mm (0.115-0.121 in.)	2.62 mm (0.104 in.)
No. 2	3.42-3.58 mm (0.135-0.141 in.)	3.12 mm (0.123 in.)
Friction plate tab width	15.9-16.0 mm (0.626-0.630 in.)	15.1 mm (0.594 in.)
Steel plate warp	–	0.1 mm (0.004 in.)
Spring free length	58.9 mm (2.32 in.)	56.0 mm (2.20 in.)
Number of clutch plates		
Friction plates No. 1	6	–
Friction plate No. 2	1	–
Steel plates	6	–

Table 2 CLUTCH AND GEARSHIFT MECHANISM TORQUE SPECIFICATIONS

Item	N•m	in.-lb.	ft.-lb.
Cam stopper bolt	10	88	–
Clutch cover bolts	10	88	–
Clutch hub nut	50	–	37
Clutch spring bolts	5.5	49	–
Shift cam Allen bolt	10	88	–

CHAPTER SEVEN

TRANSMISSION AND INTERNAL SHIFT MECHANISM

This chapter covers service to the transmission and internal gearshift assemblies. Specifications are listed in **Table 1** and **Table 2** at the end of this chapter.

When the clutch is engaged, the input (main) shaft is driven by the clutch hub, which is driven by the primary crankshaft drive gear/clutch outer housing. Power is transferred from the input shaft through the selected gear combination to the output (counter) shaft, which drives the engine drive sprocket.

To gain access to the transmission and internal shift mechanism, it is necessary to remove the engine and disassemble the crankcase as described in Chapter Five.

> NOTE
> *Suzuki terminology for the transmission shafts is different than most manufacturers. Suzuki refers to the input (main) shaft as the countershaft and the output shaft as the driveshaft. Most manufacturers, if they do not use the input/output shaft terms, refer to the input shaft as the mainshaft and the output shaft as the countershaft. Notice that this is opposite of Suzuki's parts information and keep this in mind when ordering replacement parts. In this manual, the input shaft is termed the mainshaft and the output shaft is called the countershaft.*

INTERNAL SHIFT MECHANISM

Removal

Refer to **Figure 1**.

1. Disassemble the crankcase as described in Chapter Five.

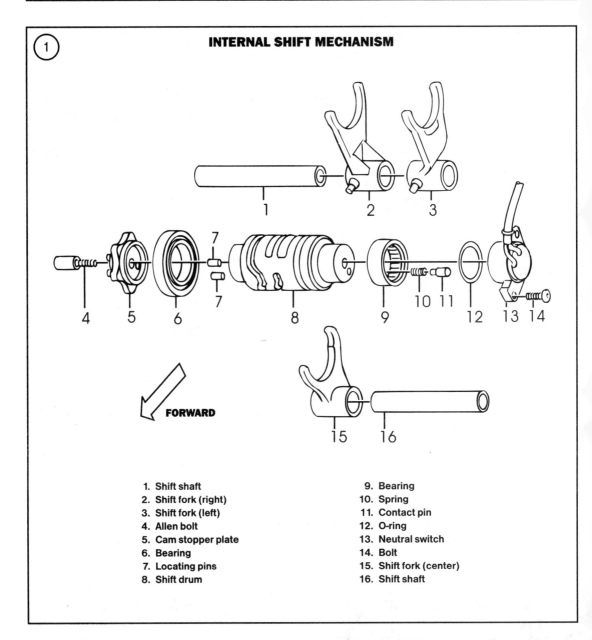

INTERNAL SHIFT MECHANISM

FORWARD

1. Shift shaft
2. Shift fork (right)
3. Shift fork (left)
4. Allen bolt
5. Cam stopper plate
6. Bearing
7. Locating pins
8. Shift drum
9. Bearing
10. Spring
11. Contact pin
12. O-ring
13. Neutral switch
14. Bolt
15. Shift fork (center)
16. Shift shaft

2. Remove the shift fork shafts (**Figure 2**).

3. Remove the shift drum (**Figure 3**).

4. Remove the shift forks (**Figure 4**).

Inspection

Refer to **Figure 1**.

1. Clean all parts in solvent and thoroughly dry them with compressed air.

2. Inspect each shift fork for signs of wear or cracking. Check for any burned marks on the fingers of the

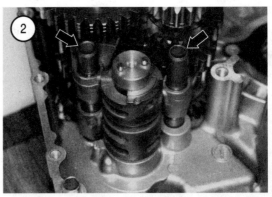

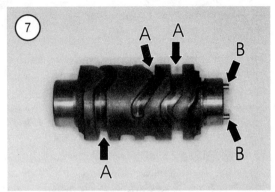

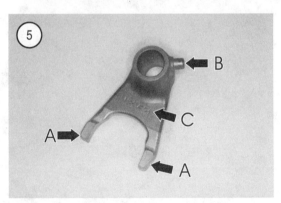

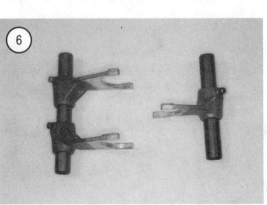

shift forks (A, **Figure 5**). This indicates that the shift fork has come in contact with the gear. Replace the fork if the fork fingers have become excessively worn.

3. Check the bore of each shift fork and the shift fork shaft for burrs, wear or pitting. Replace any worn parts.

4. Install each shift fork onto its shaft (**Figure 6**) and make sure it moves freely on the shaft with no binding.

5. Check the guide pin (B, **Figure 5**) on each shift fork for wear or damage. Replace the shift fork(s) as necessary.

6. Roll each shift fork shaft on a surface plate or a piece of plate glass. If a shaft is bent, replace it.

7. Check the grooves in the shift drum (A, **Figure 7**) for wear or roughness. If any of the groove profiles have excessive wear or damage, replace the shift drum.

8. Inspect the cam gear locating pins (B, **Figure 7**) and threaded hole in the end of the shift drum for wear or damage. Replace the shift drum if necessary.

9. Check the neutral switch contact plungers and springs (**Figure 8**) for wear or damage. If the springs have sagged, replace them.

CAUTION
Replace marginally worn shift forks.
Worn forks can cause the transmis-

sion to slip out of gear, leading to serious damage.

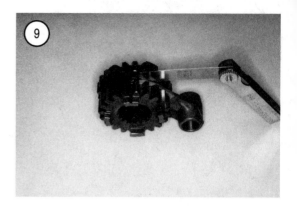

10. Install each shift fork into the groove in its respective gear. Use a flat feeler gauge and measure the clearance between the fork and the groove as shown in **Figure 9**. If the shift fork-to-groove clearance exceeds the service limit specified in **Table 2**, perform the following:

   a. Measure the thickness of the shift fork fingers with a micrometer (**Figure 10**). Replace the shift fork if the width is outside the range specified in **Table 2**.

   b. Use a vernier caliper to measure the width of the shift fork groove in the gear (**Figure 11**). Replace the gear if the groove width is outside the range specified in **Table 2**.

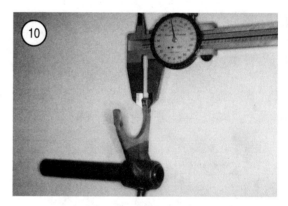

Installation

> *NOTE*
> *Lubricate all rotating and sliding surfaces with engine oil during assembly.*

1. Be sure the mainshaft and countershaft assemblies are properly installed.

2. Note the identifying number cast into each shift fork (C, **Figure 5**).

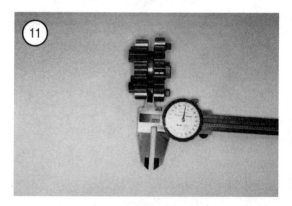

> *NOTE*
> *All shift forks have a pin that must engage the proper groove in the shift drum. Be sure to install the shift forks so the pin points toward the shift drum.*

3. Install the shift forks as follows:

   a. Install the left shift fork (identifying number 42E1-2B) into the sixth driven gear groove (A, **Figure 12**).

   b. Install the right shift fork (identifying number 42E-1E) into the fifth driven gear groove (B, **Figure 12**).

   c. Install the center shift fork (identifying number 42E-3D) into the third/fourth drive gear groove (**Figure 13**).

4. Install the shift drum (A, **Figure 14**). Position the shift drum and shift forks so the pins on the shift forks properly engage the grooves in the shift drum.

5. Install the long shift shaft (B, **Figure 14**).

6. Install the short shift shaft (C, **Figure 14**).

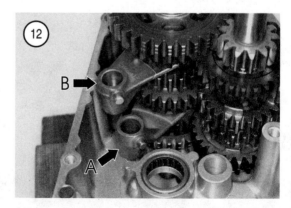

7. Rotate the transmission shafts and shift through all gears using the shift drum. Make sure the mechanism will shift into all gears. This is the time to find that something may be installed incorrectly, not after the crankcase is completely assembled.

> *NOTE*
> *This procedure is easier with the aid of a helper as the assemblies are loose and will not spin very easily. While turning the shift drum through all the gears, have the helper spin the transmission shaft.*

8. Reassemble the crankcase as described in Chapter Five.

TRANSMISSION

Removal/Installation

1. Remove the internal shift mechanism as described in this chapter.

2. Remove the washer (A, **Figure 15**) on the countershaft.

> *NOTE*
> *It may be necessary to tap the outer end (drive sprocket) of the countershaft to dislodge the countershaft from the bearing.*

3. Pull out both the countershaft assembly (B, **Figure 15**) and the mainshaft assembly (C) from the left crankcase half as shown in **Figure 16**.

4. If necessary, disassemble and inspect the transmission assemblies as described in this chapter.

5. To install the transmission, assemble the countershaft and mainshaft assemblies so all gears are meshed (**Figure 16**).

6. Install the transmission into the left crankshaft half (**Figure 15**). It may be necessary to *gently* tap the inner end of the countershaft so it will pass through the bearing in the crankcase half.

7. Install the washer (A, **Figure 15**) onto the countershaft.

8. Install the internal shift mechanism as described in this chapter.

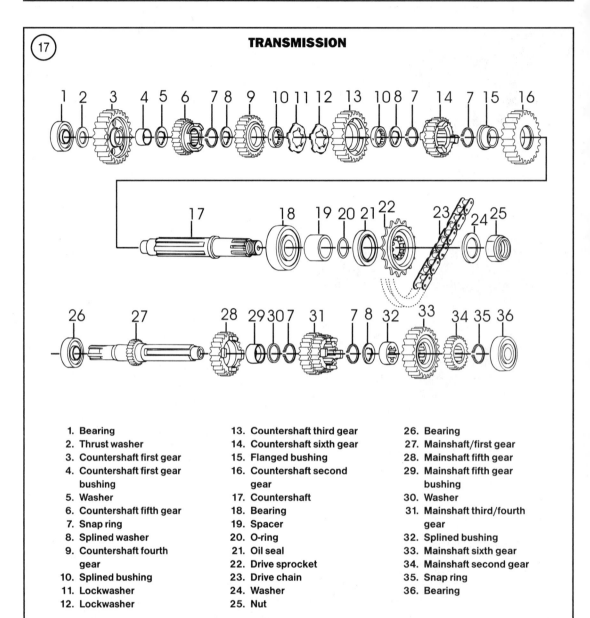

TRANSMISSION

1. Bearing
2. Thrust washer
3. Countershaft first gear
4. Countershaft first gear bushing
5. Washer
6. Countershaft fifth gear
7. Snap ring
8. Splined washer
9. Countershaft fourth gear
10. Splined bushing
11. Lockwasher
12. Lockwasher
13. Countershaft third gear
14. Countershaft sixth gear
15. Flanged bushing
16. Countershaft second gear
17. Countershaft
18. Bearing
19. Spacer
20. O-ring
21. Oil seal
22. Drive sprocket
23. Drive chain
24. Washer
25. Nut
26. Bearing
27. Mainshaft/first gear
28. Mainshaft fifth gear
29. Mainshaft fifth gear bushing
30. Washer
31. Mainshaft third/fourth gear
32. Splined bushing
33. Mainshaft sixth gear
34. Mainshaft second gear
35. Snap ring
36. Bearing

Preliminary Inspection

1. Clean and inspect the assemblies before disassembling them. Place the assembled shaft into a large can or plastic bucket and thoroughly clean the assembly with a stiff brush and petroleum-based solvent. Dry the assembly with compressed air or let it sit on rags to drip dry. Do this for both shaft assemblies.

2. Visually inspect the components for excessive wear. Check the gear teeth for chips, burrs or pitting. Remove burrs with an oilstone. Replace any damaged components.

3. Carefully check the engagement dogs. If any is chipped, worn, rounded or missing, replace the affected gear.

4. Rotate the transmission bearings in the crankcase halves by hand. Check for roughness, noise and radial play. Replace any bearing that is suspect as described in Chapter Five.

5. Slide the clutch pushrods into the mainshaft and check for binding. If binding occurs, check the pushrods for damage. Inspect the mainshaft bore for debris. Clean out the bore if necessary.

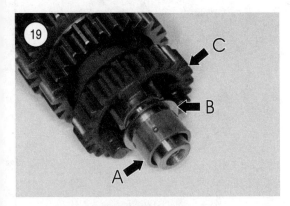

6. If the transmission shafts are satisfactory and are not going to be disassembled, apply assembly oil or engine oil to all components and reinstall them into the crankcase as described in this chapter.

NOTE
If disassembling a high mileage transmission, pay particular attention to any additional shims that may have been added by a previous owner. These may have been added to take up the tolerance of worn components and must be reinstalled in the same position, since the shims have developed a wear pattern. If new parts are going to be installed, these shims may be eliminated. This is something to determine during assembly.

Transmission Service Notes

1. After removing a part from the shaft, set it in an egg crate in the exact order of removal and with the same orientation the part had when installed on the shaft. This is an easy way to remember the correct relationship of all parts.
2. The snap rings fit tightly on the transmission shafts. It is recommended that all snap rings be replaced during assembly.
3. Snap rings will turn and fold over, making removal and installation difficult. To ease replacement, open a snap ring with a pair of snap ring pliers while at the same time holding the back of the snap ring with a pair of pliers and remove it. Repeat for installation.

Countershaft Disassembly

Refer to **Figure 17**.
1. If not cleaned during *Preliminary Inspection*, place the assembled shaft into a large can or plastic bucket. Thoroughly clean it with solvent and a stiff brush. Dry the shaft assembly with compressed air or let it sit on rags to dry.
2. Remove the thrust washer (A, **Figure 18**) and first gear (B).
3. Remove the first gear bushing (A, **Figure 19**), thrust washer (B) and fifth gear (C).
4. Remove the snap ring (A, **Figure 20**), splined washer (B) and fourth gear (C).
5. Remove the fourth gear bushing (**Figure 21**).

6. Slide off the lockwasher No. 2 (A, **Figure 22**).

7. Rotate the lockwasher No. 1 (B, **Figure 22**) in either direction to disengage its tangs from the grooves on the countershaft. Slide off the lockwasher No. 1.

8. Slide off the third gear (**Figure 23**).

9. Remove the third gear bushing (A, **Figure 24**) and splined washer (B).

10. Remove the snap ring (C, **Figure 24**) and sixth gear (D).

11. Remove the snap ring (A, **Figure 25**).

12. Slide off the second gear (B, **Figure 25**) with the flanged bushing (C).

13. Inspect the components as described in *Transmission Inspection*.

Countershaft Assembly

> *NOTE*
> *Install new snap rings during assembly to ensure proper gear alignment. Do not expand a snap ring more than necessary to slide it over the shaft.*

1. Apply a light coat of molybdenum oil to all sliding surfaces prior to installing any parts.

2. Slide the second gear (A, **Figure 26**) and flange bushing (B) onto the countershaft. The gear's engagement slots should face out, away from the threaded shaft end. The flanged end of the bushing must face the adjacent snap ring.

3. Install the snap ring (A, **Figure 25**) so the flat side is away from the bushing flange. Make sure the snap ring is correctly seated in the snap ring groove.

4. Install sixth gear (D, **Figure 24**) so its shift-fork groove faces out, away from second gear.

5. Install the snap ring (C, **Figure 24**) so it is properly seated in the snap ring groove.

6. Install the splined washer (B, **Figure 24**) and the third gear bushing (A). Make sure the oil hole in the bushing aligns with the oil hole in the countershaft. These holes must align to ensure proper gear lubrication.

7. Install third gear (**Figure 23**) so its engagement slots face in toward sixth gear.

8. Install lockwasher No.1 (A, **Figure 27**). Rotate the lockwasher in either direction so the tangs on the lockwasher engage the grooves in the countershaft.

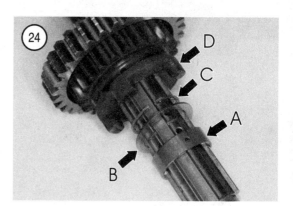

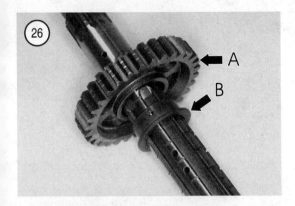

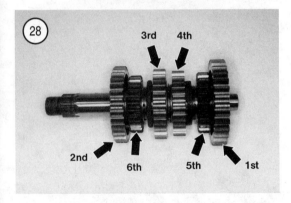

9. Install lockwasher No. 2 (B, **Figure 27**) and press it into place. The tangs on lockwasher No. 2 should engage the cutouts in lockwasher No. 1 (A).

10. Align the oil hole in the fourth gear bushing (**Figure 21**) with the oil hole in the countershaft and slide the bushing into place. This alignment is necessary for proper gear lubrication.

11. Install the fourth gear (C, **Figure 20**) so its engagement slots face out.

12. Install the splined washer (B, **Figure 20**) and the snap ring (A). Install the snap ring so the flat

side is away from the washer. Make sure the snap ring is correctly seated in the snap ring groove.

13. Install fifth gear (C, **Figure 19**) so its shift fork groove faces in toward fourth gear.

14. Slide on the thrust washer (B, **Figure 19**) and the first gear bushing (A).

15. Slide on the first gear (B, **Figure 18**) so its flat side faces out, away from fifth gear.

16. Install the thrust washer (A, **Figure 18**).

17. Refer to **Figure 28** for correct placement of all gears. Make sure all snap rings are correctly seated in the countershaft grooves.

18. Make sure each gear properly engages an adjoining gear where applicable.

Mainshaft Disassembly

Refer to **Figure 29**.

1. If not cleaned during *Preliminary Inspection*, place the assembled mainshaft into a large can or plastic bucket, and thoroughly clean the assembly with solvent and a stiff brush. Dry with compressed air or let it sit on rags to dry.

NOTE
The snap ring is recessed inside the second gear. Steps 2-4 must be performed to expose this snap ring for removal.

2. Slide the third-fourth combination gear (A, **Figure 30**) away from the sixth gear (B) to expose the snap ring (**Figure 31**) and splined washer.

3. Using angled snap ring pliers, open the snap ring (**Figure 32**) and slide the snap ring and the splined washer away from the sixth and second gears.

4. Slide the sixth and second gears toward the third-fourth combination gear to expose the snap ring (A, **Figure 33**) under the second gear. If necessary, use the sixth and second gears to tap the sixth-gear snap ring and splined washer inward until the snap ring is exposed.

5. Remove the snap ring (A, **Figure 33**), then remove second gear (B) and sixth gear (C).

6. Remove the sixth gear bushing (A, **Figure 34**), splined washer (B) and snap ring (C).

7. Slide off the third-fourth combination gear (**Figure 35**).

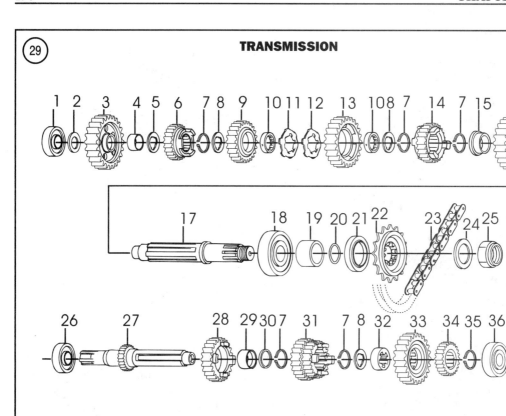

TRANSMISSION

1. Bearing
2. Thrust washer
3. Countershaft first gear
4. Countershaft first gear bushing
5. Washer
6. Countershaft fifth gear
7. Snap ring
8. Splined washer
9. Countershaft fourth gear
10. Splined bushing
11. Lockwasher
12. Lockwasher
13. Countershaft third gear
14. Countershaft sixth gear
15. Flanged bushing
16. Countershaft second gear
17. Countershaft
18. Bearing
19. Spacer
20. O-ring
21. Oil seal
22. Drive sprocket
23. Drive chain
24. Washer
25. Nut
26. Bearing
27. Mainshaft/first gear
28. Mainshaft fifth gear
29. Mainshaft fifth gear bushing
30. Washer
31. Mainshaft third/fourth gear
32. Splined bushing
33. Mainshaft sixth gear
34. Mainshaft second gear
35. Snap ring
36. Bearing

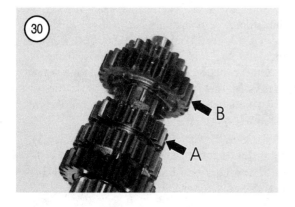

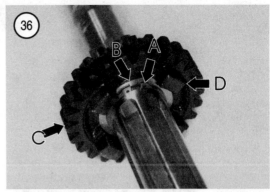

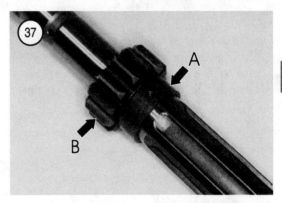

8. Remove the snap ring (A, **Figure 36**), washer (B) and fifth gear (C).

9. Remove the fifth gear bushing (A, **Figure 37**).

10. Inspect the components as described in *Transmission Inspection*.

Mainshaft Assembly

> *NOTE*
> *The first gear (B, **Figure 37**) is part of the mainshaft. If the gear is defective, replace the mainshaft.*

1. Apply a light coat of molybdenum oil to all sliding surfaces prior to installing any parts.

2. Install the fifth gear bushing (A, **Figure 37**) and fifth gear (C, **Figure 36**) onto the mainshaft. Install the gear so the engagement dogs face out, away from first gear (D, **Figure 36**).

3. Install the washer (B, **Figure 36**) and snap ring (A). Install the snap ring so its flat side faces out away from fifth gear. Make sure the snap ring is correctly seated in the snap ring groove.

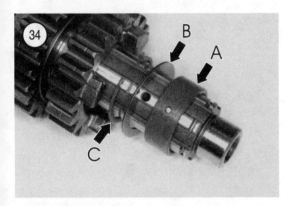

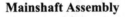

7

4. Install third-fourth combination gear with the larger diameter fourth gear (**Figure 35**) going on first.

NOTE
In Step 5 do not seat the snap ring in its respective groove at this time. It will be positioned correctly in Step 10.

5. Install the snap ring (C, **Figure 34**) but do not seat it in its respective groove in the shaft. Position the snap ring so its faces in toward third-fourth combination gear. Move the snap ring past the snap ring groove toward the third-fourth combination gear.
6. Install the splined washer (B, **Figure 34**) and slide it up against the snap ring installed in Step 5.
7. Install sixth gear (C, **Figure 33**) so its engagement dogs face in toward the third-fourth combination gear.

NOTE
After the second gear is installed on the shaft, the outermost snap ring groove in the shaft must be exposed.

8. Install the second gear so the relieved inner diameter (**Figure 38**) is toward the end of the shaft. Slide the second gear (B, **Figure 33**) toward the sixth gear (C) until the snap ring groove is exposed. If necessary, use the second and sixth gears to tap the splined washer farther down the shaft.
9. Install the snap ring (A, **Figure 33**). Make sure it is correctly seated in the mainshaft groove.
10. Slide the second and sixth gears against the snap ring at the end of the shaft to expose the snap ring and splined washer installed in Step 5.
11. Slide the splined washer toward the sixth gear.
12. Using angled snap ring pliers, move the snap ring into its respective groove (**Figure 32**). Make sure it is correctly seated in the mainshaft groove.
13. After the snap ring is installed, spin the sixth gear to make sure it rotates correctly and that the splined washer and snap ring are installed correctly. Reposition the snap ring if necessary.
14. Refer to **Figure 39** for correct placement of all gears. Make sure the snap rings are correctly seated in the mainshaft grooves. Check that each gear properly engages an adjoining gear where applicable.
15. After both transmission shafts have been assembled, mesh the two assemblies together in the

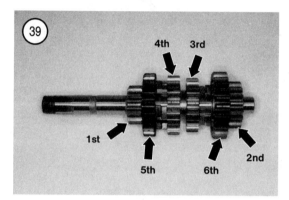

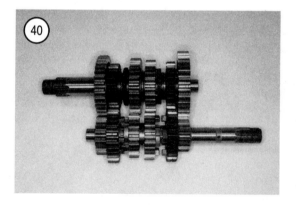

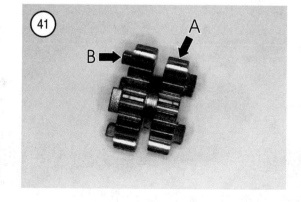

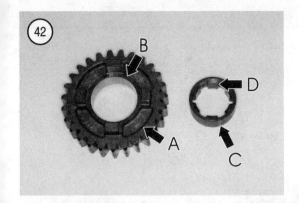

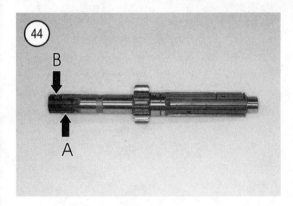

correct position (**Figure 40**). Check that each gear properly engages its mate on the opposite shaft. This is the last check prior to installing the shaft assemblies into the crankcase; make sure they are correctly assembled.

Transmission Inspection

NOTE
Replace defective gears and their mating gears on the other shaft as well, even though they may not show as much wear or damage.

1. Check each gear for excessive wear, burrs, pitting, chipped or missing teeth (A, **Figure 41**). Make sure the engagement dogs (B, **Figure 41**) on the gears are in good condition. Also inspect the engagement slots (A, **Figure 42**) for wear or damage.

2. On splined gears, check the inner splines for excessive wear or damage. Replace the gear if necessary.

3. On gears with bushings, inspect the inner surface of the gear (B, **Figure 42**) for wear, pitting or damage. Insert the bushing into the gear and check for smooth operation.

4. Check each bushing (C, **Figure 42**) for excessive wear, pitting or damage. Replace any bushing if necessary.

5. On splined bushings, check the inner splines (D, **Figure 42**) for excessive wear or damage. Replace if necessary.

6. Make sure that all gears and bushings slide smoothly on the shaft splines.

7. Inspect countershaft lockwashers No. 1 and No. 2 (**Figure 43**) for wear, cracks, or damage. Replace if necessary.

8. Inspect the washers for bending wear or damage. Replace if necessary.

9. Inspect the splines and snap ring grooves in a shaft. If any are damaged, replace the shaft.

10. Inspect the clutch hub splines (A, **Figure 44**) and clutch nut threads (B) on the end of the mainshaft. If any of the splines are damaged, the shaft must be replaced.

11. Inspect the shift fork-to-gear clearance as described in the *Internal Gearshift Mechanism* section.

Table 1 and Table 2 are on the following page.

Table 1 TRANSMISSION SPECIFICATIONS

Item	
Transmission gear ratios	
First gear	2.461 (32/13)
Second gear	1.777 (32/18)
Third gear	1.380 (29/21)
Fourth gear	1.125 (27/24)
Fifth gear	0.961 (25/26)
Sixth gear	0.851 (23/27)
Primary reduction ratio	2.088 (71/34)
Secondary reduction ratio	
All SV650, SV650S and SV650SF (2007-on)	3.000 (45/15)
SV650S (1999-2006)	2.933 (44/15)

Table 2 INTERNAL SHIFT MECHANISM SERVICE SPECIFICATIONS

Item	Standard	Service limit
Shift fork-to-groove clearance	0.1-0.3 mm (0.004-0.012 in.)	0.50 mm (0.020 in.)
Shift fork groove width	5.5-5.6 mm (0.217-0.220 in.)	–
Shift fork thickness	5.3-5.4 mm (0.209-0.213 in.)	–

CHAPTER EIGHT

FUEL, EMISSION CONTROL AND EXHAUST SYSTEMS

This chapter covers the service procedures for the fuel and emission systems. Air filter service is covered in Chapter Three. Carburetor specifications are listed in **Tables 1-6** at the end of the chapter.

The fuel system on the SV650 consists of the fuel tank, vacuum fuel valve, two carburetors, a diaphragm-type fuel pump and the air box.

The emission system components vary depending on the model. A crankcase breather system is used on all models. California models are equipped with an evaporative emissons control system and a PAIR (air supply) system.

> *WARNING*
> *Gasoline is a known carcinogen. It is extremely flammable and must be handled carefully. Wear latex gloves when working on components that may spill gasoline. If skin comes in contact with gasoline, rinse it off immediately and then thoroughly wash with soap and warm water.*

CARBURETOR OPERATION

The carburetor atomizes fuel and mixes it in correct proportions with air that is drawn in through the air intake. At the primary throttle opening (idle), a small amount of fuel is siphoned through the pilot jet by the incoming air. As the throttle is opened further, the air stream begins to siphon fuel through the main jet and needle jet. As the tapered needle is lifted, it occupies progressively less area of the needle jet and thus increases the effective flow capacity of the jet. At full throttle, the carburetor venturi is fully open and the needle is lifted far enough to permit the main jet to flow at full capacity.

The choke circuit is a bystarter system in which the choke lever on the left handlebar opens an enrichment valve rather than closing a butterfly in the venturi area, as on some carburetors. In the open position, the slow jet discharges a stream of fuel into the carburetor venturi, which enriches the mixture.

The carburetors used on motorcycles sold in the United Kingdom are equipped with a carburetor heater.

CARBURETOR

Removal/Installation

> *NOTE*
> *Remove the carburetors as an assembly. After removal from the engine, they can be separated if necessary.*

> *NOTE*
> *There are several hoses connected to the carburetors. Labeling the hoses during disassembly will aid assembly. Color-coded plugs and clips are available at most motorcycle and auto parts stores.*

1. Disconnect the negative battery cable as described in Chapter Three.
2. Disconnect the vacuum hose from the fuel valve (**Figure 1**).
3. Remove the air box as described in this chapter.
4. Disconnect the fuel hose from the fuel pump (A, **Figure 2**).
5. Disconnect the throttle position sensor connector (B, **Figure 2**).
6. Cut the cable tie that secures the starter cable to the carburetor bracket (A, **Figure 3**).
7. Unscrew the starter fitting retaining screw (B, **Figure 3**) and separate the starter fitting assembly from the rear carburetor.
8. Detach the idle speed control cable from the mounting bracket (**Figure 4**).
9. Loosen the clamp screw on the rubber intake tube (**Figure 5**) for each carburetor.

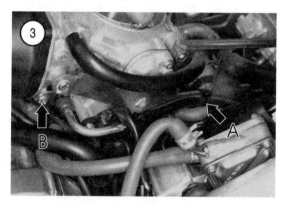

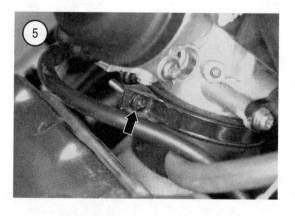

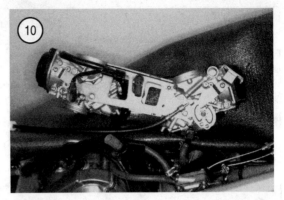

NOTE
Lift up, but do not remove, the carburetor assembly in Steps 10 and 11 for access to the starter fitting and throttle cables.

10. Lift up the carburetor assembly (**Figure 6**), then unscrew the starter fitting retaining screw (**Figure 7**) and separate the starter fitting assembly from the front carburetor.

11. Measure the height of the cable adjusters (A, **Figure 8**) so they can be reinstalled in their original locations. Loosen the locknuts securing the throttle cable fittings to the mounting bracket and remove the adjusters from the bracket.

12. Detach the throttle cables from the throttle pulley (B, **Figure 8**).

13. Detach the drain hoses from the carburetors (**Figure 9**).

14. Remove the carburetor assembly (**Figure 10**).

15. Cover the intake tubes with a clean lint-free cloth to prevent the entry of debris.

16. If the carburetor assembly is not going to be serviced, store it as follows:

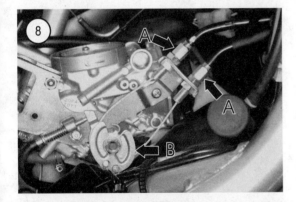

   a. Attach a fuel line to the drain outlet on each float bowl.

   b. Hold the carburetor assembly in its normal position.

   c. Open each drain screw and drain the fuel from the float bowls into a suitable container. Dispose of the fuel properly.

   d. Carefully and slowly shake the carburetor assembly to drain out as much fuel as possible.

   e. Close both drain screws and remove the fuel hoses from the float bowl fittings.

   f. Place the carburetor assembly in a clean heavy-duty plastic bag and close it off to avoid moisture and debris contamination.

8

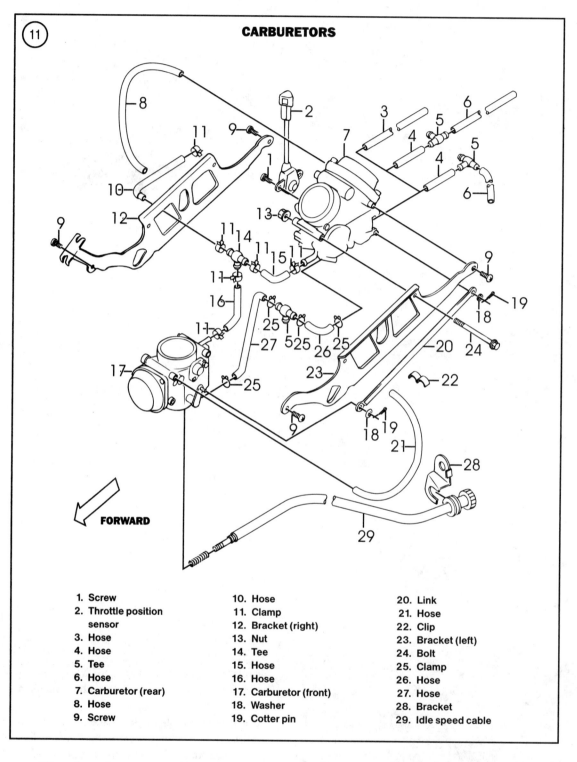

CARBURETORS

1. Screw
2. Throttle position sensor
3. Hose
4. Hose
5. Tee
6. Hose
7. Carburetor (rear)
8. Hose
9. Screw
10. Hose
11. Clamp
12. Bracket (right)
13. Nut
14. Tee
15. Hose
16. Hose
17. Carburetor (front)
18. Washer
19. Cotter pin
20. Link
21. Hose
22. Clip
23. Bracket (left)
24. Bolt
25. Clamp
26. Hose
27. Hose
28. Bracket
29. Idle speed cable

g. Place the carburetor assembly, right side up, in a sturdy cardboard box. Set the box in a safe place away from any heating equipment or ignition source.

17. Install by reversing the preceding removal steps.

a. Route the rear carburetor starter cable (**Figure 3**) so that it passes under the front carbu-

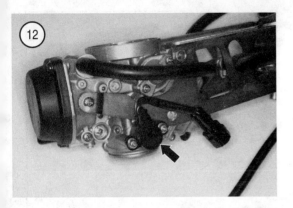

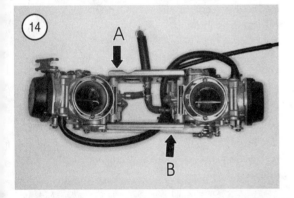

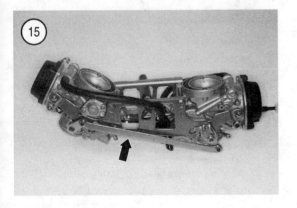

retor, then passes over the middle frame tube. Secure the cable to the carburetor bracket with a new cable tie (A, **Figure 3**).

b. Position the throttle cable adjuster on each cable in its original location. Tighten the locknuts (A, **Figure 8**) securing each adjuster to the mounting bracket.

c. Adjust the throttle cables as described in Chapter Three.

Carburetor Separation

The carburetors are joined by two brackets. All carburetor parts can be replaced without separating the carburetors. If the carburetors must be cleaned internally or if the pipe fittings must be replaced, separate the carburetors.

Refer to **Figure 11** for this procedure.

> *NOTE*
> *The photographs in the following procedure show a carburetor assembly from a California model. The number of hoses and their fitting locations vary for carburetors found on other models.*

1. Remove the carburetor assembly as described in this chapter.

> *NOTE*
> *The throttle position sensor (**Figure 12**) is preset by the manufacturer. Do not remove it. If removal is necessary, make alignment marks on the carburetor body and sensor relating to the centerline of the mounting screws so the sensor can be installed in the **exact** same position.*

2. If necessary, remove the throttle position sensor (**Figure 12**) from the rear carburetor.

3. Remove the idle speed cable retaining bracket (**Figure 13**), then remove the idle speed cable.

4. Detach the right bracket (A, **Figure 14**).

5. Detach the left bracket (B, **Figure 14**).

6. Remove the cotter pins and washers at each end of the throttle link (**Figure 15**) and remove the throttle link.

7. Separate the carburetors.

8. Reverse the procedure to reassemble the carburetors and brackets. Note the location of the fuel

hoses (A, **Figure 16** and **Figure 17**) and vent hoses (B, **Figure 16** and **Figure 17**).

Individual Carburetor Disassembly/Assembly

Refer to **Figure 18**.

To avoid accidentally mixing parts, disassemble, clean and reassemble one carburetor at a time.

1. Remove the carburetor assembly as described in this chapter.
2. Remove the two top cover screws and the top cover (**Figure 19**).
3. Remove the spring (**Figure 20**) from the piston valve/diaphragm assembly.
4. Remove the piston valve/diaphragm (**Figure 21**). Note the O-ring (**Figure 22**) that is attached to the diaphragm rim.
5. Turn the carburetor over.
6. Remove the float bowl screws, then remove the float bowl (**Figure 23**) and the float bowl O-ring (**Figure 24**).
7. Use needlenose pliers and carefully remove the float pivot pin (A, **Figure 25**) from the float and carburetor body.
8. Carefully pull straight up and remove the float assembly (B, **Figure 25**). Account for the fuel valve (**Figure 26**) hanging from the float tang.
9. Unscrew and remove the main jet (A, **Figure 27**) and the main jet holder (B).
10. Unscrew and remove the pilot jet (**Figure 28**).
11. Remove the fuel valve seat retaining screw (A, **Figure 29**), then remove the fuel valve seat (B).
12A. On U.S.A., California, Switzerland and Austria models, the pilot screw assembly is located under a plug (C, **Figure 27**) that should not to be removed. If removal is necessary, refer to the *Pilot Screw* section in this chapter.
12B. On all other models, turn the pilot screw in until it *lightly seats* while counting and recording the number of turns. Reinstall the pilot screw to this same position during assembly. Unscrew and remove the pilot screw, spring, washer and O-ring.
13. To remove the pilot air jet, perform the following:
   a. Remove the screws (A, **Figure 30**) securing the funnel (B).
   b. Remove the funnel.
   c. Unscrew and remove the pilot air jets (C, **Figure 30**).

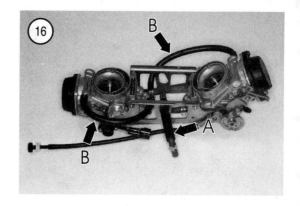

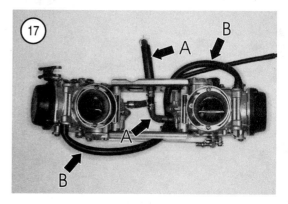

14. To disassemble the piston valve/diaphragm, perform the following:
   a. Using thin needlenose pliers, remove the stopper assembly (**Figure 31**) above the jet needle.
   b. Carefully remove the jet needle (**Figure 32**) from the piston valve.
15. Remove the coast valve cover retaining screws (**Figure 33**).
16. Remove the cover (A, **Figure 34**) and diaphragm (B).

NOTE
*The throttle position sensor (**Figure 35**) is preset by the manufacturer. Do not remove it. If removal is necessary, make alignment marks on the carburetor body and sensor so the sensor can be installed in the **exact** same position.*

NOTE
*Further disassembly is neither necessary nor recommended. Do not remove the throttle shaft and throttle valve assemblies (D, **Figure 30**). If*

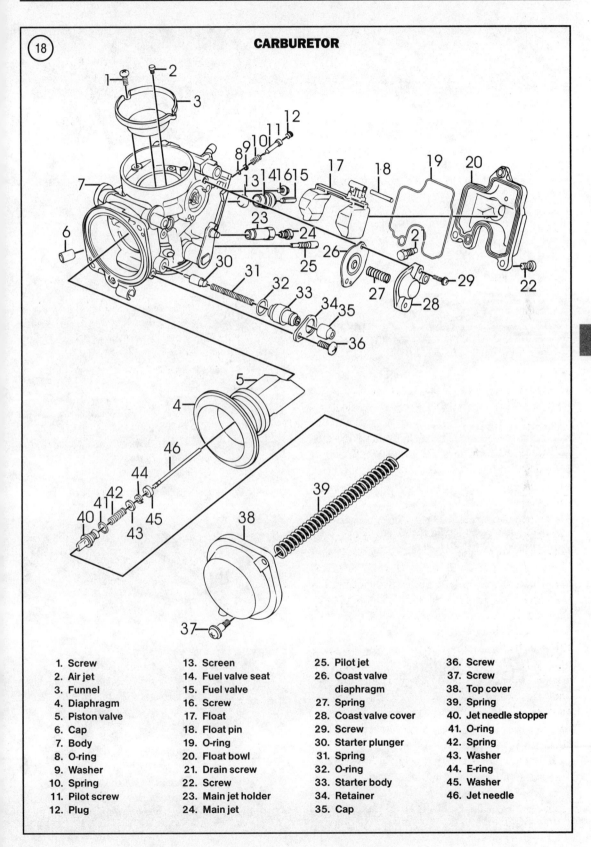

CARBURETOR

1. Screw	13. Screen	25. Pilot jet	36. Screw
2. Air jet	14. Fuel valve seat	26. Coast valve	37. Screw
3. Funnel	15. Fuel valve	diaphragm	38. Top cover
4. Diaphragm	16. Screw	27. Spring	39. Spring
5. Piston valve	17. Float	28. Coast valve cover	40. Jet needle stopper
6. Cap	18. Float pin	29. Screw	41. O-ring
7. Body	19. O-ring	30. Starter plunger	42. Spring
8. O-ring	20. Float bowl	31. Spring	43. Washer
9. Washer	21. Drain screw	32. O-ring	44. E-ring
10. Spring	22. Screw	33. Starter body	45. Washer
11. Pilot screw	23. Main jet holder	34. Retainer	46. Jet needle
12. Plug	24. Main jet	35. Cap	

8

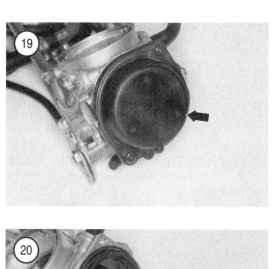

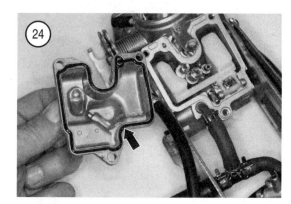

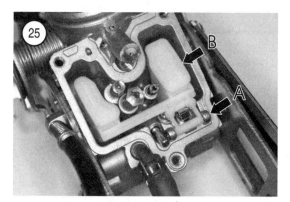

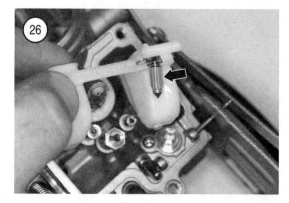

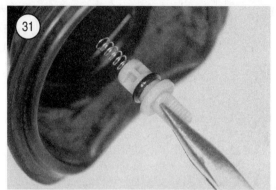

8

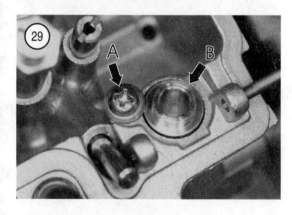

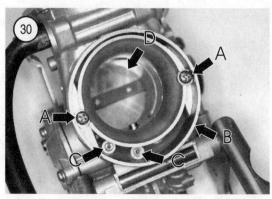

these parts are damaged, replace the carburetor, as these items are not available separately.

17. Clean and inspect all parts as described in this chapter.

18. Assemble the carburetor by reversing the preceding disassembly steps while noting the following:

   a. Make sure the washer and E-ring (**Figure 36**) are in place and installed on the jet needle. Note the parts sequence for the jet needle and stopper assemblies in **Figure 37**.

   b. Position the jet needle stopper assembly with the spring end going in first (**Figure 31**). Push the stopper assembly down until it bottoms.

   c. Install the piston valve/diaphragm into the body, and seat it in the carburetor body. Make sure the small O-ring (**Figure 38**) is positioned correctly over the vent hole. Install the top cover and tighten the top-cover screws securely.

   d. After the top cover has been installed, move the piston valve up. The piston valve should slide back down immediately with no binding. If it binds or if the movement is sluggish, the diaphragm may have seated incorrectly or may be folded over. The diaphragm rubber is very soft and may fold over during spring and top cover installation.

   e. When installing the funnel, apply ThreeBond No. 1342 to the funnel screws.

   f. Install the coasting valve diaphragm so the pin (A, **Figure 39**) enters the hole (B) in the carburetor body.

   g. Install the coasting valve cover and diaphragm so the air holes (C, **Figure 34**) in the carburetor body, diaphragm and cover are aligned.

   h. Check and adjust the fuel level as described in this chapter.

   i. After the assembly and installation are completed, adjust the carburetors as described in this chapter and in Chapter Three.

Cleaning and Inspection

> *CAUTION*
> *The carburetor bodies are equipped with plastic parts that cannot be removed. Do not dip the carburetor*

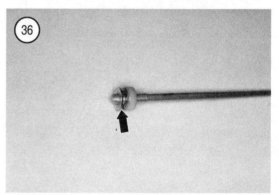

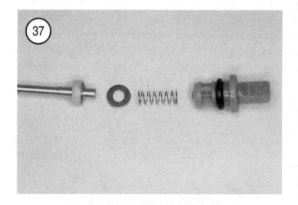

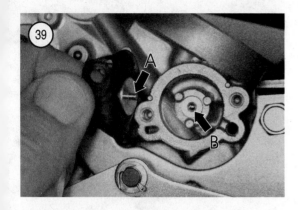

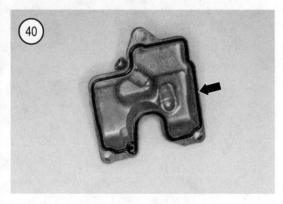

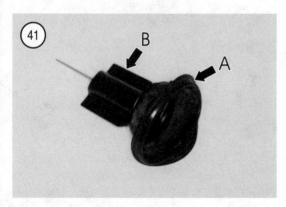

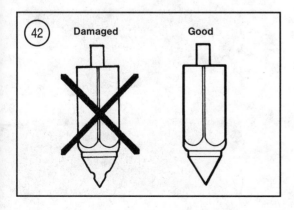

body, O-rings, float assembly, needle valve or piston valve/diaphragm into carburetor cleaner or other harsh solutions that can damage these parts. Suzuki does not recommend using a caustic carburetor cleaning solvent. Instead, clean the carburetors and related parts in a petroleum-based solvent or Simple Green. Then rinse in clean water.

1. Initially clean all parts in a mild petroleum-based cleaning solution. Wash the parts in hot soap and water, and rinse them with cold water. Blow dry the parts with compressed air.

CAUTION
*If compressed air is not available, allow the parts to air dry or use a clean lint-free cloth. Do **not** use a paper towel to dry carburetor parts. The small paper particles could plug openings in the carburetor housing or jets.*

2. Allow the carburetors to dry thoroughly before assembly. Blow out the jets and the needle jet holder with compressed air.

CAUTION
*Do **not** use wire or drill bits to clean jets. Even minor gouges in the jet can alter flow rate and alter the air/fuel mixture.*

3. Inspect the float bowl O-ring gasket (**Figure 40**). Replace the O-ring if it has become hard or is starting to deteriorate.

4. Make sure the drain screw is in good condition and does not leak. Replace the drain screw if necessary.

5. Inspect the piston valve/diaphragm (A, **Figure 41**) for cracks, deterioration or other damage. Check the piston valve sides (B) for excessive wear. Install the piston valve into the carburetor body and move it up and down in the bore. The piston valve should move smoothly with no binding or excessive play. If there is excessive play, replace the piston valve and/or carburetor body.

6. Inspect the fuel valve tapered end for steps, uneven wear or other damage (**Figure 42**). Replace if damaged.

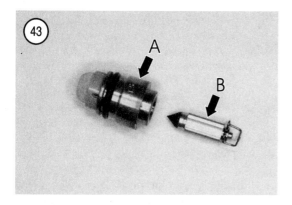

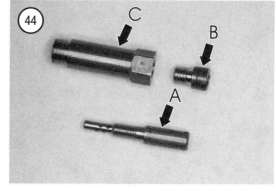

7. Inspect the fuel valve seat (A, **Figure 43**) for steps, uneven wear or other damage. Inspect the O-ring on the fuel valve for hardness or deterioration. Replace the O-ring as necessary. Insert the fuel valve (B, **Figure 43**) and slowly move it back and forth checking for smooth operation. If either part is worn or damaged, replace both for maximum performance.

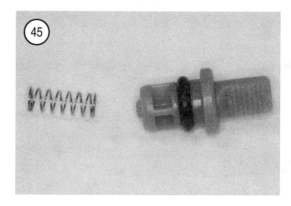

8. Inspect the pilot jet (A, **Figure 44**), main jet (B) and main jet holder (C). Make sure all holes are open and no part is worn or damaged. Replace worn parts.

9. Inspect the jet needle stopper assembly (**Figure 45**) for deterioration or damage. Inspect the O-ring for deterioration, and replace it if necessary.

10. Inspect the jet needle tapered end (**Figure 46**) for steps, uneven wear or other damage. Replace if damaged.

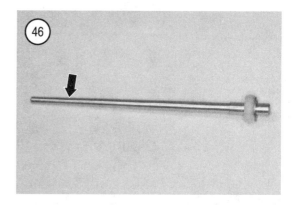

11. If removed, inspect the pilot screw O-ring. Replace the O-ring if it has become hard or is deteriorating.

12. Inspect the float (**Figure 47**) for deterioration or damage. Place the float in a container of water and push it down. If the float sinks or if bubbles appear (indicating a leak), replace the float.

13. Make sure all openings in the carburetor housing are clear. Clean them out if they are plugged in any way, and then apply compressed air to all openings.

14. Check the top cover for cracks or damage, and replace it if necessary.

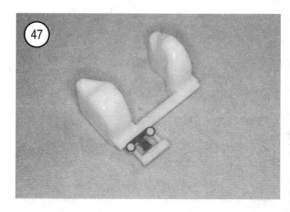

15. Make sure the throttle plate screws (A, **Figure 48**) are tight. Tighten if necessary.

16. Inspect the carburetor body for internal or external damage. If damaged, replace the carburetor assembly as the body cannot be replaced separately.

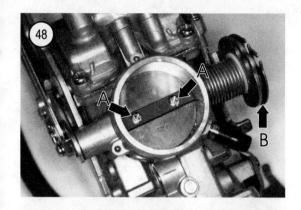

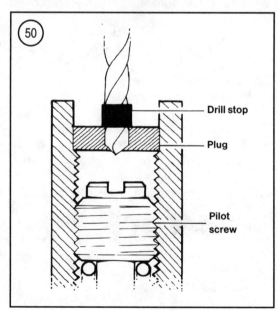

Drill stop

Plug

Pilot
screw

PILOT SCREW

Removal/Installation (U.S.A., California, Canada, Switzerland and Austria Models)

The pilot screws on these models are sealed. A plug has been installed at the outer end of the pilot screw bore (**Figure 49**) to prevent routine adjustment. The pilot screws do not require adjustment unless the carburetors are overhauled, the pilot screws are incorrectly adjusted, or the pilot screws require replacement. The following procedure describes how to remove and install the pilot screws.

1. Remove the float bowl.

NOTE
Cover the carburetor to prevent debris from entering the carburetor.

2. Set a stop 6 mm from the end of a 1/8 inch drill bit. See **Figure 50**.

3. Carefully drill a hole in the plug (**Figure 49**). Do not drill too deeply. The pilot screw will be difficult to remove if the head is damaged.

4. Screw a sheet metal screw into the plug and pull the plug from the bore.

5. Screw the pilot screw in until it *lightly seats* while counting and recording the number of turns. Reinstall the pilot screw to the same position during assembly.

6. Remove the pilot screw, spring, washer and O-ring from the carburetor body.

7. Repeat for the other carburetor. Be sure to keep each carburetor's parts separate.

8. Inspect the O-ring and the end of the pilot screw. Replace the screw and/or O-ring if damaged or worn (grooved).

NOTE
If the pilot screw was incorrectly adjusted, refer to the specifications in Tables 1-4.

8

17. Move the throttle pulley (B, **Figure 48**) back and forth from stop to stop. The throttle lever should move smoothly and return under spring tension. If it does not move freely or if it sticks in any position, replace the carburetor housing.

9. Install the pilot screw in the same position as noted during removal (Step 4) or to the specification listed in **Tables 1-4**.

10. Install a new plug by tapping it into place with a punch.

FUEL LEVEL

The fuel level in the carburetor float bowls is critical to performance. The fuel flow rate from the bowl up to the carburetor bore depends not only on the vacuum in the throttle bore and the size of the jets but also on the fuel level. Suzuki provides a specification for the fuel level measured from the top edge of the float bowl mounting screw boss on the carburetor body.

This measurement is more useful than a float height measurement because the actual fuel level can vary from motorcycle to motorcycle, even when their floats are set at the same height. A fuel level gauge (Suzuki part No. 09913-10760) is required for this inspection procedure.

The carburetors must be removed from the motorcycle, but still mounted in their mounting brackets (**Figure 51**). The fuel level is adjusted by bending the float arm tang in the proper direction.

Inspection

Rough riding, a worn needle valve or bent float arm can cause the fuel level to change. To adjust the float level, perform the following.

> *WARNING*
> *Some gasoline will drain from the carburetors during this procedure. Wipe up any spilled gasoline immediately. Work in a well-ventilated area at least 50 feet away from any open flame, including pilot lights in gas appliances. Do not allow anyone to smoke in the area.*

1. Remove the carburetors as described in this chapter, but do not remove the carburetors from their mounting brackets (**Figure 51**).
2. Mount the carburetors in a vise or other holding device so the carburetor is tilted at the angle shown in **Figure 52**.
3. Fill the float bowl of the carburetor being checked with gasoline through the carburetor fill hose.
4. Connect the fuel level gauge to the float bowl drain fitting on the carburetor and open the drain screw.
5. Hold the fuel level gauge against the carburetor so the top line is level with the mark on the carburetor (A, **Figure 52**).

6. Wait for the fuel in the gauge to settle. The fuel level on the gauge should equal the specification in **Tables 1-4**. Note the fuel level on the gauge.
7. Close the drain screw and remove the fuel level gauge from the float bowl.
   a. If the fuel level is correct, repeat Steps 2-6 for the other carburetor.
   b. If the level is incorrect, adjust the float height as described in the following procedure.

CARBURETOR FLOAT HEIGHT

Check and Adjustment

The needle valve and float maintain a constant fuel level in the carburetor float bowls. The carburetor assembly has to be removed and partially disassembled for this adjustment.

1. Remove the carburetor assembly as described in this chapter.
2. Remove the screws securing the float bowl (**Figure 53**) and remove the float bowl and the O-ring.
3. Hold the carburetor assembly so the float bowl mating surface is at a 45° angle to the workbench with the float arm just contacting the needle valve.
4. Measure the distance from the float bowl mating surface to the top of the float (A, **Figure 54**). The float height should be within the range specified in **Tables 1-4**. Note the float level dimension and carburetor number.
5. If the float height is incorrect, adjust it by performing the following:
   a. Push out, then extract the float pivot pin (**Figure 55**) from the float and carburetor body.
   b. Carefully pull straight up and remove the float assembly. Do not lose the fuel valve (**Figure 56**) hanging on the float tang.

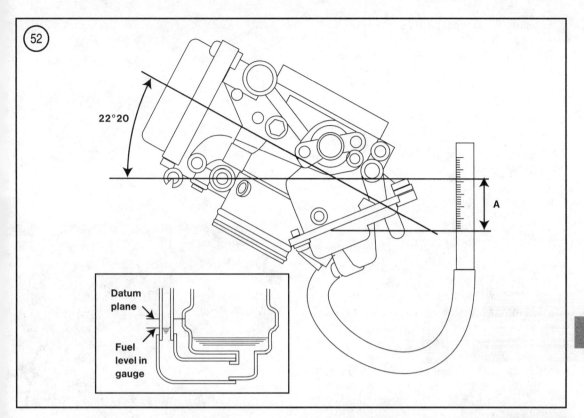

Datum plane

Fuel level in gauge

22°20

A

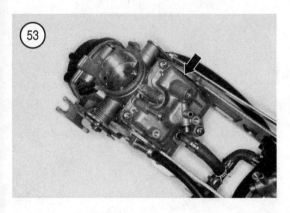

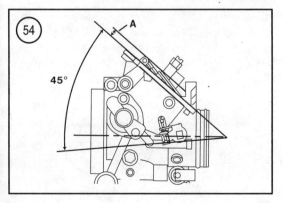

A

45°

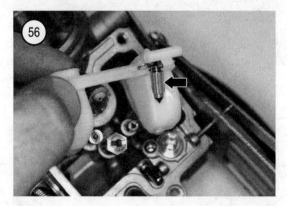

8

c. Carefully bend the float tang (**Figure 57**).

> *NOTE*
> *Decreasing the float height raises the fuel level. Increasing the float height lowers the fuel level.*

d. Install the fuel valve onto the float tang and carefully install the float assembly straight down and into place on the carburetor body.

e. Install the float pivot pin and push it in until it is seated correctly.

6. Make sure the O-ring gasket is in place and correctly seats in the float bowl.

7. Install the float bowl and screws.

THROTTLE POSITION SENSOR

Inspection/Adjustment

> *NOTE*
> *The throttle position sensor may be serviced with the carburetors installed on the engine or removed from the engine. The following illustrations show the carburetors removed for clarity.*

1. If the carburetors are installed on the engine, disconnect the electrical connector (**Figure 58**).

2. Set an ohmmeter to the R × 1k scale.

3. With the throttle lever fully closed, measure the resistance between the two terminals as shown in **Figure 59**. Record the measured value.

4. Compare the measurement to the fully closed resistance specified in **Table 6**.

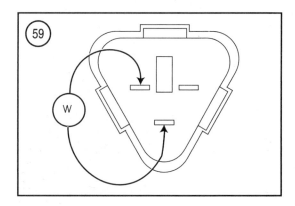

a. Replace the throttle position sensor if the resistance is outside the range specified in **Table 6**.

b. If resistance is within specification, perform Step 5.

5. With the throttle lever in the wide open position, measure the wide open resistance across the two terminals as shown in **Figure 60**. Record this value.

6. Compare the wide open resistance to the fully closed resistance measured in Step 4.

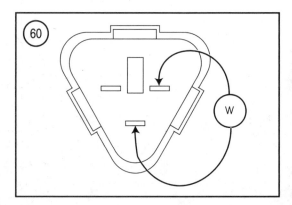

a. The wide open resistance should be 78% of the fully closed resistance. For example, if the fully closed resistance equals 5 k ohms, the wide open resistance should equal 3.9 k ohms (0.78 × 5 k = 3.9 k).

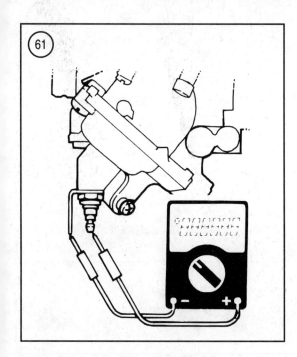

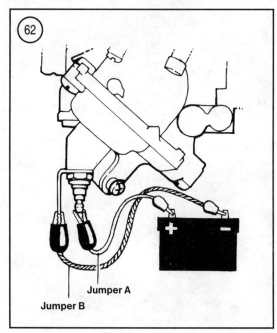

Jumper A

Jumper B

b. If wide open resistance is not 78% of the fully closed resistance, remove the carburetor assembly as described in this chapter.

7. Loosen the throttle position sensor screws and slightly rotate the sensor. Repeat Step 6.

8. Continue adjusting the angle of the throttle position sensor until the wide-open resistance equals 78% of the fully closed resistance. When it does, tighten the throttle position sensor screws to 3.5 N•m (31 in.-lb.).

CARBURETOR HEATER
(U.K. MODELS)

Removal/Installation

1. Remove the airbox as described in this chapter.

2. Disconnect the electrical lead from the carburetor heater on each carburetor.

3. Unscrew and remove the carburetor heater from the bottom of the float bowl.

4. Repeat for the remaining carburetor heaters.

5. Installation is the reverse of removal. Note the following:

   a. Apply thermo grease (Suzuki part No. 99000-59029) to the tip of the carburetor heater.

   b. Tighten the carburetor heater to 3.0 N•m (27 in.-lb.).

Carburetor Heater Inspection

1. Remove the airbox as described in this chapter.

2. Disconnect the electrical lead from the carburetor heater on the bottom of the float bowl.

3. Check the resistance of the heater coil by performing the following:

   a. Set an ohmmeter to the R × 10 scale.

   b. Connect the ohmmeter negative test lead to the spade connector on the heater, and connect the positive test lead to the heater body as shown in **Figure 61**.

   c. Replace the heater if the resistance is outside the range specified in **Table 6**.

CAUTION
Electrical arcing may occur when connecting the jumpers in the following test. Connect the jumpers in the described order so any arcing takes place away from the carburetors.

4. Use a battery to check the carburetor heater operation by performing the following:

   a. Connect one end of jumper A to the battery positive terminal, and then connect the other end of jumper A to the carburetor body as shown in **Figure 62**.

b. Connect one end of jumper B to the spade connector on the carburetor heater, and then connect the other end of jumper B to the battery negative terminal.

> *CAUTION*
> *Do not touch the carburetor heater directly. It is hot.*

c. After five minutes, check the temperature of the float bowl by hand. It should be warm. Replace the carburetor heater if the float bowl does not heat up.

d. Disconnect the jumper B from the negative battery terminal and then from the carburetor heater. Then disconnect jumper A.

5. Repeat this test for the remaining carburetor heaters.

Carburetor Heater Thermo-Switch Inspection

1. Unplug the thermo-switch connector from the wiring harness.

2. Remove the thermo-switch and immerse it in a pan of ice.

3. After the switch has remained in the ice for approximately five minutes, check the continuity between the two terminals in the thermo-switch connector (**Figure 63**).

4. The chilled switch should have zero or very low resistance. Replace the switch if it has infinite or very high resistance.

THROTTLE CABLE REPLACEMENT

> *NOTE*
> *There are two throttle cables. One is the pull cable (accelerate) and the other is the return cable (decelerate). These cables must be reinstalled in the correct position on the carburetor and connected to the correct position on the throttle grip pulley.*

1. Remove the airbox as described in this chapter.

2. At the throttle grip, loosen the throttle cable locknut (A, **Figure 64**) and turn the adjuster (B) all the way into the switch assembly to allow maximum slack in the pull cable (C). Repeat this procedure for the return cable (D, **Figure 64**).

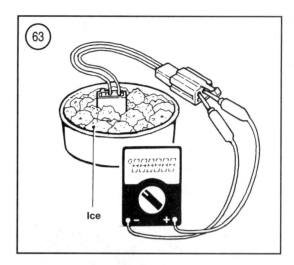

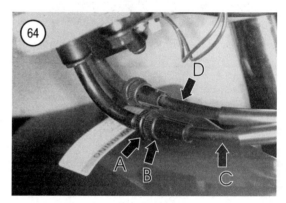

3. Remove the screws securing the right switch assembly together and separate the assembly halves (**Figure 65**).

4. Disconnect the throttle pull cable and the return cable from the throttle grip. Note that a retaining plate (A, **Figure 66**) secures the pull cable in the throttle housing and a locknut (B) secures the return cable in position.

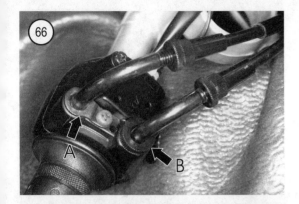

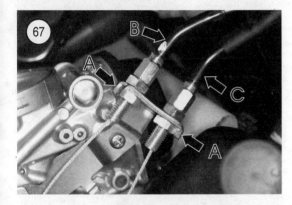

9. Lubricate the new cable as described in Chapter Three. Route the new cable along the same path noted in Step 13.

10. Reverse Steps 1-7 to install the new cables while noting the following:

   a. Connect the throttle return cable, then the pull cable onto the throttle grip and switch housing.

   b. Align the locating pin with the hole in the handlebar and install the switch onto the handlebar. Tighten the screws securely.

   c. Connect the throttle pull cable (B, **Figure 67**) onto the rear receptacle in the throttle pulley on the carburetor, then install the return cable (C) into the front receptacle in the throttle pulley on the carburetor.

   d. Operate the throttle lever and make sure the carburetor throttle linkage is operating correctly with no binding. If operation is incorrect or there is binding, carefully check that the cables are attached correctly and there are no tight bends in either cable.

   e. At the carburetor assembly, rotate the adjuster on each cable in either direction so the adjuster is at a midpoint position. Tighten the locknuts securing each throttle cable to the mounting bracket.

   f. Adjust the throttle cables as described in Chapter Three.

WARNING
An improperly adjusted or incorrectly routed throttle cable can cause the throttle to hang open. This could cause a crash. Do not ride the motorcycle until throttle cable operation is correct.

   g. Start the engine and let it idle. Turn the handlebar from side to side and listen to the engine speed. Make sure the idle speed does not increase. If it does, the throttle cables are adjusted incorrectly or the throttle cable(s) is improperly routed. Find and correct the source of the problem before riding.

5. At the front carburetor, loosen both locknuts (A, **Figure 67**) securing each throttle cable to the mounting bracket.

6. Disconnect the pull cable (B, **Figure 67**) from the throttle pulley on the carburetor, then disconnect the return cable (C). Disconnect each throttle cable from the bracket on the carburetor assembly.

7. Disconnect the throttle cable from any clips and/or cable ties that secure it to the frame.

8. Note how the cable is routed through the frame, and then remove it.

STARTER CABLE REPLACEMENT

The starter cable is constructed of one cable at the control end which actuates two cables that operate the starter valve in each carburetor.

1. Remove the airbox as described in this chapter.

2. Remove the screws securing the left switch assembly (**Figure 68**) and separate the assembly halves.

3. Disconnect the starter lever and cable from the switch housing. Disconnect the starter cable end from the lever (**Figure 69**).

4. Cut the cable tie that secures the starter cable to the carburetor bracket (A, **Figure 70**).

5. Unscrew the starter fitting retaining screw (B, **Figure 70**) and separate the starter fitting assembly from the rear carburetor.

6. Partially remove the carburetor assembly to gain access to the starter cable on the front carburetor as described in this chapter.

7. Lift up the carburetor assembly, then unscrew the starter fitting retaining screw (**Figure 71**) and separate the starter fitting assembly from the front carburetor.

8. Disconnect the starter cable from any clips and/or cable ties securing it to the frame.

9. Note the path the starter cable follows through the frame. The new cable must be routed along the same path.

10. Lubricate the new cable as described in Chapter Three.

11. Reverse Steps 1-9 to install the new cable while noting the following:

    a. Connect the cable and choke lever to the switch housing.

    b. Align the switch housing locating pin with the hole in the handlebar and fit the switch in place on the handlebar. Tighten the screws securely.

    c. Operate the choke lever and make sure the link is operating correctly without binding. If the operation is incorrect or there is binding, carefully check that the cable is attached correctly and that there are no tight bends in the cable.

    d. Start the engine and let it idle. Then turn the handlebar from side to side and listen to the engine. The engine speed should not increase when turning the handlebars. If it does, the cable is improperly routed. Correct the problem before riding.

AIR BOX

The air box is located under the fuel tank.

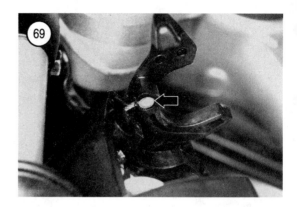

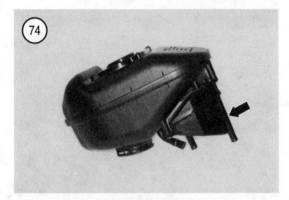

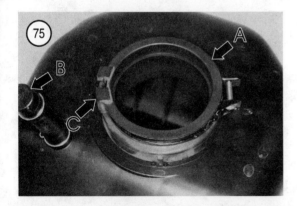

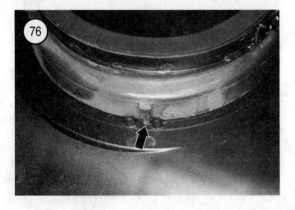

Removal/Installation

1. Raise and support the fuel tank as described in this chapter.

> *NOTE*
> *Label each hose and its air box fitting so the hose can be easily identified and reinstalled onto the correct fitting during assembly. Color-coded plugs are available at motorcycle and auto parts stores. Also plug the hoses and fittings so debris cannot enter.*

2. On California models, disconnect the PAIR cleaner hose (A, **Figure 72**) from the fitting on the air box.

3. Detach the crankcase ventilation hoses (**Figure 73**) from the fittings on the breather box.

4. Loosen the screw (B, **Figure 72**) on each carburetor clamp.

5. Pull the air box up and off the carburetor assembly.

6. Remove the air box from the engine and frame.

7. Plug the carburetor inlets to prevent debris from entering the carburetors.

8. Inspect the air box and the air inlet ducts for cracks, wear or damage. If any damage is noted, replace the air box to avoid the possibility of unfiltered air entering the engine.

9. Remove the retaining screw and separate the breather box (**Figure 74**) from the air box. Clean the breather box and replace the grommet if necessary.

10. Inspect the air box-to-carburetor tubes (A, **Figure 75**) for hardness, deterioration or damage. Replace them as necessary. Install the tube so the nub on the outside of the tube fits between the two projections on the air box (**Figure 76**).

11. Remove the drain plug (B, **Figure 75**) and clean out all residue from the plug and air box. Reinstall the drain plug.

12. Install by reversing the preceding removal steps. Note the following:

    a. When installing the clamp on an air box-to-carburetor tube, be sure the locating tabs on the clamp fit between the tabs on the tube (C, **Figure 75**).

    b. Make sure the lower section of the air box is correctly seated on each carburetor, then securely tighten the screw on each carburetor clamp. This prevents unfiltered air from en-

8

tering the carburetors and causing engine damage.

c. Make sure all hoses are securely connected to prevent air leaks.

FUEL TANK

Raising/Supporting

1. Remove the front and rear seats as described in Chapter Fifteen.
2. Remove the fuel tank stay (**Figure 77**) from the tray under the rear seat.
3. Remove the fuel tank mounting bolts (**Figure 78**) from the front of the fuel tank.
4. Raise the front of the fuel tank, insert the right-angle end of the tank stay into the steering stem and insert the other end into one of the fuel tank mounts (**Figure 79**).

Removal/Installation

> *WARNING*
> *Some fuel may spill from the fuel tank hose when performing this procedure. Because gasoline is extremely flammable and explosive, perform this procedure away from all open flames (including appliance pilot lights) and sparks. Do not smoke or allow someone who is smoking in the work area. Always work in a well-ventilated area. Wipe up any spills immediately.*

Refer to **Figure 80**.

1. Disconnect the negative battery cable as described in Chapter Three.
2. Raise and support the fuel tank as described in this chapter.

> *NOTE*
> *Label the hoses and their fittings during removal so each hose can be installed on the correct fitting during assembly.*

3. Disconnect the fuel hose (A, **Figure 81**) and the vacuum hose (B) from the fuel valve.
4. Disconnect the fuel level connector (**Figure 82**).
5. Disconnect the water drain hose and breather hose (**Figure 83**) from the fittings on the rear underside of the tank.

6. Remove the two bolts (**Figure 84**) securing the tank mounting bracket to the frame.
7. Carefully lift up the fuel tank and remove it from the frame. After the fuel tank has been inspected and serviced (if necessary), wrap the tank in a blanket or soft towels to protect the finish. Place the wrapped tank in a cardboard box and store it in an area where it will not be damaged.
8. Plug the end of the fuel lines and vacuum lines with golf tees to prevent the entry of debris and loss of fuel from the hose.
9. Inspect the fuel tank as described in this chapter.

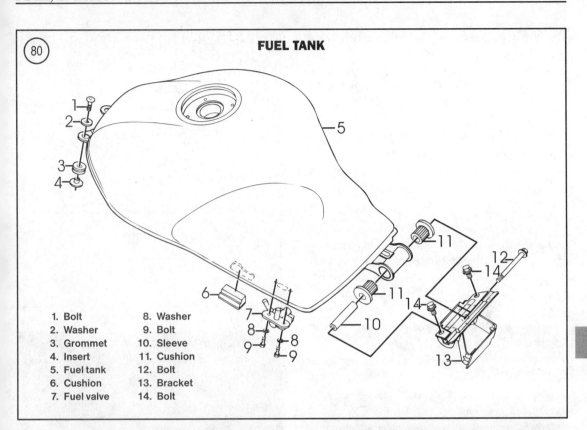

FUEL TANK

1. Bolt
2. Washer
3. Grommet
4. Insert
5. Fuel tank
6. Cushion
7. Fuel valve
8. Washer
9. Bolt
10. Sleeve
11. Cushion
12. Bolt
13. Bracket
14. Bolt

8

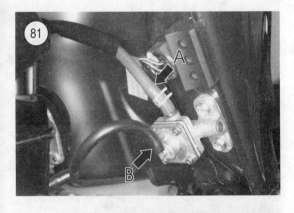

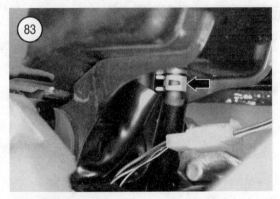

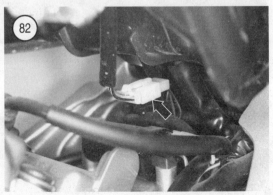

10. Install by reversing the preceding removal steps while noting the following:

    a. Be sure to reconnect the fuel hose (A, **Figure 81**), vacuum hose (B), breather hose (**Figure 83**) and water drain hose to the correct fittings.

    b. Check for fuel leakage at all hose connections after installation is completed.

    c. Tighten the fuel tank mounting bolts securely.

Inspection

1. Inspect the front rubber grommets on the mounting bracket for deterioration. Replace the grommets if necessary. Install the grommet so the large portion of the grommet contacts the flange of the metal insert as shown in **Figure 85**.

2. Inspect the rubber cushions for damage or deterioration and replace if necessary.

3. Check the fittings (**Figure 86**) on the rear of the fuel tank for damage.

4. Inspect the filler cap gaskets. If the cap gasket is damaged or deteriorating, replace the filler cap assembly. The gasket cannot be replaced separately. If the mounting flange gasket is damaged, replace it.

5. To remove the fuel filler cap, remove the screws and the filler cap assembly. Install the new filler cap and tighten the screws securely.

6. Inspect the entire fuel tank for leaks or damage. Repair or replace the fuel tank if any fuel leakage is found.

FUEL VALVE

Removal/Installation

1. Remove the fuel tank as described in this chapter. If not already drained, drain the tank and store the fuel in a can approved for gasoline storage. Place the container in a safe place.

2. Place several old blankets or soft towels on the workbench to protect the fuel tank.

3. Turn the fuel tank upside down on the workbench.

4. Remove the screws and washers securing the fuel valve (**Figure 87**) to the fuel tank.

5. Remove the valve and the O-ring. Install a new O-ring during assembly.

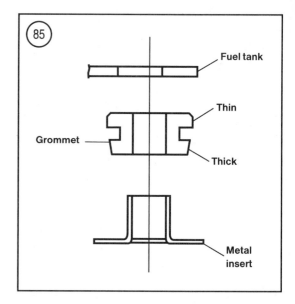

6. Fit a new O-ring seal onto the valve and install the valve onto the fuel tank. Tighten the screws securely.

7. Install the fuel tank as described in this chapter.

8. Check for fuel leakage at all hose connections after installation is completed.

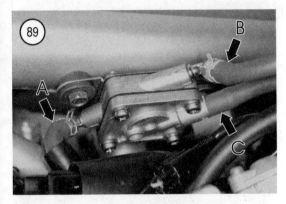

Testing

1. Remove the fuel valve as previously described.
2. Clean the fuel valve to remove any gasoline in the fuel valve. Allow the fuel valve to dry.
3. Connect a vacuum source to the vacuum fitting on the fuel valve. A Mity-Vac hand-operated pump is suitable for this purpose. The vacuum must be 51-102 mm Hg (2.0-4.0 in. Hg).
4. While operating the vacuum pump, direct low-pressure air through the fuel outlet of the fuel valve. Air should exit the fuel inlet of the fuel valve.

5. If the fuel valve does not function properly, replace the fuel valve.

FUEL PUMP

All models are equipped with a diaphragm type fuel pump mounted on the right side of the frame (**Figure 88**). Pressure pulses in the crankcase operate the fuel pump. Fuel from the fuel tank is routed to the fuel pump, which directs fuel to the carburetors. A relief valve inside the fuel pump stops output flow when the fuel level in the carburetor float bowl forces the fuel valve to close.

Removal/Installation

> *WARNING*
> *Some fuel may spill from the hoses and fuel pump when performing this procedure. Because gasoline is extremely flammable and explosive, perform this procedure away from all open flames (including appliance pilot lights) and sparks. Do not smoke or allow someone who is smoking in the work area. Always work in a well-ventilated area. Wipe up any spills immediately.*

1. Remove the air box as described in this chapter.
2. Detach the inlet fuel hose (A, **Figure 89**), outlet fuel hose (B) and vacuum hose (C) from the fuel pump. Plug the hoses to prevent fuel leakage or contamination.

> *NOTE*
> *On California models, the front fuel pump mounting bolt also serves as the rear PAIR control valve mounting bracket bolt.*

3. Remove the bolts holding the fuel pump to the frame and remove the fuel pump.
4. Replace the hose clamps as necessary.
5. Installation is the reverse of the preceding steps. Tighten the mounting bolts to 10 N•m (88 in.-lb.).

> *NOTE*
> *Fuel flow through the fuel pump is indicated by arrows on the pump inlet and outlet (**Figure 90**).*

8

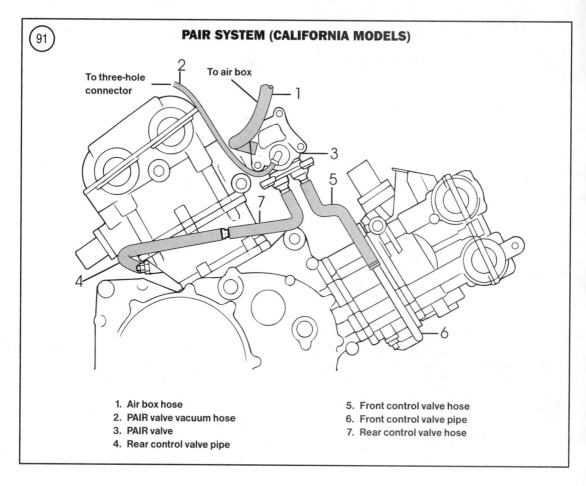

PAIR SYSTEM (CALIFORNIA MODELS)

91

To three-hole connector

To air box

2

1

3

5

7

4

6

1. Air box hose
2. PAIR valve vacuum hose
3. PAIR valve
4. Rear control valve pipe
5. Front control valve hose
6. Front control valve pipe
7. Rear control valve hose

Testing

1. Remove the air box as described in this chapter.
2. Detach the outlet fuel hose (B, **Figure 89**) from the fuel pump.
3. Connect a suitable hose to the outlet on the fuel pump and route the hose into a container.
4. Shift the transmission into neutral.
5. Operate the starter for a few seconds and check for fuel flowing from the fuel pump.
6. If no fuel flows from the fuel pump, check the fuel tank valve.
7. Be sure the crankcase pulsation (vacuum) hose to the fuel pump is not leaking.
8. If the fuel tank valve and crankcase pulsation hose operate correctly, replace the fuel pump.

PAIR (AIR SUPPLY) SYSTEM

California models are equipped with the SV650(S) PAIR system that lowers emissions output by introducing secondary air into the exhaust ports. The introduction of air raises the exhaust temperature, which consumes some of the unburned fuel in the exhaust.

The PAIR system consists of a control valve, reed valves and the vacuum and outlet hoses (**Figure 91**).

The system uses the momentary pressure variations created by the exhaust gas pulses to introduce additional air into the exhaust ports. During deceleration the control valve shuts off the airflow to the exhaust. This prevents exhaust backfire due to the rich mixture conditions on deceleration.

Removal/Installation

Refer to **Figure 92**.
1. Remove the carburetors as described in this chapter.
2. Disconnect the lower hoses (**Figure 93**) from the control valve.

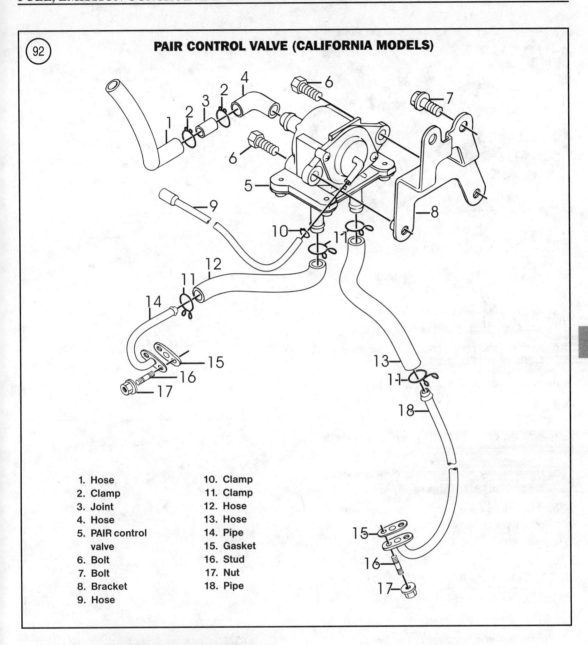

PAIR CONTROL VALVE (CALIFORNIA MODELS)

1. Hose
2. Clamp
3. Joint
4. Hose
5. PAIR control valve
6. Bolt
7. Bolt
8. Bracket
9. Hose
10. Clamp
11. Clamp
12. Hose
13. Hose
14. Pipe
15. Gasket
16. Stud
17. Nut
18. Pipe

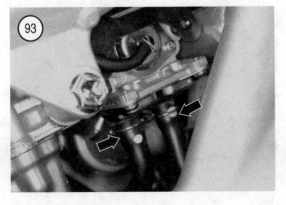

NOTE
The front fuel pump mounting bolt also serves as the rear PAIR control valve mounting bracket bolt.

3. Remove the control valve mounting bracket fasteners (A, **Figure 94**) and remove the control valve (B).

4. Reverse the removal steps to install the control valve.

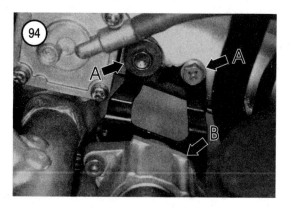

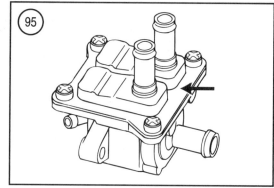

Inspection

1. Inspect the reed valve by performing the following:

    a. Remove the cover screws from the reed valve and remove the cover (**Figure 95**).

    b. Remove the reed valve from the reed-valve body.

    c. Inspect the reed valve for carbon deposits. Replace the control valve if there are deposits or the reeds are damaged.

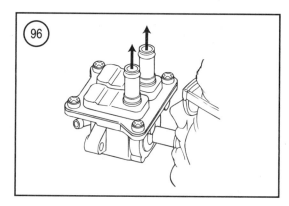

2. Inspect the control valve by performing the following:

    a. Blow air into the inlet port on the bottom of the control valve (**Figure 96**).

    b. Air should flow from the two control-valve outlet ports. Replace the control valve if it does not.

    c. Connect a vacuum pump to the vacuum fitting on the top of the control valve. See **Figure 97**.

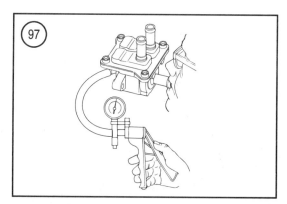

> *CAUTION*
> *Vacuum pressure applied in the following step should not exceed the value specified. The control valve could be damaged if excessive vacuum is applied.*

    d. Slowly apply vacuum to the control valve until the vacuum is within 230-400 mm Hg (9.0-15.8 in. Hg).

    e. Blow into the control valve inlet port. Air should not flow from the outlet ports when the applied vacuum is within the specified range. If it does, replace the control valve.

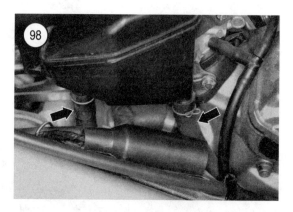

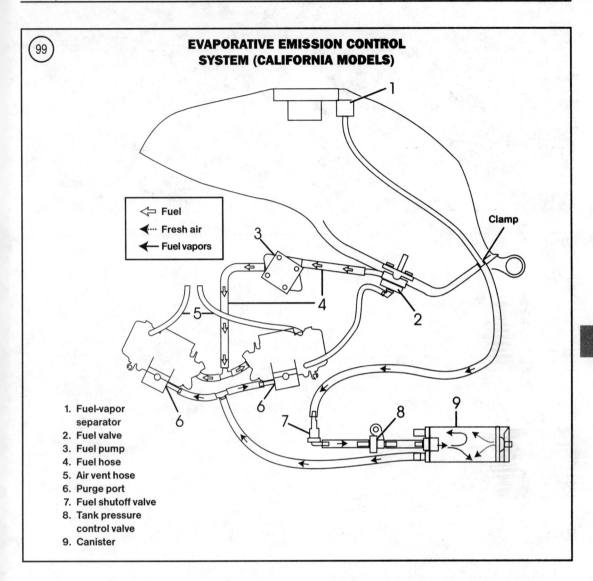

EVAPORATIVE EMISSION CONTROL SYSTEM (CALIFORNIA MODELS)

⇐ Fuel
◄··· Fresh air
◄— Fuel vapors

Clamp

1. Fuel-vapor separator
2. Fuel valve
3. Fuel pump
4. Fuel hose
5. Air vent hose
6. Purge port
7. Fuel shutoff valve
8. Tank pressure control valve
9. Canister

8

CRANKCASE BREATHER SYSTEM

All models are equipped with a closed crankcase breather system. This system routes crankcase vapors into the air box, then they are drawn into the engine and burned. Breather hoses are connected between the front cylinder and the air box, and from the rear crankcase to the air box.

Inspection and Cleaning

Inspect the breather hoses connected to the air box (**Figure 98**). Replace the hose if it is cracked or deteriorated. Make sure the hose clamps are in place and tight.

Remove the air box as described in this chapter and drain out all residue. This cleaning procedure should be done more frequently if a considerable amount of riding is done at full throttle or in the rain.

EVAPORATIVE EMISSION CONTROL SYSTEM (CALIFORNIA MODELS ONLY)

This system collects fuel system vapors in a charcoal canister when the engine is off. When the engine is started these vapors are routed to the carburetors and mixed with the intake charge and burned. Refer to **Figure 99** for a diagram of the evaporative emission control system.

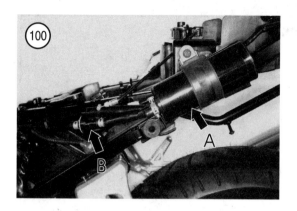

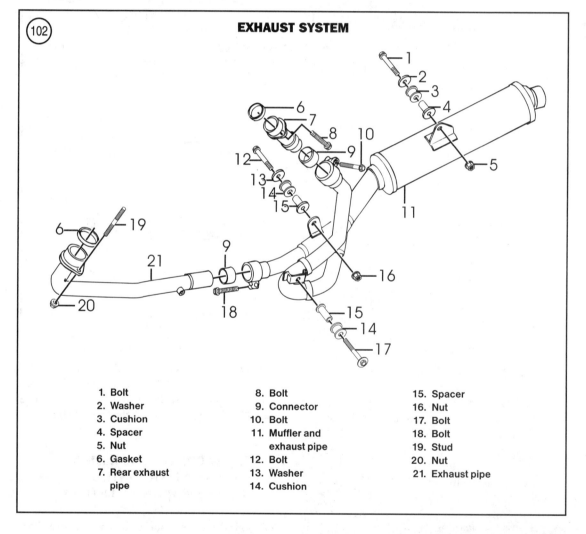

EXHAUST SYSTEM

1. Bolt	8. Bolt	15. Spacer
2. Washer	9. Connector	16. Nut
3. Cushion	10. Bolt	17. Bolt
4. Spacer	11. Muffler and	18. Bolt
5. Nut	exhaust pipe	19. Stud
6. Gasket	12. Bolt	20. Nut
7. Rear exhaust	13. Washer	21. Exhaust pipe
pipe	14. Cushion	

Make sure the hoses (**Figure 99**) are correctly routed and attached to the various components. Inspect the hoses and replace any if necessary. The charcoal canister (A, **Figure 100**) and tank pressure control valve (B) are located on the left rear frame rail.

On most models, the hoses and fittings are color coded with labels or bands. If these labels or bands are deteriorated or are missing, mark the hose and the fitting with a piece of masking tape to identify the hose. There are many vacuum hoses on these

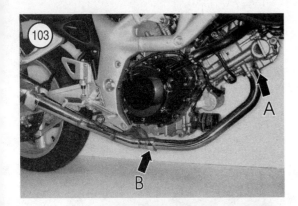

models. Without clear identifying marks, reconnecting the hoses correctly can be difficult.

Due to the various manufacturing changes made during the years, always refer to the emission control label located under the rear seat on the rear frame cover.

Tank Pressure Control Valve Testing

1. Remove the tank pressure control valve (**Figure 101**).
2. The valve is a one-way valve. Air should travel through the valve when it enters the stepped side of the valve, but not in the opposite direction.
3. Replace the valve if it does not perform correctly.
4. Install the valve so the stepped end is toward the canister (A, **Figure 100**).

EXHAUST SYSTEM

Check the exhaust system for deep dents and fractures. Repair or replace damaged parts immediately. Check the muffler frame mounting flanges for fractures and loose bolts. Check the cylinder head mounting flanges for tightness. Loose exhaust pipe connections will cause excessive exhaust noise and rob the engine of power.

Removal/Installation

The muffler is not available separately. The entire exhaust system should be removed as a unit, then serviced as needed.

Refer to **Figure 102** when performing this procedure.

1. Remove the nuts (A, **Figure 103**) securing the exhaust pipe to the front cylinder head.
2. Remove the exhaust pipe clamp bolt (B, **Figure 103**) under the engine.
3. Remove the exhaust pipe clamp bolt on the rear cylinder exhaust pipe (**Figure 104**).
4. Remove the lower rear cylinder exhaust pipe mounting bolt (**Figure 105**).
5. Remove the exhaust pipe mounting bolt below the right footpeg (**Figure 106**).
6. Drape a piece of rug as shown in **Figure 107** over the wheel and swing arm to prevent scratches when working the exhaust system loose.
7. Remove the muffler mounting bolt (**Figure 107**).

8

8. Remove the exhaust system by lowering the rear portion first, then when the front exhaust pipe lowers, twist it so it will clear the front cylinder head.

9. Check the rubber mounting grommets. Replace the rubber grommet if it is starting to harden or deteriorate.

10. Installation is the reverse of removal.

    a. Install a new gasket over the end of each exhaust pipe.

    b. Apply exhaust system sealer such as Permatex 1372 to the exhaust joints.

    c. Tighten all fasteners to 23 N•m (17 ft.-lb.).

    d. After installation is complete, start the engine and make sure there are no exhaust leaks.

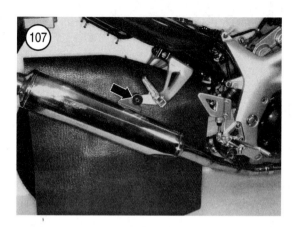

Table 1 CARBURETOR SPECIFICATIONS (U.S.A. AND CANADA MODELS)

Model No.	Mikuni BDSR39
Identification No.	20F2
Bore size	39 mm
Float height	6.5-7.5 mm (0.26-0.30 in.)
Fuel level	16.4-17.4 mm (0.64-0.68 in.)
Idle speed	1200-1400 rpm
Jet needle	6E42-52
Main jet No.	137.5
Needle jet	P-0M
Pilot jet No.	15
Pilot screw opening	Preset (3 turns out)
Throttle valve	95
Throttle cable free play	2.0-4.0 mm (0.08-0.16 in.)

Table 2 CARBURETOR SPECIFICATIONS (CALIFORNIA MODELS)

Model No.	Mikuni BDSR39
Identification No.	20F4
Bore size	39 mm
Float height	6.5-7.5 mm (0.26-0.30 in.)
Fuel level	16.4-17.4 mm (0.64-0.68 in.)
Idle speed	1200-1400 rpm
Jet needle	6E43-54
Main jet No.	137.5
Needle jet	P-0M
Pilot jet No.	15
Pilot screw opening	Preset
Throttle valve	95
Throttle cable free play	2.0-4.0 mm (0.08-0.16 in.)

Table 3 CARBURETOR SPECIFICATIONS (AUSTRALIA, BELGIUM, FINLAND, FRANCE, GERMANY, ITALY, NETHERLANDS, NORWAY, SPAIN, SWEDEN AND U.K. MODELS)

Model No.	Mikuni BDSR39
Identification No.	20F0
Bore size	39 mm
	(continued)

Table 3 CARBURETOR SPECIFICATIONS (AUSTRALIA, BELGIUM, FINLAND, FRANCE, GERMANY, ITALY, NETHERLANDS, NORWAY, SPAIN, SWEDEN AND U.K. MODELS) (continued)

Float height	6.5-7.5 mm (0.26-0.30 in.)
Fuel level	16.4-17.4 mm (0.64-0.68 in.)
Idle speed	1200-1400 rpm
Jet needle	6E38-54-2
Main jet No.	137.5
Needle jet	P-0
Pilot jet No.	17.5
Pilot screw opening	Preset (2 1/2 turns out)
Throttle valve	95
Throttle cable free play	2.0-4.0 mm (0.08-0.16 in.)

Table 4 CARBURETOR SPECIFICATIONS (AUSTRIA AND SWITZERLAND MODELS)

Model No.	Mikuni BDSR39
Identification No.	20F3
Bore size	39 mm
Float height	6.5-7.5 mm (0.26-0.30 in.)
Fuel level	16.4-17.4 mm (0.64-0.68 in.)
Idle speed	1250-1350 rpm
Jet needle	6E38-54-2
Main jet No.	137.5
Needle jet	P-2
Pilot jet No.	15
Pilot screw opening	Preset (3/4 turns out)
Throttle valve	95
Throttle cable free play	2.0-4.0 mm (0.08-0.16 in.)

8

Table 5 FUEL AND EXHAUST SYSTEM TORQUE SPECIFICATIONS

Item	N•m	in.-lb.	ft.-lb.
Carburetor heater	3.0	27	–
Exhaust fasteners	23	–	17
Fuel pump mounting bolts	10	88	–
Throttle position sensor	3.5	31	–

Table 6 FUEL AND EMISSION CONTROL SYSTEM TEST SPECIFICATIONS

Item	Specification
Carburetor heater coil resistance	12-18 ohms
Throttle position sensor	
Fully-closed resistance	3.5k-6.5k ohms
Wide-open resistance	78% of fully-closed reading

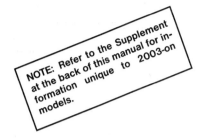

NOTE: Refer to the Supplement at the back of this manual for information unique to 2003-on models.

CHAPTER NINE

ELECTRICAL SYSTEM

This chapter covers service and test procedures for most of the electrical systems. The battery, spark plugs and ignition timing are covered in Chapter Three. Electrical system specifications are listed in **Tables 1-4** at the end of this chapter. Color wiring diagrams are located at the end of this manual.

The systems included in this chapter are:

1. Charging.
2. Ignition.
3. Starting.
4. Lighting.
5. Switches.
6. Various electrical components.
7. Cooling fan and switch.

PRELIMINARY INFORMATION

Peak Voltage and Resistance Testing

Resistance readings will vary with temperature. The resistance increases when the temperature increases and decreases when the temperature decreases.

Specifications for resistance are based on tests performed at a specific temperature (68° F [20° C]).

If a component is warm or hot, let it cool to room temperature. If a component is tested at a temperature that varies from the specification test temperature, a false reading may result.

The manufacturer specifies using the Suzuki Multi-Circuit Tester (part No. 09900-25008) and the peak voltage adapter for accurate resistance and voltage tests. Due to the specific resistance values of the semiconductors in this meter, using another meter may provide inaccurate results.

An equivalent tool is the Motion Pro IgnitionMate (part No. 08-0193). However, the test procedures in this chapter use the Suzuki Multi-Circuit Tester. If an alternative meter is being used, follow that manufacturer's instructions.

Make sure the battery of any tester being used is in good condition. The battery of an ohmmeter is the source for the current that is applied to the circuit being tested; accurate results depend on the battery having sufficient voltage.

All peak voltage specifications are minimum values. If the measured voltage meets or exceeds the specifications, the test results are acceptable. On some components the voltage may greatly exceed the minimum specification; this is normal.

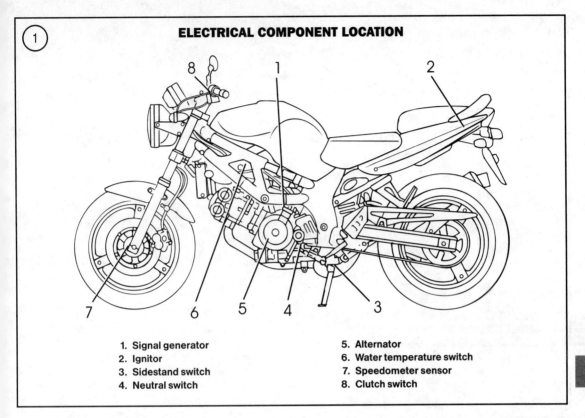

1. ELECTRICAL COMPONENT LOCATION

1. Signal generator
2. Ignitor
3. Sidestand switch
4. Neutral switch
5. Alternator
6. Water temperature switch
7. Speedometer sensor
8. Clutch switch

9

NOTE
Use caution when considering the replacement of an electrical component because it tests slightly out of specification. Resistance tests are performed on inactive circuits and are not always definitive indicators of a component's function under operating conditions.

Component Replacement

Most parts suppliers do not accept returns on electrical components. If the exact cause of any electrical system malfunction has not been determined, do not attempt to remedy the problem with guesswork and unnecessary parts replacement. If possible, have the suspect component or system tested by a professional technician before purchasing electrical components.

Electrical Component/Connector Location and Service

The location of electrical connectors can vary between model years. The position of the connectors may have been changed during previous repairs. Always confirm the wire colors to and from the connector and follow the wiring harness to the various components when performing tests.

Moisture can enter many of the electrical connectors and cause corrosion, which may cause a poor electrical connection. This may result in component failure and a possible breakdown on the road. To prevent moisture from entering into the various connectors, disconnect them and, after making sure the terminals are clean, pack the connector with dielectric grease. Do not use a substitute that may interfere with current flow. Dielectric grease is specifically formulated to seal the connector and not increase current resistance. For best results, the compound should fill the entire inner area of the connector. It is recommended that each time a connector is unplugged, it is cleaned and sealed with dielectric grease.

Ground connections are often overlooked when troubleshooting. Make sure they are corrosion-free and tight. Apply dielectric grease to the terminals before reconnecting them.

Refer to **Figure 1** and **Figure 2** for component/connector location.

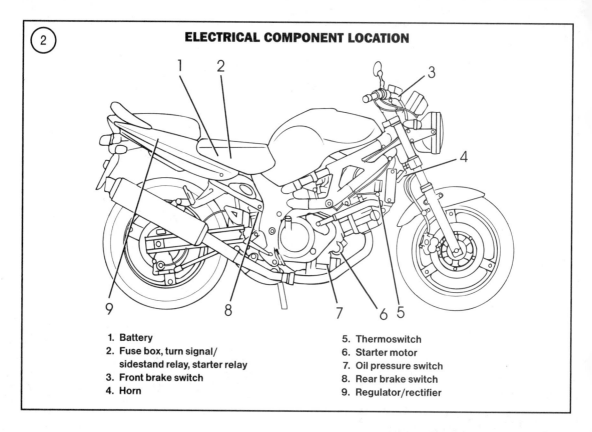

② **ELECTRICAL COMPONENT LOCATION**

1. Battery
2. Fuse box, turn signal/
   sidestand relay, starter relay
3. Front brake switch
4. Horn
5. Thermoswitch
6. Starter motor
7. Oil pressure switch
8. Rear brake switch
9. Regulator/rectifier

Negative Battery Cable

Some of the component replacement procedures and some of the test procedures in this chapter require disconnecting the negative battery cable as a safety precaution.

1. Turn the ignition switch OFF.
2. Remove the seat as described in Chapter Fifteen.
3. Remove the cover above the battery (**Figure 3**).
4. Remove the bolt and disconnect the negative battery cable (A, **Figure 4**) from the battery terminal.
5. Move the cable out of the way so it does not accidentally make contact with the battery terminal.
6. Once the procedure is completed, connect the negative battery cable to the terminal and tighten the bolt securely.
7. Install the battery cover (**Figure 3**).
8. Install the seat as described in Chapter Fifteen.

CHARGING SYSTEM

The charging system (**Figure 5**) consists of the battery, alternator and a voltage regulator/rectifier. Alternating current generated by the alternator is

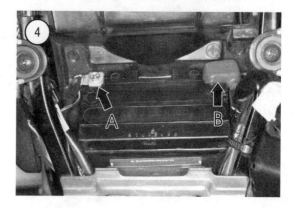

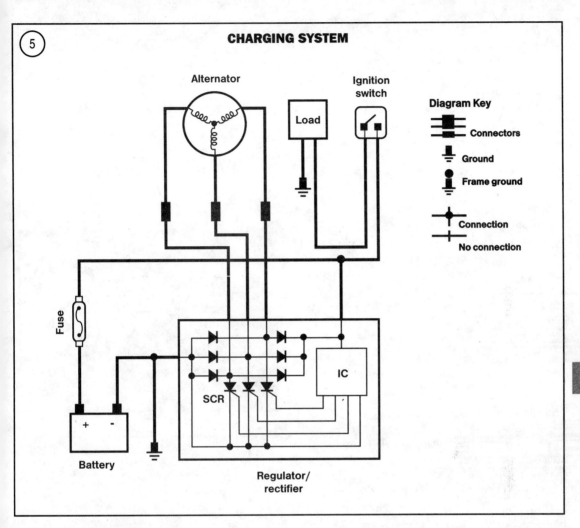

CHARGING SYSTEM

rectified to direct current. The voltage regulator maintains the voltage to the battery and additional electrical loads at a constant voltage regardless of variations in engine speed.

A malfunction in the charging system generally causes the battery to remain undercharged. To prevent damage to the alternator and the regulator/rectifier when testing and repairing the charging system, note the following precautions:

1. Always disconnect the negative battery cable, as described in this chapter, before removing a component from the charging system.

2. When it is necessary to charge the battery, remove the battery from the motorcycle and recharge it as described in Chapter Three.

3. Inspect the physical condition of the battery. Look for bulges or cracks in the case, leaking electrolyte or corrosion buildup.

4. Check the wiring in the charging system for signs of chafing, deterioration or other damage.

5. Check the wiring for corroded or loose connections. Clean, tighten or reconnect as required.

Battery Drain (Current Draw) Test

Perform this test before performing the output test.

1. Disconnect the negative battery cable as described in this chapter.

CAUTION
Before connecting the ammeter into the circuit in Step 2, set the meter to its highest amperage scale. This prevents a possible large current flow from damaging the meter or blowing the meter's fuse, if so equipped.

2. Connect the ammeter between the negative battery cable and the negative battery post (**Figure 6**). Switch the ammeter from its highest to lowest amperage scale while reading the meter. If the needle swings even the slightest amount, current is draining from the system. The battery will eventually discharge.

3. If the current drain is excessive, the probable causes are:

    a. Loose, dirty or faulty electrical system connectors in the charging system wiring harness system.

    b. Short circuit in the system.

    c. Damaged battery.

4. Isolate the current drain to a specific circuit by removing the fuses one at a time and observing the ammeter. If the current flow stops when a fuse is removed, that is the affected circuit. Further isolation can be achieved by disconnecting the connectors within that circuit.

5. After the current drain problem had been repaired, disconnect the ammeter leads and reconnect the negative battery lead.

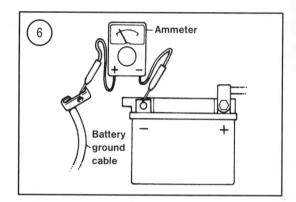

Charging System Output Test

Whenever charging system trouble is suspected, make sure the battery is fully charged and in good condition before going any further. Clean and test the battery as described in Chapter Three. Make sure all electrical connectors are tight and free of corrosion.

1. Start the engine and let it reach normal operating temperature. Shut off the engine.

2. Remove the front seat as described in Chapter Fifteen.

3. Remove the cover above the battery (**Figure 3**).

4. Connect a portable tachometer, following the manufacturer's instructions.

5. Remove the red plastic cover from the positive battery terminal (B, **Figure 4**).

6. Turn the headlight dimmer switch to the HI position.

7. Restart the engine and let it idle.

8. Connect the positive test lead of a 0-25 DC voltmeter to the positive battery terminal. Connect the negative test lead to the negative battery terminal.

9. Increase engine speed to 5000 rpm. The voltage reading should be 13.5-15.0 volts. If the voltage is outside the specified range, inspect the alternator and the voltage regulator as described in this chapter. The

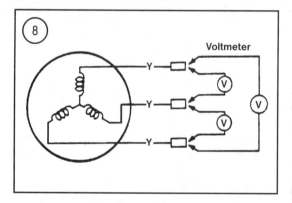

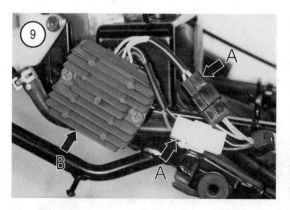

		+ Probe of tester to:				
		R	Y1	Y2	Y3	B/W
− Probe of tester to:	R		0.4 ~ 0.7	0.4 ~ 0.7	0.4 ~ 0.7	0.5 ~ 0.8
	Y1	Approx. 1.5		Approx. 1.5	Approx. 1.5	0.4 ~ 0.7
	Y2	Approx. 1.5	Approx. 1.5		Approx. 1.5	0.4 ~ 0.7
	Y3	Approx 1.5	Approx. 1.5	Approx. 1.5		0.4 ~ 0.7
	B/W	Approx. 1.5	Approx. 1.5	Approx. 1.5	Approx. 1.5	

REGULATOR/RECTIFIER TEST ⑩

R: Red, Y: Yellow, B: Black, W: White

voltage regulator/rectifier is a separate unit from the alternator and can be replaced individually.

10. If the charging voltage is too high, the voltage regulator/rectifier is probably faulty.

11. After completing the test, shut off the engine and disconnect the voltmeter and portable tachometer.

12. Install the cover (B, **Figure 4**) on the positive battery cable.

13. Install the battery cover (**Figure 3**) and the front seat as described in Chapter Fifteen.

Charging System No-Load Test

1. Remove the front seat as described in Chapter Fifteen.

2. Lift out the electrical unit module.

3. Disconnect the alternator three-wire (yellow wires) electrical connector (A, **Figure 7**).

4. Start the engine and let it idle.

NOTE
In Step 5, connect the voltmeter test leads to the alternator side of the electrical connector disconnected in Step 3.

5. Connect a 0-250 V (AC) voltmeter between each of the three terminals on the alternator side of the connector as shown in **Figure 8**.

6. Increase engine speed to 5000 rpm and check the voltage on the meter. The voltage should be greater than 70 volts.

7. Repeat this test for the remaining terminals. Take a total of three readings.

8. If the voltage in any test is less than the specified no-load voltage, shut off the engine and check the charging system wiring harness and connectors for dirt or loose-fitting terminals. Clean and repair as required. If the wiring and connectors are good, the alternator is defective and must be replaced.

9. Disconnect and remove the voltmeter and portable tachometer.

10. Reconnect the alternator connector (A, **Figure 7**). Make sure the connector is corrosion free and secure.

11. Install the electrical unit module and front seat.

VOLTAGE REGULATOR/RECTIFIER

Testing

Suzuki specifies the use of the Suzuki Multi-Circuit Tester (part No. 09900-25008) for testing the regulator/rectifier unit. If this tester is not available, have a Suzuki dealership test the unit.

NOTE
Before making this test, check the condition of the tester battery. To ensure an accurate reading, install a new battery.

1. Remove the rear fender as described in Chapter Fifteen.

2. Disconnect the two- and three-wire electrical connectors (A, **Figure 9**).

3. Connect the Suzuki Multi-Circuit Tester regulator/rectifier to the terminals indicated in **Figure 10** and check the voltage across each pair of terminals.

9

4. If any voltage reading differs from the stated value, replace the regulator/rectifier unit as described in this chapter.

5. If the voltage regulator/rectifier tests acceptable, install the rear fender as described in Chapter Fifteen.

Voltage Regulator/Rectifier Removal/Installation

1. Remove the rear fender as described in Chapter Fifteen.

2. Disconnect the negative battery cable as described in this chapter.

3. Disconnect the regulator/rectifier electrical connectors (A, **Figure 9**).

4. Remove the two mounting screws and remove the regulator/rectifier (B, **Figure 9**).

5. Install by reversing the preceding removal steps. Be sure the electrical connectors are tight and free of corrosion.

ALTERNATOR

Alternators generate alternating current. The electrical system, however, requires direct current in order to recharge the battery and operate the electrical equipment.

The alternator consists, basically, of the stator winding and the rotor. The system produces current by the rotation of the magnetized rotor around the three stator coils. The resultant three-phase alternating current is then rectified by the voltage regulator/rectifier into direct current.

Rotor Testing

The rotor is permanently magnetized and cannot be tested except by replacing it with a known good one. The rotor can lose magnetism over time or from a sharp impact. If defective, replace the rotor. It cannot be re-magnetized.

Stator Coil Continuity Test

1. Remove the front seat as described in Chapter Fifteen.

2. Lift out the electrical unit module.

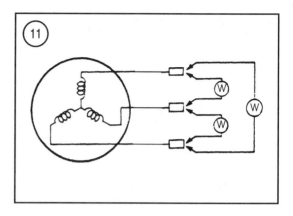

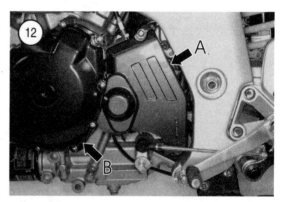

3. Start the engine and let it reach normal operating temperature. Shut off the engine.

4. Disconnect the alternator three-wire (yellow wires) electrical connector (A, **Figure 7**).

5. Check the continuity between each of the terminals on the alternator side of the connector as shown in **Figure 11**. If using an analog ohmmeter, be sure to zero the meter.

6. There should be continuity between all three terminals. If not, the alternator is defective and must be replaced.

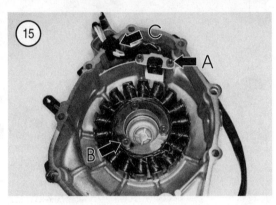

6. Remove the front seat and disconnect the alternator three-wire electrical connector (A, **Figure 7**) and the signal generator two-wire connector (B).

7. Remove the bolts securing the alternator cover (B, **Figure 12**) to the crankcase.

NOTE
Note the path of the wiring harness when withdrawing it in Step 8.

8. Remove the alternator cover while carefully withdrawing the wiring harness from the frame. Do not lose the two locating dowels behind the cover (**Figure 14**).

NOTE
The locating dowels may reside in the side of the engine or in the alternator cover.

9. Place several shop cloths on the workbench to protect the alternator cover. Turn the alternator cover upside down on these cloths.

10. Remove the bolts securing the signal generator (A, **Figure 15**) to the cover.

NOTE
Note the location of the wiring harness holder under the signal generator.

11. Remove the bolts securing the stator assembly (B, **Figure 15**) to the cover. Carefully pull the rubber grommet (C, **Figure 15**) from the cover and remove the stator and ignition signal generator assembly from the cover.

12. Install by reversing the preceding removal steps while noting the following:

   a. Apply a light coat of Threadlock 1342 or equivalent to the stator mounting bolt threads before installation. Tighten the stator retaining bolts to 10 N•m (88 in.-lb.).

   b. Properly install the wiring harness holder under the signal generator. Tighten the signal generator bolts to 5.5 N•m (49 in.-lb.).

   c. Make sure the electrical connector is free of corrosion and is tight.

   d. If removed, install the two locating dowels (**Figure 14**).

   e. Install a new gasket.

7. Next check for continuity between each terminal in the connector and ground. If there is continuity, one or more of the stator wires is shorted to ground. Replace the stator assembly.

8. Disconnect and remove the ohmmeter.

9. Reconnect the alternator electrical connector. Make sure the connector is corrosion free and tight.

10. Install the electrical unit module and front seat.

Stator Assembly Removal/Installation

The stator assembly is located within the alternator cover.

1. Remove the engine sprocket cover (A, **Figure 12**).

2. Detach the clutch release return spring (A, **Figure 13**).

3. Loosen the clutch adjusting nut (B, **Figure 13**).

4. Remove the two retaining bolts, then remove the clutch release assembly (C, **Figure 13**).

5. Loosen the clutch cable mounting nuts (D, **Figure 13**) and separate the cable from the mounting arm on the alternator cover.

f. Install a new gasket washer onto each of the indicated alternator cover bolts (**Figure 16**).

Rotor Removal/Installation

1. Remove the alternator cover as described in this chapter.
2. Place a wrench on the flats of the rotor (A, **Figure 17**), then remove the alternator rotor bolt (B) and washer.

> *CAUTION*
> *Do not attempt to remove the rotor without a puller. Doing so will ultimately lead to some form of damage to the engine and/or rotor. Pullers are available from part suppliers or dealerships (Suzuki part No. 09930-30450). If one is not available, have a dealership remove the rotor.*

3. Install the rotor removal tool (A, **Figure 18**) onto the threads of the rotor.
4. Hold the rotor with a suitable wrench (B, **Figure 18**). Turn the bolt or handle of the rotor removal tool until the rotor disengages from the crankshaft taper. Remove the rotor from the crankshaft.

> *CAUTION*
> *If the rotor is difficult to remove, strike the end of the rotor removal tool firmly with a hammer. Do **not** strike the rotor.*

> *CAUTION*
> *Do not apply excessive pressure to the puller, as this could strip the threads in the crankshaft. If the rotor is difficult to remove, have a Suzuki dealership perform the procedure.*

5. Remove the rotor removal tool.
6. Inspect the inside of the rotor (**Figure 18**) for any metal debris that may have been picked up by the magnets. These small metal bits can damage the alternator stator assembly.
7. Install by reversing the preceding removal steps while noting the following:
   a. Use aerosol parts cleaner to clean all oil residue from the crankshaft taper and the matching tapered surface in the rotor. This ensures a good fit between the rotor and the crankshaft.

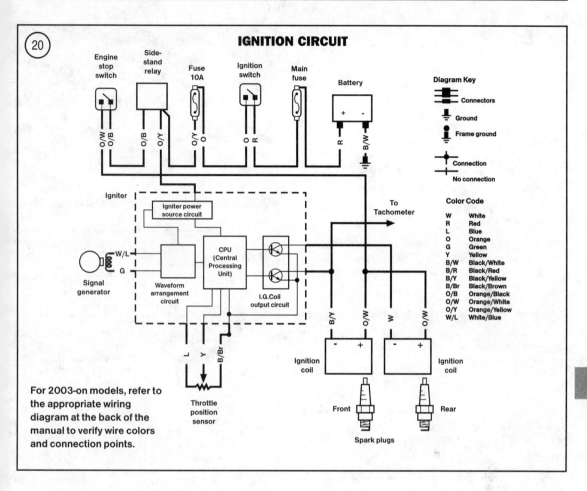

IGNITION CIRCUIT

Diagram Key

Connectors
Ground
Frame ground
Connection
No connection

Color Code

W	White
R	Red
L	Blue
O	Orange
G	Green
Y	Yellow
B/W	Black/White
B/R	Black/Red
B/Y	Black/Yellow
B/Br	Black/Brown
O/B	Orange/Black
O/W	Orange/White
O/Y	Orange/Yellow
W/L	White/Blue

For 2003-on models, refer to the appropriate wiring diagram at the back of the manual to verify wire colors and connection points.

b. Make sure the key is in place on the crankshaft (**Figure 19**).

c. Apply a light coat of engine oil to the mounting bolt threads before installation.

d. Make sure the washer is mounted on the rotor bolt, then tighten the rotor bolt to 120 N•m (88 ft.-lb.).

ELECTRONIC IGNITION SYSTEM

The engine is equipped with an electronic ignition system (**Figure 20**). The system consists of a signal generator, igniter unit, throttle position sensor, and two ignition coils and spark plugs.

The signal generator portion of the system consists of external projections on the alternator rotor and the signal generator (or pickup coil). The throttle position sensor is mounted on the carburetor assembly.

As the crankshaft rotates, the projections on the alternator rotor pass the signal generator, which sends a signal to the igniter unit. The CPU (part of the igniter) uses this signal, input from the throttle position sensor and a stored digital data map to determine the optimum ignition timing for the operating conditions.

The system includes an engine speed limiter. If the engine exceeds 10,500 rpm, the primary current to the ignition coil/spark plug caps is interrupted.

Ignition System Precautions

Certain measures must be taken to protect the ignition system. Damage to the semiconductors in the system may occur if any of the electrical connections are disconnected while the engine is running.

Troubleshooting

Refer to *Ignition System* in Chapter Two.

9

Signal Generator

Peak voltage test

Refer to *Preliminary Information* at the beginning of this chapter.

> *WARNING*
> *High voltage is present during ignition system operation. Do not touch ignition components, wires or test leads while the engine is running or cranking.*

> *NOTE*
> *All peak voltage specifications are minimum values. If the measured voltage meets or exceeds the specifications, the test results are acceptable.*

1. Remove the rear seat as described in Chapter Fifteen.
2. Disconnect the igniter connector (**Figure 21**) from the CDI unit.
3. Turn the tester's knob to voltage.
4. Connect the negative test probe to the white/blue terminal on the connector, and connect the positive test probe to the green terminal (**Figure 22**).
5. Shift the transmission into neutral and turn the ignition switch ON.
6. Press the starter button and crank the engine for a few seconds and record the highest reading.
7. If the signal generator peak voltage is less than 3.0 volts, check the peak voltage at the signal generator coupler (**Figure 23**) by performing the following:
   a. Remove the rear fender as described in Chapter Fifteen.
   b. Disconnect the two-wire signal generator connector (**Figure 24**).
   c. Connect the positive test probe to the green terminal on the signal generator side of the connector and connect the negative test probe to the white terminal. **Figure 23**.
   d. Shift the transmission into neutral and turn the ignition switch ON.
   e. Press the starter button and crank the engine for a few seconds and record the highest reading.
8. If the peak voltage measured at the signal generator connector is normal but the peak voltage at the igniter connector is less than 3.0 volts, check the wiring between the two components.

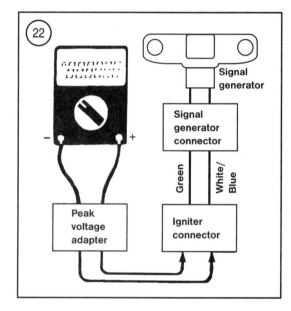

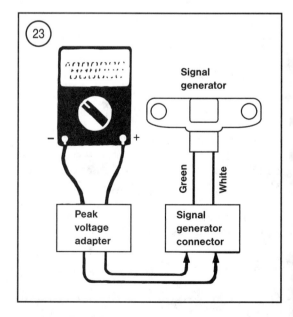

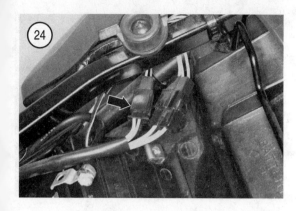

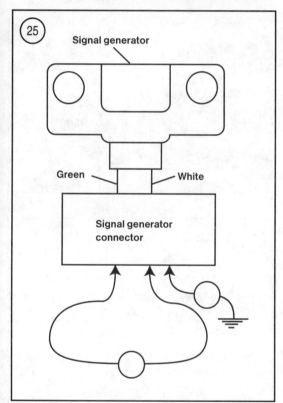

Signal generator

Green / White

Signal generator
connector

9. If the peak voltage at both the signal generator connector and the igniter connector are less than 3.0 volts, replace the signal generator.

10. If all tests are acceptable, reconnect the electrical connector. Make sure the electrical connector is free of corrosion and is tight.

11. Install the rear fender and rear seat.

Resistance test

Refer to *Preliminary Information* at the beginning of this chapter.

1. Remove the rear seat and rear frame cover as described in Chapter Fifteen.

2. Disconnect the two-wire signal generator connector (**Figure 23**).

3. Set the ohmmeter to the R × 100 scale, and check the resistance between the white and green terminals in the signal generator side of the connector (**Figure 25**). If the signal generator coil resistance is outside the range of 140-230 ohms, replace the signal generator.

4. Check the continuity between the green terminal in the signal generator connector and ground (**Figure 25**). There should be no continuity (infinite resistance). If there is continuity, replace the signal generator.

5. If all tests are acceptable, reconnect the electrical connector. Make sure the electrical connector is free of corrosion and is secure.

6. Install the rear fender and rear seat.

Signal Generator Replacement

The signal generator (A, **Figure 26**) and alternator stator (B) are located inside the alternator cover. The signal generator and stator are only available as a unit assembly. If the signal generator is faulty, replace it by following the stator replacement procedure found in this chapter.

Ignition Coil

The ignition coil is a form of transformer that develops the high voltage required to jump the spark plug gap. The only maintenance required is keeping the electrical connections clean and tight, and making sure both coils are mounted securely.

The ignition coil for the No. 1 (front) cylinder is located near the rear cylinder head adjacent to the

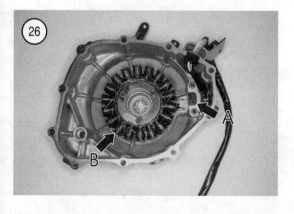

upper frame tube (**Figure 27**). The ignition coil for the No. 2 (rear) cylinder is located between the rear cylinder head and the battery (**Figure 28**).

Primary peak voltage test

The Suzuki Multi-Circuit Tester (part No. 09900-25008) with the peak voltage adapter, or the Motion Pro IgnitionMate (part No.08-0193), or an equivalent peak voltage tester is required for this test.

1. Lift and support the fuel tank.
2. Remove both spark plugs as described in Chapter Three.
3. Connect a new spark plug to each plug cap.
4. Ground both spark plugs to the crankcase.

> *WARNING*
> *High voltage is present during ignition system operation. Do not touch ignition components, wires or test leads while cranking or running the engine.*

> *NOTE*
> *All peak voltage specifications are minimum values. If the measured voltage meets or exceeds the specification, the test results are satisfactory. On some components, the voltage may greatly exceed the minimum specification.*

5. Check the peak voltage for the No. 1 cylinder by performing the following:
   a. Turn the tester knob to voltage.

> *NOTE*
> *Do not disconnect the wires from the ignition coil when performing the following test. If it is not possible to contact the coil terminal with the tester probe, pierce the wire using a needle probe.*

   b. Connect the positive test probe to the black/yellow wire or terminal on the ignition coil and connect the negative test probe to ground. See **Figure 29**.
   c. Shift the transmission into neutral and turn the ignition switch ON.
   d. Press the starter button and crank the engine for a few seconds while reading the meter.

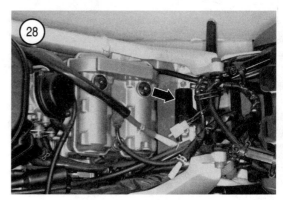

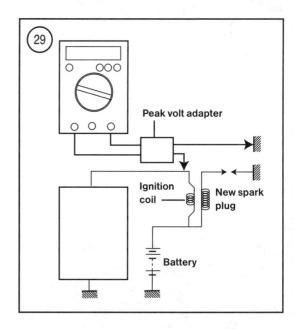

Record the highest meter reading. The minimum peak voltage is 150 volts.

6. Check the peak voltage for the No. 2 cylinder by performing Step 5, except connect the positive test probe to the white wire or terminal on the ignition coil.

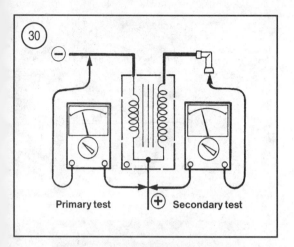

Primary test   ⊕   Secondary test

7. If the peak voltage reading on either ignition coil is less than specified, measure the resistance on that ignition coil.

Resistance test

The Suzuki Multi-Circuit Tester (part No. 09900-25008) is required for accurate resistance testing of the ignition coil/plug cap. Refer to the *Preliminary Information* section at the beginning of this chapter.

1. Disconnect all ignition coil wires (including the spark plug leads from the spark plugs) before testing.
2. Set an ohmmeter to the R × 1 scale and measure the primary coil resistance between the positive (orange/white wire) and the negative terminals (white or black/yellow wire) on the ignition coil (**Figure 30**). Specified primary coil resistance is 3.5-5.5 ohms.
3. Set the ohmmeter to the R × 1000 scale and measure the secondary coil resistance between the spark

plug lead (with the spark plug cap attached) and the positive coil terminal. Specified primary coil resistance is 20,000-31,000 ohms.
4. If either measurement does not meet specification, replace the coil. If the coil exhibits visible damage, replace it.
5. Reconnect all ignition coil wires to the ignition coil.
6. Repeat this procedure for the other ignition coil.

Removal/installation

1. Raise and support the fuel tank.
2. Disconnect the negative battery cable.
3. Disconnect all ignition coil wires (including the spark plug leads from the spark plugs).
4. Remove the screws securing the ignition coil to the frame.
5. Install by reversing the preceding removal steps. Make sure all electrical connections are corrosion-free and secure.

Igniter Unit

No test procedure is available. If all other ignition system components have been tested, replace the igniter unit and recheck ignition system operation.

> *NOTE*
> *Faulty wiring and connections cause many ignition problems. Make sure to check all wires and connections before presuming the igniter unit is faulty.*

> *NOTE*
> *Because electrical components are not returnable, ask a Suzuki dealership to check the igniter unit before purchasing a new unit.*

Replacement

1. Remove the rear seat as described in Chapter Fifteen.
2. Remove the tool kit.
3. Disconnect the connector (**Figure 31**) from the igniter.
4. Remove the rear fender as described in Chapter Fifteen.

5. Remove the three rear taillight mounting bracket bolts (**Figure 32**). Do not disconnect the taillight wire connectors. Move the taillight mounting bracket out of the way.

6. Remove the igniter mounting screws (**Figure 33**) and remove the igniter.

7. Reinstall the igniter by reversing the preceding removal steps.

STARTING SYSTEM

The starting system (**Figure 34**) consists of the starter, starter relay, clutch switch, sidestand switch, turn signal/sidestand relay, neutral switch, engine stop switch and the starter button. When the starter button is pressed, it engages the starter relay and completes the circuit, allowing electricity to flow from the battery to the starter.

The starter rotates the engine crankshaft through the starter idler gear and the starter clutch. Refer to Chapter Five for service information related to those components.

> *CAUTION*
> *Do not operate the starter for more than five seconds at a time. Let it cool approximately 10 seconds before operating it again.*

Troubleshooting

Refer to Chapter Two.

Starter Removal/Installation

1. Securely support the motorcycle on level ground.

2. Disconnect the negative battery cable as described in this chapter.

3. Pull back the rubber boot (A, **Figure 35**) from the starter electrical connector.

4. Remove the starter cable retaining nut (B, **Figure 35**) and disconnect the starter cable from the starter.

5. Remove the two bolts (C, **Figure 35**) securing the starter to the crankcase.

6. Remove the starter.

7. Thoroughly clean the starter mounting pads on the crankcase and the mounting lugs on the starter motor.

8. Inspect the O-ring (**Figure 36**) on the drive end of the starter for hardness or deterioration. Replace the O-ring if necessary. Apply clean engine oil to the O-ring before installing the starter.

9. Install the starter by reversing the removal procedure while noting the following:

    a. Install the oil pressure switch cable retainer onto the lower starter bolt (C, **Figure 35**).

    b. Tighten the starter mounting bolts to 6 N•m (53 in.-lb.).

    c. Connect the starter cable so it points at a 45° angle toward the rear of the starter. Tighten the starter cable retaining nut securely and press the rubber boot back into position.

    d. Connect the negative battery cable.

Starter Disassembly

Refer to **Figure 37** when performing this procedure.

> *NOTE*
> *While disassembling the starter, lay the parts out in the order of removal.*

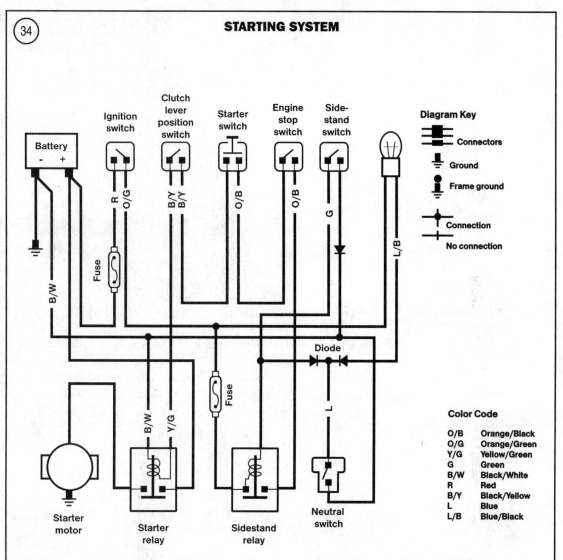

STARTING SYSTEM

Ignition switch

Clutch lever position switch

Starter switch

Engine stop switch

Side-stand switch

Battery

Fuse

B/W

R

O/G

B/Y B/Y

O/B

O/B

G

L/B

Diagram Key

Connectors

Ground

Frame ground

Connection

No connection

Diode

Fuse

B/W

Y/G

L

Diode

Starter motor

Starter relay

Sidestand relay

Neutral switch

Color Code

O/B	Orange/Black
O/G	Orange/Green
Y/G	Yellow/Green
G	Green
B/W	Black/White
R	Red
B/Y	Black/Yellow
L	Blue
L/B	Blue/Black

For 2003-on models, refer to the appropriate wiring diagram at the back of the manual to verify wire colors and connection points.

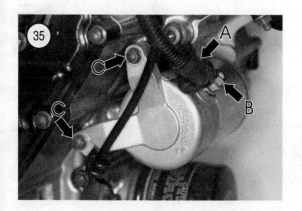

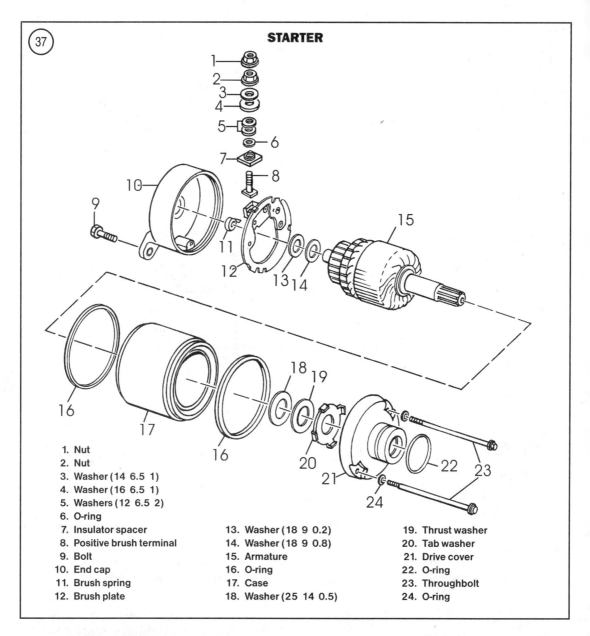

STARTER

1. Nut
2. Nut
3. Washer (14 6.5 1)
4. Washer (16 6.5 1)
5. Washers (12 6.5 2)
6. O-ring
7. Insulator spacer
8. Positive brush terminal
9. Bolt
10. End cap
11. Brush spring
12. Brush plate
13. Washer (18 9 0.2)
14. Washer (18 9 0.8)
15. Armature
16. O-ring
17. Case
18. Washer (25 14 0.5)
19. Thrust washer
20. Tab washer
21. Drive cover
22. O-ring
23. Throughbolt
24. O-ring

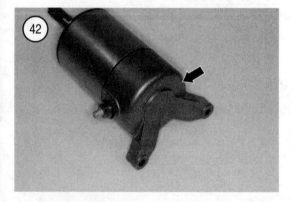

9

When removing a part from the starter, set it next to the one previously removed. This is an easy way to remember the correct relationship of all parts.

1. Remove the throughbolts (**Figure 38**) and O-ring seals.
2. Remove the drive cover (**Figure 39**) from the case.
3. Remove the tab washer (**Figure 40**).
4. Slide the washers (**Figure 41**) off the shaft.
5. Remove the end cap (**Figure 42**) from the case.
6. Slide the washers (**Figure 43**) off the armature.
7. Remove the armature (**Figure 44**) from the starter case.

NOTE
Before removing the nuts and washers, record their descriptions and order. They must be reinstalled in the same order to insulate the positive brush plate assembly from the case.

8. Remove the nut, washers, bushing and O-ring (**Figure 45**) securing the brush holder assembly to the end cap.

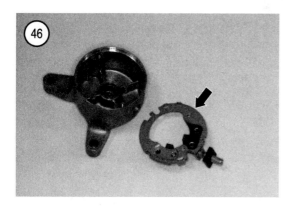

9. Pull the brush holder assembly (**Figure 46**) out of the end cap and remove it.

> *CAUTION*
> *Do not immerse the wire windings of the armature (**Figure 47**) in solvent as the insulation may be damaged. To clean the windings, wipe them with a cloth lightly moistened with solvent, then thoroughly dry.*

10. Clean all grease, dirt and carbon from all components.

11. Inspect all starter components as described in this chapter.

Starter Assembly

> *NOTE*
> *In the next step, reinstall all parts in the same order as noted during removal. This is essential to insulate the positive brush plate assembly from the case.*

1. Install the insulator spacer (7, **Figure 37**) onto the positive terminal stud and bottom the spacer on the stud.

2. Install the brush holder assembly into the end cap. Align the notches on the brush holder plate with the projections on the end cap (**Figure 48**).

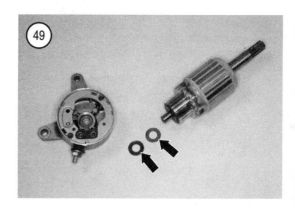

3. Install the nut, washers, bushing and O-ring (**Figure 45**) securing the brush holder assembly to the end cap. Refer to notes made during disassembly and **Figure 37** for proper sequence of parts.

4. Install the washers (**Figure 49**) onto the armature.

5. Hold the armature upright and insert the commutator end of the armature into the end cap (**Figure**

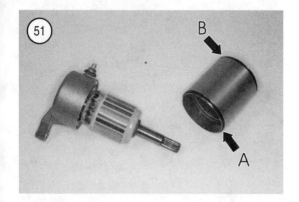

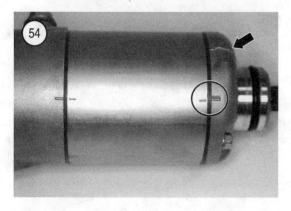

50). Do not damage the brushes during this step. Hold back the brushes as the commutator passes by them, then ensure both brushes contact the armature. Push the assembly down until it bottoms.

6. Keep the assembly in this position and slowly rotate the armature coil assembly to make sure it rotates freely with the brushes in place.

NOTE
Hold the armature and end cap together during the next step. The magnets in the case will try to pull the armature out of the end cap and disengage the brushes.

7. Install the O-ring (A, **Figure 51**) into the recess at the end of the case.

8. Install the case onto the armature and end cap. Align the marks on the case and end cap (**Figure 52**).

9. Install the washers (**Figure 41**) onto the armature shaft.

10. Install the tab washer (**Figure 53**) into the drive cover so the tabs on the washer fit into the recesses in the cover.

11. Install an O-ring (B, **Figure 51**) into the case recess.

12. Install the drive cover onto the case. Align the marks on the case and cover (**Figure 54**).

13. Install the O-rings (**Figure 55**) onto the throughbolts and apply a light coat of clean engine oil to them.

14. Install the throughbolts and tighten securely. After the throughbolts are tightened, check the seams to ensure the end covers are pulled tight against the case.

Starter Inspection

The only parts that are available separately are the brushes, the washer, the O-rings and the case bolts. If any other part of the starter motor is faulty, replace the starter motor as an assembly.

1. Inspect each brush for abnormal wear. Replace as necessary.

2. Inspect the commutator (A, **Figure 56**). The mica in a good commutator is below the surface of the copper bars. On a worn commutator, the mica and copper bars may be worn to the same level (**Figure 57**). If necessary, have the commutator serviced by a dealership or electrical repair shop.

3. Check the entire length of the armature coil for straightness or heat damage. Rotate the ball bearing and check for roughness or binding.

4. Inspect the armature shaft where it rides in the bushing (B, **Figure 56**). Check for wear, burrs or other damage. If worn or damaged, replace the starter assembly.

5. Inspect the commutator copper bars (A, **Figure 56**) for discoloration. If a pair of bars is discolored, grounded armature coils are indicated.

6. Use an ohmmeter and perform the following:
   a. Check for continuity between the commutator bars (**Figure 58**); there should be continuity between pairs of bars.
   b. Check for continuity between the commutator bars and the shaft (**Figure 59**); there should be no continuity (infinite resistance).
   c. If the unit fails either of these tests, replace the starter assembly. The armature cannot be replaced individually.

7. Use an ohmmeter and perform the following:
   a. Check for continuity between the starter cable terminal (**Figure 60**) and the end cap. There should be no continuity.
   b. Check for continuity between the starter cable terminal and the positive brushes (**Figure 61**); there should be continuity (indicated resistance).

8. Inspect the seal and needle bearing (A, **Figure 62**) in the drive cover. Inspect the seal for wear, hardness or damage. The bearing must turn smoothly without excessive play or noise. Neither the seal nor bearing is available separate from the drive cover.

9. Inspect the bushing (B, **Figure 62**) in the end cap for wear or damage. The bushing cannot be re-

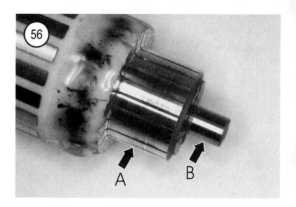

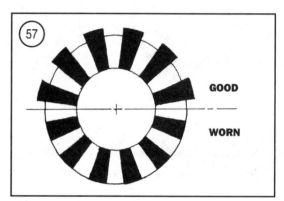

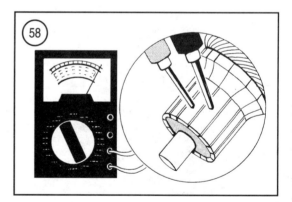

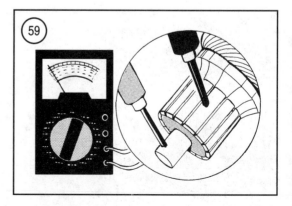

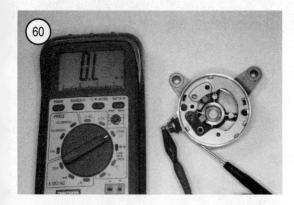

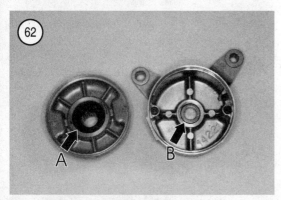

placed if damaged. The starter must be replaced, as this is not a separate part.

10. Inspect the magnets within the case. If they have picked up any small metal particles, remove the particles prior to reassembly. Then inspect for loose, chipped or damaged magnets.

11. Inspect the brush holder and springs for wear or damage. Replace if necessary.

12. Inspect the end cover and drive cover for wear or damage. If either is damaged, replace the starter.

13. Check the throughbolts for thread damage; clean up with the appropriate size metric die. Inspect the O-rings for hardness, deterioration or damage. Replace as necessary.

Starter Relay Removal/Installation

1. Remove the frame covers and front seat as described in Chapter Fifteen.

2. Disconnect the negative battery cable as described in this chapter.

3. Disconnect the starter relay primary connector (A, **Figure 63**).

4. Remove the cover (B, **Figure 63**) from the starter relay.

5. Disconnect the black starter motor lead and the red battery lead from the starter relay.

6. Install by reversing the preceding removal steps while noting the following:

   a. Install both electrical red and black cables to the relay and tighten the nuts securely.

   b. Make sure the electrical connectors are tight and that the rubber boot is properly installed to keep out moisture.

   c. Install the cover.

Testing

Refer to *Starting System* in Chapter Two for starter relay test procedures.

LIGHTING SYSTEM

The lighting system consists of a headlight (dual headlights on Model SV650S), taillight/brake light, license plate light, turn signals, instrument cluster indicator lights and assorted relays. **Table 3** lists replacement bulbs for these components.

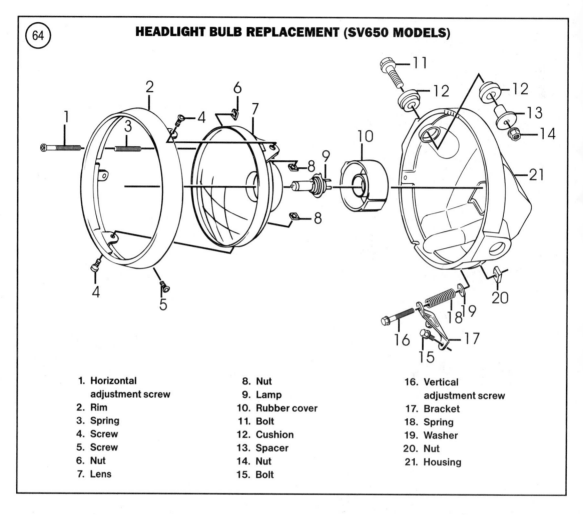

HEADLIGHT BULB REPLACEMENT (SV650 MODELS)

1. Horizontal adjustment screw	8. Nut	16. Vertical adjustment screw
2. Rim	9. Lamp	17. Bracket
3. Spring	10. Rubber cover	18. Spring
4. Screw	11. Bolt	19. Washer
5. Screw	12. Cushion	20. Nut
6. Nut	13. Spacer	21. Housing
7. Lens	14. Nut	
	15. Bolt	

Always use the correct wattage bulb as indicated in this section. A larger wattage bulb provides a dim light, and a smaller wattage bulb will burn out prematurely.

Headlight Bulb Replacement

SV650 models

Refer to **Figure 64** for this procedure.

> *WARNING*
> *If the headlight has just burned out or has just been turned off, it will be **hot**! Do not touch the bulb. Wait for the bulb to cool before removing it.*

> *CAUTION*
> *All models are equipped with a quartz-halogen bulb. Do not touch the*

*bulb glass (**Figure 65**) with bare fingers because traces of oil on the bulb will drastically reduce the life of the bulb. Clean any traces of oil or other chemicals from the bulb with a cloth moistened in alcohol or lacquer thinner.*

1. Remove the screws on both sides securing the headlight assembly in the headlight housing (A, **Figure 66**).

2. Carefully pull the headlight lens unit out of the housing.

3. Disconnect the electrical connector/socket from the headlight lens unit.

4. Remove the rubber cover.

5. Detach the bulb retaining spring.

6. Pull out the bulb.

7. Install by reversing the preceding removal steps.

SV650S models

> *WARNING*
> *If the headlight has just burned out or has just been turned off, it will be **hot**! Do not touch the bulb. Wait for the bulb to cool before removing it.*

> *CAUTION*
> *All models are equipped with quartz-halogen bulbs. Do not touch the bulb glass (**Figure 65**) with bare fingers because traces of oil on the bulb will drastically reduce the life of the bulb. Clean any traces of oil or other chemicals from the bulb with a cloth moistened in alcohol or lacquer thinner.*

1. Disconnect the electrical connector (**Figure 67**) by pulling it *straight out* from the back of the headlight assembly.

2. Pull the tab at the base and remove the rubber dust cover (**Figure 68**). Check the rubber cover for tears or deterioration; replace it if necessary.

3. Unhook the light bulb retaining clip (**Figure 69**) and pivot it out of the way.

4. Remove the defective bulb.

5. Align the three tangs on the new bulb with the notches in the headlight housing and install the bulb.

6. Hook the retaining clip (**Figure 69**) over the bulb to hold it in place.

7. Install the rubber cover so the TOP mark (**Figure 70**) on the cover sits at the top of the headlight assembly. Make sure the cover is correctly seated against the lens assembly and the bulb.

8. Correctly align the electrical connector terminals with the bulb and connect it to the bulb. Push it *straight on* until it bottoms on the bulb and the rubber cover.

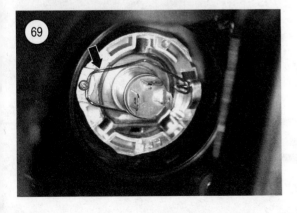

9

9. Check headlight operation.

**Headlight Lens, Housing and Bracket
Removal/Installation (SV650 Models)**

Refer to **Figure 64** for this procedure.

1. Remove the screw (A, **Figure 66**) securing the lens assembly from each side of the headlight case.

2. Place a clean shop cloth on top of the front fender.

3. Remove the headlight lens assembly (B, **Figure 66**) from the headlight housing and rest it on the front fender.

4. Disconnect the electrical connector from the bulb and remove the lens assembly.

5. To remove the lens from the trim bezel, perform the following:

   a. Remove the horizontal adjust screw and spring (**Figure 71**, typical).

   b. On each side, remove the screw, lockwasher and nut (**Figure 72**, typical) securing the lens to the trim ring.

   c. Remove the lens from the trim ring.

6A. To remove the headlight housing, perform the following:

   a. Remove the lens assembly as previously described.

   b. Remove the bolt, washer, nut, lockwasher and washer (**Figure 73**, typical) securing the headlight housing to the mounting brackets on each side.

   c. Remove the lower bracket mounting bolts (A, **Figure 74**).

   d. Move the headlight housing (A, **Figure 75**, typical) away from the steering head area and carefully move all electrical connectors and harnesses out through the openings (B) in the headlight housing.

   e. Remove the headlight housing. Do not lose the collar and rubber cushion in each mounting hole.

> *NOTE*
> *The following step is provided if the entire headlight housing and bracket assembly must be relocated for steering stem or fork service.*

6B. To relocate the headlight housing and brackets, perform the following:

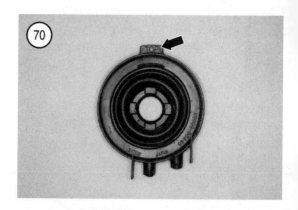

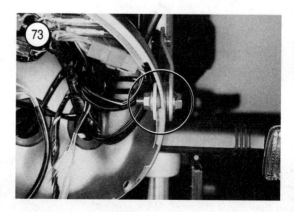

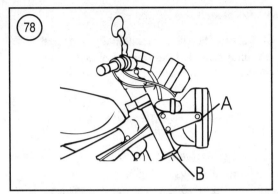

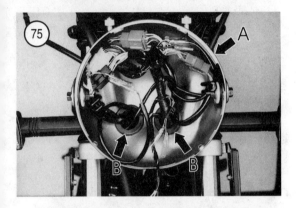

a. Remove the lower bracket mounting bolts (A, **Figure 74**).

b. Remove the headlight bracket mounting bolts (B, **Figure 74**) and move the headlight assembly out of the way.

7. Install by reversing the preceding removal steps.

Headlight Lens/Housing Removal/Installation (SV650S Models)

1. Remove the instrument panel as described in this chapter.

2. Disconnect the headlight connectors.

3. Remove the headlight housing retaining nuts (**Figure 76**) and remove the headlight housing assembly.

4. Inspect the headlight lens/housing (**Figure 77**) for damage and internal moisture. If damaged, replace the entire unit because there are no replacement parts available.

5. After installation, adjust the headlights as described below.

Headlight Adjustment

SV650 models

Adjust the headlight horizontally and vertically according to local Department of Motor Motorcycle regulations.

To adjust the headlight horizontally, turn the horizontal adjustment screw (A, **Figure 78**) on the right side of the headlight.

For vertical adjustment, turn the vertical adjustment screw (B, **Figure 78**) on the underside of the headlight.

9

SV650S models

Adjust the headlight horizontally and vertically according to local Department of Motor Motorcycle regulations.

NOTE
There are four adjustment screws, two for each headlight.

To adjust the headlight horizontally, turn the horizontal adjustment screw (A, **Figure 79**) in either direction until the aim is correct. The screws are accessible through holes in the instrument panel cover.

For vertical adjustment, turn the vertical adjustment screw (B, **Figure 79**) in either direction until the aim is correct. The screws are located just above the fairing brace below the instrument panel cover.

Position Bulb Replacement (SV650S Models)

1. Remove the lens (**Figure 80**).
2. Remove the bulb by pulling it straight out from the socket.
3. Install a new bulb.

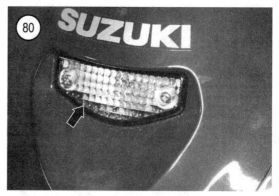

Taillight/Brake Light Bulb Replacement

1. Remove the lens (**Figure 81**).
2. Push the defective bulb into the socket, turn it counterclockwise and remove it.
3. Install a new bulb.

License Plate Light Bulb Replacement

1. Remove the cover (**Figure 82**).
2. Remove the bulb by pulling it straight out from the socket.
3. Install a new bulb.

Front and Rear Turn Signal Bulb Replacement

1. Remove the lower screw (**Figure 83**) securing the lens to the housing.
2. Partially remove the lens (**Figure 84**) from the housing and turn it around.
3. Rotate the bulb socket counterclockwise and remove it from the lens (**Figure 85**).

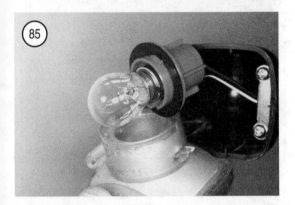

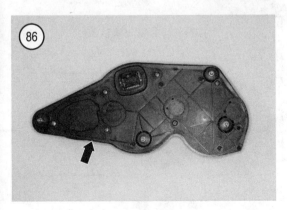

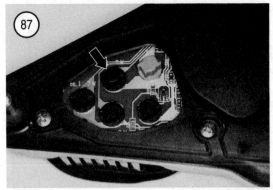

4. Push the bulb in, turn it counterclockwise, and remove it from the bulb socket. Discard the defective bulb.

5. Align the bulb pins with the bulb socket grooves. Push the bulb into the socket, turn it clockwise and release it. Check that the bulb is locked in the bulb socket.

6. Insert the bulb socket into the housing. Turn the bulb socket clockwise and lock it in place.

7. Check the turn signal light operation.

8. Install the lens into the housing. Install and tighten the lower screw.

Instrument Panel Indicator and Meter Bulb Replacement

SV650 models

1. Remove the instrument panel as described in this chapter.

2. Remove the instrument panel mounting bracket.

3. Pull out the bulb socket for the defective bulb.

4. Pull out the defective bulb.

5. Inspect the bulb socket for corrosion and clean if necessary.

6. Install a new bulb.

7. Install the bulb socket into the instrument panel.

8. Install the mounting bracket on the instrument panel, then reinstall the instrument panel.

SV650S models

1. Remove the instrument panel as described in this chapter.

2. Remove the back cover on the instrument panel (**Figure 86**).

3. Carefully rotate the bulb socket and remove it (**Figure 87**) from the printed circuit board on the instrument panel.

88 IGNITION SWITCH (EXCEPT AUSTRALIA)

Position \ Color	R	O	Gr	Br	O/R	B/W
OFF						
ON	●—●		●—●		●—●	
P	●———————●					

89 IGNITION SWITCH (AUSTRALIA)

Position \ Color	R	O	O/R	B/W
OFF				
ON	●—●		●—●	

4. Pull out the defective bulb and install a new bulb.

5. Install the bulb socket into the instrument panel. Rotate it until it is secure on the printed circuit board.

> *NOTE*
> *If a new bulb does not work, check the printed circuit board for broken circuit strips on the board. Also check the bulb socket for corrosion.*

6. Install the back cover of the instrument panel, then reinstall the instrument panel.

SWITCHES

Testing

Test switches for continuity with an ohmmeter (see Chapter One), or a test light at the switch connector plug by operating the switch in each of its operating positions and comparing the results with its switch operation diagram. For example, **Figure 88** shows a continuity diagram for an ignition switch. The horizontal line indicates which terminals should show continuity when the switch is in that position. Continuing with the example, in the PARK position there should be continuity between the red and brown terminals. With the switch in the OFF position there should be no continuity between any of the terminals.

Refer to **Table 4** for color codes. When testing switches, refer to the appropriate continuity diagrams (**Figures 88-100**) and note the following:

1. First check the fuse as described in *Fuses* in this chapter.

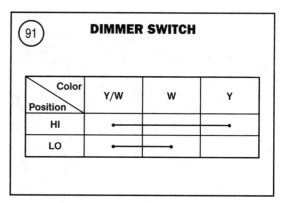

90 LIGHTING SWITCH (EXCEPT AUSTRALIA, CANADA AND U.S.)

91 DIMMER SWITCH

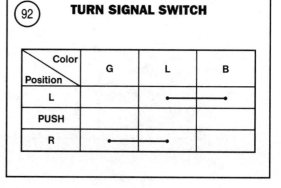

92 TURN SIGNAL SWITCH

93 PASSING LIGHT SWITCH (EXCEPT CANADA AND U.S.)

Color Position	O/R	Y
•		
PUSH	•——————•	

94 ENGINE STOP SWITCH

Color Position	O/B	O/W
•		
RUN	•——————•	

95 STARTER BUTTON

Color Position	O/W	Y/G
•		
PUSH	•——————•	

96 HORN BUTTON

Color Position	B/L	B/W
•		
PUSH	•——————•	

97 FRONT BRAKE LIGHT SWITCH

Color Position	B	B/R
OFF		
ON	•——————•	

98 REAR BRAKE LIGHT SWITCH

Color Position	O	W/B
OFF		
ON	•——————•	

99 CLUTCH SWITCH

Color Position	B/Y	B/Y
OFF		
ON	•——————•	

100 OIL PRESSURE SWITCH

Color Position	B	Ground
ON (engine is stopped)	•——————•	
OFF (engine is running)		

9

2. Make sure the battery state of charge is acceptable (Chapter Three).

3. Disconnect the switch from the circuit or disconnect the negative battery cable before performing continuity tests.

CAUTION
Do not attempt to start the engine with the battery disconnected.

4. When separating two connectors, pull the connector housings and not the wires.

5. After isolating a defective circuit, check the connectors to make sure they are clean and properly connected. Check all wires going into a connector housing to make sure each wire is properly positioned and the wire end is not loose.

6. When reconnecting electrical connector halves, push them together until they click or snap into place.

Right Handlebar Switch Housing Replacement

The right handlebar switch housing includes the engine stop switch (A, **Figure 101**), start button (B), front brake light switch (electrical connectors only; the switch is separate), and headlight switch (except U.S.A., California and Canada models).

NOTE
The engine stop and headlight switches are not available separately. If one switch is damaged, replace the right switch housing assembly. The front brake light switch can be replaced independently.

1. Disconnect the negative battery cable as described in this chapter.

2A. *SV650 models*—Perform Steps 1-3 of *Headlight Lens, Housing and Bracket Removal/Installation* in this chapter.

2B. *SV650S models*—Remove the right side section of the fairing as described in Chapter Fifteen.

3A. *SV650 models*—Inside the headlight housing, disconnect the nine-wire connector. Carefully pull out the wires leading to the right handlebar switch housing.

3B. *SV650S models*—Disconnect the nine-wire connector (**Figure 102**). Carefully pull out the wires leading to the right handlebar switch housing.

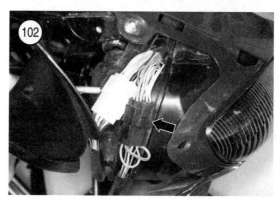

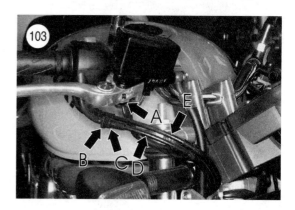

4. Remove any plastic clamps securing the wiring harness to the handlebar.

5. Disconnect the two wire connectors (A, **Figure 103**) from the front brake light switch.

6. At the throttle grip, loosen the throttle cable locknut (B, **Figure 103**) and turn the adjust nut (C) all the way into the switch assembly to allow maximum slack in both cables. Perform this on both the throttle opening (D, **Figure 103**) and closing (E) cables.

7. Remove the screws securing the right switch assembly together and separate the switch assembly.

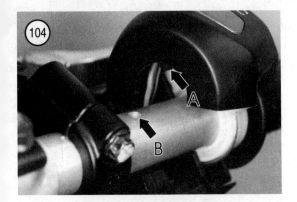

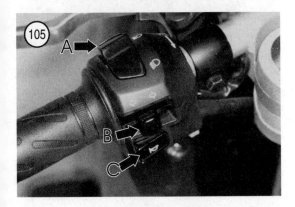

8. Disconnect the throttle opening cable, then the throttle closing cable from the throttle grip.

9. Remove the switch assembly from the handlebar and frame.

10. Install by reversing the preceding removal steps while noting the following:

    a. Connect the throttle cables onto the throttle grip and switch housing.

    b. Align the locating pin (A, **Figure 104**) with the hole (B) in the handlebar and install the switch onto the handlebar.

    c. Install the screws and tighten them securely.

    d. Make sure the electrical connectors are free of corrosion and secure.

    e. Check the operation of each switch mounted in the right handlebar switch housing.

    f. Operate the throttle lever and make sure the throttle linkage is operating correctly without binding. If operation is incorrect or if there is binding, carefully check that the cable is attached correctly and there are no tight bends in the cable.

    g. Adjust the throttle cables as described in Chapter Three.

Left Handlebar Switch Housing Replacement

The left handlebar switch housing includes the headlight dimmer switch (A, **Figure 105**), turn signal switch (B), horn button (C), clutch switch (electrical connectors only; the switch is separate), and passing button (non-U.S.A., California and Canada models).

NOTE
The three switches located within the left handlebar switch housing are not available separately. If one switch is damaged, replace the left switch housing assembly. The clutch switch is a separate unit and can be replaced independently.

1. Disconnect the negative battery cable as described in this chapter.

2A. *SV650 models*—Perform Steps 1-3 of *Headlight Lens, Housing and Bracket Removal/Installation* in this chapter.

2B. *SV650S models*—Remove the left side section of the fairing as described in Chapter Fifteen.

3A. *SV650 models*—Inside the headlight housing, disconnect the 11-wire connector. Carefully pull out the wires leading to the right handlebar switch housing.

3B. *SV650S models*—Disconnect the 11-wire connector (**Figure 106**). Carefully pull out the wires leading to the left handlebar switch housing.

4. Remove any plastic clamps securing the switch wiring harness to the frame. Carefully pull the wires out through the opening in the headlight housing.

5. Remove the screws securing the left switch assembly together and separate the switch assembly.

6. Disconnect the choke lever and cable from the switch housing.

7. Remove the switch assembly.

8. Install by reversing these removal steps while noting the following:

    a. Connect the choke cable and lever to the switch housing.

    b. Align the locating pin (A, **Figure 107**) with the hole in the handlebar (B). Install the switch onto the handlebar and tighten the screws securely.

    c. Make sure the electrical connectors are free of corrosion and are tight.

    d. Check the operation of each switch mounted in the left switch housing.

    e. Operate the choke lever and make sure the linkage is operating correctly without binding. If operation is incorrect or if there is binding, carefully check that the cable is attached correctly and that there are no tight bends in the cable.

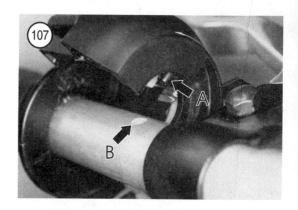

Ignition Switch Replacement

> *NOTE*
> *A **tamper-resistant** T-40 Torx bit is required to remove and install the ignition switch retaining bolts.*

1. Disconnect the negative battery cable as described in this chapter.

2. Remove the air box and disconnect the ignition switch connector (**Figure 108**).

3. Remove the upper steering stem bracket and ignition switch assembly as described in Chapter Twelve.

4. Place the upper steering stem bracket upside down on the workbench.

5. Remove the Torx bolts securing the ignition switch to the bottom of the upper steering stem bracket.

6. Install a new ignition switch and tighten the Torx bolts securely.

7. Install the upper steering stem bracket as described in Chapter Twelve.

8. Make sure the electrical connectors are free of corrosion and secure.

Neutral Switch Test

1. Lift and support the fuel tank.

2. Locate and disconnect the four-wire neutral-switch connector among the harness connectors on the left side of the frame.

3. Shift the transmission into neutral.

4. Connect an ohmmeter to the switch side of the electrical connector. Check that there is continuity between the blue terminal and ground.

5. Shift the transmission into any gear. There should be no continuity.

6. If the switch fails either of these tests, replace the switch.

7. If the switch is good, reconnect the electrical connector.

8. Return the fuel tank to its normal position.

Neutral Switch Replacement

The neutral switch is mounted on the left crankcase below the drive sprocket.

1. Remove the drive sprocket cover as described in Chapter Eleven.

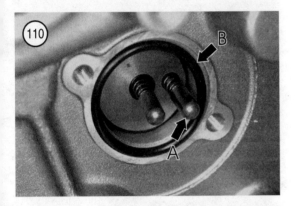

2. Locate and disconnect the neutral-switch connector as described in the previous procedure.

3. Remove the mounting screws and the neutral switch (**Figure 109**) from the crankcase.

4. Remove the spring-loaded contact pins (A, **Figure 110**) and the O-ring (B).

5. Inspect the pins and springs for damage. Replace if necessary.

6. Installation is the reverse of the preceding removal steps while noting the following:

   a. Before installation, clean the switch contacts.

   b. Install a *new* O-ring. Lubricate the O-ring with Suzuki Super Grease A or equivalent.

   c. Install the switch and tighten the mounting screws securely.

   d. Check switch operation with the transmission in neutral and reverse.

Oil Pressure Switch Testing

When the ignition switch is turned on, the low oil pressure symbol in the display should flicker and the indicator light should turn on. As soon as the engine starts, the symbol and the indicator light should go out. If there is a problem within the oil pressure system or if the oil pressure drops under the normal operating pressure range, the symbol flickers and indicator light turns on and stays on.

If the warning light is not operating correctly or does not come on when the ignition switch is in the on position (engine not running), perform the following test. The oil pressure switch (**Figure 111**) is mounted on the bottom of the engine adjacent to the oil filter.

1. Check the engine oil level as described in Chapter Three. Add oil if necessary.

2. Disconnect the electrical connector from the oil pressure switch (**Figure 111**).

3. Turn the ignition switch to the ON position.

4. Connect a jumper wire from the electrical connector to ground. The oil pressure warning light should come on.

5. If the light does not come on, perform the following:

   a. Check the oil pressure warning light bulb. Replace the bulb if necessary.

   b. Also check the wiring from the switch to the warning light assembly and between the light and the junction box.

   c. If the bulb and wiring are good, replace the switch as described below.

Oil Pressure Switch Replacement

The oil pressure switch (**Figure 111**) is mounted on the bottom of the engine adjacent to the oil filter.

1. Disconnect the electrical connector from the oil pressure switch.

2. Unscrew and remove the oil pressure switch from the crankcase.

3. Installation is the reverse of the preceding steps. Note the following:

a. Apply a light coat of silicone sealant to the switch threads before installation.

b. Install the switch and tighten to 14 N•m (124 in.-lb.).

Sidestand Switch Testing

1. Lift and support the fuel tank.

2. Locate and disconnect the four-wire neutral-switch connector among the harness connectors on the left side of the frame.

3. Locate and disconnect the two-wire sidestand connector among the harness connectors on the left side of the rear frame.

NOTE
If a Suzuki Multi-Circuit Tester is not available, perform Step 5.

4. Test the diode in the sidestand switch with a Suzuki Multi-Circuit Tester or equivalent by performing the following:

a. Set the test knob to diode test.

b. Connect the test leads to the terminals in the switch side of the connector as shown in **Figure 112**.

c. Move the sidestand to the UP position and read the voltage on the meter.

d. Move the sidestand to the DOWN position and read the voltage on the meter.

e. If the voltage is outside the range specified in **Figure 112**, replace the sidestand switch.

5. Test the continuity of the sidestand switch by performing the following:

a. Connect an ohmmeter to the terminals in the switch side of the connector terminals.

b. Move the sidestand to the UP position. The meter should show continuity.

c. Move the sidestand to the DOWN position. The meter should show no continuity.

d. If the switch fails either of these tests, replace it.

6. Reconnect the electrical connectors and install all removed items.

Sidestand Switch Replacement

1. Place the motorcycle on a suitable jack or wooden blocks on level ground.

SIDESTAND SWITCH TEST

Position \ Color	G (+ probe)	B/W (- probe)
UP	0.4-0.6 V	0.4-0.6 V
DOWN	1.4-1.5 V	1.4-1.5 V

2. Lift and support the fuel tank.

3. Locate and disconnect the two-wire sidestand connector among the harness connectors on the left side of the rear frame.

4. Move the sidestand to the UP position.

5. Remove the two bolts securing the sidestand switch (**Figure 113**) to the sidestand and remove the switch.

6. Install a new switch. Apply ThreeBond No. TB1342 to the mounting bolts and tighten them securely.

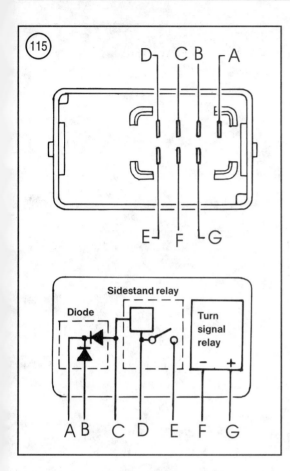

(115)

Sidestand relay

Diode

Turn signal relay

A B C D E F G

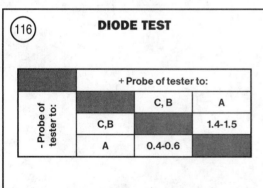

(116) **DIODE TEST**

		+ Probe of tester to:	
		C, B	A
− Probe of tester to:	C,B		1.4-1.5
	A	0.4-0.6	

7. Move the sidestand from the UP to DOWN position and check that the switch plunger has moved in.

8. Make sure the electrical connectors are free of corrosion and secure.

RELAYS

The turn-signal relay, sidestand relay and diode are combined into a single component, called the relay assembly. If the turn-signal relay, sidestand relay or the diode is faulty, replace the relay assembly.

Relay Assembly Replacement

1. Remove the front seat.
2. Remove the relay assembly (**Figure 114**) from the mounting base. Push out the tab at the end of the relay case to disengage the relay case from the mounting base latch.
3. Install the relay by reversing the removal steps.

Sidestand Relay Testing

1. Remove the relay as previously described.
2. Apply 12 volts to the relay by connecting the negative side of the battery to the C terminal in the relay assembly and connect the positive battery terminal to the D terminal. See **Figure 115**.
3. Use an ohmmeter to check the continuity between terminals D and E on the relay assembly. There should be continuity.
4. Replace the relay assembly if there is no continuity.

Turn Signal Relay Testing

If the turn signal light does not light, first look for a defective bulb. If the bulbs are good, check the turn signal switch as described in this chapter and all electrical connections within the turn signal circuit.

If all of these components are good, replace the relay unit.

Diode Testing

1. Remove the relay unit as previously described.
2. Set the Suzuki Multi Circuit Tester (part No. 09900-25008) or equivalent to diode test, and measure the voltage across the diode terminals indicated in **Figure 116**. Also see **Figure 115**.
3. Replace the relay assembly if any measurement is outside the range specified in **Figure 116**.

9

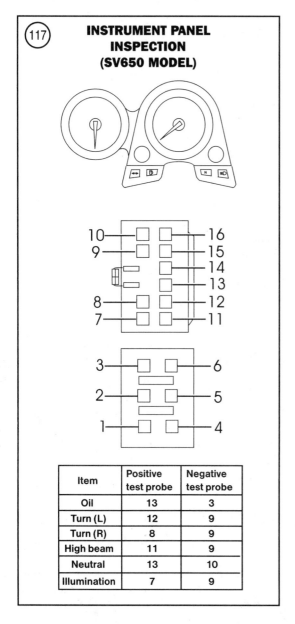

117

INSTRUMENT PANEL INSPECTION (SV650 MODEL)

Item	Positive test probe	Negative test probe
Oil	13	3
Turn (L)	12	9
Turn (R)	8	9
High beam	11	9
Neutral	13	10
Illumination	7	9

118

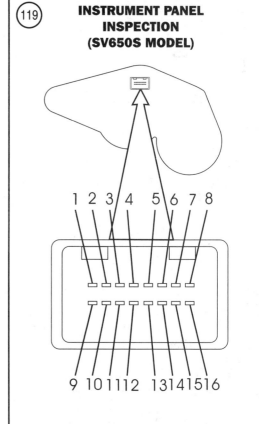

119

INSTRUMENT PANEL INSPECTION (SV650S MODEL)

Item	Positive test probe	Negative test probe
High beam	2	15
Neutral	3	1
Turn (R)	10	15
Turn (L)	9	15
Illumination	13	15
Oil	3	11

INSTRUMENT PANEL

Inspection

SV650 models

1. Disconnect the instrument panel connectors from the wiring harness.

2. Refer to **Figure 117** and check the continuity in the affected circuit.

  a. Set an ohmmeter to the diode test position and connect the test probes to the terminals indicated in the table.

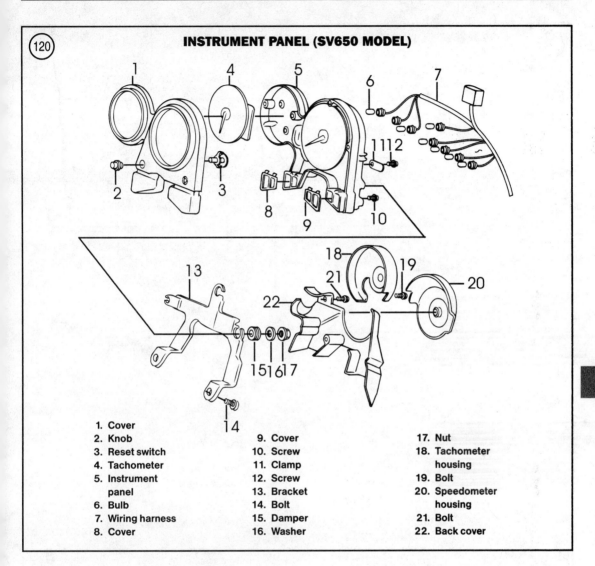

INSTRUMENT PANEL (SV650 MODEL)

1. Cover
2. Knob
3. Reset switch
4. Tachometer
5. Instrument
   panel
6. Bulb
7. Wiring harness
8. Cover
9. Cover
10. Screw
11. Clamp
12. Screw
13. Bracket
14. Bolt
15. Damper
16. Washer
17. Nut
18. Tachometer
    housing
19. Bolt
20. Speedometer
    housing
21. Bolt
22. Back cover

b. The circuit should have continuity.

3. If the circuit does not have continuity, replace the indicator bulb and repeat the continuity test.

4. If the circuit still does not have continuity, inspect the connector for loose or broken wires.

5. If this does not correct the problem, replace the instrument panel.

SV650S models

1. Remove the fairing as described in Chapter Fifteen.

2. Disconnect the instrument panel six-wire electrical connector (**Figure 118**).

3. Refer to **Figure 119** and check the continuity in the affected circuit.

a. Set an ohmmeter to the diode test position and connect the test probes to the terminals indicated in the table.

b. The circuit should have continuity.

4. If continuity does not exist between any indicated pair of terminals, inspect the related indicator bulb for that circuit. Replace the bulb as necessary and recheck the continuity. If the bulb is working, replace the meter assembly.

Removal/Installation

SV650 models

Refer to **Figure 120** when performing the following procedure.

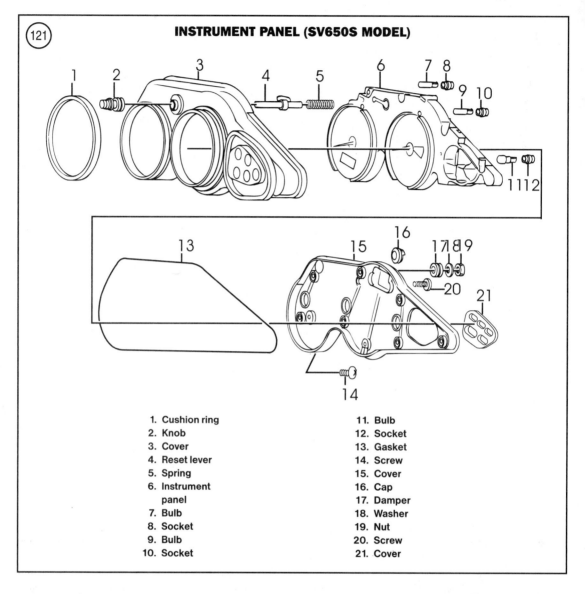

INSTRUMENT PANEL (SV650S MODEL)

1. Cushion ring
2. Knob
3. Cover
4. Reset lever
5. Spring
6. Instrument
   panel
7. Bulb
8. Socket
9. Bulb
10. Socket
11. Bulb
12. Socket
13. Gasket
14. Screw
15. Cover
16. Cap
17. Damper
18. Washer
19. Nut
20. Screw
21. Cover

1. Remove the headlight assembly as described in this chapter.

2. Disconnect the two instrument panel connectors (six-wire and ten-wire).

3. Remove the bolts (14, **Figure 120**) securing the instrument panel bracket and remove the instrument panel assembly.

4. Remove the tachometer and speedometer cover screws (19, **Figure 120**) and remove the covers.

5. Remove the back cover screws (21, **Figure 120**) and remove the back cover (22).

6. Remove the instrument panel retaining nuts (17, **Figure 120**) and separate the mounting bracket (13) and instrument panel.

7. Reverse the removal procedure to install the instrument panel.

SV650S models

Refer to **Figure 121** when performing the following procedure.

1. Remove the fairing as described in Chapter Fifteen.

2. Remove the instrument panel cover (**Figure 122**).

3. Disconnect the six-wire electrical connector (**Figure 123**) from the instrument panel.

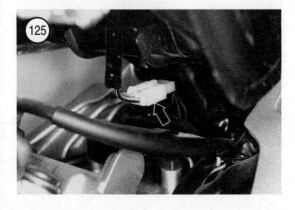

4. Remove the nuts securing the instrument panel to the front fairing mounting bracket.

5. Remove the instrument panel and store it carefully.

6. Install the instrument panel by reversing the preceding removal steps. Be sure the six-wire electrical connector is free of corrosion and fits securely.

Engine Coolant Temperature Indicator Testing

The light emitting diode (LED) in the tachometer provides engine coolant information. Check its operation by performing the following.

1. Raise and support the fuel tank.

2. Disconnect the black/green wire from the engine coolant temperature switch (**Figure 124**).

3. Connect a jumper between the black/green lead and a good engine ground. The LED in the tachometer should turn on.

4. If the meter fails the test, replace the tachometer on SV650 models or the combination meter on SV650S models.

Fuel Level Indicator Testing

1. Raise and support the fuel tank.

2. Disconnect the three-wire fuel level sensor connector (**Figure 125**).

3. Turn the ignition switch ON. The fuel level indicator should turn on for approximately three seconds after the ignition is turned on.

4. Use a jumper wire to connect the black/white terminal on the harness side of the connector to the red/black terminal on the harness side. The fuel level indicator light should flash.

5. Disconnect the jumper and watch the fuel level indicator light. It should go out within 30 seconds after disconnecting the jumper.

6. Use the jumper wire to connect the black/white terminal on the harness side of the connector to the black/light green terminal on the harness side. The fuel level indicator light should turn on.

7. Disconnect the jumper and watch the fuel level indicator light. It should go out within 30 seconds after disconnecting the jumper.

8. If the fuel level indicator does not function as described above, check the fuel level indicator bulb. If the bulb is good, replace the instrument panel.

9

Speedometer, Odometer and Tripmeter Inspection

If the speedometer, odometer or tripmeter does not function properly, inspect the speedometer sensor and the connections. If the sensor and connections are good, replace the combination meter.

Speedometer Sensor Test

SV650 models

1. Remove the headlight lens as described in this chapter.
2. Disconnect the three-wire speedometer sensor connector inside the headlight housing.
3. Support the front of the motorcycle so the front wheel can be rotated.
4. Connect four 1.5-volt batteries in series to the center connector terminal as shown in **Figure 126**.
5. Connect a 1 k ohm resistor to the outer connector terminals as shown in **Figure 126**.
6. Connect a voltmeter as shown in **Figure 126**.
7. Rotate the front wheel while observing the voltmeter. The voltage reading should be between 0-6 volts. Otherwise, replace the speedometer sensor.

SV650S models

1. Remove the airbox.
2. Disconnect the three-wire speedometer sensor connector (**Figure 127**).
3. Support the front of the motorcycle so the front wheel can be rotated.
4. Connect four 1.5-volt batteries in series to the center connector terminal as shown in **Figure 126**.
5. Connect a 1 k ohm resistor to the outer connector terminals as shown in **Figure 126**.
6. Connect a voltmeter as shown in **Figure 126**.
7. Rotate the front wheel while observing the voltmeter. The voltage reading should be between 0-6 volts. Otherwise, replace the speedometer sensor.

Oil Pressure Indicator Test

1. Raise and support the fuel tank.
2. Disconnect the black wire from the oil pressure switch (**Figure 110**).
3. Use a jumper wire to connect the black wire to a good engine ground.

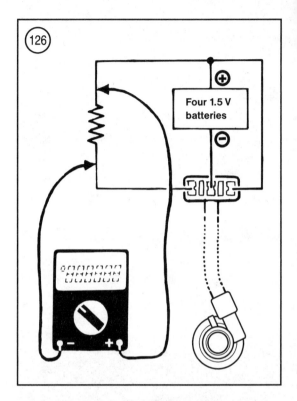

4. Turn the ignition switch ON and watch the oil pressure indicator. It should light.

5. If the indicator does not light, check the wiring and connectors between the oil pressure switch and the meter. If they are good, replace the combination meter.

HORN

Testing

1. Disconnect the negative battery cable as described in this chapter.

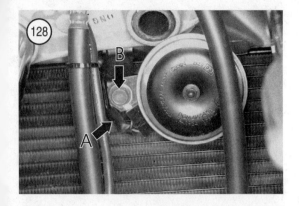

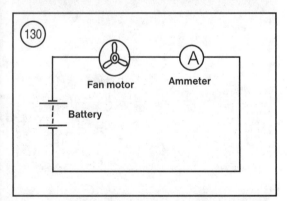

2. Disconnect the electrical connectors (A, **Figure 128**) from the horn.

3. Connect a 12-volt battery to the horn terminals. The horn should sound.

4. If it does not, replace the horn.

Removal/Installation

1. Disconnect the negative battery cable as described in this chapter.

2. Disconnect the electrical connectors (A, **Figure 128**) from the horn.

3. Remove the bolt (B, **Figure 128**) securing the horn to the mounting bracket.

4. Remove the horn.

5. Install by reversing the preceding removal steps while noting the following:

    a. Make sure the electrical connectors are free of corrosion and are tight.

    b. Test the horn to make sure it operates correctly.

COOLING SYSTEM

Fan Motor Testing

Use an ammeter and a fully charged 12-volt battery for this test.

1. Remove the airbox.

2. Locate the fan motor electrical connector (**Figure 129**) adjacent to the fuel pump.

3. Use jumper wires to connect the test battery to the motor lead of the fan motor connector. Also connect an ammeter in line as shown in **Figure 130**.

4. The fan should operate when power is applied. Replace the fan assembly if the motor does not operate.

5. With the motor running at full speed, monitor the ammeter and note the load current. Replace the fan assembly if the load current exceeds 5 amps.

Cooling Fan Switch Testing

The cooling fan switch controls the radiator fan according to the engine coolant temperature using a thermostatic element in the switch. Refer also to Chapter Ten.

1. Remove the fan switch (**Figure 131**) from the radiator as described in Chapter Ten.

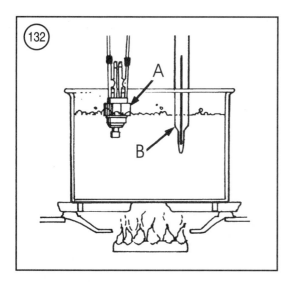

2. Fill a beaker or pan with water, and place it on a stove or hot plate.

3. Position the fan switch so that the temperature sensing tip and the threaded portion of the body are submerged as shown in A, **Figure 132**.

> *NOTE*
> *The thermometer and the fan switch must not touch the container sides or bottom. If either does, it will result in a false reading.*

4. Place a thermometer (B, **Figure 132**) in the pan of water (use a cooking thermometer that is rated higher than the test temperature).

5. If the switch has exposed terminals, attach one ohmmeter lead to the fan switch terminals as shown in A, **Figure 132**. If the switch has a non-detachable wire lead, connect the ohmmeter leads to the connector terminals. Check the resistance as follows:

   a. Gradually heat the water.

   b. When the temperature reaches 205° F (96° C), the meter should read continuity (switch on).

   c. Gradually reduce the heat.

   d. When the temperature lowers to approximately 196° F (91° C), the meter should not read continuity (switch off).

6. Replace the fan switch if it failed to operate as described in Step 5.

7. If the fan switch is good, install it onto the radiator as described in Chapter Ten.

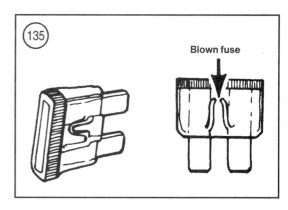

FUSES

Replacement

All models are equipped with a single 30-amp main fuse that is located next to the starter relay (**Figure 133**). The remaining fuses are located in the auxiliary fuse box (**Figure 134**) located under the front seat.

If there is an electrical failure, first check for a blown fuse. A blown fuse will have a break in the element (**Figure 135**).

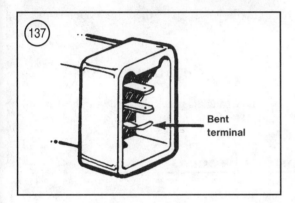

Bent
terminal

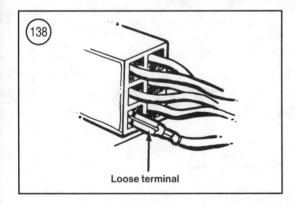

Loose terminal

Whenever the fuse blows, determine the reason for the failure before replacing the fuse. Usually, the trouble is a short circuit in the wiring. This may be caused by worn-through insulation or a disconnected wire shorted to ground. Check by testing the circuit the fuse protects.

1. To replace the main fuse, perform the following:

    a. Refer to the *Starter Relay* section in this chapter and remove the starter relay cover.

    b. Using needlenose pliers, pull out the fuse and visually inspect it.

    c. Install a new fuse and push it in all the way until it bottoms.

2. To remove the auxiliary fuses, perform the following:

    a. Remove the front seat and open the fuse panel cover.

    b. Locate the blown fuse (**Figure 136**) and install a new one of the same amperage.

NOTE
Always carry spare fuses.

    c. There are two spare fuses (10A and 15A) located in the fuse panel.

WIRING AND CONNECTORS

Circuit and Wiring Check

Many electrical troubles can be traced to damaged wiring or to contaminated or loose connectors.

1. Inspect all wiring for fraying, burning and any other visual damage.

2. Check the main fuse and make sure it is not blown. Replace it if necessary.

3. Check the individual fuse(s) for each circuit. Make sure it is not blown. Replace it if necessary.

4. Inspect the battery as described in Chapter Three. Make sure it is fully charged and that the battery electrical cable connectors are clean and securely attached to the battery terminals.

5. Connectors can be serviced by disconnecting and cleaning them with an aerosol electrical contact cleaner. After a thorough cleaning, pack multipin electrical connectors with dialectic grease to help seal out moisture.

6. Disconnect each electrical connector in the suspect circuit and check that there are no bent terminals on either side of the electrical connector (**Figure 137**). A damaged terminal will not contact its mate, and this will cause an open circuit.

7. Check each female end of the connector. Make sure the terminals on the back of each connector (**Figure 138**) are pushed all the way into the connector. If not, carefully push them in with a narrow-blade screwdriver.

8. Push the connectors together and make sure they are fully engaged and locked together (**Figure 139**).

9

9. Never pull the electrical wires when disconnecting an electrical connector. Pull the connector plastic housing instead.

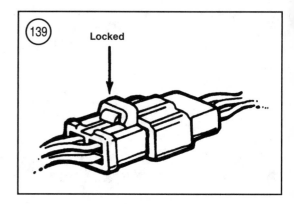

NOTE
Step 10 checks the continuity of individual circuits.

10. Check wiring continuity as follows:

a. Disconnect the negative battery cable as described in this chapter.

b. If using an analog ohmmeter, always touch test leads together and zero the needle according to manufacturer's instructions. An analog meter will yield false readings if not properly zeroed.

c. Attach the test leads to the circuit to be tested.

d. There should be continuity (indicated low resistance). If there is no continuity (infi-

nite resistance), there is an open in the circuit.

WIRING DIAGRAMS

The wiring diagrams are located at the end of this manual.

Table 1 ELECTRICAL SYSTEM SPECIFICATIONS

Alternator	
Type	Three-phase AC
No-load voltage (engine cold)	70 volts (AC) @ 5000 rpm
Maximum output	
1999-2001	300 watts @ 5000 rpm
2002	275 watts @ 5000 rpm
Regulated voltage (charging voltage)	13.5-15.0 volts @ 5000 rpm
Coil resistance	0.2-0.55 ohm
Battery	
Type	YT12A-BS Maintenance free (sealed)
Capacity	12 volt 10 amp-hour
Cooling fan current (max.)	5 amps
Ignition coil	
Primary peak voltage (min.)	150 volts
Primary resistance	3.5-5.5 ohms
Secondary resistance	20,000-31,000 ohms
Ignition system	
Type	CDI
Ignition timing	5° BTDC @ 1300 rpm
Signal generator	
Coil resistance	140-230 ohms
Peak voltage	3.0 V minimum

Table 2 ELECTRICAL SYSTEM TORQUE SPECIFICATIONS

Item	N•m	in.-lb.	ft.-lb.
Alternator rotor bolt	120	–	88
Alternator stator bolts	10	88	–
Oil pressure switch	14	124	–
Signal generator bolts	5.5	49	–
Starter mounting bolts	6	53	–

Table 3 REPLACEMENT BULBS

Item	Specification
Headlight	
SV650	60/55W
SV650S[1]	45/45W
Indicator lights[2]	1.7W
License plate	5W
Position/parking light (if equipped)	5W
Speedometer lights	
SV650	1.7W
SV650S	0.84W
Taillight/brake light	21/5W
Turn signal	21W

1. In some European countries a 55/55W bulb may be used. Check with a dealership.
2. Water temperature indicator light is LED type. On SV650, oil pressure indicator light is LED type.

Table 4 COLOR CODES

B	Black
W	White
R	Red
O	Orange
Y	Yellow
G	Green
Br	Brown
Gr	Gray

9

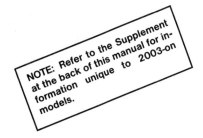

NOTE: Refer to the Supplement at the back of this manual for information unique to 2003-on models.

COOLING SYSTEM

This chapter covers repair and replacement procedures for the radiator and cap, thermostat, cooling fan and coolant reservoir. Routine maintenance operations are described in Chapter Three. Cooling system specifications are listed in **Table 1** and **Table 2** at the end of this chapter.

Refer to **Figure 1** for a diagram that depicts the coolant flow in the cooling system.

WARNING
Do not remove the radiator cap or any cooling system component that is under pressure when the engine is hot. The coolant is very hot and under pressure. Severe scalding could result if the coolant touches skin. The cooling system must be cool before removing any system component.

WARNING
If the engine is warm or hot, the fan may come on (even with the ignition off). Never work around the fan until the engine is completely cool.

WARNING
Antifreeze is an environmental toxic waste. Do not dispose of it by flushing it down a drain or pouring it onto the ground. Place old antifreeze in a suitable container and dispose of it properly. Do not store coolant where it is accessible to children or animals.

CAUTION
When adding coolant or refilling the system, use a mixture of ethylene glycol antifreeze formulated for aluminum engines and distilled water. Do not use only distilled water (even if freezing temperatures are not expected); the antifreeze inhibits internal engine corrosion and provides lubrication for moving parts.

TEMPERATURE WARNING SYSTEM

A coolant temperature indicator light (LED) is located on the face of the tachometer. If the coolant

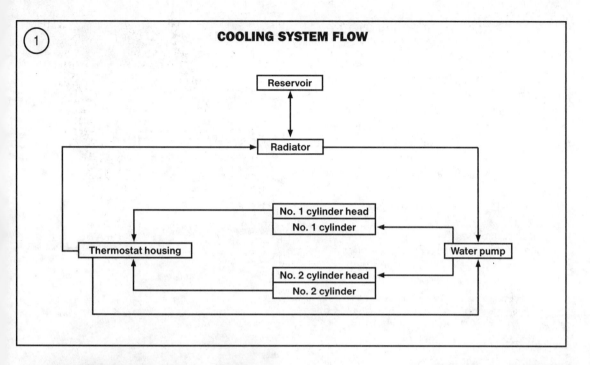

COOLING SYSTEM FLOW

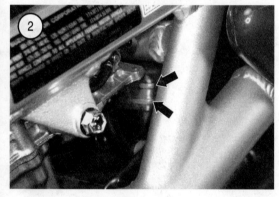

temperature is above 115° C (239° F) when the ignition switch is turned on, the indicator light on the tachometer face will illuminate.

If the coolant temperature indicator light comes on, turn the engine OFF and allow it to cool. Determine the cause of the overheating condition before operating the motorcycle. Make sure the coolant level is between the marks on the reservoir (**Figure 2**). Do not add coolant to the radiator.

HOSES AND HOSE CLAMPS

After removing any cooling system component, inspect the adjoining hose(s) to determine if replacement is necessary. Hoses deteriorate with age

and should be inspected carefully for conditions which may cause them to fail. The possibility of a hose failing should be taken seriously. Loss of coolant will cause the engine to overheat and spray from a leaking hose can injure the rider. Observe the following when servicing hoses:

1. Make sure the cooling system is cool before removing any coolant hose or component.

2. Use original equipment replacement hoses; they are formed to a specific shape and dimension for correct fit.

3. Do not use excessive force when removing a hose from a fitting. Refer to *Removing Hoses* in Chapter One.

4. If the hose is difficult to install onto the fitting, soak the hose in hot water to make it more pliable. Do not use any lubricant when installing hoses.

5. Inspect the hose clamps for damage. Always use screw adjusting type hose clamps unless otherwise specified by the manufacturer. Position the clamp head so it is accessible for future removal and does not contact other parts.

6. With the hose correctly installed, position the clamp approximately one-half inch (13 mm) from the end of the hose and tighten the clamp.

10

COOLING SYSTEM INSPECTION

1. If steam is observed at the muffler outlet, the head gasket might be damaged. If enough coolant leaks into a cylinder(s), the cylinder could hydrolock and prevent the engine from being cranked. Coolant may also be present in the engine oil. If the oil visible in the oil level gauge is foamy or milky-looking, there is coolant in the oil. If so, correct the problem before returning the motorcycle to service.

> *CAUTION*
> *If the engine oil is contaminated with coolant, change the oil and filter after performing the coolant system repair. Refer to Chapter Three.*

2. Check the radiator for clogged or damaged fins. If more than 15 percent of the radiator fin area is damaged, repair or replace the radiator.

3. Check all coolant hoses for cracks or damage. Replace all questionable parts. Make sure all hose clamps are tight, but not so tight that they cut the hoses. Refer to *Hoses* in this chapter.

4. Pressure test the cooling system as described in Chapter Three.

COOLANT RESERVOIR

Removal/Installation

1. Remove the carburetors as described in Chapter Eight.

2. Disconnect the reservoir hose (**Figure 3**) from the radiator, then drain the coolant in the reservoir out through the hose.

3. Disconnect the reservoir vent hose (**Figure 4**) from the reservoir.

4. Remove the reservoir mounting bolts and remove the reservoir.

5. Remove the fill cap and drain any residual coolant from the reservoir. Dispose of the coolant properly.

6. If necessary, clean the inside of the reservoir with a liquid detergent. Thoroughly rinse the reservoir with clean water. Be sure to remove all detergent residue from the reservoir.

7. Install by reversing the preceding removal steps.

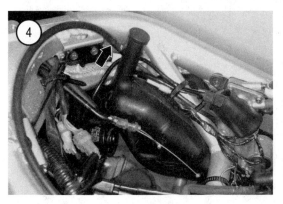

RADIATOR

> *WARNING*
> *Whenever the engine is warm or hot, the fan may start even with the ignition switch turned off. Never work around the fan or touch the fan until the engine and coolant are completely cool.*

Removal/Installation

Refer to **Figure 5**.

1. Drain the cooling system as described in Chapter Three.

2. Disconnect the reservoir hose (**Figure 3**) from the radiator, then drain the coolant in the reservoir out through the hose.

3. Remove the airbox as described in Chapter Five.

4. Move back the cover (**Figure 6**) on the cooling fan switch on the right side of the radiator. Determine if the switch is equipped with a removable connector. Later models are equipped with a switch (**Figure 7**) that cannot be disconnected from its wire lead.

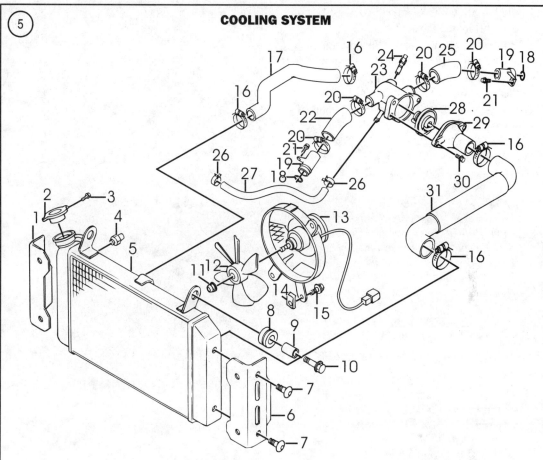

COOLING SYSTEM

1. Brace	10. Bolt	18. O-ring	25. Hose
2. Radiator cap	11. Nut	19. Fitting	26. Clamp
3. Screw	12. Fan	20. Clamp	27. Hose
4. Cooling fan switch	13. Cooling fan motor	21. Bolt	28. Thermostat
5. Radiator	and shroud	22. Hose	29. Thermostat cover
6. Brace	14. Nutplate	23. Thermostat	30. Bolt
7. Screw	15. Bolt	housing	31. Hose
8. Damper	16. Clamp	24. Coolant	
9. Bushing	17. Hose	temperature switch	

10

a. If equipped with a connector, detach the connector from the fan switch.

b. If the fan switch is not equipped with a connector, raise the fuel tank and disconnect the fan switch connector (A, **Figure 8**). Release the wire lead from any retaining straps.

5. Disconnect the cooling fan electrical connector (B, **Figure 8**). Release the wire lead from any retaining straps.

6. Disconnect the horn wiring connectors, then remove the horn and bracket.

> *NOTE*
> *Even though the cooling system has been drained, some residual coolant remains in the radiator and hoses. Place a drain pan under each hose as it is removed and wipe up any spilled coolant.*

7. Detach the upper radiator hose (A, **Figure 9**) and lower radiator hose (A, **Figure 10**) from the radiator.

> *WARNING*
> *Coolant is very slippery if spilled on concrete or a similar surface. Do not walk on spilled coolant; wipe it off the floor immediately. Also wipe off any coolant that gets on shoes.*

8. *SV650S models*—Remove the fairing mounting bolt (**Figure 11**) on each side.

9. Remove the radiator upper mounting bolts (B, **Figure 9**) on both sides and the lower mounting bolt (B, **Figure 10**).

10. Carefully remove the radiator. On SV650S models, pull out the sides of the fairing so the pins on the fairing disengage from the mounting lugs on the sides of the radiator.

11. Install the radiator by reversing the removal steps.

a. Replace any hoses if they are deteriorating or are damaged in any way, as described in this chapter.

b. Make sure the damper is in place on each radiator mount.

c. The radiator hoses are shaped hoses and must be installed properly. The paint dot on the hose end (C, **Figure 10**) of the lower hose must be on the outside of the hose when installed.

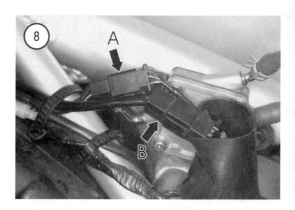

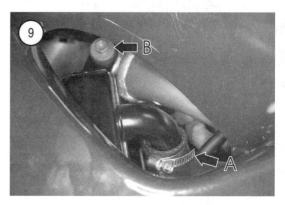

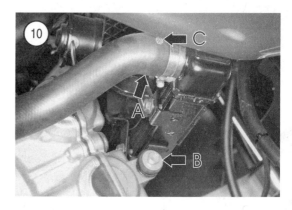

d. Make sure the cooling fan and cooling fan switch electrical connections are free of corrosion and secure.

e. Refill the cooling system with the recommended type and quantity of coolant as described in Chapter Three.

Inspection

1. Remove the cooling fan assembly (A, **Figure 12**) for inspection as described in this chapter.

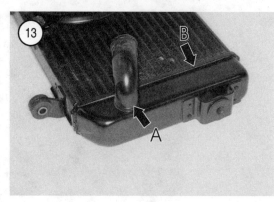

2. If compressed air is available, use short spurts of air directed to the *backside* (B, **Figure 12**) of the radiator core to blow out debris.

3. Flush the exterior of the radiator with a garden hose on low pressure. Spray both the front and the back to remove all debris. Carefully use a whisk broom or stiff paint brush to remove any stubborn dirt from the cooling fins.

CAUTION
Do not press hard on the cooling fins or tubes.

4. Carefully straighten out any bent cooling fins with a broad tipped screwdriver or putty knife.

5. Check for cracks or leakage (usually a moss-green colored residue) at all hose fittings (A, **Figure 13**) and both side tank seams (B).

6. To prevent oxidation of the radiator, touch up any areas where the paint is worn off. Use a quality spray paint and apply several *light* coats. Do not apply heavy coats as this cuts down on the cooling efficiency of the radiator.

7. Inspect the rubber dampers in the radiator mounts. Replace any that are damaged or starting to deteriorate.

8. Check for leaks at the cooling fan switch.

COOLING FAN

Removal/Installation

Replacement parts for the fan assembly are not available. If the fan motor is defective, replace the entire fan assembly.

Refer to **Figure 5** when performing this procedure.

1. Remove the radiator as described in this chapter.

2. Place a blanket or large towels on the workbench to protect the radiator.

3. Remove the screws securing the fan shroud (A, **Figure 12**) to the radiator and carefully detach the fan assembly from the radiator.

4. Test the cooling fan motor as described in Chapter Nine.

5. Install by reversing the preceding removal steps.

THERMOSTAT

Removal/Installation

Refer to **Figure 5** when performing this procedure.

1. Drain the cooling system as described in Chapter Three.

2. Disconnect the ground wire connector (**Figure 14**).

3. On models equipped with a carburetor drain hose retainer (A, **Figure 15**), disengage the hose from the retainer.

4. Loosen the hose clamp (B, **Figure 15**) and disconnect the hose from the thermostat cover.

5. Remove the bolts securing the thermostat cover
(A, **Figure 16**) and remove the cover.

6. Remove the thermostat (A, **Figure 17**) from the
thermostat housing.

7. If necessary, test the thermostat as described in
this chapter.

8. Inspect the thermostat for damage and make sure
the spring has not sagged or broken. Replace the
thermostat if necessary.

9. Clean the inside of the thermostat housing of any
debris or old coolant residue.

10. Install by reversing the preceding removal
steps while noting the following:

   a. Position the thermostat with the air bleed hole
     (B, **Figure 17**) toward the top of the cover.

   b. Install the thermostat cover so the rib is down
     (B, **Figure 16**).

   c. The radiator hose is a shaped hose and must
     be installed properly. The paint dot on the
     hose end must align with the top of the ther-
     mostat cover. Push the hose onto the thermo-
     stat cover until it contacts the rib (B, **Figure
     16**) on the bottom of the thermostat cover.

   d. Refill the cooling system with the recom-
     mended type and quantity of coolant as de-
     scribed in Chapter Three.

Testing

Test the thermostat to ensure proper operation.
Replace the thermostat if it remains open at normal
room temperature or stays closed after the specified
temperature has been reached during the test procedure.

NOTE
The thermometer and the thermostat
must not touch the container sides or
bottom. If either does, it will result in
a false reading.

Suspend the thermostat and thermometer in a pan
of water (**Figure 18**). Use a cooking thermometer
that is rated higher than the test temperature. Gradually heat the water and continue to gently stir the
water until it reaches 180° F (82° C). At this temperature the thermostat valve should open.

NOTE
Valve operation is sometimes slug-
gish; it usually takes 3-5 minutes for

the valve to operate properly and to open completely. If the valve fails to open, replace the thermostat. Be sure to replace it with a thermostat of the same temperature rating.

THERMOSTAT HOUSING

The thermostat housing contains the thermostat as well as serving as a manifold. Hoses route the coolant from the cylinders to the manifold, while a bypass hose directs coolant to the water pump when the thermostat is closed. The coolant temperature sensor is mounted on the thermostat housing. Refer to **Figure 1** for a diagram of the cooling system.

Removal/Installation

Refer to **Figure 5** when performing this procedure.

1. Drain the cooling system as described in Chapter Three.

2. Remove the carburetors as described in Chapter Five.

3. Disconnect the ground wire connector (**Figure 14**).

4. Disconnect the wire connector from the coolant temperature sensor (A, **Figure 19**).

5. Detach the bypass hose (A, **Figure 20**) from the water pump.

6. Loosen the hose clamp (B, **Figure 15**) and disconnect the hose from the thermostat cover.

7. Loosen the hose clamps (B, **Figure 19**) and disconnect the hoses from the fittings on the cylinder heads.

8. Remove the thermostat housing (**Figure 21**).

9. Reverse the removal procedure to install the thermostat housing while noting the following:

    a. The radiator hose is a shaped hose and must be installed properly. Push the hose onto the water pump until it bottoms against the stop on the pump inlet. The paint dot on the hose end (B, **Figure 20**) must be just above pump inlet centerline.

    b. Refill the cooling system with the recommended type and quantity of coolant as described in Chapter Three.

10

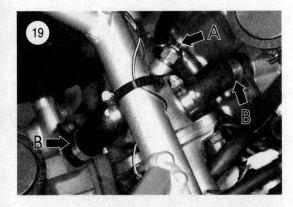

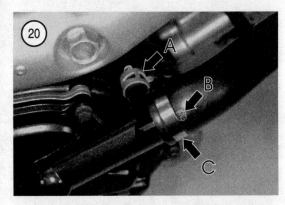

WATER PUMP

The water pump is mounted on the clutch cover. The water pump cannot be removed from the clutch cover unless the clutch cover is removed from the engine.

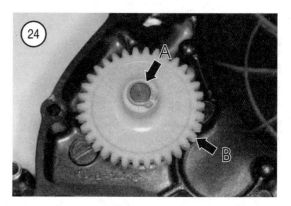

Removal/Installation

1. Drain the cooling system as described in Chapter Three.
2. Drain the engine oil as described in Chapter Three.
3. Detach the bypass hose (A, **Figure 20**) from the water pump.
4. Loosen the hose clamp (C, **Figure 20**) and disconnect the inlet hose from the water pump.

> *NOTE*
> *Different length bolts are used to retain the clutch cover. Note the length and location of the bolts during disassembly.*

5. Remove the clutch cover retaining bolts around the periphery of the cover, as well as the retaining bolt just below the water pump (**Figure 22**). Note that the three upper left bolts also retain the outer clutch cover.
6. Remove the clutch cover.
7. Remove the gasket. Do not lose the dowel pins (**Figure 23**).

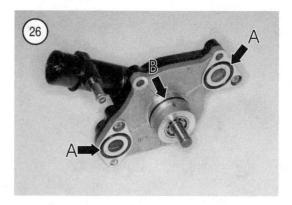

8. Remove the snap ring (A, **Figure 24**), then remove the gear (B).
9. Remove the drive pin (A, **Figure 25**) and washer (B).
10. Remove the water pump (**Figure 26**) from the clutch cover.
11. To install the water pump, reverse the removal procedure while noting the following:

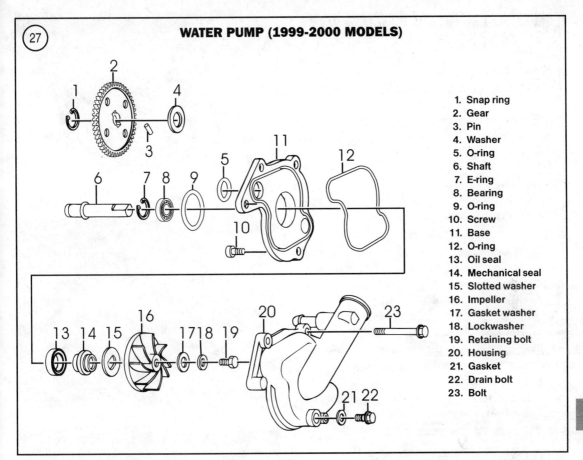

WATER PUMP (1999-2000 MODELS)

1. Snap ring
2. Gear
3. Pin
4. Washer
5. O-ring
6. Shaft
7. E-ring
8. Bearing
9. O-ring
10. Screw
11. Base
12. O-ring
13. Oil seal
14. Mechanical seal
15. Slotted washer
16. Impeller
17. Gasket washer
18. Lockwasher
19. Retaining bolt
20. Housing
21. Gasket
22. Drain bolt
23. Bolt

a. Install new O-rings around the coolant passages (A, **Figure 26**) and around the shaft housing (B).

b. Lubricate the O-ring around the shaft housing (B, **Figure 26**) using Suzuki Super Grease A or equivalent.

c. Apply Suzuki Bond No. 1207B, or equivalent, to the O-rings (A, **Figure 26**) around the water passages.

d. Tighten the water pump retaining bolts to 13 N•m (115 in.-lb.).

e. Make sure the drive slot in the gear engages the drive pin (A, **Figure 25**).

f. Install a new snap ring (A, **Figure 24**).

g. Be sure the dowel pins (**Figure 23**) are in place and install a *new* clutch cover gasket.

h. Carefully engage the water pump gears when installing the clutch cover.

i. Apply Threadlock 1342 to the clutch cover retaining bolts and tighten them to 10 N•m (88 in.-lb.).

j. The radiator hose is a shaped hose and must be installed properly. Push the hose onto the

water pump until it bottoms against the stop on the pump inlet. The paint dot on the hose end (B, **Figure 20**) must be just above pump inlet centerline.

k. Refill the cooling system with the recommended type and quantity of coolant as described in Chapter Three.

l. Refill the engine with oil as described in Chapter Three.

Disassembly/Inspection/Assembly

Two types of water pumps have been used. 1999-2000 models are equipped with a two-piece impeller and shaft assembly. 2001-on models are equipped with a single-piece impeller and shaft unit.

1999-2000 models

Refer to **Figure 27**.

1. Remove the mounting screws (**Figure 28**) and separate the base assembly from the housing.

2. Remove the retaining bolt (19, **Figure 27**), lockwasher (18) and gasket (17).

3. Lift the impeller (16, **Figure 27**) off the impeller shaft.

4. Remove the impeller shaft (6, **Figure 27**).

5. Using a chisel, raise the outer lip of the mechanical seal (**Figure 29**).

6. Using a heat gun, heat the area around the mechanical seal.

7. Using a suitable tool, pry the mechanical seal out of the base (**Figure 30**).

8. Pry out the oil seal (**Figure 31**).

9. Rotate the bearing (**Figure 32**) and check for excessive noise or roughness. If bearing operation is rough, replace the bearing by using a suitable puller or driving out the bearing.

10. Remove the seal ring, rubber seal and slotted washer from the impeller (**Figure 33**).

11. Thoroughly clean the water pump base and housing to remove all old coolant residue.

12. Check the impeller blades for corrosion or damage. If corrosion is excessive or if the blades are cracked or broken, replace the impeller.

13. Install the bearing so the numbered side is out. Drive in the bearing until it bottoms in the base.

14. Install the oil seal (**Figure 31**) so the side marked A will be toward the mechanical seal. Lubricate the seal lip using Suzuki Super Grease A or equivalent.

15. Position the mechanical seal in the base (**Figure 34**). Use a socket that matches the outside diameter of the new mechanical seal and drive the new seal into the base until it bottoms (**Figure 35**).

16. Install the E-ring onto the shaft with the flat side toward the gear end of the shaft.

17. Lubricate the shaft using Suzuki Super Grease A or equivalent.

18. Wrap tape around the impeller end of the shaft to protect the seal lip, then install the shaft. Remove the tape.

19. Install the slotted washer, rubber seal and seal ring into the impeller (**Figure 33**). Install the seal ring so the side marked A is toward the impeller.

20. Install the impeller onto the shaft.

21. Install the lockwasher (18, **Figure 27**) and gasket washer (17) onto the impeller (16). Install the lockwasher so the concave side is toward the threaded end of the bolt.

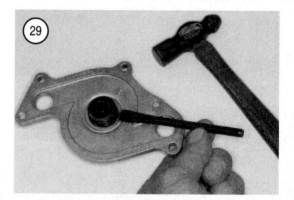

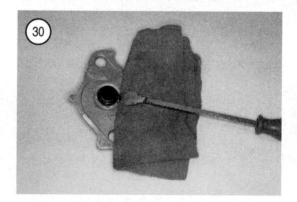

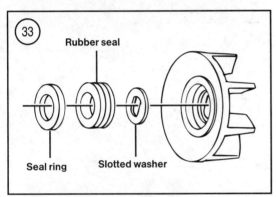

Rubber seal

Seal ring   Slotted washer

22. Apply Threadlock 1342 or equivalent to the bolt threads, then install the impeller retaining bolt. Tighten the bolt to 13 N•m (115 in.-lb.).

23. Install a new O-ring gasket onto the housing (**Figure 36**).

24. Install the housing onto the base assembly. Tighten the retaining screws (**Figure 28**) to 4.5 N•m (40 in.-lb.).

2001-on models

Refer to **Figure 37**.

1. Remove the mounting screws (**Figure 28**) and separate the base assembly from the housing.

2. Detach the E-ring (6, **Figure 37**) from the impeller shaft.

3. Lift out the impeller and shaft (**Figure 38**).

4. Using a chisel, raise the outer lip of the mechanical seal (**Figure 29**).

5. Using a heat gun, heat the area around the mechanical seal.

6. Using a suitable tool, pry the mechanical seal out of the base (**Figure 30**).

7. Pry out the oil seal (**Figure 31**).

8. Rotate the bearing (**Figure 32**) and check for excessive noise or roughness. If bearing operation is rough, replace the bearing by using a suitable puller or driving out the bearing.

9. Remove the seal ring from the impeller (**Figure 39**).

10. Thoroughly clean the water pump base and housing to remove all old coolant residue.

11. Check the impeller blades for corrosion or damage. If corrosion is excessive or if the blades are cracked or broken, replace the impeller.

12. Install the bearing so the numbered side is out. Drive in the bearing until it bottoms in the base.

10

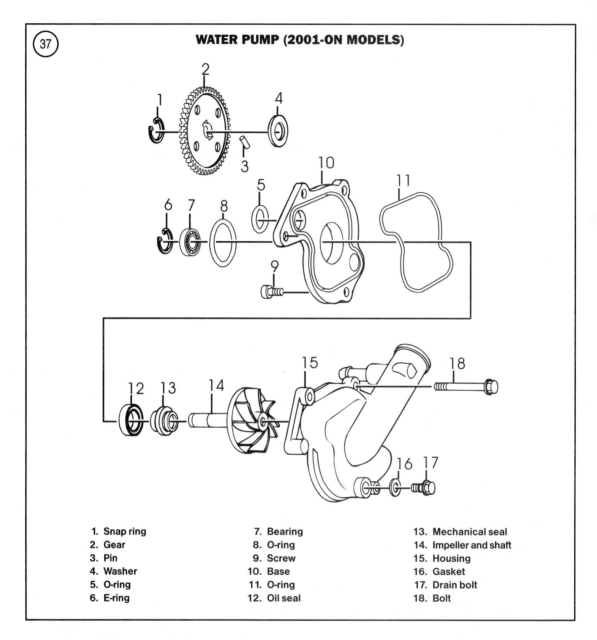

WATER PUMP (2001-ON MODELS)

1. Snap ring	7. Bearing	13. Mechanical seal
2. Gear	8. O-ring	14. Impeller and shaft
3. Pin	9. Screw	15. Housing
4. Washer	10. Base	16. Gasket
5. O-ring	11. O-ring	17. Drain bolt
6. E-ring	12. Oil seal	18. Bolt

13. Install the oil seal (**Figure 31**) so the side marked A will be toward the mechanical seal. Lubricate the seal lip using Suzuki Super Grease A or equivalent.

14. Position the mechanical seal in the base (**Figure 34**). Use a socket that matches the outside diameter of the new mechanical seal and drive the new seal into the base until it bottoms (**Figure 35**).

15. Wrap tape around the gear end of the shaft to protect the seal lip.

16. Lubricate the shaft using Suzuki Super Grease A or equivalent, then install the shaft. Remove the tape.

17. Install the original snap ring (A, **Figure 40**) into the shaft groove.

NOTE
When installing the E-ring, push the E-ring into the groove using a wood or soft tool to avoid damaging the surrounding surfaces.

18. Pull up the shaft using the snap ring (A, **Figure 40**) to expose the E-ring groove in the shaft. Install the E-ring (B) with the flat side toward the shaft end.

19. Remove the original snap ring (A, **Figure 40**).

20. Install a new O-ring gasket onto the housing (**Figure 36**).

21. Install the housing onto the base assembly. Tighten the retaining screws (**Figure 29**) to 4.5 N•m (40 in.-lb.).

COOLING FAN SWITCH

Removal/Installation

1. Drain the cooling system as described under *Coolant Change* in Chapter Three.

2. Move back the cover (**Figure 41**) on the cooling fan switch on the right side of the radiator. Determine if the switch is equipped with a removable connector. Later models are equipped with a switch (**Figure 42**) that cannot be disconnected from its wire lead.

   a. If equipped with a connector, detach the connector from the fan switch.

   b. If the fan switch is not equipped with a connector, raise the fuel tank and disconnect the fan switch connector (**Figure 43**). Release the wire lead from any retaining straps.

3. Remove the switch.

4. If necessary, test the switch as described in Chapter Nine.

5. Install by reversing the preceding removal steps while noting the following:

    a. Install a new O-ring. Apply a light coat of Suzuki Super Grease A or equivalent to the O-ring.

    b. Install the switch and tighten it to 13 N•m (115 in.-lb.).

    c. Refill the cooling system as described in Chapter Three.

    d. Start the engine and check for leaks before installing the lower fairing.

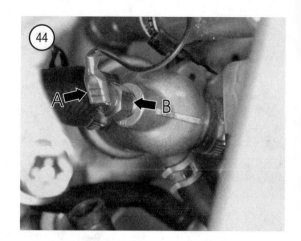

COOLANT TEMPERATURE SWITCH

Removal/Installation

1. Drain the cooling system as described under *Coolant Change* in Chapter Three.

2. Disconnect the electrical connector from the engine coolant temperature switch (A, **Figure 44**).

3. Unscrew the temperature sensor (B, **Figure 44**) from the thermostat housing and remove it.

4. Install by reversing the preceding removal steps while noting the following:

    a. Apply a light coat of Suzuki Bond 1207B or equivalent sealant to the sensor threads before installation.

    b. Tighten the switch to 10 N•m (88 in.-lb.).

    c. Refill the cooling system as described in Chapter Three.

    d. Start the engine and check for leaks before installing the lower fairing.

Table 1 COOLING SYSTEM SPECIFICATIONS

Item	Specification
Coolant capacity	1.6 L (1.7 U.S. qt., 1.4 Imp. qt.)*
Coolant type	High-quality ethylene glycol antifreeze compounded for aluminum engines
Coolant mix ratio	50/50
Radiator cap opening pressure	95-125 kPa (13.5-17.8 psi)
Thermostat opening	180° F (82° C)
*Includes reserve tank.	

Table 2 COOLING SYSTEM TORQUE SPECIFICATIONS

Item	N•m	in.-lb.	ft.-lb.
Clutch cover retaining bolts	10	88	–
Coolant temperature switch	10	88	–
Cooling fan switch	13	115	–
Water pump retaining bolts	13	115	–
Water pump impeller bolt	13	115	–
Water pump housing screws	4.5	40	–

CHAPTER ELEVEN

WHEELS, TIRES AND DRIVE CHAIN

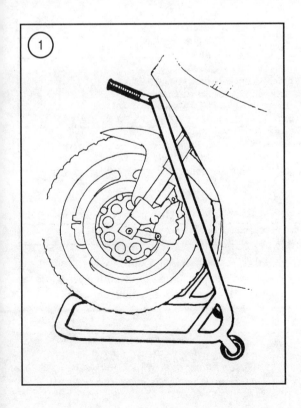

This chapter describes repair and maintenance procedures for the front and rear wheels, tires and the drive chain.

Specifications are located in **Table 1** and **Table 2** at the end of this chapter.

MOTORCYCLE STAND

Many procedures in this chapter require that the motorcycle be supported with a wheel off the ground. A motorcycle front end stand (**Figure 1**), swing arm stand or centerstand does this safely and effectively. Before purchasing or using a stand, check the manufacturer's instructions to make sure it is designed for the SV650. If the motorcycle or stand requires any adjustment or the installation of accessories (tie-downs), perform the required modification(s) before lifting the motorcycle. When using a motorcycle stand, have an assistant nearby.

> *CAUTION*
> *Regardless of the method used to lift a motorcycle, make sure the motorcycle*

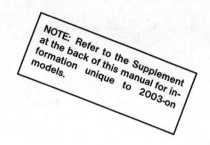

11

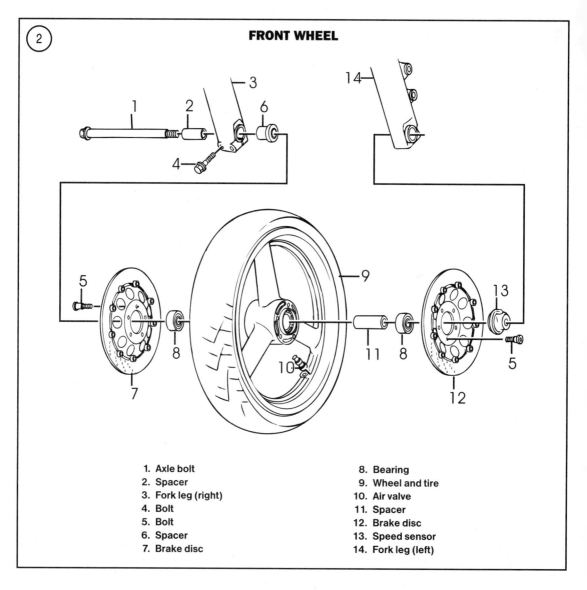

FRONT WHEEL

1. Axle bolt
2. Spacer
3. Fork leg (right)
4. Bolt
5. Bolt
6. Spacer
7. Brake disc
8. Bearing
9. Wheel and tire
10. Air valve
11. Spacer
12. Brake disc
13. Speed sensor
14. Fork leg (left)

is properly supported before walking away from it.

FRONT WHEEL

Removal

CAUTION
Use care when removing, handling and installing a wheel with disc brake rotors. The rotors can easily be damaged by side impacts due to their thin design. A rotor that is not true will cause brake pulsation. Protect the rotors if the wheels are being trans-ported for tire service. The rotors cannot be machined to repair excessive runout.

Refer to **Figure 2** when performing the following procedure.

1. Place the motorcycle on the sidestand.
2. Shift the transmission into gear to prevent the motorcycle from rolling in either direction while the motorcycle is on a jack or wooden blocks.

NOTE
Figure 3 *shows the fork leg on SV650S models, which have only one axle pinch bolt. SV650 models are equipped with two axle pinch bolts.*

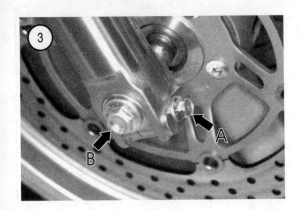

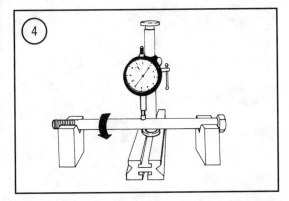

3. On the right fork leg, loosen the axle pinch bolt(s) (A, **Figure 3**), then loosen the front axle (B).

NOTE
Insert a piece of vinyl tubing or wood between the pads of each caliper once the caliper is removed. That way, if the brake lever is inadvertently squeezed, the pistons will not be forced out of the cylinder. If this does happen, the caliper may have to be disassembled to reseat the pistons and the system will have to be bled. By us-

ing a spacer, bleeding the brake is not necessary when installing the wheel.

4. Remove both brake calipers as described in Chapter Fourteen.

CAUTION
If using a jack, place a piece of wood on the jack pad to protect the motorcycle.

5. Place a suitable size jack, wooden blocks or other lifting device under the motorcycle to support the motorcycle securely with the front wheel off the ground.
6. Completely unscrew the axle from the left fork leg and remove the axle.

NOTE
Be prepared to catch the speedometer sensor when removing the front wheel. The sensor may fall out of the wheel or remain in it.

NOTE
Identify and mark all spacers so they may be returned to their original locations.

7. Pull the wheel down and forward and remove the wheel from the front fork.

CAUTION
Do not set the wheel down on the disc surface, as it may get scratched or warped. Set the tire sidewalls on two wooden blocks.

8. Inspect the wheel as described in this chapter.

Inspection

1. Remove any corrosion from the front axle with a piece of fine emery cloth. Clean the axle with solvent, and then wipe the axle clean with a lint-free cloth. Make sure all axle contact surfaces in both fork legs are clean.
2. Set the axle on V-blocks and place the tip of a dial indicator in the middle of the axle (**Figure 4**). Rotate the axle and measure axle runout. If axle runout exceeds 0.25 mm (0.010 in.), replace the axle. Do not attempt to straighten it.
3. Check the disc brake bolts (**Figure 5**) for tightness on each side. Correct tightening torque is 23 N•m (17 ft.-lb.). Tighten if necessary.
4. Check rim runout as follows:

11

a. Measure the radial (up and down) runout of the wheel rim with a dial indicator (A, **Figure 6**). If runout exceeds 2.0 mm (0.08 in.), check the wheel bearings. If the bearings are satisfactory, replace the wheel.

b. Measure the axial (side to side) runout of the wheel rim with a dial indicator (B, **Figure 6**). If runout exceeds 2.0 mm (0.08 in.), check the wheel bearings. If the bearings are satisfactory, replace the wheel.

5. Inspect the front wheel bearings as described in *Front and Rear Hubs* in this chapter.

6. Inspect the wheel rim for dents, bending or cracks. Check the rim and rim sealing surface for scratches that are deeper than 0.5 mm (0.01 in.). If any of these conditions are present, replace the wheel.

7. Clean the front axle spacers in solvent to remove old grease and dirt.

8. Inspect the brake pads (Chapter Fourteen).

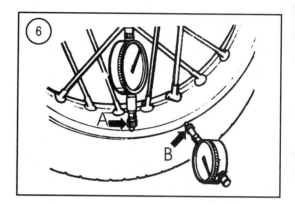

Installation

1. Make sure the bearing surfaces of each fork leg and the axle are free from burrs and nicks.

2. Position the drive lugs on the speedometer sensor (A, **Figure 7**) so they align with the recesses in the wheel hub (B), then install the sensor into the hub.

3. Correctly position the wheel so the directional arrow (**Figure 8**) on the tire points in the direction of normal wheel rotation.

4. Apply a light coat of grease to the front axle.

5. Position the wheel between the fork legs, lift the wheel and insert the front axle through the right fork leg, spacers, wheel hub, speed sensor and into the left fork leg.

6. Position the speed sensor so the boss on the sensor contacts the lug on the fork leg (**Figure 9**).

7. Screw the axle (B, **Figure 3**) into the left fork leg and tighten the axle securely.

8. Install both brake calipers as described in Chapter Fourteen.

9. Remove the jack, wooden block(s) or lifting device.

10. Have an assistant apply the front brake and tighten the axle (B, **Figure 3**) to 65 N•m (48 ft.-lb.).

11. Apply the front brake, push down hard on the handlebars and pump the fork four or five times to seat the front axle.

12. Tighten the front axle pinch bolts (A, **Figure 3**) to 23 N•m (17 ft.-lb.).

13. Shift the transmission into neutral.

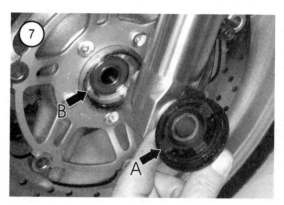

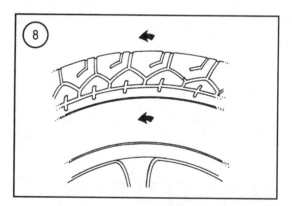

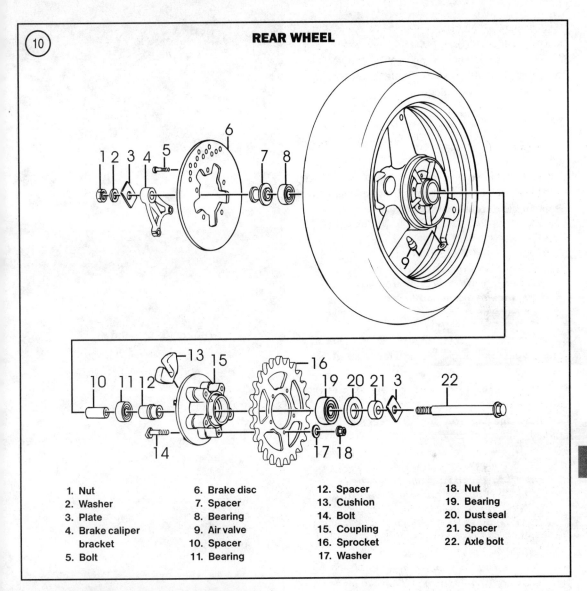

REAR WHEEL

1. Nut	6. Brake disc	12. Spacer	18. Nut
2. Washer	7. Spacer	13. Cushion	19. Bearing
3. Plate	8. Bearing	14. Bolt	20. Dust seal
4. Brake caliper	9. Air valve	15. Coupling	21. Spacer
bracket	10. Spacer	16. Sprocket	22. Axle bolt
5. Bolt	11. Bearing	17. Washer	

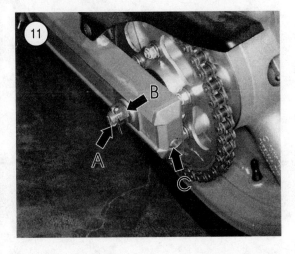

14. Roll the motorcycle back and forth several times. Apply the front brake as many times as necessary to make sure the brake pads seat against the brake discs correctly.

REAR WHEEL

Removal

Refer to **Figure 10** when performing the following procedure.

1. On all U.S. and Canada models, remove the cotter pin (A, **Figure 11**) from the rear axle nut. Install a *new* one during assembly.

2. Have an assistant apply the rear brake, and then loosen the axle nut (B, **Figure 11**).

3. Block the front wheel to prevent the motorcycle from rolling in either direction while the motorcycle is on a jack or wooden blocks.

> *CAUTION*
> *If using a jack, place a piece of wood on the jack pad to protect the motorcycle.*

4. Place a suitable size jack, wooden blocks or other lifting device under the motorcycle to support the motorcycle securely with the rear wheel off the ground.

> *WARNING*
> *If the motorcycle has just been run, the muffler will be very HOT. If possible, wait for the muffler to cool. If not, protect yourself accordingly.*

5. Loosen the adjuster (C, **Figure 11**) on each side of the swing arm to allow maximum slack in the drive chain.

6. Remove the rear axle nut (B, **Figure 11**) and the washer.

7. Remove the rear axle from the right side of the motorcycle.

> *NOTE*
> *Insert a piece of vinyl tubing or wood into the caliper in place of the brake disc. That way, if the brake pedal is inadvertently pressed, the pistons will not be forced out of the cylinders. If this does happen, the caliper may have to be disassembled to reseat the pistons and the system will have to be bled. By using a spacer, bleeding the brake is not necessary when installing the wheel.*

8. Lower the rear caliper, caliper carrier and torque link. Suspend the caliper from the frame with a bungee cord or piece of wire so there is no strain on the hydraulic hose.

9. Push the wheel forward and remove the drive chain from the rear sprocket.

> *NOTE*
> *Identify and mark all spacers when removing the rear wheel so they may be returned to their original locations.*

10. Pull the wheel rearward and remove the wheel from the swing arm.

> *CAUTION*
> *Do not set the wheel down on the disc surface, as it may get scratched or warped. Set the tire sidewalls on two wooden blocks.*

11. Inspect the wheel as described in this chapter.

Inspection

> *NOTE*
> *The rear wheel hub is equipped with a single seal that is located in the rear sprocket assembly.*

1. If still in place, remove the right (7, **Figure 10**) and left (21) axle spacers from the hub.

2. Clean the axle and spacers in solvent to remove all old grease and dirt. Make sure all axle contact surfaces are clean and free of dirt and old grease before installation. If these surfaces are not cleaned, the axle may be difficult to remove later.

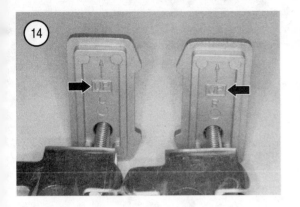

3. Place the axle on V-blocks and place the tip of a dial indicator in the middle of the axle (**Figure 4**). Rotate the axle and check the runout. If axle runout exceeds 0.25 mm (0.010 in.), replace the axle. Do not attempt to straighten it.

4. Check the rear sprocket nuts (**Figure 12**) for tightness. Correct tightening torque is 60 N•m (44 ft.-lb.). Tighten if necessary.

5. Check the disc brake bolts (**Figure 13**) for tightness. Correct tightening torque is 23 N•m (17 ft.-lb.). Tighten if necessary.

6. Check rim runout as follows:

   a. Measure the radial (up and down) runout of the wheel rim with a dial indicator (A, **Figure 6**). If runout exceeds 2.0 mm (0.08 in.), check the wheel bearings. If the bearings are satisfactory, replace the wheel.

   b. Measure the axial (side to side) runout of the wheel rim with a dial indicator (B, **Figure 6**). If runout exceeds 2.0 mm (0.08 in.), check the wheel bearings. If the bearings are satisfactory, replace the wheel.

7. Inspect the rear wheel and/or rear coupling bearings as described in *Front and Rear Hubs* in this chapter.

8. Inspect the wheel rim for dents, bending or cracks. Check the rim and rim sealing surface for scratches that are deeper than 0.5 mm (0.01 in.). If any of these conditions are present, replace the wheel.

9. Inspect the brake pads (Chapter Fourteen).

Installation

1. Make sure all axle contact surfaces on the swing arm and axle spacers are free of dirt and small burrs.

2. Apply a light coat of grease to the axle, bearings, spacers and grease seal.

3. Make sure the left (21, **Figure 10**) and right (7) axle spacers are installed on each side of the rear hub. The big end of the spacer (7) must contact the bearing.

4. Position the wheel into place and roll it forward. Install the drive chain onto the rear sprocket.

5. Remove the vinyl tubing or piece of wood from the brake caliper.

6. Move the rear brake caliper and bracket assembly onto the disc. Make sure the right axle spacer is still in place.

7. If removed, install the drive chain adjusters onto the swing arm with the UP mark (**Figure 14**) on each adjuster correctly oriented.

8. Raise the rear wheel up and into alignment with the swing arm. From the right side of the motorcycle insert the rear axle through the swing arm, the caliper bracket, the rear wheel and out through the left side of the swing arm. Push the axle all the way in until it bottoms in the swing arm.

9. Install the washer.

10. Install the rear axle nut (B, **Figure 11**). Hand-tighten the nut at this time.

11. Adjust the drive chain as described in Chapter Three.

12. Tighten the axle nut to 65 N•m (48 ft.lb.).

13. On all U.S. and Canada models, install a *new* cotter pin onto the rear axle nut (A, **Figure 11**) and bend both ends over completely.

14. Remove the jack or wooden block(s). Remove the blocks from the front wheel.

15. Roll the motorcycle back and forth the several times. Apply the rear brake as many times as necessary to make sure the brake pads are seated against the brake disc correctly.

REAR COUPLING AND REAR SPROCKET

Removal/Disassembly/Assembly/Installation

1. Remove the rear wheel as described in this chapter.

2. If still in place, remove the left axle spacer (21, **Figure 10**).

3. If the rear sprocket is going to be removed, loosen and remove the nuts (**Figure 12**) securing the rear sprocket to the rear coupling at this time.

NOTE
If the rear coupling assembly is difficult to remove from the hub, tap on the backside of the sprocket (from the op-

11

posite side of the wheel through the wheel spokes) with the wooden handle of a hammer. Tap evenly around the perimeter of the sprocket until the coupling assembly is free of the hub and the rubber dampers.

4. Pull straight up and remove the rear coupling assembly from the rear hub.

5. Remove the inner retainer (A, **Figure 15**) from the rear coupling assembly.

6. If necessary, remove the rear sprocket nuts (**Figure 12**) and separate the rear sprocket from the rear coupling.

7. Install by reversing the preceding removal steps while noting the following:

   a. Align the rear coupling bosses (B, **Figure 15**) with the rubber damper receptacles (A, **Figure 16**) and install the rear coupling.

   b. If removed, install the rear sprocket so the side with the stamping (**Figure 17**) faces out away from the rear coupling.

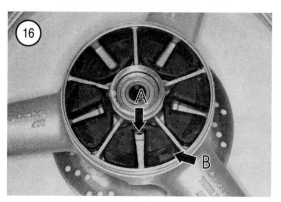

> *CAUTION*
> *On a new machine or after a new rear sprocket has been installed, check the torque on the rear sprocket nuts after 10 minutes of riding and after each 10-minute riding period until the nuts have seated to the new sprocket and remain tight. Failure to keep the sprocket nuts correctly tightened will damage the rear coupling.*

   c. Tighten the rear sprocket nuts to 60 N•m (44 ft.-lb.) after the assembly has been reinstalled in the rear wheel.

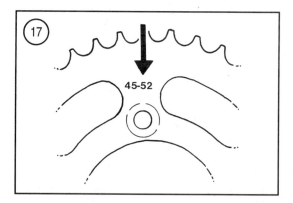

Inspection

1. Inspect the rubber dampers (B, **Figure 16**) for damage or deterioration. If damaged, replace as a complete set.

2. Inspect the raised webs (**Figure 18**) in the rear hub. Check for cracks or wear. If any damage is visible, replace the rear wheel.

3. Inspect the rear coupling assembly for cracks or damage. Replace if necessary.

4. Inspect the rear sprocket teeth. If the teeth are worn (**Figure 19**), replace the rear sprocket as described in this chapter.

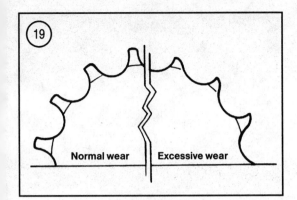

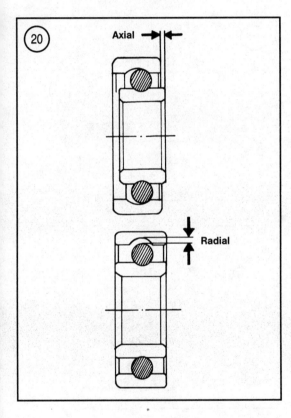

CAUTION
If the rear sprocket requires replacement, also replace the engine sprocket and the drive chain. Never install a new drive chain over worn sprockets or a worn drive chain over new sprockets. The old part wears out the new part prematurely.

5. If the rear sprocket requires replacement, also inspect the drive chain (Chapter Three) and engine sprocket (this chapter). They also may be worn and need replacing.

6. Inspect the bearing for excessive axial play (end play) and radial (side play) (**Figure 20**). Replace the bearing if it has an excess amount of free play.

7. On a non-sealed bearing, check the balls for wear, pitting or excessive heat (bluish tint). Turn the inner race by hand. The bearing must turn smoothly without excessive play or noise. Replace a questionable bearing. When replacing the bearing, compare the new and old bearing to ensure a match.

NOTE
Fully sealed bearings are available from many bearing specialty shops. Fully sealed bearings provide better protection from dirt and moisture.

FRONT WHEEL HUB

Preliminary Inspection

Inspect each wheel bearing before removing it from the wheel hub.

CAUTION
Do not remove the wheel bearings for inspection purposes. The bearings will be damaged during removal. Remove the wheel bearings only if replacing them.

1. Perform Steps 1-3 of *Disassembly* in the following procedure.

2. Turn each bearing by hand. The bearings must turn smoothly with no roughness.

3. Inspect the play of the inner race of each wheel bearing. Check for excessive axial play and radial play (**Figure 20**). Replace the bearing if it has an excess amount of free play.

4. On non-sealed bearings, check the balls for wear, pitting or excessive heat (bluish tint). Replace the bearings if necessary; always replace as a complete set. When replacing the bearings, compare the new and old bearings to ensure a match.

NOTE
Fully sealed bearings are available from many bearing specialty shops. Fully sealed bearings provide better protection from dirt and moisture that may get into the hub.

11

Disassembly

1. Remove the front wheel as described in this chapter.

2. If necessary, remove the bolts (A, **Figure 21**) securing the brake discs and remove the discs.

3. Before proceeding further, inspect the wheel bearings (B, **Figure 21**) as described in this chapter. If they must be replaced, proceed as follows.

> *WARNING*
> *Wear safety glasses while removing the wheel bearings.*

4A. A special Suzuki tool (part No. 09941-50111) can be used to remove the wheel bearings as follows:

  a. Insert the remover head (**Figure 22**) into one of the wheel bearings from the outer surface of the wheel hub.

  b. Turn the wheel over and insert the remover shaft (**Figure 22**) into the backside of the adapter. Tap the wedge and force it into the slit in the remover head (**Figure 22**). This will force the remover head against the bearing inner race.

  c. Tap on the end of the remover shaft with a hammer and drive the bearing out of the hub. Remove the bearing and the spacer.

  d. Repeat for the bearing on the other side.

4B. If the special tools are not used, perform the following:

  a. To remove the right and left bearings and spacer, insert a soft aluminum brass drift into one side of the hub.

  b. Push the inner spacer over to one side and place the drift on the inner race of the lower bearing (**Figure 23**, typical).

  c. Tap the bearing out of the hub with a hammer, working around the perimeter of the inner race. Remove the bearing and inner spacer.

  d. Repeat for the other bearing.

5. Clean the inside and outside of the hub with solvent. Dry with compressed air.

Assembly

> *CAUTION*
> *Always reinstall **new** bearings. The bearings are damaged during removal and must not be reused.*

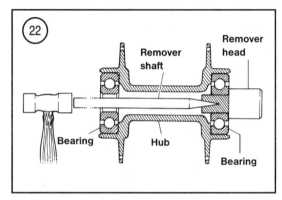

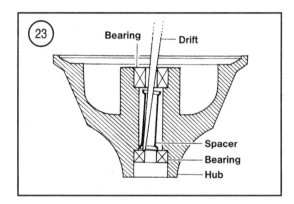

> *NOTE*
> *Replace bearings as a set. If any one bearing in a wheel is worn, replace both bearings.*

1. On non-sealed bearings, pack the bearings with a good quality waterproof bearing grease. To pack bearings, spread some grease in the palm of your hand and scrape the open side of the bearing across your palm until the bearing is packed completely full with grease. Spin the bearing a few times to determine if there are any open areas. Repack if necessary.

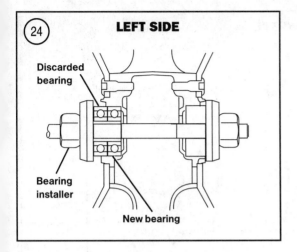

(24) LEFT SIDE

Discarded bearing

Bearing installer

New bearing

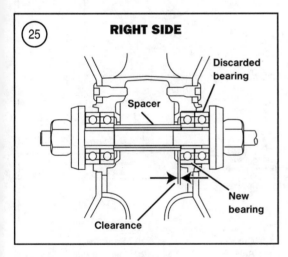

(25) RIGHT SIDE

Discarded bearing

Spacer

New bearing

Clearance

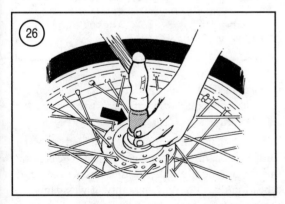

(26)

2. Blow any dirt or debris out of the hub prior to installing the new bearings.

CAUTION
Tap the bearings squarely into place.
Tap on the outer race only; do not tap

on the inner race or the bearing may be damaged. Be sure that the bearings are completely seated.

NOTE
Suzuki does not provide a specification for the slight clearance between the bearing and the spacer. The important thing is that these two parts are not pressed up against each other.

3A. A special Suzuki tool (part No.09941-34513) can be used to install the wheel bearings as follows:
   a. Install the left bearing into the hub first.
   b. Position the bearing with the sealed side facing out.

NOTE
When using a discarded bearing as a spacer, grind away a slight amount of the outside of the outer bearing race. This will prevent the old bearing from sticking in the hub bearing bore. Be sure to clean the old bearing before using it to prevent any debris from entering the hub or new bearing.

   c. Place a discarded bearing or suitable size socket against the new bearing and install the bearing installer as shown in **Figure 24**.
   d. Tighten the installer (**Figure 24**) and pull the left bearing into the hub until it is completely seated. Remove the bearing installer.
   e. Turn the wheel over (right side up) on the workbench. Apply a light coat of grease to the spacer and install it in the hub.
   f. Position the right bearing with the sealed side facing out.
   g. Place a discarded bearing or suitable size socket against the new bearing and install the bearing installer as shown in **Figure 25**.
   h. Tighten the installer and pull the right bearing into the hub until there is a *slight clearance* between the inner race and the spacer. At this time the bearing is correctly seated. Remove the bearing installer.

3B. If the special tools are not used, perform the following:
   a. Place the left bearing onto the hub with the sealed side facing out.
   b. Tap the left bearing squarely into place. Tap on the outer race only. Use a socket (**Figure 26**,

11

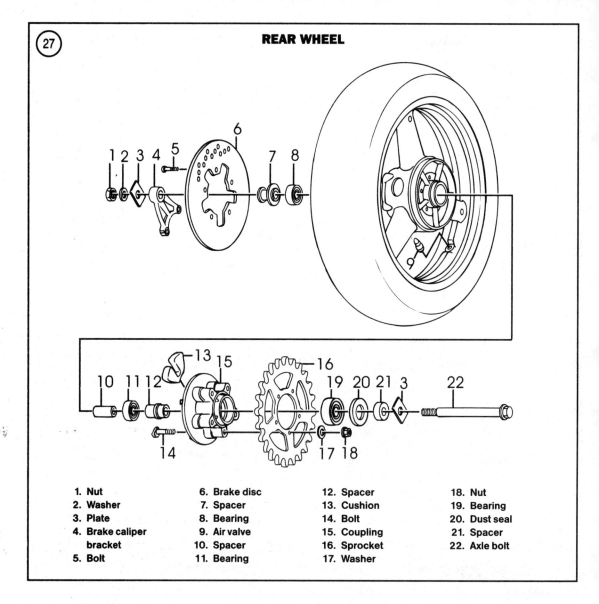

REAR WHEEL

1. Nut
2. Washer
3. Plate
4. Brake caliper bracket
5. Bolt
6. Brake disc
7. Spacer
8. Bearing
9. Air valve
10. Spacer
11. Bearing
12. Spacer
13. Cushion
14. Bolt
15. Coupling
16. Sprocket
17. Washer
18. Nut
19. Bearing
20. Dust seal
21. Spacer
22. Axle bolt

typical) that matches the outer race diameter. Do not tap on the inner race or the bearing will be damaged. Be sure the bearing is completely seated.

c. Turn the wheel over (right side up) on the workbench. Apply a light coat of grease to the spacer and install it in the hub.

d. Place the right bearing on the hub with the sealed side facing out.

e. Tap the right bearing squarely into place. Tap on the outer race only. Use a socket (**Figure 26**) that matches the outer race diameter. Do not tap on the inner race or the bearing will be damaged. Tap the right bearing into the hub

until there is a *slight clearance* between the inner race and the spacer. At this time, the bearing is correctly seated.

4. Check that both bearings are installed squarely. Turn each bearing's inner race by hand. The bearing must turn smoothly with no roughness or binding. If a bearing does not turn smoothly, it was damaged during installation. Remove and replace that bearing.

5. Use a small amount of a locking compound such as ThreeBond No. TB 1360 (red) or Loctite 271 (red) on the brake disc mounting screws prior to installation. Install the brake disc and the bolts (A, **Figure 21**). Tighten the bolts to 23 N•m (17 ft.-lb.).

6. Install the front wheel as described in this chapter.

REAR WHEEL HUB

Preliminary Inspection

Inspect each wheel bearing before removing it from the wheel hub.

CAUTION
Do not remove the wheel bearings for inspection purposes. The bearings will be damaged during removal. Remove the wheel bearings only if replacing them.

1. Perform Steps 1-3 of *Disassembly* in the following procedure.
2. Turn each bearing by hand. The bearings must turn smoothly with no roughness.
3. Inspect the play of the inner race of each wheel bearing. Check for excessive axial play and radial play (**Figure 20**). Replace the bearing if it has an excess amount of free play.

4. On non-sealed bearings, check the balls for wear, pitting or excessive heat (bluish tint). Replace the bearings if necessary; always replace as a complete set. When replacing the bearings, compare the new and old bearings to ensure a match.

NOTE
Fully sealed bearings are available from many bearing specialty shops. Fully sealed bearings provide better protection from dirt and moisture that may get into the hub.

Disassembly

Refer to **Figure 27** when performing the following procedure.
1. Remove the rear wheel as described in this chapter.
2. If still in place, remove the right and left axle spacers.
3. If still installed, remove the rear sprocket and coupling assembly from the rear hub as described in this chapter.
4. Remove the rubber dampers (**Figure 28**) from the rear hub.
5. If necessary, remove the bolts (**Figure 29**) securing the brake disc and remove the disc.
6. Before proceeding further, inspect the wheel bearings as described in this chapter. If they must be replaced, proceed as follows.

WARNING
Wear safety glasses while removing the wheel bearings.

7A. If the special tools are not used, perform the following:
  a. To remove the right and left bearings and spacer, insert a soft aluminum or brass drift into one side of the hub.
  b. Push the distance collar over to one side and place the drift on the inner race of the lower bearing.
  c. Tap the bearing out of the hub with a hammer, working around the perimeter of the inner race (**Figure 30**, typical). Remove the bearing and spacer.
  d. Repeat for the bearing on the other side.

NOTE
The Kowa Seiki Wheel Bearing Remover set can be ordered by a Suzuki

11

dealership through K & L Supply Co. in Santa Clara, CA.

7B. To remove the bearings with the Kowa Seiki Wheel Bearing Remover set, perform the following:

a. Select the correct size remover head tool and insert it into the bearing.

b. Turn the wheel over and insert the remover shaft into the backside of the adapter. Tap the shaft and force it into the slit in the adapter (**Figure 22**). This will force the adapter against the bearing inner race.

c. Tap on the end of the shaft with a hammer and drive the bearing out of the hub. Remove the bearing and the distance collar.

d. Repeat for the bearing on the other side.

8. Clean the inside and the outside of the hub with solvent. Dry with compressed air.

Assembly

> *CAUTION*
> *Always reinstall **new** bearings. The bearings are damaged during removal and must not be reused.*

> *NOTE*
> *Replace bearings as a set. If any one bearing in a wheel is worn, replace all the bearings. Replace both wheel bearings as well as the rear coupling bearing.*

1. On non-sealed bearings, pack the bearings with waterproof bearing grease. To pack the bearings, spread some grease in the palm of your hand and scrape the open side of the bearing across your palm until the bearing is completely packed full of grease. Spin the bearing a few times to determine if there are any open areas. Repack if necessary.

2. Blow any dirt or debris out of the hub before installing the new bearings.

> *CAUTION*
> *Install non-sealed bearings with the single sealed side facing outward. Tap the bearings squarely into place and tap on the outer race only. Applying pressure to the inner race will damage the bearing. Be sure the bearings are completely seated.*

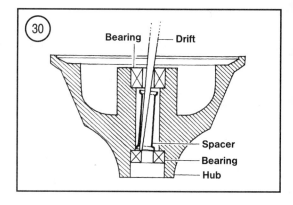

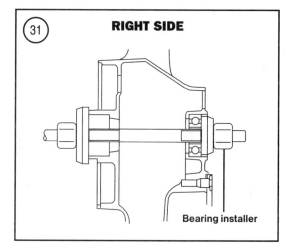

> *NOTE*
> *Suzuki does not provide a specification for the **slight clearance** between the bearing and the spacer. The important thing is that these two parts are not pressed up against each other.*

3A. A special Suzuki tool set (part No. 09924-84510) can be used to install the wheel bearings as follows:

a. Install the right bearing into the hub first.

b. Place the right bearing with the sealed side facing out, and install the bearing installer as shown in **Figure 31**.

c. Tighten the bearing installer and pull the right bearing into the hub until it is completely seated. Remove the bearing installer.

d. Turn the wheel over (left side up) on the workbench and install the spacer.

e. Place the left bearing into the hub with the sealed side facing out, and install the bearing installer as shown in **Figure 32**.

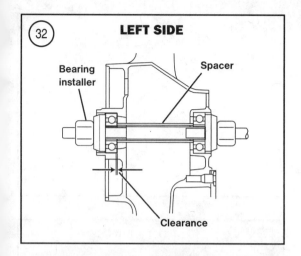

LEFT SIDE

Bearing installer

Spacer

Clearance

f. Tighten the bearing installer and pull the left bearing into the hub until there is a *slight clearance* between the inner race and the spacer.

g. Remove the bearing installer.

3B. If special tools are not used, perform the following:

a. Install the right bearing first.

b. Using a socket that matches the outer race diameter, tap the right bearing squarely into place in the hub. Tap on the outer race only (**Figure 26**, typical). Do not tap on the inner race or the bearing may be damaged. Make sure the bearing is completely seated.

c. Turn the wheel over on the workbench and install the spacer.

d. Use the same tool set-up and drive the left bearing into the hub until there is a *slight clearance* between the inner race and the distance collar.

4. If the brake disc was removed, perform the following:

   a. Apply a small amount of a locking compound such as ThreeBond No. TB1360 or Loctite No. 271 to the brake disc bolt threads before installation.

   b. Install the brake disc. Tighten the brake disc bolts (**Figure 29**) to 23 N•m (17 ft.lb.).

5. Install the right and left axle spacers.

6. Install the rubber dampers (**Figure 28**) into the rear hub.

7. Install the rear sprocket and coupling assembly into the rear hub as described in this chapter.

8. Install the rear wheel as described in this chapter.

WHEEL BALANCE

An unbalanced wheel is unsafe. Depending upon the degree of imbalance and the speed of the motorcycle, the rider may experience anything from a mild vibration to a violent shimmy that could lead to a loss of control.

The balance weights attach to the rim on the SV650. Weight kits are available from motorcycle dealerships. These kits contain test weights and strips of adhesive-backed weights that can be cut to the desired weight and attached to the rim.

Before attempting to balance the wheel, make sure the wheel bearings are in good condition and properly lubricated and that the brakes do not drag. The wheel must rotate freely.

NOTE
When balancing the wheels, do so with the brake disc(s) and the rear coupling attached. These components rotate with the wheel and they affect the balance.

1A. Remove the front wheel as described in this chapter.

1B. Remove the rear wheel as described in this chapter.

2. Mount the wheel on a stand (**Figure 33**) so the wheel can rotate freely. A suitable wooden stand can be easily fabricated.

3. Spin the wheel and let it coast to a stop. Mark the tire at the lowest point with chalk or light colored crayon.

11

4. Spin the wheel several more times. If the wheel keeps coming to rest at the same point, it is out of balance.

5. Attach a test weight to the upper (or light) side of the wheel.

6. Experiment with different weights until the wheel, when spun, comes to rest at a different position each time.

7. Remove the test weight, thoroughly clean the rim surface, then install the correct size weight onto the rim. Make sure it is secured in place so it does not fly off when riding.

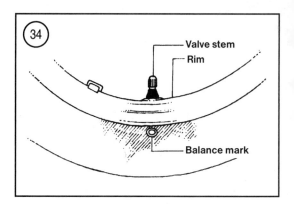

TIRE SAFETY

Tire wear and performance is greatly affected by tire pressure. Have a good tire gauge on hand and make a habit of frequent pressure checks. Refer to Chapter Three for original equipment tire specifications. If using another tire brand, follow their recommendation.

Follow a sensible break-in period when running on new tires. New tires will exhibit significantly less adhesion ability. Do not subject a new tire to hard cornering, hard acceleration or hard braking for the first 100 miles (160 km).

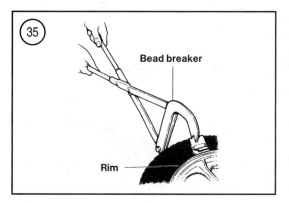

TIRE CHANGING

The original equipment cast alloy wheels are designed for use with tubeless tires only. These wheels can easily be damaged during tire removal. Take special care to avoid scratching and gouging the outer rim surface, especially when using tire irons. Insert scraps of leather between the tire iron and the rim to protect the rim from damage.

When removing a tubeless tire, take care not to damage the tire beads, inner liner of the tire or the wheel rim flange. Use tire levers or flat-handle tire irons with rounded heads.

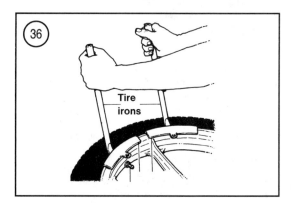

the other hand, a pneumatic tire changer can easily break the beads loose, as well as remove and install the tire without damaging the cast wheel. The following procedure is provided if this alternative is not chosen.

Tire Removal

> *CAUTION*
> *Suzuki recommends that the tires be removed with a tire changer. Due to the large and rigid tires, tire removal with tire irons can be difficult and result in rim damage. On*

> *CAUTION*
> *To avoid damage when removing the tire, support the wheel on two blocks of wood so the brake discs or*

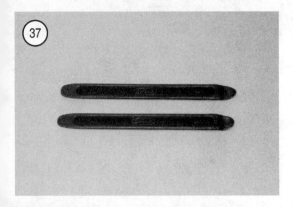

the rear sprocket does not contact the floor.

NOTE
To make tire removal easier, warming the tire will make it softer and more pliable. Place the wheel and tire assembly in the sun. If possible, place the wheel assembly in a completely closed motorcycle. At the same time, place the new tire in the same location.

1A. Remove the front wheel as described in this chapter.

1B. Remove the rear wheel as described in this chapter.

2. If not already marked by the tire manufacturer, mark the valve stem location on the tire (**Figure 34**), in order to install the tire in the same location for easier balancing.

3. Remove the valve core from the valve stem and deflate the tire.

CAUTION
The inner rim and bead area are the sealing surfaces on the tubeless tire. Do not scratch the inside of the rim or damage the tire bead.

NOTE
*Removal of tubeless tires from their rims can be very difficult because of the exceptionally tight tire bead-to-rim seal. Breaking the bead seal may require the use of a special tool (**Figure 35**). If the seal does not break loose, take the wheel to a motorcycle repair shop and have them break it loose on a tire changing machine.*

4. Press the entire bead on both sides of the tire away from the rim and into the center of the rim.

5. Lubricate both beads with soapy water.

CAUTION
*Use rim protectors (**Figure 36**) or insert scraps of leather between the tire iron and the rim to protect the rim from damage.*

NOTE
*Use only quality tire irons without sharp edges (**Figure 37**). If necessary, file the ends of the tire irons to remove rough edges.*

6. Insert a tire iron under the top bead next to the valve stem (**Figure 38**). Force the bead on the opposite side of the tire into the center of the rim and pry the bead over the rim with the tire iron.

7. Insert a second tire iron next to the first iron to hold the bead over the rim. Then work around the tire with the first tire iron, prying the bead over the rim (**Figure 39**).

11

8. Stand the wheel upright. Insert a tire iron between the second bead and the side of the rim that the first bead was pried over (**Figure 40**). Force the bead on the opposite side from the tire iron into the center of the rim. Pry the back bead off the rim working around as with the first bead.

9. Inspect the valve stem seal. It is advisable to replace the valve stem when replacing the tire.

10. Remove the old valve stem and discard it. Inspect the valve stem hole (**Figure 41**) in the rim. Remove any dirt or corrosion from the hole and wipe it dry with a clean cloth. Install a new valve stem and make sure it properly seats in the rim.

11. Carefully inspect the tire and wheel rim for any damage as described in the following.

Tire and Wheel Inspection

1. Wipe off the inner surfaces of the wheel rim. Clean off any rubber residue or any oxidation.

> *WARNING*
> *Carefully consider whether a tire should be replaced. If there is any doubt about the quality of the existing tire, replace it with a new one. Do not take a chance on a tire failure at any speed.*

2. If any one of the following is observed, replace the tire with a new one:

   a. A puncture or split with a total length or diameter exceeding 6 mm (0.24 in.).

   b. A scratch or split on the sidewall.

   c. Any type of ply separation.

   d. Tread separation or excessive abnormal wear pattern.

   e. Tread depth of less than the minimum value specified (**Table 1**) for original equipment tires. Aftermarket tire tread depth minimum may vary.

   f. Scratches on either sealing bead.

   g. The cord is cut in any place.

   h. Flat spots in the tread from skidding.

   i. Any abnormality in the inner liner.

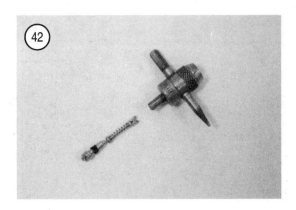

3. Inspect the valve stem hole in the rim. Remove any dirt or corrosion from the hole, and wipe it dry with a clean cloth.

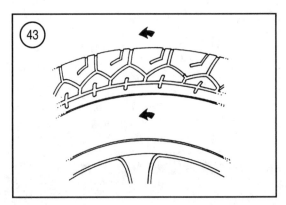

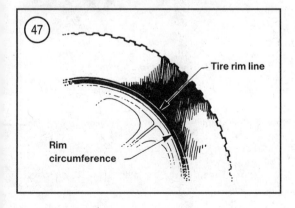

Tire Installation

1. Inspect the valve stem core rubber seal (**Figure 42**) for hardness or deterioration. Replace the valve core if necessary.

2. A new tire may have balancing rubbers inside. These are not patches and must be left in place. Most tires are marked with a colored spot near the bead (**Figure 34**) that indicates a lighter point on the tire. This should be placed next to the valve stem.

3. Lubricate both beads of the tire with soapy water.

4. When installing the tire on the rim, make sure the correct tire, either front or rear, is installed on the correct wheel. Also, install the tire so the direction arrow faces the normal direction of wheel rotation (**Figure 43**).

5. If remounting the old tire, align the mark made in Step 2 of *Removal* with the valve stem. If installing a new tire, align the colored stop near the bead (indicating the lightest point of the tire) with the valve stem. See **Figure 34**.

6. Place the backside of the tire onto the rim so the lower bead sits in the center of the rim while the upper bead remains outside the rim (**Figure 44**). Work around the tire in both directions and press the lower bead, by hand, into the center of the rim. Use a tire iron for the last few inches of bead.

7. Press the upper bead into the rim opposite the valve stem. Working on both sides of this initial point, pry the bead into the rim with a tire tool, and work around the rim to the valve stem (**Figure 45**). If the tire wants to pull up on one side, either use another tire iron or a knee to hold the tire in place. The last few inches are usually the toughest to install. If possible, continue to push the tire into the rim with by hand. Relubricate the bead if necessary. If the tire bead wants to pull out from under the rim, use both knees to hold the tire in place. If necessary, use a tire iron for the last few inches (**Figure 46**).

8. Bounce the wheel several times, rotating it each time. This forces the tire bead against the rim flanges. After the tire beads are in contact with the rim, inflate the tire to seat the beads.

9. Place an inflatable band around the circumference of the tire. Slowly inflate the band until the tire beads are pressed against the rim. Inflate the

11

tire enough to seat it. Deflate the band and remove it.

WARNING
In the next step, never exceed 400 kPa (56 psi) inflation pressure as the tire could burst, causing severe injury. Never stand directly over a tire while inflating it.

10. After inflating the tire, check to see that the beads are fully seated and that the rim lines are the same distance from the rim all the way around the tire (**Figure 47**). If the beads are seated, deflate the tire and lubricate the rim and beads with soapy water.

11. Reinflate the tire to the required pressure as listed in **Table 1**. Install the valve stem cap.

12. Balance the wheel as described in this chapter.

13A. Install the front wheel as described in this chapter.

13B. Install the rear wheel as described in this chapter.

TIRE REPAIRS

WARNING
Do not install an inner tube inside a tubeless tire. The tube will cause an abnormal heat buildup in the tire.

NOTE
Changing or patching on the road is very difficult. A can of pressurized tire sealant may inflate the tire and seal the hole, but this is only a temporary fix.

Tubeless tires have the word TUBELESS molded into the sidewall and the rims have SUITABLE FOR TUBELESS TIRES or equivalent (**Figure 48**) cast on them.

Never attempt to repair a tubeless motorcycle tire using a plug or cord patch applied from outside the tire. This type of repair might be acceptable for automobiles, but they are not safe on a motorcycle tire, especially on a high-performance motorcycle like the SV650.

If the tire is punctured, remove it from the rim, inspect the inside of the tire, and apply a combination plug/patch from inside the tire (**Figure 49**) as follows.

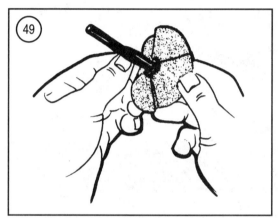

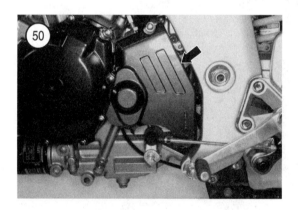

WARNING
After repairing a tubeless tire, do not exceed 30 mph (50 kph) for the first 24 hours. Do not exceed 80 mph (130 kph) on a repaired tubeless tire. The patch could work lose because of tire flex and heat, resulting in a serious accident.

1. Remove the tire from the wheel rim as described in this chapter.

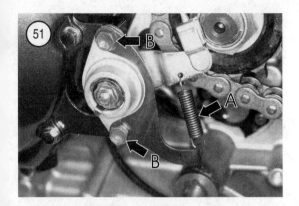

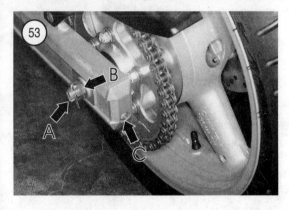

2. Inspect the rim inner flange. Smooth any scratches on the sealing surface with emery cloth. If a scratch is deeper than 0.5 mm (0.020 in.), replace the wheel.

3. Inspect the tire inside and out. Replace a tire if any of the following conditions are found:

    a. A puncture larger than 6 mm (1/4 in) diameter.

    b. A punctured or damaged sidewall.

    c. More than two punctures in the tire.

    d. Tread depth less than the minimum value specified in Chapter Three.

    e. Ply or tread separation.

    f. Flat spots.

    g. Scratches on the bead.

    h. Cuts in the cord.

4. Apply the plug/patch following the manufacturer's instructions with the patch kit.

DRIVE CHAIN

Removal/Installation

1. Remove the swing arm as described in Chapter Thirteen.

2. Remove the engine sprocket cover as described in this chapter.

3. Slide the drive chain off the engine sprocket and remove it from the motorcycle.

4. Installation is the reverse of removal.

SPROCKETS

Inspection

    Refer to *Drive Chain and Sprocket Wear Inspection* in Chapter Three.

Drive Sprocket Removal

1. Place the motorcycle on the sidestand on level ground.

2. Shift the transmission into sixth gear.

3. Remove the sprocket cover bolts, then remove the sprocket cover (**Figure 50**).

4. Detach the clutch release spring (A, **Figure 51**).

5. Remove the clutch release mechanism bolts (B, **Figure 51**) and move the mechanism out of the way.

6. Using a suitable tool, bend back the washer (A, **Figure 52**) from the sprocket nut (B).

7. On all U.S. and Canada models, remove the cotter pin (A, **Figure 53**) from the rear axle nut. Install a *new* one during assembly.

8. Loosen the axle nut (B, **Figure 53**) and the sprocket nut (B, **Figure 52**).

9. Loosen the chain adjusters (C, **Figure 53**) on both ends of the swing arm. Push the rear wheel forward until maximum chain slack is obtained.

10. Disengage the drive chain from the drive sprocket.

11

11. Remove the nut, washer and drive sprocket (**Figure 54**).

Drive Sprocket Installation

1. Install the drive sprocket, washer and nut (**Figure 54**) onto the countershaft.

> *NOTE*
> *The transmission must be in sixth gear when tightening the drive sprocket nut.*

2. Tighten the drive sprocket nut to 145 N•m (105 ft.-lb.).

3. Bend the washer (A, **Figure 52**) and flatten it against one of the flats on the sprocket nut.

4. Install the drive chain onto the drive sprocket.

5. Install the clutch release mechanism and the clutch release spring (A, **Figure 51**).

6. Install the sprocket cover (**Figure 50**).

7. Adjust the drive chain tension as described in Chapter Three.

Rear Sprocket Removal/Installation

Refer to *Rear Coupling and Rear Sprocket* in this chapter.

Table 1 WHEELS, TIRES AND DRIVE CHAIN SPECIFICATIONS

Item	New	Service limit
Front axle runout (max.)	–	0.25 mm (0.010 in.)
Rear axle runout (max.)	–	0.25 mm (0.010 in.)
Wheel rim axial runout (max.)	–	2.0 mm (0.08 in.)
Wheel rim radial runout (max.)	–	2.0 mm (0.08 in.)

Table 2 WHEELS, TIRES AND DRIVE CHAIN TORQUE SPECIFICATIONS

Item	N•m	in.-lb.	ft.-lb.
Drive sprocket nut	145	–	105
Front axle	65	–	48
Front axle pinch bolt	23	–	17
Front brake disc			
mounting bolts	23	–	17
Rear axle	65	–	48
Rear brake disc			
mounting bolts	23	–	17
Rear sprocket nut	60	–	44

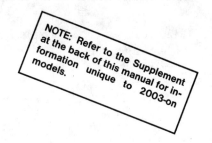

NOTE: Refer to the Supplement at the back of this manual for information unique to 2003-on models.

CHAPTER TWELVE

FRONT SUSPENSION AND STEERING

This chapter describes repair and maintenance procedures for the front fork and steering components. Front wheel removal, front hub service, tire changing, tire repair and wheel balancing are covered in Chapter Eleven. Front suspension specifications are listed in **Table 1** and **Table 2** at the end of the chapter.

HANDLEBAR

There are two different handlebar configurations used on these models, and they are covered in separate procedures. The SV650S model is equipped with separate (clip-on) handlebars on each side that can be removed separately. On all other models, the handlebar is a single continuous bar that is removed as an assembly.

SV650 Models

Removal

> *CAUTION*
> *Cover the front fender and front wheel with a heavy cloth or plastic tarp to protect them from accidental brake fluid spills. Brake fluid can mar or discolor painted or plastic surfaces. Immediately wash the surface using soapy water and rinse completely.*

> *NOTE*
> *It is not necessary to remove the fuel tank, but removal will prevent possible damage to it.*

1. Remove the fuel tank as described in Chapter Eight.

2. Unscrew the rear view mirror (A, **Figure 1**) from the master cylinder mounting bracket.

3. Remove the front master cylinder bolts and clamp. Remove the master cylinder (B, **Figure 1**) from the handlebar and lay it over the front fender. Keep the reservoir in the upright position to minimize the loss of brake fluid and to keep air from entering the brake system. It is not necessary to remove the hydraulic brake line from the master cylinder.

4. Remove the screws that hold the right handlebar switch (C, **Figure 1**) together, separate the switch and remove it from the handlebar. Lay it over the front fender.

5. Remove the balancer assembly (**Figure 2**) from the end of the right handlebar (D, **Figure 1**).

6. Disconnect the throttle cables from the grip and slide the throttle grip assembly (E, **Figure 1**) off the end of the handlebar. Move the cables out of the way. Do not crimp or damage the throttle cables.

7. Unscrew the rear view mirror (A, **Figure 3**) from the clutch lever mounting bracket.

8. Remove the balancer assembly (**Figure 2**) from the end of the left handlebar (B, **Figure 3**).

9. Remove the left hand grip (C, **Figure 3**) as described in this chapter.

10. Disconnect the clutch safety switch electrical connector from the switch.

11. Remove the screws that hold the left handlebar switch (D, **Figure 3**) together, separate the switch. Disconnect the choke cable from the choke lever (E, **Figure 3**). Remove the switch from the handlebar and lay it over the front fender. Slide the choke lever off the end of the handlebar and keep it with the switch assembly.

12. Loosen the clamp screw on the clutch lever assembly. Slide the clutch lever assembly (F, **Figure 3**) off the handlebar. Do not crimp or damage the clutch cable.

13. Remove the trim caps from the top of the handlebar upper holder Allen bolts.

14. Remove the handlebar upper holder bolts and the handlebar upper holders (**Figure 4**).

15. Remove the handlebar.

16. The knurling must be kept clean to ensure secure grip is maintained on the handlebar. Also, thoroughly clean the upper and lower handlebar holders. Make sure the knurled area of the handlebar and the handlebar holders are completely clean to prevent handlebar slippage.

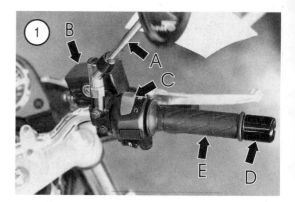

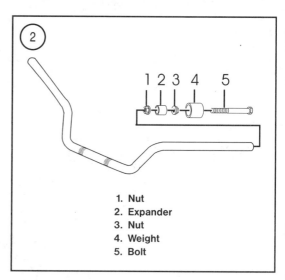

1. Nut
2. Expander
3. Nut
4. Weight
5. Bolt

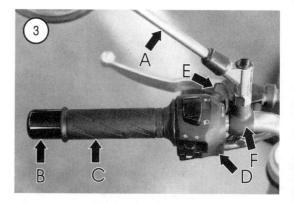

17. To remove the handlebar lower holders, perform the following:

   a. Remove the holder mounting bolt nut under the upper steering bracket, then remove the bolt.

   b. Remove the handlebar lower holder.

   c. Repeat the procedure for the remaining lower holder.

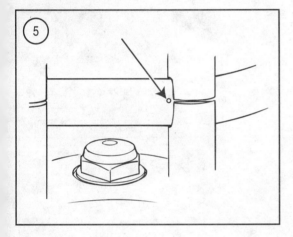

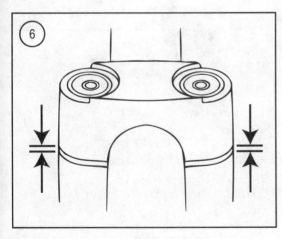

Installation

1. If removed, install the handlebar lower holder as follows:

    a. Install the handlebar lower holder on top of the upper steering bracket and align the mounting bolt holes.

    b. Install the mounting bolt and nut. Tighten the nut to 45 N•m (33 ft.-lb.).

    c. Repeat the procedure for the remaining lower holder.

2. Install the handlebar onto the lower holders, then install the upper holders, washers and bolts. Do not tighten the bolts at this time.

3. Position the handlebar so the punch mark on the handlebar aligns with the gap between the holders as shown in **Figure 5**.

4. Tighten the holder bolts so the gaps at each end of the holder are equal (**Figure 6**). Tighten the holder bolts to 23 N•m (17 ft.-lb.).

5. Install the clutch lever assembly (F, **Figure 3**) onto the left handlebar. Temporarily tighten the clamping bolt and nut.

6. Slide on the choke lever (E, **Figure 3**).

7. Install the left hand grip (C, **Figure 3**) as described in this chapter.

8. Install the balancer assembly (**Figure 2**) onto the end of the left handlebar (B, **Figure 3**). Tighten the screw securely.

9. Install the left handlebar switch (D, **Figure 3**) onto the handlebar. Index the choke lever into the switch and connect the choke cable to the lever. Install the screws securing the switch halves together and tighten securely.

10. After the hand grip and switch lever are installed, move the clutch lever assembly into a comfortable position and tighten the bolt securely.

11. Connect the clutch safety switch electrical connector to the switch.

12. Install the front master cylinder (B, **Figure 1**) onto the right handlebar. Install the holder and bolts. Align the master cylinder holder mating surface with the punched mark on the handlebar. Tighten the upper mounting bolt first, then the lower bolt, leaving a gap at the bottom. Tighten the bolts to 10 N•m (88 in.-lb.).

13. Apply a lightweight machine oil to the handlebar in the area where the throttle grip rotates.

14. Slide the throttle grip (E, **Figure 1**) onto the handlebar.

15. Install the balancer assembly (**Figure 2**) onto the end of the right handlebar (D, **Figure 1**). Tighten the screw securely.

16. Install the right handlebar switch (C, **Figure 1**) onto the handlebar. Align the switch with the throttle grip assembly. Connect the throttle cable to the

12

grip. Install the screws securing the switch halves together and tighten securely.

17. Rotate the throttle grip several times and make sure the grip moves freely from the full open to the full closed position with no binding.

18. Install the rear view mirrors, adjust and tighten securely.

19. Install the fuel tank as described in Chapter Eight.

20. After all assemblies are installed, test each one to make sure it operates correctly with no binding. Correct any problem at this time.

21. Adjust the clutch as described in Chapter Three.

SV650S Models

The individual front handlebars mount onto the fork tubes below the bottom surface of the upper steering stem bracket. It is necessary to remove the upper steering stem bracket to remove a particular handlebar.

> *NOTE*
> *This procedure covers complete removal and installation of the handlebar assembly on each side. If only one handlebar assembly requires removal, only use that portion of the procedure.*

Removal/installation

> *CAUTION*
> *Cover the fairing, front fender and front wheel with a heavy cloth or plastic tarp to protect them from accidental brake fluid spills. Brake fluid can mar or discolor painted or plastic surfaces. Immediately wash the surface using soapy water and rinse completely.*

> *NOTE*
> *It is not necessary to remove the fuel tank, but removal will prevent possible damage to it.*

1. Remove the fuel tank as described in Chapter Eight.

2. Remove the air cleaner box as described in Chapter Eight.

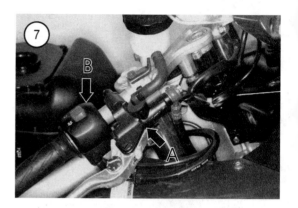

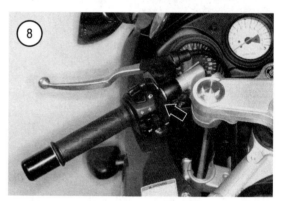

3. To remove the right handlebar, perform the following:

    a. Remove the front brake master cylinder (A, **Figure 7**) as described in Chapter Fourteen.

    b. Tie the master cylinder assembly to the frame, keeping the front brake master cylinder and reservoir in an upright position to prevent air from entering into the system.

    c. Remove the right switch assembly (B, **Figure 7**) as described in Chapter Nine.

    d. Remove the screw, cap and balancer from the end of the right handlebar.

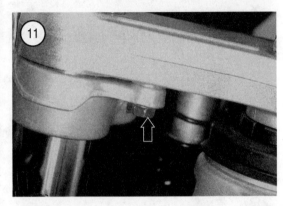

   e. Disconnect the throttle cable from the grip and slide the throttle grip assembly off the end of the handlebar. Move the cable out of the way. Make sure that the cable is not crimped or damaged.

4. To remove the left handlebar, perform the following:

   a. Remove the screw, cap and balancer from the end of the left handlebar.

   b. Remove the hand grip as described in this chapter.

   c. Remove the screws securing the left handlebar switch (**Figure 8**) together, then separate the switch. Remove it from the handlebar and lay it out of the way.

   d. Looosen the clamping bolt on the clutch lever assembly. Slide the clutch lever assembly off the end of the handlebar. Be careful that the clutch cable is not crimped or damaged.

5. Remove the air box as described in Chapter Eight.

6. Disconnect the ignition switch six-wire connector (**Figure 9**).

7. Remove the clamp bolt on the handlebar (A, **Figure 10**).

8. Remove the handlebar retaining bolt (**Figure 11**) for each handlebar.

9. Remove the steering stem cap nut (A, **Figure 12**).

10. Remove the upper fork leg clamp bolts (B, **Figure 10**).

11. Remove the upper steering stem bracket (B, **Figure 12**).

12. Remove the clamp bolt on the handlebar, then remove the handlebar from the fork leg.

13. Install by reversing the preceding removal steps while noting the following:

   a. Tighten the steering cap nut (A, **Figure 12**) to 65 N•m (48 ft.-lb.).

   b. Tighten the upper fork leg clamp bolts (B, **Figure 10**) to 23 N•m (17 ft.-lb.).

   c. Tighten the handlebar retaining bolt (**Figure 11**) to 10 N•m (88 in.-lb.).

   d. Tighten the handlebar clamp bolt (A, **Figure 10**) to 23 N•m (17 ft.-lb.).

   e. Install the switch assembly on either handlebar as described in Chapter Nine.

WARNING
After installation is completed, make sure that when the brake lever is applied it does not come in contact with the throttle grip assembly. If it does, the brake fluid may be low in the reservoir; refill it as necessary. Refer to **Bleeding the Brakes** *in Chapter Fourteen.*

Inspection (All Models)

Check the handlebar bolt holes and the entire mounting bracket for cracks or damage. Replace a bent or damaged handlebar immediately. If the motorcycle has been involved in a crash, thoroughly examine both handlebars, the steering stem and front fork for any signs of damage or misalignment. Correct any problem before operating the motorcycle.

HANDLEBAR LEFT HAND GRIP REPLACEMENT

NOTE
The original equipment right hand grip is part of the throttle grip assembly and cannot be replaced separately.

1. Remove the balancer assembly (**Figure 2**) from the end of the left handlebar (A, **Figure 13**).
2. Slide a thin screwdriver between the left hand grip (B, **Figure 13**) and handlebar. Spray electrical contact cleaner into the opening under the grip.
3. Pull the screwdriver out and quickly twist the grip to break its bond with the handlebar, then slide the grip off.
4. Clean the handlebar of all rubber or sealer residue.
5. Install the new grip, following its manufacturer's directions. Apply an adhesive, such as ThreeBond Griplock, between the grip and handlebar. When applying an adhesive, follow its manufacturer's directions regarding drying time before operating the motorcycle.
6. Install the balancer assembly (**Figure 2**) onto the left end of the handlebar (A, **Figure 13**).

STEERING STEM AND HEAD

Disassembly

Refer to **Figure 14** for this procedure:
1. On SV650S models, remove the fairing as described in Chapter Fifteen.
2. Remove the fuel tank as described in Chapter Eight.
3. Remove the speedometer and meter assembly and disconnect the electrical wires from the ignition switch as described in Chapter Nine.
4. Remove the complete front brake assembly. Refer to Chapter Fourteen.
5. Remove the handlebar on SV650 models or handlebars on SV650S models.

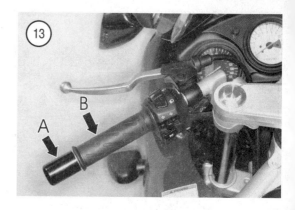

6. Remove the horn.
7. Remove the front fork as described in this chapter.
8. On SV650 models, remove the headlight bracket holders (7 and 14, **Figure 14**).
9. Remove the steering stem cap nut and washer (A, **Figure 15**) and remove the upper steering bracket assembly (B, **Figure 15**).
10. Loosen the steering stem nut (C, **Figure 15**). Use the special locknut wrench available from Suzuki (part No.09940-14911) or a fabricated tool (**Figure 16**) made from a piece of tubing or pipe, or a spanner wrench (**Figure 17**, typical).

NOTE
The steering stem nut can also be loosened by carefully tapping it loose with a punch and hammer.

NOTE
Support the weight of the steering stem assembly while removing the steering stem nut, or the assembly will drop out of the steering head.

11. Hold onto the steering stem and remove the nut (C, **Figure 15**).
•12. Lift off the dust seal (D, **Figure 15**).
13. Gently lower the steering stem out of the frame. Both bearings are caged ball bearings with no loose parts.
14. Carefully remove the upper bearing from the upper bearing race in the steering head.

CAUTION
Do not attempt to remove the lower bearing race from the steering stem unless bearing replacement is necessary. The bearing race is pressed on

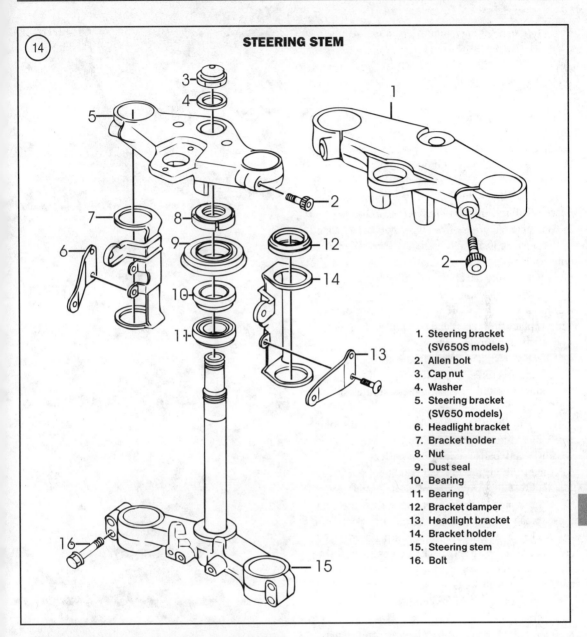

STEERING STEM

1. Steering bracket
   (SV650S models)
2. Allen bolt
3. Cap nut
4. Washer
5. Steering bracket
   (SV650 models)
6. Headlight bracket
7. Bracket holder
8. Nut
9. Dust seal
10. Bearing
11. Bearing
12. Bracket damper
13. Headlight bracket
14. Bracket holder
15. Steering stem
16. Bolt

12

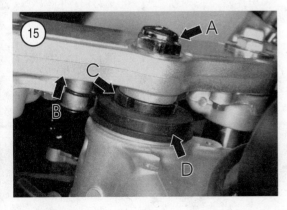

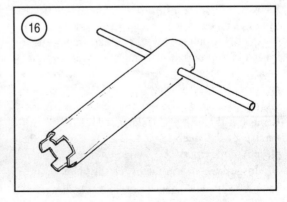

the steering stem and will be damaged during removal.

Inspection

1. Clean the upper and lower bearings in a bearing degreaser. Make certain the bearing degreaser is compatible with the rubber covers on each bearing. Hold onto the bearing so it does not spin and thoroughly dry both bearings with compressed air. Make sure all solvent is removed from the lower bearing still installed on the steering stem.

2. Wipe the old grease from the outer races located in the steering head, and then clean the outer races with a rag soaked in solvent. Thoroughly dry the races with a lint-free cloth.

3. Check the steering stem outer races for pitting, galling and corrosion. If any race is worn or damaged, replace the race(s) and bearing as an assembly as described in this chapter.

4. Check the welds around the steering head for cracks and fractures. If any damage is found, have the frame repaired at a competent frame shop or welding service.

5. Check the balls for pitting, scratches or discoloration indicating wear or corrosion. Replace the bearing if any balls are less than perfect.

6. If the bearings are in good condition, pack them thoroughly with Suzuki Super Grease A or an equivalent water-proof bearing grease. To pack the bearings, spread some grease in the palm of your hand and scrape the open side of the bearing across your palm until the bearing is packed completely full of grease. Spin the bearing a few times to determine if there are any open areas. Repack if necessary.

7. Thoroughly clean all mounting parts in solvent. Dry them completely.

8. Inspect the cap nut, washer and steering stem nut for wear or damage. Inspect the threads. If necessary, clean them with an appropriate size metric tap or replace the nut(s). If the threads are damaged, inspect the appropriate steering stem thread(s) for damage. If necessary, clean the threads with an appropriate size metric die.

9. Inspect the steering stem nut washer for damage. Replace it if necessary. If damaged, check the underside of the steering stem nut for damage. Replace it as necessary.

10. Inspect the steering stem and the lower bracket for cracks or other damage. Make sure the lower

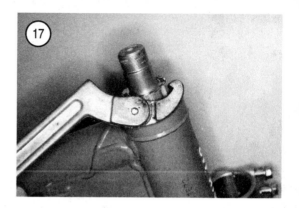
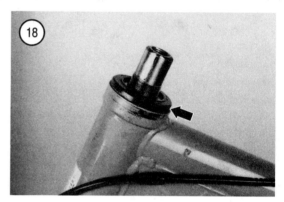

bracket clamping areas are free of burrs and the bolt holes are in good condition.

11. Inspect the upper steering bracket for cracks or other damage. Check both the upper and lower surface of the bracket. Make sure the bracket clamping areas are free of burrs and the bolt holes are in good condition.

Installation

Refer to **Figure 14**.

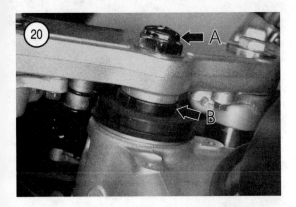

nut only finger-tight at this time. Do not tighten the cap nut until the front fork legs are in place. This will ensure proper alignment between the steering stem and the upper steering bracket.

10. Install the front fork legs, including the headlight brackets, as described in this chapter. Tighten the upper and lower fork clamp bolts to 23 N•m (17 ft.-lb.).

11. Check the movement of the front fork legs and steering stem assembly. The steering stem must turn freely from side to side, but without any free play when the fork legs are moved fore and aft.

12. Tighten the steering stem cap nut (A, **Figure 15**) to 65 N•m (48 ft.-lb.). Recheck the movement of the front end and readjust if necessary.

13. Install the horn.

14. Install the handlebar assembly as described in this chapter.

15. Install the front brake assembly. Refer to Chapter Fourteen.

16. Install the speedometer and meter assembly and connect the electrical wires to the ignition switch as described in Chapter Nine.

17. Install the fuel tank as described in Chapter Eight.

1. Make sure the steering head outer races are properly seated and clean.

2. Apply an even, complete coat of Suzuki Super Grease A or equivalent to the steering head outer races, to both bearings, and to the dust seal and cap nut.

3. Install the upper bearing into the race in the top of the steering head.

4. Carefully slide the steering stem up into the frame. Take care not to dislodge the upper bearing.

5. Hold the steering stem in position and install the dust seal (**Figure 18**, typical) on top of the upper bearing.

6. Install the steering stem nut (**Figure 19**, typical). Use the same tool setup used during disassembly and tighten the steering stem nut to 45 N•m (33 ft.-lb.).

7. Move the steering stem back and forth from lock to lock five or six times to make sure the bearings are completely seated.

8. Back off the steering stem nut 1/4 to 1/2 turn. Once again, check that the steering stem moves freely.

9. Install the upper steering bracket assembly (B, **Figure 15**), washer and cap nut (A). Tighten the cap

Adjustment

1. Raise the motorcycle with a jack and place wooden blocks under the frame to support the motorcycle securely with the front wheel off the ground.

2. Grasp each fork leg at the lower end and attempt to move the forks back and forth. If any fore and aft movement of the front end is detected, the steering stem nut must be adjusted.

3. Loosen the steering stem cap nut (A, **Figure 20**).

4. Turn the adjust nut (B, **Figure 20**) by gently tapping with a hammer and a punch. Take care not to damage the nut.

5. Tighten the steering stem cap nut to 65 N•m (48 ft.-lb.).

STEERING HEAD BEARING RACE REPLACEMENT

The upper and lower bearing outer races must not be removed unless they are going to be replaced. These races are pressed into place and will be damaged during removal. If removed, replace the outer

12

race and the bearing at the same time. Never reuse an outer race that has been removed. It is no longer true and will damage the ball bearings if reused.

NOTE
The following procedure describes simple home techniques to remove the bearing races. If removal is difficult, do not chance damage to the motorcycle or new bearing races. Have the task performed by a Suzuki dealership or a qualified specialist.

1. Remove the steering stem as described in this chapter.

2. Insert an aluminum drift into the steering head and carefully tap the lower race out from the inside (**Figure 21**, typical). Repeat for the upper race.

3. Chill the new bearing races in a freezer for a few hours to shrink the outer diameter of the race as much as possible.

4. Clean the race seats (**Figure 22**, typical) in the steering head. Check for cracks or other damage.

5. Insert the new race into the steering head with the concave side facing out and square the race with the steering head bore.

CAUTION
To avoid damage to the races and to the race seats in the steering head, install the races as described below.

6. Assemble a puller tool as shown in **Figure 23**. The block mounted at the bottom of the threaded rod is used as a T-handle to hold the rod stationary when the bearing race is being installed from the opposite end. Two nuts locked together can be used as a substitute for the handle block. Two or more *thick* washers are also required. The outer diameter of the washers must be greater than the outer diameter of the bearing races.

CAUTION
When installing the bearing outer races with the threaded rod or similar tool, do not let the rod or tool contact the face of the bearing race and damage it.

7. To install the upper race, insert the puller through the bottom of the steering stem. Seat the lower washer or plate against the steering stem.

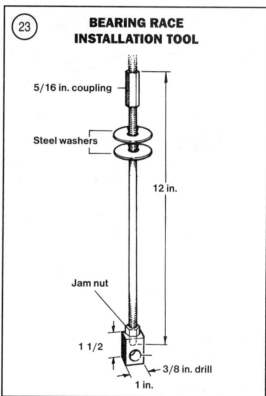

BEARING RACE INSTALLATION TOOL

5/16 in. coupling

Steel washers

12 in.

Jam nut

1 1/2

3/8 in. drill

1 in.

8. At the top of the steering stem, slide the large washer down and seat it squarely on top of the bearing race. Install the required washers and coupling nut onto the rod.

9. Hand-tighten the coupling nut and center the washer on the upper bearing race.

10. Hold the threaded rod to prevent it from turning and tighten the coupling nut (**Figure 24**) with a wrench. Continue to tighten the coupling until the race is completely drawn into the steering head. Remove the puller assembly and inspect the bearing race. It should be bottomed in the steering head.

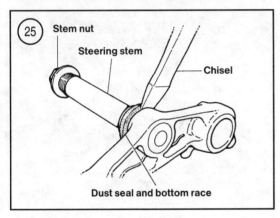

25 Stem nut
Steering stem
Chisel
Dust seal and bottom race

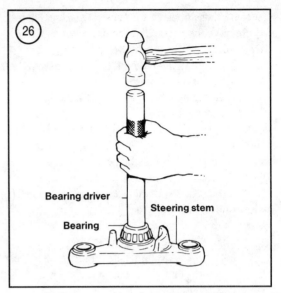

Bearing driver
Bearing
Steering stem

11. Turn the special tool over and repeat this procedure for the lower bearing race.

STEERING STEM
BEARING REPLACEMENT

Do not remove the steering stem lower bearing and lower seal unless they are going to be replaced. The lower bearing can be difficult to remove. If it cannot be removed as described in this procedure, take the steering stem to a dealership service department and have them remove it and reinstall a new bearing and seal.

Never reinstall a lower bearing that has been removed. It is no longer true and will damage the rest of the bearing assembly if reused.

1. Install the steering stem bolt onto the top of the steering stem to protect the threads.

2. Loosen the lower bearing from the shoulder at the base of the steering stem with a chisel as shown in **Figure 25**. Slide the lower bearing and grease seal off the steering stem. Discard the lower bearing and the grease seal.

3. Clean the steering stem with solvent, and dry it thoroughly.

4. Position the new grease seal with the flange side facing up.

5. Slide a new grease seal and the lower bearing onto the steering stem until it stops on the raised shoulder.

6. Align the lower bearing with the machined shoulder on the steering stem. Slide the Suzuki steering bearing installer (part No. 09941-74911), or a piece of pipe (**Figure 26**), over the steering stem until it seats against the inner portion of the *inner* race of the lower bearing. Press or drive the lower bearing onto the steering stem until it bottoms.

7. Pack the balls with wheel bearing grease.

FRONT FORK

To simplify fork service and to prevent mixing parts, service the fork assemblies individually.

If a fork problem is suspected, first drain the fork oil and refill with the proper type and quantity. If a problem still exists, such as poor damping, a tendency to bottom out or top out or leakage around the slider seal, follow the service procedures in this section.

Removal/Installation

1. On SV650S models, remove the fairing as described in Chapter Fifteen.

2. Remove the brake caliper and brake hose from each fork leg as described in Chapter Fourteen.

12

3. Remove the front wheel as described in this chapter.

4. Remove the front fender as described in Chapter Thirteen.

5. If the fork leg is going to be disassembled, loosen the cap bolt (**Figure 27**).

6. Loosen the upper (A, **Figure 28**) and lower (B) fork tube clamp bolts.

7. Carefully pull each fork leg down and out of the upper and lower steering brackets and the headlight mounting bracket. It may be necessary to rotate the fork tube slightly while pulling it down and out.

8. Install by reversing the preceding removal steps while noting the following:

    a. On SV650 models, apply a light coat of fork oil or clean engine oil to the inner surfaces of both rubber grommets (C, **Figure 28**) in the headlight mounting bracket. This will make fork tube installation easier.

    b. On SV650 models, slowly install the fork tube into the lower steering bracket, rubber grommets and headlight bracket holder. Then slide the fork tube through the upper steering bracket (D, **Figure 28**).

    c. On SV650 models, position the fork so that the top of the fork tube on U.S. and Canada models is 3.0 mm (0.12 in.) above the top surface of the top steering bracket (**Figure 29**). On all other models, position the fork so that the top of the fork tube is 6.0 mm (0.24 in.) above the top surface of the upper steering bracket (**Figure 29**).

    d. On SV650S models, position the fork so that the top of the fork tube is flush with the top edge of the upper steering bracket (**Figure 30**).

    e. Tighten the upper and lower fork clamp bolts to 23 N•m (17 ft.-lb.).

    f. If the forks were disassembled, tighten the fork cap bolt (**Figure 27**) to 23 N•m (17 ft.-lb.).

    g. If so equipped, adjust the fork spring preload as described in Chapter Three.

Disassembly

Refer to **Figure 31** for this procedure.

1. Remove the front fork legs as described in this chapter.

NOTE
When loosening the Allen bolt in the bottom of the fork tube, leave the fork cap bolt and fork spring installed un-

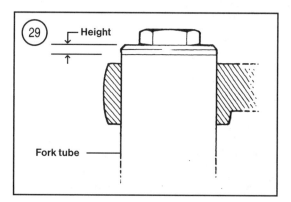

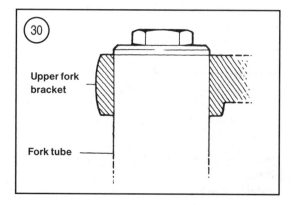

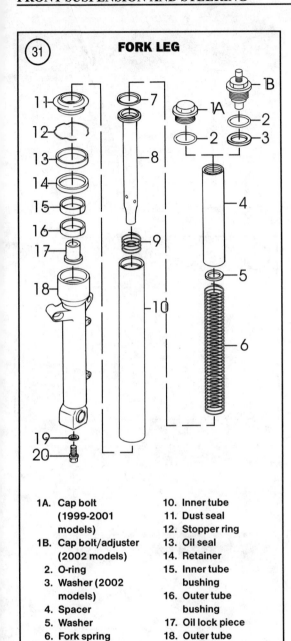

FORK LEG

1A. Cap bolt
    (1999-2001
    models)
1B. Cap bolt/adjuster
    (2002 models)
2. O-ring
3. Washer (2002
    models)
4. Spacer
5. Washer
6. Fork spring
7. Piston ring
8. Damper rod
9. Rebound spring
10. Inner tube
11. Dust seal
12. Stopper ring
13. Oil seal
14. Retainer
15. Inner tube
    bushing
16. Outer tube
    bushing
17. Oil lock piece
18. Outer tube
19. Washer
20. Allen bolt

til the Allen bolt is loosened and re-
moved. The internal spring pressure
against the damper rod assembly will
help hold it in place as the Allen bolt
is being loosened and removed.

2. Install the fork in a vise with soft jaws.

3. Have an assistant compress the fork tube assembly as much as possible and hold it compressed against the damper rod.

4. Loosen the Allen bolt at the base of the slider with an Allen wrench and an impact tool. Do not remove the Allen bolt at this time.

WARNING
Be careful when removing the fork cap bolt as the spring is under pressure. Protect eyes accordingly.

5. Slowly unscrew and remove the fork cap bolt (**Figure 32**).

6. Remove the spacer and spring.

7. Turn the fork assembly upside down over a drain pan and completely drain the fork oil. Stroke the fork several times to pump out any oil that remains. Stand the fork tube upside down in the drain pan and allow the oil to drain for several minutes.

8. Remove the Allen bolt and gasket from the base of the slider.

NOTE
The oil lock piece is often stuck to the bottom of the slider and may not come out with the damper rod. Do not lose the oil lock piece.

9. Turn the fork assembly upside down and slide out the damper rod assembly complete with the rebound spring and oil lock piece.

10. Remove the dust seal from the slider.

11. Pad the edge of the fork tube and carefully pry out the stopper ring with a flat-blade screwdriver.

NOTE
On this type of fork, force is needed to remove the fork tube from the slider.

12

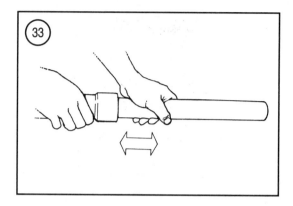

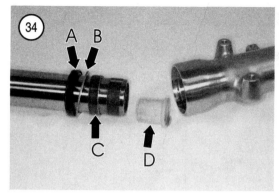

12. Install the fork tube in a vise with soft jaws.

13. There is an interference fit between the bushing in the fork slider and bushing in the fork tube. To remove the fork tube from the slider, pull hard on the fork tube using quick in-and-out strokes (**Figure 33**). Doing so will withdraw the slider bushing, oil seal retainer and oil seal from the slider.

14. Withdraw the fork tube from the slider.

> *NOTE*
> *Do not remove the fork tube bushing unless it is going to be replaced. Inspect it as described in this section.*

15. Remove the oil lock piece from the slider if it did not come out in Step 10.

16. Slide off the oil seal (A, **Figure 34**), oil seal retainer (B) and slider bushing (C) from the fork tube.

17. Remove the oil seal lock piece (D, **Figure 34**).

18. Inspect all parts as described in this chapter.

Inspection

1. Thoroughly clean all parts in solvent and dry them completely.

2. Inspect the damper rod for straightness (**Figure 35**), damage or roughness. Check for galling, deep scores or excessive wear. Replace the damper rod if necessary.

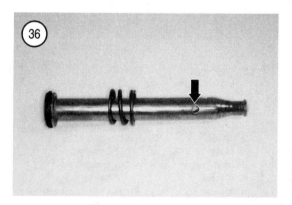

3. Make sure the oil holes (**Figure 36**) in the damper rod are clear. Clean out if necessary.

4. Inspect the piston ring (**Figure 37**) on the end of the damper rod for wear or damage. Replace if necessary.

5. Inspect the top cap bolt threads (A, **Figure 38**) for wear or damage. If damage is minimal, clean with the appropriate size metric die.

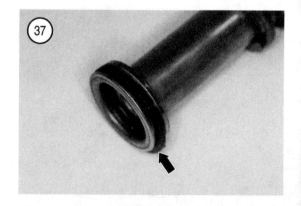

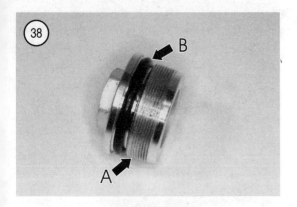

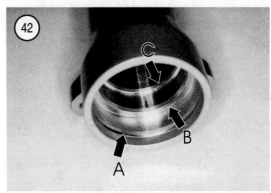

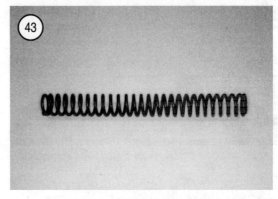

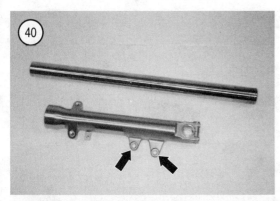

6. Check the top cap bolt O-ring (B, **Figure 38**) for hardness or deterioration. Replace if necessary to avoid an oil leak.

7. Check the fork tube for straightness. If bent or scratched, replace the fork tube.

8. Inspect the fork tube-to-top cap bolt threads (**Figure 39**) for wear or damage. If damage is minimal, clean with the appropriate size metric tap.

9. Check the slider for dents or exterior damage that may cause the fork tube to bind during riding. Replace if necessary.

10. Check the front brake caliper mounting bosses (**Figure 40**) on the fork legs. Check the front axle clamp bolt area (**Figure 41**) on the right slider for cracks or damage. Replace if necessary.

11. Check the slider stopper ring groove (A, **Figure 42**, typical) for cracks or damage. Inspect the oil seal area (B, **Figure 42**) and the slider bushing area (C) for dents or other damage and replace the slider if necessary.

12. Measure the free length of the fork spring (**Figure 43**) (not the rebound spring). If the spring length is less than 308 mm (12.13 in.), replace the spring.

12

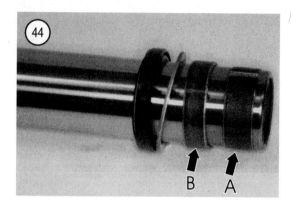

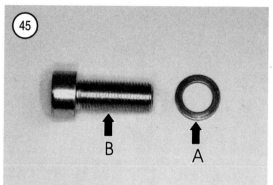

13. Inspect the slider (A, **Figure 44**) and fork tube (B) bushings. Replace them if either is scratched or scored. If the Teflon coating is worn off so the copper base material is showing on 3/4 of the total surface area, replace both bushings.

14. Inspect the gasket/washer (A, **Figure 45**) on the Allen bolt (B) and replace if necessary.

15. Replace any parts that are worn or damaged. Simply cleaning and reinstalling unserviceable components will not improve performance of the front suspension.

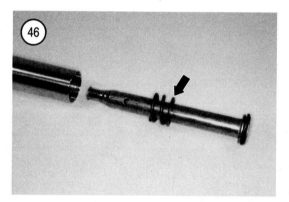

Assembly

Refer to **Figure 31** for this procedure.

> *NOTE*
> *The following illustrations depict the fork cap bolt used on 1999-2001 models. The fork cap bolt/adjuster and washer shown in **Figure 31** are used on 2002 models in place of the fork cap bolt shown.*

1. Make sure that all fork components are clean and dry. Wipe out the seal bore area (B, **Figure 42**) in the slider with a lint-free cloth.

2. Coat all parts with SAE 10 fork oil before installing.

3. Install the rebound spring (**Figure 46**) on the damper rod and install the damper rod assembly into the fork tube.

> *NOTE*
> *If a damper rod holding tool (**Figure 47**) is available to prevent damper rod movement when tightening the Allen bolt, proceed to Step 5.*

4. Temporarily install the fork spring (**Figure 48**), spacer (**Figure 49**) and fork cap bolt (**Figure 32**) to

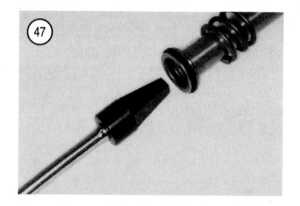

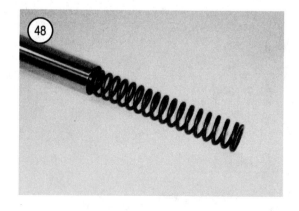

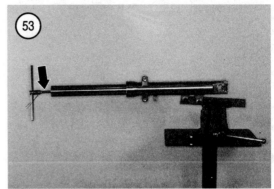

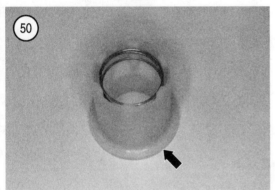

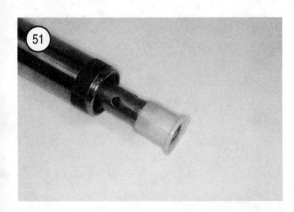

hold the damper rod in place. Only hand-tighten the fork cap bolt at this time. The tension of the fork spring will keep the damper rod in place in the fork tube and ease the assembly process.

5. Note that the oil lock piece has a flanged end (**Figure 50**).

6. Slide the oil lock piece onto the end of the damper rod assembly (**Figure 51**) so the flanged end is at the end of the damper rod.

7. Carefully install the fork tube and the damper rod assembly into the slider as shown in **Figure 52**.

8. Clean the threads of the Allen bolt (B, **Figure 45**) thoroughly with clean solvent or spray contact cleaner. Make sure that the gasket/washer is in place on the Allen bolt. Apply a couple of drops of locking compound such as Threadlocker No. 1342 to the threads on the bolt (B, **Figure 45**).

> *NOTE*
> *The fork leg may be secured in a vise by attaching a piece of metal to the brake caliper lugs as shown in **Figure 53**.*

9. Install the Allen bolt and gasket/washer (**Figure 54**) using a long Allen wrench (**Figure 55**). If avail-

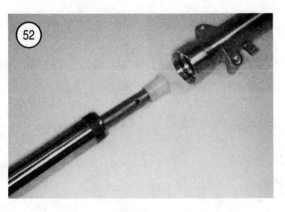

12

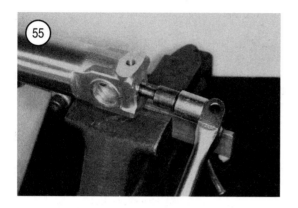

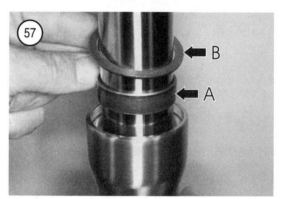

able, insert the damper rod holder tool (**Figure 53**). Tighten the Allen bolt to 30 N•m (22 ft.-lb.).

> *NOTE*
> *Install the slider bushing using an oil seal driver (**Figure 56**) or a piece of tubing and suitable plate that fits over the fork tube. Oil seal drivers are available from Suzuki dealerships and motorcycle mail order houses.*

10. Slide the fork slider bushing (A, **Figure 57**) down the fork tube and rest it on top of the fork slider.

11. Slide the oil seal retainer (B, **Figure 57**) down the fork tube and rest it on top of the slider bushing.

12. Drive the new slider bushing into the slider with the fork seal driver (or equivalent) until it bottoms (**Figure 56**). Remove the driver.

> *NOTE*
> *To avoid damage to the oil seal lips and dust seal when installing them over the top of the fork tube, place a plastic bag over the fork tube and coat it with fork oil. Then slide both seals over the fork tube and plastic bag (**Figure 58**) without damaging them.*

13. Coat the lips of the new oil seal with fresh fork oil.

14. Position the oil seal with its open groove facing upward and slide the oil seal (**Figure 59**) down the fork tube.

15. Slide the fork seal driver down the fork tube (**Figure 56**) and drive the seal into the slider until it bottoms. Make sure the groove in the slider can be seen above the top surface of the oil seal. If not, continue to drive the oil seal in until the groove is visible.

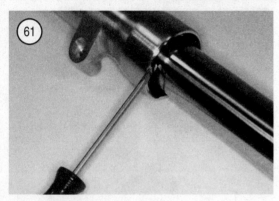

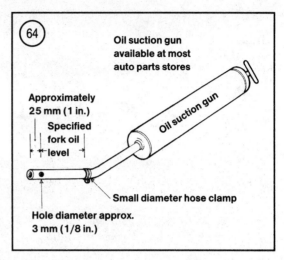

16. Slide the stopper ring (**Figure 60**) down the fork tube and rest it on top of the oil seal.

17. Carefully install the stopper ring into the slider groove (**Figure 61**). Make sure that the stopper ring is locked into the groove in the fork tube.

18. Install the dust seal into the slider. Press it in until it is completely seated (**Figure 62**).

NOTE
Measure the fork oil level, if possible, to ensure a more accurate filling. This results in a better handling motorcycle.

19. Remove the fork cap bolt, spacer, spring seat and fork spring.

20. Hold the fork assembly vertical and compress the fork tube into the slider until it bottoms.

21. Fill the fork tube with SAE 10 fork oil in the amount specified in **Table 1**. Keep the fork tube as close to vertical as possible.

22. Use an accurate ruler or the Suzuki oil level gauge (part No.09943-74111), or equivalent (**Figure 63**) to achieve the oil level specified in **Table 1**. The oil level must be measured with the fork vertical, completely compressed and with the fork spring removed.

NOTE
*An oil level measuring device can be fabricated as shown in **Figure 64**. Fill the fork tube with a few extra cubic centimeters of oil. Position the lower edge of the hose clamp against the top edge of the fork tube and draw out the excess oil. Draw out oil until the level*

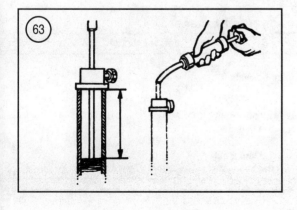

12

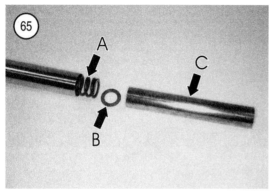

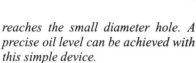

reaches the small diameter hole. A precise oil level can be achieved with this simple device.

23. Allow the oil to settle completely and recheck the oil level measurement. Adjust the oil level if necessary.

NOTE
On all models, the spring is not directional; therefore, either end can be inserted first.

NOTE
The following photographs depict the fork on its side for clarity. Keep the fork assembly vertical or some of the fork oil will drain out.

24. Install the fork spring (A, **Figure 65**), spring seat (B) and spacer (C).
25. Inspect the O-ring seal (**Figure 66**) on the fork top cap for hardness or deterioration. Replace the O-ring if necessary.
26A. On 1999-2001 models, install the fork cap bolt (**Figure 67**) hand tight at this time. Tighten the cap bolt

to 23 N•m (17 ft.-lb.) after the fork assembly has been installed. Keep the fork tube vertical until it is installed on the motorcycle to prevent the loss of fork oil.
26B. On 2002 models, install the washer (3, **Figure 31**) and fork cap bolt (1B), but tighten the cap bolt hand tight at this time. Tighten the cap bolt to 23 N•m (17 ft.-lb.) after the fork assembly has been installed. Keep the fork tube vertical until it is installed on the motorcycle to prevent the loss of fork oil. Adjust spring preload adjustment after installation as described in Chapter Three.

Table 1 FRONT SUSPENSION SPECIFICATIONS

Item	Specification	Service limit
Front fork oil		
Viscosity	Suzuki No. 10 fork oil or equivalent	–
Capacity per leg		
U.S. and California models		
1999-2001	491 ml (16.6 U.S. oz., 17.3 Imp. gal.)	–
2002	480 ml (16.2 U.S. oz., 16.9 Imp. gal.)	–
All other models		
1999-2001	489 ml (16.5 U.S. oz., 17.2 Imp. gal.)	–
2002	478 ml (16.2 U.S. oz., 16.8 Imp. gal.)	–
	(continued)	

Table 1 FRONT SUSPENSION SPECIFICATIONS (continued)

Item	Specification	Service limit
Front fork oil level		
U.S. and California models		
1999-2001	102 mm (4.02 in.)	–
2002	113 mm (4.45 in.)	–
All other models		
1999-2001	104 mm (4.09 in.)	–
2002	113 mm (4.53 in.)	–
Front fork spring free length	–	308 mm (12.13 in.)
Front fork stroke	130 mm (5.1 in.)	–

Table 2 FRONT SUSPENSION TORQUE SPECIFICATIONS

Item	N•m	in.-lb.	ft.-lb.
Front fork cap bolt	23	–	17
Front fork clamp bolts	23	–	17
Front fork damper rod bolt	30	–	22
Front master cylinder bolts	10	88	–
Handlebar			
SV650			
Upper holder bolts	23	–	17
Lower holder nut	45	–	33
SV650S			
Retaining bolt	10	88	–
Clamp bolt	23	–	17
Steering stem cap nut	65	–	48
Steering stem nut	45	–	33

12

NOTE: Refer to the Supplement at the back of this manual for information unique to 2003-on models.

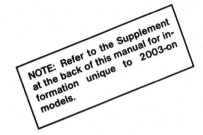

CHAPTER THIRTEEN

REAR SUSPENSION

This chapter covers procedures for the rear suspension components. Wheel removal, hub and tire service are covered in Chapter Eleven. Specifications for the rear suspension are listed in **Table 1** and **Table 2** at the end of the chapter.

The link-type suspension consists of a single adjustable shock absorber, a shock-lever and tie-rod assembly, and aluminum swing arm.

The swing arm and shock linkage rotate on caged bearings. For maximum service life, all pivot joints must be disassembled, inspected and lubricated frequently.

SHOCK ABSORBER

Removal

1. Remove the lower fairing side cover from each side as described in Chapter Fifteen.
2. Support the motorcycle securely with the rear wheel off the ground. If a motorcycle stand or jack is not available, place wooden block(s) under the engine.
3. Remove the fuel tank as described in Chapter Eight.
4. Remove the exhaust system as described in Chapter Eight.

5. Loosen the mounting hardware at the forward tie rod mount (A, **Figure 1**) and rear tie rod mount (B).
6. Remove the forward tie rod nut.
7. Remove the forward tie rod bolt from the pivot boss on the swing arm.
8. Remove the lower shock mounting bolt (**Figure 2**), and separate the lower shock mount from the shock lever.
9. Remove the upper shock mounting bolt (**Figure 3**).
10. Lower the shock absorber from the shock bracket in the frame and remove the shock through the large hole in the swing arm.

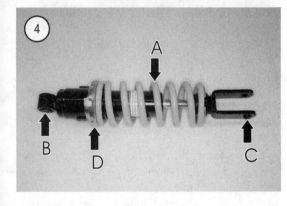

11. Inspect the shock absorber as described in this chapter.

Installation

1. Clean the mounting bolts and nuts in solvent, and dry them thoroughly.

2. Apply a light coat of waterproof grease to the shock absorber upper and lower mounts.

3. Carefully insert the shock absorber up through the swing arm opening. Rotate the shock as neces-

sary and align the upper mounting hole with the shock absorber bracket in the frame.

4. Install the upper shock mounting bolt (**Figure 3**) from the left side of the motorcycle and install the nut. Finger-tighten the nut at this time.

5. Move the shock lever up into the shock absorber lower mount and install the lower shock mounting bolt (**Figure 2**) from the left side. Finger-tighten the bolt at this time.

6. Raise the tie rods into place on either side of the swing arm pivot boss. Install the forward tie rod bolt from the left side, then install the nut (A, **Figure 1**).

> *CAUTION*
> *Do not overtighten the lower shock mounting bolt. This bolt threads directly into the shock absorber. If the threads are damaged, replace the shock absorber.*

7. Tighten the upper shock mounting nut and the lower shock mounting bolt to 50 N•m (37 ft.-lb.). Tighten the tie rod nuts to 78 N•m (57 ft.-lb.).

8. Take the motorcycle off the jack or stand, push down on the rear of the motorcycle to make sure the linkage is operating correctly with no binding.

9. Install the fuel tank and exhaust system as described in Chapter Eight.

10. Install the lower fairing side covers as described in Chapter Fifteen.

Inspection

No replacement parts are available for the original equipment shock absorber. If any part of the shock absorber is defective, replace the shock absorber assembly.

> *WARNING*
> *The shock absorber contains highly compressed nitrogen gas. Do not tamper with or attempt to open the housing. Do not place it near an open flame or other extreme heat. Do not weld on the frame near the shock. Take the unit to a Suzuki dealership where it can be deactivated and disposed of properly.*

1. Inspect the shock absorber for oil leaks.

2. Check the spring (A, **Figure 4**) for cracks or other damage.

13

3. Inspect the upper (B, **Figure 4**) and lower (C) mounts for wear or damage. If necessary, replace the upper bushing.

4. Make sure the spring preload adjust nut (D, **Figure 4**) fits properly.

5. If any of these areas are damaged, replace the shock absorber.

SWING ARM

Preliminary Inspection

The condition of the swing arm bearings can greatly affect the handling of the motorcycle. Worn bearings cause wheel hop, pulling to one side under acceleration and pulling to the other side during braking. To check the condition of the swing arm bearings, perform the following steps.

1. Remove the rear wheel as described in Chapter Eleven.

2. Remove the rear tie rod mounting hardware (B, **Figure 1**) and lower the tie rods away from the swing arm. Removal of the tie rods is not required.

3. On the right side, make sure the swing arm pivot locknut nut (A, **Figure 5**) is tight.

4. On the left side, make sure the pivot nut (**Figure 6**) is tight.

5. The swing arm is now free to move under its own weight.

NOTE
Have an assistant steady the motorcycle when performing Steps 6 and 7.

6. Grasp both ends of the swing arm and attempt to move it from side to side in a horizontal arc. If more than a slight amount of movement is felt, the bearings are worn and must be replaced.

7. Grasp both ends of the swing arm and move it up and down. The swing arm should move smoothly with no binding or abnormal noise from the bearings. If there is binding or noise, the bearings are worn and must be replaced.

8. Move the swing arm and the tie rods into position. Install the rear tie rod bolt from the left side. Install the tie rod nut and tighten to 78 N•m (57 ft.-lb.).

9. Install the rear wheel as described in this chapter.

Removal

Refer to **Figure 7**.

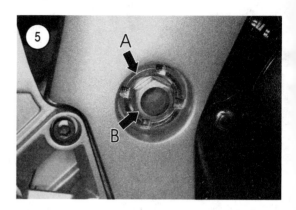

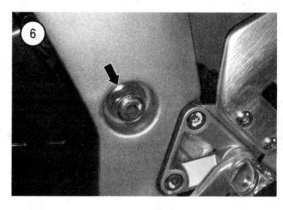

1. Remove the shock absorber as described in this chapter.

2. Remove the chain guard from the swing arm.

3. Remove the rear wheel as described in Chapter Eleven.

4. Remove the rear caliper as described in Chapter Fourteen. Place the loose end of the brake hose in a reclosable plastic bag and close it.

5. Unhook the brake hose from the clamp (A, **Figure 8**) on top of the swing arm, and carefully pull the rear brake hose out from the guide (B) on the inside surface of the swing arm.

6. On the right side, use the Suzuki swing arm pivot thrust adjuster socket wrench, (part No. 09940-14940) and remove the pivot locknut (A, **Figure 5**).

7. Tie the end of the swing arm to the frame or place a box under the end of the swing arm and support it securely.

8. Hold the pivot shaft (B, **Figure 5**) with a suitable socket.

9. On the left side, remove the pivot nut (**Figure 6**) and washer.

10. From the left side, carefully tap the pivot shaft out of the frame and swing arm. Pull the pivot shaft (**Figure 9**) from the right side of the frame.

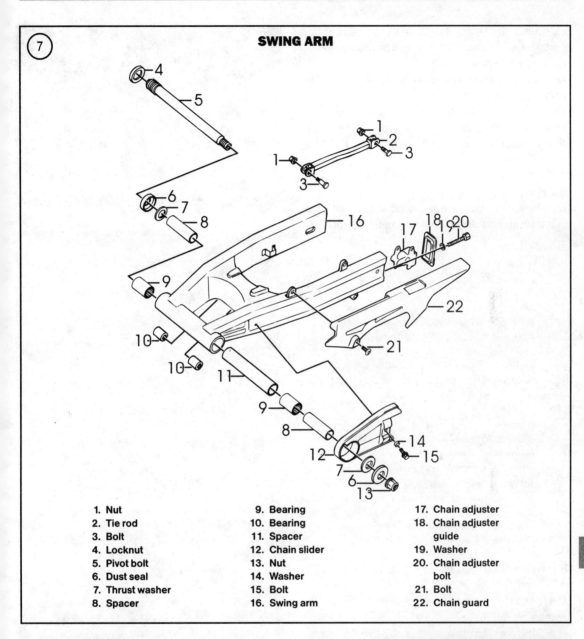

SWING ARM

1. Nut	9. Bearing	17. Chain adjuster
2. Tie rod	10. Bearing	18. Chain adjuster
3. Bolt	11. Spacer	guide
4. Locknut	12. Chain slider	19. Washer
5. Pivot bolt	13. Nut	20. Chain adjuster
6. Dust seal	14. Washer	bolt
7. Thrust washer	15. Bolt	21. Bolt
8. Spacer	16. Swing arm	22. Chain guard

13

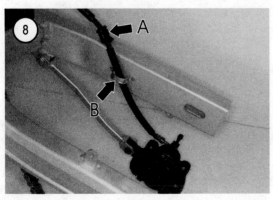

11. Lower the swing arm from the frame or from the box. Do not lose the dust seal from either side of the swing arm pivot.

12. Rotate the swing arm and remove its left arm from the drive chain.

13. If the swing arm bearings are not going to be serviced, place a strip of duct tape over each pivot. This protects the bearing assemblies and prevents the loss of any small parts.

14. If necessary, remove the mud guard flap from the swing arm.

15. Inspect the swing arm as described in this chapter. Lubricate all bearings as described in this chapter.

Installation

NOTE
Swing arm installation can be accomplished alone; however, the task is much easier with the aid of another person.

1. Lubricate the swing arm and shock linkage bearings, the pivot bolts and collars with waterproof grease before installation.

NOTE
*Refer to **Figure 7** for the correct installation direction for the pivot bolts. To ensure maximum performance and service from the rear suspension, install the bolts in the direction indicated in the illustration. If someone else serviced the swing arm, the bolt(s) may have been installed incorrectly.*

2. Make sure the dust seals are in place on all pivot points.

3. If removed, reattach the mud guard flap onto the swing arm.

4. Secure the rear brake hose above the swing arm mount in the frame so the hose will not be pinched.

5. Insert the left arm of the swing arm between the drive chain and set the swing arm in place beneath the frame.

6. Raise the swing arm and install it between the frame pivots. From the right side of the motorcycle, install the swing arm pivot shaft (**Figure 9**) through the frame and the swing arm pivots.

7. Loosely install the washer and pivot nut (**Figure 6**) onto the right end of the pivot shaft.

8. Set the thrust clearance by tightening the swing arm pivot fasteners in the order described below.

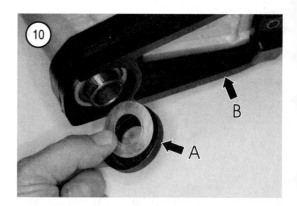

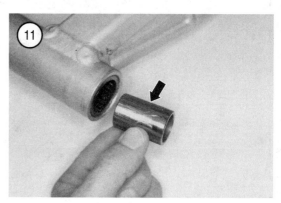

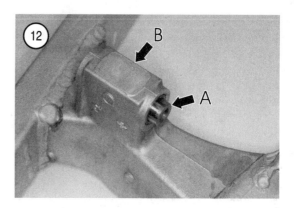

a. Tighten the swing arm pivot shaft (B, **Figure 5**) to 15 N•m (133 in.-lb.).

b. Hold the pivot shaft with a suitable socket and tighten the pivot nut (**Figure 6**) to 100 N•m (74 ft.-lb.).

c. Use the Suzuki swing arm pivot thrust adjuster socket wrench (part No. 09940-14940) and tighten the pivot locknut (A, **Figure 5**) to 90 N•m (66 ft.-lb.).

9. After tightening all of the fasteners in Step 8, move the swing arm up and down and check for smooth movement. If the swing arm is tight or loose, then the

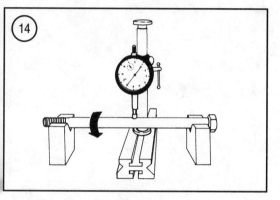

fasteners were either tightened in the wrong sequence or to the incorrect torque specification; repeat Step 8.

10. Route the rear brake hose across the swing arm and through the guide (B, **Figure 8**) on the swing arm. Make sure the hose is secured under the clamp (A, **Figure 8**) on top of the swing arm.

11. Install the chain guard onto the swing arm. Tighten the bolts securely.

12. Install the rear brake caliper (Chapter Fourteen).

13. Install the shock absorber as described in this chapter.

14. Install the rear wheel as described in Chapter Eleven.

15. Adjust the chain as described in Chapter Three.

16. Bleed the brakes as described in Chapter Fourteen.

Disassembly

Refer to **Figure 7**.

1. Remove the swing arm assembly as described in this chapter.

2. If still in place, remove the dust seal and thrust washer (A, **Figure 10**) from each side of the swing arm pivot.

3. Remove the bushing (**Figure 11**) from each needle bearing.

4. Remove the pivot collar (A, **Figure 12**) from the pivot boss on the swing arm.

5. If necessary, remove the chain slider (B, **Figure 10**) from the swing arm.

6. If necessary, remove the mounting hardware and the torque arm from the swing arm.

Inspection

1. Wash the bolts, collar and bushings in solvent, and thoroughly dry them.

2. Inspect the pivot collar and bushings for wear, scratches or score marks.

3. Check the bolts for straightness. If a bolt is bent it will restrict the movement of the swing arm.

4. Inspect the swing arm pivot bearings as follows:
   a. Use a clean lint-free rag and wipe off surface grease from the pivot area needle bearings.
   b. Turn each bearing (**Figure 13**) by hand. The bearing should turn smoothly without excessive play or noise. Check rollers for wear, pitting or rust.
   c. Inspect the bushings for wear, scratches or score marks.
   d. Reinstall the bushing (**Figure 11**) into the bearings and slowly rotate each bushing. The bushings must turn smoothly without excessive play or noise.
   e. Remove the bushings.

5. Inspect the tie-rod pivot boss (B, **Figure 12**) on the swing arm as follows:
   a. Use a clean lint-free rag and wipe off surface grease from the needle bearings.
   b. Turn each bearing by hand. The bearing should turn smoothly without excessive play or noise. Check the rollers for wear, pitting or rust.
   c. Insert the collar (A, **Figure 12**) into each bearing and slowly rotate the collar. It should turn smoothly without excessive play or noise.
   d. Remove the collar.

6. Replace any worn or damaged bearing as described in *Swing Arm Needle Bearing Replacement* in this chapter.

7. Check the welded sections on the swing arm for cracks or fractures.

8. Check the pivot shaft for straightness with V-blocks and a dial indicator (**Figure 14**). Replace

13

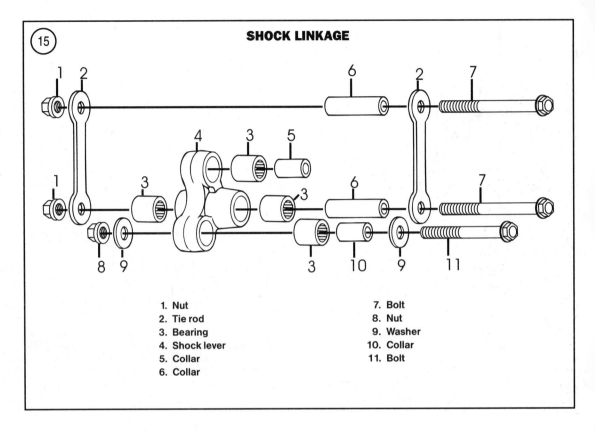

SHOCK LINKAGE

1. Nut
2. Tie rod
3. Bearing
4. Shock lever
5. Collar
6. Collar
7. Bolt
8. Nut
9. Washer
10. Collar
11. Bolt

the pivot shaft if the runout exceeds 0.3 mm (0.01 in.).

9. Inspect the drive chain slider (B, **Figure 10**) for wear or damage. Replace as necessary.

Assembly

1. If removed, install the torque arm onto the swing arm. Install the forward torque arm bolt and nut and finger-tighten the nut.

2. If removed, install the chain slider (B, **Figure 10**) onto the swing arm.

3. Lubricate the needle bearings and pivot collars and bushings with grease.

4. Install the pivot collar (A, **Figure 12**) into the tie-rod pivot boss (B) on the swing arm. Make sure the ends of the collar are flush with the end of each needle bearing.

5. Install the bushing (**Figure 11**) into the needle bearing on each side of the swing arm pivot.

6. Install the thrust washer and dust seal (A, **Figure 10**) onto each side of the swing arm pivot. Push the dust seal on until it is completely seated.

7. Install the swing arm assembly as described in this chapter.

SHOCK LINKAGE

Removal

Refer to **Figure 15**.

1. Remove the exhaust system as described in Chapter Eight.

2. Support the motorcycle securely with the rear wheel off the ground. If a motorcycle stand or jack is not available, place wooden block(s) under the engine.

3. Remove the nut and bolt (**Figure 16**) securing the tie rods to the shock lever. Swing the tie rods rearward away from the shock lever.

4. Remove the bolt (A, **Figure 17**) securing the lower shock mount to the shock lever.

5. Remove the shock lever mounting bolt (B, **Figure 17**). Pull the shock lever pivot bolt from the left side of the motorcycle and lower the shock lever (C, **Figure 17**) from the frame bracket.

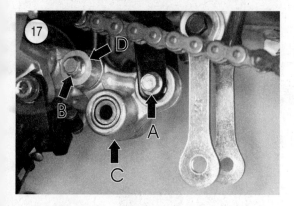

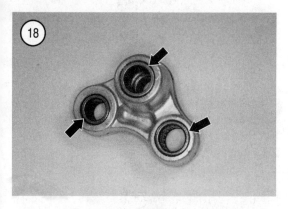

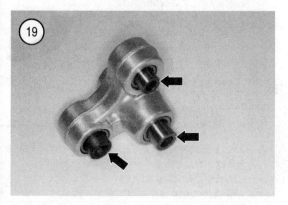

Installation

1. Apply grease to the pivot points on the lower end of the shock absorber and to the frame mounting boss.

2. Position the shock lever (C, **Figure 17**) correctly and align the shock lever forward mount within the frame bracket. Insert the shock lever pivot bolt from the left side. Be sure to install a washer (D, **Figure 17**) under the nut and bolt head. Do not tighten the nut at this time.

3. Move the shock lever up and align the lever rear pivot with the shock absorber lower mount. Loosely insert the shock mounting bolt (A, **Figure 17**) from the right side. Finger-tighten the bolt at this time.

4. Rotate the tie rods forward and align their mounting holes with the center pivot on the shock lever.

5. Install the tie rod bolt (**Figure 16**) from the right side of the motorcycle and loosely install the tie-rod mounting nut.

> *CAUTION*
> *Do not overtighten the lower shock mounting bolt. This bolt threads directly into the shock absorber. If the threads become damaged, replace the shock absorber.*

6. Tighten the mounting hardware in the following order:

   a. Tighten the lower shock mounting bolt (A, **Figure 17**) to 50 N•m (37 ft.-lb.).
   b. Tighten the tie-rod mounting nut (**Figure 16**) to 78 N•m (57 ft.-lb.).
   c. Tighten the shock lever mounting nut to 78 N•m (57 ft.-lb.).

7. Install the exhaust system as described in Chapter Eight.

Inspection

1. Inspect the shock lever pivot bearings as follows:

   a. Remove the pivot collars from the pivot.
   b. Use a clean lint-free rag and wipe off surface grease from the pivot needle bearings (**Figure 18**).
   c. Turn each bearing by hand. The bearing should turn smoothly without excessive play or noise. Check the rollers for wear, pitting or rust.
   d. Reinstall the pivot collars (**Figure 19**) into the bearings and slowly rotate each pivot collar.

13

The collars must turn smoothly without excessive play or noise.

e. Remove the pivot collars.

f. If the needle bearings must be replaced, refer to *Shock Lever Needle Bearing Replacement* in this chapter.

2. Inspect the pivot collars for wear and damage. Replace each collar as necessary.

3. Inspect the rocker arm for cracks or damage. Replace as necessary.

4. Inspect the tie rods (**Figure 20**) for bending, cracks or damage. Replace as necessary.

5. Clean the pivot bolts and nuts in solvent. Check the bolts for straightness. If a bolt is bent, it will restrict the movement of the rocker arm.

6. Before installing the pivot collars, coat the inner surface of the bearings with molybdenum disulfide grease.

BEARING REPLACEMENT

Swing Arm Needle Bearing Replacement

Do not remove the swing arm needle bearings unless they must be replaced. The needle bearings are pressed onto the swing arm. A set of blind bearing pullers is required to remove the needle bearings. The needle bearings can be installed with a homemade tool.

NOTE
If the needle bearings are replaced, replace the pivot bushings at the same time. These parts should always be replaced as a set.

1. If still installed, remove the dust seals, thrust washers and pivot bushings from the needle bearings as described in this chapter.

NOTE
In the following steps, the bearing puller grabs the inner surface of the bearing and then withdraws it from the pivot boss in the swing arm.

2. Insert the Suzuki bearing puller (part No. 09921-20220) or an equivalent blind bearing puller through the needle bearing and expand it behind the bearing.

3. Using sharp strokes of the slide hammer, withdraw the needle bearing from the pivot boss.

4. Remove the bearing puller and the bearing.

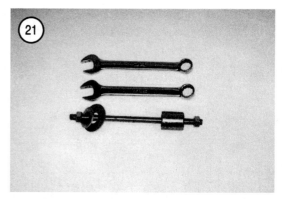

5. Withdraw the spacer located between the bearings.

6. Repeat for the bearing on the other side.

7. Remove the special tool.

8. Repeat Steps 2-7 for the shock lever pivot bearings on the bottom of the swing arm.

9. Thoroughly clean the inside of the pivot bore with solvent, then dry it with compressed air.

10. To make bearing installation easier, apply a light coat of grease to the exterior of the new bearings and to the inner circumference of the pivot bore.

NOTE
Install one needle bearing at a time. Make sure the bearing is entering the pivot boss squarely; otherwise the bearing and the pivot boss may be damaged.

11. Position the bearing with the manufacturer's marks facing out.

NOTE
The bearing can be easily installed using a homemade tool consisting of a piece of threaded rod, two thick washers, two nuts, a socket that matches

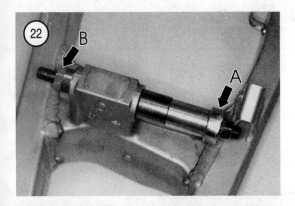

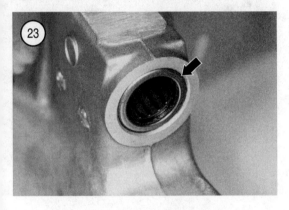

are pressed onto the shock lever. A set of blind bearing pullers is required to remove the needle bearings. The needle bearings can be installed with a homemade tool, or socket and hammer.

NOTE
If the needle bearings are replaced, replace the pivot collars at the same time. These parts should always be replaced as a set.

1. If still installed, remove the pivot collars.

NOTE
In the following steps, the bearing puller grabs the inner surface of the bearing and then withdraws it from the pivot areas of the swing arm.

2. Insert the bearing puller through the needle bearing and expand it behind the front bearing.
3. Using sharp strokes of the slide hammer, withdraw the needle bearing from the front pivot hole.

NOTE
The bearings are different sizes. Mark the bearings front, center and rear as they are removed. The center two bearings are identical.

4. Remove the special tool and the bearing.
5. At the center pivot area, repeat Step 2 and Step 3 for the bearing on each side.
6. Repeat Step 2 and Step 3 for the rear bearing.
7. Thoroughly clean out the inside of the pivot bores with solvent. Dry them with compressed air.
8. To make bearing installation easier, apply a light coat of grease to the exterior of the new bearings and to the inner circumference of the pivot bores.
9. Locate and square the new bearing in the pivot bore.
10. Install the bearings with an appropriate size drift or socket that matches the outer race diameter. Tap the bearings into place.
11. Check that the bearing is properly seated. Turn each bearing by hand. The bearing should turn smoothly.
12. Lubricate the needles of the new bearing with a waterproof bearing grease.
13. Repeat for the other bearings.
14. Before installing the pivot collars, coat the inner surface of the bearings with grease. Install the pivot collars as described in this chapter.

the outer race diameter, and two wrenches as shown in **Figure 21**.

12. Locate and square the new bearing in the pivot bore. Assemble the homemade tool through the pivot bore so the socket presses against the bearing. See **Figure 22**.
13. Hold the nut adjacent to the socket (A, **Figure 22**).
14. Tighten the nut on the opposite side (B, **Figure 22**) and pull the bearing into the pivot bore. Pull the bearing until it is flush with the outer surface of the pivot boss (**Figure 23**).
15. Disassemble the tool and reinstall it on the opposite side, then repeat for the other bearing.
16. Remove the tool.
17. Make sure the bearings are properly seated. Turn each bearing by hand; they should turn smoothly.
18. Lubricate the new bearings with grease.
19. Repeat for the other set of bearings in the swing arm.

Shock Lever Needle Bearing Replacement

Do not remove the shock lever needle bearings unless they must be replaced. The needle bearings

13

Table 1 REAR SUSPENSION SPECIFICATIONS

Item	New	Service limit
Swing arm pivot shaft runout (max.)	–	0.3 mm (0.012 in.)
Rear shock absorber spring preload		
SV650	2nd position	
SV650S	4th position	
Rear wheel travel	125 mm (4.9 in.)	–

Table 2 REAR SUSPENSION TORQUE SPECIFICATIONS

Item	N•m	in.-lb.	ft.-lb.
Shock absorber mounting bolt (upper & lower)	50	–	37
Shock lever mounting bolt	78	–	57
Swing arm			
Pivot locknut	90	–	66
Pivot nut	100	–	74
Pivot shaft	15	133	–
Tie rod nuts	78	–	57
Torque arm (both ends)	35	–	26

NOTE: Refer to the Supplement at the back of this manual for information unique to 2003-on models.

CHAPTER FOURTEEN

BRAKES

This chapter covers service, repair and replacement procedures for the front and rear brake systems. Brake specifications are located in **Table 1** and **Table 2** at the end of this chapter.

The brake system consists of dual discs up front and a single disc mounted at the rear.

BRAKE SERVICE

The disc brake system transmits hydraulic pressure from the master cylinders to the brake calipers. This pressure is transmitted from the caliper(s) to the brake pads, which grip both sides of the brake disc(s) and slow the motorcycle. As the pads wear, the pistons move out of the caliper bores to automatically compensate for wear. As this occurs, the fluid level in the reservoir goes down. This must be compensated for by occasionally adding fluid.

The proper operation of this system depends on a supply of clean brake fluid (DOT 4) and a clean work environment when any service is being performed. Any tiny particle of debris that enters the system can damage the components and cause poor brake performance.

Brake fluid is hygroscopic (easily absorbs moisture) and moisture in the system will reduce brake performance. It is a good idea to purchase brake fluid in small containers and discard any small quantities that remain. Small quantities of fluid will quickly absorb the moisture in the container. Use only fluid clearly marked DOT 4. If possible, use the same brand of fluid. Do not replace the fluid with DOT 5 (silicone) fluid. It is not possible to remove all of the old fluid and DOT 5 is not compatible with other types. Silicone type fluids used in systems for which they were not designed will cause internal seals to swell and deteriorate. Do not reuse drained fluid. Discard old fluid properly.

Proper service also includes carefully performed procedures. Do not use any sharp tools inside the master cylinders or calipers or on the pistons. Any

14

damage to these components could cause a loss in the system's ability to maintain hydraulic pressure. If there is any doubt concerning the ability to correctly and safely service the brake system, have a professional technician perform the task.

Consider the following when servicing the brake system:

1. The hydraulic components rarely require disassembly. Make sure it is necessary.

2. Keep the reservoir covers in place to prevent the entry of moisture and debris.

3. Clean parts with an aerosol brake part cleaner or isopropyl alcohol. Never use petroleum-based solvents on internal brake system components. They will cause seals to swell and distort.

4. Do not allow brake fluid to contact plastic, painted or plated parts. It will damage the surface.

5. Dispose of brake fluid properly.

6. If the hydraulic system has been opened (not including the reservoir cover), bleed the system to remove air from the system. Refer to *Bleeding the System* in this chapter.

7. Use good judgment when inspecting brake system components. If necessary, consult a professional technician for advice.

> *WARNING*
> *Do not add to or replace the brake fluid with silicone (DOT 5) brake fluid. It is not compatible with the system and may cause brake failure.*

> *WARNING*
> *Whenever working on the brake system, do **not** inhale brake dust. It may contain asbestos, which can cause lung injury and cancer. Wear a facemask that meets OSHA requirements for trapping asbestos particles, and wash hands and forearms thoroughly after completing the work.*

> *WARNING*
> *Never use compressed air to clean any part of the brake system. This will expel harmful brake pad dust. Use an aerosol brake cleaner to clean parts when servicing any component still installed on the motorcycle.*

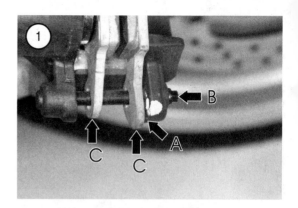

FRONT BRAKE PADS

Inspection

Inspect the front brake pads as described in Chapter Three.

Replacement

1. Review the *Brake Service* information in the preceding section.

2. Place the motorcycle on the sidestand on level ground.

3. Place a spacer between the brake lever and the throttle grip and secure it in place. That way, if the brake lever is inadvertently squeezed, the pistons will not be forced out of the cylinders.

4. Remove the caliper as described in this chapter.

5. Remove the clip (A, **Figure 1**) and pin (B).

6. Remove both brake pads (C, **Figure 1**) from the caliper assembly.

7. Clean the pad recess and the end of both sets of pistons with a soft brush. Do not use solvent, a wire brush or any hard tool that would damage the cylinders or pistons.

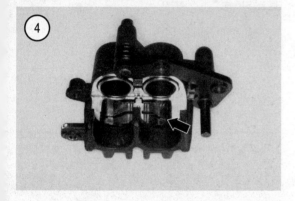

8. Carefully remove any rust or corrosion from the disc.

9. Thoroughly clean the pad pin and clip of any corrosion or road dirt.

10. Check the friction surface of the new pads for any foreign matter or manufacturing residue. If necessary, clean the pads with an aerosol brake cleaner.

NOTE
When purchasing new pads, check with the parts supplier to make sure the friction compound of the new pads is compatible with the disc material. Remove any roughness from the backs of the new pads with a fine-cut file.

11. Repeat Steps 4-10 and remove the brake pads in the other caliper assembly.

12. When new pads are installed in the calipers, the master cylinder brake fluid level will rise as the caliper pistons are repositioned. Perform the following:

   a. Clean all dirt and debris from the top of the master cylinder.

   b. Cover the area underneath the master cylinder to protect from brake fluid spills.

   c. *SV650 models*—Remove the screws securing the cover (**Figure 2**). Remove the cover and the diaphragm from the master cylinder.

   d. *SV650S models*—Unscrew the brake fluid reservoir cap (**Figure 3**). Remove the diaphragm from the reservoir.

   e. Temporarily install both old brake pads into the caliper and seat them against the pistons.

   f. Protect the caliper with a shop cloth to prevent scuffing it, then grasp the caliper and brake pad with a large pair of slip-joint pliers. Squeeze the piston back into the caliper. Repeat for each side until the pistons are completely in the caliper.

   g. Constantly check the reservoir and make sure the fluid does not overflow. Draw out excess fluid if necessary.

   h. The pistons should move freely. If they do not, remove and service the caliper as described in this chapter.

   i. Remove the old brake pads.

   j. Repeat this process for the other caliper.

13. Install the brake pad spring (**Figure 4**).

14. Install the brake pads (C, **Figure 1**) into the caliper, then install the pad mounting pin (B) and clip (A).

15. Carefully install the caliper assembly onto the brake disc. Be careful not to damage the leading edges of the pads during installation.

16. Remove the spacer from the front brake lever.

17. Pump the front brake lever to reposition the brake pads against the brake disc. Roll the motorcycle back and forth and continue to pump the brake lever as many times as it takes to refill the cylinders in the calipers and correctly position the brake pads against the disc.

WARNING
Use brake fluid clearly marked DOT 4 from a sealed container. Other types may vaporize and cause brake failure. Always use the same brand of brake fluid. Do not intermix brake fluid brands. Many brands are not compatible. Do not intermix silicone-based (DOT 5) brake fluid as it can cause brake component damage, leading to brake system failure.

NOTE
To control the small flow of hydraulic fluid, punch a small hole into the seal

14

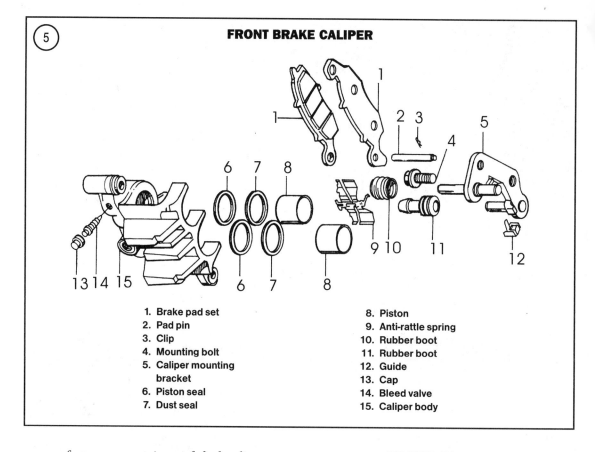

FRONT BRAKE CALIPER

1. Brake pad set
2. Pad pin
3. Clip
4. Mounting bolt
5. Caliper mounting bracket
6. Piston seal
7. Dust seal
8. Piston
9. Anti-rattle spring
10. Rubber boot
11. Rubber boot
12. Guide
13. Cap
14. Bleed valve
15. Caliper body

of a new container of hydraulic (brake) fluid next to the edge of the pour spout. This helps eliminate spillage, especially when adding fluid to the very small reservoir.

18. Refill the master cylinder reservoir, if necessary, to maintain the correct fluid level as indicated on the side of the reservoir. Install the diaphragm and cover. Tighten the cover retaining screws securely.

19. Move the reservoir top cover retaining clip back into position and tighten the mounting screw securely.

> *WARNING*
> *Do not ride the motorcycle until the brakes are operating correctly with full hydraulic advantage. If necessary, bleed the brake as described in this chapter.*

20. Bed the pads in gradually for the first two to three days of riding by using only light pressure as much as possible. Immediate hard application glazes the new friction pads and greatly reduces their effectiveness.

FRONT CALIPER

Removal/Installation

Refer to **Figure 5**.

> *CAUTION*
> *Do not spill any brake fluid on the motorcycle. Brake fluid will damage the finish on any plastic, painted or plated surface. Use soapy water to wash off any spilled brake fluid immediately.*

1. If the caliper assembly is going to be disassembled for service, perform the following:

   a. Remove the brake pads as described in this chapter.

   b. Reinstall the caliper assembly onto the brake disc and fork assembly. Tighten the caliper mounting bolts only finger-tight.

> *CAUTION*
> *During the following procedure, do not allow the pistons to come in contact with the brake disc. If this hap-*

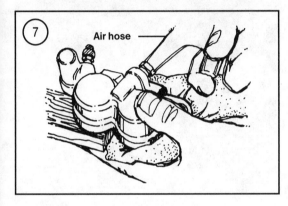

Air hose

pens, the pistons may damage the disc during caliper removal.

NOTE
By performing Step 1c, compressed air may not be necessary for piston removal during caliper disassembly.

c. Slowly apply the brake lever to push the pistons part way out of the caliper assembly for ease of removal during caliper service.

2. Remove the union bolt (A, **Figure 6**) and sealing washers attaching the brake hose to the caliper assembly. There should be two sealing washers, one on each side of the union bolt.

3. Place the loose end of the brake hose in a reclosable plastic bag to prevent brake fluid from dribbling onto the wheel or fork.

4. Remove the two caliper mounting bolts (B, **Figure 6**) and lift the brake caliper off the disc.

5. If necessary, disassemble and service the caliper assembly as described in this chapter.

6. Install by reversing the preceding removal steps while noting the following:

a. Carefully install the caliper assembly onto the disc, being careful not to damage the leading edge of the brake pads.

b. Install the two caliper mounting bolts (B, **Figure 6**) and secure the brake caliper to the front fork. Tighten the caliper mounting bolts to 39 N•m (29 ft.-lb.).

c. If disconnected, connect the brake hose to the caliper. Install a new sealing washer on each side of the union bolt (A, **Figure 6**). Tighten the union bolt to 23 N•m (17 ft.-lb.).

d. Bleed the brakes as described in this chapter.

WARNING
Do not ride the motorcycle until there is certainty that the brakes are operating properly.

Disassembly

Refer to **Figure 5**.
1. Remove the caliper and brake pads as described in this chapter.
2. Before removing the pistons, identify the pistons by marking their inner bore with a black marker so they can be reinstalled in their original cylinders.

WARNING
*Be careful when using compressed air. The piston, dirt or brake fluid can fly from the caliper at great speed and cause injury. Keep fingers out of the way. Wear safety eyewear and shop gloves and apply compressed air gradually. Do **not** use high pressure air or place the air hose nozzle directly against the fluid passageway in the caliper. Hold the air nozzle away from the inlet, allowing some of the air to escape during the procedure.*

NOTE
If the pistons were partially forced out of the caliper body during removal, Steps 3-4 may not be necessary. If the pistons or caliper bores are corroded or very dirty, a small amount of compressed air may be necessary to completely remove the pistons from the bores.

3. Place a rag or piece of wood in the path of the pistons (**Figure 7**) and place the caliper on the workbench so that the pistons face down.

14

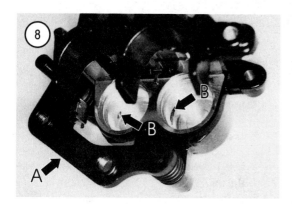

4. Blow the piston out with compressed air directed into the hydraulic fluid hole (**Figure 7**).

5. Remove the piston seals and dust seals.

6. Inspect the caliper body as described in this chapter.

Inspection

1. Carefully slide the caliper mounting bracket (A, **Figure 8**) from the caliper assembly.

2. Clean the caliper and pistons with an aerosol brake cleaner or isopropyl alcohol. Thoroughly dry the parts with compressed air.

3. Make sure the fluid passageways (B, **Figure 8**) in the base of the piston bores are clear. Apply compressed air to the openings to make sure they are clear. Clean the passages if necessary.

4. Inspect the piston and dust seal grooves (**Figure 9**) in the caliper body for damage. If any groove is damaged or corroded, replace the caliper assembly.

5. Inspect the union bolt threaded hole (**Figure 10**) in the caliper body. If worn or damaged, clean out with a metric thread tap or replace the caliper assembly.

6. Remove the bleed valve and dust cap. Inspect the bleed valve. Apply compressed air to the opening and make sure it is clear. If necessary, clean it out. Install the bleed valve, and tighten it to 7.5 N•m (66 in.-lb.).

7. Inspect the bleed valve threaded hole in the caliper body. If worn or damaged, clean the threads with a metric tap or replace the caliper assembly.

8. Remove the pad spring (**Figure 11**) from the caliper.

9. Inspect the caliper body (**Figure 12**) for damage and replace the caliper body if necessary.

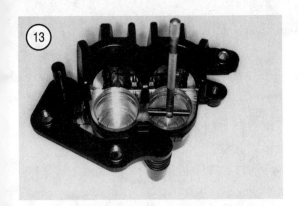

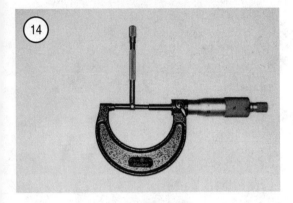

10. Inspect the caliper cylinder bores for scratches, scoring or other damage.

11. Measure the cylinder bores with a telescoping gauge (**Figure 13**) or other suitable measuring tool. If using a telescoping gauge, measure it with a micrometer (**Figure 14**). Refer to the specification listed in **Table 1**.

12. Inspect the pistons (**Figure 15**) for scratches, scoring or other damage.

13. Measure the outside diameter of the pistons with a micrometer (**Figure 16**) or vernier caliper. Refer to the specification listed in **Table 1**.

14. The piston seal helps maintain correct brake pad-to-disc clearance. If the seal is worn or damaged, the brake pads will drag and cause excessive wear and increase brake fluid temperature. It is a good practice to replace the seals whenever disassembling the caliper.

15. Inspect the mounting bracket and pins for wear or damage (**Figure 17**). Replace if necessary.

16. Inspect the brake pads for uneven wear, damage or grease contamination.

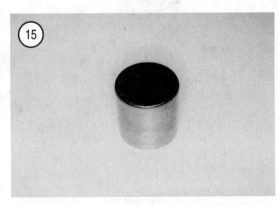

NOTE
When the brake system is operating correctly, the inboard and outboard brake pads will show approximately the same amount of wear. If there is a large difference in pad wear, the caliper is not sliding properly along the mounting bracket pins, causing one pad to drag against the disc. Worn caliper piston seals will also cause uneven pad wear.

Assembly

1. Install the brake pad anti-rattle spring (**Figure 11**) and make sure it is properly seated.

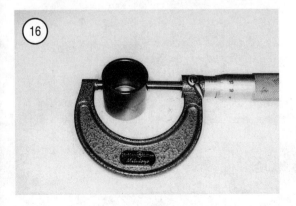

14

2. Coat the new dust seals and piston seals and piston bores with clean DOT 4 brake fluid.

3. Carefully install the new piston seals (A, **Figure 18**) into the inner grooves. Make sure the seals are properly seated in their respective grooves.

4. Carefully install the new dust seals (B, **Figure 18**) into the outer grooves. Make sure the seals are properly seated in their respective grooves.

5. Coat the pistons with clean DOT 4 brake fluid.

6. Position the pistons with the closed end facing in and install the pistons into the caliper cylinders. Push the pistons in until they bottom (**Figure 19**).

> *NOTE*
> *Prior to installing the caliper mounting bracket, apply silicone grease to the bracket pins and to the inside surfaces of the rubber boots (**Figure 20**) on the caliper assembly. This will make installation easier and will ensure that the caliper will move easily after installation on the fork slider.*

7. Carefully slide the caliper mounting bracket (**Figure 21**) onto the caliper assembly. Push the bracket on until it bottoms.

8. Install the caliper and brake pads as described in this chapter.

FRONT BRAKE MASTER CYLINDER (SV650 MODELS)

Removal/Installation

> *CAUTION*
> *Do not spill any brake fluid on the motorcycle. Brake fluid will damage the finish on any plastic, painted or plated surface. Use soapy water to wash off any spilled brake fluid immediately.*

1. Remove the rear view mirror (A, **Figure 22**) from the master cylinder clamp.

2. Clean the top of the master cylinder of all dirt and debris.

3. Remove the screws securing the cover (B, **Figure 22**). Remove the cover and the diaphragm.

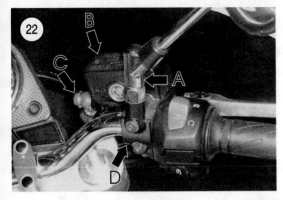

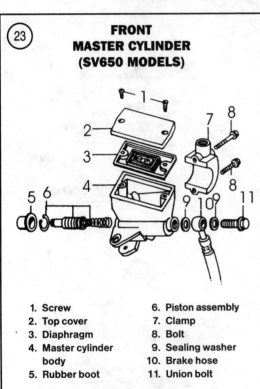

**FRONT
MASTER CYLINDER
(SV650 MODELS)**

1. Screw
2. Top cover
3. Diaphragm
4. Master cylinder
   body
5. Rubber boot
6. Piston assembly
7. Clamp
8. Bolt
9. Sealing washer
10. Brake hose
11. Union bolt

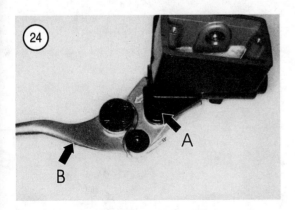

4. Use a shop syringe and draw all of the brake fluid out of the master cylinder reservoir.

5. Place a shop cloth under the union bolt (C, **Figure 22**) to catch any spilled brake fluid that will leak out.

6. Unscrew the union bolt (C, **Figure 22**) securing the brake hose to the master cylinder. Do not lose the sealing washer on each side of the hose fitting. Tie the loose end of the hose up to the handlebar and cover the end to prevent the entry of moisture and debris. Cover the loose end with a reclosable plastic bag.

7. Remove the bolts and clamp (D, **Figure 22**) securing the front master cylinder to the handlebar and remove the master cylinder.

8. Install by reversing the preceding removal steps while noting the following:

   a. Position the front master cylinder onto the right handlebar and align the mating surface with the handlebar punch mark.

   b. Position the clamp with the rear view mirror mounting hole facing up, and install the master cylinder clamp bolts (D, **Figure 22**). Tighten the upper mounting bolt first, then the lower bolt, leaving a gap at the bottom. Tighten the bolts to 10 N•m (88 in.-lb.).

   c. Place a sealing washer on each side of the brake hose fitting (C, **Figure 22**) and install the union bolt. Tighten the union bolt to 23 N•m (17 ft.-lb.).

   d. Bleed the front brakes as described under *Bleeding the System* in this chapter.

Disassembly

Refer to **Figure 23**.

1. Remove the master cylinder as described in this chapter.

2. If not already removed, remove the screws securing the cover and remove the cover and diaphragm; pour out any residual brake fluid and discard it. Never reuse brake fluid.

3. Remove the bolt (A, **Figure 24**) and nut securing the brake lever (B) and remove the brake lever.

4. Remove the rubber boot (**Figure 25**) from the area where the hand lever actuates the internal piston.

5. Using snap ring pliers, remove the internal snap ring (**Figure 26**) from the body.

14

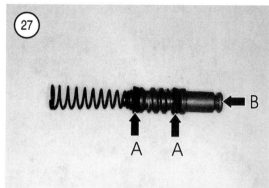

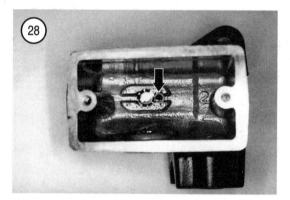

6. Remove the piston and spring assembly (**Figure 27**).

Inspection

1. Clean all parts in denatured alcohol or brake cleaning fluid. Inspect the cylinder bore and piston contact surfaces for signs of wear and damage. If either part is less than perfect, replace it.

2. Inspect the piston cups (A, **Figure 27**) for any signs of wear or damage. Cups are not available separately and must be replaced along with the new piston and spring as an assembly.

3. Check the end of the piston (B, **Figure 27**) for wear caused by the hand lever. If worn, replace the piston assembly.

4. Make sure the passage (**Figure 28**) in the bottom of the body reservoir is clear. Clean with brake fluid, then apply compressed air to make sure the passage is clear.

5. Check the reservoir cover and diaphragm for damage and deterioration and replace as necessary.

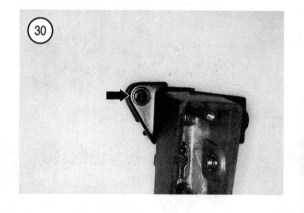

6. Inspect the threads (**Figure 29**) for the union bolt in the body. If worn or damaged, clean out with

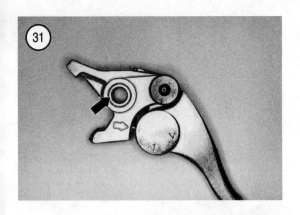

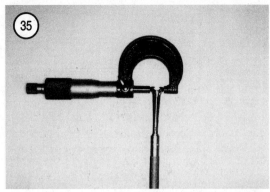

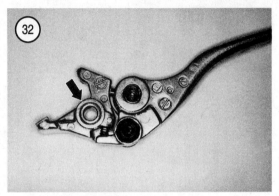

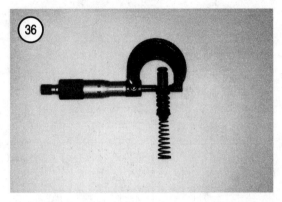

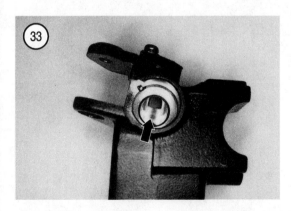

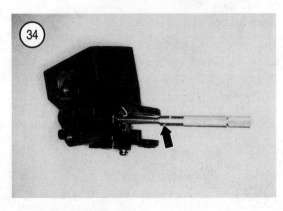

a suitable size metric thread tap or replace the master cylinder assembly.

7. Inspect the fluid viewing port for signs of hydraulic fluid leakage. If leakage has occurred, replace the master cylinder assembly.

8. Check the hand lever pivot lugs (**Figure 30**) on the master cylinder body for cracks or elongation. If damaged, replace the master cylinder assembly.

9. Inspect the hand lever pivot hole (**Figure 31**). If worn or elongated, replace the lever.

10. Inspect the adjust portion of the hand lever (**Figure 32**) in the hand lever. If worn or damaged, replace the damaged parts(s).

11. Inspect the body cylinder bore surface (**Figure 33**) for signs of wear and damage. If less than perfect, replace the master cylinder assembly. The body cannot be replaced separately.

12. Measure the cylinder bore with a small bore gauge (**Figure 34**). Measure the small bore gauge with a micrometer (**Figure 35**). Replace the master cylinder if the bore exceeds the service limit listed in **Table 1**.

13. Measure the outside diameter of the piston assembly (**Figure 36**) with a micrometer. Replace the

14

piston assembly if it is worn to, or less than, the service limit listed in **Table 1**.

Assembly

1. Soak the new, or existing, piston assembly in fresh brake fluid for at least 15 minutes to make the cups pliable. Coat the inside of the cylinder bore with fresh brake fluid prior to the assembly of parts.

> *CAUTION*
> *When installing the piston assembly, do not allow the cups to turn inside out, as they will be damaged and allow brake fluid leakage within the cylinder bore.*

2. Install the spring with the tapered end facing toward the primary cup on the piston (**Figure 37**), then install the spring and the piston assembly (**Figure 38**) into the cylinder bore.

3. Push the piston assembly into the bore and hold it in place. Install the snap ring (**Figure 26**) and make sure it seats correctly in the master cylinder body groove.

4. Install the rubber boot (**Figure 25**) and push it all the way down until it stops.

5. Install the brake lever onto the master cylinder body, then install the bolt and nut. Tighten the bolt and nut securely.

6. If removed, reinstall the brake light switch (**Figure 39**) and tighten the screw securely.

7. Install the diaphragm and cover and screws. Do not tighten the cover screws at this time, as fluid will have to be added later.

8. Install the master cylinder as described in this chapter.

FRONT BRAKE MASTER CYLINDER (SV650S MODELS)

Removal

> *CAUTION*
> *Cover the fuel tank and front fairing with a heavy cloth or plastic tarp to protect them from accidental brake fluid spills. Brake fluid damages the finish on any plastic, painted or plated surface. Immediately wash any spilled brake fluid from the motorcy-*

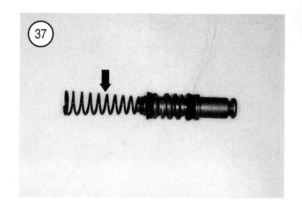

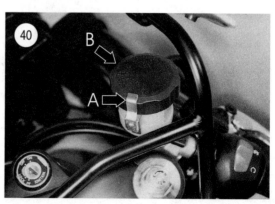

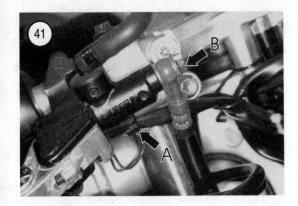

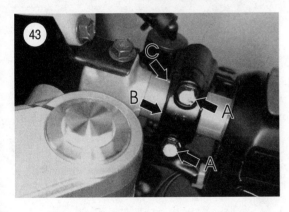

install the diaphragm, plate and cover. Tighten the cap finger-tight.

5. Disconnect the brake light switch electrical connector (A, **Figure 41**) from the brake switch.

6. Place a rag beneath the union bolt (B, **Figure 41**) and remove the bolt. Separate the brake hose from the master cylinder. Do not lose the two sealing washers, one from each side of the brake hose fitting.

7. Place the loose end of the brake hose in a reclosable plastic bag to prevent brake fluid from leaking onto the motorcycle. Tie the loose end of the hose up to the handlebar.

8. Remove the bolt (**Figure 42**) securing the master cylinder reservoir to the bracket on the upper fork bridge.

9. Remove the master cylinder clamp bolts (A, **Figure 43**) and the clamp (B).

10. Remove the master cylinder and reservoir assembly from the handlebar.

11. Drain any residual brake fluid from the master cylinder and reservoir. Dispose of the fluid properly.

12. If the master cylinder and reservoir are being removed and are not going to be serviced, place them in a reclosable plastic bag to protect them from debris.

Installation

1. Position the front master cylinder onto the right handlebar and align the mating surface with the handlebar punch mark (C, **Figure 43**).

2. Position the clamp with the UP mark facing up and install the master cylinder clamp bolts (A, **Figure 43**). Tighten the upper mounting bolt first, then the lower bolt, leaving a gap at the bottom. Tighten the bolts to 10 N•m (88 in.-lb.).

NOTE
If the reservoir was removed from the master cylinder for service, the hose may have to be repositioned on the master cylinder to prevent any binding on the hose.

3. Install the remote reservoir onto the upper fork bridge and tighten the mounting bolt securely (**Figure 42**).

4. Install the brake hose onto the master cylinder. Install a new sealing washer onto each side of the hose fitting, and tighten the union bolt (B, **Figure 41**) to 23 N•m (17 ft.-lb.).

cle. Use soapy water and rinse the area completely.

1. Clean the top of the master cylinder of all debris.

2. Remove the clip mounting screw and move the reservoir cap retaining clip (A, **Figure 40**) from the cap.

3. Remove the cap (B, **Figure 40**), diaphragm plate and diaphragm from the master cylinder reservoir.

4. Use a shop syringe and draw all the brake fluid out of the master cylinder reservoir. Temporarily re-

14

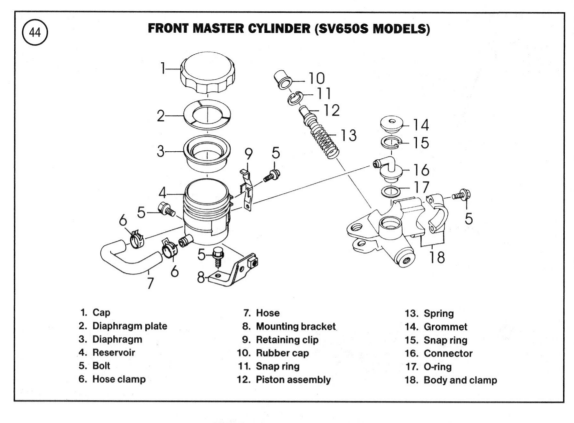

FRONT MASTER CYLINDER (SV650S MODELS)

1. Cap
2. Diaphragm plate
3. Diaphragm
4. Reservoir
5. Bolt
6. Hose clamp
7. Hose
8. Mounting bracket
9. Retaining clip
10. Rubber cap
11. Snap ring
12. Piston assembly
13. Spring
14. Grommet
15. Snap ring
16. Connector
17. O-ring
18. Body and clamp

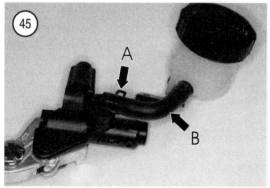

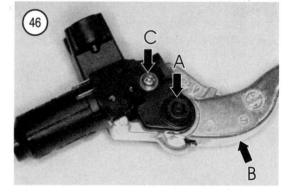

5. Reconnect the front brake light switch electrical connectors (A, **Figure 41**) onto the brake switch. Make sure the electrical connectors are locked into place.

6. Refill the master cylinder and reservoir and bleed the brake system as described in this chapter.

Disassembly

Refer to **Figure 44**.

1. Remove the master cylinder and reservoir assembly as described in this chapter.

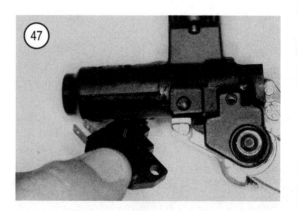

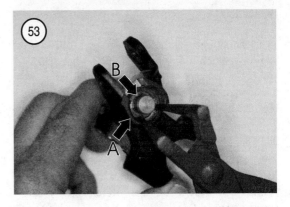

2. Release the hose clamp (**Figure 45**) and disconnect the interconnect hose from the master cylinder. Drain any residual brake fluid from both assemblies. Dispose of the fluid properly.

3. Remove the nut (A, **Figure 46**) and pivot bolt securing the hand lever to the master cylinder body. Remove the hand lever (B, **Figure 46**).

4. Remove the screw (C, **Figure 46**) securing the front brake switch. Apply the brake lever to move the lever actuating pad away from the switch plunger, and remove the switch (**Figure 47**).

5. Slide the rubber cap (**Figure 48**) up and away from the snap ring on the hose connector port on the master cylinder.

6. Using snap ring pliers, remove the internal snap ring (A, **Figure 49**) and the hose connector (B) from the master cylinder body.

7. Remove the O-ring (**Figure 50**) from the body.

8. Remove the rubber boot (**Figure 51**) from the cylinder bore on the master cylinder.

9. Press the piston (**Figure 52**) into the cylinder bore, and use snap ring pliers to remove the internal snap ring (A, **Figure 53**).

10. Remove the piston assembly (B, **Figure 53**) and the spring from the cylinder bore.

14

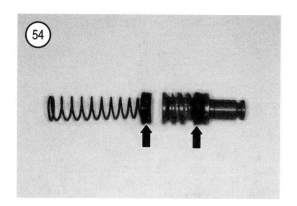

Inspection

1. Clean all parts with an aerosol brake cleaner or isopropyl alcohol. Inspect the cylinder bore surface and piston contact surfaces for wear or damage. If less than perfect, replace the master cylinder assembly. The body cannot be replaced separately.

2. Inspect the piston cups (**Figure 54**) for wear and damage. If less than perfect, replace the piston assembly. The individual cups cannot be replaced.

3. Measure the cylinder bore with a bore gauge (**Figure 55**) or vernier caliper. Refer to the specification in **Table 1**.

4. Make sure the fluid passage (**Figure 56**) in the bottom of the master cylinder body is clear. Clean it if necessary.

5. Inspect the piston contact surface (A, **Figure 57**) for wear and damage. If less than perfect, replace the piston assembly.

6. Check the end of the piston (B, **Figure 57**) for wear caused by the hand lever. If worn, replace the piston assembly.

7. Measure the outside diameter of the piston with a micrometer (**Figure 58**). Refer to the specification in **Table 1**.

8. Check the hand lever pivot lugs (**Figure 59**) on the master cylinder body for cracks or elongation. If damaged, replace the master cylinder assembly.

9. Inspect the pivot hole in the hand lever. If worn or elongated, replace the lever.

10. Inspect the threads in the master cylinder (**Figure 60**) for the union bolt. If damaged, restore the threads with a metric thread tap or replace the master cylinder assembly.

11. Inspect the hose connector and snap ring (**Figure 61**) for damage and deterioration. Replace either part as necessary.

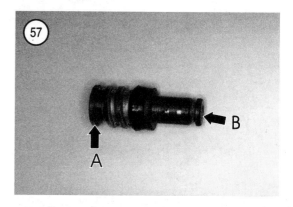

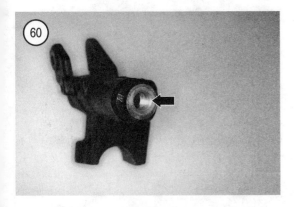

12. Check the cover, diaphragm and diaphragm plate (**Figure 62**) for damage and deterioration; replace as necessary.

13. Inspect the adjuster on the hand lever. If worn or damaged, replace the hand lever as an assembly.

14. Check the reservoir and interconnect hose (**Figure 63**) for damage and deterioration and replace as necessary.

Assembly

Refer to **Figure 44**.

1. Soak the new cups and the new piston assembly in fresh DOT 4 brake fluid for at least 15 minutes to make them pliable. Coat the inside of the cylinder bore with fresh brake fluid before the assembly of parts.

2. If removed, install the primary cup onto the spring and onto the piston cup (**Figure 54**).

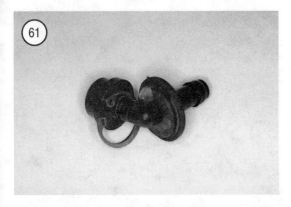

> *CAUTION*
> *When installing the piston assembly, do not allow the cups to turn inside out, as they will be damaged and allow brake fluid leakage within the cylinder bore.*

3. Position the spring with the tapered end facing the piston.

4. Install the spring and primary cup (A, **Figure 64**) and piston assembly (B) into the cylinder bore. Push them in until they bottom in the cylinder.

5. Press the piston assembly into the cylinder, and install the snap ring (C, **Figure 64**). Make sure it is correctly seated in the groove, and then slide on the rubber boot (**Figure 51**).

6. Install a new O-ring into the interconnect port (**Figure 50**) in the master cylinder body.

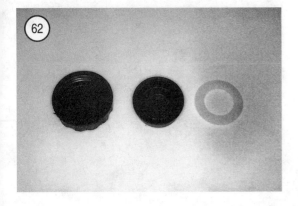

14

7. Seat the connector (B, **Figure 49**) into the interconnect port and install the circlip. Make sure the snap ring is properly seated in the groove (A, **Figure 49**).

8. Move the rubber cap down into position above the circlip, and seat it on the interconnect port (**Figure 48**).

9. Install the hand lever (B, **Figure 46**), bolt and nut (A). Tighten the bolt and nut securely, and then make sure the hand lever operates freely within the master cylinder. There should be no binding.

10. Apply the brake lever to move the lever actuating pad away from the brake switch area. Install the front brake switch (**Figure 47**) and screw (C, **Figure 46**). Tighten the mounting screw securely.

11. Release the brake lever and make sure the switch plunger moves in and out with no binding.

12. Install the interconnect hose (B, **Figure 45**) onto the connector on the master cylinder. Secure the hose in place with the hose clamp (A, **Figure 45**).

13. Install the master cylinder as described in this chapter.

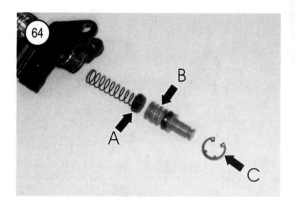

REAR BRAKE PADS

Inspection

Inspect the rear brake pads as described in Chapter Three.

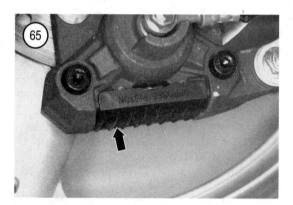

Replacement

1. Review the *Brake Service* information in this chapter.

2. Place the motorcycle on the sidestand on level ground.

3. To prevent the rear brake pedal from being applied, tie the end of the pedal up to the frame. That way, if the brake pedal is inadvertently pressed, the pistons will not be forced out of the cylinders.

4. Squeeze the sides of the pad cover and remove the cover (**Figure 65**).

5. Remove the clips (**Figure 66**).

6. Remove the anti-rattle springs (**Figure 67**), then withdraw the pad pins (**Figure 68**) from the caliper.

7. Withdraw both brake pads and shims from the caliper assembly.

8. Clean the pad recess and the end of both pistons with a soft brush. Do not use solvent, a wire brush

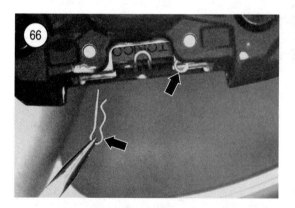

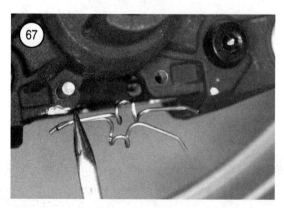

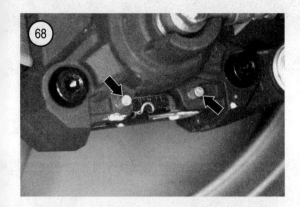

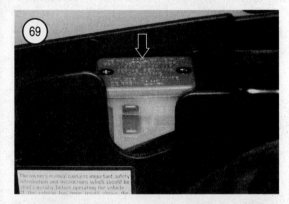

or any hard tool that would damage the cylinders or pistons.

9. Carefully remove any rust or corrosion from the disc.

10. Thoroughly clean any corrosion or road dirt from the anti-rattle springs, pad pins and clip.

11. Check the friction surface of the new pads for any debris or manufacturing residue. If necessary, clean the pads with an aerosol brake cleaner.

12. When new pads are installed in the calipers, the rear master cylinder brake fluid level will rise as the caliper pistons are repositioned. Remove the hydraulic fluid from the master cylinder reservoir by performing the following:

    a. Remove the rear frame cover as described in Chapter Fifteen.

    b. Clean the top of the master cylinder reservoir of all dirt and debris.

    c. Remove the top cover mounting screws and the top cover and diaphragm (**Figure 69**).

    d. Temporarily install one of the old brake pads into the caliper and seat it against the piston.

    e. Press the pad against the piston, and slowly push the caliper piston all the way into the caliper. Constantly check the reservoir to make sure brake fluid does not overflow. Remove fluid, if necessary, to prevent any overflow.

    f. The piston should move freely. If it does not, remove and service the caliper as described in this chapter.

    g. Remove the old brake pad and repeat this process for the piston on the other side.

13. Install the shims onto the new brake pads so the closed end of the shim faces the rear of the motorcycle as shown in **Figure 70**.

14. Install the inner brake pad (**Figure 71**) and the outer pad (**Figure 70**) into the caliper.

15. Install the anti-rattle springs (**Figure 67**) in place on both brake pads.

16. Position the front pad pin (**Figure 68**) so its clip hole points down, then insert the front pad pin through the caliper and into both pads. Make sure the pad pin is positioned under the anti-rattle springs in order to hold them in place.

17. Install the rear pad pin through the caliper and into both pads. Make sure the pad pin is positioned

14

under the anti-rattle springs and the clip hole points down.

18. Push the pins into the caliper until they bottom.

19. Install the clips (**Figure 66**) into both pad pins.

20. Note the correct assembly shown in **Figure 72**.

21. Install the pad cover (**Figure 65**), and make sure it is locked in place.

22. Untie the rear brake pedal.

23. Pump the rear brake pedal to reposition the brake pads against the brake disc. Roll the motorcycle back and forth and continue to pump the brake pedal as many times as it takes to refill the cylinders in the caliper and correctly locate the brake pads against the disc.

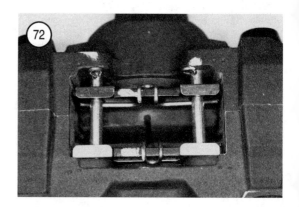

WARNING
Use brake fluid clearly marked DOT 4 from a sealed container. Other types may vaporize and cause brake failure. Always use the same brand of brake fluid. Do not intermix brands. They may not be compatible. Also do not intermix silicone based (DOT 5) brake fluid. It can cause brake component damage, leading to brake system failure.

NOTE
To control the small flow of hydraulic fluid, punch a small hole into the seal of a new container of hydraulic (brake) fluid next to the edge of the pour spout. This helps eliminate fluid spills, especially while adding fluid to the very small reservoir.

24. Refill the master cylinder reservoir, if necessary, to maintain the correct fluid level as indicated on the side of the reservoir. Install the diaphragm and the top cover. Install the screws and tighten them securely.

WARNING
Do not ride the motorcycle until the brakes are operating correctly with full hydraulic advantage. If necessary, bleed the brake as described in this chapter.

25. Bed the pads in gradually for the first two to three days of riding by using only light pressure as much as possible. Immediate hard application glazes the new friction pads and greatly reduces their effectiveness.

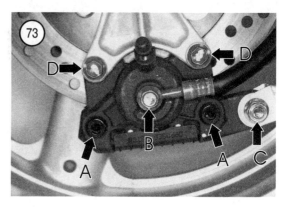

REAR BRAKE CALIPER

Removal/Installation

CAUTION
Do not spill any brake fluid on the rear wheel or swing arm. Brake fluid will damage the finish on any plastic, painted or plated surface. Wash off any spilled brake fluid immediately. Use soapy water and rinse the area completely.

CAUTION
In the following procedure, do not allow the pistons to contact the brake disc. If this happens, the pistons may damage the disc during caliper removal.

NOTE
When performing Substep b, compressed air may not be necessary for piston removal during caliper disassembly.

1. If the caliper assembly is going to be disassembled for service, perform the following:

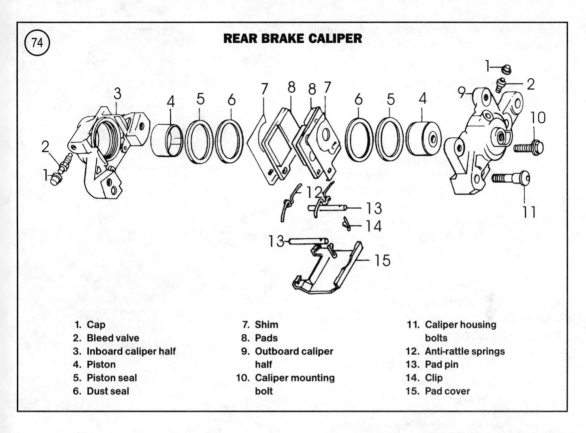

REAR BRAKE CALIPER

1. Cap	7. Shim	11. Caliper housing
2. Bleed valve	8. Pads	bolts
3. Inboard caliper half	9. Outboard caliper	12. Anti-rattle springs
4. Piston	half	13. Pad pin
5. Piston seal	10. Caliper mounting	14. Clip
6. Dust seal	bolt	15. Pad cover

a. Remove the brake pads as described in this chapter.

b. Apply the brake pedal to push the pistons partially out of the caliper assembly for ease of removal during caliper service.

c. Loosen the caliper housing bolts (A, **Figure 73**).

d. Place a drain pan under the rear caliper and remove the union bolt and sealing washers (B, **Figure 73**) securing the brake hose to the caliper assembly.

e. Place the loose end of the brake hose in a reclosable plastic bag to prevent the entry of debris and prevent brake fluid from leaking onto the motorcycle.

2. Remove the torque arm nut and bolt (C, **Figure 73**), and separate the torque arm from the caliper.

3. Remove the caliper mounting bolts (D, **Figure 73**), and lower the caliper from the caliper carrier and brake disc.

4. If necessary, disassemble and service the caliper assembly as described in this chapter.

5. Install by reversing these removal steps while noting the following:

a. Install the caliper assembly onto the disc, being careful not to damage the leading edge of the brake pads.

b. Install the caliper mounting bolts (D, **Figure 73**), and tighten them to 23 N•m (17 ft.-lb.).

c. Secure the torque arm to the rear caliper. Tighten the torque arm nut (C, **Figure 73**) to 35 N•m (26 ft.-lb.).

d. Install a new sealing washer to each side of the brake hose fitting and install the union bolt (B, **Figure 73**). Tighten the union bolt to 23 N•m (17 ft.-lb.).

e. Bleed the brake as described in this chapter.

WARNING
Do not ride the motorcycle until the brakes are operating properly.

Disassembly

Refer to **Figure 74**.

1. Remove the rear caliper and brake pads as described in this chapter.

14

2. Remove the two caliper housing bolts (**Figure 75**) loosened during the removal procedure.

3. Separate the caliper body halves. Remove the O-rings (**Figure 76**) and discard them. Install new O-rings every time the caliper is disassembled.

> *NOTE*
> *If the pistons were partially forced out of the caliper body during removal, Steps 4-6 may not be necessary. If the pistons or caliper bores are corroded or very dirty, a small amount of compressed air may be necessary to completely remove the pistons from the body bores.*

4. Place a piece of soft wood or folded shop cloth over the end of the piston and the caliper body. Turn this assembly over with the piston facing down onto the workbench top.

> *WARNING*
> *In the next step, the piston may shoot out of the caliper body with considerable force. Keep hands and fingers out of the way. Wear shop gloves and safety goggles when using compressed air to remove the pistons.*

5. Apply the air pressure in short spurts to the hydraulic fluid passageway and force the piston out of the caliper bore. Remove the piston from the bore. Repeat for the other caliper body half. Use a service station air hose if an air compressor is not available.

> *CAUTION*
> *In the following step, do not use a sharp tool to remove the dust and piston seals from the caliper cylinders. Do not damage the cylinder surface.*

6. Use a piece of wood or a plastic scraper and carefully push the dust seal and the piston seal (**Figure 77**) in toward the caliper cylinder and out of their grooves. Remove the dust and piston seals from the other caliper half, and discard all seals.

7. If necessary, remove the bleed valve (A, **Figure 78**).

8. Inspect the caliper assembly as described in this section.

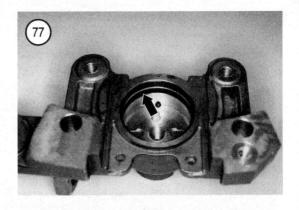

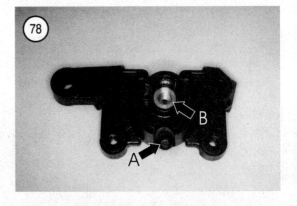

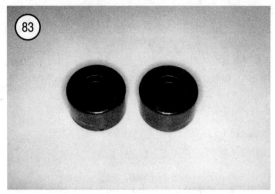

Inspection

1. Clean both caliper body halves and pistons with an aerosol brake cleaner or isopropyl alcohol. Dry the parts with compressed air.

2. Make sure the fluid passageways (**Figure 79**) in the base of the cylinder bores are clean. Apply compressed air to the openings to make sure they are clear. Clean them if necessary.

3. Make sure the fluid passageways (**Figure 80**) in the caliper body halves are clear. Apply compressed air to the openings to make sure they are clear. Clean them if necessary.

4. Inspect the piston and dust seal grooves (**Figure 81**) in both caliper bodies for damage. If damaged or corroded, replace the caliper assembly.

5. Inspect the union bolt threaded hole (B, **Figure 78**) in the outer caliper body. If worn or damaged, dress the threads with a metric tap or replace the caliper assembly.

6. Inspect the bleed valve threaded hole in the inboard caliper body. If worn or damaged, dress the threads with a metric tap or replace the caliper assembly.

7. Inspect the bleed valve. Apply compressed air to the opening and make sure it is clear. Clean the valve if necessary. Install the bleed valve into the caliper body, and tighten the valve to 7.5 N•m (66 in.-lb.).

8. Inspect both caliper bodies (**Figure 82**) for damage. Check the threads of the caliper mounting hole for wear or damage. Clean the threads with an appropriate size metric tap or replace the caliper assembly.

9. Inspect the cylinder walls and pistons (**Figure 83**) for scratches, scoring or other damage.

14

10. Measure the cylinder bores with a telescoping gauge (**Figure 84**) or vernier caliper. Refer to the specification in **Table 1**.

11. Measure the outside diameter of the pistons with a micrometer (**Figure 85**) or vernier caliper. Refer to the specification in **Table 1**.

Assembly

> *WARNING*
> *Never reuse old dust seals or piston seals. Very minor damage or age deterioration can affect brake performance.*

1. Soak the new dust and piston seals in fresh DOT 4 brake fluid.

2. Coat the piston bores and pistons with clean DOT 4 brake fluid.

> *WARNING*
> *The seal must be installed with the wide side facing out. Because the piston seal is tapered at its outer edge, the two sides are different. Stand the seal on its edge and determine the wide side. The wide side will be opposite the direction of tilt.*

3. Carefully install the new piston seal into the lower groove.

4. Carefully install the new dust seal into the upper groove. Make sure all seals are properly seated in their respective grooves (**Figure 77**).

5. Repeat Step 3 and Step 4 for the other caliper body half.

6. Position the piston with the open end facing out, and install the piston into the caliper cylinder. Push the piston in until it bottoms.

7. Repeat Step 6 for the other caliper body half (**Figure 86**). Make sure both pistons are installed correctly.

8. Coat the *new* O-rings with DOT 4 brake fluid and install the O-ring (**Figure 76**).

9. Make sure the O-ring is still in place and assemble the caliper body halves.

10. Install the two caliper housing bolts (**Figure 75**) and tighten them securely. They will be tightened to the correct torque value after the caliper is installed on the rear caliper bracket.

11. Install the bleed valve, and tighten it to 7.5 N•m (66 in.-lb.).

12. Install the caliper and brake pads as described in this chapter.

13. Tighten the two caliper housing bolts (A, **Figure 73**) to 23 N•m (17 ft.-lb.).

14. Bleed the brake as described in this chapter.

REAR MASTER CYLINDER

Removal

> *CAUTION*
> *Cover the swing arm and rear wheel with a heavy cloth or plastic tarp to protect them from accidental brake fluid*

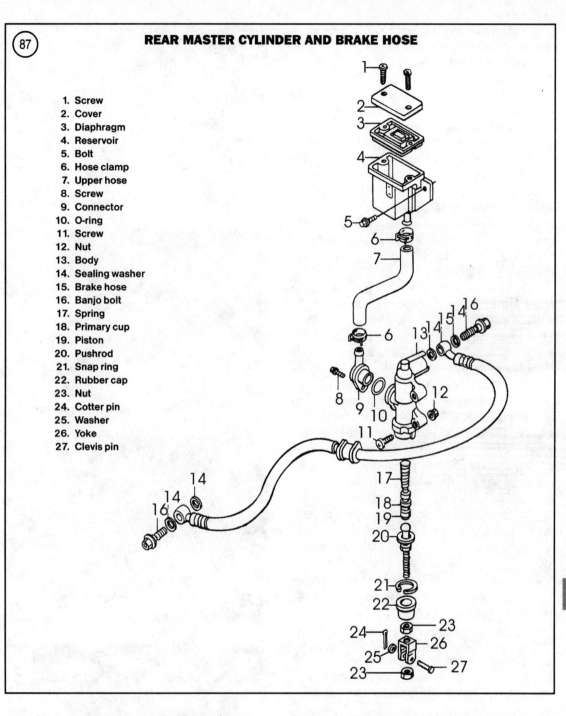

REAR MASTER CYLINDER AND BRAKE HOSE

87

1. Screw
2. Cover
3. Diaphragm
4. Reservoir
5. Bolt
6. Hose clamp
7. Upper hose
8. Screw
9. Connector
10. O-ring
11. Screw
12. Nut
13. Body
14. Sealing washer
15. Brake hose
16. Banjo bolt
17. Spring
18. Primary cup
19. Piston
20. Pushrod
21. Snap ring
22. Rubber cap
23. Nut
24. Cotter pin
25. Washer
26. Yoke
27. Clevis pin

14

spills. Brake fluid damages the finish on any plastic, painted or plated surface. Wash any spilled brake fluid off these surfaces immediately. Use soapy water and rinse the area completely.

Refer to **Figure 87**.

1. Remove the seats as described in Chapter Fifteen.

2. Remove the frame side cover as described in Chapter Fifteen.

3. Clean all debris from the top of the master cylinder reservoir.

4. Remove the top cover mounting screws, then remove the top cover (A, **Figure 88**) and diaphragm.

5. If a shop syringe is available, draw all the brake fluid out of the master cylinder reservoir.

6. Attach a hose to the bleed valve on the rear caliper and open the bleed valve.

7. Place the end of the hose over a container and let the brake fluid drain into the container. Slowly apply the rear brake pedal several times to expel most of the brake fluid from the rear hose and the master cylinder. Dispose of this brake fluid properly. Never reuse brake fluid.

8. Remove the hose and close the bleed valve.

9. Remove the bolts (**Figure 89**) securing the footrest guard and remove the guard. Reinstall the bolts to hold the master cylinder in place temporarily.

10. Remove the cotter pin from the end of the clevis pin (A, **Figure 90**), then withdraw the clevis pin securing the master cylinder pushrod to the brake pedal. Do not lose the washer behind the pushrod yoke.

11. Loosen, but do not remove, the union bolt (**Figure 91**) securing the brake hose to the inboard side of the master cylinder.

12. Place rags around the master cylinder to catch brake fluid, then loosen the hose fitting retaining screw (**Figure 92**). Separate the hose fitting (A, **Figure 93**) from the master cylinder. The O-ring (B, **Figure 93**) may remain in the master cylinder.

13. Remove the bolts (B, **Figure 90**) securing the master cylinder to the footpeg bracket. Move the master cylinder part way out of the frame.

14. Unscrew the union bolt securing the brake hose to the top of the master cylinder (**Figure 94**). Remove the sealing washer from each side of the hose fitting.

15. Remove the hose and place the loose end in a reclosable plastic bag to keep debris out of the system. Tie the loose end of the hose up to the frame.

16. Remove the master cylinder.

17. If the master cylinder will not be serviced, place it in a reclosable plastic bag to protect it from debris.

18. If necessary, remove the brake fluid reservoir after unscrewing the retaining screw (**Figure 92**).

19. Wash away any spilled brake fluid immediately.

Installation

1. If removed, install the brake fluid reservoir.

2. Correctly position the brake hose onto the top of the master cylinder. Place a sealing washer onto each side of the brake hose fitting and install the union bolt. Tighten the union bolt finger-tight.

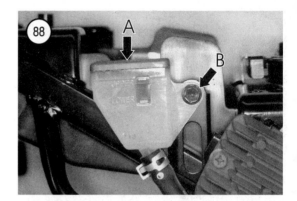

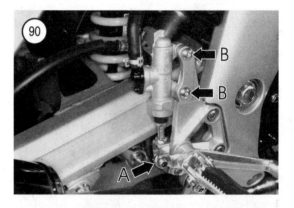

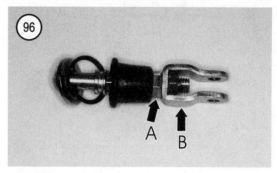

3. Install the master cylinder onto the backside of the footpeg bracket and temporarily install the mounting bolts (B, **Figure 90**). Finger-tighten the bolts.

4. Reattach the hose fitting (A, **Figure 93**) to the master cylinder. Be sure the O-ring (B, **Figure 93**) is installed on the fitting.

5. Align the master cylinder pushrod yoke with the brake pedal, and install the clevis pin (A, **Figure 90**) through both parts. Slide the washer over the end of the clevis pin. Install a *new* cotter pin, and bend the ends over completely.

6. Remove the bolts (**Figure 89**) and install the footrest guard. Reinstall the master cylinder mounting bolts. Tighten them to 10 N•m (88 in.-lb.).

7. Tighten the union bolt (**Figure 91**) to the specification in **Table 2**.

8. Bleed the rear brake as described in this chapter.

9. Install the frame side cover and seats as described in Chapter Fifteen.

Disassembly

Refer to **Figure 87**.

1. Remove the rear master cylinder as described in this chapter.

2. Slide the rubber boot (A, **Figure 95**) down the pushrod and out of the way.

3. Using snap ring pliers, remove the internal snap ring (B, **Figure 95**) securing the pushrod assembly in the master cylinder body.

4. Withdraw the pushrod assembly, the piston assembly and spring from the master cylinder body.

5. Pour out any residual brake fluid and discard it. *Never* reuse hydraulic fluid.

6. If necessary, loosen the master-cylinder-rod locknut (A, **Figure 96**), then remove the pushrod yoke (B) and nut from the pushrod.

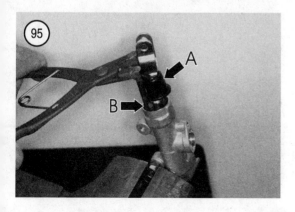

14

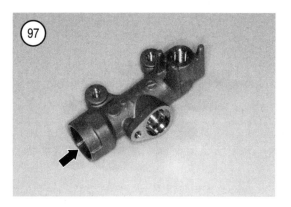

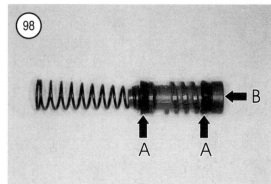

Inspection

1. Clean all parts in isopropyl alcohol or with an aerosol brake cleaner.

2. Inspect the cylinder bore surface (**Figure 97**). If it is less than perfect, replace the master cylinder assembly. The body cannot be replaced separately.

3. Inspect the piston cups (A, **Figure 98**) for wear and damage. If less than perfect, replace the piston assembly. The cups cannot be replaced separately.

4. Check the end of the piston (B, **Figure 98**) for wear caused by the pushrod. If worn, replace the piston assembly.

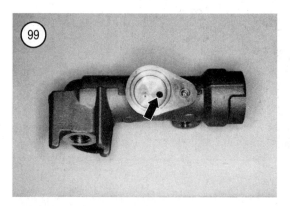

5. Make sure the fluid passageway (**Figure 99**) in the master cylinder body is clear. Clean it if necessary.

6. Measure the cylinder bore with a bore gauge (**Figure 100**) or vernier caliper. Refer to the specification listed in **Table 1**.

7. Measure the outside diameter of the piston with a micrometer (**Figure 101**). Refer to the specification in **Table 1**.

8. Check the entire master cylinder body for wear or damage. If it is damaged in any way, replace the master cylinder assembly.

9. Inspect the union bolt threads in the master cylinder body. If worn or damaged, clean the threads with a thread tap or replace the master cylinder assembly.

10. Inspect the piston pushrod assembly (A, **Figure 102**) for wear or damage. Make sure the rubber boot (B) is in good condition. Replace the boot if necessary.

11. Inspect the union bolt threads for damage. If damaged, clean the threads with a metric thread die or replace the bolt. Make sure the brake fluid hole is clear. Clean it out if necessary.

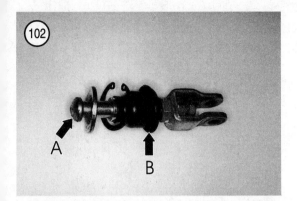

A B

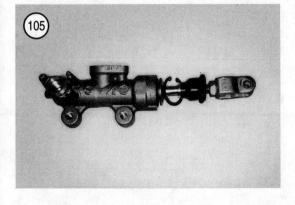

12. Check the connector for damage.

13. Remove the cover and diaphragm from the reservoir. Check all components for damage and deterioration. Replace worn components as necessary.

14. Inspect the reservoir and hose or wear or deterioration. Replace worn parts as necessary.

Assembly

Refer to **Figure 87**.

1. Soak the new cups in fresh DOT 4 brake fluid for at least 15 minutes to make them pliable. Install the new cups onto the new piston assembly.

2. Coat the inside of the cylinder bore with fresh DOT 4 brake fluid before the assembly of parts.

CAUTION
When installing the piston assembly, do not allow the cups to turn inside out, as they will be damaged and allow brake fluid leakage within the cylinder bore.

3. Position the spring with the tapered end facing the piston assembly (**Figure 103**). Install the spring and piston assembly into the cylinder together. Push the piston assembly all the way in until it bottoms in the cylinder (**Figure 104**).

4. Install the pushrod assembly (**Figure 105**) and push the piston cup assembly all the way into the cylinder.

5. Hold the pushrod assembly in this position and install the circlip. Make sure the snap ring is correctly seated in the groove.

6. Slide the rubber boot up into the body so it completely seats in the cylinder (**Figure 106**). This is necessary to keep out dirt and moisture.

14

7. If removed, install the yoke and nut onto the pushrod. Do not tighten the locknut at this time, as the brake pedal must be adjusted.

8. Install the master cylinder as described in this chapter.

9. Adjust the brake pedal height as described in Chapter Three.

BRAKE HOSE REPLACEMENT

Front Brake Hoses

Refer to **Figure 107**.

> *CAUTION*
> *Drape a heavy cloth or plastic tarp over the front fender to protect it from accidental brake fluid spills. Brake fluid will damage the finish on plastic, painted or plated sufaces. Immediately wash spilled brake fluid off the motorcycle. Use soapy water and rinse the area completely.*

1A. *SV650 models*—Remove the top cover (**Figure 108**), diaphragm plate and diaphragm from the master cylinder.

1B. *SV650S models*—Remove the cap and diaphragm from the brake fluid reservoir (**Figure 109**).

> *NOTE*
> *Place a shop cloth under the union bolts and brake hose fittings to catch any spilled brake fluid that might leak out during this procedure.*

2. Remove the union bolt (**Figure 110**) and sealing washers securing the brake hose to the left caliper.

3. Place the end of the brake hose over a container and let the brake fluid drain out into the container. Apply the front brake lever several times to force the fluid out of the brake hose. Dispose of this brake fluid properly. Never reuse brake fluid. Place the loose end of the brake hose in a recloseable plastic bag to prevent brake fluid from leaking onto the motorcycle.

4. Remove the retainer bolt (**Figure 111**) and release the hose from the retainer securing the brake hose to the fork slider.

5. Repeat Steps 4-6 for the right caliper.

6. Remove the union bolt and two sealing washers (A, **Figure 112**) from the left side of the brake hose joint and remove the left lower brake hose.

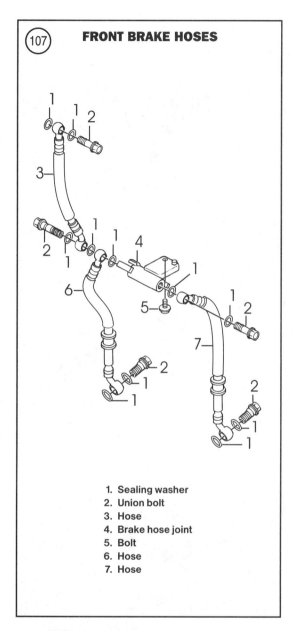

107 **FRONT BRAKE HOSES**

1. Sealing washer
2. Union bolt
3. Hose
4. Brake hose joint
5. Bolt
6. Hose
7. Hose

108

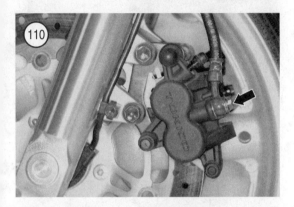

7. Disconnect the union bolt and the three sealing washer (B, **Figure 112**) from the right side of the brake hose joint and remove the right lower fork hose.

8. Remove the union bolt (**Figure 113**) and two sealing washers securing the upper brake hose to the master cylinder.

9. Carefully pull the lower end of the upper hose down and out from behind the throttle cables on the right side.

10. Wash off any spilled brake fluid that may have leaked out of the hoses during removal.

11. Install the hoses in the reverse order of removal while noting the following:

    a. Install new sealing washers on each side of the hose fittings.

    b. Use three sealing washers when securing the upper brake hose and the right lower brake hoses to the brake hose joint (B, **Figure 112**).

    c. Tighten the union bolts to 23 N•m (17 ft.-lb.).

    d. Refill the master cylinder reservoir and bleed the front brakes as described in this chapter.

WARNING
Use brake fluid clearly marked DOT 4 from a sealed container. Other types may cause brake failure. Always use the same brand name and do not intermix, as some brands are not compatible. Do not intermix silicone-based (DOT5) brake fluid, as it can cause brake component damage, which will result in brake system failure.

WARNING
Do not ride the motorcycle until making sure that the brakes are operating properly.

14

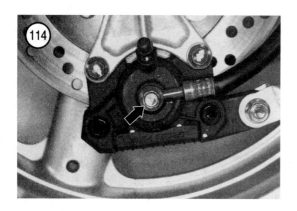

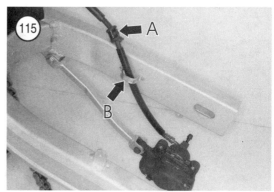

Rear Brake Hose

Refer to **Figure 87**.

> *CAUTION*
> *Cover the surrounding area with a heavy cloth or plastic tarp to protect the components from brake fluid spills. Brake fluid damages the finish on any plastic, painted or plated surface. Wash spilled brake fluid off any of these surfaces immediately. Use soapy water and rinse the area completely.*

> *NOTE*
> *The reservoir hose replacement procedure is covered under **Rear Master Cylinder** in this chapter.*

1. Remove the frame side cover as described in Chapter Fifteen.

2. Remove the rear wheel as described in Chapter Eleven.

3. Perform Steps 1-15 of *Rear Master Cylinder Removal* and disconnect the brake hose from the master cylinder.

> *NOTE*
> *Place a shop cloth under the union bolts and brake hose fittings to catch any spilled brake fluid that will leak out in the following steps.*

4. Remove the union bolt (**Figure 114**) and sealing washers attaching the brake hose to the rear caliper assembly. Do not lose the sealing washer from each side of the hose fitting.

> *NOTE*
> *Figure 115 depicts the rear wheel removed for clarity. It is not necessary to remove the wheel for this procedure.*

5. Unhook the brake hose from the clamp (A, **Figure 115**) on top of the swing arm.

6. Carefully pull the rear of the brake hose out from the guide (B, **Figure 115**) on the inner surface of the swing arm and remove the brake hose.

7. Install a new hose, new sealing washers and union bolts in the reverse order of removal while noting the following:

   a. Install new sealing washers on each side of the brake hose fittings.

   b. Tighten the union bolts to 23 N•m (17 ft.-lb.).

   c. Make sure the brake hose is correctly installed through the guide (B, **Figure 115**) on the swing arm so it does not touch the rear wheel.

   d. Refill the master cylinder reservoir and bleed the rear brake system as described in this chapter.

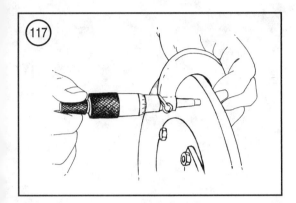

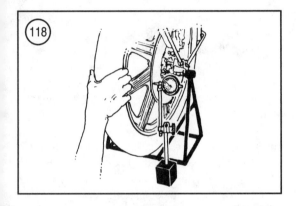

If the disc is warped, refer to *Brakes* in Chapter Two.

NOTE
It is not necessary to remove the wheel to measure the disc thickness. The measurement can be performed with the wheel installed or removed from the motorcycle.

1. Measure the thickness of the disc at several locations around the disc with a vernier caliper or a micrometer (**Figure 117**). The disc must be replaced if the thickness in any area is less than that specified in **Table 1** (or the MIN dimension stamped on the disc).

2. Make sure the disc mounting bolts are tight before running this check. Check the disc runout with a dial indicator as shown in **Figure 118**.

NOTE
When checking the front disc, turn the handlebar all the way to one side, and then to the other side.

3. Slowly rotate the wheel and watch the dial indicator. If the runout exceeds that listed in **Table 1**, replace the disc.

4. Clean the disc of any rust or corrosion, and wipe it clean with lacquer thinner. Never use an oil-based solvent that may leave an oil residue on the disc.

5. On front brake discs, inspect all fasteners (A, **Figure 119**) between the outer and the inner rings of the disc. If any are loose or damaged, replace the disc.

BRAKE DISC

The brake discs are separate from the wheel hubs and can be removed once the wheel is removed from the motorcycle.

Inspection

It is not necessary to remove the disc from the wheel to inspect it. Small nicks and marks on the disc are not important, but radial scratches deep enough to snag a fingernail reduce braking effectiveness and increase brake pad wear. If these grooves are evident and the brake pads are wearing rapidly, replace the disc.

The Suzuki specifications for the standard and service limits are listed in **Table 1**. The minimum (MIN) thickness is stamped on the disc face (**Figure 116**). If the specification stamped on the disc differs from the service limit listed in **Table 1**, use the specification on the disc when inspecting it.

When servicing the brake discs, do not have the discs reconditioned (ground) to compensate for warp. The discs are thin and grinding only reduces their thickness, causing them to warp quite rapidly.

14

Removal/Installation

1. Remove the front or rear wheel as described in Chapter Eleven.

CAUTION
Do not set the wheel down on the disc surface, as it may get scratched or warped. Set the wheel on two wooden blocks.

NOTE
Insert a piece of wood or vinyl tube between the pads in the caliper(s). That way, if the brake lever or pedal is inadvertently applied, the pistons will not be forced out of the cylinders. If this does happen, the caliper might have to be disassembled to reseat the pistons and the system will have to be bled. By using the wood or vinyl tube in place of the disc, it will not be necessary to bleed the system when installing the wheel.

2. Remove the bolts (B, **Figure 119**) securing the brake disc to the hub and remove the disc.
3. Install by reversing the preceding removal steps while noting the following:
   a. On a disc so marked, position the disc so the arrow on the disc points in the direction of tire rotation.

CAUTION
*The disc bolts are made from a harder material than similar bolts used on the motorcycle. When replacing the bolts, always use standard Suzuki brake disc bolts. Never compromise and use different bolts. They do **not** properly secure the disc to the hub.*

   b. Use a small amount of a locking compound such as ThreeBond No. TB1360 on the brake disc bolts before installation.
   c. Tighten the disc mounting bolts to 23 N•m (17 ft.-lb.).

BLEEDING THE BRAKES

Bleeding the brakes removes air from the brake system. Air in the brakes increases brake lever or pedal travel, and it makes the brakes feel soft or

spongy. Under extreme circumstances, it can cause complete loss of brake pressure.

The brakes can be bled manually or with the use of a brake bleeding tool. The manual method is described here. If there is a vacuum pump or other brake bleeding tool available, follow the instructions that came with the tool.

Only use fresh DOT 4 brake fluid when bleeding the brakes. Do not reuse old brake fluid and do not use DOT 5 (silicone based) brake fluid. Brake fluid will damage the finish on most surfaces. Protect the motorcycle from accidental spills by covering the areas beneath the calipers and master cylinders with a tarp. Immediately clean up any spilled brake fluid. Wash the affected parts with soapy water, and completely rinse the area with plenty of clean water.

NOTE
The rear caliper is equipped with two bleed valves, one for each caliper body half. Bleed the inner caliper body half first, and then the outer caliper half.

1. Check that all union bolts in the system are tight.
2. Remove the dust cap from the bleed valve on the caliper assembly.
3. Connect a length of clear tubing to the bleed valve. Place the other end of the tube into a clean container. Fill the container with enough fresh brake fluid to keep the end submerged. The tube should be long enough so its loop can be higher than the bleed valve to prevent air from being drawn into the caliper during bleeding. See **Figure 120**.

NOTE
The rear brake caliper is equipped with two bleed valves. Be sure to bleed both sides of the rear brake caliper.

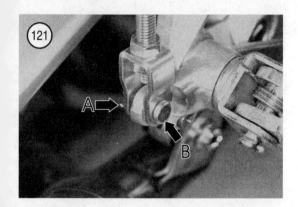

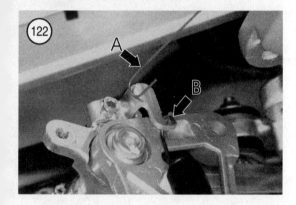

9. Repeat Steps 6-8 until the brake fluid flowing from the hose is clear and free of air. If the system is difficult to bleed, tap the master cylinder or caliper with a soft mallet.

10. Test the feel of the brake lever or pedal. It should feel firm and offer the same resistance each time it is operated. If the lever or pedal feels soft, air is still trapped in the system. Continue bleeding.

11. When bleeding is complete, disconnect the hose from the bleed valve. Tighten the caliper bleed valve to 7.5 N•m (66 in.-lb.).

12. If necessary, add brake fluid to the master cylinder to correct the fluid level.

13. Install the diaphragm, diaphragm plate (rear reservoir only) and top cover. Make sure the cover is secured in place.

NOTE
Do not ride the motorcycle until both brakes and the brake light are working properly.

14. Test ride the motorcycle slowly at first to make sure the brakes are operating properly.

REAR BRAKE PEDAL

Removal/Lubrication/Installation

NOTE
This procedure is shown with the rear wheel and swing arm removed for photographic clarity. It is not necessary to remove either of these components but it does allow more working room.

1. Remove the cotter pin (A, **Figure 121**) and the washer from the back end of the clevis pin that secure the master cylinder pushrod to the brake pedal.

2. Withdraw the clevis pin (B, **Figure 121**) and separate the pushrod yoke from the brake pedal.

NOTE
*The brake pedal is shown removed in **Figure 122** and **Figure 123** for clarity.*

3. Unhook the rear brake light switch spring (A, **Figure 122**) from the brake pedal (B).

4. Use locking pliers and disconnect the pedal return spring (A, **Figure 123**) from the brake pedal.

4. Clean all dirt or debris from the top of the front or rear master cylinder reservoir. Remove the top cover or cap, diaphragm plate (if so equipped) and the diaphragm from the reservoir.

5. Add brake fluid to the reservoir until the fluid level is about 10 mm (3/8 in.) below the top. Loosely install the diaphragm and the cover. Leave them in place during this procedure to prevent the entry of dirt.

6. Apply the front brake lever or the rear brake pedal until it stops and hold it in this position.

7. Open the bleed valve with a wrench (**Figure 120**, typical). Let the brake lever or lever move to the limit of its travel, then close the bleed valve. Do not release the brake lever (or brake pedal) while the bleed valve is open.

8. Pump the brake lever or pedal a few times and then release it.

NOTE
As brake fluid enters the system, the level in the reservoir drops. Add brake fluid as necessary to keep the fluid level 10 mm (3/8 in.) below the reservoir top so air will not be drawn into the system.

14

5. Remove the footpeg bolt (B, **Figure 123**) from the inboard side of the mounting bracket.

6. Remove the footpeg and rear brake pedal assembly. Do not lose the washer between the brake pedal and the footpeg mounting bracket.

7. Inspect the brake pedal for fractures or damage and replace if necessary.

8. Clean the footpeg bolt with solvent, and then inspect it for wear or damage. Replace if necessary.

9. Lubricate the footpeg bolt and bushing with waterproof grease.

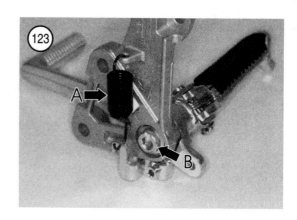

Table 1 BRAKE SPECIFICATIONS

Item	New	Service limit
Brake disc thickness		
Front	4.5 mm (0.18 in.)	4.0 mm (0.16 in.)
Rear	5.0 mm (0.20 in.)	4.5 mm (0.18 in.)
Brake disc runout (max.)	–	0.3 mm (0.012 in.)
Front brake caliper		
Cylinder bore		
inside diameter	30.230-30.306 mm (1.1902-1.1931 in.)	–
Piston outside diameter	30.150-30.200 mm (1.1870-1.1890 in.)	–
Front brake master cylinder		
(all models)		
Cylinder bore		
inside diameter	15.870-15.913 mm (0.6248-0.6265 in.)	–
Piston outside diameter	15.827-15.854 mm (0.6231-0.6242 in.)	–
Rear brake caliper		
Cylinder bore		
inside diameter	38.180-38.256 mm (1.5031-1.5061 in.)	–
Piston outside diameter	38.098-38.148 mm (1.4999-1.5019 in.)	–
Rear brake master cylinder		
Cylinder bore		
inside diameter	12.700-12.743 mm (0.5000-0.5017 in.)	–
Piston outside diameter	12.657-12.684 mm (0.4983-0.4994 in.)	–

Table 2 BRAKE TORQUE SPECIFICATIONS

Item	N•m	in.-lb.	ft.-lb.
Brake hose union bolt	23	–	17
Front brake caliper			
bleed valve	7.5	66	–
Front brake caliper			
mounting bolts	39	–	29
Front brake caliper			
union bolt	23	–	17
Front brake disc			
mounting bolts	23	–	17
Front brake master cylinder			
clamp bolts	10	88	–
(continued)			

Table 2 BRAKE TORQUE SPECIFICATIONS (continued)

Item	N•m	in.-lb.	ft.-lb.
Front brake master cylinder union bolt	23	–	17
Rear brake caliper bleed valve	7.5	66	–
Rear brake caliper mounting bolts	23	–	17
Rear brake disc mounting bolts	23	–	17
Rear brake caliper union bolt	23	–	17
Rear brake master cylinder mounting bolts	10	88	–
Rear brake master cylinder union bolt	23	–	17
Torque arm mounting bolt	35	–	26

14

NOTE: Refer to the Supplement at the back of this manual for information unique to 2003-on models.

CHAPTER FIFTEEN

BODY AND FRAME

This chapter contains removal and installation procedures for the body panels and the sidestand.

Whenever a body or frame member is removed, reinstall all mounting hardware (such as small brackets, bolts, nuts, rubber bushings, or metal collars) onto the removed part so they will not be misplaced. Frequent changes during the model year make it possible that the way it attaches to the frame may differ slightly from the one in this chapter.

The fairing (SV650S models) and frame cover parts are easily damaged and expensive to replace. After each part is removed from the motorcycle, wrap it in a blanket or towel, and place it in a cardboard box. Store it in an area where it will not be damaged.

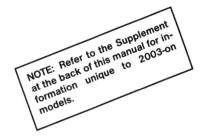

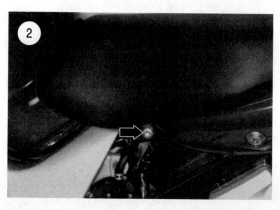

SIDE COVERS

Removal/Installation

The following procedure applies to both side covers.

1. Remove the bolt on the rear underside of the side cover (A, **Figure 1**).

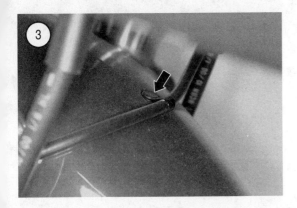

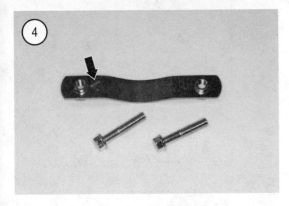

2. Remove the bolt at the front of the side cover (B, **Figure 1**) and remove the side cover.

3. To install the side cover (A, **Figure 1**), install the rear bolt first.

SEATS

Removal/Installation

1. To remove the rear seat, perform the following:
   a. On the left side of the frame cover, insert the ignition key into the lock and turn it clockwise.
   b. Lift the front of the rear seat, pull the seat forward until it clears the frame retainers, and remove the seat.
2. To remove the front seat, perform the following:
   a. Remove the frame side covers as previously described.
   b. Carefully lift up on a rear corner of the seat.
   c. Remove the mounting bolt (**Figure 2**). Repeat this on the other side.
   d. Lift the front of the seat while pulling it forward and remove it.

WARNING
*Do **not** try to repair damaged retaining hooks. These hooks are molded into the seat base and must be solid with no fractures or cracks in order to safely secure the seat. A repaired hook may create a false sense of security that may lead to a seat working loose while riding.*

3. Inspect the plastic base on the underside of each seat for cracks or damage. Make sure all molded retaining hooks and mounting tabs are not damaged. If damaged, replace the seat(s).

4. To install the front seat, perform the following:
   a. Insert the rear of the seat into the frame cover opening.
   b. Carefully lower the front of the seat and align the bolt holes with the frame. Install the mounting bolt (**Figure 2**) and tighten it securely. Repeat for the other side.
   c. Check that the seat is firmly locked in place.
5. To install the rear seat, perform the following:
   a. Slide the rear hooks into the seat retainers on the frame.
   b. Push the front of the seat down until it locks in place.
   c. Check that the seat is firmly locked in place.

WARNING
After the seats are installed, pull up firmly and move them from side to side to make sure they are securely locked into place. If the seats are not correctly locked into place, they may slide to one side or the other when riding the motorcycle. This could lead to loss of control and a possible accident.

FRONT FENDER

Removal/Installation

1. Carefully pull out the speed sensor wire retaining clamp from the fender (**Figure 3**).

2. Remove the fender retaining bolts on both sides.

3. Carefully remove the fender to prevent scratches.

4. Reinstall the front fender by reversing the removal steps. Note the triangle mark (**Figure 4**) on

15

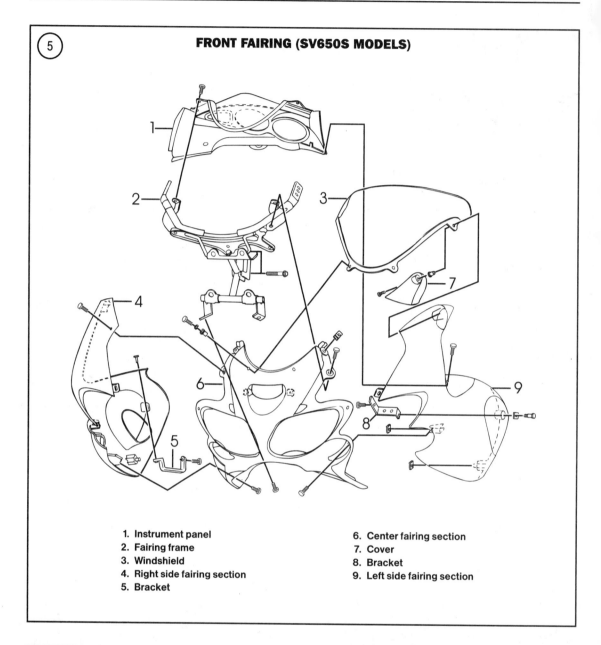

⑤ **FRONT FAIRING (SV650S MODELS)**

1. Instrument panel
2. Fairing frame
3. Windshield
4. Right side fairing section
5. Bracket
6. Center fairing section
7. Cover
8. Bracket
9. Left side fairing section

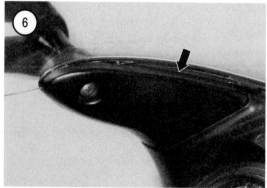

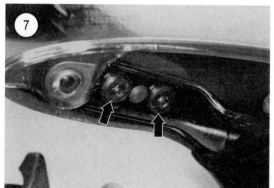

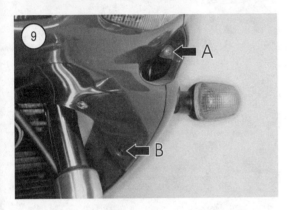

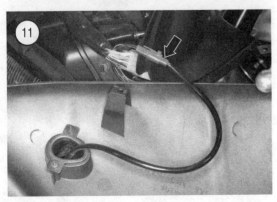

the nut plates. Install each nut plate so the end with the triangle is toward the front of the fender.

FAIRING WINDSHIELD (SV650S MODELS)

Removal/Installation

Refer to **Figure 5**.

1. Remove the inner covers (**Figure 6**) on each side.
2. Remove the nuts (**Figure 7**) securing the rear view mirror. Remove both mirror assemblies and rubber cushion.
3. Remove the four windshield retaining screws (**Figure 8**).

> *NOTE*
> *Note the location and arrangement of the windshield fasteners during disassembly.*

4. Remove the windshield. It may be necessary to depress the windshield to disengage the rubber nuts.
5. Reverse the removal procedure to install the windshield.

FAIRING (SV650S MODELS)

Removal/Installation

Refer to **Figure 5**.

1. Remove the windshield as previously described.

> *NOTE*
> *The left side fairing is shown in the following illustrations. The right side is identical.*

2. Remove the side fairing sections as follows:
   a. Hold or support the side fairing so it cannot fall and be damaged when the retaining fasteners are removed.
   b. Remove the upper screw (A, **Figure 9**) and disengage the lower plastic fastener (B). To disengage the fastener (B, **Figure 9**), push in the middle of the fastener against the pin.
   c. Remove the rear retaining bolt (**Figure 10**).
   d. Disconnect the turn signal wire connector (**Figure 11**), then remove the side fairing section.

15

3. Remove the upper retaining bolts (**Figure 12**).

4. Remove the lower retaining bolts (**Figure 13**).

5. Disconnect the position light connector (**Figure 14**), then remove the center fairing section.

6. To remove the fairing frame, proceed as follows:

    a. Remove the instrument panel as described in Chapter Nine.

    b. Remove the headlight assembly as described in Chapter Nine.

    c. Note the position of the wiring harness and remove the wiring clamps.

    d. Remove the fairing frame.

7. Install the fairing by reversing the removal procedure. Make sure all electrical connectors are free of corrosion and are secured tight. Tighten all screws and bolts securely. Do not overtighten them. The plastic fairing may fracture if the fasteners are overtightened.

REAR FRAME COVER

Removal/Installation

Refer to **Figure 15**.

1. Remove both seats as described in this chapter.

2. Remove the frame cover mounting bolts (**Figure 16**).

3. Remove the cover joint screws (**Figure 17**) and nut clips. Removing these screws allows spreading the cover assembly during removal.

4. Remove the Phillips screw (**Figure 18**) on the underside of the cover on each side.

5. Pull out the cover on each side so it detaches from the mounting grommet on each side.

6. Spread apart the cover, then lift it up and let it rest on the sub-frame.

7. Disconnect the seat lock cable (**Figure 19**).

8. Remove the rear frame cover.

9. Reverse the removal procedure to install the rear frame cover.

SIDESTAND

Removal/Installation

1. Place the motorcycle on a suitable jack or wooden blocks on level ground.

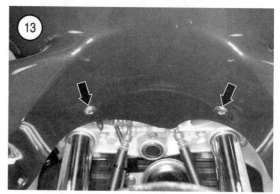

2. To replace only the springs, perform the following:

    a. Place the sidestand in the raised position. This places the return springs in their relaxed position.

    b. Use locking pliers and disconnect the springs from the mounting bracket post. Remove both springs.

    c. Reinstall the springs onto the posts.

3. To remove the sidestand assembly, perform the following:

REAR FRAME COVER

1. Bolt
2. Washer
3. Cushion
4. Hand rail
5. Center cover
6. Nutplate
7. Screw
8. Screw
9. Bolt
10. Spacer
11. Cushion
12. Left cover half
13. Right cover half
14. Screw
15. Nutplate
16. Bolt
17. Spacer
18. Cushion (upper)
19. Cushion (lower)
20. Cushion

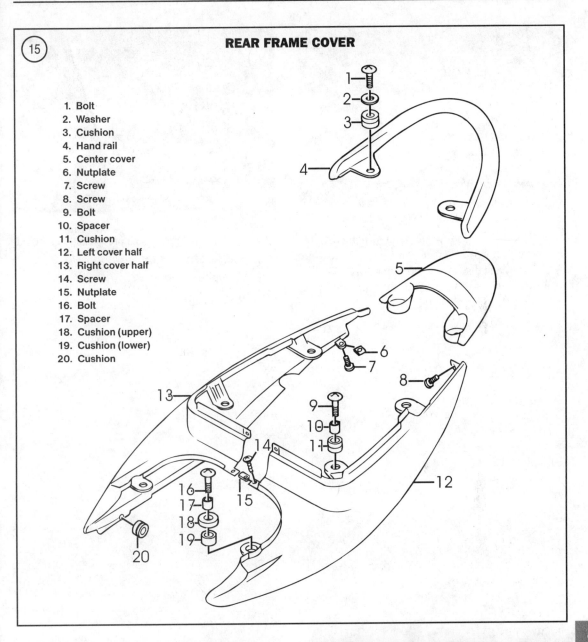

15

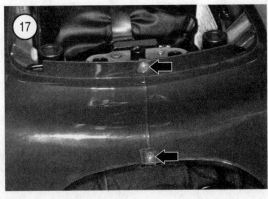

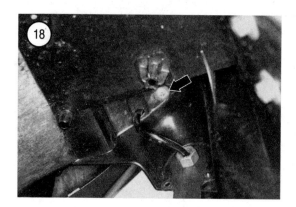

a. Locate the two-pin sidestand-switch electrical connector (one green wire, one black/white wire) and disconnect the connector.

b. Remove the bolts securing the sidestand switch and remove the switch.

c. Remove the springs as previously described.

d. Remove the bolts securing the sidestand mounting bracket to the frame.

e. Remove the sidestand.

SUPPLEMENT

2003-2009 MODEL SERVICE INFORMATION

This Supplement contains all procedures and specifications unique to the 2003-2009 models. If a specification or procedure is not included, refer to the procedure in the appropriate chapter (2-15).

This Supplement is divided into sections that correspond to the chapters in the main body of the manual.

CHAPTER ONE

GENERAL INFORMATION

Refer to **Table 1** for specifications unique to later models.

Table 1 VEHICLE DIMENSIONS AND WEIGHT

Dry weight	
SV650	
2003	167 kg (368 lb.)
2004-2006	165 kg (363 lb.)
2007-on	168 kg (370 lb.)
SV650S, SV650SF	
2003	171 kg (376 lb.)
2004-2006	169 kg (372 lb.)
2007-on	172 kg (379 lb.)
Ground clearance	
SV650	150 mm (5.9 in.)
SV650S, SV650SF	155 mm (6.1 in.)
Overall length	
SV650	
2003	2125 mm (83.7 in.)
2004-on	2080 mm (81.9 in.)
SV650S, SV650SF	
2003	2130 mm (83.9 in.)
2004-on	2085 mm (82.1 in.)
Overall width	
SV650	745 mm (29.3 in.)
SV650S, SV650SF	730 mm (28.7 in.)
Overall height	
SV650	1085 mm (42.7 in.)
SV650S, SV650SF	
2003	1175 mm (46.3 in.)
2004-on	1170 mm (46.1 in.)
Seat height	
All models	800 mm (31.5 in.)
Wheelbase	
SV650	1440 mm (56.7 in.)
SV650S, SV650SF	
2003-2006	1430 mm (56.3 in.)
2007-on	1425 mm (56.1 in.)

CHAPTER TWO

TROUBLESHOOTING

When engine or electrical problems occur, always begin troubleshooting with the self-diagnostic function built into the electronic control module (ECM). Refer to the *Fuel, Emission Control and Exhaust Systems* section in this Supplement for accessing the malfunction code(s), troubleshooting procedures and tests.

CHAPTER THREE

LUBRICATION, MAINTENANCE AND TUNE-UP

Refer to **Tables 2-4** for specifications unique to later models.

PERIODIC LUBRICATION

Engine Oil Pressure Test

The oil pressure test on later models is performed the same as earlier models. The test equipment required for later models is oil pressure gauge hose

(part No. 09915-74521), oil pressure gauge attachment (part No. 09915-74532) and high-pressure meter (part No. 09915-77331).

PERIODIC MAINTENANCE

Air Filter Replacement

Air filter replacement is similar to carbureted models. Note the following:

1. Raise the fuel tank as described in *Fuel, Emission Control and Exhaust Systems* in this Supplement.

2. Remove the screws from the perimeter of the top cover (**Figure 1**) to access the filter.

Brake Fluid Level

The rear brake master cylinder reservoir has been moved from under the seat and repositioned below the right side cover (**Figure 2**). If the reservoir must

16

be filled, remove the right side cover to access the reservoir cap screws.

PAIR System and Evaporative Emission Control System

Refer to *Fuel, Emission Control and Exhaust Systems* in this Supplement for inspection procedures for these systems.

ENGINE TUNE-UP

Idle Speed Adjustment

2003-2006 models

Idle speed adjustment is the same as for earlier models. The throttle stop screw on 2003-2006 models is similarly located on the left side of the engine **(Figure 3)**. Refer to *Fuel, Emission Control and Exhaust Systems* in this Supplement for fast idle speed adjustment.

2007-on models

There is no external adjuster on the fuel injection system. The idle speed is controlled by the electronic control module (ECM) and idle speed control (ISC) valve **(Figure 4)**. The ISC automatically adjusts the idle speed within a range of 1200-1400 rpm. Specific idle speeds within this range can be achieved by using the Suzuki Diagnosis System tool (SDS set) (part No. 09904-41010), Mode Select Switch (part No. 09930-82720) and CD-ROM software. Check with a Suzuki dealership for this equipment and the latest version of software. Refer to the tool and software instructions for using the equipment.

Throttle Valve Synchronization

2003-2006 models

1. Support the air box so the electrical connectors and intake air pressure sensor vacuum hose can be connected during the synchronization procedure. The two crankcase breather hoses **(Figure 5)** can be disconnected during the procedure.
2. Vacuum fittings are located on the bottom of each throttle body **(Figure 6)**.
3. Balance the throttle valves with the synchronizing screw (A, **Figure 7**) on the No. 2 (rear) throttle

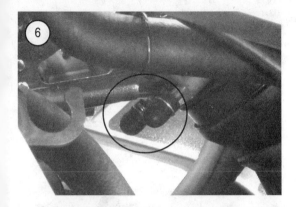

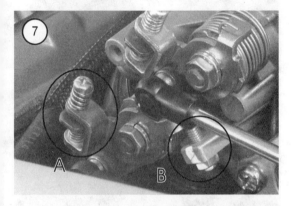

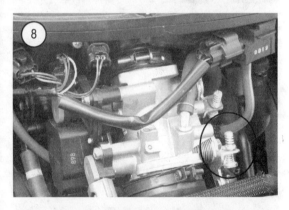

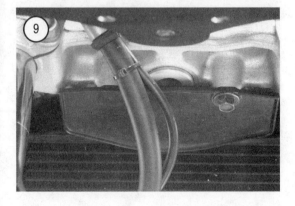

body. During adjustment of the synchronizing screw, there should be slight clearance between the throttle lever and stopper screw (B, **Figure 7**).

4. After synchronization, check throttle position (TP) sensor adjustment as described in *Fuel, Emission Control and Exhaust Systems* in this Supplement.

2007-on models

Throttle valve synchronization can be adjusted using vacuum gauges or by using the Suzuki Diagnosis System tool (SDS set) (part No. 09904-41010), CD-ROM software (part No. 99565-01010-009) and Mode Select Switch (part No. 09930-82720). Check with a Suzuki dealership for the latest version of software. Refer to the tool and software instructions for using the equipment.

The following procedure describes how to synchronize the throttle valves using a pair of vacuum gauges. After adjustment, if the idle speed is not within the 1200-1400 rpm range of the idle speed control (ISC) valve, the Suzuki Diagnosis System tool is required to preset the ISC valve. Correct idle speed cannot be achieved by adjusting the screws on the throttle bodies.

1. If necessary, raise the fuel tank and air box so the vacuum gauges can be connected to the vacuum fittings on the bottom of the throttle bodies.

2. With all engine hoses connected, start the engine and allow it to warm up.

3. Balance the throttle valves with the synchronizing screw (**Figure 8**) on the No. 2 (rear) throttle body.

4. After synchronization, check throttle position (TP) sensor adjustment as described in *Fuel, Emission Control and Exhaust Systems* in this Supplement.

SPARK PLUGS

Front Spark Plug Removal/Installation

2007-on models

1. For 2008-on SF models, remove the lower cowl (Chapter 15).

2. Remove the lower bridge cover (**Figure 9**).

3. Remove the radiator mounting bolt. (**Figure 10**). Move the radiator forward and secure it out of the way.

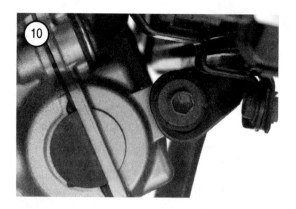

WARNING
*Do not remove or handle the radiator
if it is hot. Allow the engine to cool before servicing.*

4. Remove the front spark plug caps **(Figure 11)**.
5. Clean the spark plug wells, preferably with compressed air.
6. Remove the spark plugs. To ease removal, use the Suzuki Spark Plug Socket Wrench Set (part No. 09930-10121).
7. Refer to Chapter Three for spark plug inspection and gapping.
8. Apply a light coat of antiseize compound onto the threads of the spark plugs.
9. Install the spark plugs and tighten them to 11 N•m (96 in.-lb.).
10. Install the spark plug caps.
11. Move the radiator back into position and bolt into place.
12. Install the lower bridge cover.

Rear Spark Plug Removal/Installation

2007-on models

Remove the rear spark plugs as described in Chapter Three. Refer to **Figure 12** for the plug locations.

Table 2 RECOMMENDED LUBRICANTS AND FLUIDS	
Engine coolant	
Capacity	1.7 L (1.8 U.S. qt., 1.5 Imp. qt.)
Engine	1.5 L (1.6 U.S. qt., 1.3 Imp. qt.)
Reserve tank	250 ml (8.5 U.S. oz., 8.8 Imp. oz.)
Engine oil	
Grade	
2006-on	API SF, SG or SH, SJ with JASO MA rating
Viscosity	10W-40
	(continued)

Table 2 RECOMMENDED LUBRICANTS AND FLUIDS (continued)

Engine oil capacity	
Oil change only	2.3 L (2.4 U.S. qt., 2.0 Imp. qt.)
Oil and filter change	2.7 L (2.9 U.S. qt., 2.4 Imp. qt.)
When engine completely dry	3.1 L (3.3 U.S. qt., 2.7 Imp. qt.)
Fork Oil	
Viscosity	Suzuki No. 8 fork oil or equivalent
Capacity per leg	
SV650	490 ml (16.6 U.S. oz., 17.3 Imp. oz.)
SV650S, SV650SF	
2003	488 ml (16.5 U.S. oz., 17.2 Imp. oz.)
2004-on	485 ml (16.4 U.S. oz., 17.1 Imp. oz.)
Fuel tank capacity, including reserve	
California models	
2003-on	16 L (4.2 U.S. gal., 3.5 Imp. gal.)
All other models	
2003-on	17 L (4.5 U.S. gal., 3.7 Imp. gal.)

Table 3 MAINTENANCE AND TUNE-UP SPECIFICATIONS

Brake pedal height	
SV650	50-60 mm (2.0-2.4 in.)
SV650S, SV650SF	60-70 mm (2.4-2.8 in.)
Idle speed	1200-1400 rpm
Ignition timing	
2003-2006	
All models	7° BTDC at 1300 rpm
2007-on	
All models	8° BTDC at 1300 rpm
Fast Idle speed	1800-2400 rpm
Front fork spring preload adjusters	3rd groove from top
Rear shock absorber spring preload	
SV650	3rd position

Table 4 MAINTENANCE AND TUNE-UP TORQUE SPECIFICATIONS

	N•m	in.-lb.	ft.-lb.
Rear axle	100	–	74

16

CHAPTER FOUR

ENGINE TOP END

Service to the engine top end is the same as for earlier models. Refer to **Table 5** and **Table 6** for specifications unique to later models.

Table 5 GENERAL ENGINE SPECIFICATIONS

Ignition timing	
2003-2006	
All models	7° BTDC at 1300 rpm
2007-on	
All models	8° BTDC at 1300 rpm

Table 6 TOP END SPECIFICATIONS

	New mm (in.)	Service limit mm (in.)
Camshaft		
Lobe height		
Intake	36.060-36.105	35.76
	(1.4196-1.4214)	(1.408)
Exhaust	34.680-34.725	34.38
	(1.3654-1.3671)	(1.354)
Ring free end gap		
2003-2006		
Top	Approx. 9.5	7.6
	(0.37)	(0.30)
Second	Approx 11	8.8
	(0.43)	(0.34)
2007-on		
Top	Approx. 7	5.6
	(0.28)	(0.22)
Second	Approx 11	8.8
	(0.43)	(0.34)
Ring end gap (in cylinder bore)		
2007-on		
Top	0.20-0.30	0.70
	(0.008-0.012)	(0.028)
Second	0.30-0.45	0.70
	(0.012-0.018)	(0.028)
	(continued)	

Table 6 TOP END SPECIFICATIONS (continued)

	New mm (in.)	Service limit mm (in.)
Ring thickness		
2007-on		
Top (stepped ring)	0.76-0.81	
	(0.0299-0.0319)	
	1.08-1.10	
	(0.0425-0.0433)	
Second	0.97-0.99	
	(0.0382-0.0390)	
Piston ring groove width		
2007-on		
Top (stepped groove)	0.83-0.85	
	(0.0327-0.0335)	
	1.30-1.32	
	(0.0512-0.0520)	
Second	1.01-1.03	
	(0.0398-0.0406)	
Oil	2.01-2.03	
	(0.0791-0.0799)	

CHAPTER FIVE

ENGINE LOWER END

Refer to **Table 7** for specifications unique to later models.

ENGINE

Removal

The following removal and installation procedure outlines the basic steps necessary to remove the engine from the frame. Depending on the planned level of disassembly, consider removing top end components and those located in the crankcase covers, while the engine remains in the frame. The frame keeps the engine stabilized and tight nuts and bolts are easier to remove. Also, if the actual engine problem is unknown, it may be discovered in another assembly, other than the crankcase.

During engine removal, make note of mounting bolt directions and how cables and wire harnesses are routed. Refer to the appropriate chapters for removal, inspection and installation procedures for the components in the engine top end and crankcase covers.

Refer to **Figure 13**.

1. Support the motorcycle so it is stable and level.
2. If possible, perform a compression test (Chapter Three) and leakdown test (Chapter Two) before dismantling the engine.
3. Drain the engine oil (Chapter Three).
4. Drain the engine coolant (Chapter Three).
5. Disconnect the negative battery cable (Chapter Three).
6. On SV650S and SV650SF models, remove the seats and front fairing as described in this Supplement.
7. Remove the radiator as described in this Supplement.
8. Remove the fuel tank and fuel injection system as described in this Supplement.
9. Remove the exhaust system (Chapter Eight).

16

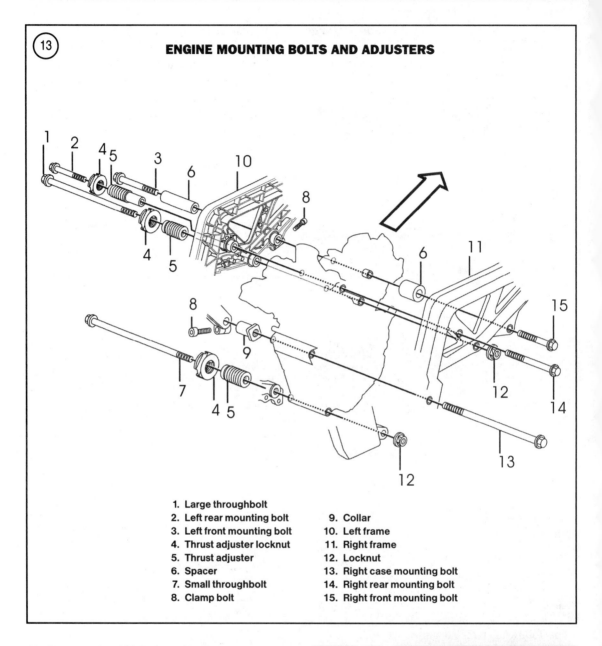

ENGINE MOUNTING BOLTS AND ADJUSTERS

1. Large throughbolt
2. Left rear mounting bolt
3. Left front mounting bolt
4. Thrust adjuster locknut
5. Thrust adjuster
6. Spacer
7. Small throughbolt
8. Clamp bolt
9. Collar
10. Left frame
11. Right frame
12. Locknut
13. Right case mounting bolt
14. Right rear mounting bolt
15. Right front mounting bolt

10. Remove the shift lever.

11. Disconnect the clutch cable (Chapter Six).

12. Remove the engine sprocket and drive chain (Chapter Eleven).

13. Remove the oil cooler as described in this Supplement.

14. Disconnect the following electrical connectors. Secure all wires out of the way.

    a. Spark plug leads.

    b. Oil pressure switch (**Figure 14**).

    c. Starter motor cable (at the starter motor).

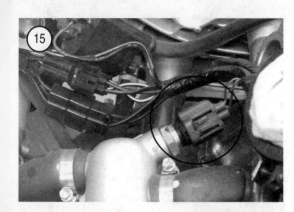

d. Engine coolant temperature (ECT) sensor (**Figure 15**).

e. Battery ground (–) cable (at the engine).

f. Alternator and crankshaft position (CKP) sensor connectors (**Figure 16**).

g. Sidestand and gear position (GP) switch connectors (**Figure 17**).

15. Place a floor jack under the engine. The jack should be padded to avoid engine damage. Raise the jack until it applies light pressure on the engine.

CAUTION
Do not contact the oil filter with the jack.

16. Remove and discard the nuts from the two through bolts.

CAUTION
The locknuts will not self-lock after they are removed from the mounting bolts.

17. Remove the left rear engine mounting bolt.

18. Remove the thrust adjuster locknuts from the two throughbolts and at the left rear engine mounting bolt location. Fully loosen the thrust adjusters, but do not remove the throughbolts at this time.

CAUTION
*The Suzuki engine mounting thrust adjuster socket wrench (part No. 09940-14990) is required to remove the thrust adjuster locknuts (**Figure 18**). The tool can be ordered from a Suzuki dealership. Do not attempt to remove the thrust adjuster locknuts with any other tool. The fasteners will be damaged.*

19. Loosen the clamp bolts.

20. Remove the left front engine mounting bolt and spacer.

21. Remove the right front engine mounting bolt and spacer.

22. Remove the right rear engine mounting bolt and collar.

23. Remove the right case mounting bolt.

24. Remove the large through bolt and slowly lower and stabilize the engine.

25. Remove the small through bolt and move the engine away from the frame.

16

26. Account for the collar (in the frame) that mates with the right rear engine mounting bolt.

Installation

Reverse the removal procedure to install the engine. Note the original direction of the bolts during installation. Install new locknuts on the mounting bolts. The locknuts will not self-lock after they are removed from the mounting bolts.

1. Install the collar and engine thrust adjusters onto the frame. Check that the the thrust adjusters are installed in the correct locations.

2. Raise the engine into position. As the engine is raised note the following:

   a. If the chain is endless (no master link), install the chain over the engine shaft as the engine is raised into the frame.

   b. As the engine is positioned in the frame, check that the collar properly seats against the crankcase (**Figure 19**).

3. Install the spacers and mounting bolts. Lightly tighten the nuts and bolts. The nuts and bolts will be tightened to their torque specification after the thrust adjusters are locked in place.

4. Tighten the thrust adjusters to 12 N•m (106 in.-lb.).

5. Tighten the thrust adjuster locknuts to 45 N•m (33 ft.-lb.).

> *CAUTION*
> *The Suzuki engine mounting thrust adjuster socket wrench (part No. 09940-14990) is required to install the thrust adjuster locknuts (**Figure 18**). The tool can be ordered from a Suzuki dealership. Do not attempt to install the thrust adjuster locknuts with any other tool. The fasteners will be damaged.*

6. Tighten the bolts to the following torque specifications:

   a. Tighten the large throughbolt to 93 N•m (69 ft.-lb.).

   b. Tighten the remaining mounting bolts to 45 N•m (33 ft.-lb.).

   c. Tighten the clamp bolts to 23 N•m (17 ft.-lb.).

7. Continue with engine assembly by reversing steps Steps 3-14 in the *Engine Removal* procedure.

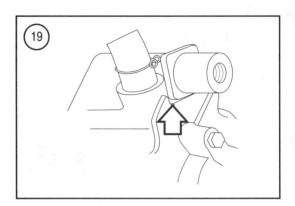

Refer to the appropriate chapters for inspection and installation procedures. Note the following:

   a. Carefully route electrical wires so they are not pinched or in contact with surfaces that get hot.

   b. Clean electrical connections and apply dielectric grease before reconnecting.

   c. If assemblies have been removed from the top end or crankcase covers, install those components.

   d. Fill the engine with engine oil (Chapter Three).

   e. Fill the cooling system with coolant (Chapter Three).

   f. Adjust the clutch free play (Chapter Three).

   g. Check throttle cable and idle speed adjustment (Chapter Three).

   h. Check rear brake pedal height. (Chapter Three).

   i. Check chain adjustment (Chapter Three).

   j. Start the engine and check for leaks.

   k. Check throttle and clutch operation.

l. If the engine top-end has been rebuilt, perform a compression check. Record the results and compare them to future checks.

OIL COOLER

Removal/Inspection/Installation

1. Drain the engine oil (Chapter Three).

2. Disconnect the oil cooler hoses at the engine (**Figure 20**). Remove the banjo bolt and seal washers at both connections. Drain any excess oil from the oil cooler and hoses.

3. Remove the oil cooler mounting bolts (**Figure 21**).

4. At the workbench, remove the oil cooler guard.

5. If the hoses must be completely removed from the oil cooler, remove the banjo bolts, seal washers and hoses. Have assistance in holding the oil cooler steady when removing the banjo bolts. Plug the oil cooler fittings to prevent the entry of debris.

6. Inspect the oil cooler assembly as follows:
   a. Wipe the exterior of the oil cooler and clean the cooling fins with compressed air.
   b. Check for damaged cooling fins. Straighten bent fins with a screwdriver. If the fins cracked or disconnected from the oil tubes, the oil cooler should be replaced.
   c. Check the seams and fittings for damage and leakage. If damage is evident, take the oil cooler to a shop specializing in radiator repair to see if the damage is repairable.
   d. Inspect the hoses. Replace hoses that are cracked or have damaged fittings.

7. Reverse this procedure to install the oil cooler. Note the following:
   a. Tighten the oil cooler mounting bolts to 10 N•m (88 in.-lb.).
   b. Install new seal washers on the banjo bolts.
   c. Position the hose fittings against the stops at the engine (**Figure 22**) and at the oil cooler.
   d. Tighten the oil cooler banjo bolts to 23 N•m (17 ft.-lb.).

Table 7 ENGINE LOWER END TORQUE SPECIFICATIONS

	N•m	in.-lb.	ft.-lb.
Connecting rod bolts			
Initial torque	21	–	15
Final torque	1/4 turn clockwise		
Engine mounting bolts			
and adjusters			
Clamp bolts	23	–	17
Engine mounting bolts			
(except large throughbolt)	55	–	41
Large throughbolt	93	–	69
Thrust adjusters	12	106	–
Thrust adjuster locknuts	45	–	33
	(continued)		

16

Table 7 ENGINE LOWER END TORQUE SPECIFICATIONS (continued)

	N•m	in.-lb.	ft.-lb.
Oil cooler			
Banjo bolts	23	–	17
Mounting bolts	10	88	–

CHAPTER SIX

CLUTCH AND EXTERNAL SHIFT MECHANISM

Service to the clutch is the same as for earlier models. Refer to **Table 8** and **Table 9** for specifications unique to later models.

Table 8 CLUTCH SERVICE SPECIFICATIONS

	New mm (in.)	Service limit mm (in.)
Friction plate No. 1 and No. 2 thickness	2.92-3.08 (0.115-0.121)	2.62 (0.103)
Friction plate tab width	13.7-13.8 (0.539-0.543)	12.9 (0.507)
Spring free length	53.1 (2.09)	50.5 (1.99)

Table 9 CLUTCH AND GEARSHIFT MECHANISM TORQUE SPECIFICATIONS

	N•m	in.-lb.	ft.-lb.
Clutch spring bolts	10	88	–

CHAPTER SEVEN

TRANSMISSION AND INTERNAL SHIFT MECHANISM

TRANSMISSION

Mainshaft Disassembly/Assembly

Service to the transmission is the same as for earlier models with the exception of the mainshaft assembly on 2004-on models. The later mainshaft has a washer and O-ring in the positions shown in **Figure 23.**

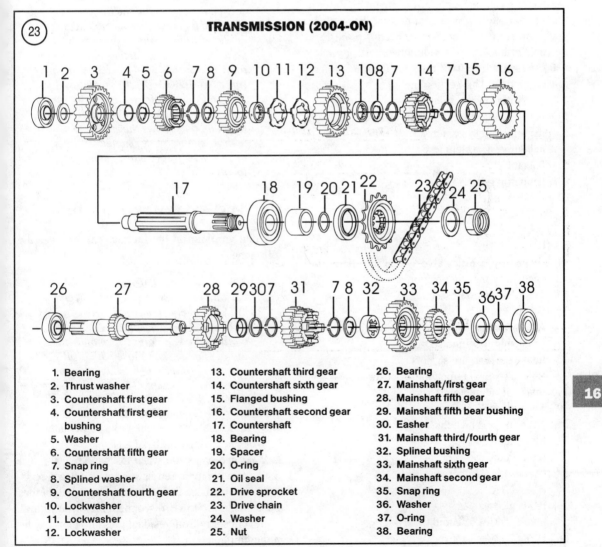

TRANSMISSION (2004-ON)

1. Bearing	13. Countershaft third gear	26. Bearing
2. Thrust washer	14. Countershaft sixth gear	27. Mainshaft/first gear
3. Countershaft first gear	15. Flanged bushing	28. Mainshaft fifth gear
4. Countershaft first gear bushing	16. Countershaft second gear	29. Mainshaft fifth bear bushing
5. Washer	17. Countershaft	30. Easher
6. Countershaft fifth gear	18. Bearing	31. Mainshaft third/fourth gear
7. Snap ring	19. Spacer	32. Splined bushing
8. Splined washer	20. O-ring	33. Mainshaft sixth gear
9. Countershaft fourth gear	21. Oil seal	34. Mainshaft second gear
10. Lockwasher	22. Drive sprocket	35. Snap ring
11. Lockwasher	23. Drive chain	36. Washer
12. Lockwasher	24. Washer	37. O-ring
	25. Nut	38. Bearing

16

CHAPTER EIGHT

FUEL, EMISSION CONTROL AND EXHAUST SYSTEMS

This section of the Supplement provides service procedures for the fuel injection system and fuel delivery system. Electrical sensors and components that affect the control of the fuel injection system by the electronic control module (ECM) are also covered in this section. The fuel injection system wiring diagrams are at the back of the manual. Refer to the appropriate wiring diagram at the back of the manual to verify wire colors, connection points, and the numbering of the ECM and harness connector.

Refer to **Tables 10-12** for specifications unique to later models. This section includes:

1. Fuel system precautions.
2. Fuel injection system self-diagnosis.
3. Fuel injection system troubleshooting.
4. Fuel delivery system tests.
5. Fuel tank.
6. Fuel pump relay.
7. Fuel pump.
8. Air box.
9. Throttle bodies.
10. Fuel injectors.
11. Secondary throttle valve synchronization.
12. Secondary throttle position sensor.
13. Throttle position sensor.
14. Fast idle speed.
15. Idle speed control valve.
16. Crankshaft position sensor.
17. Intake air pressure sensors.
18. Engine coolant temperature sensor.
19. Intake air temperature sensor.
20. Tip over sensor.
21. Gear position switch.
22. Ignition switch.
23. Ignition coils.
24. Crankcase breather system.
25. PAIR system.
26. PAIR reed valves.
27. PAIR control solenoid.
28. Heated oxygen sensor

29. Evaporative emission control system.

NOTE
Before testing or servicing the fuel injection system, read Fuel Injection System Self-Diagnosis and Fuel Injection System Troubleshooting in this section to understand the information provided by the user mode and dealer mode displays on the instrument panel. To access the dealer mode display, the Suzuki Mode Select Switch (part No. 09930-82720) is required. The self-diagnostic section also includes information on the fail-safe function, that allows the engine to run with minimum performance in order to get the motorcycle to a shop or safe location.

FUEL SYSTEM PRECAUTIONS

When working on the fuel system, observe the following:

WARNING
Gasoline and most cleaning solvents are extremely flammable. Do not smoke or use electrical tools in the vicinity of the work area. Turn off heating appliances and those with a pilot light. If gasoline can be smelled in the work area, a potential hazard exists.

1. Never work on a hot engine.
2. Wipe up fuel and solvent spills immediately.
3. Work in a well-ventilated area.
4. Wear eye protection when disconnecting the fuel system, using compressed air, solvents and degreasers.
5. Cover fuel hose fittings with a shop cloth before disconnecting. Slowly disconnect fuel hose fittings to prevent spray from residual pressure that may be in the fuel line.

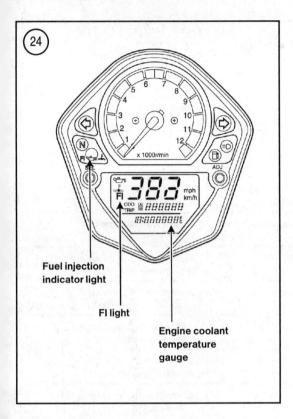

Fuel injection
indicator light

FI light

Engine coolant
temperature
gauge

6. Keep a fire extinguisher in the shop, rated for class B (fuel) and class C (electrical) fires.

FUEL INJECTION SYSTEM SELF-DIAGNOSIS

The electronic control module (ECM) includes a self-diagnostic function that monitors the sensors in the fuel injection system and some components of the ignition system. When a malfunction occurs, the ECM stores the malfunction code and displays a signal on the instrument panel. Depending on the malfunction, the engine may or may not be able to start.

The self-diagnostic function has a user mode and a dealer mode. In the user mode, basic information is displayed about the malfunction. In the dealer mode, a specific malfunction code(s) is displayed and testing can begin at that component(s). In order to access the dealer mode, the Suzuki Mode Select Switch (part No. 09930-82720) is required. The switch can be ordered from a Suzuki dealership.

In addition to the self-diagnostic function, the ECM will allow the engine to operate in a fail-safe mode for some malfunction codes. In this emergency mode, the engine will run with minimum per-formance in order to get the motorcycle to a shop or safe location.

User Mode

In the user mode, the following information will be displayed on the instrument panel for the current condition:

1. No system malfunction. The engine coolant temperature gauge (**Figure 24**) will operate normally.
2. System malfunction and engine will start.
   a. The engine coolant temperature gauge (**Figure 24**) will display the coolant temperature and the letters "FI". The displayed information will flash.
   b. The FI light (**Figure 24**) on the display will turn on.
   c. The fuel injection indicator light (**Figure 24**) on the display will turn on.
3. System malfunction and engine will not start.
   a. The engine coolant temperature gauge (**Figure 24**) will display the letters "FI". The displayed information will stay on continuously.
   b. The FI light (**Figure 24**) on the display will flash.
   c. The fuel injection indicator light (**Figure 24**) on the display will flash.
4. The instrument panel displays the letters "CHEC". This indicates that the instrument panel has not received a signal from the ECM for three seconds. This is typically caused by the following:
   a. The engine stop switch is in the off position.
   b. The ECM to instrument panel harness is making poor connection.
   c. A faulty ignition fuse.

Dealer Mode

In the dealer mode, the following information will be displayed on the instrument panel for the current condition:

1. No system malfunction. The engine coolant temperature gauge (**Figure 24**) will display the code "c00".
2. System malfunction.
   a. The engine coolant temperature gauge (**Figure 24**) will display the "c" code. If more than one malfunction is stored, the codes will be displayed in numerical order.

16

(25) **FAIL SAFE ACTION**

Failed Item	Fail-safe action	Operation Status
Intake air pressure sensor	Intake air pressure is set to 760 mmHG (29.92 in. Hg).	Engine continues operating; can restart.
Throttle position sensor	Throttle valve signal is set to its fully open position. Ignition timing is set to a preset value.	Engine continues operating; can restart.
Engine coolant temperature sensor	Engine coolant temperature is set to 80° C (176° F).	Engine continues operating; can restart.
Intake air temperature sensor	Intake air temperature is set to 40°C (104° F).	Engine continues operating; can restart.
Ignition signal, cylinder No. 1	No spark at cylinder No. 1.	Cylinder No. 2 continues operating; can restart.
Ignition signal, cylinder No. 2	No spark at cylinder No. 2.	Cylinder No. 1 continues operating; can restart.
Fuel injector No. 1	Fuel cut off to injector No. 1.	Cylinder No. 2 continues operating; can restart.
Fuel injector No. 2	Fuel cut off to injector No. 2.	Cylinder No. 1 continues operating; can restart.
Secondary throttle valve actuator	Electronic control module stops controlling secondary throttle valve.	Engine continues operating; can restart.
Secondary throttle position sensor	Electronic control module stops controlling secondary throttle valve.	Engine continues operating; can restart.
Gear position sensor	Gear position signal set to fourth gear.	Engine continues operating; can restart.
PAIR control solenoid valve	Electronic control module stops controlling solenoid valve.	Engine continues operating; can restart.
Heated oxygen sensor (California, U.K., EU, Aust.)	Feedback compensation inhibited. Air/fuel ratio fixed to normal.	Engine continues operating; can restart.
Idle speed control valve	Valve is stopped.	Engine continues operating; can restart.

b. The FI light (**Figure 24**) on the display will turn off.

Fail-Safe Function

Refer to **Figure 25** for the component operating conditions when the fail-safe function is implemented by the ECM.

FUEL INJECTION SYSTEM TROUBLESHOOTING

Read *Fuel Injection System Self-Diagnosis* in this section before beginning troubleshooting. Read this section and understand how to use the Mode Select Switch (part No. 09930-82720) to troubleshoot and reset the self-diagnostic function.

Refer to the appropriate wiring diagram at the back of the manual to verify wire colors, connection points, and the numbering of the ECM and harness connector.

Although not required for troubleshooting components, the SDS (Suzuki Diagnosis System) tool set (part No. 09904-41010) and CD-ROM software can be used to actively check the fuel injection system. Check with a Suzuki dealership for this equipment and the latest version of software. Refer to the tool and software instructions for using the equipment.

Dealer Mode Troubleshooting Procedure

Perform the following steps when troubleshooting the fuel injection system and using the mode select switch.

1. Note the user mode information displayed on the instrument panel.
2. Connect the Suzuki Mode Select Switch (part No. 09930-82720) to the connector located under the rear seat (**Figure 26**). Put the switch in the off position.
3. Start or crank the engine for five seconds or more.
4. Turn on the mode select switch and record the malfunction code(s) displayed on the instrument panel.
5. Turn off the ignition and mode select switch when all codes are recorded.

CAUTION
Always record the malfunction code(s) before disconnecting the battery, ECM, ECM ground wire harness or main fuse. Disconnecting these parts will erase any self-diagnostic

code(s) stored in the instrument panel.

6. Refer to **Figure 27** to identify the component related to the malfunction code.
7. Refer to the testing procedures in this section for the malfunctioning component. Refer to the fuel injection wiring diagram at the back of the manual as needed.
8. When troubleshooting is completed, reset the self-diagnostic function as described in this section.

Resetting the Self-Diagnostic Function

After troubleshooting is completed, reset the self-diagnostic function as follows:
1. Turn on the the ignition switch.
2. Turn on the mode select switch.
3. Turn the ignition switch off and then on.
4. View the instrument panel display. The code "c00" should be displayed in the engine coolant temperature gauge (**Figure 24**).
5. Turn off the ignition switch and mode select switch.
6. Disconnect the mode select switch.

FUEL DELIVERY SYSTEM TESTS

If the fuel injection system is suspected to be causing poor engine performance, and no malfunction codes are displayed, verify the condition of the fuel delivery system components before disassembling the throttle bodies. Perform the following tests to verify that the fuel pump, fuel pressure regulator, fuel filter and fuel pump relay are operating correctly.

Fuel Pump Operation Test

1. Turn the ignition switch on and listen for fuel pump operation. It is normal for the pump to turn off after three seconds of operation when the engine is not running.
2. Turn off the ignition switch.
3. If the fuel pump did not operate, inspect the following:
   a. Fuel pump and fuel pump relay electrical connections.
   b. Fuel pump relay operation.
   c. Tip-over sensor operation.

MALFUNCTION CODES

Malfunction code	Related item	Detected failure	Probable cause
c00	No error	–	–
c12	Crankshaft position sensor	The ECM has not received a signal from the CKP sensor 3 seconds after it received the start signal.	Faulty CKP sensor, wiring or connector.
c13, c17	Intake air pressure sensor	The sensor's voltage is outside the range of 0.1-4.8 volts.	Faulty IAP sensor, wiring or connector.
c14	Throttle position sensor	The sensor's voltage is outside the range of 0.1-4.8 volts.	Faulty TP sensor, wiring or connector.
c15	Engine coolant temperature sensor	The sensor's voltage is outside the range of 0.1-4.6 volts.	Faulty ECT sensor, wiring or connector.
c21	Intake air temperature sensor	The sensor's voltage is outside the range of 0.1-4.6 volts.	Faulty IAT sensor, wiring or connector.
c23	Tip over sensor	The sensor's voltage is outside the range of 0.2-4.6 volts 2 seconds after the ignition switch has been turned on.	faulty TO sensor, wiring or connector.
c24 (No. 1), c25 (No. 2)	Ignition system malfunction	The ECM does not receive a proper signal from an ignition coil.	Faulty ignition coil, wiring or connector.
c28	Secondary throttle valve actuator	Signal voltage from the ECM is not reaching the STVA, the ECM is not receiving a signal from the STVA, or load voltage is not reaching the actuator motor.	Faulty STVA wiring or connector.
c29	Secondary throttle position sensor	The sensor's voltage is outside the range of 0.1-4.8 volts.	Faulty STP sensor, wiring or connector.
c31	Gear position switch	The gear position switch voltage is less that 0.2 volts.	Faulty gear position switch wiring, connector or faulty shift cam.
c32 (No. 1) c33 (No. 2)	Fuel injector	The ECM receives signal from CKP, but fuel injecto signal is continously interrupted.	Faulty fuel injector, wiring or connector. Faulty power supply to the injector.
c40	Idle speed control valve (ISC)	Erratic voltage to motor drive, or idle speed higher than normal.	ISC circuit open or shorted to ground. Power circuit open. ISC valve fixed open. ISC valve hose disconnected.
c40	Idle speed control valve (ISC)	Idle speed lower than desired.	Clogged air passage. ISC valve locked. Incorrect reset of ISC valve.

(continued)

(27) (continued)

MALFUNCTION CODES (continued)

Malfunction code	Related item	Detected failure	Probable cause
c40	Idle speed control valve (ISC)	Idle speed higher than desired.	Poor ISC valve connection. ISC valve locked. Incorrect preset of ISC valve.
c41	Fuel pump relay	Load voltage flows to the fuel pump when the relay is off; load voltage does not flow to the fule pump when the relay is on.	Faulty fuel pump relay, wiring or connector. Faulty power source to the fuel pump relay or injectors.
c42	Ignition switch signal	The ECM does not receive a signal from the ignition switch	Faulty ignition switch, wiring or connector.
c44	Heaty oxygen sensor	1. The sensor's signal is not reaching the ECM. 2. The heat does not operate so its signal does not reach the ECM.	1. Faulty HO_2 sensor; the sensor circuit is open or shorted to ground. 2. Fault HO_2 sensor, its wiring connector; battery voltage not flowing to the sensor.
c49	PAIR solenoid valve	The ECM does not receive a signal from the valve.	Faulty PAIR solenoid valve, wiring or connector.

(28)

Fuel Pressure Test Special Tools

To perform the fuel pressure test, use the following Suzuki tools or equivalents. The tools can be ordered from a Suzuki dealership.

1. Fuel pressure gauge adapter (part No. 09940-40211).

2. Fuel pressure gauge hose attachment (part No. 09940-40220).

3. Oil pressure gauge (part No. 09915-77331).

4. Oil pressure gauge hose (part No. 09915-74521).

Fuel Pressure Test

WARNING
Wear eye protection when performing the pressure test. Cover the fuel hose fitting when disconnecting to prevent spray from residual pressure that may be in the fuel line.

1. Raise the fuel tank as described in this section.
2. Place a shop cloth below the fuel hose connection at the throttle body fuel delivery pipe (**Figure 28**). Slowly disconnect the hose and direct the residual fuel onto the shop cloth.
3. Assemble and install the special test tools between the fuel pump and the throttle body fuel delivery pipe (**Figure 29**).
4. Turn the ignition switch on and check the fuel pressure. It should should be approximately 300 kPa (43 psi).
5. Turn off the ignition switch.
6. If fuel pressure is below the specification, inspect the following:
    a. Fuel system leak.
    b. Clogged fuel filter.

16

c. Faulty pressure regulator.

d. Faulty fuel pump.

7. If fuel pressure is above the specification, inspect the following:

a. Fuel check valve.

b. Faulty pressure regulator.

8. Disconnect the test equipment and connect the fuel hose to the throttle body fuel delivery pipe. Drain and dry all test equipment.

Fuel Pump Discharge Test

A graduated container is required to measure the fuel pump discharge quantity. The container should have a capacity of at least 1 liter (1 U.S. qt., 0.83 Imp. qt.).

> *WARNING*
> *Wear eye protection when performing the discharge test. Cover the fuel hose fitting when disconnecting to prevent spray from residual pressure that may be in the fuel line.*

1. Raise the fuel tank as described in this section.

2. Place a shop cloth below the fuel hose connection at the throttle body fuel delivery pipe (**Figure 28**). Slowly disconnect the hose and direct the residual fuel onto the shop cloth.

3. Place the end of the fuel delivery hose into the container.

4. Remove the wiring connector from the electronic control module (ECM) (**Figure 30**).

5. Locate the yellow/black wire in the connector.

6. Identify the terminal for the yellow black wire in the end of the connector.

7. Attach a jumper wire to the yellow/black wire terminal.

8. Touch the jumper wire to the positive terminal on the battery and allow the fuel pump to operate for 10 seconds.

> *NOTE*
> *The battery must be fully charged to achieve an accurate discharge amount.*

9. Measure the amount of discharged fuel.

a. If the amount of fuel is 168 ml (5.7 U.S. oz., 5.9 Imp. oz.) or greater, the fuel pump is in good condition.

b. If the amount of fuel is less than 168 ml (5.7 U.S. oz., 5.9 Imp. oz.), check the fuel pump

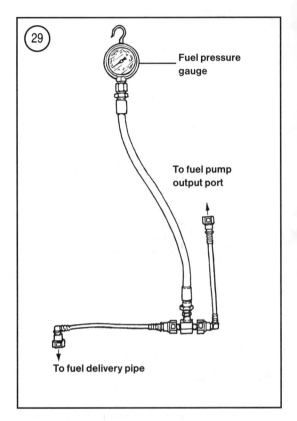

Fuel pressure gauge

To fuel pump output port

To fuel delivery pipe

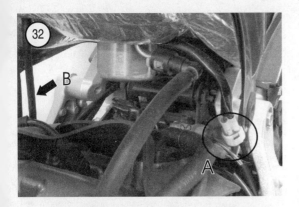

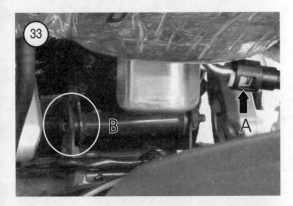

filter for clogs. If the filter is clean, replace the fuel pump.

10. Disconnect the jumper wire and reconnect the ECM. Connect the fuel hose to the throttle body fuel delivery pipe.

FUEL TANK

Raising/Removal/Installation

Removal of the fuel tank is similar for all models.

1. Support the motorcycle so it is stable and secure.
2. Remove the front seat as described in this Supplement.
3. Remove the fuel tank mounting bolts and spacers (**Figure 31**).
4. Raise the front of the tank and support it with the tank prop.
5. Disconnect the fuel pump wire harness (A, **Figure 32**).
6. Place a shop cloth below the fuel hose connection at the fuel pump (A, **Figure 33**) Slowly disconnect the hose and direct the residual fuel onto the shop cloth.
7. Remove the vent hose and fuel drain hose (B, **Figure 32**). Mark each hose so it can be installed on its correct fitting.
8. Stabilize the fuel tank and remove the pivot bolt (B, **Figure 33**).
9. Remove the fuel tank from the motorcycle.
10. Reverse this procedure to install the fuel tank.

FUEL PUMP RELAY

The fuel pump (FP) relay (**Figure 34**) is located under the front seat and behind the battery.

Continuity and Operation Test

An ohmmeter is required to check continuity in the fuel pump relay. If necessary, refer to the appropriate wiring diagram at the back of the manual for numbering of the ECU connector.

1. Remove the relay from the mounting tab and pull back the rubber cover (**Figure 35**). Pull the relay from the wiring harness
2. Check for continuity between terminals A and B (**Figure 36**) on the relay. There should not be continuity.

16

3. Connect a 12-volt battery to the C and D terminals on the relay (**Figure 36**). Connect the positive battery terminal to terminal C and the negative battery terminal to terminal D.

4. Check for continuity between the A and B relay terminals. There should be continuity while voltage is applied to terminals C and D.

　a. If the relay does not fail either test, inspect the wire harness and connectors for shorts, poor connections and open circuits. For 2003-2006 models, inspect the wires in the ECM connector at positions 9 and 32. For 2007-on models, inspect the wires in the ECM connector at positions 9 and 34. If the harness and connectors are in good condition, test the fuel injectors as described in this section. If both fuel injectors fail at the same time, the "c41" malfunction code will be displayed. If the fuel injectors and harness are in good condition, the ECM is malfunctioning.

　b. If the relay fails either test, replace the fuel pump relay.

FUEL PUMP

The fuel pump is located inside the fuel tank. The pump unit also includes the fuel filter, fuel level switch and pressure regulator. If necessary, refer to *Fuel Delivery System Tests* in this section before removing the fuel pump from the fuel tank.

Removal/Installation

1. Remove the fuel tank as described in this section.
2. Drain the fuel from the tank.

> *WARNING*
> *Drain the fuel into an approved container. Perform the draining procedure a safe distance away from the work area.*

3. Place the fuel tank on a padded work surface
4. Bend the tabs upward that secure the heat shield (**Figure 37**).
5. Evenly loosen the fuel pump mounting bolts (**Figure 38**), working in a crossing pattern.
6. Remove the fuel pump from the tank.
7. Reverse this procedure to install the fuel pump. Note the following:

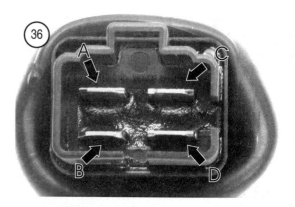

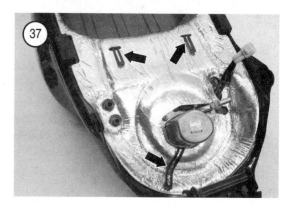

　a. Install a new O-ring into the groove on the fuel tank (**Figure 39**). Lightly lubricate the O-ring with grease.
　b. Apply Suzuki Thread Lock 1342 or equivalent to the mounting bolts.
　c. Evenly tighten the mounting bolts in a several passes, working in a crossing pattern. On the last pass, tighten the mounting bolts to 10 N•m (88 in.-lb.).

Disassembly/Inspection/Assembly

Refer to **Figure 40**.

1. Clean the exterior of the pump. Prevent any debris from entering the pump as it is disassembled.

2. Disconnect the fuel level switch lead (A, **Figure 41**). Mark the lead and the mounting plate so the lead can be correctly installed during assembly.

3. Disconnect the fuel pump positive lead (B, **Figure 41**). Mark the lead and the mounting plate so the lead can be correctly installed during assembly.

4. Remove screws and special nuts (**Figure 42**) securing the fuel pump leads and the fuel level switch.

Mark the leads and the mounting plate so the leads can be correctly installed during assembly.

5. Pull the fuel pump assembly from the mounting plate (**Figure 43**).

6. Remove the fuel pump holder (**Figure 44**).

7. Remove the rubber damper (**Figure 45**).

8. Remove the fuel filter (**Figure 46**).

9. Remove the clip (**Figure 47**).

10. Remove the pressure regulator (**Figure 48**).

11. Pull the fuel pump from the fuel pump case rubber bushing (**Figure 49**).

12. Inspect the fuel pump assembly as follows:

   a. Inspect all parts for damage and deterioration.

   b. Clean the fuel filter with compressed air (**Figure 50**). Do not use excessive air pressure.

   c. Inspect the rubber bushing (**Figure 49**) for damage.

   d. Inspect the wire leads and fuel pipe fitting (**Figure 51**). Check the fitting for cleanliness and the wires for broken insulation.

   e. If necessary, test the fuel level switch as described in this section.

13. Reverse this procedure to assemble the fuel pump. Note the following:

   a. Install new O-rings on the fuel pipe fitting and pressure regulator. Lightly lubricate the O-rings with engine oil.

   b. Lightly lubricate the rubber bushing with engine oil.

   c. Check that all wire leads are correctly positioned and tightened. Prevent wire insulation from rubbing on adjacent parts.

14. Install the fuel pump unit as described in this section.

Fuel Level Switch Test

1. Inspect the switch and lead (**Figure 52**) for damage.

2. Connect a 12-volt battery and a 3.4 watt test lamp to the switch as shown in **Figure 53**. The test lamp should turn on after several seconds.

3. With the battery and test lamp connected, submerge the switch in a container of water as shown in **Figure 53**. The test lamp should turn off.

4. Replace the switch if it fails either test.

AIR BOX

Removal/Installation

2003-2006 models

1. Support the motorcycle so it is stable and secure.

2. Raise the fuel tank as described in this section.

3. Disconnect the intake air temperature (IAT) sensor and breather hoses (**Figure 54**).

4. Disconnect the intake air pressure (IAP) sensor and vacuum hose (A, **Figure 55**).

5. Loosen the air box clamp from the front throttle body (**Figure 56**) and rear throttle body (B, **Figure 55**).

6. Disconnect the PAIR system hose and wiring coupler (**Figure 57**).

7. Remove the air box from the throttle body assembly (**Figure 58**).

8. Reverse this procedure to install the air box. Removal/Installation

2007-on models

1. Support the motorcycle so it is stable and secure.

2. Raise the fuel tank as described in this section.

3. Disconnect the intake air pressure (IAP) sensor vacuum hoses and couplers (**Figure 59**).

16

FUEL PUMP

(40)

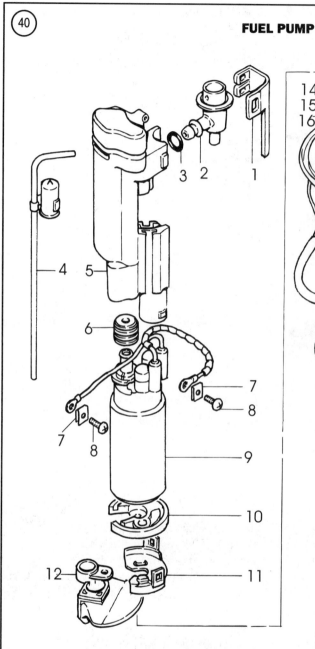

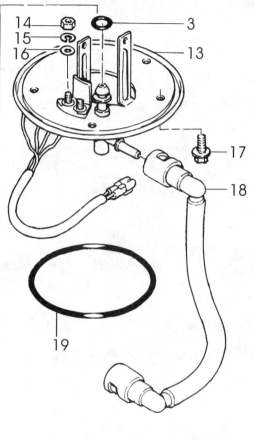

1. Safety clip
2. Pressure regulator
3. O-ring
4. Fuel level switch
5. Fuel pump case/cartridge
   filter assembly
6. Bushing
7. Special nut
8. Screw
9. Fuel pump
10. Fuel pump damper
11. Fuel pump holder
12. Fuel filter
13. Fuel pump base
14. Nut
15. Lockwasher
16. Washer
17. Bolt
18. Fuel line
19. O-ring

16

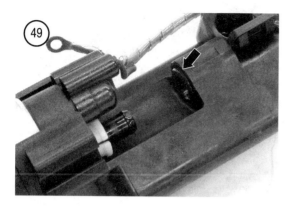

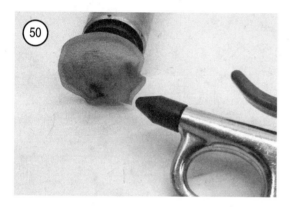

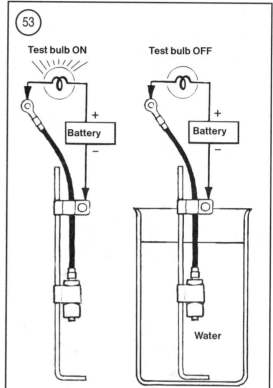

Test bulb ON   Test bulb OFF

Battery   Battery

Water

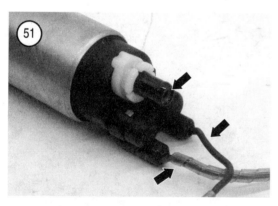

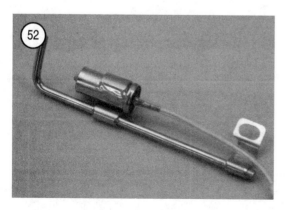

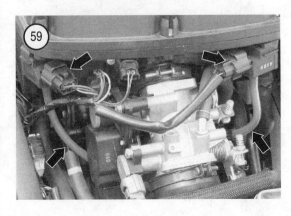

4. Disconnect the intake air temperature (IAT) sensor (**Figure 60**).

5. Loosen the air box clamp from the front throttle body (**Figure 61**) and rear throttle body (**Figure 62**).

6. Lift the air box and disconnect the PAIR hose, idle speed control (ISC) valve hose and Pair coupler (**Figure 63**).

7. Disconnect the crankcase breather hoses (**Figure 64**).

8. Remove the air box from the throttle body assembly (**Figure 65**).

9. Reverse this procedure to install the air box.

16

THROTTLE BODIES

There are two throttle bodies in the fuel injection system. Each throttle body is equipped with two throttle valves. The secondary throttle valve (STV), located at the top of the throttle body, is controlled by the electronic control module (ECM). The ECM opens and closes the secondary valve to vary the volume and speed of incoming air passing to the throttle valve.

NOTE
If necessary, refer to Fuel Injectors in this section to test the injectors before removing the throttle body assembly from the engine.

Removal/Installation

2003-2006 models

1. Remove the fuel tank as described in this section. Instead of removing the fuel hose at the fuel pump, remove the fuel hose at the throttle body fuel delivery pipe (A, **Figure 66**). Place a shop cloth below the fuel hose connection, then disconnect the hose. Direct the residual fuel onto the shop cloth.

2. Remove the air box as described in this section.

3. Disconnect the following wire connectors. Since the connectors are similar to one another, mark each connector so it can be installed in its original position.

   a. Throttle position (TP) sensor (B, **Figure 66**).

   b. Secondary throttle position (STP) sensor (C, **Figure 66**).

   c. Secondary throttle valve actuator (STVA) and fuel injectors (D, **Figure 66**).

4. Disconnect the throttle stop screw (**Figure 67**).

5. Loosen the clamp screw on each throttle body (**Figure 68**).

6. Disconnect the throttle cables as follows:

   a. Mark the pull cable (upper cable) and return cable (lower cable) (A, **Figure 69**) so they can be installed in their correct positions on the bracket and drum.

   b. Loosen the cable locknuts and turn the adjusters in until the cables can be removed from the bracket.

   c. Remove the cable ends from the throttle body drum (B, **Figure 69**).

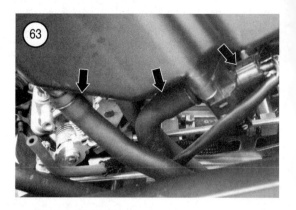

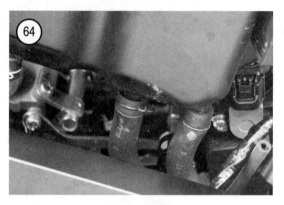

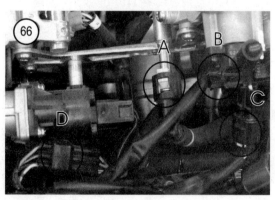

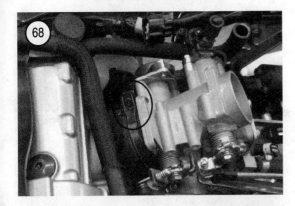

CAUTION
During or after cable removal, pre-vent the throttle valves from snapping shut. Damage may occur to the throt-tle valves or throttle bodies.

7. Remove the throttle body assembly from the engine.

8. Reverse this procedure to install the throttle body assembly. Note the following:

   a. At the engine, install and adjust the throttle ca-bles so there is no clearance between the adjuster and locknut. Tighten the locknuts to secure each throttle cable to the mounting bracket.

   b. Adjust the throttle cables at the handlebar (Chapter Three).

2007-on models

1. Remove the fuel tank as described in this sec-tion.

2. Remove the air box as described in this section.

3. Remove the fuel hose at the throttle body fuel delivery pipe (**Figure 70**). Place a shop cloth below the fuel hose connection, then disconnect the hose. Direct the residual fuel onto the shop cloth.

4. Disconnect the following wire connectors:

   a. Throttle position (TP) sensor (A, **Figure 71**).

   b. Secondary throttle position (STP) sensor (B, **Figure 71**).

   c. Secondary throttle valve actuator (STVA) (C, **Figure 71**). Access the connector through the side of the frame.

5. Disconnect the injector couplers (**Figure 72**).

6. Remove the idle speed control (ISC) valve hose from the throttle bodies (**Figure 73** and **Figure 74**).

7. Loosen the clamp screw at the base of each throt-tle body (**Figure 75**).

16

8. Disconnect the throttle cables as follows:

   a. Mark the pull cable (upper cable) and return cable (lower cable) (**Figure 76**) so they can be installed in their correct positions on the bracket and drum.

   b. Loosen the cable locknuts and turn the adjusters in until the cables can be removed from the bracket.

   c. Remove the cable ends from the throttle body drum.

> *CAUTION*
> *During or after cable removal, prevent the throttle valves from snapping shut. Damage may occur to the throttle valves or throttle bodies.*

9. Remove the throttle body assembly from the engine.

10. Reverse this procedure to install the throttle body assembly. Note the following:

   a. At the engine, install and adjust the throttle cables so there is no clearance between the adjuster and locknut. Tighten the locknuts to secure each throttle cable to the mounting bracket.

   b. Adjust the throttle cables at the handlebar (Chapter Three).

Disassembly/Assembly

2003-2006 models

Read the entire procedure before disassembling the throttle bodies. Do not remove or disassemble parts if the special tools and test equipment listed is not available. Refer to **Figure 77**.

> *CAUTION*
> *The throttle bodies are precision components that are accurately assem-*

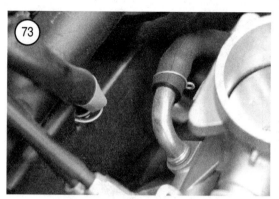

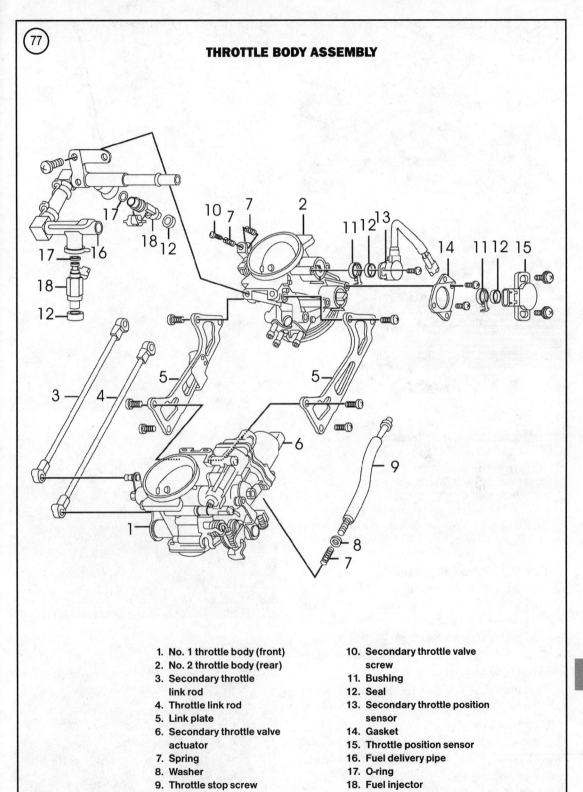

THROTTLE BODY ASSEMBLY

1. No. 1 throttle body (front)
2. No. 2 throttle body (rear)
3. Secondary throttle link rod
4. Throttle link rod
5. Link plate
6. Secondary throttle valve actuator
7. Spring
8. Washer
9. Throttle stop screw
10. Secondary throttle valve screw
11. Bushing
12. Seal
13. Secondary throttle position sensor
14. Gasket
15. Throttle position sensor
16. Fuel delivery pipe
17. O-ring
18. Fuel injector

16

*bled and adjusted at the factory. Suzuki does not recommend the removal of the secondary throttle valve actuator or adjustment of the actuator screw (**Figure 78**). Do not remove or adjust the throttle stop screw on the No. 2 (rear) throttle body (**Figure 79**). Do not remove or loosen the link plates or throttle valves (**Figure 80**).*

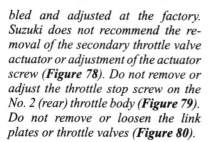

1. Remove the intake air pressure (IAP) sensor and hose (**Figure 81**). Note that the end of the sensor marked with a **D** faces the throttle body (**Figure 82**). The sensor must be installed in this direction. If no mark is visible, mark the sensor before removal.

2. Disconnect the secondary throttle valve actuator (STVA) (A, **Figure 83**).

3. Disconnect the injectors (B, **Figure 83**). Note that the No. 1 injector (front) connector is marked with an **F**.

4. Remove the throttle link rod (A, **Figure 84**) and secondary throttle link rod (B). Before removal, check for play in the rod fittings. If the rods are loose and do not operate the throttle valves simultaneously, replace the rods. Note that the throttle link rod is longer than the secondary rod.

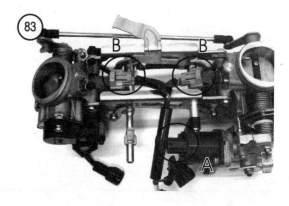

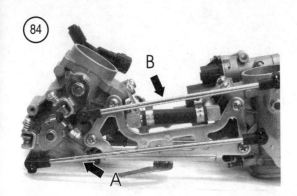

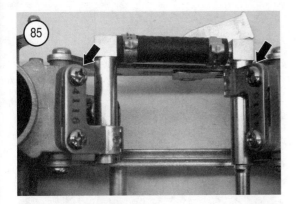

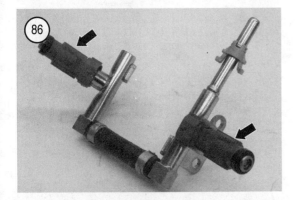

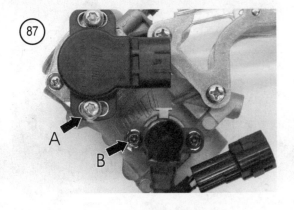

5. Remove the screws securing the fuel delivery pipe **(Figure 85)**. Pull the fuel delivery pipe and injectors out of the throttle bodies

6. Pull the injectors **(Figure 86)** from the fuel delivery pipe.

7. If practical, or necessary, remove the throttle position (TP) sensor (A, **Figure 87**) and secondary throttle position (STP) sensor (B) as follows:

NOTE
Anytime the throttle position (TP) sensor is removed from the throttle body, the most accurate method for checking sensor adjustment after installation is with the Suzuki Mode Select Switch (part No. 09930-82720). The mode select switch is used to access and display the self-diagnostic screen on the instrument panel. The displayed alignment bars will indicate when the sensor is exactly adjusted.

NOTE
Anytime the secondary throttle position (STP) sensor is removed from the throttle body, the most accurate method for checking sensor adjustment after installation is with an ohmmeter.

a. A special Torx driver or equivalent, is required to remove the sensor screws. Use the Suzuki Torx driver (part No. 09930-11950) to remove the TP sensor and the Suzuki Torx driver (part No. 09930-11960) to remove the STP sensor. The drivers can be ordered from a Suzuki dealership.

b. *Accurately* scribe a mark on the sensors and throttle body **(Figure 88)** so the sensors can be aligned and locked in their original positions during assembly. Although accurate

16

alignment of the scribe marks is possible during assembly, it is possible that the output of the sensors may slightly differ from their previous output. Using the test equipment described for each sensor is the only way to assure accurate adjustment of the sensors and maximum engine performance.

c. Remove the sensors. Account for the seal and bushing under each sensor, and the gasket under the throttle position sensor.

8. Remove the throttle stop screw as follows:

a. Accurately measure the exposed thread length on the screw (**Figure 89**). Record the measurement.

b. Remove the throttle stop screw, spring and washer.

9. Remove the fast idle lever as follows:

a. Remove the lever retaining nut (**Figure 90**).

b. Remove the lever assembly (**Figure 91**).

c. Remove the bushing and washer from the shaft (**Figure 92**).

10. Clean and inspect the parts as described in this section.

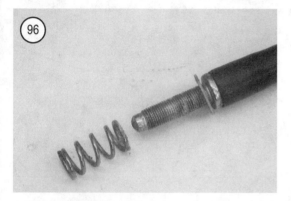

11. Reverse this procedure to assemble the throttle bodies. Install new O-rings and seals. Note the following:

a. On the fast idle lever shaft, install the concave side of the washer and the grooved end of the bushing facing out (**Figure 92**).

b. Lightly lubricate the friction point on the fast idle lever (**Figure 93**) with molydisulfide grease before assembling the spring and lever (**Figure 91**).

c. Hook the spring ends to the posts when installing the spring and fast idle lever (**Figure 94**).

d. Fully seat the plastic washer on the fast idle lever and shaft (**Figure 95**).

e. Lightly lubricate the spring ends and the tip of the throttle stop screw with grease (**Figure 96**). Adjust the screw to the measurement recorded during disassembly.

f. If the throttle position sensors are removed, lightly lubricate each sensor seal and mating shaft end with grease.

g. Install the seal and bushing onto the throttle position (TP) sensor (**Figure 97**). Engage the sensor and rotate it counterclockwise (**Figure 98**). Align the reference marks on the sensor and throttle body before tightening the mounting screws to 3.5 N•m (31 in.-lb.). Check that the throttle valve operates smoothly.

h. To install the secondary throttle position (STP) sensor (**Figure 99**), engage the boss in the sensor with the notch in the shaft (**Figure 100**). Align the reference marks on the sensor and throttle body before tightening the mounting screws to 2 N•m (18 in.-lb.). Check that the secondary throttle valve operates smoothly.

i. Lightly lubricate each injector O-ring and seal (**Figure 101**) with engine oil. Install the injectors on the fuel delivery pipe and install

16

the assembly. Push the injectors straight into the throttle bodies. Avoid twisting the injectors. Tighten the fuel delivery pipe screws (**Figure 85**) to 5 N•m (44 in.-lb.).

j. Install the throttle link rod and secondary throttle link rod. The throttle link rod is the longest rod.

12. Inspect the secondary throttle valve (STV) synchronization as described in *Secondary Throttle Valve Synchronization* in this section.

13. If removed during disassembly, check the secondary throttle position (STP) sensor adjustment as described in *Secondary Throttle Position Sensor* in this section.

14. Install the throttle body assembly as described in this section. After installation:

a. Inspect the throttle valve synchronization as described in *Throttle Valve Synchronization* in this section.

b. If removed during disassembly, check the throttle position (TP) sensor adjustment as described in *Throttle Position Sensor* in this section.

2007-on models

Read the entire procedure before disassembling the throttle bodies. Do not remove or disassemble parts if the special tools and test equipment listed is not available. Refer to **Figure 102**.

CAUTION
*The throttle bodies are precision components that are accurately assembled and adjusted at the factory. Suzuki does not recommend the removal of the secondary throttle valve actuator. Do not remove or adjust the stop screw on the front throttle body (**Figure 103**) or rear throttle body (**Figure 104**). Do not remove or loosen the link plates or throttle valves.*

1. Remove the remaining vacuum hoses.

2. Remove the throttle link rod and secondary throttle link rod. Before removal, check for play in the rod fittings. If the rods are loose and do not operate the throttle valves simultaneously, replace the rods. Note that the throttle link rod is longer than the secondary rod.

3. Remove the screws securing the fuel delivery pipe. Pull the fuel delivery pipe and injectors out of the throttle bodies.

4. Pull the injectors from the fuel delivery pipe. Mark the injectors so they can be installed in their original position (front or rear throttle body). The No. 1 injector (front) connector *may be* marked with an **F**.

5. If practical, or necessary, remove the throttle position (TP) sensor and secondary throttle position (STP) sensor as follows:

NOTE
Anytime the throttle position (TP) sensor is removed from the throttle body, the most accurate method for checking sensor adjustment after installation is with the Suzuki Mode Select Switch (part No. 09930-82720). The mode select switch is used to access and display the self-diagnostic screen on the instrument panel. The displayed alignment bars will indicate when the sensor is exactly adjusted.

NOTE
Anytime the secondary throttle position (STP) sensor is removed from the throttle body, the most accurate method for checking sensor adjustment after installation is with an ohmmeter.

THROTTLE BODY ASSEMBLY (2007-ON)

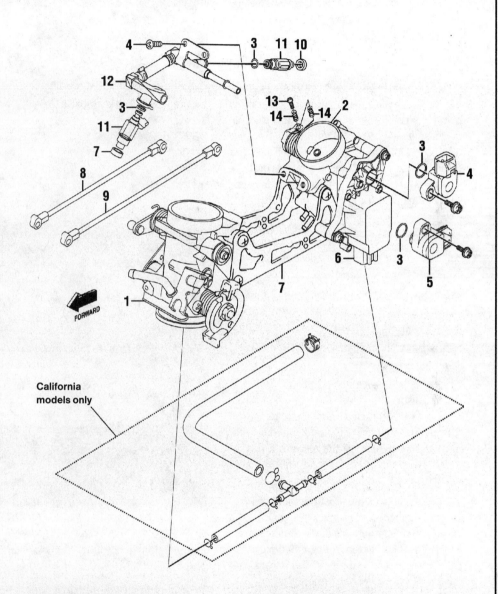

California models only

1. No. 1 throttle body (front)
2. No. 2 throttle body (rear)
3. O-ring
4. Secondary throttle position sensor
5. position sensor
6. Secondary throttle valve actuator
7. Link plate
8. Secondary throttle link rod
9. Throttle link rod
10. Seal
11. Fuel injector
12. Fuel delivery pipe
13. Secondary throttle valve screw
14. Spring

16

a. A special Torx driver or equivalent, is required to remove the sensor screws. Use the Suzuki Torx driver (part No. 09930-11950) to remove the TP sensor and the Suzuki Torx driver (part No. 09930-11960) to remove the STP sensor. The drivers can be ordered from a Suzuki dealership.

b. *Accurately* scribe a mark on the sensors and throttle body so the sensors can be aligned and locked in their original positions during assembly. Although accurate alignment of the scribe marks is possible during assembly, it is possible that the output of the sensors may slightly differ from their previous output. Using the test equipment described for each sensor is the only way to assure accurate adjustment of the sensors and maximum engine performance.

c. Remove the sensors. Account for the O-ring under each sensor.

6. Clean and inspect the parts as described in this section.

7. Reverse this procedure to assemble the throttle bodies. Install new O-rings. Note the following:

a. If the throttle position sensors are removed, lightly lubricate each sensor seal and mating shaft end with grease.

b. To install the secondary throttle position (STP) sensor , fully close the secondary throttle valve (STV), then engage the parts. Align the reference marks on the sensor and throttle body before tightening the mounting screws to 3.5 N•m (30 in.-lb.). Check that the secondary throttle valve operates smoothly.

c. To install the throttle position (TP) sensor, fully close the throttle valve, then engage the parts. Align the reference marks on the sensor and throttle body before tightening the mounting screws to 3.5 N•m (30 in.-lb.). Check that the throttle valve operates smoothly.

d. Lightly lubricate each injector O-ring and seal with engine oil. Install the injectors on the fuel delivery pipe and install the assembly. Push the injectors straight into the throttle bodies. Avoid twisting the injectors. Tighten the fuel delivery pipe screws to 5 N•m (44 in.-lb.).

e. Install the throttle link rod and secondary throttle link rod. The throttle link rod is the longest rod.

8. Inspect the secondary throttle valve (STV) synchronization as described in *Secondary Throttle Valve Synchronization* in this section.

9. If removed during disassembly, check the secondary throttle position (STP) sensor adjustment as described in *Secondary Throttle Position Sensor* in this section.

10. Install the throttle body assembly as described in this section. After installation:

a. Inspect the throttle valve synchronization as described in *Throttle Valve Synchronization* in this section.

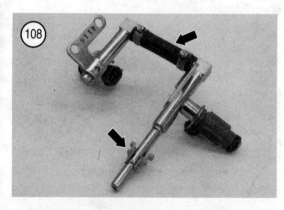

b. If removed during disassembly, check the throttle position (TP) sensor adjustment as described in *Throttle Position Sensor* in this section.

Cleaning/Inspection

The following procedure shows the parts used on the 2003-2006 fuel injection system. Although the 2007-on fuel injection system differs in appearance, this procedure can be used for inspection and cleaning of the later system.

Use a commercial cleaner specifically for fuel systems. These cleaners contain solvents that remove fuel residues and buildup. Use a cleaner that is harmless to rubber and plastic parts. Follow the manufacturer's instructions.

Do not submerge or spray the throttle position sensors and secondary throttle valve actuator with solvent. Because of heat and age, O-rings will lose their flexibility and do not seal properly. It is standard practice to replace O-rings and seals when rebuilding the throttle bodies.

1. Clean the throttle body assembly with solvent and compressed air.

2. Inspect the assembly for damage and loose parts.

3. Operate the throttle valves and secondary throttle valve shafts (**Figure 105**). The shafts must turn smoothly and have no play or wear.

4. Inspect the bushing and seal for each throttle position sensor (**Figure 106**).

5. Inspect the throttle stop screw, spring and washer for damage (**Figure 96**).

6. Inspect the fast idle lever assembly for worn or damaged parts (**Figure 107**).

7. Inspect the fuel delivery pipe lock and hose for cracks or damage (**Figure 108**).

8. Inspect the fuel injectors for carbon and buildup on the nozzle (**Figure 109**).

16

FUEL INJECTORS

The "c32" code represents the No. 1 throttle body fuel injector (A, **Figure 110**) and the "c33" code represents the No. 2 throttle body fuel injector (B). When testing, always check both fuel injectors when either code is shown on the instrument panel.

Continuity and Resistance Tests

An ohmmeter is required to check continuity and resistance at the fuel injector terminals (**Figure 111**). Do not remove the fuel injectors from the throttle body assembly to perform the tests.

1. Do not turn on the ignition switch during the test.

2. Remove the air box as described in this section.

3. Disconnect the wire connectors from the fuel injectors.

4. Test each fuel injector for continuity as follows:

    a. Connect an ohmmeter lead to one of the fuel injector terminals and the other lead to the throttle body, engine or frame ground.

    b. Check for continuity. There should be no continuity between the fuel injector and ground.

    c. Repeat substep a and substep b for the remaining terminal.

    d. If continuity exists at either terminal, replace the fuel injector.

5. Test each fuel injector for resistance as follows:

    a. Connect an ohmmeter lead to each terminal in the fuel injector.

    b. Measure and record the resistance reading.

    c. Compare the resistance measurement with the specification in **Table 11**.

    d. If the measurement is within specification, the fuel injector is in good condition.

    e. If the measurement is not within specification, replace the fuel injector.

6. For 2003-2006 models, test the fuel injector wire harness and connectors for continuity. Disconnect and test only the harness section that connects the fuel injectors and secondary throttle valve actuator (STVA) to the main harness.

    a. If there is continuity for all wires and connectors, the harness is in good condition.

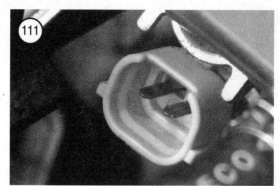

    b. If there is not continuity in any wire or connector, repair or replace the harness

Input Voltage Test

A voltmeter is required to measure input voltage to the fuel injectors. If necessary, refer to the appropriate wiring diagram at the back of the manual for numbering of the ECU connector.

1. Check that the ignition switch is turned off.

2. Remove the air box as described in this section.

3A. For 2003-2006 models, disconnect the wire connector that powers the secondary throttle valve actuator (STVA) and the fuel injectors (**Figure 112**).

3B. For 2007-on models, disconnect the wire connector that powers the faulty fuel injector (**Figure 113**).

4. Connect the voltmeter to the harness side of the connector and measure input voltage as follows:

   a. Check that all wires are secure in the connector.

   b. Identify the yellow/red wire terminal in the connector.

   c. Connect the voltmeter positive lead to the yellow/red wire terminal and the negative lead to the engine or frame ground.

   d. Turn on the ignition switch and read the voltage measurement. Turn off the ignition switch and record the measurement.

NOTE
The injector voltage is measurable for three seconds after the ignition switch is turned on. If necessary, turn off the ignition switch and repeat substep d to read the voltage.

   e. Compare the input voltage measurement with the specification in **Table 11**.

   f. If the measurement is within specification, inspect the green/white and green/black wires in the harness for shorts, poor connections and open circuits. For 2003-2006 models, inspect the wires in the ECM connector at positions 5 (front injector) or 6 (rear injector). For 2007-on models, inspect the wires in the ECM connector at positions 51 (front injector) or 42 (rear injector). If the wires and harness are in good condition, the ECM is malfunctioning.

   g. If the measurement is not within specification, inspect the fuel pump relay.

SECONDARY THROTTLE VALVE SYNCHRONIZATION

The secondary throttle valve (STV) synchronization procedure can be performed with the throttle bodies removed or installed on the motorcycle. The purpose of the procedure is to identically set both secondary throttle valves so the valves are parallel to the top surface of their respective throttle body.

1. If the throttle body assembly is installed on the motorcycle, do the following:

   a. Remove the air box as described in this section

   b. Do not turn on the ignition switch during the adjustment procedure.

2. Begin adjustment at the No. 1 (front) throttle body as follows:

   a. Measure the distance from the top of the throttle body to the STV surface (A, **Figure 114**). Make the measurement at a point 90 degrees to the axis of the STV shaft and centered with the STV. Record the measurement.

   b. Repeat the measurement at the point directly opposite (B, **Figure 114**) the first measurement point . Record the measurement.

   c. Compare the two measurements. If the measurements are not identical, turn the shaft on the secondary throttle valve actuator (STVA) (C, **Figure 114**) to open/close the STV. Continue to measure and adjust the position of the STV until the two measurements are identical.

3. Adjust the No. 2 (rear) throttle body. Do the following:

   a. Measure the distance from the top of the throttle body to the STV surface (A, **Figure 115**).

16

Make the measurement at a point 90 degrees to the axis of the STV shaft and centered with the STV. Record the measurement.

b. Repeat the measurement at the point directly opposite (B, **Figure 115**) the first measurement point. Record the measurement.

c. Compare the two measurements. If the measurements are not identical, turn the adjustment screw (C, **Figure 115**) to open/close the STV. Continue to measure and adjust the position of the STV until the two measurements are identical.

4. Check secondary throttle position (STP) sensor adjustment as described in this section.

SECONDARY THROTTLE POSITION SENSOR "c29"

Adjustment

2003-2006 models

The Suzuki Torx wrench (part No. 09930-11960) or equivalent is required to loosen the STP sensor screws (**Figure 90**). A voltmeter is required to measure voltage in the sensor.

Always check STP sensor adjustment after the secondary throttle valves have been synchronized.

1. If the throttle body assembly is installed on the motorcycle, disconnect the wire connector at the secondary throttle valve actuator (STVA) (**Figure 116**).

2. Connect the voltmeter probes to the STP connector as follows:

a. Check that all wires are secure in the connector.

b. Identify the yellow and black wires entering into the connector.

c. Insert one voltmeter lead in contact with the yellow wire and the other lead in contact with the black wire.

3. Check and adjust the STP sensor as follows:

a. Turn on the ignition.

b. At the No. 1 (front) throttle body, turn the shaft on the secondary throttle valve actuator (STVA) (**Figure 117**) until the secondary throttle valve (STV) is fully open. Record the voltage reading.

c. Turn off the ignition.

d. Compare the voltage reading with the specification in **Table 11**.

e. If the measurement is within specification, adjustment is not necessary.

f. If the measurement is not within specification, loosen the sensor mounting screws and rotate the sensor until the correct specification is achieved. Tighten the mounting screws to 2 N•m (18 in.-lb.). Repeat substep a and substep b to verify proper adjustment.

g. If the correct specification cannot be achieved, replace the STP sensor.

4. Reconnect the wire connectors.

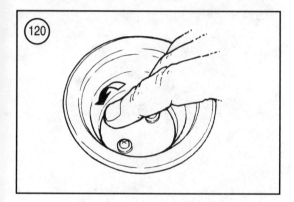

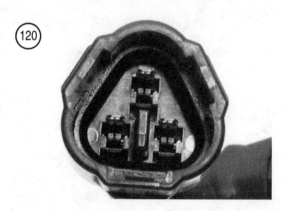

2007-on models

The Suzuki Torx wrench (part No. 09930-11950) or equivalent is required to loosen the STP sensor screw. A voltmeter is required to measure voltage in the sensor.

Always check STP sensor adjustment after the secondary throttle valves have been synchronized.

1. If the throttle body assembly is installed on the motorcycle, disconnect the wire connector at the secondary throttle valve actuator (STVA) (**Figure 118**). Access the connector through the side of the frame.

2. Connect the voltmeter probes to the STP connector (**Figure 119**) as follows:
    a. Check that all wires are secure in the connector.
    b. Identify the yellow and black wires entering into the connector.
    c. Insert one voltmeter lead in contact with the yellow wire and the other lead in contact with the black/brown wire.

3. Check and adjust the STP sensor as follows:
    a. Turn on the ignition.
    b. At the No. 2 (rear) throttle body, close the secondary throttle valve actuator (STVA) (**Figure 120**) by hand. Record the voltage reading.
    c. Turn off the ignition.
    d. Compare the voltage reading with the specification in **Table 11**.
    e. If the measurement is within specification, adjustment is not necessary.
    f. If the measurement is not within specification, loosen the sensor mounting screws and rotate the sensor until the correct specification is achieved. Tighten the mounting screws to 2 N•m (18 in.-lb.). Repeat substep a and substep b to verify proper adjustment.
    g. If the correct specification cannot be achieved, replace the STP sensor.

4. Reconnect the wire connectors.

Continuity Test

2003-2006 models only

An ohmmeter is required to check continuity in the STP sensor (**Figure 99**).

1. If the throttle body assembly is installed on the motorcycle, do the following:
    a. Do not turn on the ignition switch during the test.
    b. Raise the fuel tank as described in this section.
    c. Disconnect the wire connector at the STP sensor.

2. Connect the ohmmeter to the sensor connector as follows:
    a. Check that all wires are secure in the connector.
    b. Identify the yellow wire terminal in the connector (**Figure 121**).

16

c. Connect one ohmmeter lead to the yellow wire terminal and the other lead to the throttle body, engine or frame ground.

3. Check for continuity. There should be no continuity between the sensor and ground. If continuity exists, replace the STP sensor. If there is no continuity, continue with the Input Voltage Test.

Input Voltage Test

A voltmeter is required to measure input voltage to the STP sensor. For 2003-2006 models, refer to **Figure 99** and **Figure 122**. For 2007-on models, refer to **Figure 118 and Figure 119**. If necessary, refer to the appropriate wiring diagram at the back of the manual for numbering of the ECU connector.

1. Check that the ignition switch is turned off.

2. Raise the fuel tank as described in this section.

3. Disconnect the wire connector at the STP sensor.

4. Connect the voltmeter to the harness side of the connector and measure input voltage as follows:

a. Check that all wires are secure in the connector.

b. Identify the red wire terminal in the connector.

c. Connect the voltmeter positive lead to the red wire terminal and the negative lead to the engine or frame ground.

d. Turn on the ignition switch and read the voltage measurement. Turn off the ignition switch and record the measurement.

e. Identify the black/brown wire terminal in the connector.

f. Connect the voltmeter positive lead to the red wire terminal and the negative lead to the black/brown wire terminal.

g. Turn on the ignition switch and read the voltage measurement. Turn off the ignition switch and record the measurement

h. Compare both input voltage measurements with the specification in **Table 11**.

i. If the measurements are within specification, the wire harness, connectors and electronic control module (ECM) are in good condition.

j. If the measurements are not within specification, inspect the wire harness and connectors for shorts, poor connections and open circuits. For 2003-2006 models, inspect the wires in the ECM connector at positions 10 and 34. For 2007-on models, inspect the

wires in the ECM connector at positions 5 and 12. If the harness and connectors are in good condition, continue with the *Output Voltage Test*.

Output Voltage Test

Perform the continuity test and input voltage test in this section before the output voltage test. A voltmeter and the Suzuki needle probe set (part No. 09900-25009) or equivalent are required to measure output voltage of the STP sensor. For 2003-2006 models, refer to **Figure 99**. For 2007-on models, refer to **Figure 118.**

1. Check that the ignition switch is turned off.

2. Remove the air box as described in this section.

3. Check that all wires and connections are clean and secure in both halves of the STP sensor connector. The connector halves must be locked together to perform the test.

4. Connect the voltmeter and needle probes to the harness side of the STP sensor connector as follows:

a. Identify the yellow and black/brown wires in the connector (**Figure 123**).

b. At the back side of the connector, insert a needle probe into the yellow wire connector. Connect the voltmeter positive lead to this probe.

c. At the back side of the connector, insert a needle probe into the black/brown wire connector. Connect the voltmeter negative lead to this probe.

5A. 2003-2006 models, at the No. 1 (front) throttle body, disconnect the wire connector from the secondary throttle valve actuator (STVA) (**Figure 116**).

5B. 2007-on models, at the No. 2 (rear) throttle body, disconnect the wire connector from the secondary throttle valve actuator (STVA) (**Figure 118**). Access the connector through the side of the frame.

6. Measure the voltage as follows:

a. Turn on the ignition switch.

b. At the No. 1 (front) throttle body, turn the shaft on the secondary throttle valve actuator (STVA) (Figure 95) until the secondary throt-

tle valve (STV) is fully open. Record the voltage reading.

c. Turn the shaft on the secondary throttle valve actuator (STVA) until the secondary throttle valve (STV) is fully closed. Record the voltage reading.

d. Turn off the ignition switch.

e. Compare the voltage measurements with the specifications in **Table 11**.

f. If the measurements are within specifications, the STP sensor is in good condition.

g. If the measurements are not within specification, replace the STP sensor.

THROTTLE POSITION SENSOR "c14"

Adjustment

All models

The Suzuki Torx wrench (part No. 09930-11950) or equivalent is required to loosen the TP sensor screws (**Figure 124 or Figure 125**). The most accurate method for checking sensor adjustment is with the Suzuki Mode Select Switch (part No. 09930-82720). The mode select switch is used to access and display the self-diagnostic screen on the instrument panel. The displayed alignment bars will indicate when the sensor is exactly adjusted.

Always check TP sensor adjustment after the throttle valves have been synchronized.

1. Warm up the engine and set the idle speed at 1300 rpm. Turn off the engine.

2. Raise the fuel tank as described in this section.

3. Connect the Suzuki Mode Select Switch as described in *Fuel Injection System Troubleshooting* in this section.

4. Turn on the mode select switch and view the malfunction code and alignment bars on the instrument panel. The code and screen displayed should appear as in **Figure 126**. Note the following:

a. If the center alignment bar is illuminated the sensor is correctly adjusted.

b. If the upper or lower alignment bar is illuminated, loosen the sensor mounting screws and turn the sensor until the center bar is illuminated. Tighten the mounting screws to 3.5 N•m (31 in.-lb.).

c. Check that the center bar remains illuminated.

16

5. Turn off and disconnect the mode select switch.

6. If necessary reset the idle speed to 1300 rpm.

Input Voltage Test

All models

A voltmeter is required to measure input voltage to the TP sensor (**Figure 124 or Figure 125**). If necessary, refer to the appropriate wiring diagram at the back of the manual for numbering of the ECU connector.

1. Check that the ignition switch is turned off.

2. Raise the fuel tank as described in this section.

3. Disconnect the wire connector at the TP sensor.

4. Connect the voltmeter to the harness side of the connector and measure input voltage as follows:

   a. Check that all wires are secure in the connector.

   b. Identify the red wire terminal in the connector (**Figure 127** or **Figure 128**).

   c. Connect the voltmeter positive lead to the red wire terminal and the negative lead to the engine or frame ground.

   d. Turn on the ignition switch and read the voltage measurement. Turn off the ignition switch and record the measurement.

   e. Identify the black/brown wire terminal in the connector (**Figure 127** or **Figure 128**).

   f. Connect the voltmeter positive lead to the red wire terminal and the negative lead to the black/brown wire terminal.

   g. Turn on the ignition switch and read the voltage measurement. Turn off the ignition switch and record the measurement

   h. Compare both input voltage measurements with the specification in **Table 11**.

   i. If the measurements are within specification, the wire harness, connectors and electronic control module (ECM) are in good condition.

   j. If the measurements are not within specification, inspect the wire harness and connectors for shorts, poor connections and open circuits. For 2003-2006 models, inspect the wires in the ECM connector at positions 10 and 34. For 2007-on models, inspect the wires in the ECM connector at positions 5 and 12. If the harness and connectors are in good condition continue the TP sensor tests.

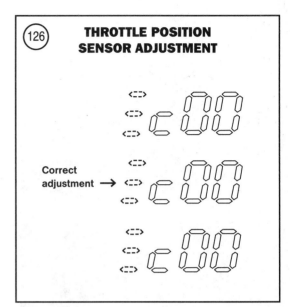

THROTTLE POSITION
SENSOR ADJUSTMENT

Correct
adjustment →

Continuity and Resistance Tests

2003-2006 models only

Perform the input voltage test in this section before the continuity test. An ohmmeter is required to

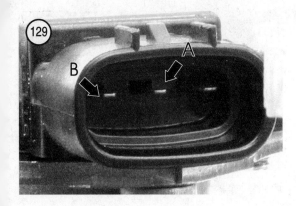

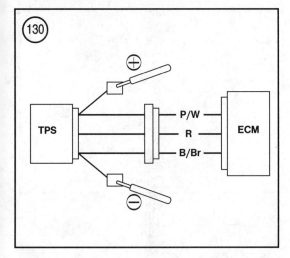

check continuity and resistance in the TP sensor (**Figure 124**).

1. If the throttle body assembly is installed on the motorcycle, do the following:

   a. Do not turn on the ignition switch during the test.

   b. Raise the fuel tank as described in this section.

   c. Disconnect the wire connector at the TP sensor.

2. Connect the ohmmeter to the sensor and check for continuity as follows:

   a. Connect one ohmmeter lead to the center terminal (A, **Figure 129**) and the other lead to the throttle body, engine or frame ground.

   b. Check for continuity. There should be no continuity between the sensor and ground. If continuity exists, replace the TP sensor.

3. Connect the ohmmeter to the sensor and measure resistance as follows:

a. Connect one ohmmeter lead to the center terminal (A, **Figure 129**) and the other lead to the left terminal (B). Check that the plug is oriented as shown so the correct terminals are tested.

b. Measure and record the resistance reading with the throttle closed.

c. Measure and record the resistance reading with the throttle fully open.

d. Compare the resistance measurements with the specifications in **Table 11**.

e. If the measurements are within specifications, continue the TP sensor tests.

f. If the measurements are not within specifications, perform the adjustment procedure in this section. If the sensor cannot be adjusted properly, replace the TP sensor.

Output Voltage Test

All models

Perform the input voltage test in this section before the output voltage test. A voltmeter and the Suzuki TPS test wire harness (part No. 09900-28630) or equivalent are required to measure output voltage of the TP sensor (**Figure 128**). If necessary, refer to the appropriate wiring diagram at the back of the manual for numbering of the ECU connector.

1. Check that the ignition switch is turned off.

2. Raise the fuel tank as described in this section.

3. Connect the test harness between the throttle position sensor and the wire harness (**Figure 130**).

4. Connect the positive meter probe to the pink/white wire connector.

5. Connect negative meter probe to the black/brown wire connector.

6. Measure the voltage as follows:

   a. Turn on the ignition switch.

   b. Measure and record the voltage reading with the throttle closed.

   c. Measure and record the voltage reading with the throttle fully open.

   d. Turn off the ignition switch.

   e. Compare the voltage measurements with the specifications in **Table 11**.

   f. If the measurements are within specifications, the TP sensor is in good condition.

16

g. If the measurements are not within specification, inspect the wire harness and connectors for shorts, poor connections and open circuits. For 2003-2006 models, inspect the wire in the ECM connector at position 19. For 2007-on models, inspect the wires in the ECM connector at position 21. If the harness and connectors are in good condition replace the TP sensor.

SECONDARY THROTTLE VALVE ACTUATOR "c28"

Operation Test

All models

1. Check that the ignition switch is turned off.
2. Raise the fuel tank and remove the air box lid so the secondary throttle valves can be viewed.
3. Check that all wires and connections are clean and secure in the STVA connector.
4. Check STVA operation as follows:
   a. Turn on the ignition switch and observe the operation of the secondary throttle valve (STV) (A, **Figure 131**) in each throttle body.
   b. The secondary throttle valves should fully open, then move to a partially open position (**Figure 132**).
   c. Turn off the ignition switch.
   d. If the secondary throttle valves operated correctly, the STVA unit is in good condition.
   e. If the secondary throttle valves operated correctly, but were not identically positioned, perform the STV synchronization procedure in this section. After synchronization, repeat the operation test.
   f. If the secondary throttle valves did not operate correctly, perform the continuity and resistance tests in this section to verify the condition of the STVA.

Continuity and Resistance Tests

2003-2006 models

Perform the operation test in this section before the continuity and resistance tests. An ohmmeter is required to check continuity and resistance in the STVA (B, **Figure 131**). If necessary, refer to the ap-

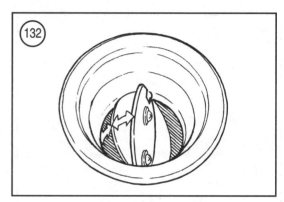

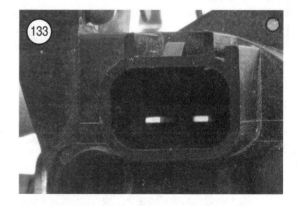

propriate wiring diagram at the back of the manual for numbering of the ECU connector.

1. If the throttle body assembly is installed on the motorcycle, do the following:

   a. Do not turn on the ignition switch during the test.

   b. Remove the air box as described in this section.

   c. Disconnect the connector at the STVA (**Figure 116**).

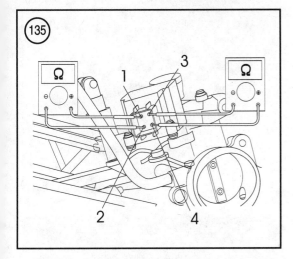

2. Connect the ohmmeter to the STVA and check for continuity as follows:

   a. Connect one ohmmeter lead to either STVA terminal (**Figure 133**) and the other lead to the throttle body, engine or frame ground.

   b. Check for continuity. There should be no continuity between the STVA and ground. If continuity exists, replace the STVA. If no continuity exists, check the STVA resistance.

3. Connect the ohmmeter to the STVA and measure resistance as follows:

   a. Connect the ohmmeter leads to the STVA terminals (**Figure 133**).

   b. Measure and record the resistance.

   c. Compare the resistance measurement with the specification in **Table 11**.

   d. If the measurement is within specification, the STVA is in good condition. Inspect the wire harness and connectors for shorts, poor connections and open circuits. Inspect the wires in the ECM connector at positions 20

and 22. If the harness and connectors are in good condition the ECM is malfunctioning.

   e. If the measurement is not within specification, replace the STVA.

2007-on models

Perform the operation test in this section before the continuity and resistance tests. An ohmmeter is required to check continuity and resistance in the STVA (**Figure 134**). If necessary, refer to the appropriate wiring diagram at the back of the manual for numbering of the ECU connector.

1. Remove the throttle bodies as described in this section.

2. Check for continuity between each terminal on the STVA (**Figure 135**) and ground. There should be no continuity between the STVA and ground. If continuity exists, replace the STVA. If no continuity exists, check the STVA resistance.

3. Connect the ohmmeter to the STVA and measure resistance as follows:

   a. Connect the ohmmeter leads to the STVA terminals 1 and 2 (**Figure 135**).

   b. Measure and record the resistance.

   c. Connect the ohmmeter leads to the STVA terminals 3 and 4 (**Figure 135**).

   d. Measure and record the resistance.

   e. Compare the resistance measurements with the specification in **Table 11**.

   f. If the measurements are within specification, the STVA is in good condition. Inspect the wire harness and connectors for shorts, poor connections and open circuits. Inspect the wires in the ECM connector at positions 35, 37, 44 and 46. If the harness and connectors are in good condition the ECM is malfunctioning.

   g. If the measurement is not within specification, replace the STVA.

FAST IDLE SPEED

2003-2006 Models Only

Operation

The fast idle speed is controlled by the secondary throttle valve actuator (STVA). The STVA turns a cam (A, **Figure 136**) that pushes the fast idle lever (B) and raises the idle speed. During operation, the STVA lowers the fast idle speed, depending on ambient temperature and engine coolant temperature. When the engine coolant reaches approximately 40-50° C (104-122° F), the fast idle system is canceled and the engine idles at normal idle speed.

Adjustment

A voltmeter and the Suzuki needle probe set (part No. 09900-25009) or equivalent are required to measure output voltage of the throttle position (TP) sensor (**Figure 124**) so the fast idle speed can be adjusted.

1. Check that the ignition switch is turned off.
2. Remove the air box as described in this section.
3. Disconnect the connector at the secondary throttle valve actuator (STVA) (**Figure 116**).
4. Check that all wires and connections are clean and secure in the TP sensor and connector. The connector must be locked to the TP sensor to perform the test.
5. Connect the voltmeter and needle probes to the connector as follows:
   a. Identify the pink/white and black/brown wires in the connector.
   b. At the back side of the connector, insert a needle probe into the pink/white wire connector. Connect the voltmeter positive lead to this probe.
   c. At the back side of the connector, insert a needle probe into the black/brown wire connector. Connect the voltmeter negative lead to this probe.
6. Measure and adjust the voltage as follows:
   a. Refer to **Table 11** for the required fast idle TP sensor output voltage.
   b. Turn on the ignition switch.
   c. At the No. 1 (front) throttle body, turn the shaft on the secondary throttle valve actuator (STVA) (**Figure 117**) until the secondary throttle valve (STV) is fully open. Note the TP sensor output voltage reading.
   d. If the voltage reading meets the required specification, the TP sensor is correctly adjusted.
   e. If the voltage reading does not meet the required specification, turn the fast idle adjustment screw (**Figure 137**) until the TP sensor is correctly adjusted.

   f. Turn off the ignition switch.

7. At engine startup, check the idle speed as described in *Lubrication, Maintenance and Tune-Up* in this Supplement.

> *NOTE*
> *If the fast idle speed does not cancel after the engine is at operating temperature, test the engine coolant temperature (ECT) sensor and wiring harness.*

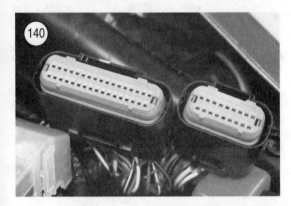

**IDLE SPEED CONTROL VALVE
"c40"**

2007-On Models Only

Continuity and resistance tests

An ohmmeter is required to check continuity and resistance in the idle speed control (ISC) valve (**Figure 138**). Refer to the appropriate wiring diagram at the back of the manual for numbering of the ECM connector.

1. Check that the ignition switch is turned off.

WARNING
In the following step, if the ignition switch has been turned on, do not disconnect the ISC valve coupler for at least five seconds after turning the ignition switch off.

2. Disconnect the ISC valve connector (**Figure 139**) and the ECM connector (**Figure 140**). To ease handling of the ISC valve, remove the two bolts securing it to the frame.

3. Check the harness for continuity between the specified terminals in the ISC valve connector (**Figure 139**) and the ECM connector.

  a. Check for continuity between the ISC connector terminal 1 and terminal 49 in the ECM connector.

  b. Check for continuity between the ISC connector terminal 2 and terminal 10 in the ECM connector.

  c. Check for continuity between the ISC connector terminal 3 and terminal 47 in the ECM connector.

  d. Check for continuity between the ISC connector terminal 4 and terminal 38 in the ECM connector.

  e. Check for continuity between the ISC connector terminal 5 and terminal 10 in the ECM connector.

  f. Check for continuity between the ISC connector terminal 6 and terminal 40 in the ECM connector.

  g. There should be continuity for each of the checks. If continuity does not exist for any of the checks, inspect the wire harness and connectors for shorts, poor connections and open circuits.

  h. If the harness and connectors are in good condition, continue the tests.

4. Check for continuity between the terminals on the ISC valve (**Figure 141**) as follows:

  a. Check for continuity between terminal 1 and terminal 2.

  b. Check for continuity between terminal 3 and terminal 4.

  c. There should be no continuity between the terminals checked. If continuity exists, replace the ISC valve.

  d. If there is no continuity between the checked terminals, continue the tests.

16

5. Check for resistance between the terminals on the ISC valve (**Figure 141**) as follows:
   a. Check for resistance between terminal 1 and terminal 2. Measure and record the resistance.
   b. Check for resistance between terminal 3 and terminal 4. Measure and record the resistance.
   c. Compare the resistance measurements with the specification in **Table 11**.
   d. If the measurements are not within specification, replace the ISC valve.

ISC Valve Replacement Preset

Anytime the ISC valve is removed from the fuel injection system, it must be preset before starting the engine. The Mode Select Switch (part No. 09930-82720) is used to preset the ISC valve.

1. Install the ISC valve into the fuel injection system.
2. Connect the mode select switch to the dealer mode coupler (**Figure 142**).
3. Turn the mode select switch to the ON position.
4. Turn on the ignition switch.
5. Turn off the ignition switch.
6. Wait for at least 10 seconds so the ISC valve can preset itself.
7. Turn the mode select switch to the OFF position and disconnect it from the dealer mode coupler.

CRANKSHAFT POSITION SENSOR
"c12"

The crankshaft position (CKP) sensor (also called the signal generator in Chapter Nine of this manual) is located inside the alternator cover. The sensor can be tested at the wire connector (**Figure 143**) located under the rear frame cover.

Continuity and Resistance Tests

An ohmmeter is required to check continuity and resistance in the CKP sensor.

1. Do not turn on the ignition switch during the test.
2. Remove the rear frame cover as described in this Supplement.
3. Disconnect the CKP wire connector (**Figure 143**). The sensor harness contains a green wire and either a blue or white wire. Refer to the appropriate wiring diagram at the back of the manual to verify wire colors for the model being serviced.

4. Check that both wires and terminals are clean and secure in the harness leading to the sensor.
5. Connect the ohmmeter to the sensor connector and check for continuity as follows:
   a. Connect one ohmmeter lead to the green wire terminal and the other lead to the engine or frame ground.
   b. Check for continuity.
   c. Repeat the procedure and check for continuity in the other wire.
   d. There should be no continuity between either wire and ground. If continuity exists, replace the CKP sensor.
6. Connect the ohmmeter to the sensor connector and measure resistance as follows:
   a. Connect the ohmmeter leads to the wire terminals.
   b. Measure and record the resistance reading.
   c. Compare the resistance measurement with the specification in **Table 11**.
   d. If the measurement is within specification, perform the peak voltage test to verify the condition of the CKP sensor.
   e. If the measurement is not within specification, replace the TP sensor.

Peak Voltage Test

Perform the continuity and resistance tests in this section before the peak voltage test. A voltmeter and peak voltage adapter is required to measure peak voltage of the CKP sensor. The peak voltage adapter is part of the Suzuki multi-circuit tester (part No. 09900-25008). An equivalent adapter is the Motion Pro Ignition Mate (part No. 08-0193). Follow the manufacturer's instructions when using either adapter. If necessary, refer to the appropriate wiring diagram at the back of the manual for numbering of the ECU connector.

1. Check that the ignition switch is turned off.
2. Shift the transmission into neutral.
3. Remove the rear frame cover as described in this Supplement.
4. Disconnect the CKP wire connector (**Figure 143**). The sensor harness contains a green wire and either a blue or white wire. Refer to the appropriate wiring diagram at the back of the manual to verify wire colors for the model being serviced.
5. Check that both wires and terminals are clean and secure in the harness leading to the sensor.

6. Connect the voltmeter to the sensor side of the connector and measure peak voltage as follows:

a. Identify the green wire terminal in the connector. Connect the voltmeter negative lead to this terminal.

b. Connect the voltmeter positive lead to the terminal of the other wire.

WARNING
When cranking the engine in the following step, high voltage is present in the ignition system. Do not touch wires or test leads while cranking the engine.

c. Turn on the ignition switch and crank the engine several times. Read the voltage measurements while the engine is cranking. Turn off the ignition switch and record the highest voltage measurement. Repeat this step and determine the highest voltage measurement.

d. Compare the peak voltage measurement with the specification in **Table 11**.

e. If the measurement is within specification, the CKP sensor is in good condition.

f. If the measurement is not within specification, inspect the wire harness and connectors for shorts, poor connections and open circuits. For 2003-2006 models, inspect the wires in the ECM connector at positions 26 and 30. For 2007-on models, inspect the wires in the ECM connector at positions 8 and 27. If the harness and connectors are in good condition the ECM is malfunctioning.

INTAKE AIR PRESSURE SENSORS
"c13" or c17

For 2003-2006 models, there is one intake air pressure (IAP) sensor, located at the rear of the air box (**Figure 144**). The c13 trouble code will appear when this sensor malfunctions.

For 2007-on models, there are two intake air pressure sensors, located at the rear of the air box (**Figure 145**). The c13 trouble code will appear when the sensor for the rear cylinder (right side of air box) malfunctions. The c17 trouble code will appear when the sensor for the front cylinder (left side of air box) malfunctions.

16

Input Voltage Test

A voltmeter is required to measure input voltage to the IAP sensor(s). If necessary, refer to the appropriate wiring diagram at the back of the manual for numbering of the ECU connector.

1. Check that the ignition switch is turned off.
2. Raise the fuel tank as described in this section.
3. Disconnect the wire connector at the IAP sensor.
4. Connect the voltmeter to the harness connector and measure input voltage as follows:

   a. Check that all wires are secure in the connector.
   b. Identify the red wire terminal in the connector (**Figure 146**).
   c. Connect the voltmeter positive lead to the red wire terminal and the negative lead to the engine or frame ground.
   d. Turn on the ignition switch and read the voltage measurement. Turn off the ignition switch and record the measurement.
   e. Identify the black/brown wire terminal in the connector (**Figure 146**).
   f. Connect the voltmeter positive lead to the red wire terminal and the negative lead to the black/brown wire terminal.
   g. Turn on the ignition switch and read the voltage measurement. Turn off the ignition switch and record the measurement.
   h. Compare both input voltage measurements with the specification in **Table 11**.
   i. If the measurements are within specification, the wire harness, connectors and electronic control module (ECM) are in good condition.
   j. If the measurements are not within specification, inspect the wire harness and connectors for shorts, poor connections and open circuits. For 2003-2006 models, inspect the wires in the ECM connector at positions 10 and 34. For 2007-on models, inspect the wires in the ECM connector at positions 5 and 12. If the harness and connectors are in good condition perform the Output Voltage Test.

Output Voltage Test

Perform the input voltage test in this section before the output voltage test. A voltmeter and the Suzuki needle probe set (part No. 09900-25009) or equivalent are required to measure output voltage

of the IAP sensor(s) (**Figure 147**). If necessary, refer to the appropriate wiring diagram at the back of the manual for numbering of the ECU connector.

1. Warm up the engine to operating temperature.
2. Check that the ignition switch is turned off.
3. Raise the fuel tank as described in this section.
4. Check that all wires and connections are clean and secure in the IAP sensor and connector. The connector must be locked to the sensor to perform the test.
5. Connect the voltmeter and needle probes to the connector as follows:

   a. Identify the green/black and black/brown wires in the connector. For 2007-on models, these wire colors are for the front cylinder sensor. If testing the rear cylinder sensor, use the green/yellow and black brown wires.
   b. At the back side of the connector, insert a needle probe into the green/black wire connector. Connect the voltmeter positive lead to this probe. For 2007-on models, a green/black wire is used for the front cylinder sensor. If testing the rear cylinder sensor, use the green/yellow wire.

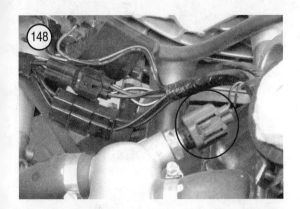

c. At the back side of the connector, insert a needle probe into the black/brown wire connector. Connect the voltmeter negative lead to this probe.

6. Measure the voltage as follows:

a. Start the engine and allow it to idle.

b. Measure and record the voltage.

c. Turn off the ignition switch.

d. Compare the voltage measurement with the specification in **Table 11**.

e. If the measurement is within specification, the IAP sensor is in good condition.

f. If the measurement is not within specification, inspect the wiring, sensor and vacuum hose for damage, leaks and clogs. For 2003-2006 models, inspect the wire in the ECM connector at position 16. For 2007-on models, inspect the wires in the ECM connector at positions 3 (front cylinder) and 22 (rear cylinder). If the harness and connectors are in good condition, replace the IAP sensor(s).

ENGINE COOLANT TEMPERATURE SENSOR "c15"

The engine coolant temperature (ECT) sensor is located on the thermostat housing (**Figure 148**). If necessary, refer to the appropriate wiring diagram at the back of the manual for numbering of the ECU connector.

Input Voltage Test

A voltmeter is required to measure input voltage to the ECT sensor. If necessary, refer to the appropriate wiring diagram at the back of the manual for numbering of the ECU connector.

1. Check that the ignition switch is turned off.

2. Remove the throttle body assembly as described in this section.

3. Disconnect the wire connector at the ECT sensor.

4. Connect the voltmeter to the harness connector and measure input voltage as follows:

a. Check that all wires are secure in the connector.

b. Identify the black/blue wire terminal in the connector (**Figure 149**).

c. Connect the voltmeter positive lead to the black/blue wire terminal and the negative lead to the engine or frame ground.

d. Turn on the ignition switch and read the voltage measurement. Turn off the ignition switch and record the measurement.

e. Identify the black/brown wire terminal in the connector (**Figure 149**).

f. Connect the voltmeter positive lead to the black/blue wire terminal and the negative lead to the black/brown wire terminal.

g. Turn on the ignition switch and read the voltage measurement. Turn off the ignition switch and record the measurement

h. Compare both input voltage measurements with the specification in **Table 11**.

i. If the measurements are within specification, the wire harness, connectors and electronic control module (ECM) are in good condition.

j. If the measurements are not within specification, inspect the wire harness and connectors for shorts, poor connections and open circuits. For 2003-2006 models, inspect the wires in the ECM connector at positions 34

16

and 36. For 2007-on models, inspect the wires in the ECM connector at positions 19 and 12. If the harness and connectors are in good condition, perform the Resistance Test.

Resistance Test

Perform the input voltage test in this section before the resistance test. The following test requires that the sensor be placed in heated water, to simulate actual operating conditions. Read and understand the procedure so the proper equipment is on hand to safely and accurately perform the test. An ohmmeter is required to measure resistance in the ECT sensor.

1. Remove the sensor from the thermostat housing.
2. Refer to **Table 11** and note the four temperatures and corresponding resistance measurements for the sensor.
3. Test the sensor as follows:
   a. Fill a container with water that is 20° C (68° F).
   b. Connect an ohmmeter to the sensor terminals and suspend it in the water. Measure and record the meter reading.
   c. Repeat substep a and substep b, progressively increasing the water temperature in the container.
4. Compare all temperatures and measurements to the specifications in **Table 11**.
   a. If the sensor is within the resistance specification for each temperature, the ECT is in good condition and the ECM is malfunctioning.
   b. If the sensor is not within the resistance specification for each temperature, replace the ECT sensor.

INTAKE AIR TEMPERATURE SENSOR "c21"

The intake air temperature (IAT) sensor is located at the rear of the air box. For 2003-2006 models, refer to **Figure 150**. For 2007-on models, refer to **Figure 151**.

Input Voltage Test

A voltmeter is required to measure input voltage to the IAT sensor.
1. Check that the ignition switch is turned off.

2. Raise the fuel tank as described in this section.
3. Disconnect the wire connector at the IAT sensor.
4. Connect the voltmeter to the harness connector and measure input voltage as follows:
   a. Check that all wires are secure in the connector.
   b. Identify the dark green wire terminal in the connector (**Figure 149**).
   c. Connect the voltmeter positive lead to the dark green wire terminal and the negative lead to the engine or frame ground.
   d. Turn on the ignition switch and read the voltage measurement. Turn off the ignition switch and record the measurement.
   e. Identify the black/brown wire terminal in the connector (**Figure 149**).
   f. Connect the voltmeter positive lead to the dark green wire terminal and the negative lead to the black/brown wire terminal.
   g. Turn on the ignition switch and read the voltage measurement. Turn off the ignition switch and record the measurement
   h. Compare both input voltage measurements with the specification in **Table 11**.

i. If the measurements are within specification, the wire harness, connectors and electronic control module (ECM) are in good condition.

j. If the measurements are not within specification, inspect the wire harness and connectors for shorts, poor connections and open circuits. For 2003-2006 models, inspect the wires in the ECM connector at positions 14 and 34. For 2007-on models, inspect the wires in the ECM connector at positions 2 and 12. If the harness and connectors are in good condition, perform the *Resistance Test*.

Resistance Test

Perform the input voltage test in this section before the resistance test. The following test requires that the sensor probe be placed in heated water, to simulate actual operating conditions. Read and understand the procedure so the proper equipment is on hand to safely and accurately perform the test. An ohmmeter is required to measure resistance in the IAT sensor.

1. Remove the sensor (**Figure 152** or **Figure 153**) from the air box.
2. Refer to **Table 11** and note the four temperatures and corresponding resistance measurements for the sensor.
3. Test the sensor as follows:
   a. Fill a container with water that is 20° C (68° F).
   b. Connect an ohmmeter to the sensor terminals and suspend the probe in the water. Measure and record the meter reading.
   c. Repeat substep a and substep b, progressively increasing the water temperature in the container.
4. Compare all temperatures and measurements to the specifications in **Table 11**.
   a. If the sensor is within the resistance specification for each temperature, the IAT is in good condition and the ECM is malfunctioning.
   b. If the sensor is not within the resistance specification for each temperature, replace the IAT sensor.

TIP OVER SENSOR
"c23"

The tip over (TO) sensor is located in front of the battery (**Figure 154**).

Resistance Test

An ohmmeter is required to check resistance in the TO sensor.

1. Do not turn on the ignition switch during the test.
2. Remove the right side cover as described in this Supplement.
3. Remove the sensor and disconnect the wire connector.
4. Check that the wires and terminals are clean and secure in the connector (**Figure 155**).

16

5. Connect the ohmmeter to the connector and check for resistance as follows:

    a. Connect one ohmmeter lead to the red wire terminal and the other lead to the black/brown wire terminal.

    b. Measure and record the resistance reading.

    c. Compare the resistance measurement with the specification in **Table 11**.

    d. If the measurement is within specification, perform the voltage test to verify the condition of the TO sensor.

    e. If the measurement is not within specification, replace the TO sensor.

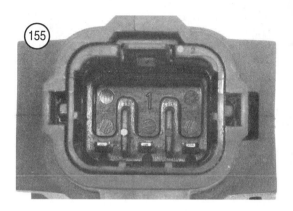

Voltage Test

Perform the resistance test in this section before the voltage test. A voltmeter and the Suzuki needle probe set (part No. 09900-25009) or equivalent are required to measure voltage in the TO sensor. If necessary, refer to the appropriate wiring diagram at the back of the manual for numbering of the ECU connector.

1. Check that the ignition switch is turned off. If necessary, refer to the appropriate wiring diagram at the back of the manual for numbering of the ECU connector.

2. Remove the right side cover as described in this Supplement.

3. Check that all wires and connections are clean and secure in the TO sensor and connector. The connector must be locked to the sensor to perform the test.

4. Connect the voltmeter and needle probes to the connector (A, **Figure 156**) as follows:

    a. Identify the brown/white and black/brown wires in the connector.

    b. At the back side of the connector, insert a needle probe into the brown/white wire connector. Connect the voltmeter positive lead to this probe.

    c. At the back side of the connector, insert a needle probe into the black/brown wire connector. Connect the voltmeter negative lead to this probe.

5. Measure the voltage as follows:

    a. Position the sensor so it is level and the arrow on the sensor points up (B, **Figure 156**).

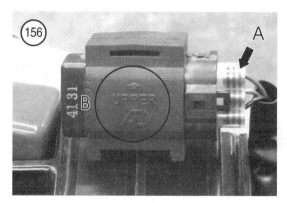

    b. Turn on the ignition switch and read the voltage measurement. Turn off the ignition switch and record the measurement.

    c. Tilt the sensor 65° to the left (**Figure 157**).

    d. Turn on the ignition switch and read the voltage measurement. Turn off the ignition switch and record the measurement.

    e. Tilt the sensor 65° to the right.

    f. Turn on the ignition switch and read the voltage measurement. Turn off the ignition switch and record the measurement.

    g. Compare all voltage measurements with the specifications in **Table 11**.

    h. If the voltages meet the specifications in **Table 11**, the TO sensor is in good condition.

    i. If the voltages do not meet the specifications in **Table 11**, inspect the wire harness and connectors for shorts, poor connections and open circuits. For 2003-2006 models, inspect the wires in the ECM connector at positions 10, 34 and 41. For 2007-on models, inspect the wires in the ECM connector at positions 5, 12 and 20. Repeat the voltage test. If the voltages do not meet specification, replace the TO sensor. If voltage readings continue to be out of

specification after sensor replacement and wire harness inspection, the ECM is malfunctioning.

GEAR POSITION SWITCH "c31"

The gear position (GP) switch is located near the shift lever. The wire connector (**Figure 158**) is located above the switch and under the fuel tank.

Continuity Test

An ohmmeter is required to check continuity in the GP switch.

1. Do not turn on the ignition switch during the test.
2. Raise the fuel tank as described in this section.
3. Shift the transmission into neutral.
4. Disconnect the wire connector (**Figure 158**).
5. Connect the ohmmeter to the connector half leading to the GP switch as follows:
   a. Check that all wires are secure in the connector.

b. Identify the blue and black/white wire terminals in the connector.
   c. Connect an ohmmeter lead to each wire terminal.
6. Check for continuity. There should be continuity in neutral. If there is no continuity in neutral, replace the switch.
7. Shift the transmission into all gears and check for continuity. There should be no continuity in any gear position except neutral. If continuity exists in any position except neutral, replace the GP switch.

Voltage Test

A voltmeter and the Suzuki needle probe set (part No. 09900-25009) or equivalent are required to measure GP switch voltages. If necessary, refer to the appropriate wiring diagram at the back of the manual for numbering of the ECU connector.

1. Check that the ignition switch is turned off.
2. Raise the fuel tank as described in this section.
3. Check that all wires and connections are clean and secure in the connector (**Figure 158**). The connector must be locked together to perform the test.
4. Connect the voltmeter to the connector as follows:
   a. Identify the pink and black/white wires in the connector.
   b. At the back side of the connector, insert a needle probe into the pink wire connector. Connect the voltmeter positive lead to this probe.
   c. At the back side of the connector, insert a needle probe into the black/white wire connector. Connect the voltmeter negative lead to this probe.
   d. Secure the voltmeter so it does not have to be handled during the test.
5. Refer to **Table 11** and note the required voltage for each gear position.
6. Place the engine stop switch in the run position.
7. Place the side stand in the up position.
8. Measure the voltage for each gear as follows.
   a. Turn on the ignition switch.
   b. Shift the transmission into first gear
   c. Measure and record the voltage reading.
   d. Repeat substep b and substep c for all remaining gears.
   e. Turn off the ignition switch and lower the side stand.

16

f. If the voltages meet the specifications in **Table 11**, the switch is in good condition.

g. If the voltages do not meet the specifications in **Table 11**, inspect the wire harness and connectors for shorts, poor connections and open circuits. For 2003-2006 models, inspect the wires in the ECM connector at positions 26 and 31. For 2007-on models, inspect the wire in the ECM connector at position 1. Repeat the voltage test. If the voltages do not meet specification, replace the GP switch. If voltage readings continue to be out of specification after switch replacement and wire harness inspection, the ECM is malfunctioning.

IGNITION SWITCH
"c42"

Continuity Test

An ohmmeter is required to check continuity in the ignition switch and wiring harness. Inspect the ignition switch, wire harness and connectors for shorts, poor connections and open circuits. If the switch and harness are in good condition, the electronic control module (ECM) is malfunctioning.

IGNITION COILS
"c24 or c25"

The ignition coils are located under the fuel tank. The No. 1 cylinder coil (c24) is at the left side of the engine and the No. 2 cylinder coil (c25) is at the right side.

Resistance Tests

An ohmmeter is required to check resistance in the coils.

1. Do not turn on the ignition switch during the test.
2. Raise the fuel tank as described in this section.
3. Disconnect the spark plug leads and the coil wire couplers.
4. Connect the ohmmeter to the coil and measure primary resistance as follows:

a. Connect the ohmmeter leads to the positive terminal (black/orange or orange/white wire) and the negative terminal (black or white/blue wire) (**Figure 159**).

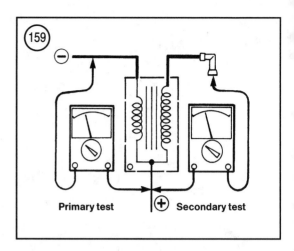

Primary test · Secondary test

b. Measure and record the resistance reading.

5. Connect the ohmmeter to the coil and spark plug cap and measure secondary resistance as follows:

a. Connect the ohmmeter leads to the positive terminal (black/orange or orange/white wire) and the spark plug cap (**Figure 159**).

b. Measure and record the resistance reading.

6. Compare the resistance measurements with the specification in **Table 11**.

a. If the measurements are within specification, perform the peak voltage test to verify the condition of the coil.

b. If the measurements are not within specification, replace the coil.

Peak Voltage Test

Perform the resistance tests in this section before the peak voltage test. A voltmeter and peak voltage adapter is required to measure peak voltage of the coils. The peak voltage adapter is part of the Suzuki multi-circuit tester (part No. 09900-25008). An equivalent adapter is the Motion Pro Ignition Mate (part No. 08-0193). Follow the manufacturer's instructions when using either adapter.

1. Check that the ignition switch is turned off.
2. Shift the transmission into neutral.
3. Remove the air box as described in this section.
4. Attach a new spark plug to each spark plug cap and ground the plugs on the engine.

CAUTION
To prevent possible damage to the electrical system, the spark plugs must be grounded.

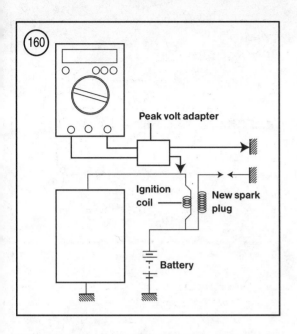

5. Connect the voltmeter and needle probes to the coil positive wire connector as follows:

a. The positive wire for the coils may be black, black/white or white/blue. Insert the positive needle probe into the back side of this connector (**Figure 160**). The black, black/white or white/blue wire must remain connected to the coil to perform the test.

b. Connect the voltmeter negative lead to ground.

WARNING
When cranking the engine in the following step, high voltage is present in the ignition system. Do not touch wires or test leads while cranking the engine.

c. Turn on the ignition switch and crank the engine several times. Read the voltage measurements while the engine is cranking. Turn off the ignition switch and record the highest voltage measurement.

d. Compare the peak voltage measurement with the specification in **Table 11**.

e. If the measurement is within specification, the coil is in good condition.

f. If the measurement is not within specification, replace the coil.

CRANKCASE BREATHER SYSTEM

All models are equipped with a positive crankcase ventilation system. This system routes blow-by gasses from the crankcase to the air box. The gasses are mixed with intake air and passed through the throttle bodies and into the combustion chamber.

A breather hose is connected at the rear of the front cylinder and at the rear of the crankcase. The hoses are individually routed to the air box.

PAIR SYSTEM

All models are equipped with an exhaust emission control system (**Figure 161**). This system reduces emissions by introducing fresh air into the exhaust port to burn remaining combustible gasses. The flow of fresh air into the system is regulated by the PAIR control solenoid. This valve is controlled by the electronic control module (ECM). The ECM opens or closes the valve based on the signals received from the throttle position (TP) sensor, engine coolant temperature (ECT) sensor, intake air temperature (IAT) sensor and intake air pressure (IAP) sensor.

Fresh air that is passed through the PAIR control solenoid enters the engine through the PAIR reed valves. The reed valves are one-way valves that prevent backflow in the fresh air hose. Inspect the PAIR reed valves and PAIR control solenoid valve as described in this section.

PAIR REED VALVES

Tests

A PAIR reed valve is located on each cylinder head cover (**Figure 161**).

1. Disconnect the fresh air hose from the reed valve fitting

2. Blow air through the fitting and reed valve. Air should pass through the reed valve.

3. Apply suction to the hose fitting. Air should not pass through the reed valve.

4. If the reed valve fails either test, inspect the reed valve for cleanliness. If the reed valve fails either test after cleaning, replace the reed valve.

16

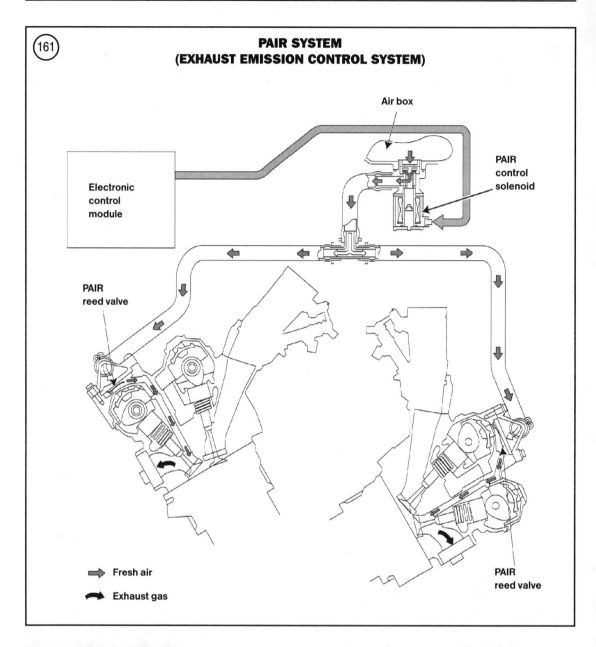

**PAIR SYSTEM
(EXHAUST EMISSION CONTROL SYSTEM)**

Air box

PAIR
control
solenoid

Electronic
control
module

PAIR
reed valve

PAIR
reed valve

➡ Fresh air

➡ Exhaust gas

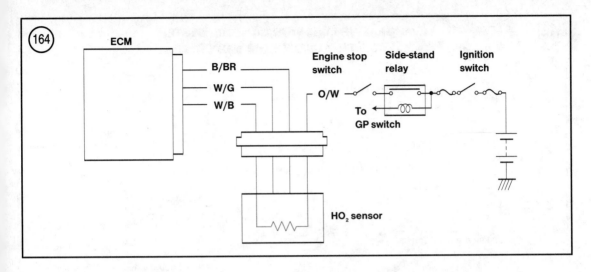

PAIR CONTROL SOLENOID
"c49"

The pair control solenoid is located on the bottom of the air box. For 1999-2006 models, refer to **Figure 162**. For 2007-on models, refer to **Figure 163**.

Resistance Test

Perform the PAIR reed valve tests in this section before the resistance test. An ohmmeter is required to check resistance in the PAIR solenoid.

1. Remove the air box as described in this section.
2. Check that all wires and connections are clean and secure in the connector.
3. Check for resistance as follows:
   a. Connect the ohmmeter leads to the wire terminals.
   b. Measure and record the resistance reading.
   c. Compare the resistance measurement with the specification in **Table 11**.
   d. If the measurement is within specification, perform the voltage test as described in this section.
   e. If the measurement is not within specification, replace the solenoid.

Voltage Test

Perform the resistance test in this section before the voltage test. A voltmeter and the Suzuki needle probe set (part No. 09900-25009) or equivalent are required to measure voltage in the solenoid.

1. With the solenoid wires connector coupled to the wiring harness, test voltage as follows:
   a. At the back side of the connector, insert the positive needle probe into the brown wire connector.
   b. Connect the remaining lead to ground.
   c. Turn on the ignition.
   d. Measure the voltage reading.
   e. The measurement should be battery voltage.
   f. If the measurement is battery voltage, the solenoid is in good condition. Inspect the wire harness and connectors for shorts, poor connections and open circuits. If the harness and connectors are in good condition, the electronic control module (ECM) is malfunctioning.

HEATED OXYGEN SENSOR
"c44"

2007-on California Models Only

The heated oxygen sensor is located in the exhaust system. The electrical connector for the sensor is located behind the right side cover, near the brake fluid reservoir. All electrical tests are performed at this connector.

A volt/ohmmeter and the Suzuki needle probe set (part No. 09900-25009) or equivalent are required to check continuity, resistance and voltage in the HO2 sensor circuit and wiring harness. Refer to **Figure 164**. Refer to the appropriate wiring dia-

16

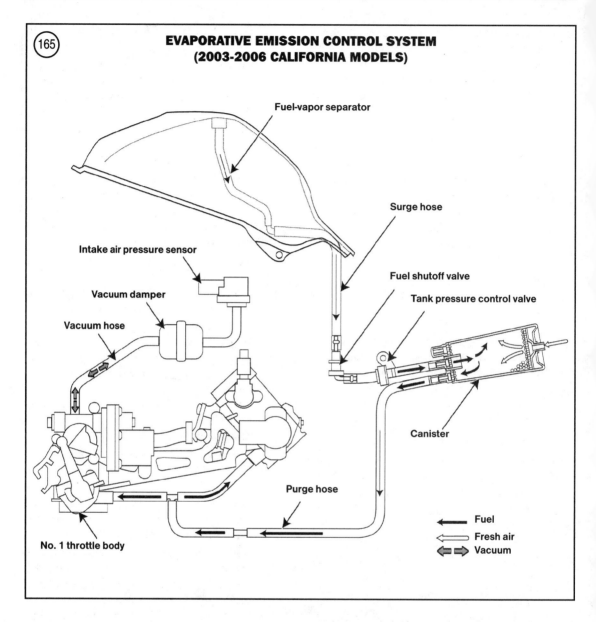

**EVAPORATIVE EMISSION CONTROL SYSTEM
(2003-2006 CALIFORNIA MODELS)**

(165)

Fuel-vapor separator

Surge hose

Intake air pressure sensor

Fuel shutoff valve

Tank pressure control valve

Vacuum damper

Vacuum hose

Canister

Purge hose

Fuel

Fresh air

Vacuum

No. 1 throttle body

gram at the back of the manual for numbering of the ECU connector.

Continuity Tests

If necessary, refer to the appropriate wiring diagram at the back of the manual for numbering of the ECU connector.

1. Check that the ignition switch is turned off.

2. Disconnect the HO_2 sensor connector.

3. Using an ohmmeter, check for continuity between the white/green wire and ground. There should be no continuity.

4. Check for continuity between the white/green wire and black/brown wire. There should be no continuity.

5. Disconnect the harness connector at the ECM. Check the harness for continuity between the white/green wire and and terminal 6 in the connector. There should be continuity.

6. Check the harness for continuity between the black/brown wire and and terminal 12 in the connector. There should be continuity.

7. Check the harness for continuity between the white/black wire and and terminal 17 in the connector. There should be continuity.

a. If all continuity tests are okay, perform the resistance tests to verify the condition of the sensor.

b. If any of the continuity tests failed, check the white/green and black/brown wires for shorts or breaks.

Resistance Test

1. Check that the ignition switch is turned off.
2. Disconnect the HO_2 sensor connector.
3. Using an ohmmeter, check for resistance between the two white terminals.

a. Measure and record the resistance reading.

b. Compare the resistance measurement with the specification in **Table 11**.

c. If the measurement is within specification, perform the voltage tests as described in this section.

d. If the measurement is not within specification, replace the sensor.

Voltage Tests

The following voltage tests will measure HO2 sensor heater voltage, and sensor output voltage at idle and at 5000 rpm. An voltmeter and the Suzuki needle probe set (part No. 09900-25009) or equivalent are required to check voltage in the HO2 sensor circuit and wiring harness. Refer to **Figure 164**. Refer to the appropriate wiring diagram at the back of the manual for numbering of the ECU connector.

1. Connect the HO2 sensor coupler to the wiring harness.
2. Measure heater voltage as follows:

a. At the back side of the connector containing the white/black wire, insert the positive needle probe.

b. Ground the negative probe.

c. Turn on the ignition and measure the voltage. The voltage should be battery voltage.

d. Turn off the ignition switch.

e. If the measurement is battery voltage, continue the voltage tests.

f. If the measurement is not battery voltage, recheck the wiring for an intermittent short or break.

3. Start and warm up the engine.
4. With the engine at idle speed, measure the sensor idle speed voltage as follows:

a. At the back side of the connector containing the white/green wire, insert the positive needle probe.

b. At the back side of the connector containing the black/brown wire, insert the negative needle probe.

c. Measure and record the voltage reading.

d. Turn off the ignition switch.

e. Compare the voltage measurement with the specification in **Table 11**.

f. If the measurement is within specification, continue the voltage tests.

g. If the measurement is not within specification, replace the sensor.

5. Measure the sensor high-speed voltage as follows:

a. Use a suitable clamp to pinch shut the hose leading to the PAIR solenoid valve. The hose is visible at the T-fitting at the right side of the frame, below the fuel tank.

b. At the back side of the connector containing the white/green wire, insert the positive needle probe.

c. At the back side of the connector containing the black/brown wire, insert the negative needle probe.

d. Start the engine and temporarily raise the speed to 5000 rpm while observing the voltmeter.

e. Measure and record the voltage reading.

f. Compare the voltage measurement with the specification in **Table 11**.

g. If the measurement is within specification, recheck the wiring for an intermittent short or break. If the sensor and all wiring are in good condition, the ECM is faulty.

h. If the measurement is not within specification, replace the sensor.

EVAPORATIVE EMISSION CONTROL SYSTEM

California Models Only

The evaporative emission control system (**Figure 165** or **Figure 166**) prevents fuel vapor from entering the atmosphere. When the engine is not running, fuel vapor from the fuel tank is routed to the canister. At engine startup, the vapor is drawn through the throttle bodies and into the combustion chamber.

16

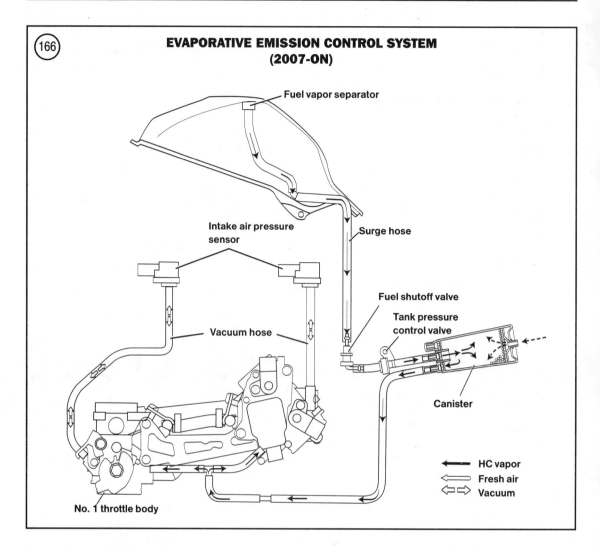

EVAPORATIVE EMISSION CONTROL SYSTEM (2007-ON)

Fuel vapor separator

Intake air pressure sensor

Surge hose

Fuel shutoff valve

Tank pressure control valve

Vacuum hose

Canister

No. 1 throttle body

HC vapor
Fresh air
Vacuum

Inspection and Test

1. Inspect the hoses and components of the emission control system for damage. Replace hoses that are loose or cracked.

2. Test the tank pressure control valve as follows:

   a. Remove the tank pressure control valve from the surge hose.

   b. Blow air through the inlet fitting (A, **Figure 167**). Air should pass through the valve.

   c. Blow air through the outlet fitting (B, **Figure 167**). Air should not pass through the valve.

   d. If the valve fails either test, replace the valve.

3. Install the tank pressure control valve with the stepped side (A, **Figure 167**) facing the canister.

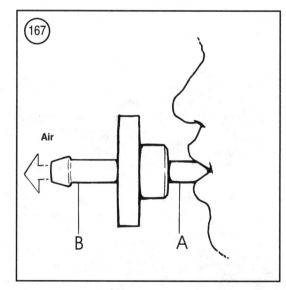

Air

B   A

Table 10 FUEL INJECTION SYSTEM SPECIFICATIONS

Identification number	
California models	
2003-2006	17G1
2007-on	17G3
All other models	
2003-2006	17G0
2007-on	17G2
Bore diameter	39 mm
Idle speed	1200-1400 rpm
Fast speed	
2003-2006	1800-2400 rpm
2007-on	1800-2200 rpm

Table 11 FUEL INJECTION AND EMISSION SYSTEMS SPECIFICATIONS

Crankshaft position (CKP) sensor	
Peak voltage	3.7 volts minimum
Resistance	130-240 ohms
Engine coolant temperature (ECT) sensor	
Input voltage	4.5-5.5 volts
Resistance	2450 ohms at 20° C (68° F)
	1148 ohms at 40° C (104° F)
	587 ohms at 60° C (140° F)
	322 ohms at 80° C (176° F)
Fuel injector	
Input voltage	Battery voltage
Resistance	11-13 ohms at 20° C (68° F)
Gear position (GP) switch voltage	1.0 volts or more for all gears
Heated oxygen sensor	
2007-on Calif., U.K., EU, Aust., models only	
Output voltage at idle	0.3 volts or less
Output voltage at 5000 rpm	0.6 volts and more
Heated oxygen sensor resistance	
2007-on Calif., U.K., EU, Aust., models only	6.5-9.5 ohms at 23° C (73° F)
Idle speed control (ISC) valve resistance	
2007-on models only	29-31 ohms at 20° C (68° F)
Ignition coil	
Primary peak voltage	150 volts minimum
Primary resistance	2.0-5.0 ohms
Secondary resistance	24,000-37,000 ohms
Intake air pressure (IAP) sensor	
Input voltage	4.5-5.5 volts
Output voltage	Approximately 2.5-2.7 volts at idle speed
Intake air temperature (IAT) sensor	
Input voltage	4.5-5.5 volts
Resistance	2500 ohms at 20° C (68° F)
PAIR solenoid valve resistance	
2003-2006	20,000-24,000 ohms at 20° C (68° F)
2007-on	18,000-22,000 ohms at 20°-30° C (68°-86° F)
Secondary throttle position (STP) sensor	
Input voltage	4.5-5.5 volts
Output voltage	
Closed	Approximately 0.6 volts
Open	Approximately 4.5 volts
	(continued)

16

Table 11 FUEL INJECTION AND EMISSION SYSTEMS SPECIFICATIONS (continued)

Secondary throttle position (STP) sensor (continued)	
Resistance (2003-2006 models only)	
Closed	Approximately 0.6 ohms
Open	Approximately 4.5 ohms
Secondary throttle valve actuator (STVA) resistance	
2003-2006	7-14 ohms
2007-on	7 ohms
Throttle position (TP) sensor	
Input voltage	4.5-5.5 volts
Output voltage	
Closed	Approximately 1.1 volts
Open	Approximately 4.3 volts
Fast idle speed	1.21 volts
Resistance (2003-2006 models only)	
Closed	Approximately 1.1 ohms
Open	Approximately 4.3 ohms
Tip over (TO) sensor	
Resistance	19,100-19,700 ohms
Voltage	Approximately 0.4-1.4 volts upright
	Approximately 3.7-4.4 volts tilted 65°

Table 12 FUEL AND EXHAUST SYSTEM TORQUE SPECIFICATIONS

	N•m	in.-lb.	ft.-lb.
Fuel delivery pipe screws	5	44	–
Fuel pump mounting bolts	10	88	–
Heated oxygen sensor			
(Calif., U.K., EU, Aust., models only)	25	–	18
Secondary throttle position sensor mounting screws			
2003-2006	2	18	–
2007-on	3.5	31	
Throttle position sensor			
mounting screws	3.5	31	–

CHAPTER NINE

ELECTRICAL SYSTEM

Refer to **Table 13** and **Table 14** for specifications unique to later models. Refer to the appropriate wiring diagram at the back of the manual to verify wire colors and connection points.

Because some sensors, switches and components of the ignition system are recognized by the fuel injection self-diagnostic system, they are tested in the *Fuel, Emission Control and Exhaust Systems* section in this Supplement. Failure of these components will display a malfunction code on the instrument panel.

CHARGING SYSTEM

Charging System No-Load Test

The following information is unique to later models when testing the alternator.

1. Remove the rear frame cover as described in this Supplement to access the alternator connector (**Figure 168**).

2. The alternator wires are black in both halves of the connector. The male half leads to the alternator.

VOLTAGE REGULATOR/RECTIFIER

Testing

The following information is unique to later models when testing the regulator/rectifier.

1. Remove the air box as described in this Supplement to access both regulator/rectifier connectors (**Figure 169**).

2. Refer to **Figure 170** for the required voltages.

ALTERNATOR

Stator Coil Continuity Test

The following information is unique to later models when testing the alternator.

1. Remove the rear frame cover as described in this Supplement to access the alternator connector (**Figure 168**).

2. The alternator wires are black in both halves of the connector. The male half leads to the alternator.

ELECTRONIC IGNITION SYSTEM

Crankshaft Position Sensor/Signal Generator

Early models refer to this component as the signal generator. Refer to *Fuel, Emission Control and Exhaust Systems* in this Supplement for testing the crankshaft position (CKP) sensor. This part is related to the fuel system and self-diagnostic codes.

16

(170)

REGULATOR/RECTIFIER TEST

Volts

- Probe of tester to:	+ Probe of tester to:				
		B/R	B1	B2	B3	B/W
B/R		0.4 ~ 0.7	0.4 ~ 0.7	0.4 ~ 0.7	0.5 ~ 1.2
B1	Approx. 1.5		Approx. 1.5	Approx. 1.5	0.4 ~ 0.7
B2	Approx. 1.5	Approx. 1.5		Approx. 1.5	0.4 ~ 0.7
B3	Approx. 1.5	Approx. 1.5	Approx. 1.5		0.4 ~ 0.7
B/W	Approx. 1.5	Approx. 1.5	Approx. 1.5	Approx. 1.5	

B/W: Black/White, B/R: Black/Red, B: Black

Ignition Coils

Refer to *Fuel, Emission Control and Exhaust Systems* in this Supplement for testing the ignition coils. This part is related to the fuel system and self-diagnostic codes.

Electronic Control Module (ECM)/Igniter Unit

Early models refer to this component as the igniter. The ECM is located next to the battery (A, **Figure 171**). There is no test procedure specifically for the ECM. Check the wiring harnesses and other components connected to the ECM before replacing the module.

STARTING SYSTEM

Starter Relay

The starter relay (B, **Figure 171**) is located under the seat.

LIGHTING SYSTEM

Taillight/Brake Light/License Plate Light

The taillight and brake light are LEDs. If the LEDs fail to operate and the wiring harness is in good condition, replace the entire taillight and

(171)

brake light assembly (**Figure 172**). The license plate light is a 5-watt bulb.

SWITCHES

Ignition Switch Replacement

Replacement of the ignition switch on later models does not require the removal of the upper steering stem bracket.

Gear Position Switch/Neutral Switch

On early models, a neutral switch sends a signal when the transmission is in neutral. On later models, the neutral switch has been replaced with a gear position (GP) switch. This switch sends a signal to the ECM for all gear positions. Refer to *Fuel, Emission*

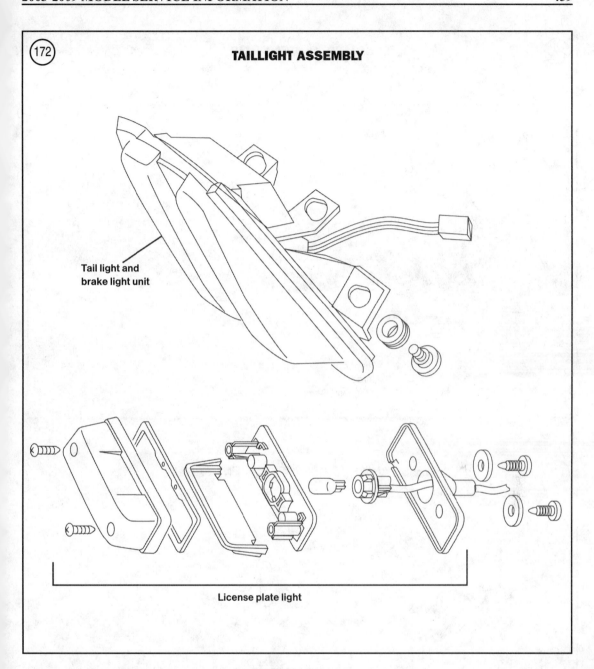

TAILLIGHT ASSEMBLY

Tail light and brake light unit

License plate light

Control and Exhaust Systems in this Supplement for testing the gear position switch. This part is related to the fuel system and self-diagnostic codes.

INSTRUMENT PANEL

Removal/Installation

The gauges and LEDs in the combination meter (**Figure 173** and **Figure 174**) are not available as individual part numbers. If the instrument panel does not illuminate or malfunctions, the meter case can be disassembled and the combination meter can be replaced. Inspect the instrument panel as follows:

1. For SV650 models do the following:
   a. Remove the headlight.
   b. Remove the retainers and cover (**Figure 175**).
   c. Disconnect the wiring harness from the instrument panel (A, **Figure 176**).

16

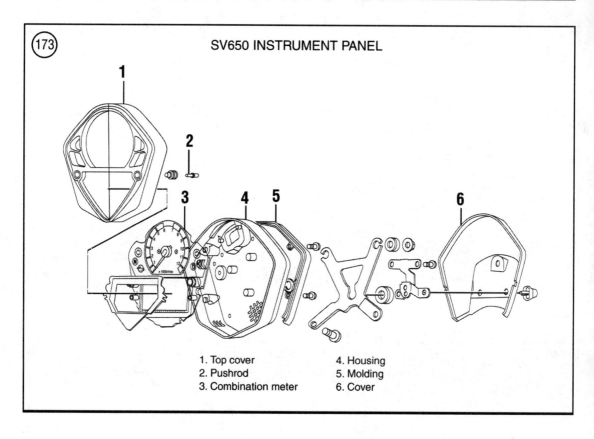

⑴⑺⑶ SV650 INSTRUMENT PANEL

1. Top cover
2. Pushrod
3. Combination meter
4. Housing
5. Molding
6. Cover

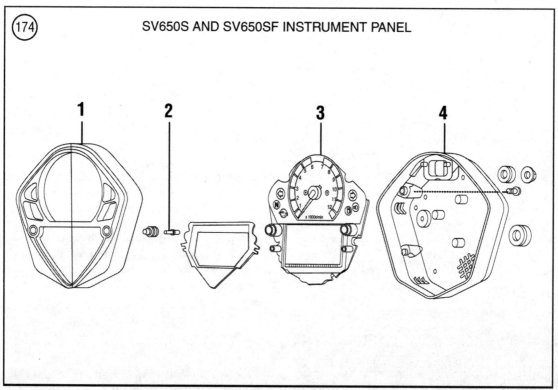

⑴⑺⑷ SV650S AND SV650SF INSTRUMENT PANEL

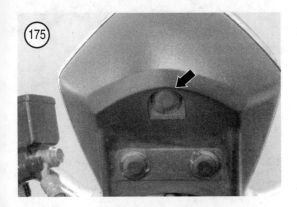

d. Remove the retaining nuts (B, **Figure 176**) and disengage the instrument panel from the motorcycle.

2. For SV650S and SV650SF models do the following:

    a. Remove the front fairing as described in this Supplement.

    b. Disconnect the wiring harness from the instrument panel (**Figure 177**).

    c. Remove the retaining nuts (**Figure 178**) and disengage the instrument panel from the motorcycle.

3. If necessary, disassemble the instrument panel and install a new combination meter. During assembly of the instrument panel note the following:

    a. Install the pushrods with the short end facing up.

    b. On the SV650 instrument panel, check that the molding is seated with the parts.

4. Reverse the procedure to install the instrument panel.

5. Reset the tachometer as described in this section.

Resetting the Tachometer

The tachometer must be reset whenever the battery or instrument panel wiring harness has been disconnected for more than 40 seconds. Reset the tachometer after reconnecting the battery/harness.

1. If the tachometer needle is in its normal position, turn on the ignition switch and observe the action of the tachometer needle. The tachometer needle should move approximately 90° clockwise and then fall to the normal resting position.

2. If the tachometer needle is pointing straight up, turn on the ignition switch and observe the action of the tachometer needle. The tachometer needle should move approximately 90° clockwise and then fall to the normal resting position.

3. If necessary, repeat the reset procedure until the needle falls to the resting position. If the needle will not reset itself, inspect the wiring harness and connectors. If the harness and connectors are in good condition, replace the combination meter.

Engine Coolant Temperature Indicator Testing

Refer to *Fuel, Emission Control and Exhaust Systems* in this Supplement for testing the engine cool-

16

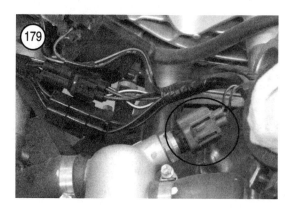

ENGINE COOLANT TEMPERATURE INDICATOR TESTING

	2450 ohms or higher	587 ohms or higher	100 ohms or less	0 ohms
Resistance				
Coolant indicator light	Off	Off	On	On
Coolant temperature warning indicator	Off	Off	On	On
Engine coolant temperature gauge	–	60°C (140° F)	120-129°C (248-265° F) Flicker	HI Flicker

ant temperature (ECT) sensor (**Figure 179**). The sensor must be in good condition to accurately test the indicators on the instrument panel. Also check that the wire harness and connectors between the test point and the instrument panel are in good condition.

1. Check that the ignition switch is off.

2. Install a variable resistor/meter between the terminals in the ECT connector (**Figure 180**).

3. Turn on the ignition switch.

4. Refer to **Figure 181** and set the resistor to each of the resistance settings shown. For each setting, observe the instrument panel and note whether the indicators shown in **Figure 182** are operating as required.

5. If any indicators are not operating as required, the combination meter should be replaced.

Fuel Level Indicator Light Testing

1. Raise the fuel tank as described in this Supplement.

2. Disconnect the fuel pump wire harness (**Figure 183**).

3. In the connector half leading to the instrument panel (**Figure 184**), use a jumper wire to connect the yellow/black wire terminal to the black/white wire terminal.

4. Turn on the ignition switch. After five seconds the fuel level indicator light should turn on.

5. Turn off the ignition switch. It takes about 30 seconds for the light to turn off.

6. If the light did not turn on, inspect the wiring harness and connectors. If the harness and connectors are in good condition, replace the combination meter.

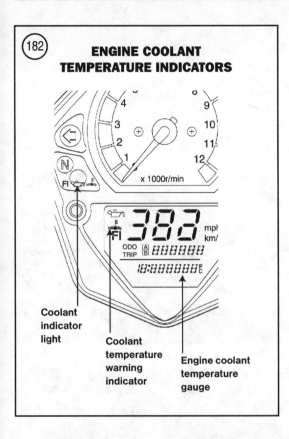

ENGINE COOLANT TEMPERATURE INDICATORS

Coolant indicator light

Coolant temperature warning indicator

Engine coolant temperature gauge

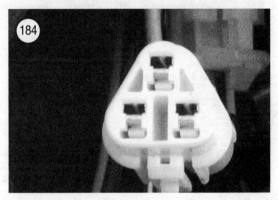

Table 13 ELECTRICAL SYSTEM SPECIFICATIONS

Alternator	
No-load voltage (engine cold)	60 volts (AC) minimum at 5000 rpm
Maximum output	375 watts at 5000 rpm
Regulated voltage (charging voltage)	14.0-15 volts at 5000 rpm
Coil resistance	0.2-0.7 ohm
Ignition timing	
2003-2006	
All models	7° BTDC at 1300 rpm
2007-on	
All models	8° BTDC at 1300 rpm

Table 14 REPLACEMENT BULBS

Headlight (all models)	55W/60W
License plate	5W
Turn signal light	21W
Instrument panel lights	
Coolant temperature indicator light	LED
Fuel indicator light	LED
Fuel injection indicator light	LED
High beam indicator light	LED
Neutral indicator light	LED
Oil pressure indicator light	LED
Speedometer light	LED
Tachometer light	LED
Taillight/brake light	LED
Turn signal indicator light	LEDs

16

CHAPTER TEN

COOLING SYSTEM

Refer to **Table 15** and **Table 16** for specifications unique to later models.

Refer to the *Fuel, Emission Control and Exhaust Systems* section in this Supplement for testing the engine coolant temperature (ECT) sensor. This part is related to the fuel system and self-diagnostic codes.

RADIATOR

Removal/Installation

Service to the cooling system is the same as for earlier models with the exception of the radiator. Because of slight alterations in the mounting of parts, the recommended removal and installation procedure for the radiator is revised.

1. On SV650S and SV650SF models, remove the bodywork surrounding the radiator as described in this Supplement.

2. Drain the engine coolant (Chapter Three).

3. Disconnect the left and right hoses from the radiator (A, **Figure 185**).

4. Disconnect the reservoir hose from the radiator (B, **Figure 185**).

5. Disconnect the horn leads.

6. Disconnect the cooling fan motor and the fan switch (C, **Figure 185**).

7. Remove the lower radiator mounting bolt (D, **Figure 185**).

8. Remove the upper mounting bolt at each side of the frame (**Figure 186**).

9. Remove the radiator from the motorcycle.

10. If necessary, remove the cooling fan, fan switch and horn from the radiator.

11. Reverse this procedure to install the radiator. Note the following:

    a. Replace hoses that are hard, cracked or show signs of deterioration, both internally and ex-

ternally. Hold each hose and flex it in several directions to check for damage. For a hose that is difficult to install on a fitting, dip the hose end in hot water until the rubber has softened, then install the hose.

    b. Install clamps in their original positions.

    c. Check that the fan switch is installed and tight.

    d. Fill and bleed the cooling system (Chapter Three).

    e. Start the engine and allow it to warm up. Check for leaks.

Table 15 COOLING SYSTEM SPECIFICATIONS

Coolant capacity (includes reserve tank)	1.7 L (1.8 U.S. qt., 1.5 Imp. qt.)
Thermostat opening	
2003-2006	88° C (190° F)
2007-on	7° C (170° F)
Cooling fan switch	
Off temperature (approximate)	92° C (198° F)
On temperature (approximate)	98° C (208° F)

Table 16 COOLING SYSTEM TORQUE SPECIFICATIONS

	N•m	in.-lb.	ft.-lb.
Engine coolant temperature sensor	18	–	13

CHAPTER ELEVEN

WHEELS, TIRES AND DRIVE CHAIN

Refer to **Table 17** for the specification that is unique to later models.

FRONT WHEEL

Removal/Installation

Removal and installation of the front wheel is the same as for earlier models with the exception of the front axle. The later axle is shouldered and eliminates the two spacers at the right side of the early axle.

REAR WHEEL

Removal/Installation

Removal and installation of the rear wheel is the same as for earlier models with the exception of the brake caliper bracket. The brake caliper on later models is mounted above the swing arm (A, **Figure 187**). The caliper does not have to be removed from its mounting bracket when the axle is removed. Although the caliper bracket engages with the swing arm, the caliper assembly should be secured in place until the rear wheel is installed. Refer to **Table 17** for the recommended rear axle torque specification.

Other changes to the rear axle assembly include a redesigned chain adjuster plate (B, **Figure 187**) and right-hand spacer (**Figure 188**). Removal and installation of these parts has not changed.

REAR WHEEL HUB

Disassembly/Assembly

On later models, a dust seal covers the right-hand wheel bearing (**Figure 188**). Replace both hub seals whenever the hub bearings are serviced. Pack the seals with waterproof grease prior to installation.

16

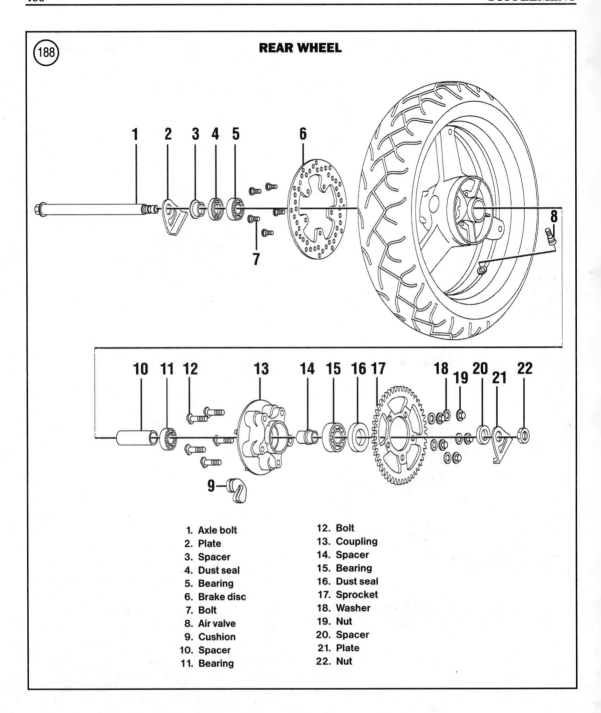

REAR WHEEL

(188)

1. Axle bolt
2. Plate
3. Spacer
4. Dust seal
5. Bearing
6. Brake disc
7. Bolt
8. Air valve
9. Cushion
10. Spacer
11. Bearing
12. Bolt
13. Coupling
14. Spacer
15. Bearing
16. Dust seal
17. Sprocket
18. Washer
19. Nut
20. Spacer
21. Plate
22. Nut

Table 17 WHEELS TIRES AND DRIVE CHAIN TORQUE SPECIFICATIONS

	N•m	in.-lb.	ft.-lb.
Rear axle	100	–	74

CHAPTER TWELVE

FRONT SUSPENSION AND STEERING

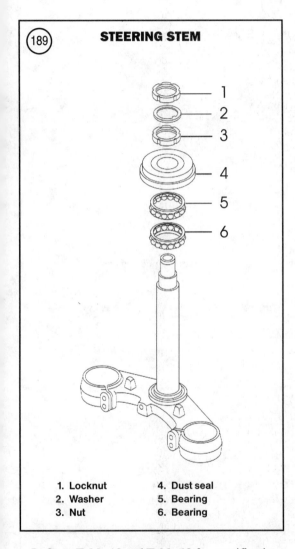

STEERING STEM

1. Locknut
2. Washer
3. Nut
4. Dust seal
5. Bearing
6. Bearing

Refer to **Table 18** and **Table 19** for specifications unique to later models.

STEERING STEM AND HEAD

Disassembly/Installation/Adjustment

Removal and installation of the steering stem is the same as for earlier models with the exception of

the steering stem washer and locknut (**Figure 189**). The washer and locknut secure the adjustment of the steering stem nut. To remove or install the locknut and nut, use the Suzuki steering stem nut wrench (part No. 09940-14911) and steering stem nut wrench socket (part No. 09940-14960). The tools can be ordered from a Suzuki dealership.

FRONT FORK

Removal/Installation

On all models, when installing the fork legs, position each fork leg so the top of the fork tube (not the cap) is flush with the top of the upper steering bracket.

Disassembly/Inspection/Assembly

Service to the fork leg is the same as for earlier models with the exception of a revised cap bolt (**Figure 190**) and oil lock piece. If fork oil leakage is evident at the cap bolt adjuster, remove the clip and disassemble the cap bolt. A replaceable O-ring is installed on the adjuster.

The oil lock piece, which is fitted to the end of the inner tube has been redesigned. The lock piece is now tapered and not shouldered. During assembly of the fork leg, install the tapered end of the of the lock piece into the inner tube.

16

Table 18 FRONT SUSPENSION SPECIFICATIONS

	Specification	Service limit
Front fork oil		
Viscosity	Suzuki No. 8 fork oil or equivalent	–
Capacity per leg		
SV650	490 ml (16.6 U.S. oz., 17.3 Imp. oz.)	–
SV650S, SV650SF		
2003	488 ml (16.5 U.S. oz., 17.2 Imp. oz.)	–
2004-on	485 ml (16.4 U.S. oz., 17.1 Imp. oz.)	–
Front fork oil level		
SV650	92 mm (3.62 in.)	–
SV650S, SV650SF		
2003	94 mm (3.7 in.)	–
2004-on	96 mm (3.78 in.)	–
Front fork spring free length		
SV650	429 mm (16.89 in.)	420 mm (16.5 in.)
SV650S, SV650SF	437.4 mm (17.22 in.)	428 mm (16.8 in.)
Front fork stroke		
SV650S, SV650SF		
2004-on	125 mm (4.9 in.)	–

Table 19 FRONT SUSPENSION TORQUE SPECIFICATIONS

	N•m	in.-lb.	ft.-lb.
Front fork damper rod bolt	20	–	15
Steering stem locknut	80	–	59
Steering stem cap nut	90	–	66

CHAPTER THIRTEEN

REAR SUSPENSION

Refer to **Table 20** for specifications unique to later models.

Table 20 REAR SUSPENSION SPECIFICATIONS

Rear shock absorber spring preload adjuster	
2003-on	
SV650	3rd position
Rear wheel travel	137 mm (5.4 in.)

CHAPTER FOURTEEN

BRAKES

On 2003-on models, the rear brake caliper has been changed to a single-piston caliper **Figure 191**. The caliper is positioned above the swing arm, unlike early models that have the caliper mounted below the swing arm. Also, the rear brake master cylinder reservoir has been moved from under the seat and repositioned below the right side cover.

Refer to **Table 21** for specifications unique to later models.

REAR BRAKE PADS

Replacement

Inspect the rear brake pads (Chapter Three). The brake pads can be replaced with the caliper mounted on the motorcycle. Refer to **Figure 192**.

> *CAUTION*
> *In the following step, monitor the level of fluid in the master cylinder reservoir. Brake fluid will back flow to the reservoir as the caliper piston is pressed into its bore. Do not allow brake fluid to spill from the reservoir, or damage can occur to painted and plastic surfaces. Immediately clean*

up any spills, flooding the area with water.

1. Grasp the caliper and press it firmly toward the brake disc. This will push the caliper piston down into its bore, creating room for the new pads.
2. Remove the pad pin plug and loosen the pad pin (A, **Figure 193**).
3. Remove the brake caliper mounting bolt (B, **Figure 193**).
4. Pivot the brake caliper forward and remove the pad pin and brake pad assemblies. Check that the insulator and metal shim on the back of each pad is also removed.

> *NOTE*
> *Do not operate the brake pedal with the pads removed. The piston in the caliper can come out of the bore.*

5. Clean the interior of the caliper and inspect for leakage or damage.
6. Inspect the pad pin and plug. Replace the parts if worn, corroded or damaged.
7. Inspect the pads for contamination, scoring and wear.
   a. Replace the pads if they are worn to the wear indicator groove.
   b. If the pads are worn unevenly, the caliper is probably not sliding correctly on the slide pin and sleeve. The caliper must be free to *float* on the pin and sleeve. Buildup or corrosion on the parts can hold the caliper in one position, causing brake drag and excessive pad wear.
8. Assemble the pads. On the back side of the pad, install the insulator and metal shim. The tabs on the shim should fit over the pad.
9. Install the pad assemblies on each side of the disc, seating the pads against the pad retainer and pad spring.

16

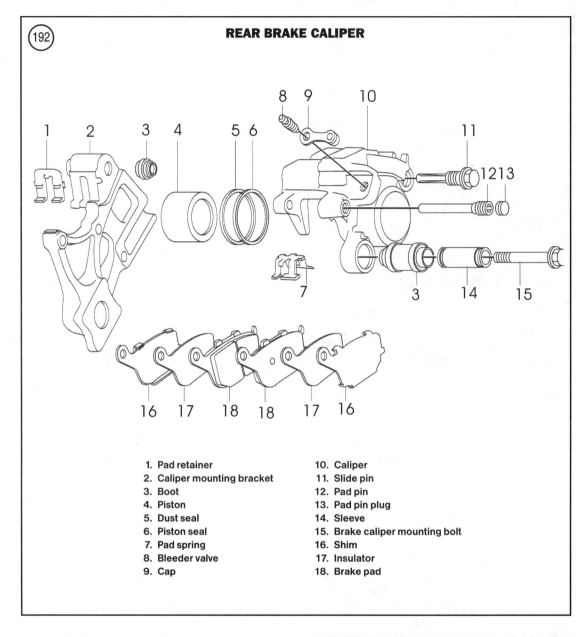

REAR BRAKE CALIPER

1. Pad retainer
2. Caliper mounting bracket
3. Boot
4. Piston
5. Dust seal
6. Piston seal
7. Pad spring
8. Bleeder valve
9. Cap
10. Caliper
11. Slide pin
12. Pad pin
13. Pad pin plug
14. Sleeve
15. Brake caliper mounting bolt
16. Shim
17. Insulator
18. Brake pad

10. Install the pad pin, guiding it through the holes in the pads. Lightly tighten the pad pin. The pin will be torqued in a later step.

11. Pivot the brake caliper back and install the brake caliper mounting bolt. Tighten the brake caliper mounting bolt to 23 N•m (17 ft.-lb.).

12. Tighten the pad pin to 18 N•m (13 ft.-lb.).

13. Install the pad pin plug.

14. Operate the brake pedal several times to seat the pads.

15. Check the brake fluid reservoir and replenish or remove fluid, as necessary.

16. With the rear wheel raised, check that the wheel spins freely and the brake operates properly.

REAR BRAKE CALIPER

Removal/Installation

Use the following procedure to remove the caliper from the motorcycle. Refer to **Figure 192**.

1. If the caliper will be removed from the brake hose, or disassembled, drain the system as described in *Brake System Draining* in this Supplement.

2. Remove the brake pads as described in *Rear Brake Pad Replacement* in this Supplement.

3. Remove the banjo bolt and seal washers from the brake hose. Have a shop cloth ready to absorb excess brake fluid that drips from the hose.

b. Wrap the hose end to prevent brake fluid from damaging other surfaces. Wipe the caliper fitting of any brake fluid.

4. Pivot the caliper forward (**Figure 194**) and away from the mounting bracket.

5. Drain excess brake fluid from the caliper.

6. Repair the caliper as described in this section.

7. Reverse this procedure to install the caliper. Note the following:

    a. Install new seal washers on the banjo bolt.

    b. Position the brake hose fitting so it is seated in the notch on the caliper.

    c. If the caliper was rebuilt, or the brake hose disconnected from the caliper, fill and bleed the brake system(Chapter Fourteen).

Repair

Use the following procedure to disassemble, inspect and assemble the brake caliper, using new seals. Refer to **Figure 192**.

1. Remove the brake pads and caliper as described in this section.

2. Remove the slide pin and brake caliper mounting bolt (**Figure 195**).

3. Remove the pad spring, sleeve and boot (**Figure 196**).

4. Remove the piston from the caliper bore using compressed air. To perform this technique, an air nozzle is tightly held in the brake hose fitting and air pressure ejects the piston. Do not attempt to pry the piston out of the caliper. Read the following procedure entirely before beginning removal.

    a. Place the caliper on a padded work surface.

    b. Close the bleeder valve (A, **Figure 197**) so air cannot escape.

    c. Place a strip of wood, or similar pad, in the caliper. The pad will cushion the piston when it comes out of the caliper.

16

WARNING
Wear eye protection when using compressed air to remove the piston. Keep fingers away from the piston discharge area. Personal injury can occur if an attempt is made to stop the piston with the fingers.

d. Lay the caliper so the piston will discharge downward.

e. Insert an air nozzle into the brake hose fitting (B, **Figure 197**). If the nozzle does not have a rubber tip, wrap the nozzle with tape. This will allow the nozzle to seal tightly and prevent thread damage.

f. Place a shop cloth over the entire caliper to catch any spray that may discharge from the caliper.

g. Apply pressure and listen for the piston to discharge from the caliper.

5. Remove the bleeder valve and cap from the caliper.

6. Remove the dust seal and piston seal from the bore (**Figure 198**).

7. Inspect the caliper assembly.

a. Clean all parts that will be reused with fresh brake fluid or isopropyl (rubbing) alcohol. Use a wood or plastic-tipped tool to clean the caliper seal and boot grooves. Use clean brake fluid to aid in cleaning the piston, bore and seal grooves.

b. Inspect the cylinder bore and piston for wear, pitting or corrosion.

c. Measure the inside diameter of the caliper bore (**Figure 199**). Refer to **Table 21** for specifications.

d. Measure the outside diameter of the piston (**Figure 200**). Refer to **Table 21** for specifications.

e. Inspect the slide pin, sleeve and boot for wear, pitting or corrosion. The pin must be in good condition to allow slight pad movement when installed.

f. Inspect the bleeder valve, pad pin and plug for wear, pitting and corrosion.

g. Clean and inspect the caliper mounting bracket, boot and pad retainer (mounted on the motorcycle) for wear, pitting or corrosion. The retainer must be in good condition to allow slight pad movement when installed.

h. Inspect the pads for contamination, scoring and wear. Replace the pads if they are worn to

the wear indicator groove. If the pads are worn unevenly, the caliper is probably not sliding correctly on the slide pin and sleeve. The caliper must be free to *float* on the pins. Buildup or corrosion on the pins can hold the caliper in one position, causing brake drag and excessive pad wear.

NOTE
Use new brake fluid (rated DOT 4) to lubricate the parts in the following steps.

8. Install the new piston seal and dust seal as follows:

    a. Soak the seals in brake fluid for 15 minutes.

    b. Coat the caliper bore and piston with brake fluid.

    c. Seat the piston seal and the dust seal in the caliper grooves. The piston seal goes in the back groove.

    d. Install the piston, with the open side facing out. Twist the piston past the seals, then press the piston to the bottom of the bore.

9. Install the slide pin. Tighten the slide pin to 27 N•m (20 ft.-lb.).

10. Install the bleeder valve and cap.

11. Apply silicone brake grease to the sleeve and slide pin, and to the interior of the boots. Install the boot and sleeve onto the caliper.

12. Check that the boot and pad retainer are seated on the mounting bracket.

13. Install the caliper and pads as described in this section.

REAR MASTER CYLINDER

Removal/Installation

The rear brake master cylinder reservoir has been moved from under the seat and repositioned below the right side cover (**Figure 201**).

BRAKE SYSTEM DRAINING

To drain the brake fluid from the system, have an 8 mm wrench, tip-resistant container and a length of clear tubing that fits tightly on the bleeder valve.

> *CAUTION*
> *Brake fluid can damage painted and finished surfaces. Use water to immediately wash any surface that becomes contaminated with brake fluid.*

1. Attach one end of the tubing to the bleeder valve (A, **Figure 202**) and place the other end into the container.

2. Open the bleeder valve so fluid can pass into the tubing.

3. Pump the brake pedal to force the fluid from the system.

4. When the system no longer drips fluid, close the bleeder valve.

5. Dispose the brake fluid in an enviroN•mentally-safe manner.

6. If the caliper will be disassembled, loosen the brake hose banjo bolt (B, **Figure 202**) while the caliper is stable on the swing arm, then lightly tighten the bolt. It will be removed in the *Rear Brake Caliper Removal* procedure in this Supplement.

Table 21 BRAKE SPECIFICATIONS

	New	Service limit
Rear brake master cylinder bore	14.000-14.043 mm	–
	(0.5512-0.5529 in.)	–
Rear brake master cylinder piston diameter	13.957-13.984 mm	–
	(0.5495-0.5506 in.)	–

CHAPTER FIFTEEN

BODY AND FRAME

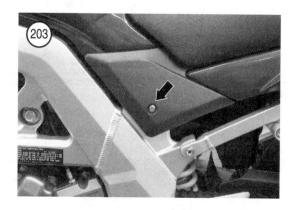

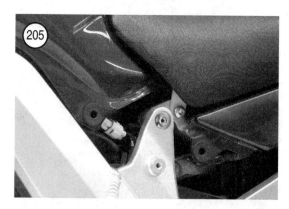

Use the following removal and installation procedures for the side covers, seats, hand rail, rear frame
cover, taillight covers, front fender, front fairing
and lower cowl.

SIDE COVERS

Removal/Installation

1. Remove the screw from the cover (**Figure 203**).

2. Grasp the left and right sides of the cover and
carefully pull outward to disengage the friction
prongs on the back of the cover.

3. To install the cover:

   a. Align the friction prongs with the rubber
     grommets.

   b. On the outside of the cover, press the prong
     locations to seat the cover into place.

   c. Install the screw.

REAR SEAT

Removal/Installation

1. Insert the ignition key into the seat release (**Figure 204**) and turn the key clockwise to release the
seat.

2. Lift the seat and move it away from the rear
fender.

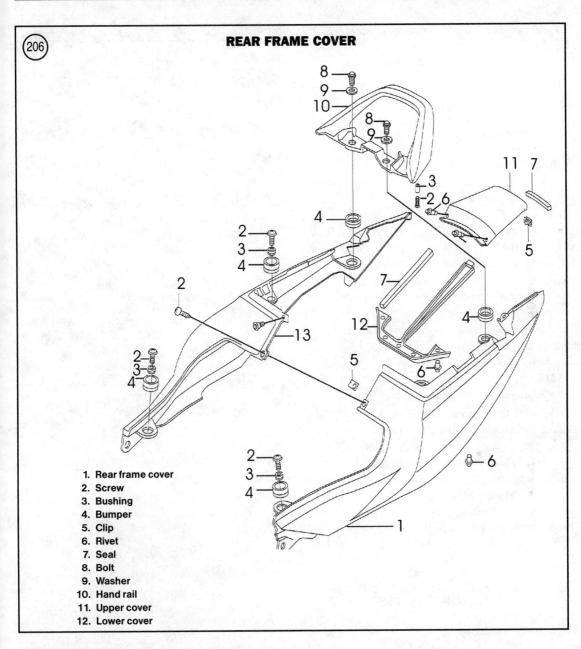

REAR FRAME COVER

(206)

1. Rear frame cover
2. Screw
3. Bushing
4. Bumper
5. Clip
6. Rivet
7. Seal
8. Bolt
9. Washer
10. Hand rail
11. Upper cover
12. Lower cover

3. Remove the ignition key from the seat release.
4. To install the seat:
   a. Align the seat in the mounting holes.
   b. Push down on the seat to lock it into position.

FRONT SEAT

Removal/Installation

1. Remove the side covers and rear seat as described in this Supplement.

2. Remove the bolt (**Figure 205**) from the left and right side of the front seat.

3. Reverse this procedure to install the front seat.

HAND RAIL

Removal/Installation

Refer to **Figure 206**.

1. Remove the rear seat as described in this Supplement.

16

2. Remove the bolts (**Figure 207**) securing the hand rail.

3. Reverse this procedure to install the hand rail.

REAR FRAME COVER

Removal/Installation

Refer to **Figure 206**.

1. Remove the side covers, rear seat, front seat and hand rail as described in this section.

2. Remove the screws and plastic rivet from the front section of the frame cover (**Figure 208**). To remove the rivet, raise the center stake (**Figure 209**) so the flanges can pass through the hole.

3. Remove the screws from the rear section of the tail cover and disconnect the tail light connector (**Figure 210**).

4. Remove the plastic rivets from the underside of the tail cover (**Figure 211**).

5. Disconnect the cable from the seat lock (**Figure 212**).

6. Remove the rear frame cover.

7. Reverse this procedure to install the rear frame cover. Note the following:

   a. Check that wire harnesses are not pinched when the tail cover is installed.

   b. Install the plastic rivets with the stake pulled out (**Figure 209**). When the rivet is seated in the joined parts, press the stake flush to the top of the rivet. Check that the parts are secure. Replace rivets that are fatigued or broken.

TAILLIGHT COVERS

Removal/Installation

Refer to **Figure 206**.

1. Remove the rear frame cover as described in this Supplement.

2. Remove the plastic rivets (**Figure 213**) securing the lower cover. To remove the rivets, raise the center stake (**Figure 209**) so the flanges can pass through the hole. When the rivets are removed, disengage the tab at the opposite end of the lower cover. Remove the cover.

3. Remove the bolts (**Figure 214**) securing the upper cover. When the bolts are removed, disengage

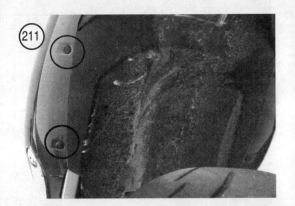

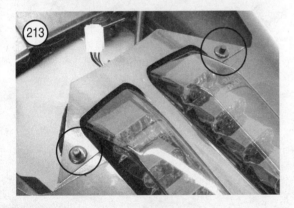

the hooks at the opposite end of the upper cover. Remove the cover.

4. Reverse this procedure to install the taillight covers. Note the following:

    a. Check that wire harnesses are not pinched when the cover are installed.

    b. Install the plastic rivets with the stake pulled out (**Figure 209**). When the rivet is seated in the joined parts, press the stake flush to the top of the rivet. Check that the parts are secure. Replace rivets that are fatigued or broken.

FRONT FENDER

Removal/Installation

1. Remove the front and rear bolts from each side of the fender (**Figure 215**). Note that the rear bolts are located inside the fender.

2. When installing the fender, finger-tighten all bolts before final tightening.

FRONT FAIRING (SV650S AND SV650SF MODELS)

Removal/Installation

For 2008-on SF models, remove the lower cowl before removing the front fairing. Refer to **Figure 216**.

1. Remove the bolts securing the mirrors (**Figure 217**).

2. Remove the fairing inner cover as follows:

    a. Remove the plastic rivet (**Figure 218**) from the left and right side of the of the fairing inner cover. To remove the rivet, raise the cen-

16

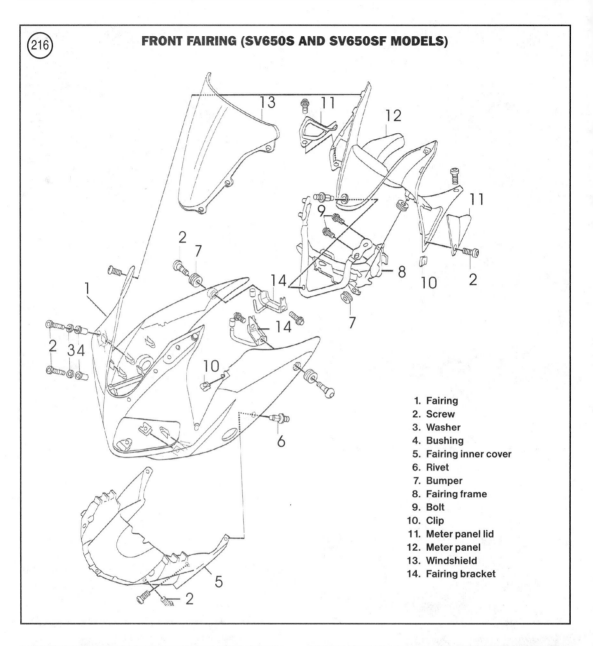

FRONT FAIRING (SV650S AND SV650SF MODELS)

216

1. Fairing
2. Screw
3. Washer
4. Bushing
5. Fairing inner cover
6. Rivet
7. Bumper
8. Fairing frame
9. Bolt
10. Clip
11. Meter panel lid
12. Meter panel
13. Windshield
14. Fairing bracket

217

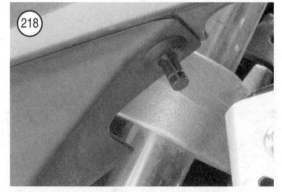

218

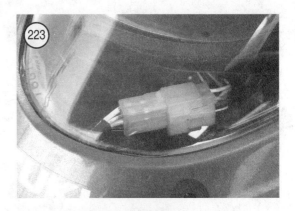

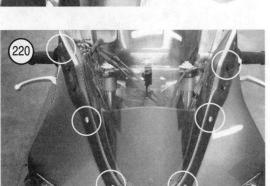

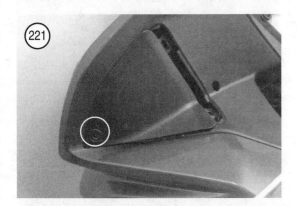

ter stake (**Figure 209**) so the flanges can pass through the hole.

b. Remove the screws (**Figure 219**) from the left and right side of the fairing inner cover.

c. Remove the cover.

3. Remove the screws and washers (**Figure 220**) securing the windshield. Where used, account for the bushings that pass through the windshield.

4. Remove the screw securing each meter panel lid (**Figure 221**). Disengage and remove the lids.

5. Remove the fairing as follows:

a. Remove the screws (**Figure 222**) from the left and right side of the fairing.

b. Stand in front of the fairing. Grasp the left and right sides of the fairing and carefully pull outward to disengage the friction prongs on the back of the fairing. When the fairing disengages, do not pull it away from the motorcycle. The wiring harness is still connected.

c. Disconnect the wiring harness (**Figure 223**) and move the fairing away from the motorcycle.

6. Remove the plastic rivet (**Figure 224**) securing the meter panel.

16

7. Remove the bolts (**Figure 225**) securing the fairing frame.

8. Disconnect the combination meter (**Figure 226**) and remove it from the motorcycle.

9. Reverse this procedure to install the front fairing assembly. Note the following:

    a. Check that wire harnesses are not pinched when the parts are installed.

    b. Install the plastic rivets with the stake pulled out (**Figure 209**). When the rivet is seated in the joined parts, press the stake flush to the top of the rivet. Check that the parts are secure. Replace rivets that are fatigued or broken.

LOWER COWL (SV650SF MODELS)

A two-piece lower cowl is fitted to 2008-on SF models (**Figure 227**).

Removal/Installation

1. Remove the plastic rivets from the front and bottom of the cowl (**Figure 228**). Only two of the bottom rivets need to be removed, if they are removed from the same panel of the cowl. The rivets in the other panel can stay in place. To remove the rivets, raise the center stake (**Figure 209**) so the flanges can pass through the hole.

2. Remove each panel as follows:

    a. Remove the bolts shown in **Figure 229**. Account for the collars and rubber grommets when the bolts are removed.

    b. Remove the bolt from the fairing that secures the top of the lower cowl (**Figure 230**).

    c. Carefully pull outward on the fairing so the lower cowl can be removed.

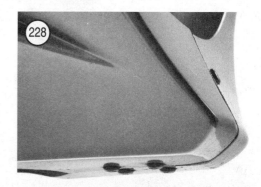

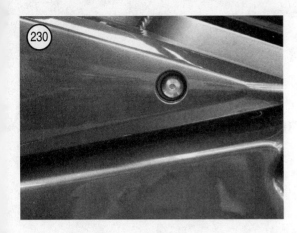

d. Repeat these steps to remove the remaining lower cowl.

3. Reverse this procedure to install the lower cowls. Note the following:

a. Install the plastic rivets with the stake pulled out (**Figure 209**). When the rivet is seated in the joined parts, press the stake flush to the top of the rivet. Check that the parts are secure. Replace rivets that are fatigued or broken.

b. Do not tighten the bolts until all rivets are installed and the cowl has been inspected for a good fit.

16

INDEX

17

17

17

2003-2006 and 2007-ON ECM CONNECTORS CONFIGURATION DETAILS

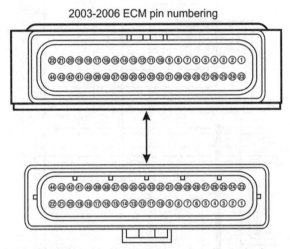

2003-2006 ECM pin numbering

2003-2006 ECM wiring harness connector pin numbering

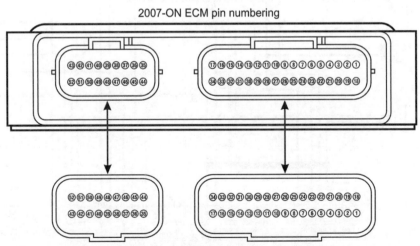

2007-ON ECM pin numbering

2007-ON ECM wiring harness connectors pin numbering

17

1999-2000 SV650 USA AND CANADA MODELS

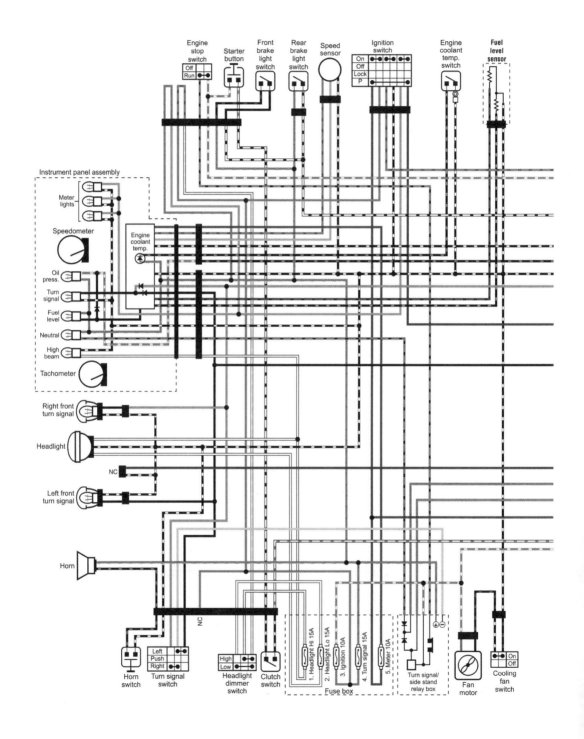

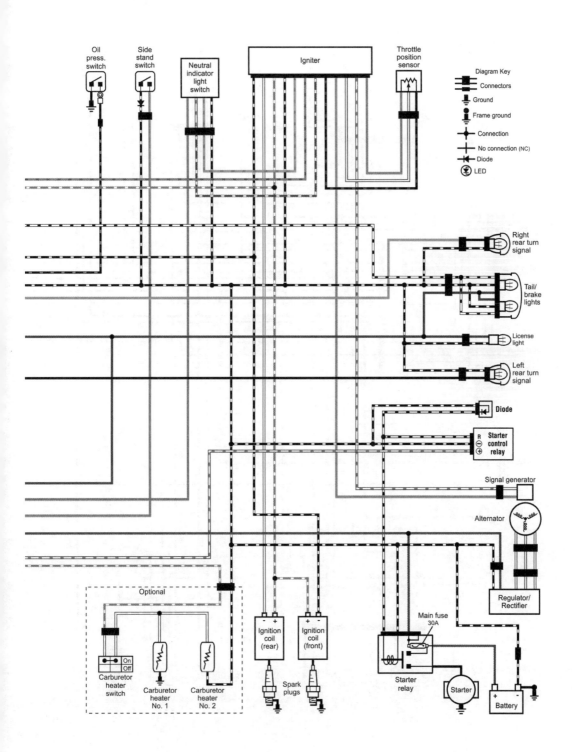

18

1999-2000 SV650 AUSTRALIA MODELS

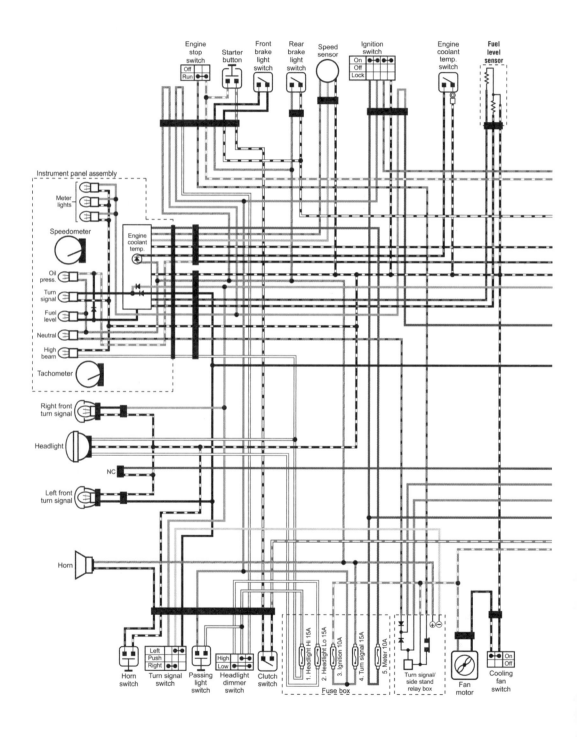

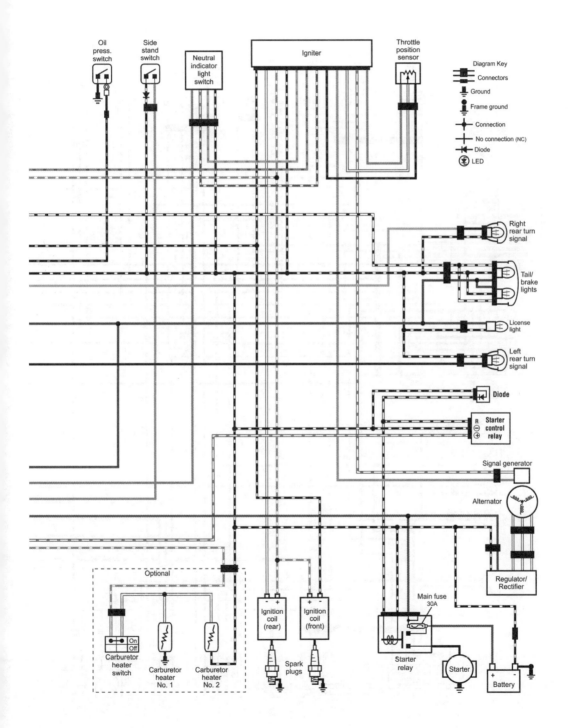

1999-2000 SV650 UK & EUROPE MODELS

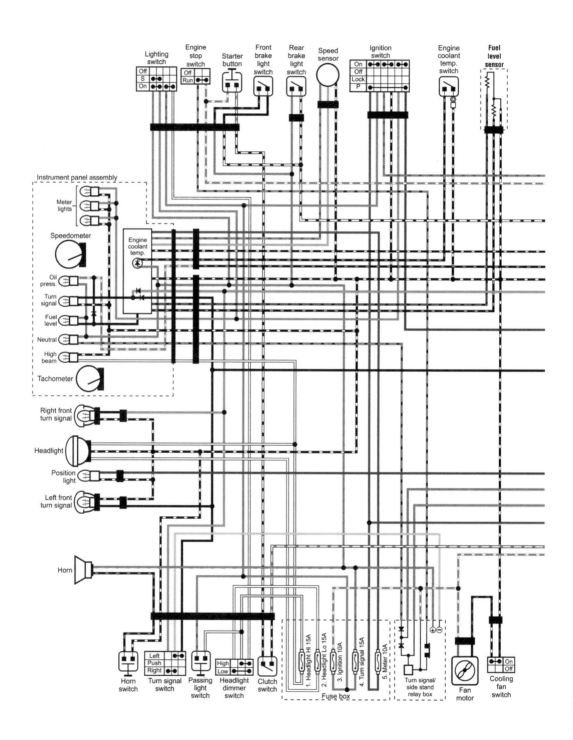

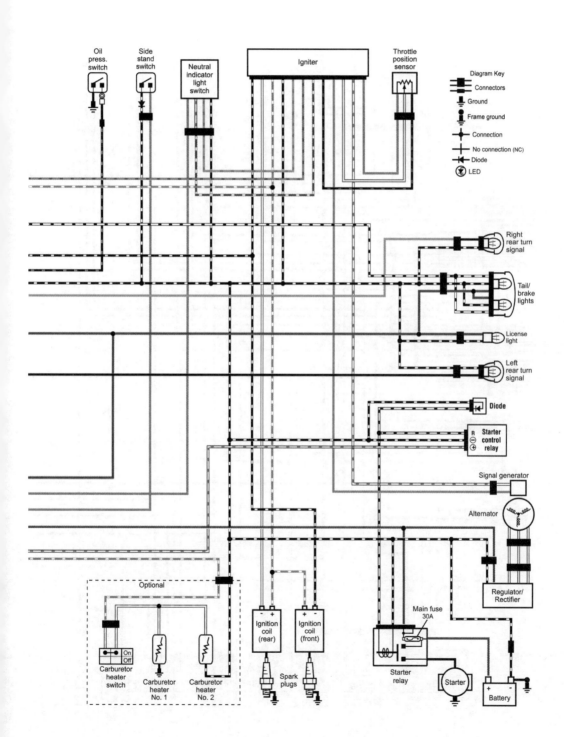

2001 SV650K1 USA AND CALIFORNIA MODELS

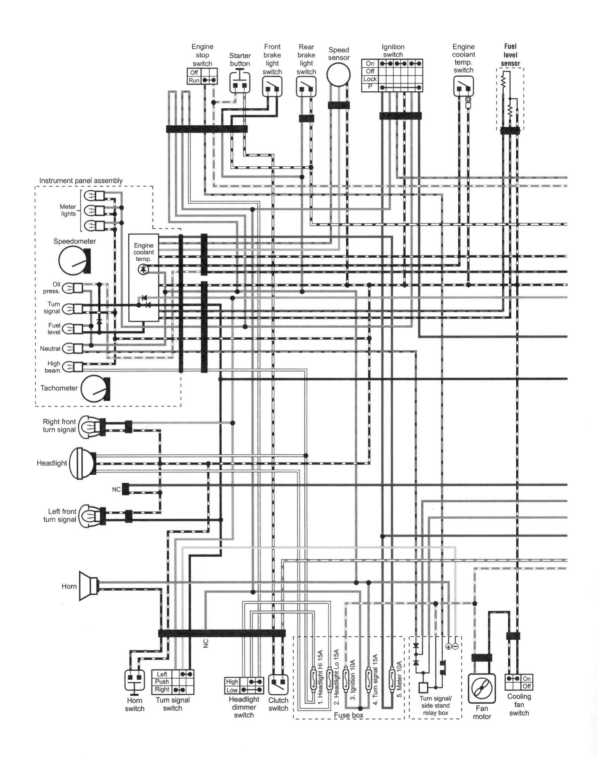

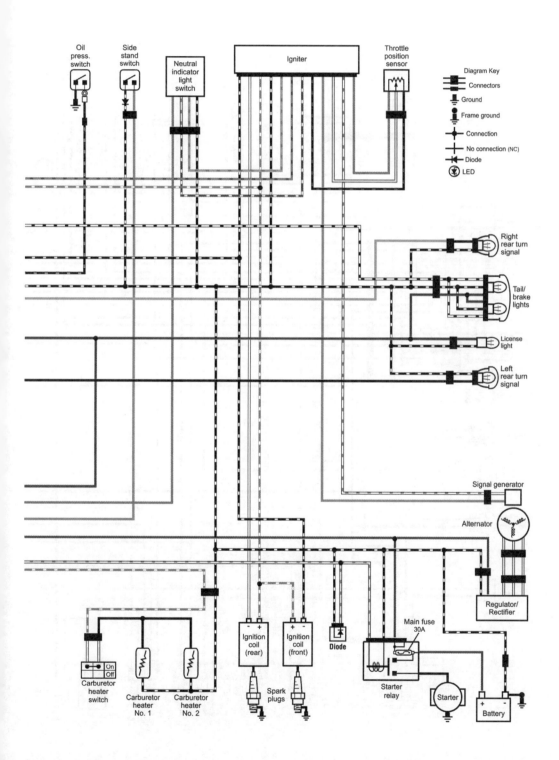

2001 SV650 UK & EUROPE MODELS

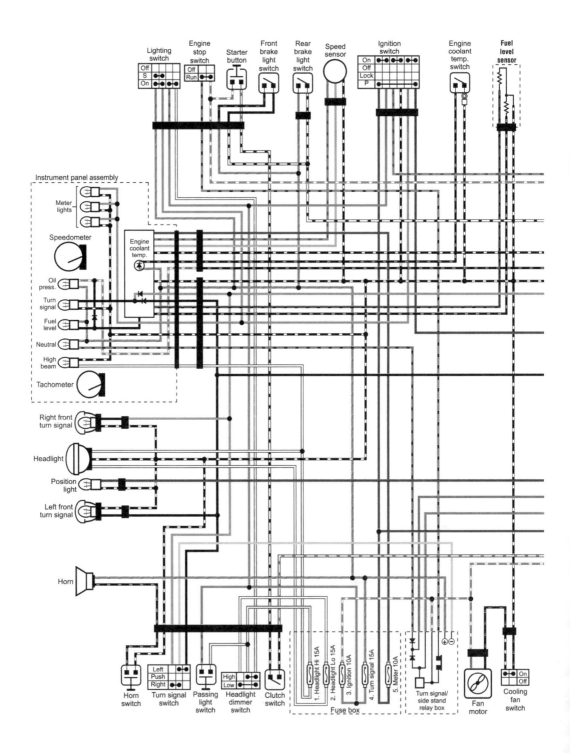

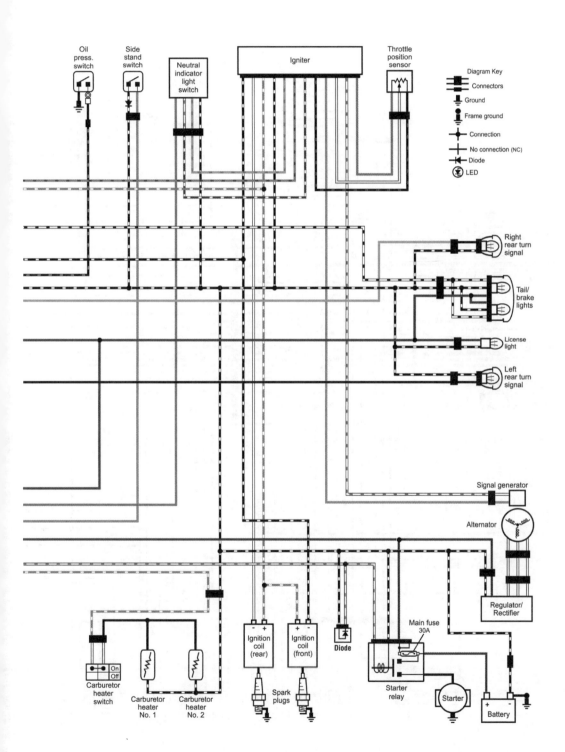

2001 SV650SK1 USA AND CANADA MODELS

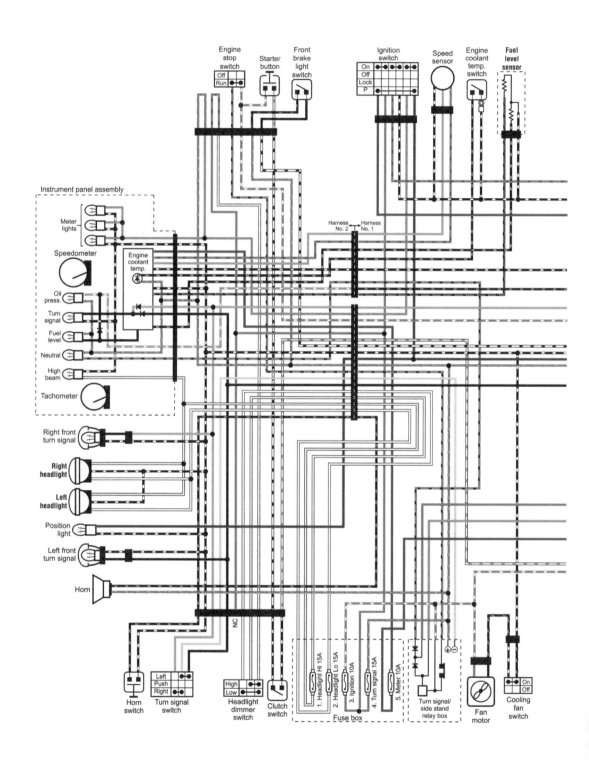

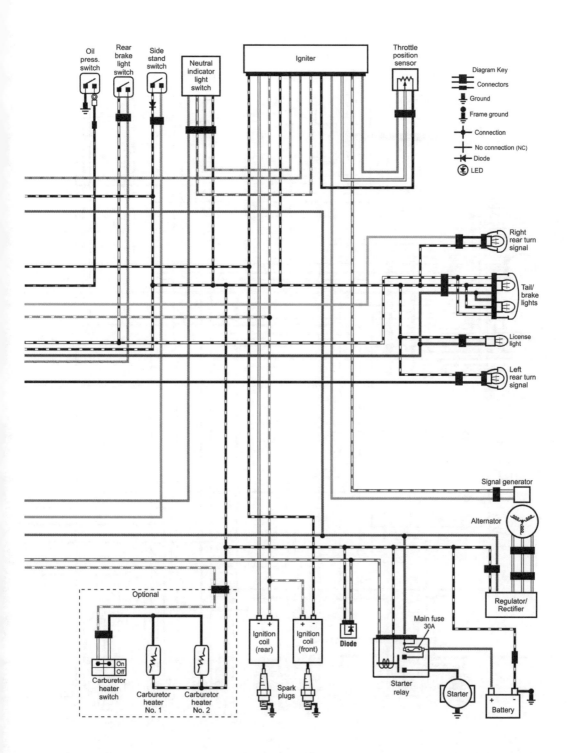

18

2002 SV650K2 UK & EUROPE MODELS

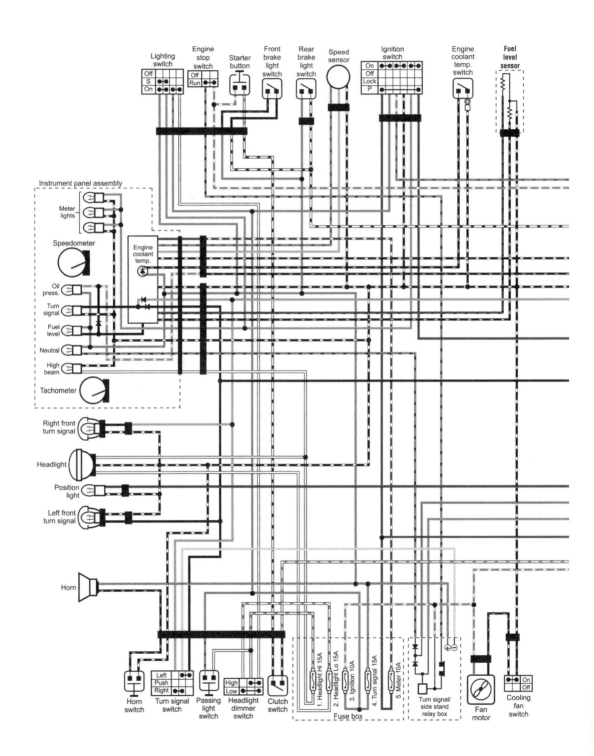

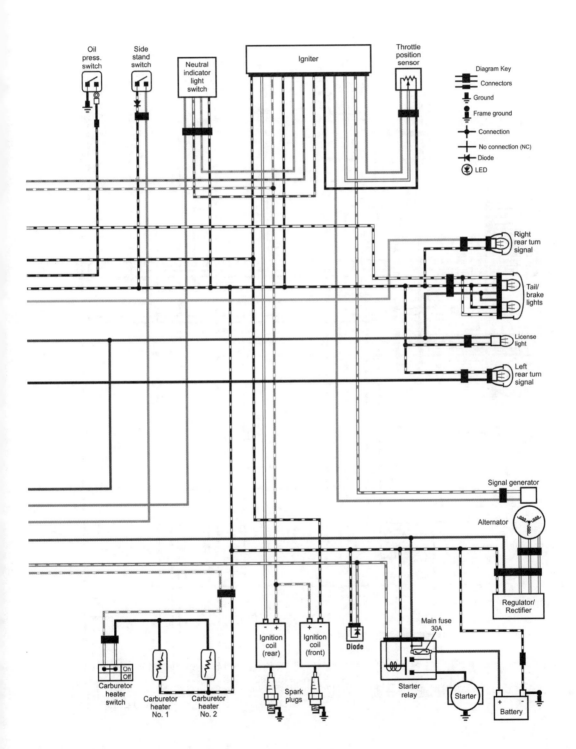

2002 SV650K2 AUSTRALIA MODELS

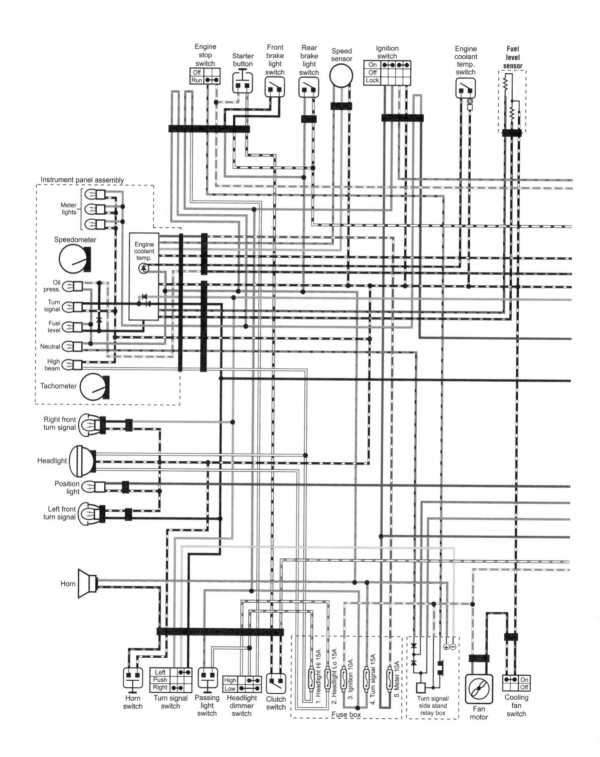

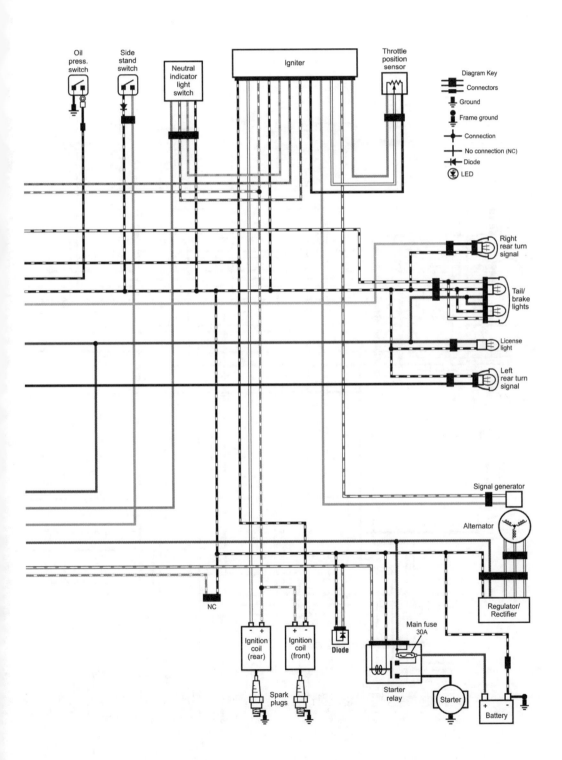

2002 SV650K2 USA/CALIFORNIA MODELS

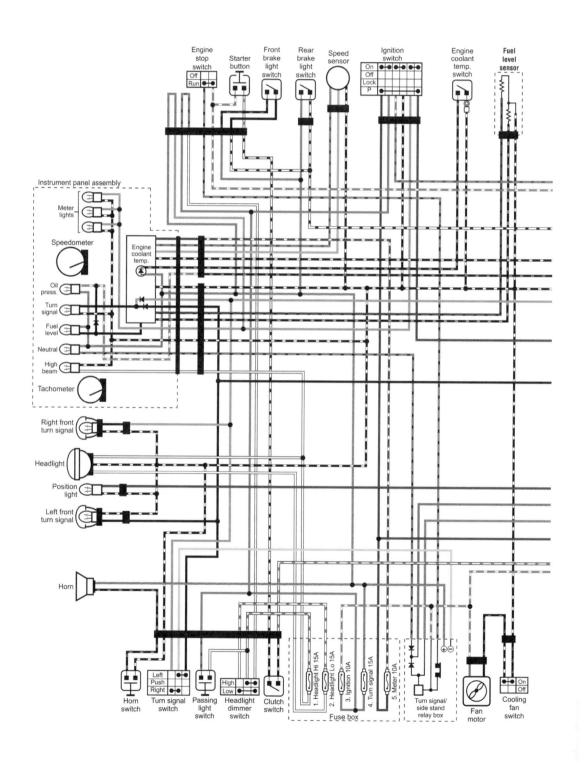

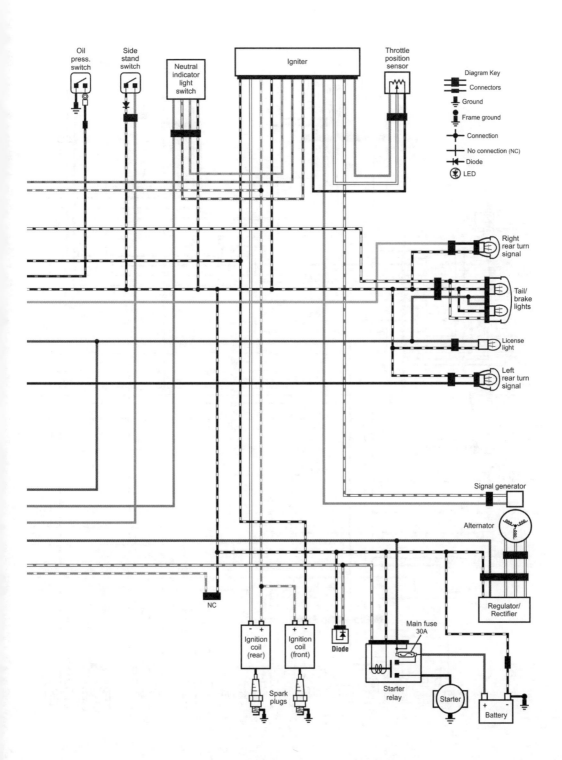

18

2002 SV650SK2 EUROPE MODELS

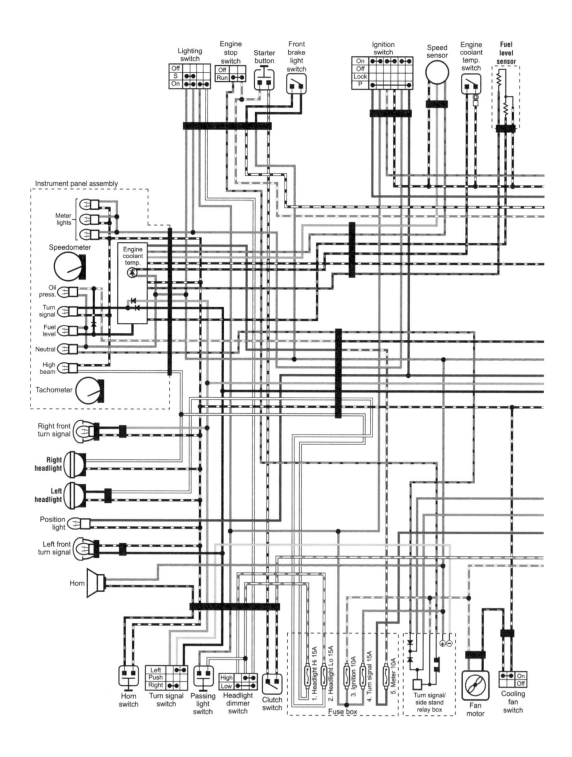

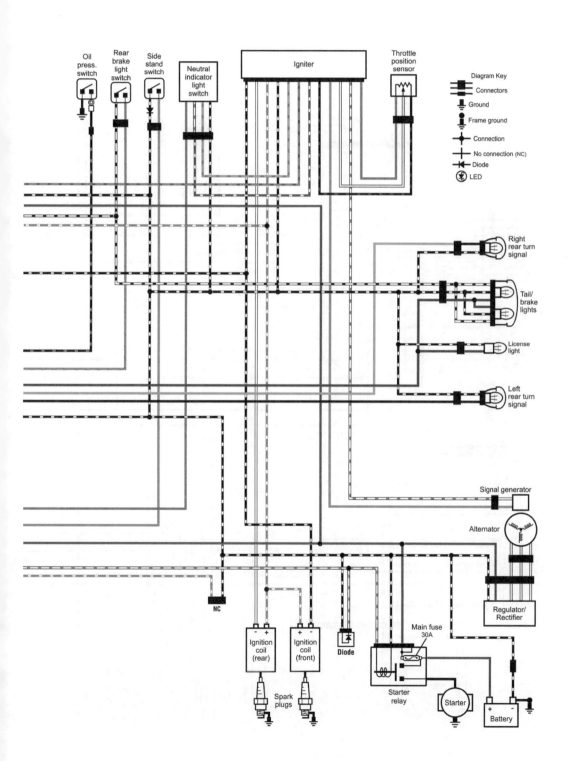

2002 SV650SK2 UK MODELS

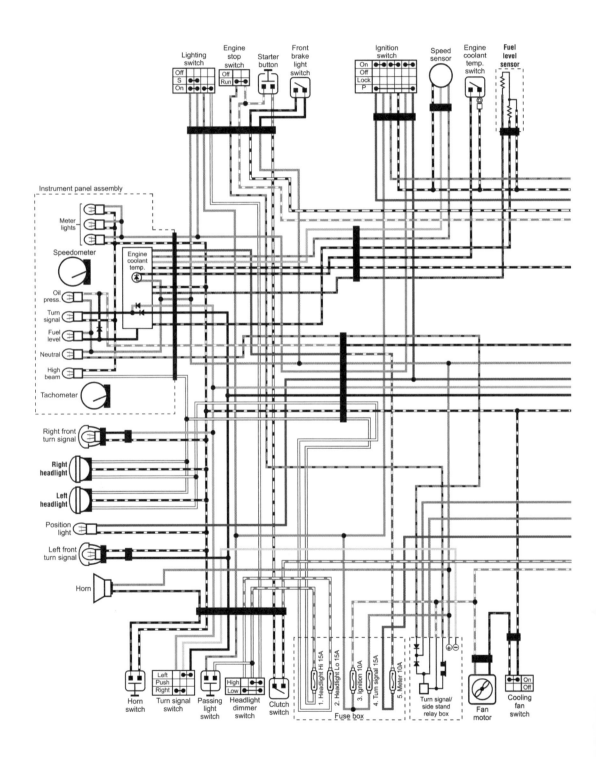

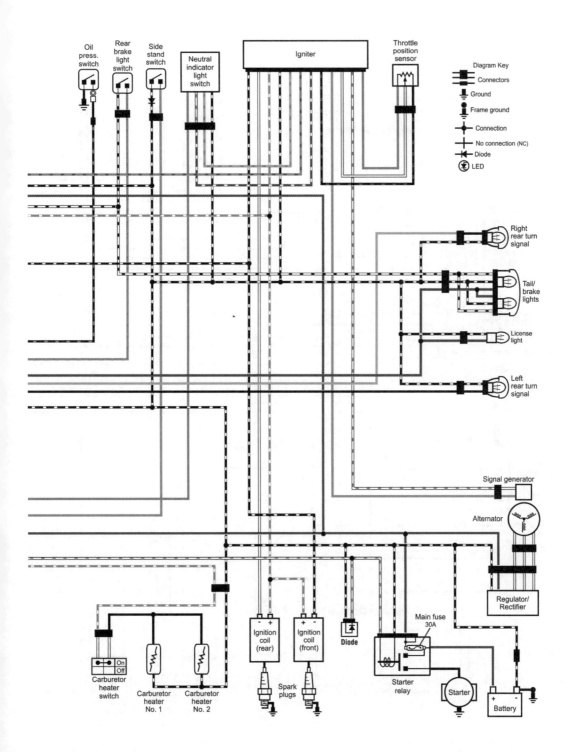

2002 SV650SK2 AUSTRALIA MODELS

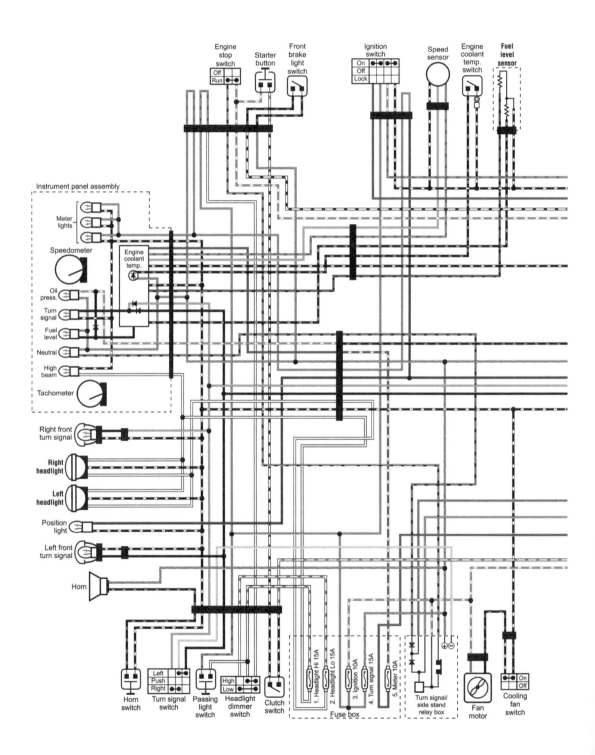

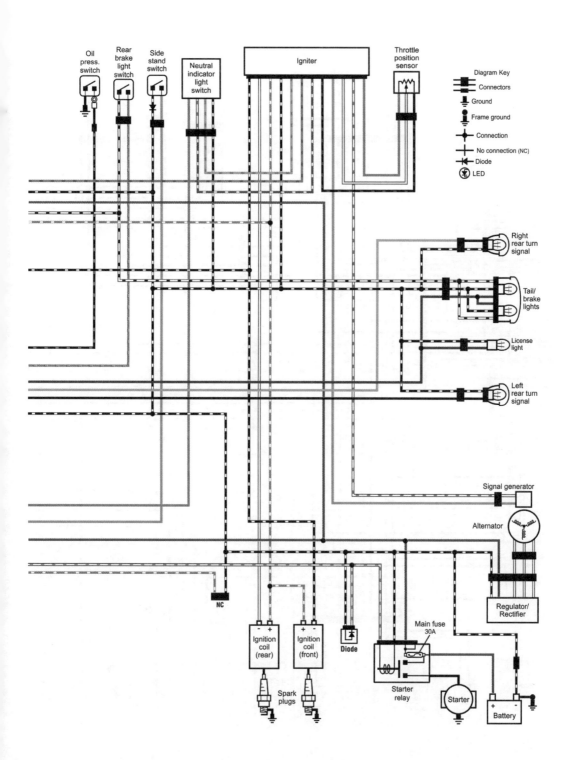

2002 SV650SK2 USA/CALIFORNIA AND CANADA MODELS

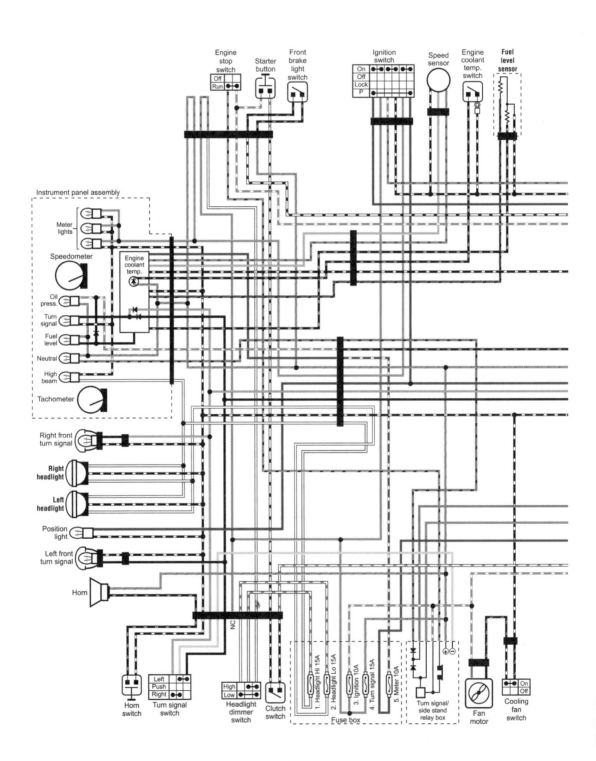

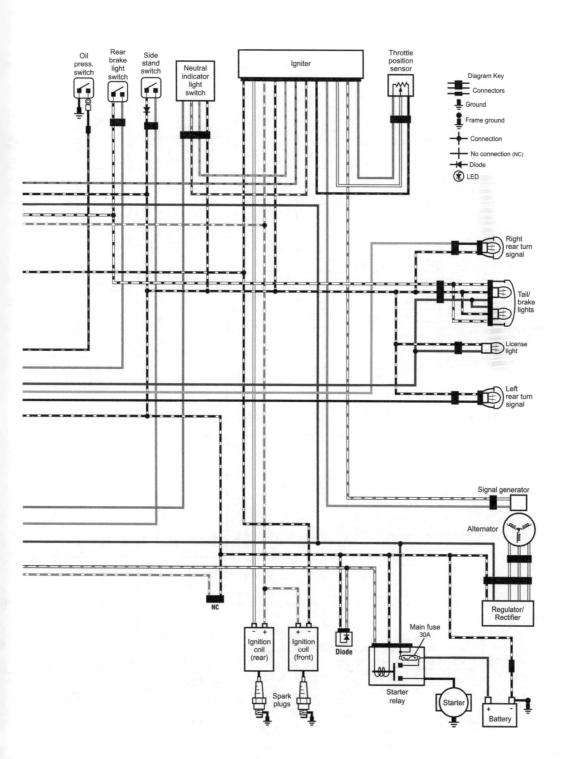

2003-2004 SV650 USA/AUSTRALIA/CANADA/CALIFORNIA MODELS

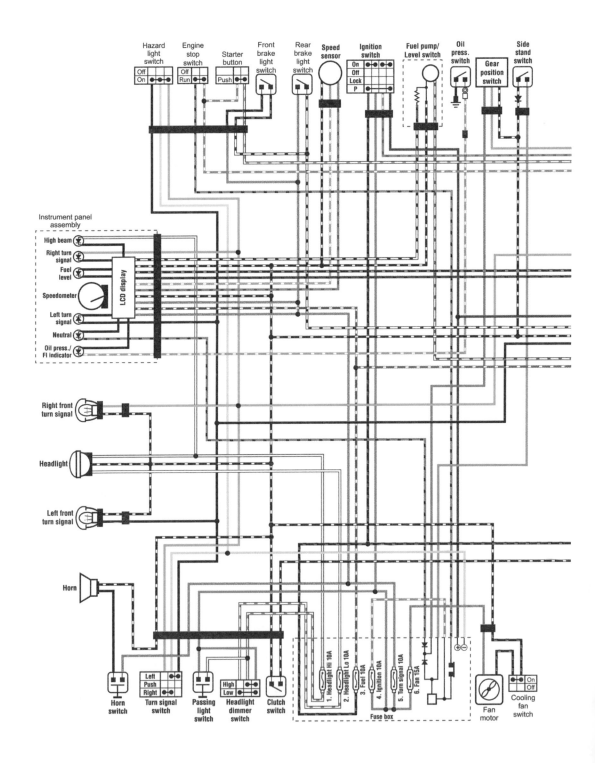

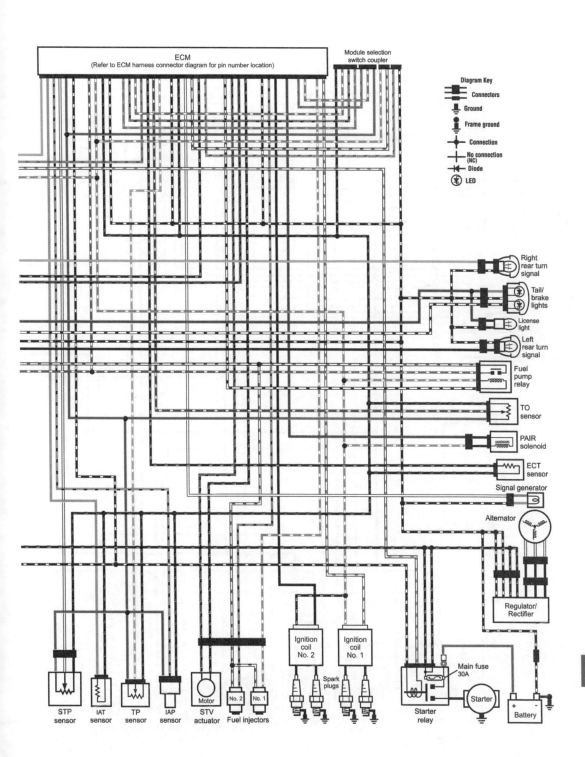

2005-2006 SV650 USA/CANADA/CALIFORNIA MODELS

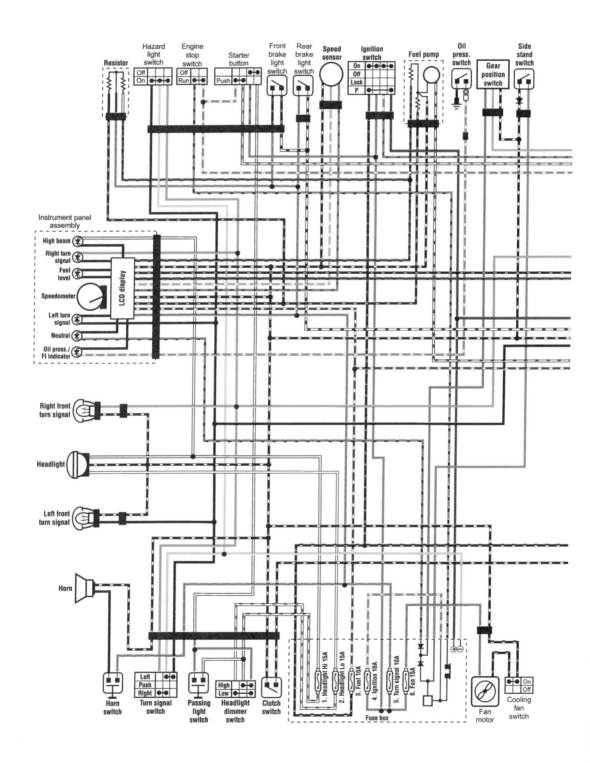

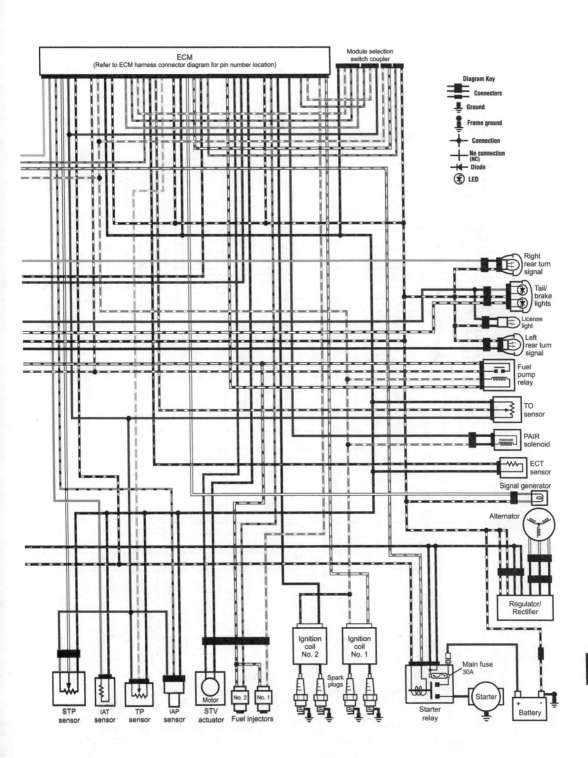

2003-2006 SV650S USA/CANADA/CALIFORNIA MODELS

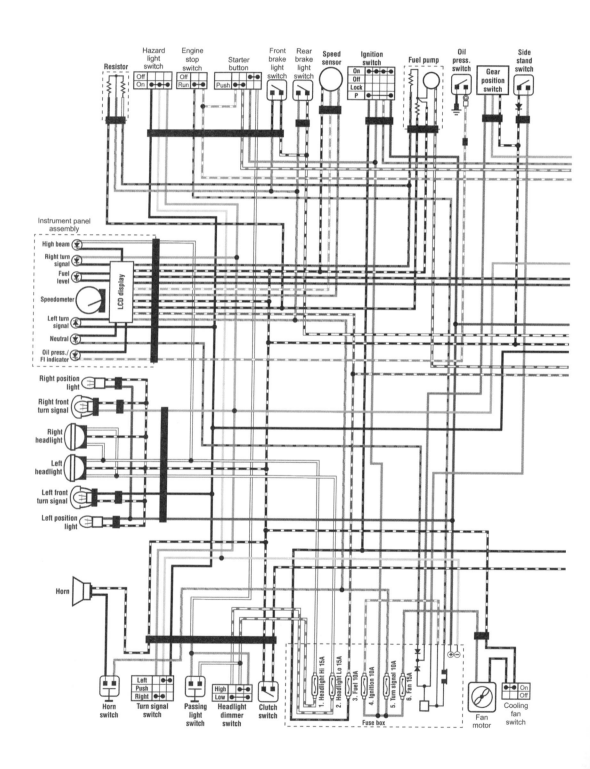

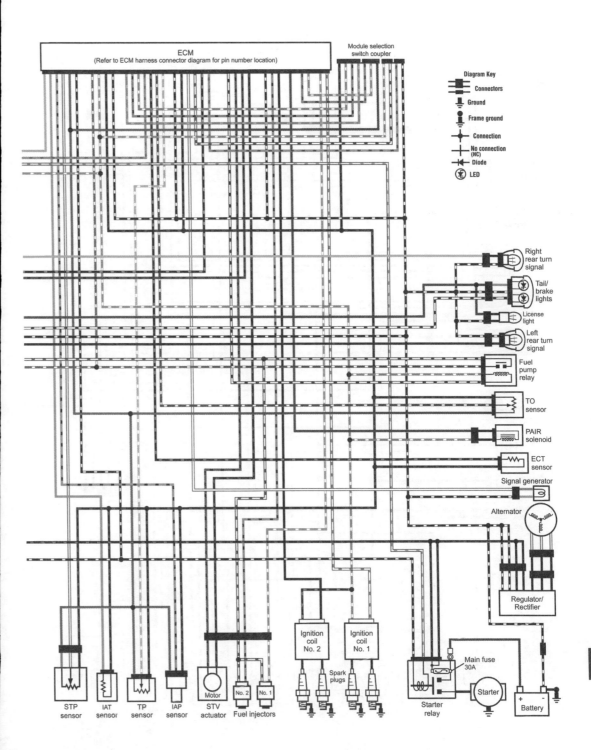

2007 SV650K7 UK/EUROPE/AUSTRALIA/CALIFORNIA MODELS

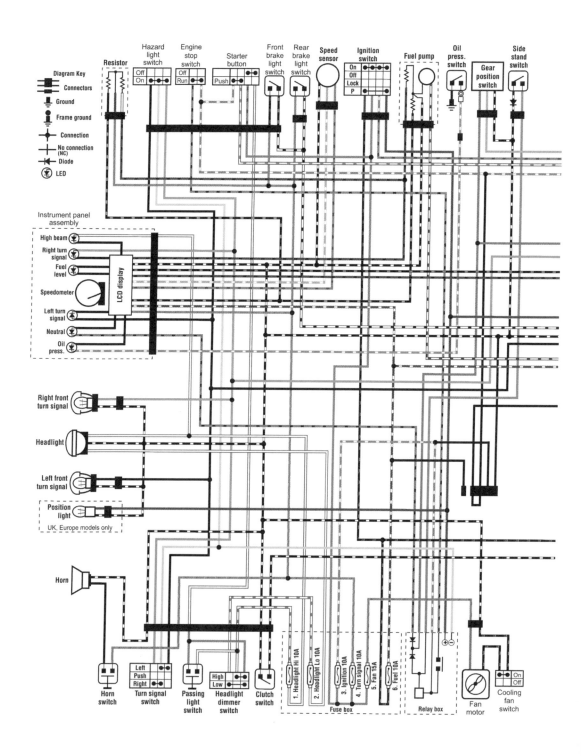

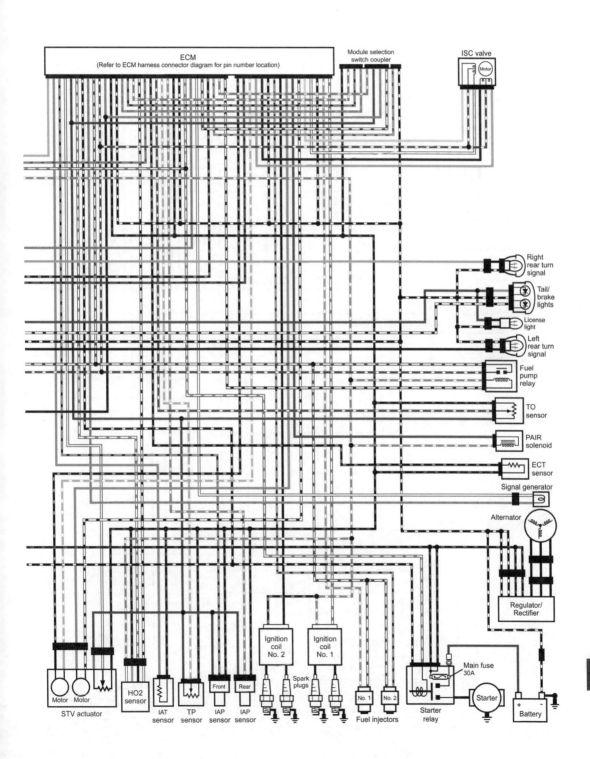

2007 SV650K7 USA/CANADA MODELS

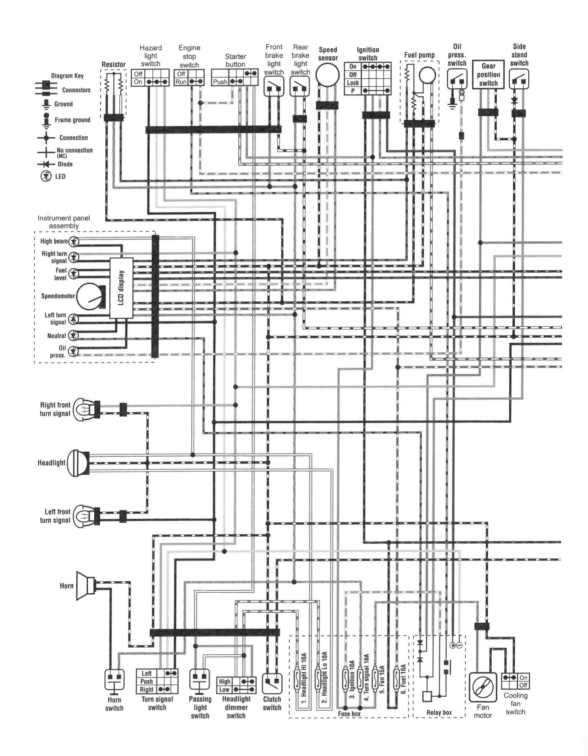

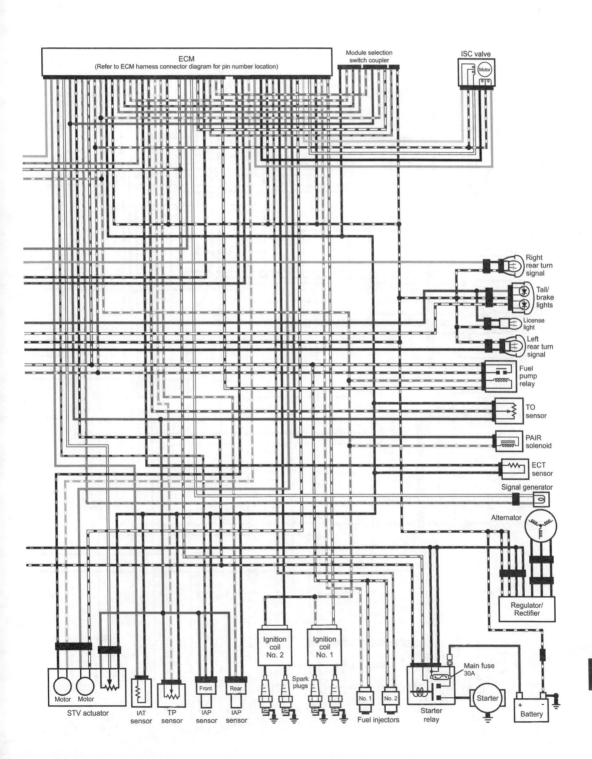

2007 SV650SK7 UK/EUROPE/AUSTRALIA/CALIFORNIA MODELS

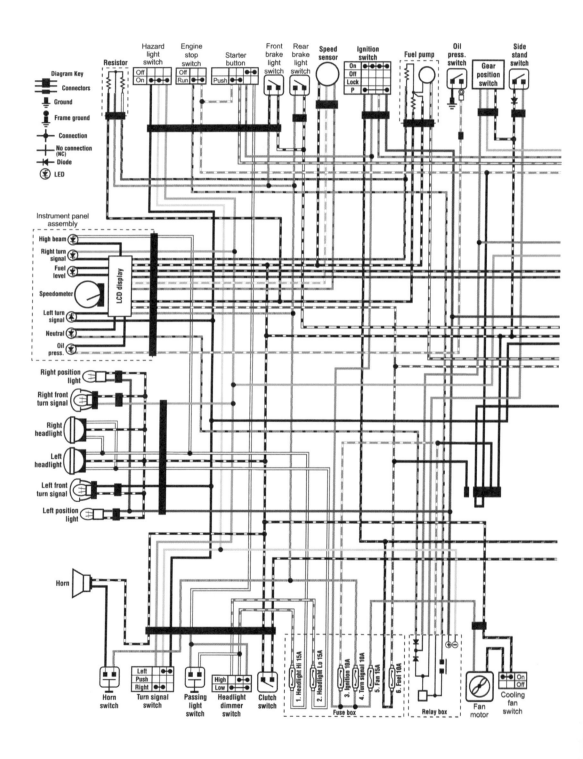

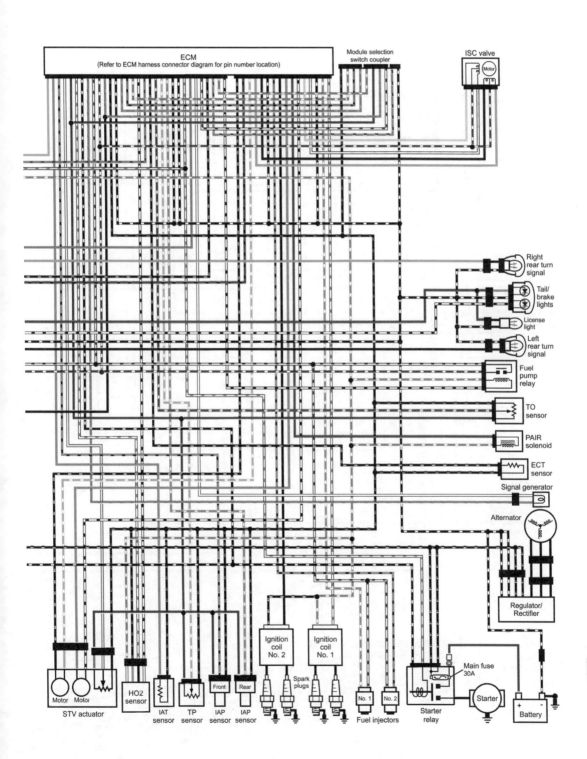

2007 SV650SK7 USA/CANADA MODELS

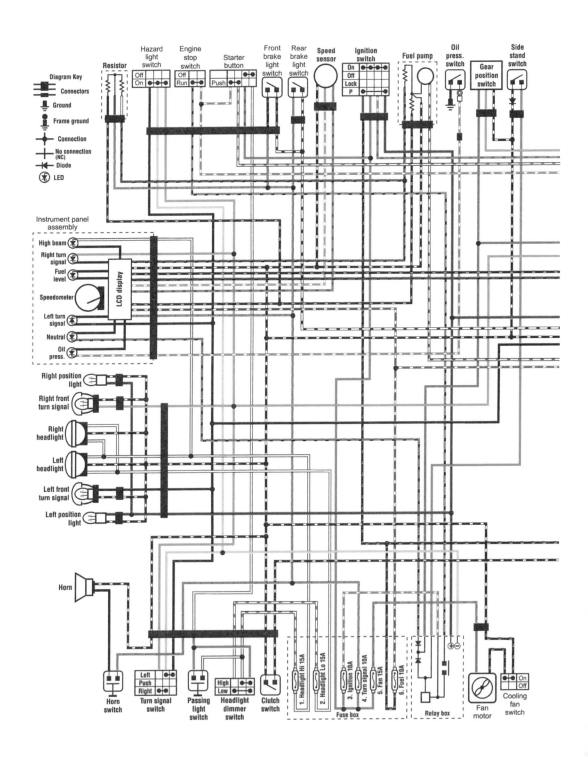

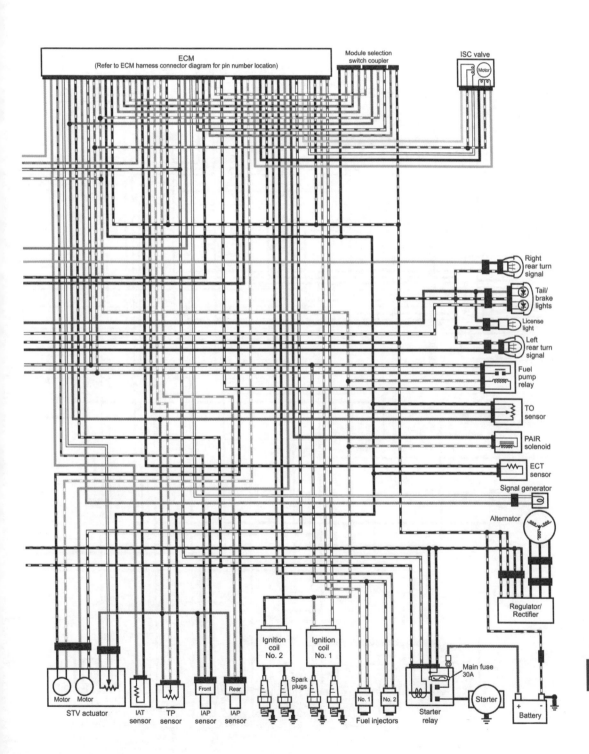

18

2007 SV650AK7 UK/EUROPE/AUSTRALIA/CALIFORNIA (ABS) MODELS

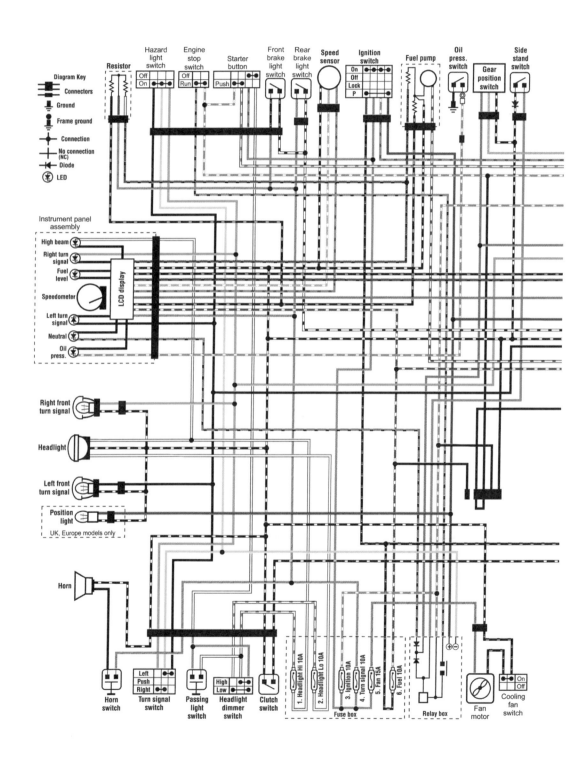

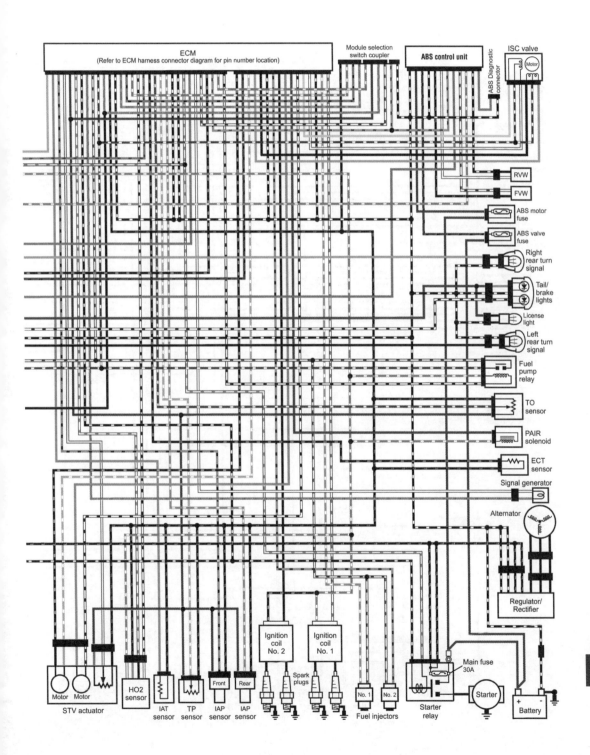

2007 SV650AK7 USA/CANADA (ABS) MODELS

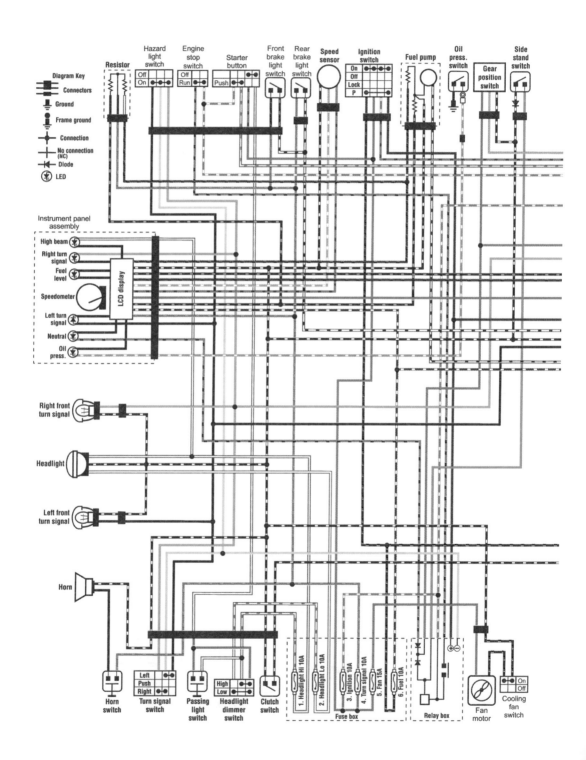

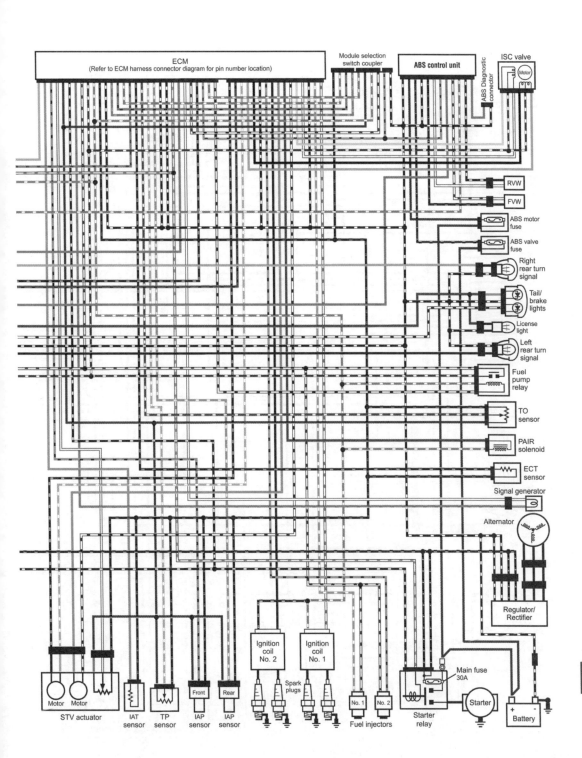

2007 SV650SAK7 UK/EUROPE/AUSTRALIA/CALIFORNIA (ABS) MODELS

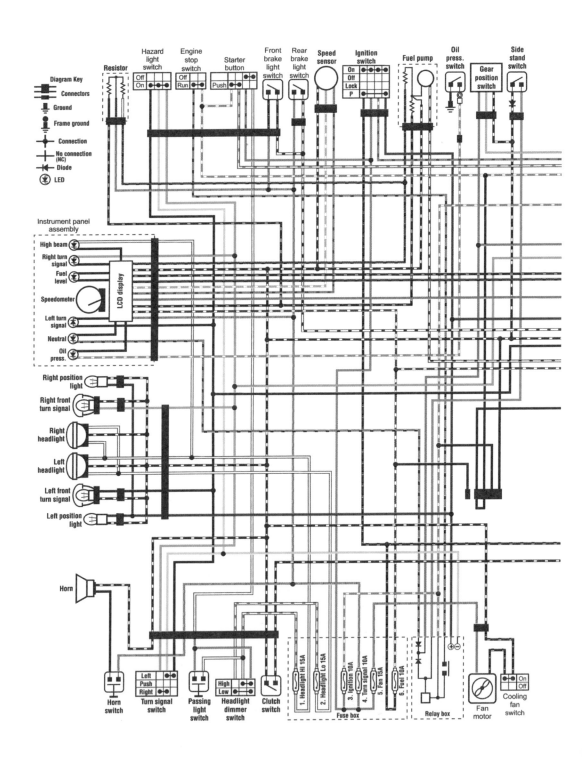

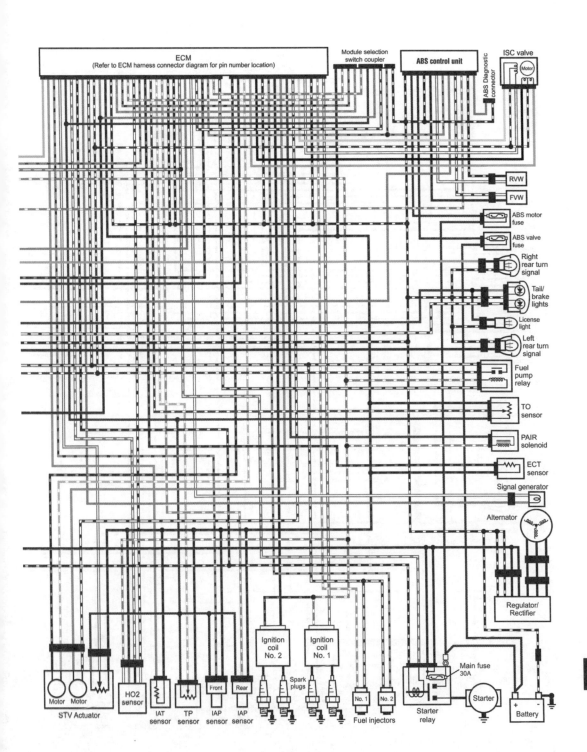

2007 SV650SAK7 USA/CANADA (ABS) MODELS

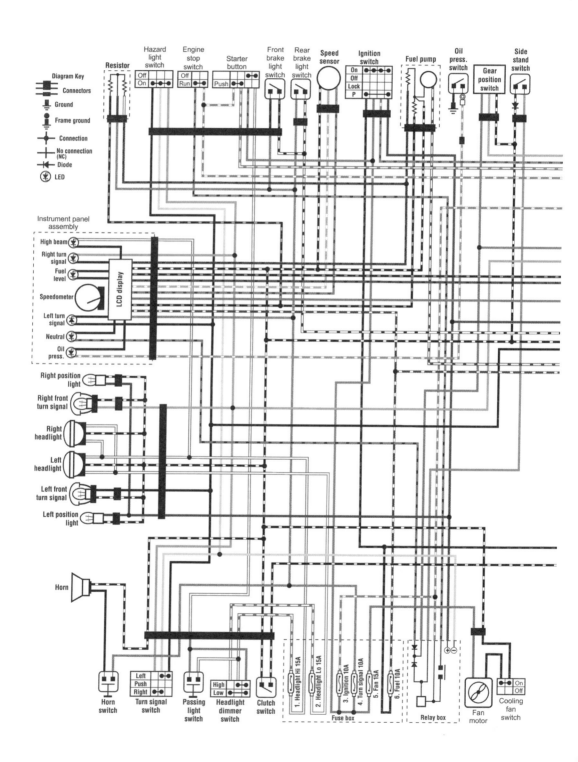

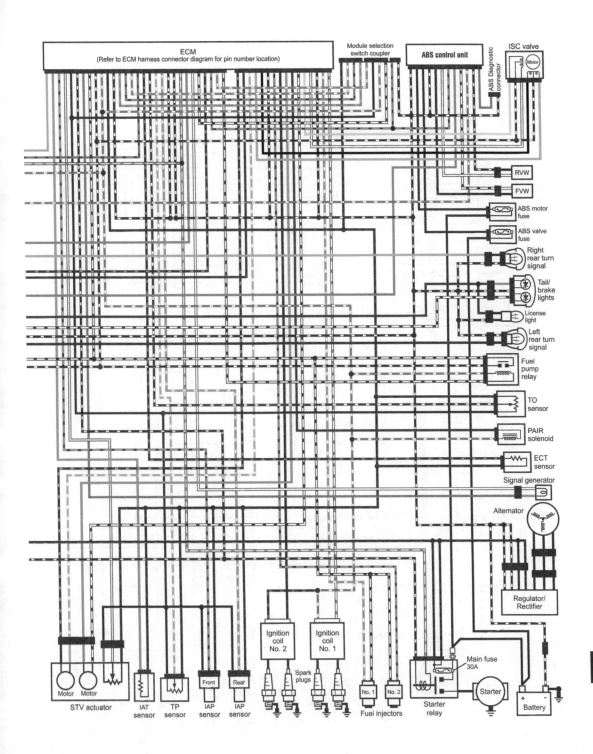

2008-ON SV650SK8 USA/CANADA MODELS

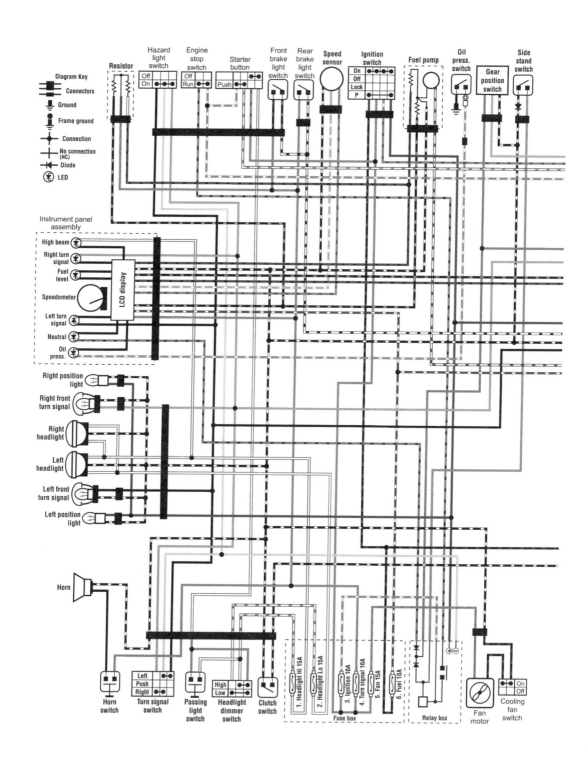

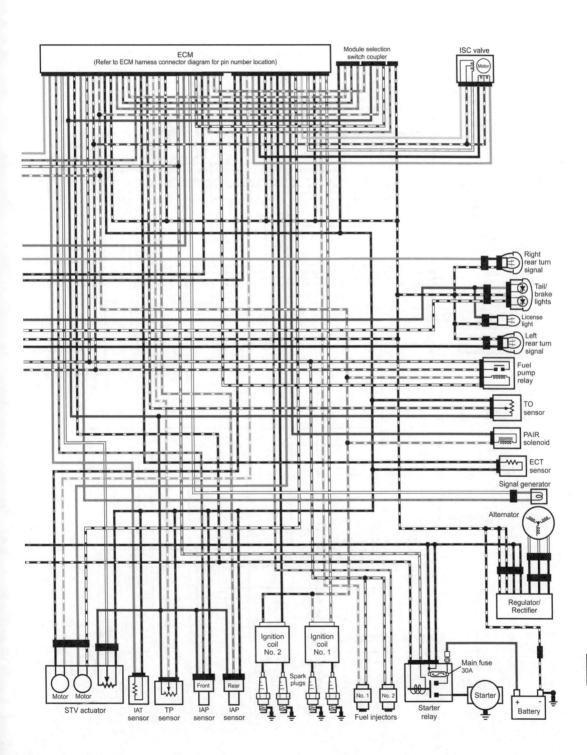

2008-ON SV650AK8 USA/CANADA (ABS) MODELS

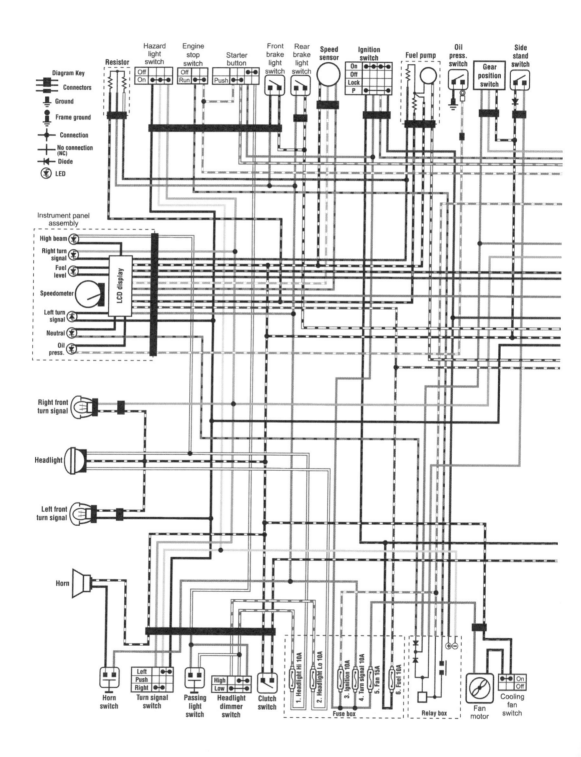

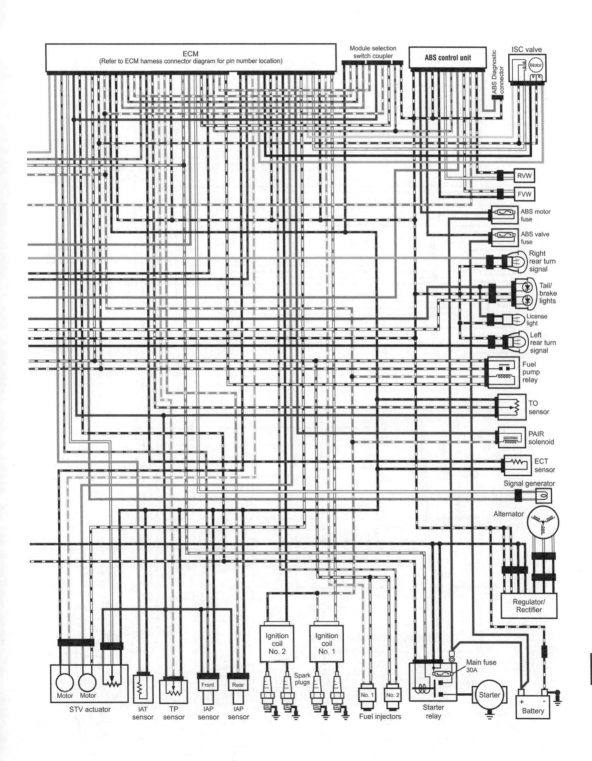

ECM
(Refer to ECM harness connector diagram for pin number location)

Module selection switch coupler

ABS control unit

ABS Diagnostic connector

ISC valve

Motor

RVW

FVW

ABS motor fuse

ABS valve fuse

Right rear turn signal

Tail/brake lights

License light

Left rear turn signal

Fuel pump relay

TO sensor

PAIR solenoid

ECT sensor

Signal generator

Alternator

Regulator/Rectifier

Ignition coil No. 2

Ignition coil No. 1

Spark plugs

Main fuse 30A

Motor Motor

STV actuator

IAT sensor

TP sensor

IAP sensor

IAP sensor

Front Rear

No. 1 No. 2

Fuel injectors

Starter relay

Starter

Battery

18

2008-ON SV650SAK8 USA/CANADA (ABS) MODELS

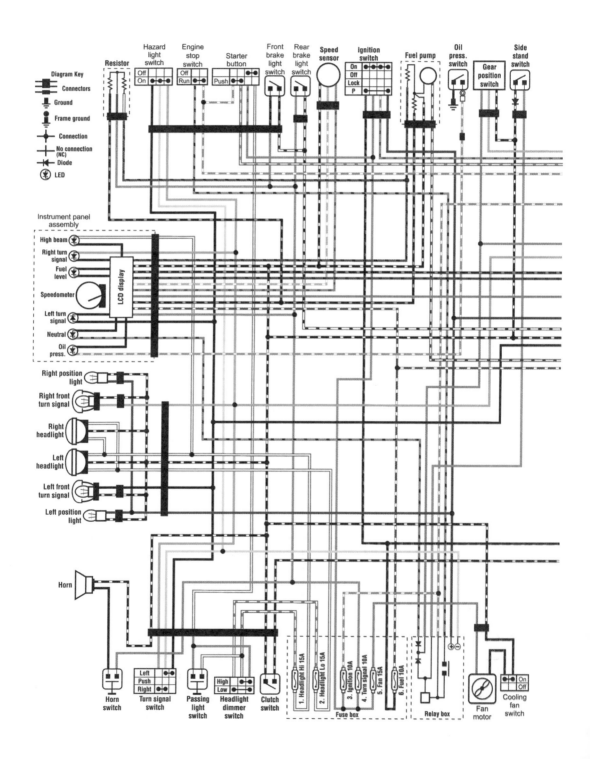

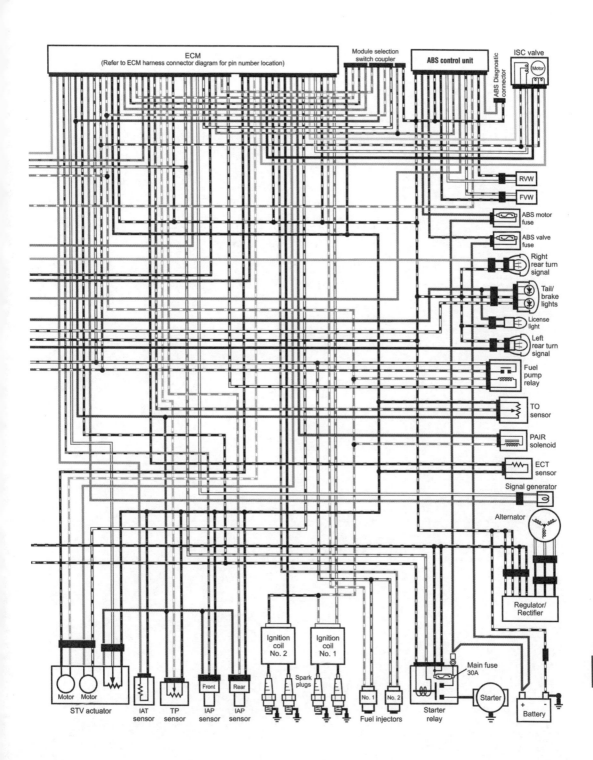

NOTES

MAINTENANCE LOG

Date	Miles	Type of Service

BMW

M308	500 & 600cc Twins, 55-69
M502-3	BMW R50/5-R100GS PD, 70-96
M500-3	BMW K-Series, 85-97
M501-3	K1200RS, GT & LT, 98-10
M503-3	R850, R1100, R1150 & R1200C, 93-05
M309	F650, 1994-2000

HARLEY-DAVIDSON

M419	Sportsters, 59-85
M429-5	XL/XLH Sportster, 86-03
M427-4	XL Sportster, 04-13
M418	Panheads, 48-65
M420	Shovelheads, 66-84
M421-3	FLS/FXS Evolution, 84-99
M423-2	FLS/FXS Twin Cam, 00-05
M250	FLS/FXS/FXC Softail, 06-09
M422-3	FLH/FLT/FXR Evolution, 84-98
M430-4	FLH/FLT Twin Cam, 99-05
M252	FLH/FLT, 06-09
M426	VRSC Series, 02-07
M424-2	FXD Evolution, 91-98
M425-3	FXD Twin Cam, 99-05
M254	Dyna Series, 06-11

HONDA

ATVs

M316	Odyssey FL250, 77-84
M311	ATC, TRX & Fourtrax 70-125, 70-87
M433	Fourtrax 90, 93-00
M326	ATC185 & 200, 80-86
M347	ATC200X & Fourtrax 200SX, 86-88
M455	ATC250 & Fourtrax 200/250, 84-87
M342	ATC250R, 81-84
M348	TRX250R/Fourtrax 250R & ATC250R, 85-89
M456-4	TRX250X 87-92; TRX300EX 93-06
M446-3	TRX250 Recon & Recon ES, 97-07
M215-2	TTRX250EX Sportrax and TRX250X, 01-12
M346-3	TRX300/Fourtrax 300 & TRX300FW/Fourtrax 4x4, 88-00
M200-2	TRX350 Rancher, 00-06
M459-3	TRX400 Foreman 95-03
M454-5	TRX400EX Fourtrax & Sportrax 99-13
M201	TRX450R & TRX450ER, 04-09
M205	TRX450 Foreman, 98-04
M210	TRX500 Rubicon, 01-04
M206	TRX500 Foreman, 05-11

Singles

M310-13	50-110cc OHC Singles, 65-99
M315	100-350cc OHC, 69-82
M317	125-250cc Elsinore, 73-80
M442	CR60-125R Pro-Link, 81-88
M431-2	CR80R, 89-95, CR125R, 89-91
M435	CR80R &CR80RB, 96-02
M457-2	CR125R, 92-97; CR250R, 92-96
M464	CR125R, 1998-2002
M443	CR250R-500R Pro-Link, 81-87
M432-3	CR250R, 88-91 & CR500R, 88-01
M437	CR250R, 97-01
M352	CRF250R, CRF250X, CRF450R & CRF450X, 02-05
M319-3	XR50R, CRF50F, XR70R & CRF70F, 97-09
M312-14	XL/XR75-100, 75-91
M222	XR80R, CRF80F, XR100R, & CRF100F, 92-09
M318-4	XL/XR/TLR 125-200, 79-03
M328-4	XL/XR250, 78-00; XL/XR350R 83-85; XR200R, 84-85; XR250L, 91-96
M320-2	XR400R, 96-04
M221	XR600R, 91-07; XR650L, 93-07
M339-8	XL/XR 500-600, 79-90
M225	XR650R, 00-07

Twins

M321	125-200cc Twins, 65-78
M322	250-350cc Twins, 64-74
M323	250-360cc Twins, 74-77
M324-5	Twinstar, Rebel 250 & Nighthawk 250, 78-03
M334	400-450cc Twins, 78-87
M333	450 & 500cc Twins, 65-76
M335	CX & GL500/650, 78-83
M344	VT500, 83-88
M313	VT700 & 750, 83-87
M314-3	VT750 Shadow Chain Drive, 98-06
M440	VT1100C Shadow, 85-96
M460-4	VT1100 Series, 95-07
M230	VTX1800 Series, 02-08
M231	VTX1300 Series, 03-09

Fours

M332	CB350-550, SOHC, 71-78
M345	CB550 & 650, 83-85
M336	CB650, 79-82
M341	CB750 SOHC, 69-78
M337	CB750 DOHC, 79-82
M436	CB750 Nighthawk, 91-93 & 95-99
M325	CB900, 1000 & 1100, 80-83
M439	600 Hurricane, 87-90
M441-2	CBR600F2 & F3, 91-98
M445-2	CBR600F4, 99-06
M220	CBR600RR, 03-06
M434-2	CBR900RR Fireblade, 93-99
M329	500cc V-Fours, 84-86
M349	700-1000cc Interceptor, 83-85
M458-2	VFR700F-750F, 86-97
M438	VFR800FI Interceptor, 98-00
M327	700-1100cc V-Fours, 82-88
M508	ST1100/Pan European, 90-02
M340	GL1000 & 1100, 75-83
M504	GL1200, 84-87

Sixes

M505	GL1500 Gold Wing, 88-92
M506-2	GL1500 Gold Wing, 93-00
M507-3	GL1800 Gold Wing, 01-10
M462-2	GL1500C Valkyrie, 97-03

KAWASAKI

ATVs

M465-3	Bayou KLF220 & KLF250, 88-10
M466-4	Bayou KLF300, 86-04
M467	Bayou KLF400, 93-99
M470	Lakota KEF300, 95-99
M385-2	Mojave KSF250, 87-04

Singles

M350-9	80-350cc Rotary Valve, 66-01
M444-2	KX60, 83-02; KX80 83-90
M448-2	KX80, 91-00; KX85, 01-10 & KX100, 89-09
M351	KDX200, 83-88
M447-3	KX125 & KX250, 82-91; KX500, 83-04
M472-2	KX125, 92-00
M473-2	KX250, 92-00
M474-3	KLR650, 87-07
M240-2	KLR650, 08-12

Twins

M355	KZ400, KZ/Z440, EN450 & EN500, 74-95
M241	Ninja 250R (EX250), 88-12
M360-3	EX500, GPZ500S, & Ninja 500R, 87-02
M356-5	Vulcan 700 & 750, 85-06
M354-3	Vulcan 800, 95-05
M246	Vulcan 900, 06-12
M357-2	Vulcan 1500, 87-99
M471-3	Vulcan 1500 Series, 96-08
M245	Vulcan 1600 Series, 03-08

Fours

M449	KZ500/550 & ZX550, 79-85
M450	KZ, Z & ZX750, 80-85
M358	KZ650, 77-83
M359-3	Z & KZ 900-1000cc, 73-81
M451-3	KZ, ZX & ZN 1000 &1100cc, 81-02
M452-3	ZX500 & Ninja ZX600, 85-97
M468-2	Ninja ZX-6, 90-04
M469	Ninja ZX-7, ZX7R & ZX7RR, 91-98
M453-3	Ninja ZX900, ZX1000 & ZX1100, 84-01
M409-2	Concours, 86-06

POLARIS

ATVs

M496	3-, 4- and 6-Wheel Models w/250-425cc Engines, 85-95
M362-2	Magnum & Big Boss, 96-99
M363	Scrambler 500 4X4, 97-00
M365-5	Sportsman/Xplorer, 96-13
M366	Sportsman 600/700/800 Twins, 02-10
M367	Predator 500, 03-07

SUZUKI

ATVs

M381	ALT/LT 125 & 185, 83-87
M475	LT230 & LT250, 85-90
M380-2	LT250R Quad Racer, 85-92
M483-2	LT-4WD, LT-F4WDX & LT-F250, 87-98
M270-2	LT-Z400, 03-08
M343-2	LT-F500F Quadrunner, 98-02

Singles

M369	125-400cc, 64-81
M371	RM50-400 Twin Shock, 75-81
M379	RM125-500 Single Shock, 81-88
M386	RM80-250, 89-95
M400	RM125, 96-00
M401	RM250, 96-02
M476	DR250-350, 90-94
M477-4	DR-Z400E, S & SM, 00-12
M272	DR650, 96-12
M384-5	LS650 Savage/S40, 86-12

Twins

M372	GS400-450 Chain Drive, 77-87
M484-3	GS500E Twins, 89-02
M361	SV650, 1999-2002
M481-6	VS700-800 Intruder/S50, 85-09
M261-2	1500 Intruder/C90, 98-09
M260-3	Volusia/Boulevard C50, 01-11
M482-3	VS1400 Intruder/S83, 87-07

Triple

M368	GT380, 550 & 750, 72-77

Fours

M373	GS550, 77-86
M364	GS650, 81-83
M370	GS750, 77-82
M376	GS850-1100 Shaft Drive, 79-84
M378	GS1100 Chain Drive, 80-81
M383-3	Katana 600, 88-96 GSX-R750-1100, 86-87
M331	GSX-R600, 97-00
M264	GSX-R600, 01-05
M478-2	GSX-R750, 88-92; GSX750F Katana, 89-96
M485	GSX-R750, 96-99
M377	GSX-R1000, 01-04
M266	GSX-R1000, 05-06
M265	GSX1300R Hayabusa, 99-07
M338	Bandit 600, 95-00
M353	GSF1200 Bandit, 96-03

YAMAHA

ATVs

M499-2	YFM80 Moto-4, Badger & Raptor, 85-08
M394	YTM200, 225 & YFM200, 83-86
M488-5	Blaster, 88-05
M489-2	Timberwolf, 89-00
M487-5	Warrior, 87-04
M486-6	Banshee, 87-06
M490-3	Moto-4 & Big Bear, 87-04
M493	Kodiak, 93-98
M287-2	YFZ450, 04-13
M285-2	Grizzly 660, 02-08
M280-2	Raptor 660R, 01-05
M290	Raptor 700R, 06-09
M291	Rhino 700, 2008-2012

Singles

M492-2	PW50 & 80 Y-Zinger & BW80 Big Wheel 80, 81-02
M410	80-175 Piston Port, 68-76
M415	250-400 Piston Port, 68-76
M412	DT & MX Series, 77-83
M414	IT125-490, 76-86
M393	YZ50-80 Monoshock, 78-90
M413	YZ100-490 Monoshock, 76-84
M390	YZ125-250, 85-87 YZ490, 85-90
M391	YZ125-250, 88-93 & WR250Z, 91-93
M497-2	YZ125, 94-01
M498	YZ250, 94-98; WR250Z, 94-97
M406	YZ250F & WR250F, 01-03
M491-2	YZ400F, 98-99 & 426F, 00-02; WR400F, 98-00 & 426F, 00-01
M417	XT125-250, 80-84
M480-3	XT350, 85-00; TT350, 86-87
M405	XT/TT 500, 76-81
M416	XT/TT 600, 83-89

Twins

M403	650cc Twins, 70-82
M395-10	XV535-1100 Virago, 81-03
M495-7	V-Star 650, 98-11
M284	V-Star 950, 09-12
M281-4	V-Star 1100, 99-09
M283	V-Star 1300, 07-10
M282-2	Road Star, 99-07

Triple

M404	XS750 & XS850, 77-81

Fours

M387	XJ550, XJ600 & FJ600, 81-92
M494	XJ600 Seca II/Diversion, 92-98
M388	YX600 Radian & FZ600, 86-90
M396	FZR600, 89-93
M392	FZ700-750 & Fazer, 85-87
M411	XS1100, 78-81
M461	YZF-R6, 99-04
M398	YZF-R1, 98-03
M399	FZ1, 01-05
M397	FJ1100 & 1200, 84-93
M375-2	V-Max, 85-07
M374-2	Royal Star, 96-10

VINTAGE MOTORCYCLES

Clymer® Collection Series

M330	Vintage British Street Bikes, BSA 500-650cc Unit Twins; Norton 750 & 850cc Commandos; Triumph 500-750cc Twins
M300	Vintage Dirt Bikes, V. 1 Bultaco, 125-370cc Singles; Montesa, 123-360cc Singles; Ossa, 125-250cc Singles
M305	Vintage Japanese Street Bikes Honda, 250 & 305cc Twins; Kawasaki, 250-750cc Triples; Kawasaki, 900 & 1000cc Fours